# TECHNICAL RISK MANAGEMENT

PRENTICE HALL INTERNATIONAL SERIES IN INDUSTRIAL AND SYSTEMS ENGINEERING

*W. J. FABRYCKY AND J. H. MIZE, EDITORS*

AMOS AND SARCHET    *Management for Engineers*
AMRINE, RITCHEY, MOODIE, AND KMEC    *Manufacturing Organization and Management, 6/E*
ASFAHL    *Safety and Health Management, 3/E*
BABCOCK    *Managing Engineering and Technology 2/E*
BADIRU    *Comprehensive Project Management*
BADIRU    *Expert Systems Applications in Engineering and Manufacturing*
BANKS, CARSON, AND NELSON    *Discrete-Event System Simulation, 2/E*
BLANCHARD    *Logistics Engineering and Management, 4/E*
BLANCHARD AND FABRYCKY    *Systems Engineering and Analysis, 2/E*
BROWN    *Technimanagement: The Human Side Of The Technical Organization*
BURTON AND MORAN    *The Future Focused Organization*
BUSSEY AND ESCHENBACH    *The Economic Analysis of Industrial Projects, 2/E*
BUZACOTT AND SHANTHIKUMAR    *Stochastic Models of Manufacturing Systems*
CANADA AND SULLIVAN    *Economic and Multi-Attribute Evaluation of Advanced Manufacturing Systems*
CANADA, SULLIVAN, AND WHITE    *Capital Investment Analysis for Engineering and Management, 2/E*
CHANG AND WYSK    *An Introduction to Automated Process Planning Systems*
CHANG, WYSK, AND WANG    *Computer Aided Manufacturing*
DELAVIGNE AND ROBERTSON    *Deming's Profound Changes*
EAGER    *The Information Payoff: The Manager's Concise Guide to Making PC Communications Work*
EBERTS    *User Interface Design*
EBERTS AND EBERTS    *Myths of Japanese Quality*
ELSAYED AND BOUCHER    *Analysis and Control of Production Systems, 2/E*
FABRYCKY AND BLANCHARD    *Life-Cycle Cost and Economic Analysis*
FABRYCKY AND THUESEN    *Economic Decision Analysis, 2/E*
FISKWICK    *Simulation Model Design and Execution: Building Digital Worlds*
FRANCIS, MCGINNIS, AND WHITE    *Facility Layout and Location: An Analytical Approach, 2/E*
GIBSON    *Modern Management of the High-Technology Enterprise*
GORDON    *Systematic Training Program Design*
GRAEDEL AND ALLENBY    *Industrial Ecology*
HALL    *Queuing Methods: For Services and Manufacturing*
HANSEN    *Automating Business Process Reengineering*
HAMMER    *Occupational Safety Management and Engineering, 4/E*
HAZELRIGG    *Systems Engineering*
HUTCHINSON    *An Integrated Approach to Logistics Management*
IGNIZIO    *Linear Programming in Single- and Multiple-Objective Systems*
IGNIZIO AND CAVALIER    *Linear Programming*
KROEMER, KROEMER, KROEMER-ELBERT    *Ergonomics: How to Design for Ease and Efficiency*
KUSIAK    *Intelligent Manufacturing Systems*
LAMB    *Availability Engineering and Management for Manufacturing Plant Performance*
LANDERS, BROWN, FANT, MALSTROM, SCHMITT    *Electronic Manufacturing Processes*
LEEMIS    *Reliability: Probabilistic Models and Statistical Methods*
MICHAELS    *Technical Risk Management*
MUNDEL AND DANNER    *Motion and Time Study: Improving Productivity, 7/E*
OSTWALD    *Engineering Cost Estimating, 3/E*
PINEDO    *Scheduling: Theory, Algorithms, and Systems*
PRASAD    *Concurrent Engineering Fundamentals, Vol. I: Integrated Product and Process Organization*
PULAT    *Fundamentals of Industrial Ergonomics*
SHTUB, BARD, GLOBERSON    *Project Management: Engineering Technology and Implementation*
TAHA    *Simulation Modeling and SIMNET*
THUESEN AND FABRYCKY    *Engineering Economy, 8/E*
TURNER, MIZE, CASE, AND NAZEMETZ    *Introduction to Industrial and Systems Engineering, 3/E*
TURTLE    *Implementing Concurrent Project Management*
WALESH    *Engineering Your Future*
WOLFF    *Stochastic Modeling and the Theory of Queues*

# TECHNICAL RISK MANAGEMENT

## Jack V. Michaels, Ph.D.

*For book and bookstore information*

http://www.prenhall.com

Prentice Hall PTR
Upper Saddle River, NJ 07458

*Library of Congress Cataloging-in-Publication Data*

Michaels, Jack V.
    Technical risk management / Jack V. Michaels
       p.   cm.
    Includes index.
    ISBN 0-13-155756-4
    1. Technology--Risk assessment. I. Title.
T174.5.M53  1996
658.15'5--dc20                         95-48013
                                            CIP

*Editorial /production supervision: bookworks / Karen Fortgang*
*Cover design director: Jerry Votta*
*Cover design: Design Source*
*Manufacturing manager: Alexis R. Heydt*
*Acquisitions editor: Bernard Goodwin*
*Page layout/formatting: Bear Type & Graphics*

© 1996 by Prentice Hall P T R
Prentice-Hall, Inc.
A Simon & Schuster Company
Upper Saddle River, NJ 07458

The publisher offers discounts on this book when ordered in bulk quantities.
For more information, contact:

    Corporate Sales Department
    Prentice Hall P T R
    One Lake Street
    Upper Saddle River, New Jersey 07458
    Phone: 800-382-3419
    FAX: 201-236-7141
    E-mail: corpsales@prenhall.com

All rights reserved. No part of this book may be
reproduced, in any form or by any means,
without permission in writing from the publisher.

Printed in the United States of America

10  9  8  7  6  5  4  3  2  1

ISBN 0-13-155756-4

Prentice-Hall International (UK) Limited, *London*
Prentice-Hall of Australia Pty. Limited, *Sydney*
Prentice-Hall Canada Inc., *Toronto*
Prentice-Hall Hispanoamericana S.A., *Mexico*
Prentice-Hall of India Private Limited, *New Delhi*
Prentice-Hall of Japan, Inc., *Tokyo*
Simon & Schuster Asia Pte. Ltd., *Singapore*
Editora Prentice-Hall do Brasil, Ltda., *Rio de Janeiro*

This book is dedicated to the memory of
> Gabriel Greenhause
> Peter S. Megani
> Dr. Seymour O. Zeiberg

esteemed colleagues and friends, each in a very special way.

> *God's finger touched him and he slept.*
> **Alfred Lord Tennyson**

# CONTENTS

**Foreword xvii**
**Preface xix**
**Acknowledgements xxi**
**About the Author xxiii**

**1 INTRODUCTION 1**
   1.1  Definitions 2
   1.2  Technical Risk Management Overview 4
        *1.2.1  Technical Risk Management Absolutes 4*
        *1.2.2  Allied Disciplines 6*
        *1.2.3  User Requirements 7*
        *1.2.4  Window of Opportunity 8*
        *1.2.5  Best Practices 10*
        *1.2.6  Scientific Method 11*
        *1.2.7  Example of the Built-Up Cube Problem 12*
   1.3  Organization of the Book 14
   1.4  Abbreviations, Symbology, and Conventions 16
   1.5  Exercises 17
        *1.5.1  Planning Disasters 18*
        *1.5.2  Scientific Method 18*
        *1.5.3  Greek Alphabet 18*
   1.6  References 18

**2 RISK FUNDAMENTALS 20**
   2.1  Definitions 21
   2.2  Risk Principles 23
        *2.2.1  Risk Benefit-Equity Principle 23*
        *2.2.2  Risk Cost-Effectiveness Principle 24*
        *2.2.3  Example of Balancing Risk Principles 24*
   2.3  Risk Morphology 26
        *2.3.1  Quantified Risk Measures 28*
        *2.3.2  Example of Quantified Risk Measures 28*
        *2.3.3  Hazards and Perils 29*

## CONTENTS

- 2.3.4 Risk Systems 30
- 2.3.5 Example of Production Hazards and Perils 31
- 2.3.6 Risk Hierarchy 32
- 2.3.7 Example of Pareto Analysis of Risk Cost 34
- 2.3.8 Risk Categories 36
- 2.3.9 Example of Subjective Engineering 37

2.4 Probabilistic Nature of Risk 38
- 2.4.1 Risk Time 39
- 2.4.2 Risk Cost 39
- 2.4.3 Example of Risk Exposure at the Component Level 40
- 2.4.4 Risk Network 42
- 2.4.5 Dependent Network 42
- 2.4.6 Independent Network 43
- 2.4.7 Hybrid Network 43
- 2.4.8 Example of Risk Network in Manufacturing 44

2.5 Risk Dominance 46
- 2.5.1 Risk Order 47
- 2.5.2 k-Factor 48
- 2.5.3 Example of Risk Time Dominance 49
- 2.5.4 Risk Applicability 51
- 2.5.5 Example of Risk Exposure in Investment 52
- 2.5.6 Example of Risk Exposure in Construction 54

2.6 Summary 56

2.7 Exercises 57
- 2.7.1 Risk Principles 57
- 2.7.2 Risk Continuum 57
- 2.7.3 Risk Hierarchy 58
- 2.7.4 Multiprocess Risk Probability 58
- 2.7.5 Risk Network 59
- 2.7.6 Risk Dominance 59
- 2.7.7 Risk Exposure in Product Development 60
- 2.7.8 Risk Exposure in Manufacturing Process 60
- 2.7.9 Risk Exposure in Investment 60
- 2.7.10 Risk Exposure in Construction 61
- 2.7.11 Scientific Method 61
- 2.7.12 Probability and Statistics 61

2.8 References 62

## 3 RISK METRICS 64

3.1 Definitions 66

3.2 Risk Determinant Categories 66
- 3.2.1 Products and Processes 67
- 3.2.2 Example of Risk Exposure in Highway and Roadway Construction 69
- 3.2.3 Risk Formulation 71
- 3.2.4 Example of Risk Cost Estimate in Development 72

3.3 Issues of Realism and Credibility 74
- 3.3.1 Aggregation vs. Disaggregation 76

# CONTENTS ix

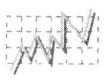

      3.3.2   *Probabilistics vs. Deterministics* 76
      3.3.3   *Example of Estimating Cost at Completion* 79
      3.3.4   *Example of Confidence in Estimating Cost at Completion* 80
  3.4  Selection and Tailoring Process 82
      3.4.1   *Methodology* 83
      3.4.2   *Linearity of Scale* 84
      3.4.3   *Example of Tailoring Risk Determinant Factors* 84
      3.4.4   *Product Categories* 86
  3.5  Attribute Weighting 89
      3.5.1   *Majority Rule* 89
      3.5.2   *Constant Weighting* 90
      3.5.3   *Binary Weighting* 91
      3.5.4   *Example of Attribute Weighting* 91
  3.6  Rating Schema 93
      3.6.1   *Attribute Checklist* 94
      3.6.2   *Truth Table* 95
      3.6.3   *Example of Truth Table Design* 97
      3.6.4   *Lookup Table* 100
  3.7  Risk Determinant Factors 101
      3.7.1   *Management Attribute Factor* 102
      3.7.2   *Extrinsic Attribute Factor* 102
      3.7.3   *Product and Process Maturity Factors* 103
      3.7.4   *Product and Process Quality Factors* 103
      3.7.5   *Product and Process Complexity Factors* 104
      3.7.6   *Product and Process Concurrency Factors* 106
      3.7.7   *Composite Factor* 106
  3.8  Summary 107
  3.9  Exercises 107
      3.9.1   *Metrics* 108
      3.9.2   *Scientific Method* 108
      3.9.3   *Confidence Level in Risk Exposure* 108
      3.9.4   *Risk Determinant Factor Categories* 108
      3.9.5   *Risk Determinant Factors for Trade Study* 108
      3.9.6   *Comparative Realism and Credibility* 108
      3.9.7   *Reverse Engineering* 109
      3.9.8   *Attribute Weighting* 110
      3.9.9   *Risk Exposure in Cost Trades* 110
      3.9.10 *Number Systems* 110
  3.10 References 111

# 4 RISK BASELINES 112
  4.1  Definitions 113
  4.2  Product Network 115
      4.2.1   *PERT and CPM* 116
      4.2.2   *Network Coding* 118
      4.2.3   *Critical Path Definition* 119
      4.2.4   *Task Flow Analysis* 119

## 4.3 Baseline Time Estimate 133

- 4.2.5 Network Utilization 122
- 4.2.6 Example of Task Flow Analysis 122
- 4.2.7 Network Utilization 125
- 4.2.8 Example of Network Compression 127
- 4.2.9 Precedence Diagramming 128
- 4.2.10 Example of Precedence Diagramming 129

### 4.3 Baseline Time Estimate 133

- 4.3.1 Standards 133
- 4.3.2 Universal Standard Data 133
- 4.3.3 Standard Data for Job Families 134
- 4.3.4 Example of Standard Data for Job Families 135
- 4.3.5 Learning Curves 139
- 4.3.6 Learning Curve Formulation 140
- 4.3.7 Learning Curve Applications 142
- 4.3.8 Example of Learning Curve Selection 143
- 4.3.9 Probabilistic Nature of Learning Curves 145
- 4.3.10 Example of Learning Curve Confidence Interval 147
- 4.3.11 Learning Curve Discontinuity 149
- 4.3.12 Example of Learning Curve Discontinuity 150

### 4.4 Baseline Cost Estimate 152

- 4.4.1 Cost Scenario 152
- 4.4.2 Should Cost, Could Cost, Would Cost 153
- 4.4.3 Cost Categories 153
- 4.4.4 Cost Element Structure 154
- 4.4.5 Work Breakdown Structure 155
- 4.4.6 Generation Breakdown 157
- 4.4.7 Cost Estimating Methodology 157
- 4.4.8 Expert Opinion Estimate 159
- 4.4.9 Analogy Estimate 160
- 4.4.10 Parametric Estimate 160
- 4.4.11 Example of Parametric Estimate 162
- 4.4.12 Example of Parametric Estimate as a Function of Power Output and Volume 164
- 4.4.13 Industrial Engineering Estimate 164

### 4.5 Time Value of Money 165

- 4.5.1 Time Value of Money Formulation 167
- 4.5.2 Number of Decimal Places 168
- 4.5.3 Present Value of a Future Payment 171
- 4.5.4 Future Value of a Present Payment 171
- 4.5.5 Present Value of Uniform Series of Payments 172
- 4.5.6 Future Value of Uniform Series of Payments 173
- 4.5.7 Single Payment in Uniform Series of Payments for Present Value 173
- 4.5.8 Single Payment in Uniform Series of Payments for Future Value 175
- 4.5.9 Economic Analysis 176
- 4.5.10 Present Value Method 176
- 4.5.11 Annual Equivalent Value Method 176
- 4.5.12 Benefit-Cost Ratio Method 177

CONTENTS xi

   4.5.13 Internal Rate of Return Method 177
   4.5.14 Example of Trial and Error Solution for Internal Rate of Return 178
   4.5.15 Escalation and Inflation 179
   4.5.16 Price Indexes 180
   4.5.17 Example of Forecasting Producer Price Index 183
 4.6 Summary 185
 4.7 Exercises 186
   4.7.1 Constructing Precedence Diagrams 186
   4.7.2 Balancing Production Lines 186
   4.7.3 Deriving Standard Data for Job Families 186
   4.7.4 Learning Curves in Service Products 187
   4.7.5 Learning Curve Selection 187
   4.7.6 Learning Curve Confidence Interval 187
   4.7.7 Learning Curve Discontinuity 187
   4.7.8 Parametric Estimate 188
   4.7.9 Cost Projections 188
   4.7.10 Benefit-Cost Ratio 189
   4.7.11 Internal Rate of Return 189
   4.7.12 Cost of Inflation 189
   4.7.13 Coefficient of Determination 189
 4.8 References 189

## 5 RISK FORMULATION 191
 5.1 Definitions 193
 5.2 Perspective on Risk Determinant Factors 193
 5.3 Management Attribute Factors 196
   5.3.1 Management Attribute Checklists 197
   5.3.2 Management Attribute Factor Formulation 198
   5.3.3 Example of Management Attribute Factor for Funding
      and Budgeting Policy 202
 5.4 Extrinsic Attribute Factors 204
   5.4.1 Extrinsic Attribute Checklist 204
   5.4.2 Example of Tailoring Extrinsic Attribute Factor Checklist 205
   5.4.3 Extrinsic Attribute Factor Formulation 205
   5.4.4 Example of Composite Effect of MAF and EAF 206
 5.5 Hardware Factors 208
   5.5.1 Hardware Product Maturity Factor 208
   5.5.2 Example of Hardware Product Maturity Factor 210
   5.5.3 Hardware Product Quality Factor 211
   5.5.4 Example of Hardware Product Quality Factor 215
   5.5.5 Hardware Product Complexity Factor 219
   5.5.6 Example of Hardware Product Complexity Factor 220
   5.5.7 Hardware Product Concurrency Factor 221
   5.5.8 Example of Expanded Hardware Product Concurrency Factor 222
   5.5.9 Hardware Process Maturity Factor 223
   5.5.10 Example Hardware Process Maturity Factor 224

xii            CONTENTS

      5.5.11 Hardware Process Quality Factor 226
      5.5.12 Example of Hardware Process Quality Factor 228
      5.5.13 Example of Composite Hardware Product and Process
             Quality Factors 229
      5.5.14 Hardware Process Complexity Factor 233
      5.5.15 Example of Composite Hardware Process Maturity, Quality,
             and Complexity Factors 234
      5.5.16 Hardware Process Concurrency Factor 236
      5.5.17 Example of Composite Hardware Process Maturity, Quality,
             Complexity, and Concurrency Factors 237

5.6   Software Factors 239
      5.6.1  Computer Operation 239
      5.6.2  Software Program 241
      5.6.3  Software Management Attribute Factor 241
      5.6.4  Software Product and Process Maturity Factors 243
      5.6.5  Example of Composite Software Product and Process
            Maturity Factors 244
      5.6.5  Software Product or Process Quality Factor 245
      5.6.7  Software Product or Process Complexity Factor 246
      5.6.8  Software Product or Process Concurrency Factor 247
      5.6.9  Example of Composite Software Product and Process Maturity,
            Quality, Complexity, and Concurrency Factors 248

5.7   Service Factors 250
      5.7.1  Service Product or Process Maturity Factors 251
      5.7.2  Service Product or Process Quality Factor 251
      5.7.3  Service Product Quality Factor Example 253
      5.7.4  Service Product or Process Complexity Factor 254
      5.7.5  Service Product or Process Concurrency Factor 254

5.8   Summary 255
5.9   Exercises 256
      5.9.1  Risk Determinant Factor Dominance 256
      5.9.2  Hardware Risk Determinant Factors 256
      5.9.3  Extrinsic Attribute Checklist 256
      5.9.4  Composite Management Attribute and Extrinsic Attribute Factors 257
      5.9.5  Risk Cost Estimate 257
      5.9.6  Revised Risk Cost Estimate 257
      5.9.7  Hardware Product Complexity Factor 257
      5.9.8  Generation Breakdowns and Lists of Part Numbers 257
      5.9.9  Hardware Product and Process Complexity Factors 257
      5.9.10 Risk Exposure in Total Procurement Package 258
      5.9.11 Software Risk Determinant Factors 258
      5.9.12 Software Management Attribute Factor 258
      5.9.13 Composite Software Risk Exposure 258
      5.9.14 Service Risk Determinant Factors 259
      5.9.15 Risk Exposure in Service Products 259
      5.9.16 Service Product or Process Concurrency Factor 259
      5.9.17 Risk Cost Retrospective 259

5.10  References 260

# 6 RISK MODELS 261

- 6.1 Definitions 262
- 6.2 Perspective on Risk Models 264
    - 6.2.1 Selection Criteria 264
    - 6.2.2 Example of Cost as Function of Material 266
    - 6.2.3 Example of Cost as Function of Weight 266
    - 6.2.4 Example of Cost as Function of Volume 267
    - 6.2.5 Application Guidelines 268
- 6.3 Art of Simulation 269
    - 6.3.1 Normal Distribution 270
    - 6.3.2 Tests of Hypothesis 271
    - 6.3.3 Example of Test of Hypothesis with Large Sample 273
    - 6.3.4 Degrees of Freedom 274
    - 6.3.5 Sampling Distributions 275
    - 6.3.6 Student's t Distribution 275
    - 6.3.7 Example of Test of Hypothesis with Small Sample 276
    - 6.3.8 Simulation Approaches 277
    - 6.3.9 Random Numbers 278
    - 6.3.10 Monte Carlo Method 280
    - 6.3.11 Example of the Monte Carlo Method 282
- 6.4 Aggregation vs. Disaggregation 286
    - 6.4.1 Aggregate Modeling 287
    - 6.4.2 Example of Aggregate Modeling 288
    - 6.4.3 Disaggregate Modeling 289
    - 6.4.4 Example of Disaggregate Modeling 291
- 6.5 Summary 293
- 6.6 Exercises 293
    - 6.6.1 Parametric Relationship 293
    - 6.6.2 Law of Large Numbers 294
    - 6.6.3 Central Limit Theorem 294
    - 6.6.4 Area Under Normal Probability Density Curve 294
    - 6.6.5 Area in Tails of Normal Probability Density Function 294
    - 6.6.6 Degrees of Freedom 294
    - 6.6.7 Mean and Standard Deviation 294
    - 6.6.8 Confidence Limits 295
    - 6.6.9 Sampling Distributions 295
    - 6.6.10 Area Under Student's t Probability Density Curve 295
    - 6.6.11 Student's t Distribution 295
    - 6.6.12 Test of Hypothesis 295
    - 6.6.13 Random Numbers 295
    - 6.6.14 Monte Carlo Method 295
    - 6.6.15 Simulation 295
    - 6.6.16 Aggregate Model 296
    - 6.6.17 Disaggregation 296
    - 6.6.18 Disaggregate Modeling 296
- 6.7 References 297

## 7 RISK CONTROL 298
- 7.1 Definitions 301
- 7.2 Organizational Guidelines 302
  - 7.2.1 Technical Risk Management Plan 303
  - 7.2.2 Roles and Responsibilities 303
  - 7.2.3 Configuration Control 303
  - 7.2.4 Performance Tracking and Reporting 303
- 7.3 Procedural Guidelines 304
  - 7.3.1 Funding 304
  - 7.3.2 Design 304
  - 7.3.3 Configuration Control 305
  - 7.3.4 Test 305
  - 7.3.5 Production 305
  - 7.3.6 Facilities 306
  - 7.3.7 Support 306
  - 7.3.8 Management 306
- 7.4 Motivational Guidelines 306
  - 7.4.1 Award Structure 307
  - 7.4.2 Incentive Structure 308
- 7.5 Risk Perspectives 310
  - 7.5.1 Risk Priorities 310
  - 7.5.2 Deliberate Haste 310
  - 7.5.3 Risk Control Teamwork 310
  - 7.5.4 Calculated Risks 311
  - 7.5.5 Margin for Error in Opinion Polls 311
  - 7.5.6 Managing Conceptual Programs 314
- 7.6 Risk Examples 315
  - 7.6.1 Main Battle Tank 315
  - 7.6.2 Pegasus 316
  - 7.6.3 Ford Motor Company 316
  - 7.6.4 Presidential Election 317
  - 7.6.5 Why Companies Fail 317
  - 7.6.6 Why Buildings Fall Down 318
  - 7.6.7 Reengineering the Defense Industry 319
- 7.7 Risk Principles 320
- 7.8 Summary 322
- 7.9 Exercises 323
  - 7.9.1 Lloyd's of London 323
  - 7.9.2 Corporate Losses 323
  - 7.9.3 Standardized Risk Measure 323
  - 7.9.4 Consumer Price Index 324
  - 7.9.5 Short-Term Interest Rates 324
  - 7.9.6 Conflicting Requirements 325
  - 7.9.7 Nuclear Energy 325
  - 7.9.8 Sample Space 326
- 7.10 References 326

**Epilogue 328**

**A  Glossary 332**

**B  Technical Risk Management in the Department of Defense 341**
  B.1  *Acquisition Policy 341*
  B.2  *Technical Risk Management Plan 348*

**C  Solutions to Exercises 351**

**Index 422**

# FOREWORD

Reflecting on the recent celebration of the 500th anniversary of Columbus's discovery of the "New World," it is instructive to remember that this voyage almost didn't make it out of the planning stage because of a faulty risk-benefit assessment.

Columbus had proposed the voyage to Ferdinand and Isabella in 1486. The monarchs promptly set up a special commission of "learned men" to study the elaborate proposal, which they found vague and somewhat arcane. After four years of stormy and unsatisfying discussions with the master mariner, the commission finally rejected the proposal.

To their credit, Ferdinand and Isabella did not abandon Columbus and soon recalled him to the court, not to discuss his plan again, but to name his price for carrying it out. The price was enormous. Columbus insisted on being knighted, appointed grand admiral and viceroy, and given 10 percent of all transactions within his admiralty. Stunned by his audacity and affronted by his unwillingness to compromise, the king and queen dismissed Columbus. Eventually, they relented and accepted all of Columbus's demands, and one of the world's great adventures got under way. I put forth this well-known example because it seems to me all the parties involved would have benefited by some basic exposure to the concept of technical risk management. Columbus could have presented his proposals as containing an element of risk, but considering the potential payoff, well worth the investment. Ferdinand and Isabella could have measured Columbus's demands against the "price of doing nothing." And the commission of "experts" would have had an intellectual framework within which they could evaluate, to some degree, the technical feasibility of a proposal they couldn't quite grasp. If the parties had studied technical risk management, perhaps today we would celebrate 1486, not 1492.

In any case, five centuries after Columbus's voyage, the need for technical risk management continues to manifest itself. Most key players in today's increasingly global economy acknowledge that competitiveness with excellence is essential for survival and growth. As we move into a new millennium, those organizations that master the art of affordable quality will dominate the new world.

At the forefront of engineering skills dedicated to achieving affordable quality is technical risk management. Other concepts have vital roles to play: design to cost makes design converge on cost rather than cost on design; concurrent engineering seeks to integrate design, manufacturing, and product support to shorten the development cycle and reduce the attendant cost; total quality management strives to improve quality and productivity at every level in an organization; and quality function deployment heeds the voice of the customer in design and production processes. But it is technical risk management that helps keep programs on course within specifications, schedule, and cost.

In this book, Dr. Michaels does an excellent job of capturing the fundamentals of technical risk management. He has folded into this book many of the necessary tools and techniques for its practice. The examples and exercises comprise a broad spectrum of role models for the problems managers and engineers face every day in both the private and public sectors. The applications he cites were evolved over decades of increasingly complex and difficult engineering projects, providing new ways to conserve resources while enhancing profitability. Careful study of and adherence to the principles in this book should certainly lead to the achievement of engineering excellence at affordable cost. I commend the text as a valuable addition to the knowledge base of an essential and increasingly important engineering discipline.

Norman R. Augustine
President
Lockheed Martin Corporation

# PREFACE

*Technical Risk Management* is for people who are concerned about bringing high-technology products to the marketplace within allotted time and financial specifications. This includes those who are in marketing, administration, and management as well as those in analysis, design, manufacturing, and marketing. The products can be hardware, software, and service; there is no restriction on the nature of the product.

The title, *Technical Risk Management*, should differentiate this book from those dealing with casualty risk and insurance. The word technical is used in the broad sense to describe the many factors that serve as the framework for the success or failure of ventures in the public and the private sectors.

The cardinal sin in technical writing is forgetting that the reader has nowhere near the author's familiarity with the subject matter. In undertaking the book, I chose to be guilty of explaining the obvious rather than leaving the reader in the dark. Toward this end, I enlist the aid of an ethereal colleague whose name is Analyst.

Analyst helps me guide you through the mazes of words and numbers. We illustrate theoretical relationships with simple exercises and coalesce these relationships with more detailed examples at key points in the chapter. We provide a summary and a number of exercise problems at the end of each chapter as review. There are step-by-step solutions to the problems in Appendix C.

The book is mathematically correct yet does not obfuscate relatively simple notions with complex relationships. We cover theoretical relationships sufficiently to ensure a firm grasp of risk fundamentals and how to address risk problems. To ensure understanding, each chapter includes definitions of key terms used in that chapter. We give these definitions when we first use the terms and repeat them in the glossary in Appendix A.

We stress problem formulation and solution as the learning vehicle. Although not scientific in the rigorous sense, the book emulates the scientific method by going from statements of perceived problems to the formulation of problems in the manner needed to ensure that the right problems are solved and solved properly.

> *For now, do what I tell you. Conviction will come later.*
> *Analyst*

We wrote *Technical Risk Management* in response to the longstanding need for a book of its nature. For example, the risk management needs of the U.S. Department of Defense are as great now as they were decades ago, despite the military's longstanding formalism in addressing risk. We follow this formalism with a significant difference. The military approach is primarily doctrinal, stressing what risk management is and why risk management is needed. The approach in this book is primarily procedural, providing step-by-step methodology and guidance for solving the kind of problems you may face in your daily endeavors. The examples and exercise problems can serve as role models for you.

You should find *Technical Risk Management* easy to read, helpful from the tutorial point of view, and valuable as a reference. Be sure to read the Epilogue that starts on page 328. It will help put what you learned in the proper perspective. For that matter, read it now; it is only four pages long.

Dr. Jack V. Michaels<br>
3515 Idle Hour Drive<br>
Orlando, Florida 32822-3037

# ACKNOWLEDGMENTS

This book is the beneficiary of the pioneering effort of many colleagues whom I recognize for their contribution to the state of the art. I thank them for their suggestions regarding the work.

I am grateful to the Martin Marietta Corporation and the Defense System Management College for insight into their risk management techniques and for source material. I also thank Management Science for supplying the material used in Section 4.5 of the book.

Above all, I am grateful to Betty L. Michaels for her penetrating insight, her infinite patience, and her unending support during the composition of the manuscript. I thank my colleagues Anthony A. Flowers for his critical review of the technical content and Doris M. Huston for her assistance in preparing the manuscript in final form.

# ABOUT THE AUTHOR

Jack V. Michaels, Ph.D, PE, CVS, is Executive Director of Management Science, publishers of technical and business texts and training aids, and Past Editor of Value World, the Journal of the Society of American Value Engineers. Formerly, he was an Instructor at Florida Southern College and Senior Member of the Professional Staff at Martin Marietta Corporation. On two separate occasions, he received the corporation's prestigious "Author of the Year Award" for his publications.

His recent publications include *Understanding the Time Value of Money* (Management Science, 1996) and *Design to Cost* (Wiley 1989-coauthor). Dr. Michaels has a Ph.D Degree in Engineering, MS Degree in Engineering Management, and Bachelor Degrees in Electrical Engineering and Business Administration. He is a Certified Value Specialist in the Society of American Value Engineers and a Registered Professional Engineer in the State of Florida.

# TECHNICAL RISK MANAGEMENT

# CHAPTER 1

# INTRODUCTION

> A dollar of risk avoidance is worth many dollars of risk recovery.
> **Analyst**

Risk recovery is expensive. In this book, we show you how to estimate risk exposure in your undertakings so that you may make cogent decisions on how much to invest in avoiding risk. We suggest a ratio of about four to one. For every four dollars of risk exposure, invest one dollar in risk avoidance. We offer guidance on getting the most out of your investment.

**Risk management** is the executive function of controlling hazards and the consequential perils that organizations encounter in their various undertakings. The essence of risk management is to reduce risk exposure rather than recover from perils that materialize. On this basis, a sound risk management plan stresses risk avoidance as the first line of defense and relies on risk recovery with corrective action or insurance only as a backup.

It follows that technical risk management is the executive function of controlling hazards and perils of a technical nature. Table 1.1 lists a number of perils in the categories of commercially insurable and noninsurable (except at extremely high cost) from the perspective of insurance underwriters. One key distinction between risk management and technical risk management is the reduced dependence of the latter on insurance as a risk countermeasure in bringing products to the marketplace.

Performance bonds and warranties provide some insurance for organizations as customers and users of products. The limited nature of warranties, however, rarely results in adequate cost compensation and leads to issues of negligence (*i.e.*, legal liability) in cases of product malfunction and negligence. Premiums for negligence insurance are quite high (*e.g.*, medical malpractice).

Government agencies and property developers frequently require performance and schedule bonds in large undertakings. Fiduciary organizations obtain financial bonds for personnel handling and disbursing funds. Manufacturers attempt to limit their liability to product replacement, but occasionally purchase insurance against product malfunction. Health and other professional practitioners usually purchase insurance against negligence.

*Table 1.1    Insurability of Perils*

**Insurable Perils**
**Property**: Loss to property from perils that cause destruction or loss of use of the property.
**Personal**: Loss of life, incapacitation, or loss of income from the perils of death or physical injury.
**Performance**: Financial loss from lack of completion of contractual obligation within performance, schedule, and cost specification.
**Negligence**: Loss to property and person, or financial loss from the perils of negligent behavior in the use of motor vehicles, occupancy of buildings, employment, manufacture of products, or from fraudulent behavior, professional nonfeasance, misfeasance, or malfeasance, or other misconduct.

**Noninsurable Perils**
**Production**: Loss from the perils of failure of machinery to function properly, failure to resolve technical problems, exhaustion of raw material and other resources, strikes, absenteeism, or labor unrest.
**Market**: The occurrence of loss from perils of seasonal or cyclical demand, style changes, consumer indifference, or competition from other products.
**Political**: The occurrence of loss from perils of unreasonable or punitive taxation, environmental restrictions, restrictions on free trade, civil disorders, political changes, or war.

For the most part, consequential perils of hazards in the technical arena fall in the commercially uninsurable category. Your best countermeasure for these perils is a technical risk management program over the life cycle of the products of concern.

## 1.1
## DEFINITIONS

The language of technical risk management contains terms with specific meanings. There is immediacy in understanding these terms and abbreviations in undertaking the respective chapters. Therefore, we give definitions of terms and abbreviations in the first section of each chapter and repeat them in the glossary in Appendix A.

Table 1.2 gives definitions of terms and abbreviations used in this chapter. Note, in particular, the terms *hazard, peril, corrective-action cost, corrective-action time, risk cost, risk time,* and *risk exposure*. The point is that perils are events that occur as consequences of hazardous conditions, and recovery from the consequences of perils requires corrective action. Corrective action results in the unforeseen expenditure of time and money.

Hazards and perils are governed by the law of conditional probability. Given a certain hazard, there is a certain probability of occurrence of the consequential peril. Perils have associated probability of occurrence and corrective-action time and cost. Multiplying the former by the latter yields risk time and risk cost. Risk time and risk cost are the probabilistic measures of risk exposure in perils.

Note the definitions of *quality, form, fit,* and *function* and their relationship with the concept of functionality. Note the terms *functional worth* and *return-on-investment* and their relationship to the concepts of affordability and profitability.

The perspective on affordability and profitability varies from suppliers to consumers. Technical risk management and the allied disciplines described in Section 1.2.2 share the challenge of achieving the optimal balance of affordability and profitability, along with the requisite quality and functionality, from the viewpoint of both suppliers and consumers.

## 1.1 Definitions

*Table 1.2   Definitions of Terms and Abbreviations in Chapter 1*

**Affordability**: Characteristic of a system or product with a selling price that approaches its functional worth and is within the limit of what the customer is both able and willing to pay.
**Commitment to excellence**: Philosophy of doing things right the first time.
**Corrective action**: Action taken to offset performance degradation, or schedule or cost perturbations in programs due to perils so that the programs may continue as planned. Also called *work-around* or *risk recovery*.
**Fit**: Property of products given by the static and dynamic interfaces with other components of the systems or products.
**Form**: Property of products given by the attributes of shape, weight, material, and packaging.
**Function**: Property of products given by the operations performed by the products.
**Functional worth**: Cost of least expensive way to perform the intended function.
**Functionality**: Form, fit, and function of products relative to the intended use for the products.
**Hazard**: Condition or action that may result in perilous conditions.
**IR&D**: Independent research and development.
**Life cycle cost**: Cost of product acquisition, operation, support, and disposal.
**Limited warranty**: Guaranty covering product replacement but not extending to the cost consequences of product malfunction.
**Management science**: Body of techniques used to model and improve operations that include decision theory, utility and game theory, queuing theory, forecasting, linear and dynamic programming, distribution modeling, network modeling, inventory modeling, and simulation. Also called *operations research*.
**NASA**: National Aeronautics and Space Administration.
**Peril**: Undesirable event resulting from a hazard.
**Peril probability**: Probability of occurrence of a given peril.
**Peril recovery**: Corrective-action cost and time to recover from a given peril.
**Product**: A system, product, or service.
**Profitability**: Return on investment that is commensurate with the resources expended on producing products.
**Quality**: Degree to which products provide reliable functionality over expected periods of time with expected levels and frequencies of maintenance and repair.
**Risk**: Uncertainty surrounding the loss from a given peril.
**Risk avoidance**: Action taken to reduce risk exposure. Also called *risk reduction*.
**Risk cost**: Product of corrective-action cost for recovery from peril and probability of needing corrective action.
**Risk exposure**: Sum of risk costs and risk times for a given product.
**Risk management**: Executive function of controlling those hazards whose consequential perils cause property loss, personal loss, or legal liability.
**Risk morphology**: Form and structure of hazards and perils contributing to risk exposure.
**Risk recovery**: Corrective action taken to offset performance degradation, or schedule or cost perturbations in programs due to a materialized peril so that the programs may continue as planned. Also called *work-around*.
**Risk time**: Product of corrective-action time for recovery from peril and probability of needing corrective action.
**ROI**: Return-on-investment.
**Scientific method**: Formalized reasoning process that consists of observation, problem formulation, formulation of hypotheses, test of hypotheses, verification.
**Supplier**: Producer or supplier of systems, products, or services.
**Technical risk management**: Executive function of controlling technical hazards and perils.
**User**: Customer or user.
**Window of opportunity**: Period of time for pursuing an opportunity without loss of potential.

## 1.2 TECHNICAL RISK MANAGEMENT OVERVIEW

Table 1.3 lists the major elements and steps comprising the process of **technical risk management**. You should not view risk identification, risk quantification, and risk control as sequential phases. You can undertake as many of the elemental steps simultaneously and in various orders depending on your need.

*Table 1.3   Technical Risk Management Processes*

| Risk Identification | Risk Quantification | Risk Control |
|---|---|---|
| • Establish investigation scope. | • Derive risk hierarchy. | • Establish risk organization. |
| • Indoctrinate personnel. | • Select risk metrics. | • Fund organization and reserve. |
| • Interface allied disciplines. | • Select risk formulation. | • Promulgate best practices. |
| • Define user requirements. | • Establish risk model. | • Implement audit trail. |
| • Establish baseline model. | • Calculate risk exposure. | • Initiate motivational program. |
| • Identify hazards and perils. | • Estimate contingency reserve. | • Reward performance. |

### ■ 1.2.1 Technical Risk Management Absolutes

Table 1.4 lists several absolutes for successful technical risk management. Above all, you must follow a formal methodology from start to finish. Allow no change without full concurrence of all disciplines and document every step along the way. Equally important is the need to indoctrinate and motivate personnel in the technical risk management process. Be sure to involve personnel in the allied disciplines described in Section 1.2.2.

*Table 1.4   Technical Risk Management Absolutes*

- Obtain the full commitment and support of top management.
- Implement technical risk management within the window of opportunity.
- Maintain closed-loop, real-time command, and control.
- Indoctrinate and motivate personnel and suppliers.
- Publicize and reward performance.

Not only do you need top management's commitment and support; it must be visible to your people. We have rarely seen technical risk management fail when people knew that top management wanted it to succeed. On the other hand, we have rarely seen it succeed when people did not know the feelings of top management. Top management should participate in the technical risk management process and, as a minimum, attend progress review sessions and performance recognition ceremonies.

The essence of technical risk management is the reduction of **risk exposure** to a cost-effective level. This is part of rational management's concern for cost-effective operation of entire organizations. Learning from mistakes is the key. [1]

## 1.2 Technical Risk Management Overview

The annals of commerce and industry are replete with accounts of repeated mistakes by organizations that knew better, bringing to mind George Santayana's words, "Remember the past or be condemned to repeat it."

An amazingly large number of organizations in both the public and private sectors vacillate in annual funding for **independent research and development (IR&D)** tasks, then wonder why there is so little return-on-investment from IR&D. Patience is a sound business practice as well as a virtue.

Technical risk management identifies uncertainties in achieving performance, schedule, and cost goals; quantifies uncertainties in terms of risk exposure; and takes action to eliminate uncertainties to the greatest extent possible. This process is **risk avoidance**.

**Return-on-investment (ROI)** should determine the extent to which you pursue risk avoidance. Total risk avoidance would be not only extremely costly but also nearly impossible to achieve. **Risk recovery** connotes the **corrective action** or work-around used to offset the effects of **hazards** and **perils** that cannot be avoided.

The need for vehicular travel in snow is an example of such a hazard; one of the consequential perils is being in an accident. The risk avoidance measure in this case is the use of snow tires or chains. The risk recovery measure would be towing and repairs, which would cost much more than the cost of snow tires and chains combined.

Thus, the challenge is to implement an appropriate degree of risk avoidance with consideration of the ROI in the products of concern. In general, you will find risk avoidance to be orders of magnitude more cost-effective than risk recovery accomplished with work-around or other corrective action.

As a case in point, consider the spacecraft *Galileo*, **National Aeronautics and Space Administration's (NASA)** mission to the planet Jupiter. *Galileo* has been plagued by a malfunctioning main antenna since the launch of the spacecraft in October 1989.

The main antenna has not opened properly because a trio of inch-long pins have jammed against the central mast, preventing the ribs of the umbrella-like antenna from unfolding completely. The consequences are degraded communication with the ground station. In a recent news release, NASA revealed that, in the interest of economy, it had decided to ship the spacecraft to the launch site by truck rather than by aircraft. NASA now believes that the shock and vibration which the spacecraft experienced during transportation shook loose most of the powder lubricant that was to have allowed the pins to slide out once *Galileo* was deployed in space. NASA reached this conclusion following the launch of four of its Tracking and Data Relay Spacecraft with similar antennas, which had been air transported to the launch site. The antennas functioned properly over the expected lifetime of the spacecraft.

The cost saving from shipping *Galileo* by truck was about $210,000. It is impossible to estimate the additional operation and support cost on the *Galileo* program to compensate for the malfunctioning antenna; however, the ratio of risk recovery cost to risk avoidance cost is unquestionably great.

More recently, one badly positioned bolt on the space shuttle *Atlantis* doomed the $379 million tethered satellite experiment. The experiment had been designed to fly a satellite at the end of a 12-mile cord. Because of the way the bolt was installed, the deployment mechanism jammed repeatedly, never allowing the satellite to travel more than 850 feet from *Atlantis*.

Still more recently, a design error marred the optical performance of the space telescope *Hubble*. Repairing *Hubble* was the primary mission of the crew of the space shuttle *Endeavor* during the December 1993 mission. The crew replaced a defective mirror assembly and restored *Hubble's* performance.

The quality of observational data from *Hubble* is most impressive, to the delight of the scientific community. NASA estimates the cost of $321 million for a space shuttle mission. Assuming a fully operational mirror assembly costs $2.5 million, the ratio of risk recovery cost to risk avoidance cost in this instance is about 128:1.

### ■ 1.2.2 Allied Disciplines

The ill-fated *Apollo 1* and *Challenger 10* and the misadventures of *Galileo* and *Hubble* illustrate the consequences of escalating schedule and economic issues over environmental and design factors. In the case of *Galileo*, the more logical approach would have been to equip the trucks carrying the spacecraft with shock and vibration sensors and to use the data as the basis for the launch decision. Practitioners of technical risk management and the allied disciplines listed in Table 1.5 attempt to follow this approach.

*Table 1.5    Benefits of Allied Disciplines*

---

**Concurrent engineering**: Systematic approach to the concurrent design of products and their related manufacturing and support, requiring developers to consider simultaneously all elements of the product life cycle from conception to disposal in order to shorten the development cycle. [2, 3]

**Design of experiments**: Also called "robust design" and "Taguchi Method." Methodology intended to identify important and unimportant variables in product or process designs, reduce the variation on the important variables through close tolerancing, and open up tolerances on the unimportant variables to reduce cost. [4, 5, 6]

**Design to cost**: Organized activity intended to make design converge on cost instead of allowing cost to converge on design, to elevate cost to the same level of concern as performance and schedule, and to mandate affordability from the perspective of customers. [7]

**Quality function deployment**: Overall concept that provides the means of translating user requirements, stated in the user's terms, into appropriate technical requirements for each stage of product development, production, and support. [8, 9]

**System engineering**: Iterative process wherein functional and performance requirements are identified and translated successively into lower-level functional and performance requirements, and then synthesized into schemes for implementation that can fulfill requirements. [10, 11]

**Total quality management**: Continuous process of improvement involving everyone and everything in an organization in a totally integrated effort aimed at improved performance at every level and increased customer and user satisfaction. [12, 13]

**Value engineering**: Also called "value analysis" and "value management." Systematic application of techniques to identify the functions of products or services, establish their functional worth, and provide essential functions reliably at the lowest overall cost. [14, 15, 16]

---

We call these disciplines "allied" because their concurrent performance supposedly yields synergistic benefits in the quality, functionality, affordability, and profitability of products. For example, consider the approach and objectives of concurrent engineering, design to cost, technical risk management, and value engineering.

Proponents of concurrent engineering cite the shrinking window of opportunity for cost-effective design (v., Section 1.2.4) as the basis for their advocacy. By bringing together all the disciplines involved in bringing products to the marketplace during the conceptual phase of programs, develop-

## 1.2 Technical Risk Management Overview

ment cycles are shortened and products are optimized. Overall, the cost of development, production, and support would be less than the classical, serial approach to development and production.

The essence of design to cost is to elevate cost to the same level of concern as performance and schedule in order to achieve optimal balance of functionality, quality, affordability, and profitability. Technical risk management strives to prevent the erosion of such optimality as programs reach fruition.

Value engineering, which is concerned with the functional worth of products rather than the existing form of their implementation, seeks answers to such questions as: What is the essential job to be done? How should the job be done? How long should the job take? and How much should the job cost? Realistic answers to such questions ensure product success in the marketplace.

On the down side, there is risk in assuming that adequate resources will be available for the simultaneous, up-front conduct of these allied disciplines. In addition to the competition for funding, there is a natural tendency to avoid expenditures until they are absolutely necessary. This is the reason why the U.S. Department of Defense, in its acquisition directives, requires concurrent performance of technical risk management and design to cost from the start of major programs. [17]

### ■ 1.2.3 User Requirements

In many instances, users of products are not the customers purchasing the products. The user's perspectives may differ significantly from those of the customer and lead to problems in the transactions of interest. Failure to recognize the user's requirements, as well as those of the customer, will adversely affect product acceptance.

We often use the words *quality, functionality, affordability,* and *profitability* interchangeably with the words *reliability, performance, schedule,* and *cost* in expressing user requirements. The former words are more global in their meaning and encompass issues of preference and motivation among those who produce and sell products and those who buy and use them.

**Quality** is the degree to which **products** provide reliable functionality over expected periods of time with expected levels and frequencies of maintenance and repair. **Functionality** connotes the form, fit, and function of products relative to the intended use.

**Affordability** is the characteristic of a product with a selling price that approaches its functional worth and is within the limit of what the customer is both able and willing to pay. **Profitability** is the ROI that is commensurate with the resources expended in producing the product.

The very important concept of the functional worth of a product is key to understanding affordability from the customer's perspective. **Functional worth** is the cost of the least expensive way to perform the intended function of a product. The functional worth of a picture hanger is the cost of a nail, the least expensive way to hang a picture; that of a reusable waterproof container is the cost of a resealable plastic bag.

Functional worth is dependent on what the product does (*i.e.,* functionality); its availability at the time it is needed; and what it costs. The functional worth of a product may vary as time elapses. Occasionally, there may be only one known way to perform a function and, in that case, the functional worth is whatever you have to pay for the function to be performed. As Henry Ford allegedly said, "You can have any color you want so long as it's black."

Differences in perspective are quite commonplace in the military marketplace. In weapon systems acquisition, the customers are usually the procurement commands such as the U.S. Army

Materiel Command. The interim user would be a training and combat doctrine command such as the U.S. Army Combat Development Command. The ultimate user would be some combat organization such as an infantry division.

The Materiel Command, with the major share of the initial funding responsibility, is concerned primarily with the affordability of weapon systems. The Combat Development Command, not sharing the funding responsibility until a milestone called "Initial Operational Capability" has been achieved, is more concerned with quality and functionality, and, frequently, there is contention between the two commands.

Concern for quality and functionality ultimately rests with the combat organizations who deploy the weapon systems following a milestone called "Required Operational Capability." The funding responsibility returns to the Materiel Command as the ultimate customer.

In the background are the **suppliers** of weapon systems who are concerned, in the near term, with the profitability in the weapons systems and, in the long term, with the quality, functionality, and affordability of their products for future business. Customers and **users** share the concern for profitability, from a motivational viewpoint, since they need these suppliers to support deployed weapon systems as well as develop countermeasures against future threats.

Analogous situations exist in industrial and commercial organizations in their roles as both suppliers and users. Although the primary concern as suppliers is profitability, they should strike a balance with quality, functionality, and affordability commensurate with the balance they expect as users of products they purchase.

For example, airlines are both customers and users of aircraft in their primary role of supplying transportation. Airlines desire quality and functionality but demand affordability and profitability as they alternate between roles. Passengers and shippers desire affordability as customers but demand quality and functionality as users.

### ■ *1.2.4 Window of Opportunity*

There is a **window of opportunity** early in the life cycle of programs where prompt action will effect significant risk avoidance with relatively small investment in capital or other resources. Figure 1.1 illustrates the exponentially diminishing optimal period for cost-effective risk avoidance.

Typically, 40 to 70 percent of product and process designs in the high-technology arena have been ordained by the end of the conceptual phase of a given program. This point is indicated by the crossover of the two curves in Figure 1.1. The area between the two curves to the left of this point is the window of opportunity for cost-effective implementation of risk-avoidance measures as well as improvements in product designs and production processes.

Beyond this point, risk avoidance opportunities decrease exponentially, leaving risk recovery as the primary tool for risk management. The window of opportunity shrinks exponentially as programs mature; potential problems become self-fulfilling prophecies. In addition, the cost of implementing risk avoidance or corrective action increases exponentially.

> *Risk avoidance is corrective action with the greatest return-on-investment.*
> ***Analyst***

## 1.2 Technical Risk Management Overview

As we stated in Section 1.2.2, the shrinking window of opportunity is basis for advocating concurrent engineering during the conceptual phase of programs. The issue of committing sufficient resources to do the job is the stumbling block. [18]

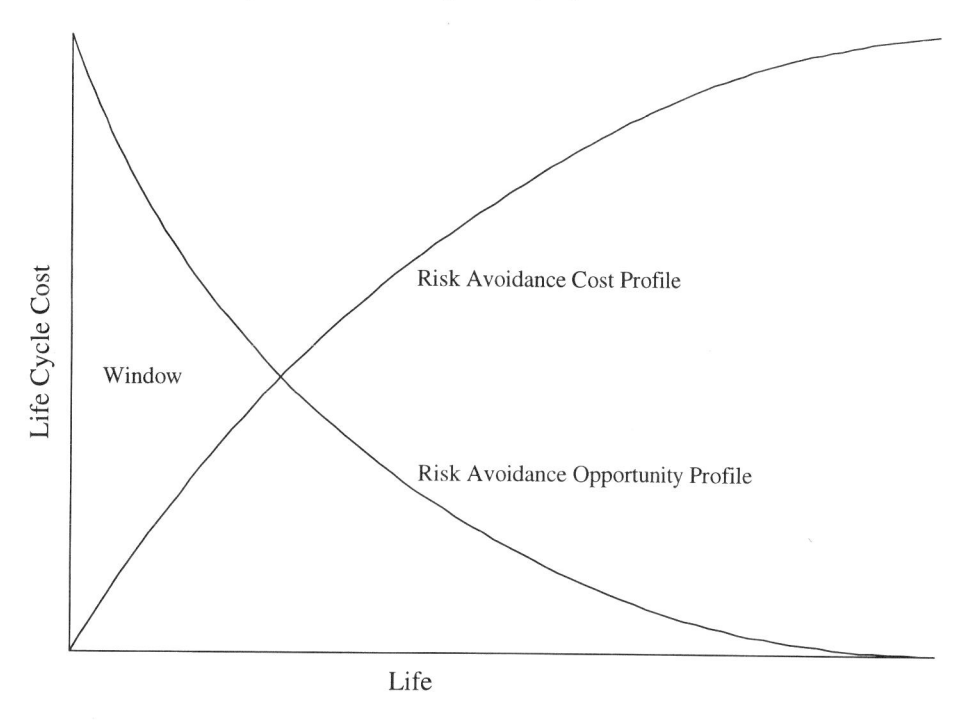

**Figure 1.1** Window of Opportunity

Table 1.6 reveals the continuum of decisions that management should address while the window of opportunity remains open. There is need for deliberate haste, because the window closes early in program life cycles.

The decision categories in Table 1.6 are extremely interrelated and serve to compound the difficulty in making timely, concurrent decisions. As a consequence, there is a strong tendency to make the decisions in the sequence given in the table rather than attempt to make the decisions concurrently. The window of opportunity may close on the continuum of decisions before completion, but the problems that begged for resolution remain.

> *There once lived a king with an aversion to bad news. Whenever a messenger arrived with bad news, he would suffer decapitation. The king quickly ran out of messengers, but he never ran out of bad news.*
>
> **Parable of the King's Messenger**

*Table 1.6    Continuum of Decisions*

**Product Decisions**
    System architecture
        Piece parts technology
            Fabrication and assembly technology
                Materials selection
                      Pricing structure

**Process Decisions**
    Make or buy
        Manufacturing processes
            Tooling and testing philosophy
                Quality assurance philosophy
                      Facilitization

**Program Decisions**
    Procurement strategy
        Warranty and support philosophy
            Product improvement

### ■ 1.2.5 Best Practices

The concept of best practices, which is under the stewardship of the U.S. Navy's Best Manufacturing Practices Program in Arlington, Virginia, evolved from the work of the Defense Science Board Task Force on Transition from Development to Production. [19]

    The effort attempts to enlighten both government and industry by identifying specific practices in current use and their potentially adverse consequences in terms of cost, schedule, performance, and readiness. It then identifies proven best practices which avoid or alleviate these consequences, and provides sufficient information to understand their rationale and adopt the practices.

    Representatives of the Best Manufacturing Practices Program have surveyed a large number of organizations for their adherence to best practices. Table 1.7, which is the checklist for addressing technical risk management, is one of the many checklists used in the survey. The risk metrics and formulation we evolve in Chapters 3 and 5 build from Items 1 through 3 in the table. Item 4 provides the rationale for our discussion of aggregate vs. disaggregate modeling in Chapters 4 and 6.

*Table 1.7    Best Practices Technical Risk Management Checklist [19]*

1. Is a specific technical risk assessment and reporting program in place?
2. Are periodic formal reports provided to all levels of management on the technical status, corrective actions, and subsequent program impact?
3. Have technical risk indicators been generated for design, test, manufacturing, cost, and management?
4. Have all top-level technical requirements been allocated to the lowest design and test levels?

## 1.2 Technical Risk Management Overview

ment cycles are shortened and products are optimized. Overall, the cost of development, production, and support would be less than the classical, serial approach to development and production.

The essence of design to cost is to elevate cost to the same level of concern as performance and schedule in order to achieve optimal balance of functionality, quality, affordability, and profitability. Technical risk management strives to prevent the erosion of such optimality as programs reach fruition.

Value engineering, which is concerned with the functional worth of products rather than the existing form of their implementation, seeks answers to such questions as: What is the essential job to be done? How should the job be done? How long should the job take? and How much should the job cost? Realistic answers to such questions ensure product success in the marketplace.

On the down side, there is risk in assuming that adequate resources will be available for the simultaneous, up-front conduct of these allied disciplines. In addition to the competition for funding, there is a natural tendency to avoid expenditures until they are absolutely necessary. This is the reason why the U.S. Department of Defense, in its acquisition directives, requires concurrent performance of technical risk management and design to cost from the start of major programs. [17]

### ■ 1.2.3 User Requirements

In many instances, users of products are not the customers purchasing the products. The user's perspectives may differ significantly from those of the customer and lead to problems in the transactions of interest. Failure to recognize the user's requirements, as well as those of the customer, will adversely affect product acceptance.

We often use the words *quality, functionality, affordability,* and *profitability* interchangeably with the words *reliability, performance, schedule,* and *cost* in expressing user requirements. The former words are more global in their meaning and encompass issues of preference and motivation among those who produce and sell products and those who buy and use them.

**Quality** is the degree to which **products** provide reliable functionality over expected periods of time with expected levels and frequencies of maintenance and repair. **Functionality** connotes the form, fit, and function of products relative to the intended use.

**Affordability** is the characteristic of a product with a selling price that approaches its functional worth and is within the limit of what the customer is both able and willing to pay. **Profitability** is the ROI that is commensurate with the resources expended in producing the product.

The very important concept of the functional worth of a product is key to understanding affordability from the customer's perspective. **Functional worth** is the cost of the least expensive way to perform the intended function of a product. The functional worth of a picture hanger is the cost of a nail, the least expensive way to hang a picture; that of a reusable waterproof container is the cost of a resealable plastic bag.

Functional worth is dependent on what the product does (*i.e.*, functionality); its availability at the time it is needed; and what it costs. The functional worth of a product may vary as time elapses. Occasionally, there may be only one known way to perform a function and, in that case, the functional worth is whatever you have to pay for the function to be performed. As Henry Ford allegedly said, "You can have any color you want so long as it's black."

Differences in perspective are quite commonplace in the military marketplace. In weapon systems acquisition, the customers are usually the procurement commands such as the U.S. Army

Materiel Command. The interim user would be a training and combat doctrine command such as the U.S. Army Combat Development Command. The ultimate user would be some combat organization such as an infantry division.

The Materiel Command, with the major share of the initial funding responsibility, is concerned primarily with the affordability of weapon systems. The Combat Development Command, not sharing the funding responsibility until a milestone called "Initial Operational Capability" has been achieved, is more concerned with quality and functionality, and, frequently, there is contention between the two commands.

Concern for quality and functionality ultimately rests with the combat organizations who deploy the weapon systems following a milestone called "Required Operational Capability." The funding responsibility returns to the Materiel Command as the ultimate customer.

In the background are the **suppliers** of weapon systems who are concerned, in the near term, with the profitability in the weapons systems and, in the long term, with the quality, functionality, and affordability of their products for future business. Customers and **users** share the concern for profitability, from a motivational viewpoint, since they need these suppliers to support deployed weapon systems as well as develop countermeasures against future threats.

Analogous situations exist in industrial and commercial organizations in their roles as both suppliers and users. Although the primary concern as suppliers is profitability, they should strike a balance with quality, functionality, and affordability commensurate with the balance they expect as users of products they purchase.

For example, airlines are both customers and users of aircraft in their primary role of supplying transportation. Airlines desire quality and functionality but demand affordability and profitability as they alternate between roles. Passengers and shippers desire affordability as customers but demand quality and functionality as users.

### ■ *1.2.4 Window of Opportunity*

There is a **window of opportunity** early in the life cycle of programs where prompt action will effect significant risk avoidance with relatively small investment in capital or other resources. Figure 1.1 illustrates the exponentially diminishing optimal period for cost-effective risk avoidance.

Typically, 40 to 70 percent of product and process designs in the high-technology arena have been ordained by the end of the conceptual phase of a given program. This point is indicated by the crossover of the two curves in Figure 1.1. The area between the two curves to the left of this point is the window of opportunity for cost-effective implementation of risk-avoidance measures as well as improvements in product designs and production processes.

Beyond this point, risk avoidance opportunities decrease exponentially, leaving risk recovery as the primary tool for risk management. The window of opportunity shrinks exponentially as programs mature; potential problems become self-fulfilling prophecies. In addition, the cost of implementing risk avoidance or corrective action increases exponentially.

> *Risk avoidance is corrective action with the greatest return-on-investment.*
> ***Analyst***

### 1.2.6 Scientific Method

As an executive-driven process, technical risk management has also been called **commitment to excellence**. It entails doing things right the first time they are undertaken. Commitment to excellence ensures that the technical and financial goals of supplier and customer will be realized to the benefit of both.

The **scientific method** is inherent in the commitment to excellence. It is a formalized reasoning process that consists of: observation; formulation of problems; formulation of hypotheses regarding the causes of the problems; test of hypotheses; and verification of hypotheses.

The taxonomy of risk exposure in Table 1.8 is an example of the scientific method in problem formulation. We attempt to state perceived problems in precise, concise, and complete mathematical descriptions. Note the logical flow from the hazards statement to equating **risk cost** and **risk time** to risk exposure.

*Table 1.8   Taxonomy of Risk Exposure*

- Hazards are by-products of actions following decisions.
- Hazards produce consequential perils.
- Perils are probabilistic events.
- **Peril recovery** requires corrective action.
- Corrective action imposes additional time and cost.
- Product of corrective-action time and **peril probability** yields risk time.
- Product of corrective-action cost and peril probability yields risk cost.
- Risk time and risk cost equal risk exposure.

Figure 1.2 shows the flow of activities in the scientific method. You can see the iterative nature (*i.e.*, feedback loop) of the scientific method from the observation of an event to verification of the hypothesis regarding the cause of the event. The challenge is to formulate the problem and hypothesis with the least number of iterations.

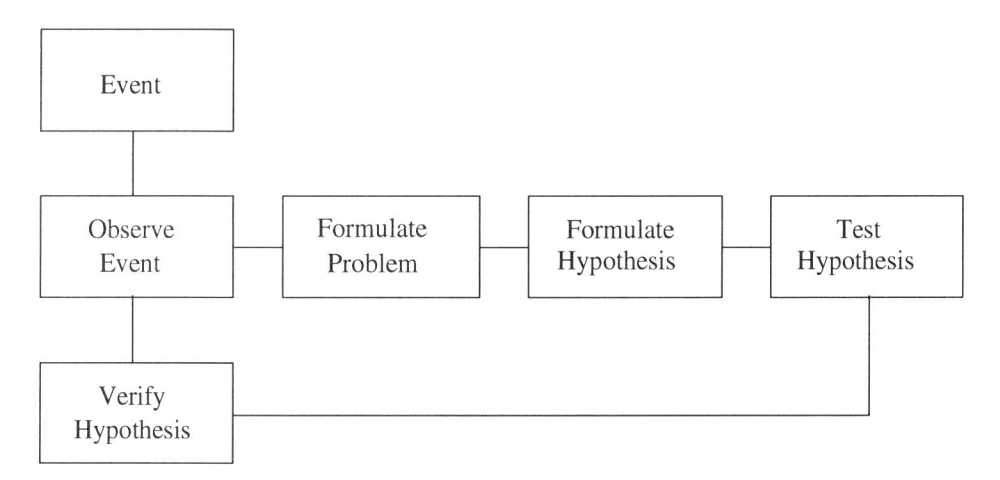

**Figure 1.2**   Scientific Method

**Management science**, also called "operations research," is a depository of techniques that have become the modern-day tool kit for the scientific method. The essence of management science is quantitative methods for decision making. Management science methods are adaptable to a wide range of problems in technical risk management, and include decision theory, game theory, linear programming, and forecasting. [20]

Decision theory determines alternate approaches for product implementation. Game theory is used to choose among approaches where external forces are at play or to select business strategies where competition is a factor.

Linear programming is one of the best-known tools of management science. A general statement of its objective is that it is used to determine an optimal allocation of an organization's limited resources among competing demands. There are innumerable problems in business and industry that can be approached as allocation problems and solved with linear programming.

Forecasting has as its objective the prediction of future events or condition. You would use forecasting to attempt an accurate but simplified representation of future reality. The essential challenge is to include those factors that are critical and exclude those that are not.

The forecasting process is systematic and definitive, but uses techniques that are dependent on human judgment. Choice may be made today; however, the consequences of decisions based on the forecasts occur sometime in the future. The quality of decisions depends in large measure on the quality of the forecasts.

For example, in planning highway projects, planners use forecasting. Increasing traffic congestion and number of accidents, however, would suggest otherwise.

### ■ *1.2.7 Example of the Built-Up Cube Problem*

There is an unfortunate tendency to short-circuit the scientific method with intuition when facing problems of a complex nature, inevitably leading to uneconomical utilization of time and money. To demonstrate the consequences of this tendency, consider the configuration shown in Figure 1.3 that consists of 64 unit cubes. The dimensions of the configuration are 4 unit cubes by 4 unit cubes by 4 unit cubes.

The question asked is, "How many built-up cubes of various dimensions can you compose within the confines of the illustration?"

You would initially determine the forms of built-up configurations which are possible with 64 unit cubes. Four possible forms of built-up configurations are possible. These are: 1 unit cube by 1 unit cube by 1 unit cube; 2 unit cubes by 2 unit cubes by 2 unit cubes; 3 unit cubes by 3 unit cubes by 3 unit cubes; and 4 unit cubes by 4 unit cubes by 4 unit cubes. It is obvious that the 1 by 1 by 1 configuration could occupy 64 positions and that the 4 by 4 by 4 configuration could occupy only one position. The number of positions which could be occupied by the other two configurations are not as obvious. You could count the number of possible positions which could be occupied by built-up cubes of the various sizes possible. The effort, however, becomes increasingly more difficult as the number of unit cubes increases.

At this point, let us invite Analyst to take over. In accordance with the scientific method, Analyst first establishes the technical approach to solving the problem.

## 1.2 Technical Risk Management Overview

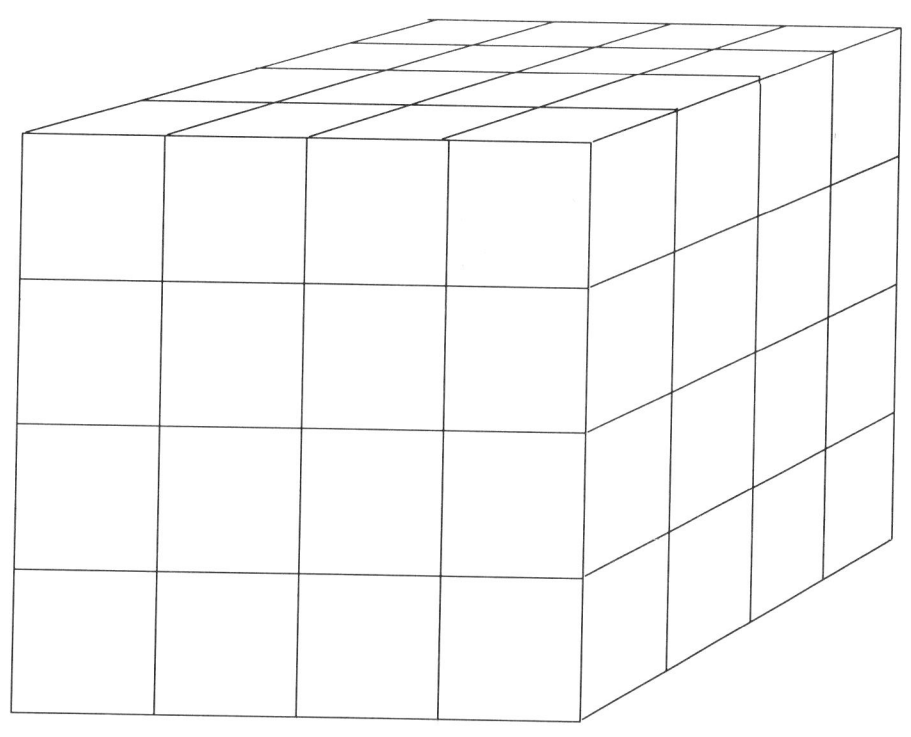

**Figure 1.3** Configuration of 64 Unit Cubes

The steps Analyst follows are the following:

1. Derive the hypothesis governing the number of positions.
2. Verify the hypothesis by counting the number of positions.

Analyst hypothesizes that every dimensional increase in the built-up cube configuration causes an equal decrease in the number of positions which the built-up cube can occupy along each of the three axes. For example, the 1 by 1 by 1 configuration can occupy 4 positions in each of the three axes for a total of (4)(4)(4), or 64 positions. The 2 by 2 by 2 configuration can occupy $(4-1)(4-1)(4-1)$, or 27 positions, and the 3 by 3 by 3 configuration can occupy $(4-2)(4-2)(4-2)$, or 8 positions.

Analyst derives the following relationship for the number of positions that $n$ cubes could occupy:

$$n = x^3 + (x-1)^3 + (x-2)^3 + \ldots + (x-n+1)^3. \tag{1.1}$$

Substituting $n = 4$ in Equation 1.1, Analyst obtains

$$\begin{aligned} n &= 4^3 + (4-1)^3 + (4-2)^3 + (4-3)^2 \\ &= 4^3 + 3^3 + 2^3 + 1^3 \\ &= 100. \end{aligned} \tag{1.2}$$

Analyst verifies the hypothesis by counting the number of positions which can be occupied by built-up cubes with the various dimensions. Analyst obtains the same total of 100 positions.

Can you imagine how much more difficult an intuitive solution would have been if there were more than 64 unit cubes in Figure 1.3? Would you care to estimate the number of built-up cubes you could form with a configuration of 8 by 6 by 4 unit cubes?

## 1.3
## ORGANIZATION OF THE BOOK

Figure 1.4 illustrates the organization of the book and the subject matter of the chapters and appendixes. The chapters encompass the elements of the technical risk-management processes you saw earlier in Table 1.3. Each chapter addresses pertinent relationships and includes a variety of examples and exercises that can serve as role models for a broad spectrum of problems. Appendix C contains step-by-step solutions to these exercises.

The chapters build from risk fundamentals and metrics through risk baselines, formulation, models, and control. By the end of the last chapter, you should have a good understanding of the elements of technical risk management and a firm grasp of the methodology.

**Chapter 2 RISK FUNDAMENTALS** offers definitions of risk principles, explores the relationship between hazards and perils, and illustrates the concept of risk morphology that encompasses risk causatives and risk determinants. The chapter explores the probabilistic nature of risk and illuminates the interrelationships of risk time, risk cost, and risk network, and the concepts of risk dominance, and first-order and second-order risk determinant factors.

**Chapter 3 RISK METRICS** involves the risk determinant factors for estimating the risk exposure in the production of products, which are characterized as hardware, software, and service. Numerous examples illustrate the applications of the factors.

**Chapter 4 RISK BASELINES** provides the baseline for the risk models in Chapter 5. The subjects include: baseline time estimate; baseline cost estimate; cost estimating; and learning curves. Fiscal reality is the essence of credible estimates. Thus, Chapter 4 includes the subjects of time value of money and price indexes, which the U.S. Bureau of the Census updates monthly and annually in the *Statistical Abstract of the United States*. [21]

**Chapter 5 RISK FORMULATION** presents the kit of tools used in deriving risk determinant factors and estimating risk exposure in the development and production of hardware, software, and service products. Chapter 5 develops the formulation for management and extrinsic factors and product and process risk determinant factors.

**Chapter 6 RISK MODELS** applies this kit of tools to the transformation of baseline models into risk models for estimating risk exposure in terms of risk time and risk cost. Chapter 6 includes the subjects of model categories, art of simulation, risk determinant factors, and disaggregate, aggregate, and hybrid modeling.

Aggregate models provide results that are equivalent to those provided by top-down estimating approaches. Disaggregate models provide results that are equivalent to those from bottom-up estimating. Hybrid models employ combinations of both.

**Chapter 7 RISK CONTROL** offers some guidance to the high-technology community on the art of surviving in the third millennium. The chapter provides organizational and procedural

## 1.3 Organization of the Book

guidelines for cost-effective risk control. The chapter gives motivational schema for your employees and contractors. The section on risk perspectives suggests a philosophy and outlook for risk control practitioners. It includes a discussion of risk exposure in opinion surveys and how to manage conceptual programs. The chapter presents some risk examples and offers some principles for risk control that you may want to consider on your next assignment.

|  |  |
|---|---|
| 1 Introduction | Definitions, Overview, Scientific Method, Organization of Book, Abbreviations, Symbology, and Conventions, Exercises, References. |
| 2 Risk Fundamentals | Definitions, Risk Principles, Risk Morphology, Probabilistic Nature of Risk, Risk Dominance, Summary, Exercises, References. |
| 3 Risk Metrics | Definitions, Issues of Realism and Credibility, Selection and Tailoring Process, Attributes Weighting, Rating Schema, Risk Determinant Factors, Summary, Exercises, References. |
| 4 Risk Baselines | Definitions, Product network, Baseline Time Estimate, **Baseline** Cost Estimate, Time Value of Money, Summary, Exercises, References. |
| 5 Risk Formulation | Definitions, Perspective on Risk Determinant Factors, Management Attribute Factor, Extrinsic Attitude Factor, Hardware Factors, Software Factors, Service Factors, Summary, Exercises, References. |
| 6 Risk Models | Definitions, Model Categories, Art of Simulation, Aggregation Versus Disaggregation, Summary, Exercises, References. |
| 7 Risk Control | Definitions, Risk Observations, Risk Lessons, Risk Discipline, Motivational Guidelines, Organizational Guidelines, Summary, Exercises, References. |
| Epilogue | Getting Started in Technical Risk Management; Dealing with Apathy and Opposition. |
| Appendixes | Glossary, Technical Risk Management in The Department of Defense, Solutions to Exercises. |

**Figure 1.4** Organization of Book

Each chapter concludes with a summary, exercises, and a list of references. The summary serves to review the key points and relationships developed in the chapter. The exercises can serve as role models for the kind of problems that you encounter in your everyday activities.

Whether we like it or not, many programs go forth without formal technical risk management. As a matter of fact, many programs go forth with no concern for risk at all. The **EPILOGUE** offers some guidance on getting started in technical risk management and dealing with apathy and opposition that you will most assuredly encounter.

The language of technical risk management contains terms with specific meanings which you should understand as you read the respective chapters. We give definitions in the first section of each chapter. Take a moment to peruse the definitions before launching into the chapter. We repeat the definitions in **Appendix A GLOSSARY**.

**Appendix B TECHNICAL RISK MANAGEMENT IN THE DEPARTMENT OF DEFENSE (DoD)** is not intended just for those interested in contracting in the military marketplace. Components of the DoD have been at the forefront of technical risk management and allied disciplines such as design to cost and value engineering for many years and are worthy of emulation. Be sure to read the section on the technical risk management plan.

The book concludes with **Appendix C SOLUTIONS TO EXERCISES**. Step-by-step solutions to chapter exercises are given in this appendix. Please accept the challenge to solve the exercises on your own before looking at the solutions.

## 1.4 ABBREVIATIONS, SYMBOLOGY, AND CONVENTIONS

The book makes frequent use of abbreviations from Latin expressions with the intent of aiding the narrative flow. Table 1.9 gives the abbreviations and the meanings of the expressions.

*Table 1.9    Abbreviations Used in Text*

| Abbreviation | Latin Expression | Meaning |
|---|---|---|
| ca. | *Circa* | About |
| e.g. | *Exempli gratia* | For example |
| etc. | *Et cetera* | And so forth |
| f.f. | *Folium* | Following pages |
| i.e. | *Id est* | That is |
| n.b. | *Nota bene* | Note well |
| q.e. | *Quod est* | Which is |
| v. | *Vide* | See |
| viz. | *Videlicet* | Namely |

We also make frequent use of the Greek alphabet in examples and problems in the text. To paraphrase George Bernard Shaw, "Nobody can say a word against Greek. It stamps a book at once as an authoritative work."

Table 1.10 gives the names of the letters of the Greek alphabet along with the upper-case and lower-case symbols for the respective letters. Note that there are only 24 letters in the Greek alphabet as opposed to 26 in the English alphabet.

Do you know which English letters do not have Greek roots? The exercise in Section 1.5.3 also asks this question. You will find the answer in Appendix C or in an unabridged dictionary.

## 1.5 Exercises

The book follows the symbolic conventions given in Table 1.11 for the mathematical formulation in equations and in the narrative of the text. Symbols appear in bold type. With respect to probability and statistics, we use lower-case Greek letters for parameters of populations and the equivalent lower-case English letters for statistics of samples. For example, the Greek letter $\mu$ denotes the mean of a population; the English letter $m$ denotes the mean of a sample. The Greek letter denotes the standard deviation of a population; the English letter $s$ denotes the standard deviation of a sample. The Greek upper-case letter denotes summation.

*Table 1.10    Greek Alphabet*

| Alpha | A | $\alpha$ | Nu | N | $\nu$ |
| Beta | B | $\beta$ | Xi | $\Xi$ | $\xi$ |
| Gamma | $\Gamma$ | $\gamma$ | Omicron | O | o |
| Delta | $\Delta$ | $\delta$ | Pi | $\Pi$ | $\pi$ |
| Epsilon | E | $\varepsilon$ | Rho | P | $\rho$ |
| Zeta | Z | $\zeta$ | Sigma | $\Sigma$ | $\sigma$ |
| Eta | H | $\eta$ | Tau | T | $\tau$ |
| Theta | $\Theta$ | $\theta$ | Upsilon | Y | $\upsilon$ |
| Iota | I | $\iota$ | Phi | $\Phi$ | $\phi$ |
| Kappa | K | $\kappa$ | Chi | X | $\chi$ |
| Lambda | $\Lambda$ | $\lambda$ | Psi | $\Psi$ | $\psi$ |
| Mu | M | $\mu$ | Omega | $\Omega$ | $\omega$ |

*Table 1.11    Symbols Used in Text*

| **Parameter or Statistic** | **Population** | **Sample** |
| --- | --- | --- |
| Coefficient of correlation | $\rho$ | $r$ |
| Coefficient of determination | $\rho^2$ | $r^2$ |
| Error | $\varepsilon$ | $e$ |
| Mean | $\mu$ | $m$ |
| Regression constant | $\alpha$ | $a$ |
| Regression coefficient | $\beta$ | $b$ |
| Standard deviation | $\sigma$ | $s$ |
| Variance | $\sigma^2$ | $s^2$ |

# 1.5 EXERCISES

We select exercise problems to reinforce key points and relationships in each chapter. Appendix C gives step-by-step solutions. We include three problems in this chapter to set the stage for you. You will find them interesting. You will also find their solutions at the beginning of Appendix C.

### ■ 1.5.1 Planning Disasters

Planning disasters are projects that go awry, costing monumental sums of money without fulfilling their intended purposes. Identify three such planning disasters and cite the driving forces behind the disasters.

### ■ 1.5.2 Scientific Method

In the example of Section 1.2.7, Analyst calculated the number of positions that various configurations of unit cubes could occupy. Given a built-up cube with the dimensions of eight unit cubes by six unit cubes by four unit cubes and following Analyst's technical approach, calculate the number of positions that various configurations of these unit cubes could occupy.

### ■ 1.5.3 Greek Alphabet

Which English letters do not have roots in the Greek alphabet? What are the roots of these letters?

## 1.6
## REFERENCES

You can obtain referenced government documents from the issuing organizations and from:

    Superintendent of Documents, U.S. Government Printing Office, Washington, DC 20402. Telephone: (202) 783-3238.
    National Technical Information Service, U.S. Department of Commerce, Springfield, VA 22161. Telephone: (703) 487-4650.

1. Tricia Welsh, *Best and Worst Corporate Reputations*, FORTUNE, February 7, 1994.
2. Institute of Defense Analysis, IDA Paper P-2318, *An Examination of Various Methods Used in Support of Concurrent Engineering*, 1990.
3. James L. Nevins, Daniel E. Whitney, et al., *Concurrent Design of Products and Processes*, McGraw-Hill Publishing Company, 1989.
4. Madhav S. Phadke, *Quality Engineering Using Robust Design*, Prentice Hall, 1989.
5. Genichi Taguchi and Don Clausing, *Robust Quality*, HARVARD BUSINESS REVIEW, January–February 1990.
6. Phillip J. Ross, *Taguchi Techniques for Quality Engineering*, McGraw-Hill Book Company, 1988.
7. Jack V. Michaels and William P. Wood, *Design to Cost*, John Wiley & Sons, Inc., 1989.
8. Defense System Management College, *Defense Manufacturing Management Guide for Program Managers*, Third Edition, DSMC Press, Fort Belvoir, Virginia.
9. John R. Hauser and Don Clausing, *The House of Quality*, HARVARD BUSINESS REVIEW, May–June 1988.
10. Defense System Management College, *System Engineering Guide*, DSMC Press, Fort Belvoir, Virginia, 1990.

## 1.6 References

11. Benjamin S. Blanchard, *System Engineering Management*, John Wiley & Sons, Inc., 1991.
12. Defense System Management College, *Manufacturing Guide for Program Managers*, DSMC Press, Fort Belvoir, Virginia, 1990.
13. Department of Defense Guide, DoD 5000.51.G, *Total Quality Management, A Guide for Implementation*, January 1990.
14. Lawrence D. Miles, *Techniques of Value Analysis and Engineering*, Second Edition, McGraw-Hill Book Company, 1972.
15. Arthur E. Mudge, *Value Engineering; A Systematic Approach*. McGraw-Hill Book Company, 1981.
16. Theodore C. Fowler, *Value Analysis in Design*, Van Nostrand Rheinhold, 1990.
17. Department of Defense Directive, DoDD 5000.1, *Defense Acquisition*, February 23, 1991.
18. DoD 4275-M, *Transition from Development to Production*, U.S. Department of Defense, 1995.
19. Department of the Navy NAVSO P6071, *Best Practices*, Reliability, Maintainability, and Quality Assurance Directorate, 1986.
20. Kamlesh Mathur and Daniel Solow, *Management Science: The Art of Decision Making*, Prentice Hall, 1994.
21. U.S. Bureau of the Census, *Statistical Abstract of the United States: 1994* (114th Edition), Washington, DC, 1994.

> *I go to seek a great perhaps.*
> **François Rabelais**

# CHAPTER 2

# RISK FUNDAMENTALS

> The more things change, the more they are the same.
> **Alphonse Karr**

Effective risk management depends on the ability to differentiate risk causes from risk indicators, quantify risk consequences, set priorities for combating risk, and take preventive measures in a timely fashion.

Figure 2.1 illustrates the organization of the chapter. Section contents are listed alongside the respective sections. As we stated in the introduction, the language of technical risk management contains terms with specific meanings that you need to know before undertaking the respective chapters.

**Section 2.1 Definitions** provides definitions of terms and abbreviations used in Chapter 2. You will find these definitions the first time they are used in the chapter and again in the glossary in Appendix A.

**Section 2.2 Risk Principles** discusses the issue of conflicting principles for combating risk (*viz.*, risk benefit-equity principle and risk cost-effectiveness principle). Such issues are important whenever the public is involved and we give an interesting example of such an issue.

**Section 2.3 Risk Morphology** introduces risk from a systematic viewpoint and shows that every decision made or action taken is fraught with elements of risk in a framework of cause and effect. We explore the relationship between hazards and perils and show the hierarchical nature of hazards and perils in the context of risk systems. We illustrate these relationships with several examples, one of which uses Pareto analysis.

**Section 2.4 Probabilistic Nature of Risk** brings in the probabilistic concepts of risk time and risk cost, and shows how these elements combine to form risk networks. We show the evolution of networks from simple series configurations to series-parallel, and series-parallel-parallel configurations. We illustrate the summation of individual elements of risk time and cost elements for the cases of dependence and independence among the activities comprising the network.

**Section 2.5 Risk Dominance** introduces the concept of risk determinants and illustrates the concept of first-order and second-order determinants. We show that first-order determinants modify

*2.1 Definitions* 21

the contribution to risk exposure from second-order determinants. We introduce the *k*-factor as the measure of the degree of dominance and discuss the applicability of various risk determinants as a function of product categories.

|  |  |
|---|---|
| 2.1 Definitions | Key Terms and Abbreviations. |
| 2.2 Risk Principles | Risk Benefit-Equity Principle; Risk Cost-Effectiveness Principle. |
| 2.3 Risk Morphology | Quantified Risk Measures; Hazards and Perils; Risk Systems; Risk Hierarchy; Risk Categories. |
| 2.4 Probabilistic Nature of Risk | Risk Time; Risk Cost; Risk Network; Dependent Network; Independent Network; Hybrid Network. |
| 2.5 Risk Dominance | Risk Order; *k*-factor; Risk Applicability. |
| 2.6 Summary | Review of Highlights. |
| 2.7 Exercises | Role Models. |
| 2.10 References | Data Sources. |

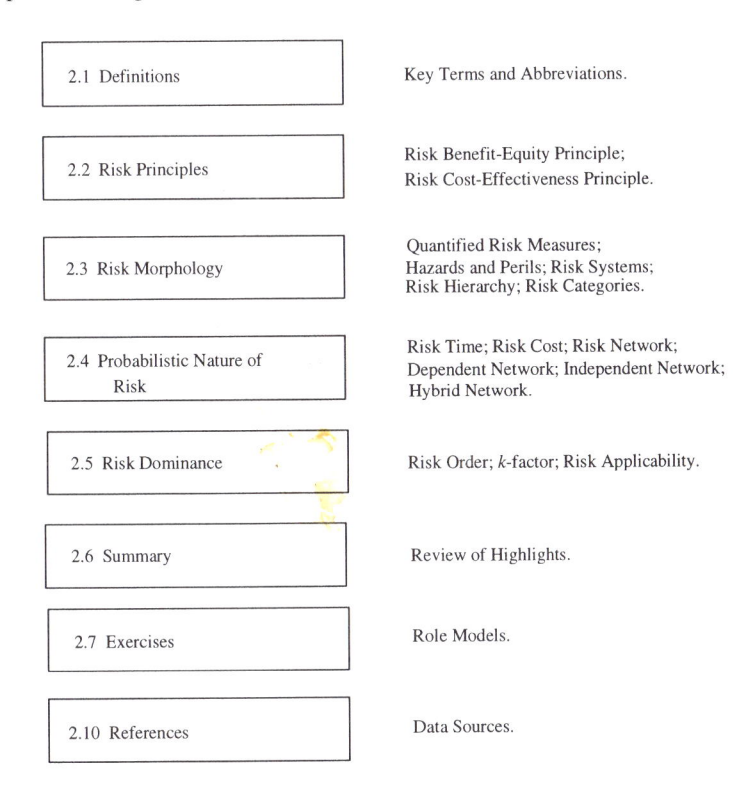

**Figure 2.1** Organization of Chapter 2

Chapter 2 concludes with **Section 2.6 Summary**, **Section 2.7 Exercises**, and **Section 2.8 References**. The summary serves to highlight the contents of the chapter, and the exercises reinforce the highlights. We urge you to try the exercises before resorting to the solutions in Appendix C.

# 2.1
# DEFINITIONS

Table 2.1 gives definitions of terms used in this chapter. Note the terms *critical path* and *dummy activity* in relationship to *network*. Note also the meaning of the terms relating to risk: *risk avoidance, risk cost, risk determinant factor, risk dominance, risk exposure, risk management, risk morphology, risk network, risk recovery, risk reduction,* and *risk time*.

There are a large number of definitions relating to risk determinants and risk determinant factors. Risk determinant factors have scalar properties (*viz.*, 0 to 1.0). They are used to quantify risk exposure in terms of risk time and risk cost. Note the relationship between hazard and peril, and how peril relates to risk exposure. Note the role of extrinsic factors and intrinsic factors in determining the risk exposure.

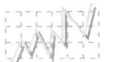

Note the terms *mean*, *standard deviation*, and *variance*, which are elements of probability and statistics. Proficiency in probability and statistics is useful in technical risk management and we include an exercise in Section 2.7 that will allow you to test your proficiency.

*Table 2.1* Definitions of Terms and Abbreviations in Chapter 2

**BCE**: Baseline cost estimate.
**BTE**: Baseline time estimate.
**Cause and effect diagram**: Depiction of risk network.
**Critical path**: Path whose activities require the most time to complete of all the paths comprising the network.
**Dummy activity**: Activity inserted in a path of a network to complete the path in a depiction of the network.
**Extrinsic attributes**: External forces such as inflation and regulatory statutes, which are peripheral to given organizations and, as such, are largely beyond the control of organizations.
**Factorial**: Product of a positive integer and all positive integers less than that integer. By definition, factorials 1 and 0, denoted by 1! and 0!, are both equal to 1.
**Failure rate**: Number of failures per unit time of a particular item.
**Hazard**: Condition or action that may result in perilous conditions.
**HDI**: Human development index.
**Human development index**: Measure of the quality of life based on longevity, literacy, and command over resources needed for a decent living.
**Intrinsic attributes**: Properties of management, products, and processes of organizations.
**Limited warranty**: Guarantee for a specified time period to replace or reimburse a particular failed item but not the cost of incidental or consequential damage.
**Mean**: Average value of data comprising a probability distribution.
**Mean-time-between-failures**: Average time interval of successive failures of a particular item.
**Measure of effectiveness**: Quantitative measure of the effectiveness of a given strategy.
**Network**: System of activities and events annotated with time.
**NFA**: Need for aid.
**Outcome**: An event with a unique probability of occurrence.
**Pareto's law**: The bulk of wealth, influence, and power in the world resides mostly in the hands of a few people (*i.e.*, the vital few), and if distributed evenly among all the people of the world (*i.e.*, the trivial many), would inevitably return to the hands of the few.
**Peril**: Undesirable event that may result from a hazard.
**PODR**: Point of diminishing return.
**PROCMF**: Process maturity factor.
**PRODMF**: Product maturity factor.
**QFAP**: Quality, functionality, affordability, and profitability.
**RCE**: Risk cost estimate.
**RDF**: Risk determinant factor.
**Risk avoidance**: Action taken to reduce risk exposure. Also called *risk reduction*.
**Risk cost**: Product of corrective-action cost and corrective-action probability of occurrence.
**Risk determinant factor**: Quantified attribute that serves as measure of risk exposure.
**Risk exposure**: Vulnerability of operations to risk elements as predicted by the risk determinant factor and quantified in terms of risk time and risk cost.

## 2.2 Risk Principles

*Table 2.1   Definitions of Terms and Abbreviations in Chapter 2 (Cont.)*

---

**Risk management**: Executive function of controlling the hazards faced by organizations in their various undertakings.
**Risk morphology**: Form and structure of hazards contributing to risk exposure.
**Risk network**: Hierarchy of hazards and perils, or causes and effects.
**Risk order**: Degree of dominance of one risk over another.
**Risk recovery**: Corrective action taken to offset performance, schedule, or cost perturbations in programs due to a materialized peril so that programs may continue as planned. Also called *work-around* and *corrective action*.
**Risk reduction**: Action taken to prevent risk incidents (*i.e.*, the materialization of risk elements) by choosing from alternative approaches on a return-on-investment basis.
**Risk time**: Product of corrective-action time for recovery from peril and probability of needing corrective action.
**Root-sum-of-squares**: Square root of the sum of the squares of a series of numbers.
**RTE**: Risk time estimate.
**Standard deviation**: Measure of dispersion about the mean of a probability distribution. Square root of variance.
**Variance**: Measure of dispersion in data comprising a probability distribution. Square of standard deviation.
**VOA**: Value of aid.

---

# 2.2 RISK PRINCIPLES

You can reduce most risks to an acceptable level, provided you have sufficient resources to devote to their management. Limited resources, however, lead to issues of priority and allocation of resources in selecting approaches to risk management.

> *Choosing the right road is easy when you know what lies at the end.*
> **Analyst**

Issues of priority and allocation of resources arise from the conflict between two opposing principles for risk management. These are risk benefit-equity and risk cost-effectiveness.

### ■ 2.2.1 Risk Benefit-Equity Principle

Today's approach to public safety stems from the risk benefit-equity principle. It is the underlying rationale for the operation of numerous agencies ranging from the Federal Aviation Administration and Environmental Protection Administration to municipal police and fire departments.

The risk benefit-equity principle holds that risk and benefit for a particular peril should be shared as equally as possible by the population of interest. Population is used in the broad sense to encompass property and products as well as people. This principle is applied almost universally in the public sector and to some extent in private sector business dealings with the public.

## ■ 2.2.2 Risk Cost-Effectiveness Principle

The risk cost-effectiveness principle dictates that resources should be deployed for maximum **risk reduction** per unit cost in the particular activity of interest. For example, an electric power utility would attempt to balance cost and return-on-investment from investing in pollution control equipment.

The social, political, and economic implications of a view so diametrically opposed to the risk benefit-equity principle are obvious. These implications pervade both the public and private sectors, influencing almost every action taken. Although risk cost-effectiveness may be the primary concern in the financial, industrial, commercial, and military communities, the issue of risk benefit-equity cannot be ignored because of legal constraints or civil pressure.

The equivalent thrust in the domain of technical risk management is the need for balanced quality, functionality, affordability, and profitability viewed from the perspective of producers and suppliers as well as customers and users of products. Never lose sight of the public's influence on the success of products entering the marketplace.

> *An equitable balance of risk benefit-equity and risk cost-effectiveness is necessary for risk management to prevail in the long term.*
> ***Analyst***

## ■ 2.2.3 Example of Balancing Risk Principles

A certain charitable organization wishes to expend the sum of $100 million on improving the quality of life in Central America. Central America consists of seven small nations: Belize, Costa Rica, Guatemala, El Salvador, Honduras, Nicaragua, and Panama. The population of Central America in 1992 was estimated at more than 31 million.

The organization is unsure of how to allocate the money among the seven nations, but does wish to observe the risk benefit-equity principle in rendering aid. The organization requests Analyst to address the problem scientifically. Table 2.2 gives the technical approach Analyst uses in carrying out the assignment.

*Table 2.2   Technical Approach for Balancing Risk Principles Example*

1. Determine the populations of the nations.
2. Select a measure for quality of life in these nations.
3. Use the reciprocal of the measure for quality of life as the *per capita* measure for needing aid.
4. Calculate the product of population and the *per capita* measure for needing aid to use as the **measure of effectiveness (MOE)** for granting aid.
5. Use the ratio of the individual values of MOE to the sum of all values of MOE as factors for allocating money to the individual nations of Central America.

Table 2.3 lists the populations of the nations of Central America. The population of Belize (about 212,000) is combined with the population of its southern neighbor, Guatemala, for administrative purposes.

Belize, the northernmost nation in Central America, is bordered by Mexico on the north, Guatemala on the south and west, and the Caribbean Sea on the east. The former British colony was

## 2.2 Risk Principles

known as British Honduras until it was granted independence on September 21, 1981, ending more than 300 years of British colonial presence on the American mainland.

For the measure of quality of life, Analyst turns to the work of the United Nations and selects the **human development index (HDI)**, which is based on longevity, literacy, and command over resources needed for a decent living. Column three of Table 2.3 lists the values of HDI for the nations of Central America.

The smaller the value of HDI, the greater is the need for aid. Similarly, the greater the population at any given value of HDI, the greater is the need for aid. The **need for aid (NFA)**, in the fourth column of Table 2.3, is the product of the population and the reciprocal of HDI. The larger the population or the smaller the value HDI, the greater is the need for aid. For example, the value of NFA for Belize and Guatemala is 10,322 ÷ 0.608, or $16,976.974 million.

*Table 2.3* Central America Data for Balancing Risk Principles Example [1]

| Nation | Population Thousands | HDI* | NFA** $ Million | VOA*** $ Million |
|---|---|---|---|---|
| Belize and Guatemala | 10,322 | 0.608 | 16,976.974 | 35.66664 |
| Costa Rica | 2,921 | 0.916 | 3,188.865 | 6.69943 |
| El Salvador | 5,830 | 0.651 | 8,955.453 | 18.81436 |
| Honduras | 5,469 | 0.563 | 9,714.032 | 20.40805 |
| Nicaragua | 4,290 | 0.743 | 5,773.890 | 12.13027 |
| Panama | 2,640 | 0.883 | 2,989.807 | 6.28123 |
| Totals | 31,472 | -- | 47,599.021 | 100.00000 |

*Human Development Index
**Need for Aid
***Value of Aid
Adapted by permission of the Institute for Risk Research, University of Waterloo, Waterloo, Ontario, Canada N2L 3G1 from N. C. Lind, J. S. Nathwani, and E. Siddall, *Managing Risk in the Public Interest*, 1991.

Calculation of the **value of aid (VOA)** awarded the respective nations uses relative values of NFA. Equation 2.1 is the relationship for calculating individual values of VOA.

$$VOA = Budget \frac{NFA}{\Sigma NFA} \tag{2.1}$$

where the budget is the amount of aid money available.

Column five of Table 2.3 lists the amounts of VOA for the respective nations. The need for aid is greater in Honduras than in the other Central American nations. The amount of VOA calculated with Equation 2.1 ranges from $35.66664 million for Belize and Guatemala to $6.28123 million for Panama.

Equation 2.2 gives the calculation of VOA for Belize and Guatemala.

$$VOA = \$100,000,000 \frac{\$16,976.974}{\$47,599.021}$$
$$= \$35,666,400. \tag{2.2}$$

where $100,000,000 is the dollar amount of money available for aid, $16,976.974 the value of NFA for Belize and Guatemala, and $47,599.021 the total value of NFA.

## 2.3
## RISK MORPHOLOGY

**Risk morphology** consists of the antecedents, form, and structure of risk exposure. The antecedents of risk exposure are decisions, or lack of decisions, and subsequent actions.

**Risk exposure** is a function of the degree of uncertainty regarding perils surrounding the actions taken. Table 1.6 in the previous chapter gives the continuum of decisions faced by modern-day management. These decisions are fraught with varying degrees of risk exposure.

Decision making is an iterative process that remains constant in purpose and only changes in emphasis as programs mature. Interactive decision making requires a substantial amount of judgment and simultaneity of action, all of which contribute to risk exposure.

Certain events are inevitable, unless management literally intervenes and does so from the very start of programs. Left to its own resources, engineers will design future products in substantially the same way as they designed previous products. Manufacturing personnel will continue to design tooling and produce products as they always have.

Table 2.4 supplements the technical risk management absolutes in Table 1.4. The last absolute is the hallmark of prudent management.

*Table 2.4    Technical Risk Management Absolutes*

- Risk exposure is inherent in the decision process.
- Risk exposure is a probabilistic function of the uncertainty in the decision process and subsequent actions.
- There exist alternative courses of actions that offer varying degrees of risk exposure.
- Management can minimize risk exposure by choosing lower risk alternatives.
- Return-on-investment is the measure of effectiveness for choosing among alternatives.
- Return-on-investment is the ratio of risk recovery cost to risk avoidance cost.
- Maintain cash reserve for contingencies.

Management should not direct specific product and process design approaches. Management should, however, make it clear from the start that approaches violating principles of risk management are unacceptable and that performance will be rewarded commensurately.

Figure 2.2 shows the risk morphology for a product decision. The output of the process is risk exposure expressed in terms of risk time and risk cost. The measure of risk exposure is the probabilistic need to expend risk time and risk cost.

The input is the technical approach described by the attributes of maturity, quality, complexity, and concurrency for the product design and manufacturing process. These attributes are compounded by the attributes of schedule and funding adequacy.

The foregoing attributes are the sources of risk exposure. For example, the inadequacy of schedule and funding for a given technical approach is a **hazard**. The consequential **peril** is the need for corrective action. Risk time and risk cost are the products of corrective-action time and cost and the probability of needing corrective action.

## 2.3 Risk Morphology

Scheduling and funding attributes in Figure 2.2 are part of a broader set of management attributes that contribute to risk exposure. In addition, there are external forces with extrinsic attributes that combine with the former to comprise the operational environment.

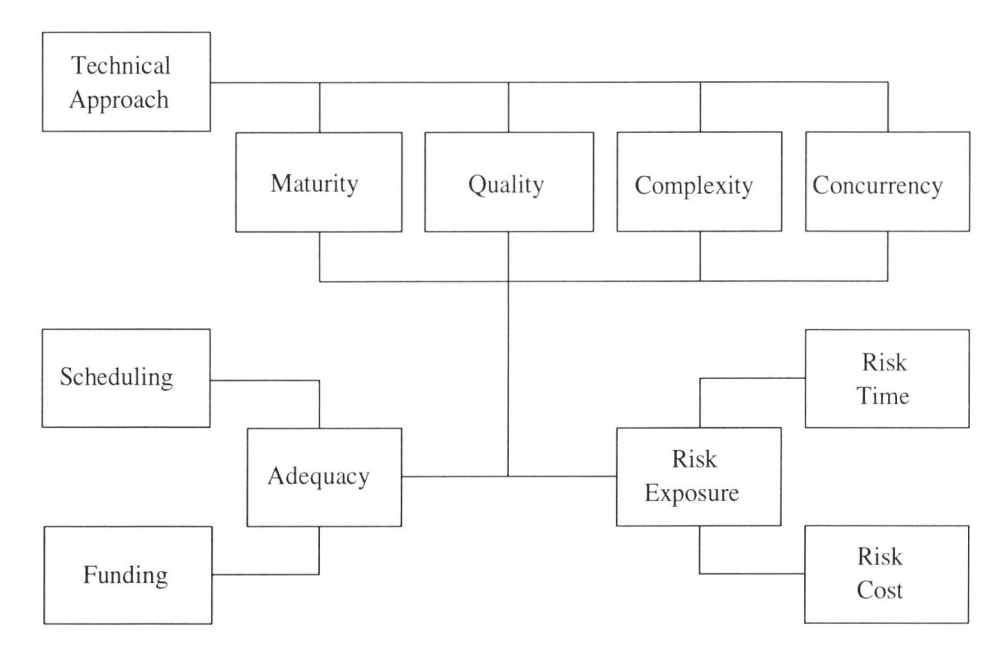

**Figure 2.2** Risk Morphology for Product Decision

Table 2.5 lists various attributes of the technical approach and the operational environment. Whatever the management attributes, they influence the entire product line of a given company. Although extrinsic attributes vary somewhat by products produced, they do establish the operating environment for the whole company. We reveal the full contribution to risk exposure of management and extrinsic attributes in the next chapter.

*Table 2.5* Technical Approach Attributes

> **Management attributes**: Funding and investment policy, customer and user policy, program continuity policy, and personnel retention policy.
> **Extrinsic attributes**: Inflation, escalation, regulatory statutes, labor relations, public attitudes, and physical environment that can contribute to risk exposure.
> **Product maturity**: Maturity and production readiness of the product design.
> **Product quality**: Producibility, reliability, and testability of the product design.
> **Product complexity**: Magnitude of the generation breakdown, in levels and expanse of levels, for the product design.
> **Product concurrency**: Concurrency of interdependent product design activities.
> **Process maturity**: Maturity and production readiness of the process design.
> **Process quality**: Uniformity of process in producing products.
> **Process complexity**: Population of assemblies, subassemblies, details, and parts comprising the product.
> **Process concurrency**: Concurrency of interdependent production operations.

## 2.3.1 Quantified Risk Measures

There is a tendency to describe the risk exposure as certain, extremely high, very high, high, medium, low, very low, extremely low, or impossible. Verbal expressions such as the foregoing are difficult to deal with mathematically and you should express risk exposure quantitatively in the manner suggested by Table 2.6. The verbal expressions "certain" and "impossible" are mathematical impossibilities, but we have received such responses in surveys.

How would you transform the verbal expression of a medium to high risk to a quantified expression? Simply interpolate midway between 0.50 and 0.75 for 0.625.

*Table 2.6   Verbal Expressions vs. Quantified Measures of Risk Exposure*

| **Verbal Expression** | **Quantified Measure** | **Verbal Expression** | **Quantified Measure** |
|---|---|---|---|
| Certain | 1.00 | Medium | 0.50 |
| Extremely High | 0.99 | Low | 0.25 |
| Very High | 0.90 | Very Low | 0.10 |
| High | 0.75 | Impossible | 0 |

## 2.3.2 Example of Quantified Risk Measures

The Alpha Corporation receives an invitation to bid on the construction of a bridge in about 25 percent less time than is usually allowed. The corporation surveys its subcontractors on the risk exposure they perceive in accelerating their part of the project. Table 2.7 lists the subcontractors' opinions of their perception of risk exposure. It appears to the Alpha Corporation that the company's subcontractors' perception of risk exposure is somewhere between very high and extremely high.

*Table 2.7   Survey Data for Quantified Measures of Risk Exposure Example*

| High | Very High | Medium | Very High |
|---|---|---|---|
| Medium | Certain | High | Medium |
| Medium | Medium | Extremely High | High to Very High |
| Certain | Extremely High | Very High | |

The Alpha Corporation retains Analyst to convert the responses into a quantitative consensus on risk exposure. Table 2.8 gives the technical approach Analyst follows in carrying out the assignment.

*Table 2.8   Technical Approach for Quantified Measures of Risk Exposure Example*

1. Convert the verbal expressions in Table 2.7 to quantified measures of risk exposure in accordance with Table 2.6.
2. Calculate the average of the quantified values.
3. Convert the average quantified value back to a verbal expression of the consensus of perceived risk exposure.

Table 2.9 gives the worksheet for this example. Analyst uses interpolation to quantify risk exposure of high to very high. The quantified measure is $(0.75 + 0.90) \div 2$, or 0.825.

## 2.3 Risk Morphology

The sum of the quantified expressions in Table 2.9 is 11.505 and the average value is 11.505 ÷ 15, or 0.767. This falls within the quantified measures for "high" and "very high" and closer to "high" in Table 2.6.

Analyst provides the findings to Alpha but does not elaborate on the consensus of the subcontractors' opinions that the two opinions of certainty are impossible states. Analyst leaves that prerogative to the client.

*Table 2.9*    *Worksheet for Quantified Measures of Risk Exposure Example*

| | | | |
|---|---|---|---|
| High | 0.75 | Medium | 0.50 |
| Very High | 0.90 | Medium | 0.50 |
| Medium | 0.50 | Extremely High | 0.99 |
| Very High | 0.90 | High to Very High | 0.825 |
| Medium | 0.50 | Certain | 1.00 |
| Certain | 1.00 | Extremely High | 0.99 |
| High | 0.75 | Very High | 0.90 |
| Medium | 0.50 | | |
| | | | |
| Sum: | | | 11.505 |
| | | | |
| Average: | | | 0.767 |

> *Experts should provide only facts. Allow managers to form the opinions.*
>                                                                        ***Analyst***

### ■ 2.3.3 Hazards and Perils

You have seen risk exposure expressed in terms of risk time and risk cost. You can also define risk exposure in terms of hazards and perils. A hazard is that condition that may cause a peril to materialize whereas a peril is an event that will result in a loss. Risk time and cost are measures of perils.

For example, road condition and traffic density are hazards whose consequential perils include automotive accident. Automotive accident is, in itself, a hazard whose consequential perils include injury, property damage, traffic jams, singly or in any combination of the three. The latter are called "outcomes of perils" but are, in themselves, perils.

Hazards are thus characterized as having one or more possible perils, each with a unique probability of occurrence. Similarly, perils of a particular hazard are characterized as having one or more possible **outcomes**, each with a unique probability of occurrence. As stated, the hazard causing the peril of an automotive accident could include road condition and traffic density, plus factors such as excessive or low speed and careless or reckless driving, or any combination of the foregoing.

In the industrial world, hazards could include defective parts and material, poor workmanship, and tolerance build-up among the component subassemblies. The outcome of these hazards could include such perils as reduced output and increased rework and scrap.

Hazards and perils are probabilistic in nature. You should be concerned for the probability of occurrence of the various consequential perils given the occurrence of some causative hazard. For example, given the probability of defective assemblies and the corrective-action time and cost to rectify the problem, you can quantify risk time and risk cost as the products of probability of defective assemblies and of corrective-action time and cost.

### ■ 2.3.4 Risk Systems

The relationship between hazards and perils is a risk system as shown in Figure 2.3. Adverse effects on quality, functionality, affordability, or profitability may be due to any or all combinations of hazards and perils.

The number of possible hazard-peril combinations is a measure of the complexity of risk systems of interest. There are 4 hazards and 4 peril combinations in the simple looking risk system in Figure 2.3, but we can form 60 hazard-peril combinations from the configuration. The 60 combinations are called "partitions."

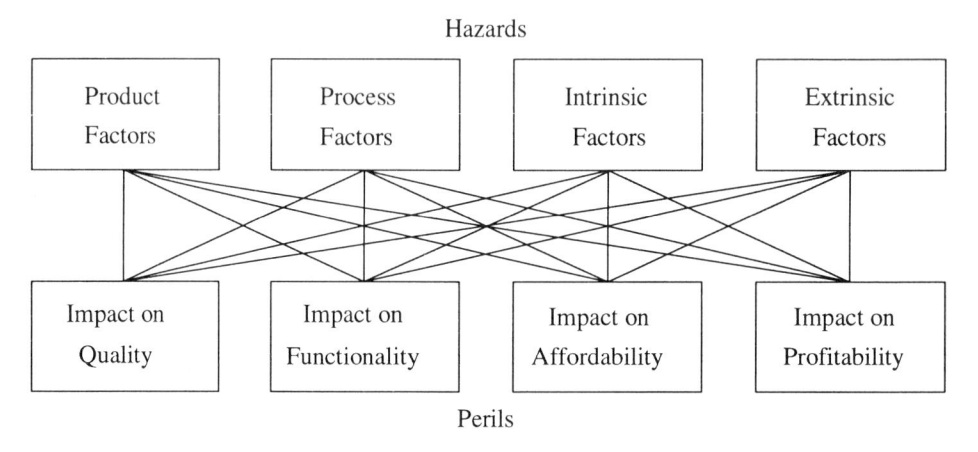

Hazards

| Product Factors | Process Factors | Intrinsic Factors | Extrinsic Factors |
|---|---|---|---|

| Impact on Quality | Impact on Functionality | Impact on Affordability | Impact on Profitability |
|---|---|---|---|

Perils

**Figure 2.3** Risk System of Hazards and Perils

A partition consists of all variations of possible combinations for the given configuration. In the illustration, each of the four hazards can combine with one, two, three, and four of the perils Similarly, any two, three, and all four of the hazards can combine with one, two, three, and four of the perils. We can calculate the number of partitions, hazards, or perils with combinatorial equations which use factorials.

The **factorial** of a positive integer (*i.e.*, a positive whole number) is the product of that integer and all positive integers less than that integer. We denote the factorial of five by 5! and calculate it with (5)(4)(3)(2)(1) for 120.

Try calculating the factorials of six, seven, eight, nine, ten, and eleven. The factorial of 11, or 11!, equals (11)(10)(9)(8)(7)(6)(5)(4)(3)(2)(1), or 39,916,800.

We denote the factorials of one and zero by 1! and 0! By mathematical convention, both 1! and 0! are equal to 1.

Hazards are the independent variables, and perils are the dependent variables in risk systems. The four hazards in Figure 2.3 can occur in combinations of 1, 2, 3, and 4. These combinations comprise the hazard partition for the system of: $r = 1$ and $n = 4$; $r = 2$ and $n = 4$; $r = 3$ and $n = 4$; and $r = 4$ and $n = 4$.

## 2.3 Risk Morphology

We calculate the number of combinations $c$ which can be formed from $n$ items taken $r$ at a time with Equation 2.3.

$$c = \frac{n!}{r!(n-r)!} \tag{2.3}$$

where $n!$ and $r!$ denote the factorials of $n$ and $r$.

We solve Equation 2.3 for each of the combinatorial elements and sum the number of combinations for the elements.

Substituting $r = 1$ and $n = 4$ in Equation 2.3, we obtain

$$\begin{aligned} c &= \frac{4!}{1!(4-1)!} \\ &= \frac{24}{1(6)} \\ &= 4. \end{aligned} \tag{2.4}$$

For $r = 2$ and $n = 4$, we obtain

$$\begin{aligned} c &= \frac{4!}{2!(4-2)!} \\ &= \frac{24}{2(2)} \\ &= 6. \end{aligned} \tag{2.5}$$

For $r = 3$ and $n = 4$, we obtain

$$\begin{aligned} c &= \frac{4!}{3!(4-3)!} \\ &= \frac{24}{6(1)} \\ &= 4. \end{aligned} \tag{2.6}$$

For $r = 4$ and $n = 4$, we obtain

$$\begin{aligned} c &= \frac{4!}{4!(4-4)!} \\ &= \frac{24}{24(1)} \\ &= 1. \end{aligned} \tag{2.7}$$

Next, we sum the foregoing number of combinations, obtaining 4 + 6 + 4 + 1, or 15. When multiplied by four (*i.e.*, the number of hazards), the number of possible combinations becomes (15)(4), or 60.

### ■ 2.3.5 Example of Production Hazards and Perils

There is concern in a certain company for the integrity of its products from the viewpoint of product quality, functionality, affordability, and profitability. The company ascertains that there are six perils that can adversely effect these attributes in twenty-four of its products. Realizing that the possible number of combinations is large, but not knowing how to calculate the number, the company retains Analyst to do so. Analyst uses the technical approach in Table 2.10 to carry out the assignment.

*Table 2.10   Technical Approach for Production Hazards and Perils Example*

1. Partition the 6 factors that effect the integrity of quality, functionality, affordability, and profitability.
2. Multiply the above answer by 4 (*i.e.*, for quality, functionality, affordability, and profitability).
3. Multiply the above answer by 24 (*i.e.*, for the number of products).

The assignment is essentially an exercise in combinatorial mathematics. Analyst applies Equation 2.3 six times and compiles the number of combinations in Table 2.11. Analyst is relieved that the client has not requested analysis of the 6,048 combinations.

*Table 2.11   Compilation of Number of Combinations for Production Hazards and Perils Example*

For $b = 6$ and $r = 1$, $c = 6$.
For $b = 6$ and $r = 2$, $c = 15$.
For $b = 6$ and $r = 3$, $c = 20$.
For $b = 6$ and $r = 4$, $c = 15$.
For $b = 6$ and $r = 5$, $c = 6$.
For $b = 6$ and $r = 6$, $c = 1$.
Number of partitions: $6 + 15 + 20 + 15 + 6 + 1 = 63$.
Product of 63 and 4 (*i.e.*, the attributes of quality, functionality, affordability, and profitability): $63 \times 4 = 252$.
Product of 252 and 24 (*i.e.*, the number of products): $252 \times 24 = 6,048$.

### ■ 2.3.6 Risk Hierarchy

Hazards are the independent variables (*i.e.*, the drivers) in risk systems, and perils are the dependent variables. Hazards and perils are hierarchical in nature and degenerate into sequentially lower orders as indicated in Table 2.12. This poses a problem of choice since greater sensitivity of perils to risk often occurs at the lower hierarchical levels.

It is convenient to consider a given hazard and its associated peril in the framework of cause and effect. Figure 2.4 is the top-level **cause and effect diagram** relating variability in product, process, intrinsic and extrinsic factors to effects on **quality, functionality, affordability, and profitability (QFAP)**.

*Table 2.12   Hierarchy of Hazards and Perils*

| Hazards | Perils |
|---|---|
| Inadequate resources | Marginal design |
| Marginal design | Tolerance build-up |
| Tolerance build-up | Lot rejection |
| Lot rejection | Need for corrective action |
| Need for corrective action | Cost overrun |
| Cost overrun | Reduced profitability |
| Reduced profitability | Program cancellation |

## 2.3 Risk Morphology

**Figure 2.4** Top-Level Cause and Effect Diagram

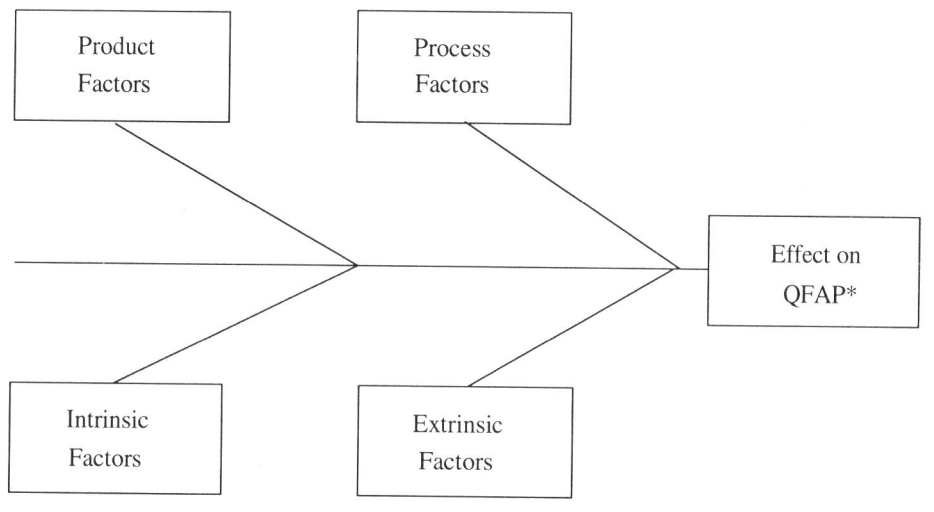

*QFAP: Quality; Functionality; Affordability; Profitability

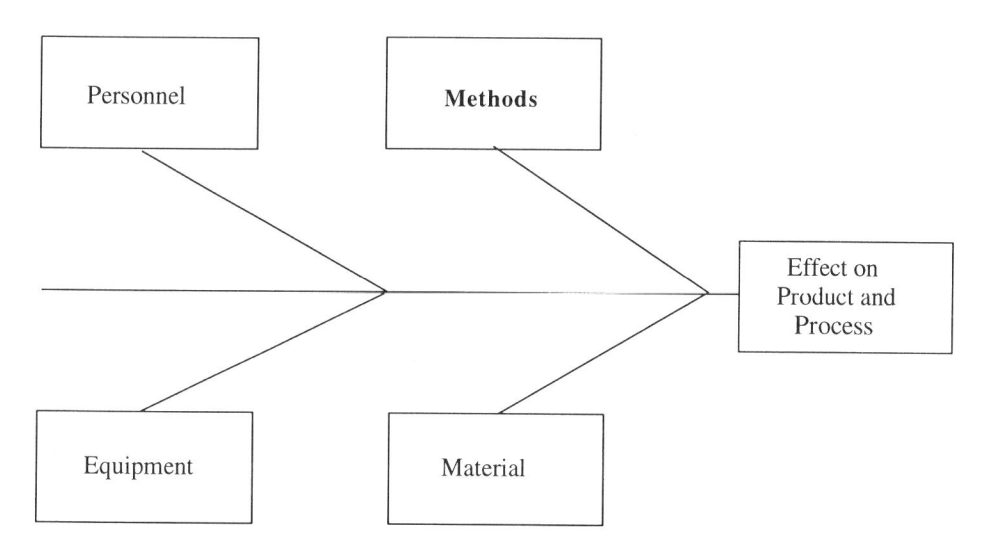

**Figure 2.5** Lower-Level Cause and Effect Diagram

Figure 2.4 is the universal top-level cause and effect diagram for QFAP in that the four categories of causes apply to almost every product and process. Figure 2.5 is the next lower-level cause and effect diagram for product and process factors. Note the fishbone appearance of the diagram. This appearance becomes more pronounced in still lower-level cause and effect diagrams.

You should consider hazard and peril combinations at all levels in the hierarchy. The number of combinations grows rapidly as you proceed down the hierarchy and you need to select those combinations that offer the greatest return-on-investment for your effort.

In investigations of this kind, you will find that not too many of the items in question account for the bulk of the effect. This is referred to as **Pareto's law** or Pareto's principle. Pareto analysis is the application of Pareto's principle.

Pareto analysis can be used to determine the point of diminishing return for any form of analysis where there is more than one specimen to investigate. Pareto analysis is used extensively in inventory control.

For example, in a bill of material for a typical high-technology product, about 20 percent of the items account for about 80 percent of the cost. The 20 percent represents the vital few, the remainder of the items the trivial many. [2]

### ■ 2.3.7 Example of Pareto Analysis of Risk Cost

Beta Industries, a manufacturer of home appliances, conducted risk analysis of its new product line and discerned varying degrees of risk exposure in 20 of the products. The estimated risk costs for these products are listed in Table 2.13.

> *Vilfredo Pareto (1848–1923), an Italian economist, postulated that if all the wealth, influence, and power in the world, which reside mostly in the hands of a few people, were distributed evenly among all the people of the world, the wealth, influence, and power would inevitably return to the hands of the few. The expressions* the vital few, *usually taken at about 20 percent of the items of interest, and* the trivial many, *usually taken at about 80 percent, stem from Pareto's work.*
>
> ***Analyst***

*Table 2.13   Data for Pareto Analysis of Risk Cost Example*

| $475,000 | $155,000 | $465,000 | $220,000 |
| 245,000 | 250,000 | 480,000 | 70,000 |
| 495,000 | 90,000 | 245,000 | 480,000 |
| 125,000 | 70,000 | 100,000 | 80,000 |
| 90,000 | 490,000 | 80,000 | 100,000 |

The company asks Analyst to conduct a Pareto analysis to determine the point of diminishing return for analysis of designs and processes for new products. Table 2.14 gives the technical approach which Analyst uses in carrying out the assignment.

*Table 2.14   Technical Approach for Pareto Analysis of Risk Cost Example*

1. Rank risk costs in descending order.
2. Calculate the cumulative risk cost by risk cost item.
3. Calculate the percentage of cumulative risk cost by rank order of risk-cost items.
4. Plot percentage of risk cost versus risk cost items.
5. Locate the point of diminishing return.

## 2.3 Risk Morphology

Analyst prepares the worksheet given in Table 2.15. Risk costs are rank-ordered in descending order, and the cumulative risk cost and percentage of total cumulative risk cost are calculated for each line item in the table. You can discern the point of diminishing return (PODR) in the table where the step changes in the percentage of total cumulative risk cost from about 10 percent in Rank Orders 1 through 6 decreases to about 5 percent or less in Rank Orders 7 through 20.

Analyst then plots the percentage of total cumulative cost as a function of rank order as shown in Figure 2.6. This is the so-called *Pareto curve*. Analyst also plots the 20-80 curve (*i.e.*, the vital few vs. trivial many curve) in the figure as a frame of reference.

The PODR is quite pronounced in Figure 2.6. You can see it after Rank Order 6 where the steps of the percentage of total cumulative risk cost change from about 10 percent to about 5 percent or less.

You can say that six of the products account for about 60 percent of the risk cost. The six products are 30 percent of the twenty products. If the data were to follow the Pareto curve, or 20-80 curve in the figure, you would be able to say that 20 percent of the products (*i.e.*, four out of twenty) accounted for 80 percent of the risk cost.

*Table 2.15  Worksheet for Pareto Analysis of Risk Cost Example*

| Rank Order | Risk Cost | Cumulative Risk Cost | Cumulative Percentage of Risk Cost |
|---|---|---|---|
| 1 | $495,000 | $ 495,000 | 10.3 |
| 2 | 490,000 | 985,000 | 20.5 |
| 3 | 485,000 | 1,465,000 | 30.5 |
| 4 | 475,000 | 1,945,000 | 40.5 |
| 5 | 470,000 | 2,415,000 | 50.3 |
| 6 | 465,000 | 2,880,000 | 60.0 |
| 7 | 250,000 | 3,130,000 | 65.2 |
| 8 | 245,000 | 3,375,000 | 70.3 |
| 9 | 235,000 | 3,620,000 | 75.4 |
| 10 | 230,000 | 3,840,000 | 80.0 |
| 11 | 155,000 | 3,995,000 | 83.2 |
| 12 | 125,000 | 4,120,000 | 85.8 |
| 13 | 100,000 | 4,220,000 | 87.9 |
| 14 | 100,000 | 4,320,000 | 90.0 |
| 15 | 90,000 | 4,410,000 | 91.9 |
| 16 | 90,000 | 4,500,000 | 93.8 |
| 17 | 80,000 | 4,580,000 | 95.4 |
| 18 | 80,000 | 4,660,000 | 97.1 |
| 19 | 70,000 | 4,730,000 | 98.5 |
| 20 | 70,000 | 4,800,000 | 100.0 |

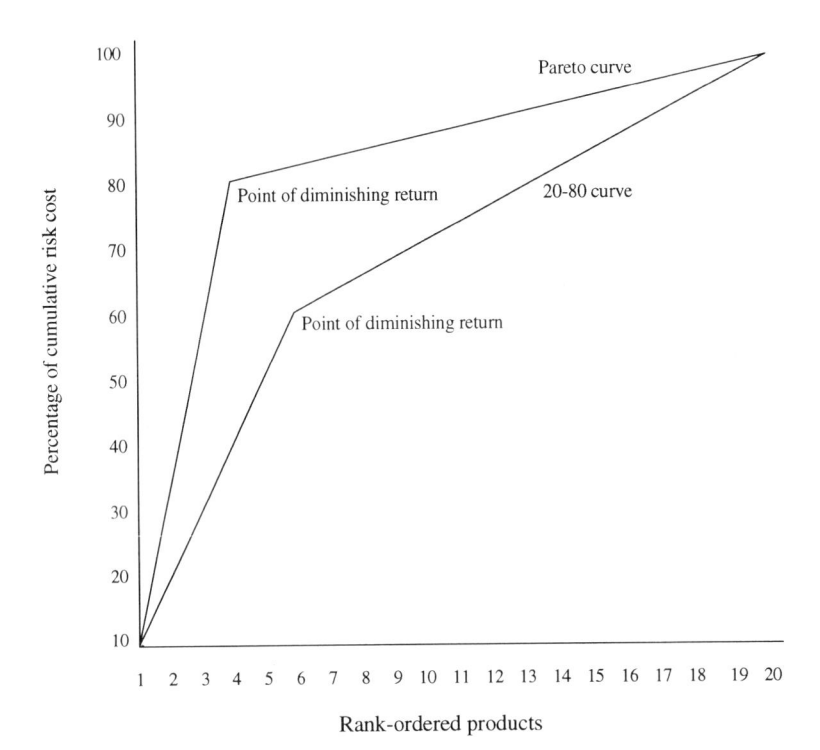

**Figure 2.6** Point of Diminishing Return

Analyst informs the manufacturer that the PODR occurs after Rank Order 6, which is the sixth product. The cumulative risk cost is $2,880,000 and the cumulative percentage of risk cost is 60.0 percent. According to Pareto's principle, the cumulative risk cost would be $3,840,000 at the cumulative percentage of 80 percent.

The Beta Company decides to limit the investigation for risk reduction to the first six products on the basis of the PODR.

### ■ 2.3.8 Risk Categories

Risks may be categorized as objective or subjective. An objective risk is one which can be described by statistics based on the variations of actual losses from expected losses. These statistics (*e.g.*, mortality tables) are used by the insurance industry to establish rates. Objective risks in such instances usually involve rather large groups of insured individuals and properties.

A subjective risk is a reflection of individual attitudes and states of mind, and is subject to individual perception of the risk consequences. Some people are risk-takers; some are risk-averters. There are significant attitudinal differences in each group. Attitudes toward risks change drastically in extraordinary circumstances wherein ordinary people do extraordinary things.

Finally, distinctions can be drawn between risks that are speculative or pure in nature. In a pure risk, there is no uncertainty (*i.e.*, question) that peril will produce a loss, but there may be uncertainty as to whether a hazard leading to the peril will occur.

## 2.3 Risk Morphology

In a speculative risk, there is uncertainty about the outcome of an action under consideration or events which are forecasted. Typical speculative risks are profit or loss resulting from the introduction of a new product line, victory or defeat in battle from choosing military strategies, and capital gain or loss from predicting stock market trends.

The concern in speculative risks is the uncertainty relating to both perils and hazards, whereas the concern in pure risks is primarily the uncertainty relating to hazards. This distinction is significant because pure risks are generally insurable whereas speculative risks must be handled with technical risk management.

### ■ 2.3.9 Example of Subjective Engineering

The 1957 launch of *Sputnik* (*n.b.*, The name means *traveling companion* in Russian) marked the beginning of the space race between the United States and the former Soviet Union. The significance of *Sputnik* was not lost on American political leaders.

On October 1, 1958, NASA began functioning as an integrated civilian organization for space activity. Manned space flight has been the most challenging and exciting aspect of space exploration from the very start.

Soon after the creation of NASA, the United States and the Soviet Union began work on manned space vehicles. The U.S.S.R. launched the world's first manned spacecraft, *Vostok*, piloted by Cosmonaut Yuri Gagarin on April 12, 1961. The spacecraft was a three-ton sphere and a two-ton service module.

Although the U.S. and U.S.S.R. followed divergent paths in their manned space flight programs, they both employed subjective engineering in large measures. Subjective engineering relies on engineering judgment and tests to minimize risk and limit the use of probabilistic techniques in analyzing the interactions of subsystems, human activities, and environmental conditions.

Building from familiar capability with proven reliability is another attribute of subjective engineering. The U.S.S.R.'s early success was built from a launch vehicle three times as powerful as those possessed by the U.S. However, there is a limit to how much can be built from old technology, and the attempt to use *Soyuz* as the vehicle for travel to the moon did not succeed. The Soviet Union subsequently canceled the lunar program.

In 1961, President John F. Kennedy declared that the goal of the U.S. manned space flight program was to land a man on the moon before the end of the decade. The need to venture into new disciplines was key in the ultimate success of U.S. manned space flight. NASA implemented the *Mercury*, *Gemini*, and *Apollo* series of programs that proceeded in rapid fashion. Successful landing on the moon took place on July 20, 1969.

Unfortunately, the event was marred by earlier tragedy. Disaster struck on January 27, 1967, when fire erupted in the *Apollo 1* command module from an electrical short circuit. Dense fumes from burning plastic suffocated the crew who was simulating flight routines. The peril had not been foreseen.

> **Crew of the Ill-Fated *Apollo 1***
>
> Roger B. Chaffee
> Virgil I. "Gus" Grissom
> Edward H. White II

NASA instituted many design and policy changes in the program. The first manned flight was aboard *Apollo 7* on October 11, 1968. The crew members were Donn F. Eisele, Walter Cunningham, and Walter M. Schirra, Jr. *Apollo 11* made the first lunar landing on July 20, 1969. The crew members were Edwin E. Aldrin, Jr., Michael Collins, and Neil Armstrong, who was the first to set foot on the moon.

The Space Shuttle program began formally on January 5, 1972. There followed a series of successes until the 25th Mission, the tenth mission of *Challenger*. On January 28, 1986, the flight of *Challenger 10* ended less than two minutes after lift off when a fireball engulfed the spacecraft within full view of observers. All hands were lost.

> **Crew of the Ill-Fated *Challenger 10***
>
> **Gregory Jarvis**
> **Christa McAuliffe**
> **Ronald McNair**
> **Ellison Onizuka**
> **Judith Resnik**
> **Francis Scobee**
> **Michael Smith**

The commission investigating the disaster attributed the problem to cold-temperature failure of an O-ring in one of the solid-fuel booster engines. The faulty seal allowed flames to attack the main liquid-fuel tank and a strut linking the tank to the booster. The collapsing strut allowed the upper end of the booster to swing into the liquid-fuel tank and the whole shuttle burned explosively.

The commission criticized NASA's management practices, inadequate quality control, over-ambitious schedules. The political atmosphere exacerbated the situation. [4]

The political atmosphere threatened the existence of the Space Shuttle program, which had become the major part of NASA. The prevailing attitude at NASA was that risk is best countered by careful engineering design and test. NASA had not conducted probabilistic risk assessment (PRA) and so failed to collect the statistical data that might have predicted the O-ring malfunction.

NASA now recognizes the value of PRA as a tool for understanding system vulnerability and now operates under a policy that requires disciplined and documented management of risk. NASA has established an ongoing risk management program and conducts periodic workshops to train personnel in risk assessment.

## 2.4
## PROBABILISTIC NATURE OF RISK

Technical performance, schedule, and cost issues that become the sources of risk have their roots in uncertainty: namely, how should a job be done; how long should it take; and how much should it cost. The laws of probability govern the magnitude of risk exposure in the foregoing issues, and probability and statistics allow inferences about the magnitude of the exposure.

As we stated in the previous chapter, the essence of **risk management** is the avoidance of hazards and perils. A hazard or a peril is an event whose outcome is governed by a random variable

## 2.4 Probabilistic Nature of Risk

from a probability distribution, which may be known or assumed, but whose occurrence is uncontrollable. A technical hazard or peril is an undesirable event occurring in the course of development, production, or operation of a product which requires corrective action for activities to continue as planned. In mathematical terms, a risk incident is the joint probability of the occurrence of the event and the occurrence of a given consequence of the event.

Consequential perils of interest in technical risk management impose risk time and risk cost. Risk time and risk cost are derived by multiplying corrective-action time and corrective-action cost and the probability of occurrence of the peril. The resultant products are the risk exposure from the particular peril.

### ■ 2.4.1 Risk Time

**Risk time (RT)** relates the probabilistic nature of risk to the impact on schedule time caused by corrective action. There are two approaches to calculating risk time depending on whether you use an aggregate or disaggregate approach to modeling risk exposure.

Both approaches start with a baseline time estimate (**BTE**) for the activity. In the aggregate approach, risk probability is estimated for the overall activity and the BTE is factored by the risk probability to yield RT. RT is added to BTE to yield risk time estimate (**RTE**). The magnitude of RTE runs higher in the aggregate approach than in the disaggregate approach.

Consider a product in development with a risk probability estimated as medium and a BTE of 24 months. Medium risk probability equates to a quantified risk probability measure of 0.5 ($v.$, Table 2.6).

The value of RT is (24 months)(0.5), or 12 months. The RTE for the product is 24 months + 12 months, or 36 months.

In the disaggregate approach, risk probability is pinpointed to a specific assembly, subassembly, or component of the product. The greater the granularity, the greater the degree of disaggregation and, usually, the greater the realism and credibility.

Consider an assembly in the product with the same risk probability of medium and an estimated corrective-action time of 12 months. The assembly RT is (12 months)(0.5), or 6 months. The RTE for the product containing the assembly is 24 months + 6 months, or 30 months.

The values of RTE obtained in both the aggregate and disaggregate approaches are probabilistic. Judging the risk as medium is an expression of probability; multiplying BTE by expressions of probability yields probabilistic estimates.

The disaggregate approach is more amenable to deterministic estimating of RTE insofar as risk has already been pinpointed to a particular area in the product. Instead of judging the risk on a top-down basis, you would attempt to determine what could go wrong in the development from the bottom-up and estimate the corrective-action time on this basis.

### ■ 2.4.2 Risk Cost

**Risk cost (RC)** relates the probabilistic nature of risk to the cost of corrective action. As with risk time, there are two approaches to the calculation of risk cost depending again on whether you use an aggregate or disaggregate approach to modeling risk cost.

Both approaches start with a baseline cost estimate (BCE) for the activity of interest. In the aggregate approach, you first estimate the risk probability for the overall activity. Then you multiply BCE by the quantified risk probability measure to obtain RC. You add RC to BCE to obtain the risk cost estimate (RCE).

Consider a product in a development task with a BCE of $500,000 and risk probability of medium, or 0.5. The value of RC is ($500,000)(0.5), or $250,000, and the value of RCE is $500,000 + $250,000, or $750,000.

In the disaggregate approach for estimating RC, you pinpoint the risk probability and corrective-action cost to a specific assembly, subassembly, or component of the product. Consider an assembly in the product with a risk probability of medium and an estimated corrective-action cost of $100,000. The assembly RC is ($100,000)(0.5), or $50,000. The RCE for the product containing the assembly is $500,000 + $50,000, or $550,000.

Again, the value of RC used in both the aggregate and disaggregate approaches is probabilistic. As we stated previously, the disaggregate approach is more amenable to deterministic estimates of RCE.

The aggregate approach is less amenable to deterministic estimates of RC because of the lack of granularity in the BCE. Disaggregate-based deterministic estimates take much more work, but generally are worth the effort. These estimates usually have significantly more realism and credibility than aggregate-based estimates of any kind.

### ■ 2.4.3 Example of Risk Exposure at the Component Level

Gamma Products, Inc. manufactures a product line of X-ray equipment. At the heart of each product is the X-ray tube used to produce electromagnetic radiations of extremely short wavelength that can penetrate solids.

> *The first efficient X-ray tube was developed by the American scientist William D. Coolidge in 1913 and one form of the tubes used today is still called the "Coolidge tube."*
> **Analyst**

Gamma manufactures its own X-ray tubes in lots of 1,000. The tubes are rugged devices consisting of an evacuated glass envelope, a cathode (*i.e.*, source of electrons), an anode (*i.e.*, target for the electrons), and a source of high electric voltage used to focus and drive the electron beam from cathode to anode. The emission of electrons by the cathode can be controlled independently of the applied high voltage. The bombardment by the focused electron beam on the anode induces the anode to emit X-rays. The anode is usually fabricated from copper, molybdenum, or tungsten, which is coated with a thin film of gold.

Cooling for the larger tubes is provided by oil or water circulating through the anode, and by conduction, convection, and radiation for smaller tubes. Reliability analysis indicates that the **mean-time-between-failures** (**MTBF**) of the X-ray tubes manufactured by Gamma is at least 10,000 hours.

Gamma estimates that, on the average, service calls involving the replacement of X-ray tubes cost an average of $1,250. Gamma provides its customers with a **limited warranty** that includes on-site replacement of failed components for a period of 2,000 hours of operational life or two

## 2.4 Probabilistic Nature of Risk

years, whichever is less. Gamma wishes to increase the warranty period to 3,000 operational hours, or three years, whichever is less, to promote sales.

> *A limited warranty covers only replacement cost of the particular failed item and not the cost of incidental or consequential damage for a specified time period.*
> **Analyst**

Gamma retains Analyst to estimate the risk cost, on a per-lot basis, over the extended warranty period. Table 2.16 gives the approach followed by Analyst in carrying out the assignment.

If the X-ray equipment was used every day of the week for 24 hours, the limit of 3,000 operational hours would be reached in 125 days. On the basis of 8 hours per day, 5 days per week, the limit of 3,000 operational hours would be reached in 75 weeks. Therefore, Analyst uses 3,000 operational hours, along with *MTBF* = 10,000 hours, in the calculations. Equation 2.8 is the relationship for calculating the probability of no failure ($P(0)$) until after time $t$.

*Table 2.16   Technical Approach for Risk Exposure at Component Level Example*

1. Determine whether 3,000 hours or 3 years is the warranty period to use in the analysis.
2. Use the exponential probability distribution to model X-ray tube failures.
3. Calculate the probability of a failure before the end of the warranty period.
4. Derive per-unit risk cost by multiplying the average X-ray tube replacement cost by the probability of a failure.
5. Derive the per-lot risk cost by multiplying the per-unit risk cost by the lot size.

$$P_0 = e^{-\lambda t} \tag{2.8}$$

where $\lambda$ denotes **failure rate** and is the reciprocal of *MTBF* or

$$\lambda = \frac{1}{MTBF} \tag{2.9}$$

For *MTBF* = 10,000 hours, $\lambda$ is 1 ÷ 10,000, or 0.0001 failure per hour. The probability of no failure before $t$ = 3,000 hours is

$$P_0 = e^{-(0.001)(3,000)}$$
$$= 0.7408. \tag{2.10}$$

The probability of one or more failures before 3,000 hours is simply 1 − 0.7408, or 0.2592.

You multiply the tube replacement cost and 0.2592 to obtain the per-unit risk cost of $1,250(0.2592), or $324. The per-lot risk cost is the product of $324 and the lot size of 1,000 for $324(1,000), or $324,000.

Analyst provides this information to Gamma Products, Inc. with the reminder that risk cost is a probabilistic value subject to variation. Gamma adds 10 percent to the estimate for its management reserve.

> *Dig the well before you are thirsty.*
> **Old Chinese saying**

### ■ 2.4.4 Risk Network

Schedule control is a major element of program management in complex programs. The concern of schedule control is the integrity of the flow of activities and the time that the activities should consume.

We will address schedule control techniques such as programmed review and evaluation technique (PERT) and critical path method (CPM) in subsequent chapters. Our interest now is in the concept of networks.

The conglomeration of activities and time is a **network**. Figure 2.7 illustrates a typical depiction of a **risk network**. Shaded circles are called "milestones" or "events." The lines connecting the milestones are "activities."

### ■ 2.4.5 Dependent Network

Where activities lie on the same path in a network, as in the upper part of Figure 2.7, the relationship is one of dependence because subsequent activities are dependent on the completion of prior activities on the path. In this case, the individual elements of risk time or cost are additive. In addition, there is possible dependence at the end of the path on the output of the other paths in the lower part of Figure 2.7.

For example, consider four elements of risk cost with individual values of $12,000, $20,000, $18,000, and $14,000 for activities lying on the same path in the network. The total risk cost would be the arithmetic sum of the four individual values, or $64,000.

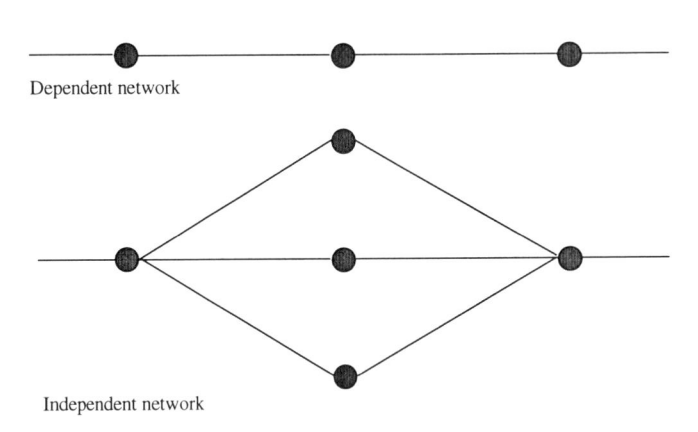

**Figure 2.7** Dependence in Risk Networks

## 2.4 Probabilistic Nature of Risk

### ■ 2.4.6 Independent Network

Where activities lie on different paths, as in the lower part of Figure 2.7, the relationship is one of independence because any given activity is not dependent on the completion of another. In this case, we use the **root-sum-of-squares** (**RSS**) method to sum the individual elements.

Next consider the same four activities if they were lying on four different paths in the network. The total risk cost would no longer be the arithmetic sum of the four individual elements of risk cost, but rather the RSS of the individual elements of risk cost.

Equation 2.11 gives the relationship for calculating the RSS of a series of numbers.

$$RSS = \sqrt{a^2 + b^2 + c^2 + \ldots + n^2} \tag{2.11}$$

where $a$, $b$, $c$, and $n$ denote the numbers in the series.

Substituting the four elements of risk cost with individual values of $12,000, $20,000, $18,000, and $14,000 in Equation 2.11, we obtain

$$RSS = \sqrt{(12{,}000)^2 + (20{,}000)^2 + (18{,}000)^2 + (14{,}000)^2}$$
$$= \$29{,}462. \tag{2.12}$$

which is appreciably less than the previously calculated value of $64,000.

Now you calculate the RSS of 2, 2, 2, and 2. The square of 2 is 4 and 4 + 4 + 4 + 4 is 16. The square root of 16 is 4. This is one of the interesting properties of the number 2.

### ■ 2.4.7 Hybrid Network

The networks shown in Figure 2.8 are commonplace. The configuration in the upper part of the illustration is a parallel-series network meaning that paths are in parallel and consist of activities which are in series.

The configuration in the lower part of Figure 2.8 is a parallel-series-parallel network because a section of the middle path (*i.e*, activity c) is in parallel with a section of the bottom path (*i.e.*, activity b) via activity l. In addition, a section of the middle path (*i.e*, activity g) is in parallel with a section of the bottom path (*i.e.*, activities h and j) also via activity l. The parallel-series-parallel network in part b adds another path to the network in part a. This has special significance when considering the composite risk cost of the overall network.

There is the question of whether to include the risk cost of activities d, h, and j in the middle path or the bottom path of the network of Figure 2.8. Usually, we include the risk cost in whatever path results in the greater composite risk cost for the overall network.

Individual risk times have an effect on overall schedules only if the individual risk times lie on the **critical path** of the network. In that event, the cumulative sum of the risk times adds to the overall schedule time (*i.e.*, BTE).

When the individual risk times lie on noncritical paths of the flow of activities, then the cumulative sum of the individual risk times on any given noncritical path adds to the overall time of that particular path only. When the new overall time of a given path exceeds that of the original critical path time, then it becomes the critical path.

Parallel-series network

Parallel-series-parallel network

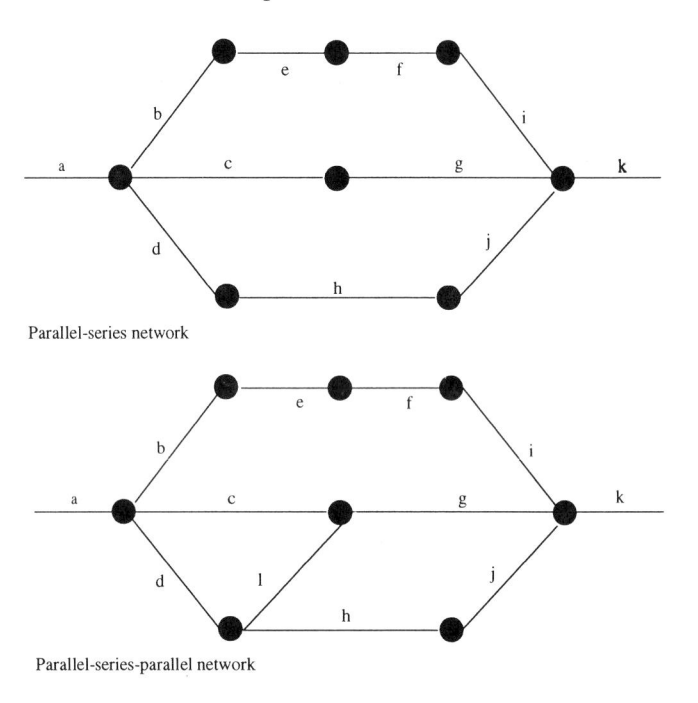

**Figure 2.8** Hybrid Risk Networks

It is relatively common to find networks with more than one critical path. You must exercise care in alleviating problems in any one of the paths where activities on the path are dependent on each other.

The introduction of risk time in the flow of activities increases cost. In the critical path, you need to consider the additional time over which direct cost such as labor will be expended. In addition, you need to consider the prolonged schedule over which additional indirect cost such as overhead will be expended. In noncritical paths, you only need to consider the expenditure of additional direct cost. Use the RSS approach for independent relationships among elements of risk cost. Use the additive approach for dependent relationships among individual elements of cost.

### ■ 2.4.8 Example of Risk Network in Manufacturing

Delta Industries manufactures commercial and private jet aircraft. Figure 2.9 is the network depicting final assembly and checkout of a certain aircraft model.

The activities in Figure 2.9 comprise a parallel-series network similar to the top part of Figure 2.8. The start and finish activities a and j have no risk time or risk cost. Again, values of risk time and risk cost along any given path are additive.

## 2.4 Probabilistic Nature of Risk

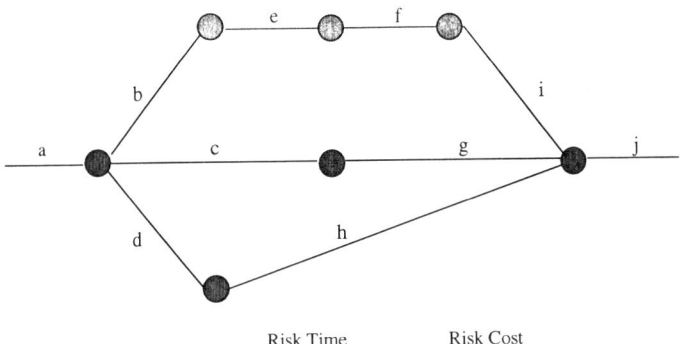

| Activity | Risk Time Months | Risk Cost Dollars |
|---|---|---|
| a | — | — |
| b | 1 | 75,000 |
| c | 2 | 125,000 |
| d | 1 | 50,000 |
| e | 1 | 65,000 |
| f | 1 | 50,000 |
| g | 2 | 110,000 |
| h | — | — |
| i | — | — |
| j | — | — |

**Figure 2.9** Risk Network in Manufacturing Example

Activities in the network are annotated with values of risk time and risk cost Analyst estimated on a previous occasion. Activity a in the figure is the starting activity. Note that the top path in the network has three dependent activities (*viz.*, b, c, and f).

Activity i is called a **dummy activity** that we use to connect the path to ending activity k. The middle path has two dependent activities (*viz.*, c and g) and the bottom path none. Activity h is a dummy that connects the bottom path to the ending activity k.

The company is concerned about the overall risk exposure in final assembly and checkout phase and retains Analyst to calculate the composite risk time and risk cost. Table 2.17 gives the approach Analyst uses in carrying out the assignment.

*Table 2.17*   *Technical Approach for Risk Network in Manufacturing Example*

---
1. Enumerate the paths through the network.
2. Calculate the composite values of the activities on the same paths.
3. Calculate the RSS for the composite values of all the paths in the network.
---

Analyst uses the worksheet in Table 2.18 to calculate the composite values of risk time and risk cost. The network configuration is parallel-series with three paths.

The activities comprising the paths are in the first column of Table 2.18. The respective calculations of risk time and risk cost are in the second and third columns of the table. The composite values of risk time and risk cost values of the three paths in the network are as follows:

Top path: 3 months and $190,000

Middle path: 4 months and $235,000

Bottom Path: 1 month and $50,000.

Which path is the critical path in the network? How much slack do the other paths have?

Table 2.18  Worksheet for Risk Network in Manufacturing Example

| Path | Risk Time | Risk Cost |
|---|---|---|
| b, e, g | (1 + 1 + 1) months = 3 months | $(75,000 + 65,000 + 50,000) = $190,000 |
| c, f | (2 + 2) months = 4 months | $(125,000 + 110,000) = $235,000 |
| d | 1 month | $50,000 |

The critical path in the network is the one requiring the most time to complete. The middle path in the network is the critical path. The critical path risk time is 4 months.

The slack time in the top path is 4−3, or 1 month; the slack time in the bottom path is 4−1, or 3 months. This means that you can delay the work in the top and bottom paths by 1 month and 3 months with no negative effect.

Analyst determines that the three paths in the network are independent of each other; meaning that composite values of risk time and risk cost for the overall network should be derived using the RSS method.

Analyst substitutes the values from Table 2.18 in Equation 2.11 and obtains

$$RSS = \sqrt{(3 \text{ months})^2 + (4 \text{ months})^2 + (1 \text{ month})^2}$$
$$= 5.0990 \text{ months} \quad (2.13)$$

for risk time, and

$$RSS = \sqrt{(190,000)^2 + (235,000)^2 + (50,000)^2}$$
$$= \$306,309 \quad (2.14)$$

for risk cost.

Analyst provides the composite risk time and risk cost values of 5.0990 months and $306,309 to Delta Industries.

## 2.5
## RISK DOMINANCE

As we stated previously, risk exposure is a function of hazards and their consequential perils. Section 2.3.3 illuminated the hierarchy of hazards and risks. Certain hazards and risks dominate others in establishing risk exposure in any given hierarchy. That is to say, the more dominant influence will mitigate the effect of the less dominant hazards or perils.

## 2.5 Risk Dominance

For example, the hazards of design immaturity and design complexity have the consequential peril of excessive manufacturing defects. The hazard of design immaturity dominates the hazard of design complexity.

You will experience fewer defects in a complex product whose design is fully mature than in a simple product whose design is completely immature. In other words, the more often you do the same job, the less mistakes you will make, irrespective of the quality, complexity, and concurrency of the elements of the job.

This is the rationale for the dominance of product and process maturity factors over the other product and process factors. We define this relationship of dominance by risk order, first-order or second-order. We quantify the degree of dominance of first-order hazards over second-order hazards by *k*-factors.

### ■ 2.5.1 Risk Order

The metrics of risk exposure use a system of **risk determinant factors** (**RDF**). Dominant risk determinant factors are first-order. The derivative risk determinant factors which are dominated by first-order risk determinant factors are second-order.

Technical risk management is concerned with the adequacy of certain **intrinsic attributes** of the management of organizations, the products which these organizations produce, and the processes used to produce the products. There is also concern for the attributes of the environment in which these organizations function.

Intrinsic attributes are part of the particular program and are largely within the span of control of program management. The environments in which organizations function is described by the **extrinsic attributes**, which are largely beyond the control of program management. Table 2.19 lists the attributes and their order of dependency.

*Table 2.19    Order of Attributes*

|  |  **Intrinsic Attributes** |  |
|---|---|---|
| Management | Funding and Investment Policy | First-Order |
|  | Program Continuity Policy | First-Order |
|  | Personnel Retention Policy | First-Order |
| Product | Maturity | First-Order |
|  | Quality | Second-Order |
|  | Complexity | Second-Order |
|  | Concurrency | Second-Order |
| Process | Maturity | First-Order |
|  | Quality | Second-Order |
|  | Complexity | Second-Order |
|  | Concurrency | Second-Order |
|  | **Extrinsic Attributes** |  |
| External | Inflation | First-Order |
|  | Regulatory Statutes | First-Order |
|  | Labor Relations | First-Order |
|  | Public Attributes | First-Order |
|  | Physical Environment | First-Order |

### 2.5.2 k-Factor

As we stated previously, the adequacy of both intrinsic and extrinsic attributes serve as risk determinants that we quantify into a system of risk determinant factors. Figure 2.10 shows the influence of the value of the *k*-factor on second-order risk determinant factors. The abscissa in the figure is used to enter the value of the second-order risk determinant factor. The value of *k*-factor is that of the appropriate first-order risk determinant factor. The ordinate in the figure gives the resultant value of the factored second-order risk determinant factor.

The abscissa in Figure 2.10 is the second-order risk determinant factor. The ordinate is the product of the second-order risk determinant factor (RDF) and the respective values of the *k*-factor. For example, at the intersection of second-order RDF = 0.8 and the plot *k* = 0.5, Figure 2.10 reads 0.4 on the ordinate.

The value 0.4 is simply the product of 0.5 and 0.8. As you would expect, the slope of the plot of the *k*-factor increases with increasing values of *k*. The values of the *k*-factor range from 0 to 1.0, with 0 signifying no dominance and 1 maximum dominance.

We usually equate the *k*-factor to the value of the risk determinant factor for either product maturity or process maturity. The rationale is that the greater the maturity of a given product or process, as indicated by a smaller value of the first-order risk determinant factor, the smaller would be the influence of second-order risk determinants on risk exposure.

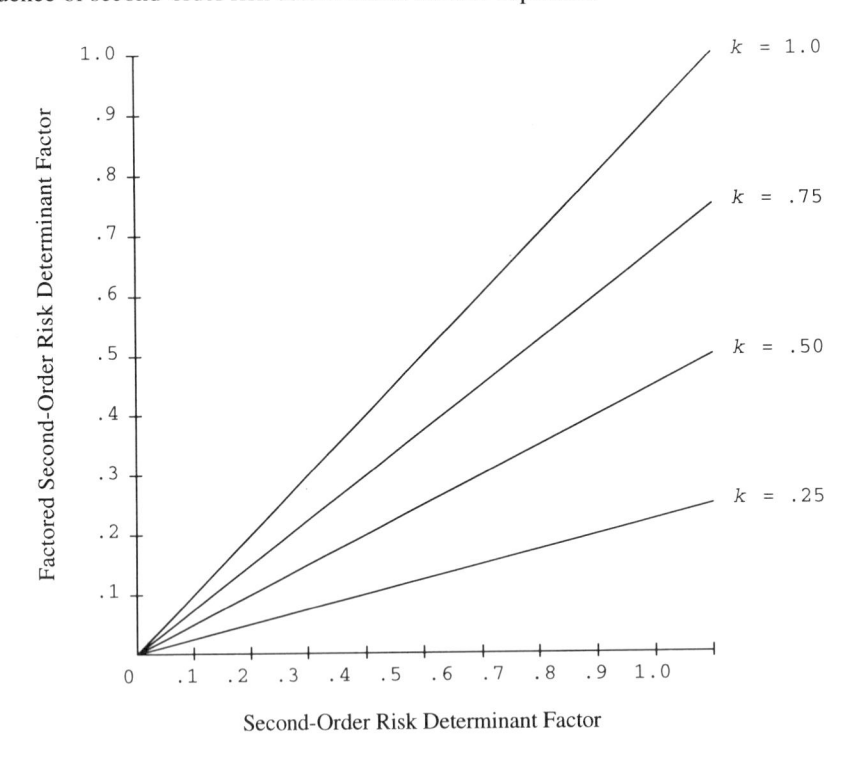

**Figure 2.10** Influence of *k*-Factors on Second-Order Risk Determinant Factors

## 2.5 Risk Dominance

We use the value of the product maturity factor as the $k$-factor for product quality factor, product complexity factor, and product concurrency factor. We use the value of the process maturity factor as the $k$-factor for process quality factor, process complexity factor, and process concurrency factor.

Since the $k$-factor describes the dependent relationship between first-order and second-order risk determinant factors, the first-order and factored second-order risk determinant factors are additive in estimating risk exposure. Consider an item with a product maturity factor of 0.2, product quality factor of 0.4, product complexity factor of 0.6, and product concurrency factor of 0.8. The composite risk determinant factor ($\Sigma$RDF) would be

$$\Sigma RDF = 0.2 + (0.2)(0.4) + (0.2)(0.6) + (0.2)(0.6)$$
$$= 0.56 \qquad (2.15)$$

You should note that by using the product maturity factor and process maturity factor to arrive at values of the $k$-factor, you are in essence looking to the past to predict the future.

> *What is past is prologue.*
> **William Shakespeare**

### ■ 2.5.3 Example of Risk Time Dominance

Epsilon Enterprises, Inc. distributes a broad line of giftware which it packages under its own label. Figure 2.11 is the network depicting the activities starting with the receipt of items from the company's suppliers to the shipment of packaged merchandise to the company's customers.

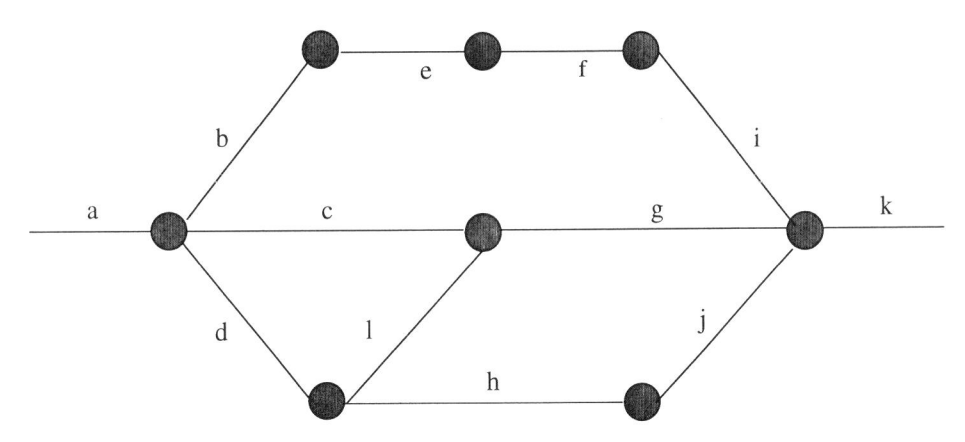

**Figure 2.11** Network for Risk Time Dominance Example

Table 2.20 gives the risk times and $k$-factors which Analyst had estimated in a previous assignment. The last column lists the products of risk times and $k$-factors.

*Table 2.20  Data for Risk Time Dominance Example*

| Activity | Risk Time Days | k-factor | Factored Risk Time, Days |
|---|---|---|---|
| a | - | - | - |
| b | 1 | 0.2 | 0.2 |
| c | 3 | 0.1 | 0.3 |
| d | 1 | 0.4 | 0.4 |
| e | 2 | 0.2 | 0.4 |
| f | 1 | 0.4 | 0.4 |
| g | 3 | 0.5 | 1.5 |
| h | 2 | 0.3 | 0.6 |
| i | - | - | - |
| j | - | - | - |
| k | - | - | - |
| l | 4 | 0.5 | 2.0 |

Epsilon retains Analyst to estimate the composite risk delay which the company may experience. Table 2.21 give the technical approach Analyst uses in carrying out the assignment.

Analyst enumerates the four paths through the network in Table 2.22, the worksheet for the example. Analyst then calculates the composite risk time by path. Activity a in Figure 2.11 is the starting activity. Activities i and j are dummy activities that connect the paths to activity k, the ending activity.

Note that the value of risk time ranges from 1.0 day to 3.9 days. How much slack time is there in each of the three noncritical paths of the network? How much negative slack time is there in the critical path?

*Table 2.21  Technical Approach for Risk Time Dominance Example*

1. Enumerate the paths through the network.
2. Calculate the composite risk delay values of the activities on the same paths.
3. Identify the critical path.

*Table 2.22  Worksheet for Risk Time Dominance Example*

| Path | Composite Factored Risk Delay, Days |
|---|---|
| a, b, e, f, i, k | - + 0.2 + 0.4 + 0.4 + - + - = 1.0 |
| a, c, g, k | - + 0.3 + 1.5 + - = 1.8 |
| a, d, l, g, k | - + 0.4 + 2.0 + 1.5 + - = 3.9 |
| a, d, h, j, k | - + 0.4 + 0.6 + - + - = 1.0 |

There are 3.9 – 1.0, or 2.9 days of slack time in the first noncritical path; 3.9 – 1.8, or 2.1 days of slack time in the second noncritical path; and 3.9 – 1.0, or 2.9 days of slack time in the third path. There is 1.8 – 3.9, or –2.1 days of (negative) slack time in the critical path.

Analyst advises the client that the critical path in the network consists of activities a, d, l, g, and k, and that the composite factored risk delay is 3.9 days. The longest factored risk delay (*i.e.*, 2

## 2.5 Risk Dominance

days) is in activity l which covers in-house printing of labels. Epsilon's management decides to contract for printing in the future.

### ■ 2.5.4 Risk Applicability

Table 2.23 cross-references categories of products and applicable risk determinant factors. Note that all risk determinant factors are deemed applicable to hardware and software products, whereas only product-related factors are designated for service; the rationale being that the product is the process of providing service.

*Table 2.23    Risk Applicability*

| Risk Determinant Factor | Hardware | Software | Service |
|---|---|---|---|
| Management Attributes | ✔ | ✔ | ✔ |
| Product Maturity | ✔ | ✔ | ✔ |
| Product Quality | ✔ | ✔ | ✔ |
| Product Complexity | ✔ | ✔ | ✔ |
| Product Concurrency | ✔ | ✔ | ✔ |
| Process Maturity | ✔ | ✔ | |
| Process Quality | ✔ | ✔ | |
| Process Complexity | ✔ | ✔ | |
| Process Concurrency | ✔ | ✔ | |
| Extrinsic Attributes | ✔ | ✔ | ✔ |

The designations in Table 2.23 are judgmental. There are a multitude of products and risk determinant factors that need to be adapted to the specific needs of the products of interest.

Hardware products include component parts of products and systems comprised of many products produced by a broad range of industries. Buildings and highways are products in the construction industry.

Software includes both the programs which users need to operate products and systems, and the programs which suppliers need to provide services. In addition, *software* includes the programs needed by producers to produce hardware and software items.

Service covers a broad spectrum of products that encompasses the larger share of the gross domestic product of the United States. Service institutions include diversified service companies, commercial banking companies, diversified financial companies, savings institutions, life insurance companies, transportation companies, and utilities. [3]

The implications of the risk determinant factors change from product to product. Product maturity factor is a measure of the production readiness of hardware and software products, as well as a measure of experience in service.

Product quality factor is used as a measure of producibility, reliability, and testability in hardware, software, and service products. Product complexity factor and product concurrency factor serve as essentially the same measures in hardware, software, and service.

Process maturity factor, process quality factor, process complexity factor, and process concurrency factor serve as essentially the same measures in hardware and software products, but are not applicable to service products wherein the product and process are one and the same. The contribution of personnel to risk exposure in service products is accommodated by the management attribute factor. In addition, management attribute factor and extrinsic attribute factor serve as measures in all product categories.

### 2.5.5 Example of Risk Exposure in Investment

A client asks Analyst to estimate the risk exposure from investing in the mutual fund whose yield data are given in Table 2.24.

*Table 2.24  Mutual Fund Data for Risk Exposure in Investment Example*

| Year | Percent | Year | Percent |
|------|---------|------|---------|
| 1975 | 9.65    | 1984 | 11.78   |
| 1980 | 12.56   | 1985 | 9.83    |
| 1981 | 13.20   | 1986 | 8.37    |
| 1982 | 12.11   | 1987 | 7.91    |
| 1983 | 11.46   | 1988 | 8.56    |

Table 2.25 gives the technical approach Analyst uses in carrying out the assignment. The question of how good is a good investment is usually answered by comparison to the yield of U.S. Treasury instruments. Table 2.26 lists the percentage yield of U.S. Treasury instruments for periods of three years, five years, and ten years from 1975 through 1988.

Table 2.27 gives suggested values of **product maturity factor** (**PRODMF**) as functions of the **standard deviation** (**s**) divided by the **mean** (**m**). You can derive in-between values of PRODMF with interpolation.

*Table 2.25  Technical Approach for Risk Exposure in Investment Example*

1. Select U.S. Treasury 10-year note data as the basis for the analysis.
2. Subtract the mutual fund yield by year in Table 2.24 from the 10-year Treasury note yield by year in Table 2.26.
3. Calculate the standard deviation of the difference in values.
4. Select the product maturity factor from the values in Table 2.27 as the measure of risk exposure.

*Table 2.26  Treasury Note Data for Risk Exposure in Investment Example [5]*

|               | 1975 | 1980  | 1981  | 1982  | 1983  |
|---------------|------|-------|-------|-------|-------|
| 3-Year Notes  | 7.49 | 11.55 | 14.44 | 12.92 | 10.45 |
| 5-Year Notes  | 7.77 | 11.48 | 14.24 | 13.01 | 10.80 |
| 10-Year Notes | 7.99 | 10.81 | 13.91 | 13.00 | 11.11 |

|               | 1984  | 1985  | 1986 | 1987 | 1988 |
|---------------|-------|-------|------|------|------|
| 3-Year Notes  | 11.89 | 9.64  | 7.06 | 7.68 | 8.26 |
| 5-Year Notes  | 12.24 | 10.13 | 7.31 | 7.94 | 8.47 |
| 10-Year Notes | 12.44 | 10.75 | 7.68 | 8.39 | 8.98 |

Adapted by courtesy of the U.S. Bureau of the Census from *Statistical Abstract of the United States*: 1990 (110th Edition).

## 2.5 Risk Dominance

**Table 2.27** *Product Maturity Factors for Risk Exposure in Investment Example*

| PRODMF | $s \div m$ | PRODMF | $s \div m$ |
|---|---|---|---|
| 0.1 | <1 | 0.6 | ≥5<6 |
| 0.2 | ≥1<2 | 0.7 | ≥6<7 |
| 0.3 | ≥2<3 | 0.8 | ≥7<8 |
| 0.4 | ≥3<4 | 0.9 | ≥8<9 |
| 0.5 | ≥4<5 | 1.0 | ≥9 |

PRODMF: Product maturity factor.
$s \div m$: Standard deviation divided by the mean.
<: Less than.
≥: Equal to or more than.

Investment risk ratings in contemporary literature are given typically as very low to very high. We prefer the ratings in Table 2.27 where PRODMF corresponds to risk exposure that is extremely low and PRODMF = 1.0 to risk exposure that is extremely high. An average risk exposure could have a mean ($m$) of about 2 and standard deviation ($s$) of about 0.5 for $s \div m = 2 \div 0.5$, or 4. This value corresponds to PRODMF = 0.5.

Analyst calculates the yearly difference between the yields of the mutual fund and U.S. Treasury notes as the first step in calculating the value of $s$. These calculations are given in the fourth column of the worksheet in Table 2.28.

The mean ($m$) of the differences in Table 2.28 is 1.03 ÷ 10, or 0.103. Analyst uses Equation 2.17 to calculate the variance ($s^2$) of the variates $x_i$ (i.e., differences) with sample size $n = 10$.

**Table 2.28** *Worksheet for Risk Exposure in Investment Example*

| Year | Mutual Fund | 10-Year Notes | Difference |
|---|---|---|---|
| 1975 | 9.65 | 7.99 | 1.66 |
| 1980 | 12.56 | 10.81 | 1.75 |
| 1981 | 13.20 | 13.91 | −0.71 |
| 1982 | 12.11 | 13.00 | −0.89 |
| 1983 | 11.46 | 10.45 | 1.01 |
| 1984 | 11.78 | 12.44 | −0.66 |
| 1985 | 9.83 | 10.75 | −0.92 |
| 1986 | 8.37 | 7.68 | 0.69 |
| 1987 | 7.91 | 8.39 | −0.48 |
| 1988 | 8.56 | 8.98 | −0.42 |

Sum of differences: 1.03

$$s^2 = \frac{\Sigma(x_i - m)^2}{n - 1} \tag{2.16}$$

Substituting values of $x_i$, $m$, and $n$ in Equation 2.16, Analyst obtains

$$s^2 = [(1.66 - 0.103)^2 + (1.75 - 0.103)^2 + (-0.71 - 0.103)^2 + (-0.89 - 0.103)^2 + (1.01 - 0.103)^2$$
$$+ (0.66 - 0.103)^2 + (-0.92 - 0.103)^2 + (0.69 - 0.103)^2 + (-0.48 - 0.103)^2 + (0.42 - 0.103)^2] \div (10 - 1)$$
$$= 1.133. \tag{2.17}$$

54  Chapter 2 • RISK FUNDAMENTALS

The standard deviation is simply the square root of the **variance**, or 1.064 percent.

The value of $s \div m$ is $1.133 \div 1.03$, or 1.10. In accordance with Table 2.27, the corresponding value of PRODMF is between 0.1 and 0.2. For every $100 invested, the risk exposure in terms of risk cost is at between $100(0.1), or $10.00, and $100(0.2), or $20.00. Analyst interpolates between PRODMF = 0.1 and 0.2 and obtains

$$PRODMF = 0.1 + 0.1(1.10 - 1)$$
$$= 0.110 \qquad (2.18)$$

The precise value of risk cost is $100(0.110), or $11.00.

### ■ 2.5.6 Example of Risk Exposure in Construction

The subject of this example is a major construction project in a western city of the United Kingdom. The value of the project is 104 million British pounds (£104 million). [6]

The project encounters a number of costly delays and the owner engages Analyst to estimate the risk exposure in terms of risk cost. Table 2.29 is the technical approach Analyst follows in carrying out the assignment.

*Table 2.29  Technical Approach for Risk Exposure in Construction Example*

1. Obtain BCE and RDF by work packages.
2. Assume dependence among values of RDF for given work packages, calculate values of composite risk determinant factors (CRDF), and products of BCE and CRDF.
3. Select the work packages whose products of BCE and CRDF are 80 to 85 percent of the total of all products of BCE and CRDF.
4. Calculate and sum the values of risk cost for the work packages from Item 3.

There are four areas of concern: the complexity of the design; level of technological innovation; complexity of off-site construction; and complexity of on-site construction. Table 2.30 is the worksheet Analyst uses to list staff members' baseline cost estimates (**BCE**) and risk determinant factor (**RDF**) estimates by project work packages..

*Table 2.30  Worksheet for Risk Exposure in Construction Example [6]*

| Work Package | BCE £M | RDF-1 | RDF-2 | RDF-3 | RDF-4 | CRDF | Factored BCE |
|---|---|---|---|---|---|---|---|
| Demolition | 2 | - | - | - | 0.5 | 0.5 | 1.0 |
| Piling | 4 | 0.4 | 0.3 | - | 0.6 | 1.3 | 5.2 |
| Diaphragm Wall | 3 | 0.6 | 0.4 | - | 0.6 | 1.6 | 4.8 |
| Substructure | 12 | 0.7 | 0.5 | - | 0.8 | 2.0 | 24.0 |
| Steel Frame | 16 | 0.8 | 0.4 | 0.6 | 0.7 | 2.5 | 40.0 |
| Superstructure | 3 | 0.5 | 0.4 | - | 0.3 | 1.2 | 3.6 |
| Fire Protection | 4 | 0.4 | 0.3 | - | 0.4 | 1.1 | 4.4 |

## 2.5 Risk Dominance

*Table 2.30* Worksheet for Risk Exposure in Construction Example [6] (Cont.)

| Work Package | BCE £M | RDF-1 | RDF-2 | RDF-3 | RDF-4 | CRDF | Factored BCE |
|---|---|---|---|---|---|---|---|
| Drylining | 5 | 0.6 | 0.4 | - | 0.3 | 1.3 | 6.5 |
| Cladding | 34 | 0.9 | 0.8 | 0.9 | 0.5 | 3.1 | 105.4 |
| Glazed Atrium | 3 | 0.7 | 0.7 | 0.8 | 0.6 | 2.8 | 8.4 |
| Electrical | 11 | 0.8 | 0.6 | 0.7 | 0.5 | 2.6 | 28.6 |
| Mechanical | 15 | 0.7 | 0.6 | 0.5 | 0.4 | 2.2 | 33.0 |
| Lifts | 4 | 0.4 | 0.7 | 0.6 | 0.4 | 2.1 | 8.4 |
| Air Handling Pods | 3 | 0.6 | 0.7 | 0.8 | 0.3 | 2.4 | 7.2 |
| Toilet Pods | 3 | 0.6 | 0.7 | 0.7 | 0.3 | 2.3 | 6.9 |
| Suspended Ceilings | 2 | 0.7 | 0.5 | 0.5 | 0.7 | 2.4 | 4.8 |
| Raised Floors | 1 | 0.3 | 0.4 | 0.6 | 0.5 | 1.8 | 1.8 |
| Totals: | 125 | | | | | | 294.0 |

RDF-1: Complexity of design risk determinant factor.
RDF-2: Level of technological innovation risk determinant factor.
RDF-3: Complexity of off-site construction risk determinant factor.
RDF-4: Complexity of on-site construction risk determinant factor.
CRDF: Composite risk determinant factor.
Factored BCE: Product of baseline cost estimate and composite risk determinant factor.
Adapted by permission of AACE International, P.O. Box 1557, Morgantown, WV 26507-1557 from David H. Buchan, *Risk Analysis—Some Practical Suggestions*, Cost Engineering, January 1994.

The sixth column in Table 2.30 lists values of composite risk determinant factor that Analyst derives by adding the respective values of risk determinant factors. Analyst adds the values of RDF because the work packages are dependent on each other.

The total for all the work packages is £228.9 million. The sum for the substructure, steel frame, cladding, glazed atrium, electrical, mechanical, and lifts work packages is 24.0, 40.0, 40.3, 8.4, 28.6, 33.0, 8.4, or £158.7 million.

Analyst questions the BCE of £134 million for cladding. Staff members inform Analyst that the high cost of cladding is due to using 1,100 panels of which no more than six types are used more than once.

With the concurrence of the owner, Analyst limits the risk cost estimate to the substructure, steel frame, cladding, glazed atrium, electrical, mechanical, and lifts work packages. The respective values of CRDF are 2.0, 2.5, 3.1, 2.8, 2.6, 2.2, and 2.1.

The maximum possible value for CRDF is four, the number of RDF inputs to the values of CRDF. Analyst divides the CRDF values by four, and obtains the following values normalized with respect to unity:

Substructure CRDF: $2.0 \div 4 = 0.50$

Steel frame CRDF: $2.5 \div 4 = 0.625$

Cladding CRDF: $3.1 \div 4 = 0.775$

Glazed atrium CRDF: $2.8 \div 4 = 0.70$

Electrical CRDF: 2.6 ÷ 4 = 0.65
Mechanical CRDF: 2.2 ÷ 4 = 0.55
Lifts CRDF: 2.1 ÷ 4 = 0.525.

Analyst multiplies the values of CRDF and the respective values of factored BCE, and obtains the following values of RC:

Substructure RC: (0.50)(£12 million) = £6 million
Steel frame RC: (0.625)(£12 million) = £7.5 million
Cladding RC: (0.775)£13 million) = £10.075 million
Glazed atrium RC: (0.70)(£3 million) = £2.1 million
Electrical RC: (0.65)(£11 million) = £7.15 million
Mechanical RC: (0.55)(£15 million) = £8.25 million
Lifts RC: (0.525)(£4 million) = £2.1 million.

The total RC equals £43.175 million. RCE is the sum of BCE and RC. The project RCE is £125 million + £43.175 million, or £168.175 million. The biggest driver is the cladding RC of £10.075 million.

Analyst provides the findings to the owner. The owner directs the architect to redesign the cladding for lower cost and to review the other work packages for possible cost saving.

## 2.6
## SUMMARY

There are numerous terms in the vocabulary of technical risk management with very precise meanings. **Section 2.1 Definitions** provided definitions of the key terms used in this chapter.

**Section 2.2 Risk Principles** discussed the issue of conflicting principles for combating risk: the risk benefit-equity principle and the risk cost-effectiveness principle.

The risk benefit-equity principle mandates that both the risk and the benefit of avoiding any particular calamity should be shared as equally as possible by the population of interest. The risk cost-effectiveness principle mandates that risk reduction resources should be deployed for maximum risk reduction cost for a given activity. The section included an interesting example based on foreign aid.

**Section 2.3 Risk Morphology** introduced risk from a systematic viewpoint and showed that every decision made or action taken is fraught with elements of risk. The relationship between hazards and perils was explored along with the concepts of cause and effect, risk system, and risk hierarchy. The categories of risk were discussed from the viewpoints of objectivity and subjectivity.

**Section 2.4 Probabilistic Nature of Risk** brought in the probabilistic concepts of risk time and risk cost, and showed how these elements combine to form risk networks. The summation of idual risk delay and cost elements was demonstrated for the cases of dependence and independ among the elements.

ction **2.5 Risk Dominance** reiterated the basic definitions of risk, hazards, and perils, risk risk incidents, and risk exposure to illustrate the concept of first-order and second-order nant factors. It was shown that first-order risk determinant factors exert an influence on the contribution to risk exposure from second-order risk determinant factors. The use of the $k$-factor was demonstrated with two detailed examples.

The applicability of the various risk determinant factors as a function of product categories was discussed. The categories are hardware, software, and service. Detailed examples and exercises illustrated the application to product development, investment, manufacturing, and construction.

## 2.7 EXERCISES

These exercise problems have been selected to reinforce key points and relationships in the preceding sections of the chapter. Step-by-step solutions to the problems are given in Appendix C of the book, but we urge you to attempt the exercises before resorting to the solutions.

### ■ 2.7.1 Risk Principles

There is much concern about the depletion of the ozone layer from use of chlorofluorocarbons (CFC). Under the terms of the Montreal Protocol international agreement, the United States and a number of other industrialized nations have pledged to halt production of CFC by the year 2000. In a series of working sessions, these nations developed an orderly phase-out plan for the chlorofluorocarbons by the turn of the century.

In a recent press release, however, NASA reported that ozone-depleting chemicals over Canada, the United States, and Europe have reached an alarming level. As a consequence, the ozone layer is being depleted at a much faster rate than had been believed. This news has aroused the environmental community.

The news also prompted the President of the United States to order the phase-out of ozone-depleting chemicals by the year 1995, rather than wait until the year 2000 which had been mandated in the international agreement.

Another press release described a state-of-the art advance in the circuit card assembly (**CCA**) manufacturing process that eliminates the use of freon and attendant emission of ozone-depleting chlorofluorocarbons.

The new process uses water-based fluxes in soldering CCAs, and for clean-up uses water, rather than freon used with rosin fluxes. The Environmental Protection Agency has hailed the new process as a major stride toward arresting the depletion of the ozone layer and reducing cancer-causing levels of ultraviolet radiation from the sun.

On the other hand, the Department of Defense (**DoD**) insists that freon cleaning is an indispensable ingredient in the production of high-quality weapon systems. Despite the imminence of the ban, the DoD has not yet relaxed the requirement on its contractors for freon cleaning.

Identify the conflicting risk principles in this situation and the protagonists who are engaged in the conflict. Discuss the significance of the foregoing to DoD contractors and the defense budget.

### ■ 2.7.2 Risk Continuum

In a certain production facility, there are six hazards involving inspection, of which any two can induce the peril of a faulty part eluding inspection. Calculate the number of combinations which are possible in the problem of interest.

Increase the number of hazards to seven and note the increase in the number of combinations. Next, increase the number of perils to three and note how the number of combinations have multiplied.

### ■ 2.7.3 Risk Hierarchy

Many breaches of computer security have come to light in recent years, the most notable being the notorious Equity Funding Corporation of America case which involved insurance company fraud. This case points out some major reasons why computer fraud is growing, why it can be so successful, and why its existence is often difficult either to predict or detect. In the first place, the computer is usually a substitute for a manual system for recording and updating financial records which are the object of fraudulent intent. In the second place, the integrity of computer systems, whose output appears to be comprehensive and accurate, are rarely questioned and, if questioned, difficult to challenge. It is clear that computer fraud constitutes a major technical risk. [7]

The peril in this case was the fraudulent conversion of the company's assets by some individuals. Hazards, which may be the root of similar perils in other areas where computers are employed, include: (1) fire, flood, other natural disasters; (2) power outages and emergency power failure; (3) equipment failure; (4) human error; (5) labor relation problems; and (6) acts of sabotage.

Develop a hierarchial system of hazards and perils for this particular case along the lines of Table 2.12.

### ■ 2.7.4 Multiprocess Risk Probability

Table 2.31 gives suggested values of **process maturity factor** (**PROCMF**) as a function of the level of maturity in the related process. Consider three processes used on the same product, one of which has been used to produce and test similar LRIP first articles and two of which have had similar LRIP rate tooling proofed. Calculate the composite multiprocess PROCMF with the assumptions of dependence and independence among the processes.

*Table 2.31* Process Maturity Factors for Exercise in Section 2.7.4

| Factor | Level of Process Maturity |
|--------|---------------------------|
| 0.0 | Similar rate units produced and tested |
| 0.1 | Similar rate first-article produced and tested |
| 0.2 | Similar rate tooling proofed |
| 0.3 | Similar LRIP first-article produced and tested |
| 0.4 | Similar LRIP tooling proofed |
| 0.5 | Similar prototype produced and tested |
| 0.8 | Similar brassboard produced and tested |
| 0.9 | Similar breadboard produced and tested |
| 1.0 | No similar experience possessed |

Rate: Full production rate.
LRIP: Low rate of initial production.

Under what circumstances would the assumptions of dependence and independence among the three processes be valid?

## 2.7 Exercises

### ■ 2.7.5 Risk Network

Independent Research and Development (IRAD) by contractors, under the auspices of various government agencies, is one of the more cost-effective means for advancing the state of the art in a broad spectrum of areas. However, the path from start to finish in IRAD programs is somewhat tenuous.

IRAD programs, which are negotiated yearly, are typified by constant reviews, redirection, and even termination. Over the past several decades, we have participated in hundreds of IRAD of which more than 25 percent were terminated before their scheduled completion.

Table 2.32 gives the precedence data for a hypothetical IRAD program. The IRAD program consists of ten tasks that are being proposed by an aerospace company to a certain agency. The tasks are interrelated and therefore comprise a network. Tasks a and j are the starting and finish tasks.

Table 2.32 also gives corresponding baseline time estimates and the design status for the programs which were started during the previous year. Assume product maturity factors of 0.8 for brassboard status and 0.9 for breadboard status. Use the technical approach for the example in Section 2.4.7 to construct the risk network. Calculate path risk cost estimates and the composite network risk cost estimate.

*Table 2.32   Precedence Data for Exercise in Section 2.7.5*

| Activity | Precedent | Successor | BTE | Design Status |
|---|---|---|---|---|
| a | None | b, c, d, e | N/A | N/A |
| b | a | f | 1 month | Brassboard |
| c | a | g | 2 months | Brassboard |
| d | a | h | 4 months | Breadboard |
| e | a | i | 3 months | Breadboard |
| f | b | j | 1 month | Brassboard |
| g | c | h | 2 months | Brassboard |
| h | d | j | 1 month | Brassboard |
| i | e | j | 1 month | Brassboard |
| j | f | None | N/A | N/A |

BTE: Baseline time estimate.
N/A: Not applicable.

Which path is the critical path of the network? How much slack is there in the noncritical paths?

Repeat the exercise with the assumption that the tasks are dependent on each other and they overlap 50 percent. How does your finding change with the assumption of independence among the tasks?

### ■ 2.7.6 Risk Dominance

Alpha-Omega Company has a contract to produce several million quartz clocks which will be used as a give-away in an advertising campaign. The unit cost of the clocks is estimated to be $0.75. The product and process quality, complexity, and concurrency factors are estimated to be 0.9.

Alpha-Omega has already produced millions of quartz clocks of a similar design, and the product and process maturity factors are estimated to be 0.1. Estimate the unit risk cost of the quartz clocks.

Repeat the exercise with the assumption that Alpha-Omega has only completed a prototype of the clock and that the product and process maturity factors are estimated to be 0.5.

### ■ 2.7.7 Risk Exposure in Product Development

Risk exposure is significantly lower in developing and producing products with low values of PRODMF and PROCMF irrespective of the values of the other risk determinant factors. Consider a product with a development cost of $1.5 million and production cost of $3.0 million, and PRODMF and PROCMF equal to 0.8.

Estimate the risk exposure in terms of risk cost for PRODMF and PROCMF. What are the other pertinent risk determinant factors? Calculate the increase in risk cost if you were to consider these risk determinant factors equal to 0.8. Repeat the exercise with PRODMF and PROCMF equal to 0.5 and the other risk determinant factors equal to 0.8.

### ■ 2.7.8 Risk Exposure in Manufacturing Process

Consider an item with a PROCMF of 0.2, process quality factor (PROCQF) of 0.4, process complexity factor (PROCCF) of 0.6, and process concurrency factor (PROCYF) of 0.8. Calculate the ($\Sigma$RDF) for the manufacturing process.

Would you assume dependence or independence among these factors and how would the assumptions affect results?

Repeat the calculation for PROCMF = 0.3 and the other risk determinant factors unchanged, and again for PROCMF = 0.2, and PROCQF = 0.6, PROCCF = 0.8, and PROCYF = 1.0. Describe the sensitivity of the value of $\Sigma$RDF to changes in the value of PROCMF compared to changes in the value of the other risk process determinant factors.

### ■ 2.7.9 Risk Exposure in Investment

Table 2.33 is an updated version of Table 2.24. Using U.S. Treasury 10-year note yield data from the current edition of the *Statistical Abstract of the United States*, recalculate the risk exposure in the example of Section 2.5.5. [8]

Repeat the exercise with U.S. Treasury 3-year note yield data. Compare the results from using 10-year and 3-year note data with the mutual fund data in Table 2.33. How has the risk exposure changed from the example in Section 2.5.5? Which U.S. Treasury instrument yield has the greatest variability? Which U.S. Treasury instrument would you recommend as an investment on the basis of risk exposure? State your reasons for the recommendation.

*Table 2.33* Mutual Fund Data for Exercise in Section 2.7.9

| Year | Percent | Year | Percent |
|------|---------|------|---------|
| 1984 | 11.78   | 1989 | 9.75    |
| 1985 | 9.83    | 1990 | 9.30    |
| 1986 | 8.37    | 1991 | 8.68    |
| 1987 | 7.91    | 1992 | 8.90    |
| 1988 | 8.56    | 1993 | 6.10    |

## 2.7 Exercises

### ■ 2.7.10 Risk Exposure in Construction

Review the example of risk exposure in construction in Section 2.5.6. Calculate the risk cost for the other work packages in the example.

Under what circumstance would you assume dependence or independence among these work packages? What approach would you use to derive composite risk determinant factors as functions of your assumptions? Derive the composite risk determinant factors for both assumptions.

### ■ 2.7.11 Scientific Method

Revise the configuration of 24 circles in Figure 2.12 to consist only of circles at locations on the axes that are prime numbers. Determine how many rectangles or squares can be formed from the revised configuration with the four corners of each rectangle or square on four of the circles in the figure.

Review the example in Section 1.2.6 and the exercise in Section 1.5.2 of the previous chapter. Apply the methodology used therein to the solution of this exercise.

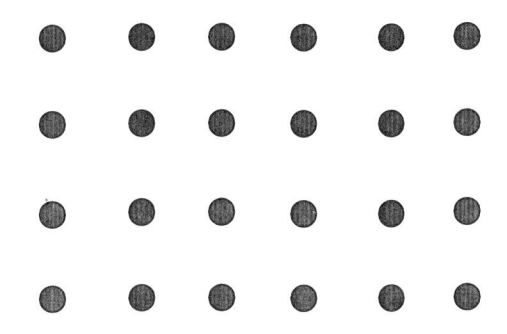

**Figure 2.12**   Configuration for Exercise in Section 2.7.11

Here are two hints that may help you.

1. Look beyond the perpendicularity of the abscissa and ordinate in Figure 2.12 in depicting the orientation of the rectangles and squares.
2. Derive parametric expressions for the number of positions that rectangles and squares can move on the abscissa and ordinate the way we did in the example of Section 1.2.6.

Reword this exercise so that it applies to the number of triangles that can be formed with the three corners of the triangle on three of the circles in the figure.

### ■ 2.7.12 Probability and Statistics

Proficiency with probability and statistics is useful in technical risk management. Test your knowledge with this exercise.

1. Define *combinations, permutations, populations, samples, parameters, statistics, large samples, small samples, continuous variables, discrete variables, normal distribution, student's* t *distribution, probability density functions,* and *probability distribution functions.*

2. Define the central limit theorem and the law of large numbers.
3. Define *mean, median, mode, variance,* and *standard deviation.*
4. Define and enumerate tests of hypothesis.
5. What are the statistical measures of central tendency and dispersion?
6. Calculate the mean, median, mode variance, and standard deviation for the sample data in Table 2.34. [9]

*Table 2.34   Sample Data for Exercise in Section 2.7.12*

| 16 | 41 | 29 |
| 14 | 36 | 20 |
| 25 | 12 | 18 |
| 42 | 49 | 17 |
| 23 | 26 | 35 |
| 10 | 15 | 42 |
| 33 | 25 | 19 |
| 18 | 42 | 27 |

7. Which statistical distribution would you use to model the sample data in Table 2.34? State your reason.
8. Calculate the 95 percent confidence limits about the mean of the sample data in Table 2.34.

## 2.8
## REFERENCES

You can obtain referenced government documents from the issuing organizations and from:

Superintendent of Documents, U.S. Government Printing Office, Washington, DC 20402. Telephone: (202) 783-3238.

National Technical Information Service, U.S. Department of Commerce, Springfield, VA 22161. Telephone: (703) 487-4650.

1. N. C. Lind, J. S. Nathwani, and E. Siddall, *Managing Risk in the Public Interest*, Institute for Risk Research, University of Waterloo, 1991.
2. Jack V. Michaels and William P. Wood, *Design to Cost*, John Wiley & Sons, Inc., 1989.
3. *The Service 500*, FORTUNE, May 30, 1994.
4. Committee on Shuttle Criticality Review and Hazard Analysis, *Post-Challenger Evaluation of Space Shuttle Risk Assessment*, National Research Council, 1988.
5. U.S. Bureau of the Census, *Statistical Abstract of the United States: 1990* (110th Edition), Washington, DC, 1991.
6. David H. Buchan, *Risk Analysis—Some Practical Suggestions*, Cost Engineering, January 1994.

## 2.8 References

7. David Hertz and Howard Thomas, *Practical Risk Analysis: An Approach through Case Histories*, John Wiley & Sons, Inc., 1984.
8. U.S. Bureau of the Census, *Statistical Abstract of the United States: 1994* (114th Edition), Washington, DC, 1994.
9. Irwin Miller, John E. Freund, Richard A. Johnson, *Probability and Statistics for Engineers*, Fourth Edition, Prentice Hall, 1990.

> *The longest and shortest journeys both begin with the first step.*
> **Confucius**

# CHAPTER 3

# RISK METRICS

> The winds that blow, ask them which leaf of the tree will be the next to go.
> **Old Japanese saying**

This chapter builds on risk fundamentals introduced in Chapter 2 and addresses the risk metrics we use to quantify risk exposure in the consequential perils of hazards. The metrics of risk exposure are probabilistic in nature, serving as measures of the probability of occurrence of perils. Technical risk management uses the probabilistic concepts of risk time and risk cost.

In this context, **risk metrics** are a system of attributes describing risk exposure in terms of risk time and risk cost. Attributes derived for specific products are called *risk determinants*. Specific values (*i.e.*, quantified values) of these determinants are called *risk determinant factors*. These factors operate on baseline time estimates and baseline cost estimates to yield **risk time estimates** (**RTE**) and **risk cost estimates** (**RCE**). RTE and RCE are quantified measures of risk exposure.

Risk metrics provide the language of technical risk management and follow the rules of the scientific method. In addition to the approach to problem solution, the scientific method mandates explicit, complete, and unambiguous terminology in problem statements, hypotheses, and definitions.

> *Baseline time estimate plus risk time equals risk time estimate.*
> *Baseline cost estimate plus risk cost equals risk cost estimate.*
> ***Taxonomy of Risk Exposure***

Figure 3.1 illustrates the organization of the chapter. Section contents are listed alongside the respective sections.

**Section 3.1 Definitions** provides the definitions of terms and abbreviations used in the chapter. These definitions are given when the terms are first used in the chapter and repeated in the glossary in Appendix A.

**Section 3.2 Risk Determinant Categories** expands on the concepts in Chapter 2. In this section, we address risk determinants as functions of product and process risk determinant categories. We also introduce the formulation to quantify risk exposure.

# Chapter 3 • Risk Metrics

|  |  |
|---|---|
| 3.1 Definitions | Key Terms and Abbreviations. |
| 3.2 Risk Determinant Categories | Products and Processes; Risk Formulation. |
| 3.3 Issues of Realism and Credibility | Probabililistics vs. Deterministics; Aggregation vs. Disaggregation. |
| 3.4 Selection and Tailoring Process | Methodology; Linearity of Scale; Product Categories. |
| 3.5 Attributes Weighting | Majority Rule; Constant Weighting; Binary Weighting. |
| 3.6 Rating Schema | Attributes Checklists; Truth Table; Lookup Table. |
| 3.7 Risk Determinant Factors | Management Attribute Factor; Extrinsic Attribute Factor; Product and Process Maturity Factors; Product and Process Quality Factors; Product and Process Compelxity Factors; Product and Process Concurrency Factors; Composite Factor |
| 3.8 Summary | Review of Highlights. |
| 3.9 Exercises | Role Models. |
| 3.10 References | Data Sources. |

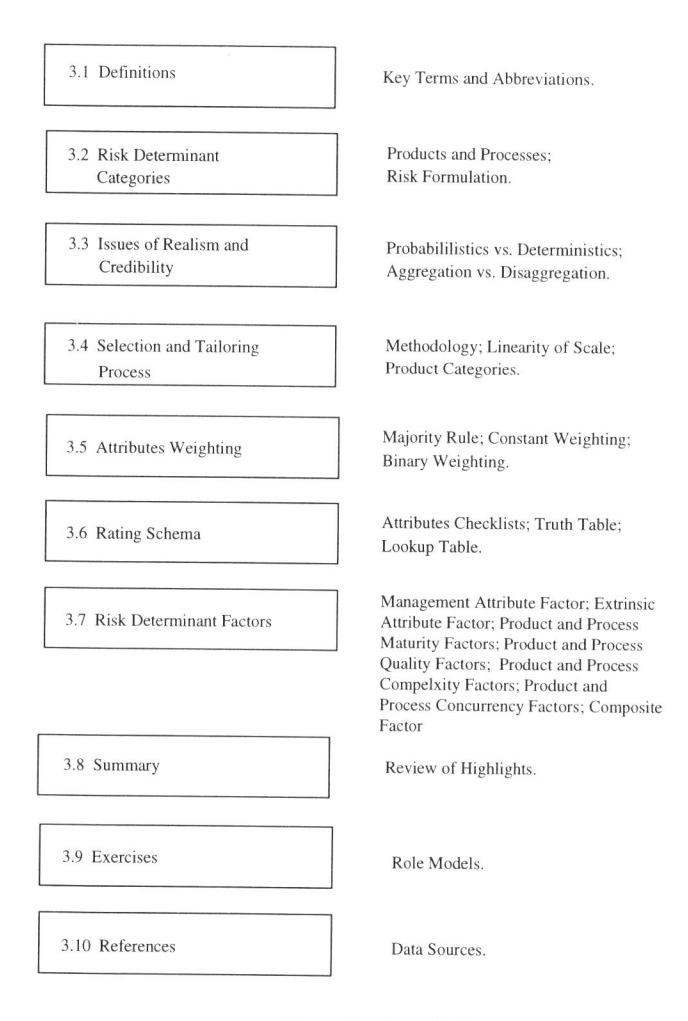

**Figure 3.1** Organization of Chapter 3

**Section 3.3 Issues of Realism and Credibility** is a key section of the book as well as of Chapter 3. The importance of perceived as well as actual realism and credibility is underscored in the discussion of aggregation vs. disaggregation and probabilistics vs. deterministics in estimating risk exposure.

**Section 3.4 Selection and Tailoring Process** explores the selection and tailoring of risk determinant factors as functions of product categories. The factors considered are derived from management and extrinsic attributes, and attributes for product and process maturity, product and process quality, product and process complexity, and product and process concurrency.

**Section 3.5 Attribute Weighting** illustrates the manner in which risk determinant factors are derived from the various attributes describing products, processes, management, and external conditions surrounding the foregoing. The process is weighting and uses majority rule, constant weighting, and binary weighting. The section includes the truth table for defining attribute states and lookup table for assigning values to attribute states.

**Section 3.6 Rating Schema** completes the kit of tools one uses to derive risk determinant factors. The section discusses linear vs. nonlinear scaling and illustrates the use of checklists and lookup tables. We include an interesting truth table example.

**Section 3.7 Risk Determinant Factors** addresses the derivation of the various risk determinant factors. These include the management attribute factor, extrinsic attribute factor, product factor, and process factor. The discussion of composite factors covers the interaction among the foregoing factors.

Chapter 3 concludes with **Section 3.8 Summary**, **Section 3.9 Exercises**, and **Section 3.10 References**. The summary serves to highlight the contents of the chapter, and the exercises reinforce the highlights.

## 3.1
## DEFINITIONS

Table 3.1 gives definitions of key terms used in this chapter. Note the difference in meaning of *aggregation* and *disaggregation*, *heuristics* and *specifics*, and *probabilistics* and *deterministics*. Note also the meaning of *baseline, baseline cost estimate, baseline time estimate, risk cost, risk cost estimate, risk time*, and *risk time estimate*. Risk cost, risk cost estimate, risk time, and risk time estimate are deterministic-probabilistic estimates.

Note the various attributes of risk determinant factors and processes (*viz.*, maturity, quality, complexity, and concurrency) and their relationship with risk exposure. The magnitudes of risk determinant factors are statements of the probability of occurrence of perils.

Note the broad definition of *process* and *product* and the adjectives *tangible* and *intangible* that differentiate hardware and software products from service products. Note also the meaning of and the relationship between logical statement and truth table and between constant weighting and binary weighting.

## 3.2
## RISK DETERMINANT CATEGORIES

**Risk determinants** describe the risk exposure in developing, producing, and bringing products to the marketplace. The determinants are reflective of the organizations producing the products and of the environments within which the organizations operate.

Table 3.2 lists the risk determinant categories encountered in technical risk management. Not every risk determinant is applicable to every product and you should exercise care in selecting and tailoring determinants to the products of interest.

Quantified risk determinants are **risk determinant factors**. We usually derive risk determinant factors on a scale of 0 to 1.0 with low values signifying less risk exposure than high values.

## 3.2 Risk Determinant Categories

The process of converting risk determinant factors from risk determinants is attribute weighting. We give specific schema in Section 3.6. We discuss applications of risk determinant factors in estimating risk exposure in the subsequent chapters.

### ■ 3.2.1 Products and Processes

We categorize **products** as hardware, software, and service. Hardware products are tangible, in the context of having quantifiable value determined by the cost to produce the products. They include real estate as well as classical electrical and mechanical hardware products. Software products are also tangible with quantifiable values. [1]

*Table 3.1   Definition of Terms and Abbreviations in Chapter 3*

**Aggregation**: Act of assembling distinct components of products into an aggregate for the purpose of top-down estimating the time and cost to produce the products.
**Application program**: Software that provides computational functions on computers.
**Attribute**: Characteristic of risk determinants.
**Baseline cost estimate**: Initial estimated cost to complete the development and production of products.
**Baseline time estimate**: Initial estimated time to complete the development and production of products.
**BCE**: Baseline cost estimate.
**Binary weighting**: Method of weighting answers to questions with the use of binary numbers.
**Bit**: Binary digit.
**BTE**: Baseline time estimate.
**Caveat emptor**: Latin for *let the buyer beware*.
**Constant weighting**: System of weights that change at a uniform rate from question to question in a sequence of questions.
**Deterministics**: Method of solution using a sequence of causes.
**Disaggregation**: Disassembling products into their component (*i.e.*, disaggregate) parts for the purpose of estimating the time and cost to produce the products.
**DOS**: Disk operating system.
**Extrinsic attribute**: Source of risk exposure from such as inflation and statutory regulation that are external to given program and largely beyond control of the program.
**Extrinsic attribute factor**: Quantified extrinsic attribute on a scale of 0 to 1.0.
**GB**: Generation breakdown.
**Heuristics**: Method of solution in which one proceeds along empirical lines using rules of thumb.
**Intangible property**: Nonphysical property such as cash on hand, investments, accounts receivable, and prepaid services.
**MAF**: Management attribute factor.
**Majority rule**: If majority of answers to question is "yes," the logical statement of the question is "yes." Conversely, if majority is "no," the statement is "no."
**Operating system**: Software used to run a specific suite of computer hardware.
**Probabilistics**: Method of solution based on probability of outcomes.
**Process**: Methodology, facility, equipment, and personnel for supplying a specific process.
**Process complexity**: Expanse of components comprising the product.
**Process concurrency**: Concurrency of independent production activities.
**Process maturity**: Production readiness of process design.
**Process quality**: Uniformity of process in producing products of consistent quality.
**PROCCF**: Process complexity factor.
**PROCMF**: Process maturity factor.
**PROCQF**: Process quality factor.
**PROCYF**: Process concurrency factor.

***Table 3.1**  Definition of Terms and Abbreviations in Chapter 3   (Cont.)*

**PRODCF**: Product complexity factor.
**PRODMF**: Product maturity factor.
**PRODQF**: Product quality factor.
**Product**: Tangible or intangible product, or number of products called "system," including tangible hardware, tangible software products, and intangible service products.
**Product complexity**: Expanse of the generation breakdown for the product design.
**Product concurrency**: Concurrency of interdependent product design activities.
**Product maturity**: Maturity and production readiness of the product design.
**Product quality**: Producibility, reliability, and testability of the product design.
**RCE**: Risk cost estimate.
**Risk cost**: Product of probability of occurrence of a risk incident and the cost of corrective action to recover from the risk incident; a probabilistic-deterministic estimate.
**Risk cost estimate**: Sum of baseline cost estimate and risk cost.
**Risk determinant**: Attribute that serves as predictor of a risk element.
**Risk determinant factor**: Quantified measure of a risk determinant.
**Risk exposure**: Vulnerability to risk incidents resulting from hazard-peril combinations.
**Risk metrics**: System of measurements for quantifying risk exposure.
**Risk time**: Product of probability of occurrence of a peril and the time for corrective action to recover from the risk incident; a probabilistic-deterministic estimate.
**RTE**: Risk time estimate.
**Scientific method**: Formalized reasoning process that consists of observation, problem formulation, formulation of hypotheses, test of hypotheses, verification.
**Service**: Intangible product including transportation, investment, and other business and personal services.
**Specifics**: Use of specific details of individual elements of cost based on historical data from the same or similar products. Provides maximum realism and credibility but requires maximum expenditure of resources.
**Truth table**: Rendition of logical statements in binary form.

***Table 3.2**  Risk Determinant Categories*

| Management Attributes | Extrinsic Attributes |
|---|---|
| Product Maturity | Process Maturity |
| Product Quality | Process Quality |
| Product Complexity | Process Complexity |
| Product Concurrency | Process Concurrency |

Software products include application programs and operating systems. **Application programs** are a class of software products (*e.g.*, word processing and spreadsheet programs) that provide computational functions on the broad spectrum of computers.

**Operating systems** are defined as software used to run a computer mechanized process using a specific suite of computer hardware (*e.g.*, automatic testing and communication network control). Operating system software is used also to run computers (*e.g.*, **disk operating system** (**DOS**)). Computers are, in essence, computer-mechanized processes.

Service products are intangible, in the context of **intangible property**. The economic value of service products is a function of the functional worth to the customer. If there is only one supplier of a particular **service**, however, the economic value is determined by the supplier's cost to provide the service.

## 3.2 Risk Determinant Categories

Service products include financial services, transportation, and public safety as well as such classical items as custodial and health-related services. In general, service products, like most intangible property, have no resale value.

### ■ 3.2.2 Example of Risk Exposure in Highway and Roadway Construction

Highway and roadway construction are interesting product areas for examining the approach to estimating **risk exposure**. Highway construction connotes the construction of multilane, limited access, super thoroughfares that transcend long distances, whereas roadway construction connotes the construction or improvement of roads within local areas.

Highway and roadway construction share a number of common risk determinants; however, each is exposed to some which are unique. Consider, first, the highway construction process that begins with a survey of the intended route.

It has become the practice to use aerial photography in surveying candidate routes and collect data for estimating the impact of the geological and physical features of the terrain on construction time and cost. This is a vital element in finalizing route selection.

Photo-interpretation of aerial surveys demands a high degree of skill and familiarity with terrain of a similar nature. The potential is great for either underestimating or overestimating the impact of terrain on construction time and cost which compromises the selection of a given route and increases the risk exposure in the construction effort.

Issues of environmental and endangered species protection, and economic issues such as displacement of homes and businesses, have become key factors in the selection of given routes. Resistance to the acquisition of the right of way is a major source of risk exposure.

The accommodation of existing traffic introduces an element of risk exposure which is primarily unique to roadway construction in local areas, but also causes hindrances in highway projects at intersections and interconnections with existing highways and roadways. The amount of traffic is a variable with a wide parametric range.

The highway construction process requires a large conglomeration of specialized equipment and skilled operators. The availability of equipment and operators is another source of risk exposure. Familiarity and experience with the geological and physical features of the terrain mitigates risk exposure to a degree.

Inclement weather is another source of risk exposure common to both highway and roadway construction. The practice, on large projects, is to retain the services of private weather forecasting organizations to lessen the impact of inclement weather. It is difficult to recover from lost time even when it is anticipated. The logical approach is to allow extra time in the construction schedule based on a long-range weather forecast for the particular regions where work will be done or temporarily divert operations to regions where there is less rainfall. This strategy, however, increases the cost of construction.

Inadequate drainage is the nemesis of highways and roadways. A high degree of risk exposure is inherent in the assumed climatic conditions on which you base the drainage design.

The problem of drainage is closely related to the selection of highway and roadway foundations. In the past, foundations were prepared from crushed rock or concrete. More recently, it has become the practice to stabilize the subsoil, provided the subsoil is reasonably uniform.

The combination of climatic conditions, design of drainage, and choice of foundation is another major source of risk exposure. For example, if a foundation of crushed lime rock were to become excessively wet from rain before it was compacted and treated, it would be literally impossible to compact the lime rock sufficiently for the foundation.

The principle of no work—no pay applies almost universally to direct elements of cost, such as labor and subcontractors, in the construction industry. Indirect elements of cost, manifest in equipment rental, overhead, and administration.

Gulf Construction Company has a contract to construct a roadway in the city of Mobile, Alabama. The period of performance is twelve months beginning in January of the year following the award of contract. The schedule requires the foundation of the roadway to be placed over a period of five days in the month of May.

In the past, many of the roadways in Mobile suffered severe degradation because of foundation wash-out due to inadequate soil stabilization. Consequently, the contract specifies crushed lime rock for the foundation because nonuniformity of the subsoil in the area where the roadway is to be built precludes soil stabilization.

The rainfall threshold is 0.01 inch per day for placing a foundation of crushed lime rock of the grade available in the Mobile area. The hazard is rainfall exceeding 0.01 inch per day; the peril is increased cost from lost time.

Gulf Construction had suffered substantial financial losses from inclement weather on two previous contracts. The company had received a quotation of $15,000 for inclement weather insurance and wished to compare the quotation to the potential loss in the new contract. The company retains Analyst to estimate the risk exposure in terms of risk cost. Table 3.3 gives the approach followed by Analyst in carrying out the assignment. Analyst determines that 5.74 days is the average number of days that rainfall during the month of May exceeded 0.01 inch over the past 50 years in Mobile. [2]

Although this is a simple assignment, Analyst needs to be careful about the sample space and expected value of the number of days with excessive rainfall. Initially, the sample space is 31 days because there are 31 days in the month of May. After one day passes, with or without excessive rainfall, the sample space is 30 days, the number of days left in the month. The successive sample spaces are 29 days, 28 days, and 27 days.

Initially, the expected value of the number of days with excessive rainfall in the month of May is 5.74 days. After one day of excessive rainfall, the expected value of the number of days decreases to 4.74 days. After two days with excessive rainfall, the sample space is 3.74 days. Subsequent sample spaces are 2.74 days, 1.74 days, and 0.74 day.

**Table 3.3** *Technical Approach for Risk Exposure in Highway and Roadway Construction Example*

1. Determine average number of days in May with rainfall exceeding 0.01 inch per day.
2. Calculate rainfall exceeding 0.01 inch per day over five days in May.
3. Obtain the baseline cost estimate of indirect elements of cost.
4. Calculate the risk cost.

Equation 3.1 is the relationship for calculating the probability of a day with excessive rain in the month of May in the Mobile, Alabama, area.

$$P = \frac{5.74 \text{ days}}{31 \text{ days}}$$
$$= 0.185. \tag{3.1}$$

## 3.2 Risk Determinant Categories

Equation 3.2 is the relationship for calculating the probability of a day with excessive rain in the month of May in Mobile, Alabama, area, given that it has already rained on one day.

$$P = \frac{4.74 \text{ days}}{30 \text{ days}}$$

$$= 0.158. \tag{3.2}$$

Note the change from Equation 3.1 to Equation 3.2 in the sample spaces and in the expected values of the number of days with excessive rainfall. Now, you calculate the probability of a day with excessive rainfall, given it has already rained on two days, three days, and four days in the month of May in Mobile, Alabama.

The probability of a day with excessive rainfall, given that it has already rained on two days in the month, is $3.74 \div 29$, or 0.129. The probability of a day with excessive rainfall, given that it has already rained on three days in the month, is $2.74 \div 28$, or 0.098. The probability of a day with excessive rainfall, given that it has already rained on four days in the month, is $1.4 \div 27$, or 0.052.

Analyst determines that the **baseline cost estimate** of indirect elements of cost in Gulf Construction will be $25,000 per day during the month of May. This is the cost that will continue irrespective of whether or not the company places the roadway foundation.

The values of the **risk cost** are the products of the probability of rainfall exceeding 0.01 inch on each of the five days and $25,000. Table 3.4 is the worksheet Analyst uses for the calculations. The risk exposure is the sum of the individual risk cost for each of the five days and totals $15,475.

Analyst provides this information to Gulf Construction, stressing that the estimate of $15,475 is the expected value of the risk exposure. The company elects to forego the weather insurance that would cost $15,000, or $475 less. Look at Section 3.3.4, and the exercise relating to confidence intervals in Section 3.9.3, and decide what you would do in the same situation.

*Table 3.4  Worksheet for Risk Exposure in Highway and Roadway Construction Example*

| | | |
|---|---|---|
| **Day 1:** | (0.184)($25,000) = | $4,600 |
| **Day 2:** | (0.158)($25,000) = | 3,900 |
| **Day 3:** | (0.129)($25,000) = | 3,225 |
| **Day 4:** | (0.098)($25,000) = | 2,450 |
| **Day 5:** | (0.052)($25,000) = | 1,300 |
| **Total:** | | $15,475 |

### 3.2.3 Risk Formulation

We quantify risk exposure in terms of **risk time** and risk cost. We use essentially the same formulation with all classes of products and all categories of risk determinants.

The preferred method for using risk determinant factors is as multipliers of estimated corrective-action time and cost for given risk incidents. The results are factored values of corrective-action time and corrective-action cost (*viz.*, risk time and risk cost).

You should always use this method unless the product of interest is conceptual and you have only a gross estimate of the time and money needed to develop and produce the product. In that event, you may use the risk determinant factor as a multiplier of the baseline time estimate and baseline cost estimates.

The **baseline time estimate** and baseline cost estimate are the estimated time and estimated cost to complete the development and production of the initial baseline in the absence of perils. Risk determinant factors operate on these baseline estimates to yield risk time and cost estimates. Equations 3.3 and 3.4 are the preferred relationships to use.

$$RTE = BTE + (CAT)(RDF). \tag{3.3}$$

$$RCE = BCE + (CAT)(RDF). \tag{3.4}$$

where **RTE** and **RCE** denote the risk time estimate and risk cost estimate, **BTE** and **BCE** the baseline time estimate and baseline cost estimate, **CAT** and **CAC** the corrective-action time and corrective-action cost, and **RDF** the appropriate risk determinant factor for the product.

In situations where corrective-action time and cost cannot be estimated, as with conceptual products, you use the alternative relationships, given by Equations 3.5 and 3.6.

$$RTE = BTE(1 + RDF). \tag{3.5}$$

$$RCE = BCE(1 + RDF). \tag{3.6}$$

Consider a conceptual product with a BCE of $2,500. One of the product's assembly has already been tested as a brassboard with a BCE of $500. The BCE of the rest of the product is therefore $2,500 − $500, or $2,000.

Assume the potential CAC is $250 and the RDF is 0.4 for the brassboard assembly and the CAC is $1,000 and RDF is 1.0 for the rest of the product. Substituting these values in Equations 3.4 and 3.5 yields

$$\begin{aligned} RCE &= \$500 + (\$250)(0.4) \\ &= \$600 \end{aligned} \tag{3.7}$$

for the brassboard assembly, and

$$\begin{aligned} RCE &= \$2,000 + (\$1,000)(1.0) \\ &= \$3,000 \end{aligned} \tag{3.8}$$

for the rest of the product. The value of RCE for the product is therefore $600 + $3,000, or $3,600.

Now assume that the brassboard assembly does not exist in the conceptual product. In this case, you would apply Equation 3.6, with the BCE of $2,500 and RDF of 1.0, and obtain

$$\begin{aligned} RCE &= \$2,500(1 + 1) \\ &= \$5,000. \end{aligned} \tag{3.9}$$

Equation 3.9 gives a significantly greater value of risk cost (*i.e.*, $5,000) than the sum of the values provided by Equations 3.7 and 3.8 together (*i.e.*, $3,600). Which value would you select? Do you think that you can be too conservative when dealing with conceptual products?

> *Who dares nothing, need hope for nothing.*
> **Johann von Schiller**

### ■ 3.2.4 Example of Risk Cost Estimate in Development

The challenge is to remain realistic and credible in the eyes of management as programs mature, yet not prejudice yourself in the competition for carry-on funding by being too conservative.

## 3.2 Risk Determinant Categories

A program director at Zeta Corporation, manufacturer of military communication products, faces such a challenge. Under this individual's direction, a development program that began as a conceptual undertaking three years ago has advanced to the fabricated-breadboard stage.

The initial estimate of cost to complete the program was $30 million. The sum of $10 million has been expended to date and Zeta's management contends that $10 million of the remaining $20 million would be sufficient to complete the program. The program director contends that the entire $20 million would be needed.

Zeta management agrees to retain Analyst for a brief investigation of the issue. Table 3.5 gives the technical approach followed by Analyst in carrying out the assignment.

Analyst selects **product maturity factor** (**PRODMF**) for the key risk determinant factor. Table 3.6 gives the schema derived by Analyst for rating the PRODMF of a hardware product. Note that the value for a conceptual product is 1.0, signifying that the company has not validated a similar functional design by analysis.

***Table 3.5*** *Technical Approach for Risk Cost Estimate in Development Example*

1. Select the key risk determinant factor to use in the assignment.
2. Derive values of the selected risk determinant factor.
3. Calculate the risk cost in the original estimate to complete.
4. Derive the original baseline cost estimate.
5. Obtain estimate of the revised baseline cost at the current time.
6. Obtain estimate of potential corrective-action cost.
7. Estimate the risk cost at the current time.
8. Compare the current risk cost estimate to the remaining funds.

***Table 3.6*** *Product Maturity Factor*

| PRODMF | Event |
|---|---|
| 0.0 | Similar production first-article product tested successfully. |
| 0.1 | Similar production first-article produced. |
| 0.2 | Similar prototype tested successfully. |
| 0.3 | Similar prototype fabricated. |
| 0.4 | Similar brassboard tested successfully. |
| 0.5 | Similar brassboard fabricated. |
| 0.6 | Similar breadboard tested successfully. |
| 0.7 | Similar breadboard fabricated. |
| 0.8 | Similar functional design completed. |
| 0.9 | Similar functional design validated by analysis. |
| 1.0 | Similar functional design not validated by analysis. |

PRODMF: Product design maturity factor.
First-article: First item produced and qualified with validated technical data packages and certified production tooling.
Prototype: Item produced and qualified with validated technical data packages and development tooling.
Brassboard: Item identical in form, fit, and function to its production counterpart but has not been qualified.
Breadboard: Item identical to production item only in function.

The rating schema is linear. PRODMF = 0.5 signifies that the company has fabricated a similar breadboard. PRODMF = 0 signifies that the company has tested successfully a similar production first-article.

To calculate the original baseline cost estimate when PRODMF equaled 0, Analyst rearranges Equation 3.6 and substitutes *PRODMF* for *RDF* as follows:

$$BCE = \frac{RCE}{1 + PRODMF} \tag{3.10}$$

where BCE is the baseline cost estimate to be calculated.

Substituting *RCE* = $30,000,000 and *PRODMF* = 1.0 in Equation 3.10 yields

$$BCE = \frac{30,000,000}{1 + 1}$$

$$= \$15,000,000. \tag{3.11}$$

Analyst obtains estimates of $9,000,000 for the work remaining (*i.e.*, BCE) and $3,000,000 for potential corrective-action cost (CAC). The company has fabricated a similar breadboard. From Table 3.6, PRODMF = 0.7 for this event. Substituting these values in Equation 3.4, Analyst obtains

$$RCE = \$9,000,000 + (\$3,000,000)(0.7)$$

$$= \$11,100,000. \tag{3.12}$$

The risk cost estimate is $1.1 million more than the amount of $10 million which Zeta's management contends is sufficient to complete the program. Analyst provides the foregoing analysis to Zeta, whose management allocates the additional $11.1 million to complete the job.

# 3.3
# ISSUES OF REALISM AND CREDIBILITY

Realism and credibility are essential ingredients in describing risk exposure and estimating resources for combating risk. Realism ensures a valid baseline for assessing alternative approaches and true pictures of the potential cost growth and delay embodied in these approaches. Realism is imparted by the adequacy and reliability of substantiating data.

Credibility ensures that recommendations are believable and is an essential element in gaining support of management, employees, and customers. Credibility is imparted by the perceived adequacy and reliability of substantiating data. The importance of well-documented data bases cannot be overstated.

> *The job is not finished until the paper work is done.*
> *Analyst*

Without credibility, it is futile to seek management support for technical risk management or, for that matter, the support of any other engineering specialty such as concurrent engineering,

## 3.3 Issues of Realism and Credibility

design to cost, quality function deployment, total quality management, or value engineering. It is equally futile, in the absence of credibility, to seek the support of the people who are essential for the success of undertakings. It is literally impossible to achieve long-term success in a business undertaking without perceived credibility. [3]

The more credible risk determinant factors are based on specific details of labor, material, other direct cost, and indirect cost. This approach is industrial engineering estimating or bottom-up estimating in the development domain.

Industrial engineering, or bottom-up estimates, require detailed design definition, technical expertise, and sufficient time and money to implement the estimates. Ideally, risk determinant factors are based on data from undertakings of the same or similar nature and address single, specific elements of cost. Such industrial engineering estimates offer the highest degree possible of realism and credibility.

Issues of realism and credibility arise more frequently in programs of a conceptual nature where detailed design definition is lacking. In these situations, expert opinion, analogy, and parametric estimating are used to build credibility. This approach offsets lack of detail with judgment and experience as well as probabilistic relationships. There is a good probability that an estimate for a given product will be valid if it is based on the cost of products of a similar nature. [4]

In actuality, expert opinion estimates are variants of estimates by analogy wherein you compare products to products of a similar nature produced by others as well as yourself. Expert opinion estimates are often encountered in instances of intense competition. Companies retain experts with insight into customer's funding profiles to glean proposal-winning prices that frequently bear little relationship to the actual cost of the proposed product. We have seen many instances where departments within companies retained experts at the last minute to share the blame for poor decisions.

The foregoing approaches to estimating risk exposure are tradeoffs of aggregation vs. disaggregation and probabilistics vs. deterministics. Table 3.7 lists issues of realism and credibility resulting from these trades.

***Table 3.7*** *Issues of Realism and Credibility*

> **Aggregation**: Assembling distinct elements of cost into an *aggregate* (*e.g.*, building cost is an aggregate of building material cost, labor cost, other direct cost, and indirect cost). Realism, credibility, and estimating time and money are inverse functions of the degree of *aggregation* employed in the estimates.
> **Disaggregation**: Decomposing elements of cost into their component elements (*i.e., disaggregates*). Realism, credibility, and estimating time and money are direct functions of the degree of *disaggregation* employed in the estimates.
> **Probabilistics**: Method of solution which is based on the probability of outcomes. Realism and credibility are functions of the degree of disaggregation involved. Requires less estimating time and money than other approaches.
> **Deterministics**: Method of solution which is based on the sequence of causes. Realism and credibility are also functions of the degree of disaggregation involved. Requires more estimating time and money than other approaches.
> **Heuristics**: Method of solution in which one proceeds along empirical lines using rules of thumb. The realism, credibility, and estimating time and cost of the approach depends on the extent to which rules of thumb are based on related historical data and the degree of aggregation employed.
> **Specifics**: Use of specific details of individual elements of cost based on historical data from the same or similar products. The approach provides maximum realism and credibility but requires greater expenditure of resources.

Note the comment on the tradeoff of heuristics vs. specifics, which is somewhat similar in substance to the comment on the tradeoff of probabilistics vs. deterministics. The term heuristics denotes a method of solution in which you proceed along empirical lines using rules of thumb.

Realism and credibility depend on the extent to which these rules are based on related historical data and the degree of aggregation employed. We caution you against using heuristics without adequate substantiation. Doing so will invariably get you into all kinds of trouble.

### ■ 3.3.1 Aggregation vs. Disaggregation

Realism and credibility are adversely impacted by the degree of aggregation used in baseline time and cost estimates as well as in risk time and cost estimates.

Aggregation is the act of assembling distinct parts of products into an aggregate for the purpose of estimating the time and cost to produce the products on a gross, top-down basis. Disaggregation is the reverse process whereby products are disassembled into their component (*i.e.*, disaggregate) parts for the purpose of estimating the time and cost to produce the products on a detailed, bottom-up basis.

It is difficult to attain realism and credibility in risk time and risk cost estimates without close adherence of the estimates to either the work breakdown structure (WBS) or the generation breakdown (GB) for the products of interest. Thus, realism and credibility are direct functions of the degree of disaggregation employed in the estimates, irrespective of which estimating methodology one may choose to use. The greater the adherence to the WBS or GB, the greater is the realism and perception of credibility in baseline and risk exposure estimates.

On the other side of the issue, the greater the adherence to the WBS or GB, the greater are the resources needed to derive risk exposure estimates. The challenge, in products of a conceptual nature, is to strike the cost-effective level of disaggregation.

Top-down and bottom-up estimating approaches are used progressively as programs mature. Figure 3.2 illustrates the salient differences between the two approaches and the challenge of evolving a cost element structure that couples the top to the bottom and preserves the integrity of both approaches. Top-down estimates serve to allocate costs to lower levels in the products. Bottom-up estimates serve to validate the original estimates.

Costs are estimated with the use of cost estimating relationships which are within the framework of the appropriate cost element structure. Cost element structures should permit management to avoid minutiae yet permit analysts to understand issues. The flow should relate aggregate to disaggregate costs and maintain its integrity as programs mature.

In the aggregate form, cost element structures should allow alternative design concepts, production philosophies, and business strategies to be evaluated with the confidence that nothing has been overlooked. Above all, cost element structures and cost estimating relationships should be maintained strictly under configuration control to ensure traceability from the aggregate to the disaggregate costs and to separate the cost of requirement changes from cost growth.

### ■ 3.3.2 Probabilistics vs. Deterministics

In a philosophical context, probabilism is the doctrine that certainty in knowledge is impossible and that probability is a sufficient basis for belief and action. Determinism is the doctrine that everything is entirely determined by a sequence of causes.

## 3.3 Issues of Realism and Credibility

People and even business organizations willingly accept probabilistic approaches to solving problems of a philosophical or global nature. In profit-oriented organizations, however, determinism usually prevails over probabilism. It is literally impossible, however, to derive estimates of risk exposure or, for that matter, cost estimates of any kind, on a purely deterministic basis.

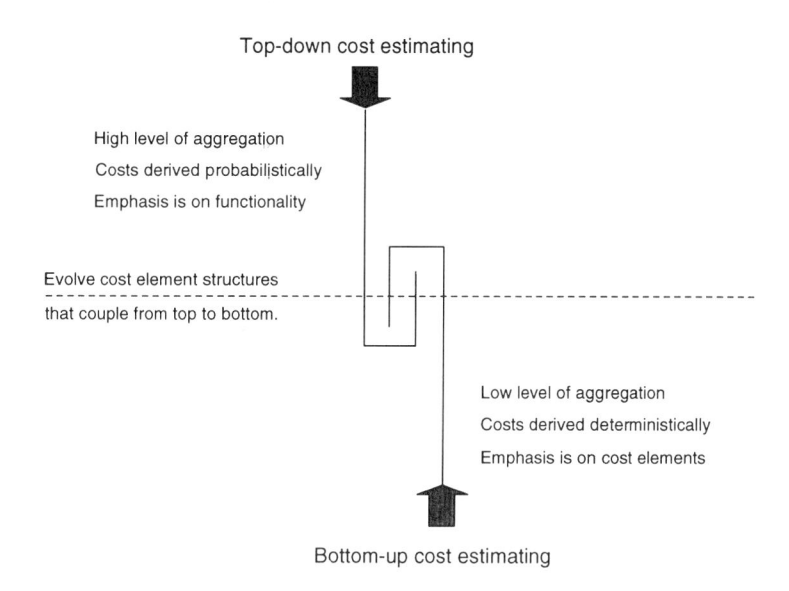

```
                    Top-down cost estimating
                              ↓

        High level of aggregation
        Costs derived probabilistically
        Emphasis is on functionality


        Evolve cost element structures
        - - - - - - - - - - - - - - - - - - - - - - - - - - - - - - - - - - - - - -
        that couple from top to bottom.


                                        Low level of aggregation
                                        Costs derived deterministically
                                        Emphasis is on cost elements

                              ↑
                    Bottom-up cost estimating
```

**Figure 3.2**   The Cost Element Structure Challenge

> *Where money is involved, the more deterministic the approach to solving the problem, the more realistic and credible is the perception of the solution.*
>
> ***Analyst***

There is even a strong probabilistic element in the application of learning curves in estimating production costs. Consider the learning curve theory that production efficiency improves as an increased quantity of items are produced uninterruptedly. The learning curve theory is valid, but the magnitude of improvement is probabilistic. For example, a production line operating on a learning curve of 80 percent is really on a curve of 80 percent plus or minus some amount.

It is the practice, nonetheless, to cite industrial engineering estimates of cost or time to complete, and corrective-action time or cost as being deterministic, and the other approaches for estimating as probabilistic. Thus, an industrial engineering estimate of risk exposure, in terms of risk time or risk cost, or both, starts with a deterministic baseline estimate complete, to which you add the product of a deterministic corrective-action estimate and a probabilistic risk determinant factor. The foregoing is referred to as the "deterministic-deterministic-probabilistic approach."

Figure 3.3 illustrates the flow in the various approaches for estimating risk exposure. Beginning with Part a, the approaches are shown in the descending order of realism and credibility and also in the inverse order of effort required to prepare the estimates.

Part a of the figure shows the estimating flow in the deterministic-deterministic-probabilistic approach. Both the baseline estimate and corrective-action estimate are derived from the bottom-up (*i.e.*, industrial engineering), whereas the risk determinant factor is derived probabilistically. As stated, this approach imparts the most realism and credibility but requires the most estimating effort.

[Bottom-up baseline estimate] ⊕ [Bottom-up corrective-action estimate] ⊙ [Risk determinant factor] = [Risk exposure]

Part a. Deterministic-deterministic-probabilistic approach.

[Bottom-up baseline estimate] ⊕ [Top-down corrective-action estimate] ⊙ [Risk determinant factor] = [Risk exposure]

Part b. Deterministic-probabilistic-probabilistic approach.

[Top-down baseline estimate] ⊕ [Bottom-up corrective-action estimate] ⊙ [Risk determinant factor] = [Risk exposure]

Part c. Probabilistic-deterministic-probabilistic approach.

[Top-down baseline estimate] ⊕ [Top-down corrective-action estimate] ⊙ [Risk determinant factor] = [Risk exposure]

Part d. Probabilistic-probabilistic-probabilistic approach.

[Bottom-up baseline estimate] ⊙ [1+Risk determinant factor] = [Risk exposure]     ⊕ Addition   ⊙ Multiplication

Part e. Deterministic-probabilistic approach.

[Top-down baseline estimate] ⊙ [1+Risk determinant factor] = [Risk exposure]

Part f. Probabilistic-probabilistic approach.

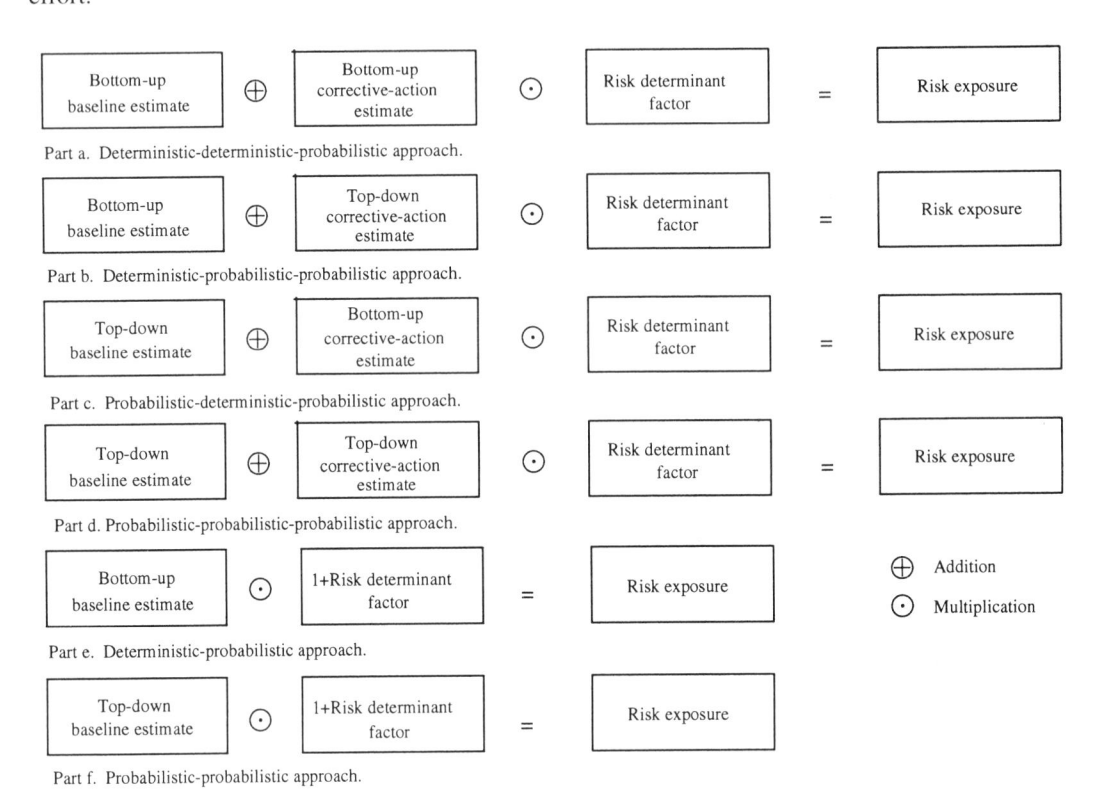

**Figure 3.3** Risk Exposure Estimating Approaches

Part b shows the flow in the deterministic-probabilistic-probabilistic approach for estimating risk. This approach is favored by designers who are prone to relate to their experience in corrective-action estimates, and you frequently hear statements like, "This problem is similar to that one which took so long and cost so much to fix." These people are estimating by analogy, which is probabilistic, and frequently do not realize it.

Where consequences of risk incidents are severe in conceptual programs, flow is encountered in the probabilistic-deterministic-probabilistic approach in Part c. This signifies that a significant amount of risk analysis is being devoted to the concept of interest.

Under less severe circumstances, flow is encountered in the probabilistic-probabilistic-probabilistic approach of Part d, especially in conceptual programs. Flow is encountered in the deterministic-probabilistic approach in Part e less frequently than the flow in the probabilistic-probabilistic approach in Part f.

## 3.3 Issues of Realism and Credibility

> *There is never enough time or money to do the job properly the first time. Somehow, however, there is always enough the second time around.*
>
> *Analyst*

### ■ 3.3.3 Example of Estimating Cost at Completion

In the long run, estimating approaches with the deterministic-deterministic-probabilistic flow are the most economical in time and money. Unfortunately, this realization usually comes after considerable time and money have been expended on the other approaches. [3]

Tau Air Systems, Inc. contemplates the introduction of a new air compressor for industrial use. Although, the estimated development cost appears compatible with the desired return-on-investment, there remain issues of realism and credibility.

Table 3.8 summarizes the analysis leading to the risk cost estimate for the product. The first of two estimates was prepared on a bottom-up, deterministic-deterministic-probabilistic basis; the second on a top-down, probabilistic-probabilistic-probabilistic basis to serve as a check on the first.

**Table 3.8** *Data for Estimating Cost at Completion Example*

|  | Bottom-Up | Top-Down |
|---|---|---|
| Baseline cost estimate | $8.0 million | $6.0 million |
| Corrective-action cost | $2.0 million | - |
| Risk determinant factor | 0.2 | 0.2 |
| Risk cost estimate | $8.4 million | $7.2 million |

Management's concern is twofold. The design baseline was prepared five years ago and the baseline cost estimate may not reflect the costs when the product will be introduced. In addition, the two risk cost estimates in Table 3.8 are $1.2 million apart. The company retains Analyst to investigate the difference.

Table 3.9 gives the approach Analyst follows in carrying out the assignment. Analyst validates that the proper formulation was used (*viz.*, Equations 3.3 and 3.4) for both risk cost estimates.

**Table 3.9** *Technical Approach for Estimating Cost at Completion Example*

1. Establish the validity of the formulation used in the estimates.
2. Establish the validity of the risk determinant factor used in the formulation.
3. Check the accuracy of the calculations.
4. Establish the validity of cost data from the 1988 baseline cost for the earlier baseline cost estimate.

Analyst validates that the proper formulation was used in the bottom-up and top-down estimates. Equation 3.13 is the relationship used by the company for the risk cost estimate in the bottom-up, deterministic-deterministic-probabilistic approach.

$$RCE = BCE + (CAC)(RDF) \qquad (3.13)$$

where RCE and BCE denote risk cost estimate and baseline cost estimate, CAC estimate of corrective-action cost, and RDF risk determinant factor.

Equation 3.14 is the relationship used by the company for RCE in the top-down, probabilistic-probabilistic approach.

$$RCE = BCE(1 + RDF) \qquad (3.14)$$

Analyst validates that the company used the proper risk determinant factor (*viz.*, product maturity factor) and that the value of 0.2 is proper for the product's current level of maturity.

Analyst also verifies the company's calculations. Applying Equations 3.13 and 3.14, Analyst obtains

$$RCE = \$8,000,000 + (\$2,000,000)(0.2)$$
$$= \$8,400,000 \qquad (3.15)$$

for the bottom-up, deterministic-deterministic-probabilistic approach, and

$$RCE = \$6,000,000(1 + 0.2)$$
$$= \$7,200,000 \qquad (3.16)$$

for the top-down, probabilistic-probabilistic approach.

These values check those in Table 3.8. Analyst notes, however, that the effect of inflation over the five years since the cost baseline estimate was prepared, is not considered in the table. The annual change in Producer Price Index (PPI) for capital equipment for the years 1985, 1986, 1987, 1988, and 1989 are 1.0, 1.4, 2.1, 2.5, and 5.2 percent. Compounding these percentages on an annual basis, Analyst obtains

$$\Delta PPI = (1 + 0.01)(1 + 0.014)(1 + 0.021)(1 + 0.025)(1 + 0.052)$$
$$= 1.126 \qquad (3.17)$$

where $\Delta PPI$ denotes change in PPI, which increased by 26 percent over the five-year period.

Multiplying the risk cost estimates of \$8,400,000 and \$7,200,000 by the factor of 1.126, Analyst obtains \$10,584,000 and \$9,072,000. The difference of \$1,512,000 is significantly greater than the difference of \$12 million between the bottom-up and top-down estimates of five years ago.

Analyst provides the information to Tau Air Systems. Tau decides to redo both the bottom-up estimate and top-down estimate. Tau requests Analyst to calculate the 95 percent confidence limits about the mean of the old-updated and new risk cost estimates.

### ■ 3.3.4 Example of Confidence in Estimating Cost at Completion

Table 3.10 is the technical approach Analyst follows in carrying out the additional assignment. The assignment is a straightforward application of statistics. [5]

## 3.3 Issues of Realism and Credibility

Table 3.11 is the worksheet Analyst uses. The first column in the table lists the two old estimates updated by the PPI compounding factor of 1.226 (v., Equations 3.15 and 3.16) and the new bottom-up and top-down estimates.

**Table 3.10** Technical Approach for Confidence in Estimating Cost at Completion Example

1. Acquire data sample.
2. Select governing probability distribution.
3. Derive mean and standard deviation of data sample.
4. Derive appropriate statistic for calculating confidence limits.
5. Calculate the confidence limits about the mean of risk cost.

**Table 3.11** Worksheet for Confidence in Estimating Cost at Completion Example

| Risk Cost Estimate | $x_i$ | $(x_i - m)^2$ |
|---|---|---|
| Old-updated bottom-up | $10,584,000 | 49,617,562,500 |
| Old-updated top-down | 9,072,000 | 1,662,165,562,500 |
| New bottom-up | 11,235,000 | 763,439,062,500 |
| New top-down | 10,554,000 | 37,152,562,500 |
| Total: | $41,445,000 | 2,512,374,750,000 |

Mean: $41,445,000 ÷ 4 = $10,361,250
Variance: 2,512,378 ÷ (4 − 1) = 837,458,250,000
Standard deviation: $915,127

Because of the small sample size, Analyst selects the Student's *t* distribution as the governing probability distribution. This also means that the *t*-statistic is used in the relationship for confidence limits.

Equation 3.18 is the relationship Analyst uses to calculate the 95 percent confidence limits (CL) about the mean of the risk cost estimates.

$$CL = m \mp \frac{st}{\sqrt{n}} \quad (3.18)$$

where $m$ denotes mean, $s$ standard deviation, $t$ the *t*-statistic, $n$ sample size.

Equation 3.19 is the relationship Analyst uses for calculating the mean ($m$).

$$m = \frac{\Sigma x_i}{n} \quad (3.19)$$

where $x_i$ denotes variates (*i.e.*, four risk cost estimates in Table 3.9).

From Table 3.11, the value of $m$ is $10,361,250.

The standard deviation is the square root of the variance. Equation 3.20 is the relationship for calculating the value of the variance ($s^2$) of the sample.

$$s^2 = \frac{\Sigma (x_i - m)^2}{n - 1} \qquad (3.20)$$

where $\Sigma(x_i - m)^2$ denotes summation of the squares of the deviations of variates from the mean.

From Table 3.11, the value of $s^2$ is 837,458,250,000. The value of the standard deviation is the square root of $s^2$, or $915,127.

Analyst next derives the *t*-statistic for confidence of 95 percent to use in Equation 3.18. Confidence of 95 percent is synonymous with a confidence level of 0.95. The equivalent significance level is 1 − 0.95, or 0.05.

Analyst also needs to know the number of degrees of freedom, which is one less than the sample size. For a sample size of four, $\upsilon = 4 - 1$, or 3.

Analyst now enters Table 3.12 at $\upsilon = 3$, and reads the area under the curve of 3.182 in the $\alpha = 0.05$ column. This is the value of the *t*-statistic to use in Equation 3.18.

**Table 3.12** Area Under Student's t Probability Density Curve from $-t$ to $+t$

| $\upsilon$ | $\alpha = 0.1$ | 0.05 | 0.02 | 0.01 | 0.001 |
|---|---|---|---|---|---|
| 1 | 6.314 | 12.706 | 31.821 | 63.657 | 636.619 |
| 2 | 2.920 | 4.303 | 6.965 | 9.925 | 31.598 |
| 3 | 2.353 | 3.182 | 4.541 | 5.841 | 12.941 |
| 4 | 2.132 | 2.776 | 3.747 | 4.604 | 8.610 |
| 5 | 2.015 | 2.571 | 3.365 | 4.032 | 6.859 |
| 6 | 1.943 | 2.447 | 3.143 | 3.707 | 5.959 |
| 7 | 1.895 | 2.365 | 2.998 | 3.499 | 5.405 |
| 8 | 1.860 | 2.306 | 2.898 | 3.355 | 5.041 |
| 9 | 1.833 | 2.262 | 2.821 | 3.250 | 4.781 |
| 10 | 1.812 | 2.228 | 2.764 | 3.169 | 4.587 |

Analyst substitutes $m = \$10,361$, $s = \$915$, $t = 3.182$, and $n = 4$ in Equation 3.18, and obtains

$$CL = \$10,361,250 \mp \frac{\$915,127 \, (3.182)}{\sqrt{4}}$$

$$= \$8,905,283 \quad \$11,817,217. \qquad (3.21)$$

The interest is in the upper limit of $11,817,217 serving as the risk cost estimate (RCE). Analyst provides the findings to Tau. In light of the magnitude of RCE, the competition, and the temperament of the current marketplace, the company decides not to proceed with the development of the product.

## 3.4
## SELECTION AND TAILORING PROCESS

The process of selecting risk determinants for specific categories of products is shown in Figure 3.4. Note the sequence of decisions from hardware to software to service products as indicated by the decision milestones in the figure.

## 3.4 Selection and Tailoring Process

The upper-case letters in circles indicate the proper risk determinants to use for hardware, software, and service products. Note the omission of process risk determinants in the case of service products. We show in Chapter 5, that product and process are synonymous in service products.

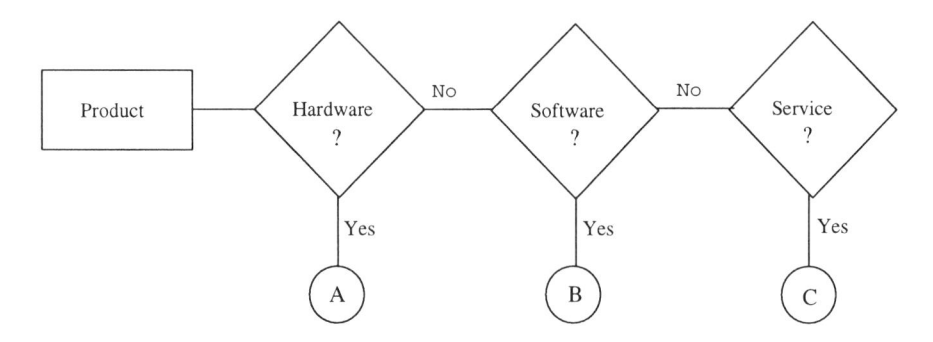

**Risk Determinant Factors**

A: Management and extrinsic attributes, hardware product and process maturity, quality, and complexity, and concurrency.

B: Management and extrinsic attributes, software product and process maturity, quality, complexity, and concurrency.

C: Management and extrinsic attributes, service product maturity, quality, complexity, and concurency.

**Figure 3.4** Risk Determinant Factors Selection

### ■ 3.4.1 Methodology

Risk determinants are the sources of risk exposure. Risk determinant factors are quantified measures of risk determinants on a scale of 0 to 1.0. The greater the risk determinant factor value, the greater the risk exposure.

Table 3.13 gives general guidelines for estimating risk exposure. The admonition to document data sources, bases of estimates, cost estimating relationships, and data outputs is put at the head of the list. Despite the importance, most investigators neglect this task until they near the end of the estimating effort.

**Table 3.13** *General Guidelines for Estimating Risk Exposure*

> 1. Document data sources, bases of estimates, cost estimating relationships, and data outputs.
> 2. Use disaggregation instead of aggregation to the extent possible.
> 3. Use the deterministic approach vs. the probabilistic approach to the extent possible.
> 4. Tailor risk determinant factors to the exigencies of the products of interest.

Most people do a poor job of defining cost data sources, as well as justifying their bases of estimates and cost estimating relationships. They tend to concentrate on cost data outputs. You should strive for documentation balanced in detail and be sure to cite references which are recognized authorities with respect to pertinent elements of cost. A typical example would be a compendium of construction costs per square feet for various elements of various kinds of buildings.

Customers scrutinize bases for cost estimates with more rigor than they do any other part of technical or cost proposals. The best bases of estimates are cost documentation from similar jobs that customers audited and approved for payment. Develop cumulative statistics for schedule and cost adherence on these jobs.

With regard to Step 2 in Table 3.13, you should use disaggregation instead of aggregation to the extent possible irrespective of whether the deterministic approach or probabilistic approach is followed. Use balance, however, in your approach. Don't use disaggregation for a small part of a product when you use aggregation everywhere else.

With regard to Step 3 in Table 3.13, you should use the deterministic approach instead of the probabilistic approach to the extent possible in the preparation of baseline estimates and risk estimates. The fact that risk determinant factors are probabilistic makes it all the more important that you use the deterministic approach in preparing corrective-action estimates which are factored by the risk determinant factors. An all probabilistic approach should be your course of last resort.

With regard to Step 4 in Table 3.13, the admonition to tailor risk determinant factors to the exigencies of products of interest means that you should predict whether risk incidents will be greater in earlier or later stages of development for the products and modify the numerical values of appropriate risk determinant factors to match the aforementioned distribution of risk incidents.

### ■ 3.4.2 Linearity of Scale

The risk determinant factor values that we gave in Table 3.6 are quite typical of what investigators encounter in technical risk management. The table is linear in scale in that the step increments are constant (*viz.*, 0.1 per step). A plot of the values would appear as a straight line.

Tailoring risk determinant factors to the exigencies of products of interest would cause a plot of the values in Table 3.6 to depart from this linearity. In some situations, you may prefer a nonlinear relationship such as logarithmic or exponential. Figure 3.5 shows values of PRODMF plotted on logarithmic and exponential scales vs. linear scales.

To avoid computational difficulty, the plot on the logarithmic scale is obtained by taking the common logarithm of the numbers 1 through 10 rather than 0 through 1.0. The power-function plot is obtained by raising the numbers 0 through 1.0 to the power of 2.

Figure 3.5 shows that, under logarithmic scaling, mid-values of PRODMF are weighted more than the extreme values (*i.e.*, values close to 0 and 1.0), whereas under exponential scaling, mid-values of PRODMF are weighted less than the extreme values.

You would use logarithmic scaling if more risk incidents were expected over a given program, and exponential if less were expected. The effect in Figure 3.5 can be accentuated by using a power greater than 2 in the exponential scaling and by adding to the mid-values in the logarithmic scaling. You are encouraged to modify the scaling on the basis of your experience in similar products.

### ■ 3.4.3 Example of Tailoring Risk Determinant Factors

Reverse engineering is a relatively common practice to circumvent patents in high technology. High-technology specima are submitted to a form of *post-mortem* to glean the detailed essence of

## 3.4 Selection and Tailoring Process

the designs. People go to extraordinary lengths in reverse engineering including X-rays to penetrate encapsulated packages.

The objectives of reverse engineering range from gaining competitive insight to gaining competitive advantage without the need for large expenditures. Occasionally, the intent is to replicate designs with sufficient changes to avoid patent infringement suits by the company that developed the product.

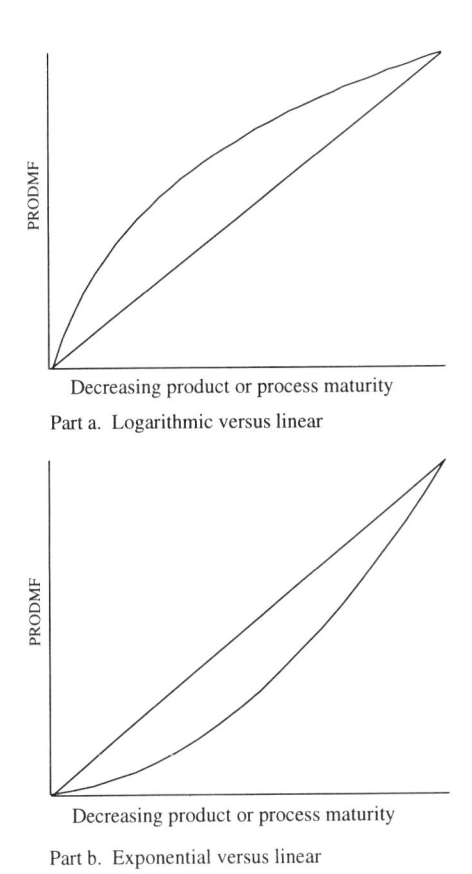

Decreasing product or process maturity

Part a. Logarithmic versus linear

Decreasing product or process maturity

Part b. Exponential versus linear

**Figure 3.5** Logarithmic and Exponential Risk Determinant Factor Plots

This odious practice of circumventing patents is called "wrinkling" and is one way in which fringe operations stay in business. Personal computer clones are a good example of the practice. Unfortunately, it is the customer, not the supplier of clones, who bears the consequences of poor service and inadequate technical support.

The usual rationalization expressed by such organizations is that wrinkling makes products more affordable to a broader segment of the buying public and prompts the original producers to be more efficient in their operations. Issues of warranty are usually ignored. This is a classical case both of **caveat emptor** and of the end justifying the means. [6]

> *No matter the exigency, never let the need justify the means for its satisfaction.*
> **Analyst**

Occasionally, organizations practice reverse engineering with the objective of calibrating some phase of their own operations. Such is the case with Iota Industries, Inc. that seeks a convenient methodology for tailoring risk determinant factors to reflect the company's way of doing business. Iota retains Analyst to develop the methodology.

Specifically, Iota desires a scheme for tailoring values of product maturity factor. Table 3.14 gives the technical approach Analyst follows in carrying out the assignment.

Table 3.15 lists cost and risk analysis data that Analyst collects on three of the company's recently completed contracts for development, fabrication, and installation of digital communication systems, each consisting of three assemblies. The data in Table 3.16 are for the assemblies used in the three systems.

***Table 3.14*** *Technical Approach for Tailoring Risk Determinant Factors Example*

1. Obtain history on cost and risk analysis in at least three recently completed contracts.
2. Calculate the quotient of risk cost estimate values and actual cost at completion values by dividing the former by the latter.
3. Tailor values of PRODMF by dividing the values by the respective quotients.*

*Quotients are numbers that result from dividing one number by another.

Analyst factors each value of CAC in Table 3.15 by the respective value of PRODMF and added to BCE to yield the RCE for each line item. RCE is thus the predicted cost at completion as opposed to the actual cost at completion (ACAC). Analyst prepares the worksheet in Table 3.15, first listing the values of RCE and ACAC by subsystems and then the quotient of RCE and ACAC. Next, Analyst multiplies the PRODMF values by the respective quotients to obtain the values of tailored product maturity factor (TPRODMF) in the last column of the table. Analyst provides the data to Iota Industries, Inc.

Departing from the role of providing only facts and not judgment, Analyst suggests that the tailoring does not appear to warrant the effort expended on the somewhat complicated methodology. Table 3.16 is the worksheet Analyst would use.

> *The simpler the approach to the problem, the greater the perceived credibility of the solution.*
> **Analyst**

## ■ 3.4.4 Product Categories

There are a multitude of hardware, software, and service products. You often need to tailor risk determinant factors to the specific needs of the products of interest.

## 3.4 Selection and Tailoring Process

Table 3.17 cross-references product categories to risk determinant factors. The designations are judgmental. You should apply whatever seems appropriate for your products.

Note the absence of checkmarks for process maturity, quality, complexity, and concurrency factors for service. The process is the product where service is concerned. We choose to use product maturity, quality, complexity, and concurrency factors for service, but you may use the equivalent process factors if you so desire. At any rate, the maturity factor is the dominant risk determinant factor..

*Table 3.15* Data for Tailoring Risk Determinant Factors Example

| GB | BCE $M | CAC $M | PRODMF | RCE $M | ACAC $M |
|---|---|---|---|---|---|
| Assembly A | 875 | 200 | - | 993 | 1,075 |
| A1 | 170 | 45 | 0.6 | 197 | 215 |
| A2 | 165 | 45 | 0.4 | 183 | 210 |
| A3 | 190 | 35 | 0.8 | 218 | 225 |
| A4 | 180 | 40 | 0.6 | 204 | 220 |
| A5 | 170 | 35 | 0.6 | 191 | 205 |
| Assembly B | 850 | 120 | - | 908 | 970 |
| B1 | 165 | 15 | 0.4 | 179 | 200 |
| B2 | 160 | 25 | 0.4 | 170 | 185 |
| B3 | 185 | 25 | 0.6 | 200 | 210 |
| B4 | 175 | 25 | 0.6 | 190 | 200 |
| B5 | 165 | 10 | 0.4 | 169 | 175 |
| Assembly C | 825 | 95 | - | 856 | 920 |
| C1 | 160 | 20 | 0.2 | 164 | 180 |
| C2 | 155 | 15 | 0.4 | 161 | 170 |
| C3 | 180 | 15 | 0.2 | 183 | 195 |
| C4 | 170 | 20 | 0.4 | 178 | 190 |
| C5 | 160 | 25 | 0.4 | 170 | 185 |

GB: Generation breakdown
$M: $Million
PRODMF: Product maturity factor
ACAC: Actual cost at completion
BCE: Baseline cost estimate
CAC: Corrective-action cost
RCE: Risk cost estimate

The management attribute factor is applicable to all product categories with minor tailoring. This fact is indicated by the checkmarks in the three columns of Table 3.17.

The extrinsic attribute factor serves as the same measure in all product categories, accommodating such forces as inflation, regulatory statutes, physical environments, labor relations, and, not the least of all, public attitudes. Only minor tailoring is required for individual product categories.

Product and process maturity factors are measures of production readiness of hardware and software. The product maturity factor is also a measure of experience in service products. The process maturity factor does not apply to service products since the products constitute the processes.

Product and process quality factors serve as measures of producibility, reliability, and testability in producing hardware and software products, and of the uniformity of production processes. On the other hand, product quality factors are measures of quality and thoroughness in service and of return-on-investment. Process quality factors are again not necessary in service products since the products constitute the processes.

*Table 3.16* Worksheet for Tailoring Risk Determinant Factors Example

| GB | RCE $M | ACAC $M | Quotient | PRODMF | TPRODMF |
|---|---|---|---|---|---|
| Assembly A | 993 | 1,075 | - | - | - |
| A1 | 197 | 215 | 0.916 | 0.6 | 0.655 |
| A2 | 183 | 210 | 0.871 | 0.4 | 0.459 |
| A3 | 218 | 225 | 0.969 | 0.8 | 0.826 |
| A4 | 204 | 220 | 0.927 | 0.6 | 0.647 |
| A5 | 191 | 202 | 0.932 | 0.6 | 0.644 |
| Assembly B | 908 | 970 | - | - | - |
| B1 | 179 | 200 | 0.895 | 0.4 | 0.447 |
| B2 | 170 | 185 | 0.919 | 0.4 | 0.435 |
| B3 | 200 | 210 | 0.952 | 0.6 | 0.630 |
| B4 | 190 | 200 | 0.950 | 0.6 | 0.632 |
| B5 | 169 | 175 | 0.966 | 0.4 | 0.414 |
| Assembly C | 856 | 920 | - | - | - |
| C1 | 164 | 180 | 0.911 | 0.2 | 0.320 |
| C2 | 161 | 170 | 0.947 | 0.4 | 0.422 |
| C3 | 183 | 195 | 0.938 | 0.2 | 0.213 |
| C4 | 178 | 190 | 0.937 | 0.4 | 0.427 |
| C5 | 170 | 185 | 0.919 | 0.4 | 0.435 |

GB: Generation breakdown  
$M: $Million  
Quotient: RCE ÷ ACAC  
TPRODMF: Tailored PRODMF  
RCE: Risk cost estimate  
ACAC: Actual cost at completion  
PRODMF: Product maturity factor  

*Table 3.17* Risk Determinant Factors vs. Product Categories

|  | Hardware | Software | Service |
|---|---|---|---|
| Management Attribute Factor | ✔ | ✔ | ✔ |
| Extrinsic Attribute Factor | ✔ | ✔ | ✔ |
| Product Maturity Factor | ✔ | ✔ | ✔ |
| Product Quality Factor | ✔ | ✔ | ✔ |
| Product Complexity Factor | ✔ | ✔ | ✔ |
| Product Concurrency Factor | ✔ | ✔ | ✔ |
| Process Maturity Factor | ✔ | ✔ |  |
| Process Quality Factor | ✔ | ✔ |  |
| Process Complexity Factor | ✔ | ✔ |  |
| Process Concurrency Factor | ✔ | ✔ |  |

Product complexity and concurrency factors serve as essentially the same measures in all product categories with minor tailoring. Process complexity and concurrency factors are required in only hardware and software products since service and investment products constitute the processes.

## 3.5
## ATTRIBUTE WEIGHTING

Attribute weighting is an extension of the task of tailoring risk determinant factors insofar as the weighting alters the linearity of scale of the risk determinant factors based on the weighted **attributes**. The weighting process is facilitated through the use of checklists. Checklists consist of sequences of questions which are phrased so that they can be answered by either yes or no. The consensus of the answers that are used to describe attributes of products then serve as the bases for deriving risk determinant factors.

The usual approaches to obtaining a consensus of answers include the majority rule, constant weighting, or **binary weighting**. In its simplest form, the majority rule treats questions in a given series as being of equal importance. In its weighted form, the majority rule treats some questions as being more important than others.

The importance of questions, under the progressive and binary weighting approaches, is imparted by the position of questions in their respective sequences. In general, the binary approach is more conservative than the progressive approach as a measure of the contribution of attributes to risk exposure.

### ■ 3.5.1 Majority Rule

The **majority rule** appears in both simple and weighted forms. Under the simple majority rule, a consensus of answers is achieved whenever there is a majority of either yes or no answers.

Under the weighted majority rule, a consensus of answers is achieved whenever either the sum of the weighted yes answers or the sum of the weighted no answers is greater than the other.

One of the problems with the simple majority rule is the need to pose an odd number of questions to avoid the possibility of ties between yes and no answers. In addition, the simple majority rule does not recognize the relative importance of the question in given sequences.

Consider, for example, sequences of five questions for which answers are received from two different sources. One sequence of answers could be yes, yes, yes, no, no, and the second no, no, yes, yes, yes. Under the simple majority rule, both sequences would constitute a consensus of yes answers even if the importance of the answers to the first two questions far outweighed the importance of the answers to the three last questions.

In such instances, the weighted majority rule provides a consensus based on the relative importance of questions as well as reducing the possibility of ties from equal numbers of yes or no answers. If the questions in the aforementioned sequence were weighted 4, 3, 2, 1, the weighted sum of all yes would be 5 + 4 + 3 + 2 + 1, or 15. The consensus yes results from weighted sums equal to or greater than one-half of 15, or 7.5. The consensus no results from weighted sums less than 7.5.

For example, if the answers were yes, yes, yes, no, no, the weighted sum would be 5 + 4 + 3 + 0 + 0, or 12, and the result would be the consensus yes. If the answers were no, no, yes, yes, yes, the weighted sum would be 0 + 0 + 3 + 2 + 1, or 6, and the consensus would be no. Ties could still arise if the weighted sum of the answers were equal to 7.5.

You can prevent this possibility by modifying the rule so that the weighted sum for a yes consensus would be equal to or greater than 7.5 and the weighted sum for no consensus to be less than 7.5. Alternatively, you can let the weighted sum of the yes consensus be greater than 7.5 and the weighted sum for a no consensus be equal to or less than 7.5.

### ■ 3.5.2 Constant Weighting

**Constant weighting** connotes a system of weights that change at a uniform rate from question to question in a sequence of questions. Uniform weighting avoids the aforementioned problem of ties from equal numbers of yes and no answers by the quantitative rating schema used in the approach.

Consider a hypothetical sequence of four questions which are listed in the descending order of importance (*i.e.*, the most important question being first in the list and the least important last). The first question could be assigned Weight 4, the second question Weight 3, the third question Weight 2, and the fourth and last question Weight 1.

The sum of these four weights, 4 + 3 + 2 + 1, or 10, is the largest possible sum which can be formed, given yes answers to all four questions. Assume that the answers to the four questions are yes, no, yes, no. The sum of the weights of these positive-answer (*i.e.*, yes) questions is 4 + 0 + 2 + 0, or 6. The positive-answer rating is simply the sum of the positive-answer weights divided by the largest-possible sum of all weights, which is 6 ÷ 10, or 0.6.

Weighting sequences, such as 1, 2, 3, 4 and 4, 3, 2, 1, are arithmetic progressions. An arithmetic progression is a sequence of numbers in which each number is equal to the sum of the preceding number and a constant.

The creation of an arithmetic progression begins by selecting a constant, $c$, with a value judged to be indicative of the increase in importance between sequential questions in the series. Equation 3.22 is the relationship for an arithmetic progression (AP).

$$AP = a, (a + c), (a + 2c), \ldots, (a + nc - 1) \tag{3.22}$$

where $a$ denotes the first term in the series, $c$ the constant, and $n$ the number of terms in the series.

Consider a sequence of seven questions and answers listed in the order of importance. Let $c = 1$. Substituting $c = 1$ and $n = 7$ in Equation 3.22 yields

$$AP = 1, (1 + 1), (1 + 2), (1 + 3), (1 + 4), (1 + 5), (1 + 6), (1 + 7 - 1) = 1, 2, 3, 4, 5, 6, 7. \tag{3.23}$$

These values are also the sequence numbers of the eight questions of interest. The last question in the series is considered seven times more important than the first. Questions are more frequently listed in the descending order of importance, for which you use Equation 3.23 in reverse, as follows:

$$AP = (1 + 7 - 1), (1 + 6), (1 + 5), (1 + 4), (1 + 3), (1 + 2), (1 + 1), 1 = 7, 6, 5, 4, 3, 2, 1. \tag{3.24}$$

## 3.5 Attribute Weighting

These values are the reverse order of the sequence numbers of the seven questions of interest. Now, the first question in the series is considered seven times more important than the last. The value $c = 1$ connotes that the importance of the last question in a series of $n$ questions is $n$ times more than the first in a sequence of increasing importance. The value $c = 2$ connotes that the importance of the last question is $2n$ times more than the first question.

### ■ 3.5.3 Binary Weighting

You can weight a series of questions and answers by expressing the answers as a binary number. For example, the binary number ($n_2$) for a hypothetical series of answers to seven questions could be

$$n_2 = 0011100 \tag{3.25}$$

where the subscript notation $n_2$ signifies a number to the base 2 (*i.e.*, a binary number), and 1 and 0 denote yes and no answers to the questions.

The right-hand term of Equation 3.25 is a seven-bit number. **Bit** is the abbreviation for binary digit. The first position from the left is that of the most-significant bit in the number; the last position is that of the least-significant bit.

The decimal value of the bit positions, starting from the left, are $2^6$, $2^5$, $2^4$, $2^3$, $2^2$, $2^1$, and $2^0$. Therefore, the equivalent decimal value ($n_{10}$) of the binary number 0011100 in Equation 3.25 is

$$n_{10} = 0\bullet 2^6 + 0\bullet 2^5 + 1\bullet 2^4 + 1\bullet 2^3 + 1\bullet 2^2 + 1\bullet 2^1 + 2^0 = 32 + 16 + 16 + 8 = 56. \tag{3.26}$$

If the binary number were to consist of seven 1's (*i.e.*, a 1 in each of the seven positions), the equivalent decimal value of the word would be

$$n^2 = 1\bullet 2^6 + 1\bullet 2^5 + 1\bullet 2^4 + 1\bullet 2^3 + 1\bullet 2^2 + 1\bullet 2^1 + 1\bullet 2^0 = 64 + 32 + 16 + 8 + 4 + 2 + 1 = 127. \tag{3.27}$$

The equivalent decimal value of 127 is the weight of the answers yes, yes, yes, yes, yes, yes, yes. The weight of the answers no, no, yes, yes, yes, no, no (*i.e.*, $0011100_2$) is 56 from Equation 3.26. The weight of the answers yes, yes, yes, yes, yes, yes, yes (*i.e.*, $1111111_2$) is 127 from Equation 3.27. You can use the two weights to calculate the risk determinant factor for the answers no, no, yes, yes, yes, no, no, as follows:

$$RDF = \frac{127 - 56}{127}$$

$$= 0.559. \tag{3.28}$$

### ■ 3.5.4 Example of Attribute Weighting

Delta Products uses the product maturity factor rating schema in Table 3.18 for estimating the risk exposure in developing new products. A number of cost overruns causes the comptroller of the corporation to suspect the adequacy of the schema. Table 3.19 gives the cost history leading to this perception.

## Table 3.18  Product Maturity Factor Rating Schema

| PRODMF | Event |
|---|---|
| 0.0 | Similar production first article tested successfully. |
| 0.1 | Similar production first article produced. |
| 0.2 | Similar prototype tested successfully. |
| 0.3 | Similar prototype fabricated. |
| 0.4 | Similar brassboard tested successfully. |
| 0.5 | Similar brassboard fabricated. |
| 0.6 | Similar breadboard tested successfully. |
| 0.7 | Similar breadboard fabricated. |
| 0.8 | Similar functional design completed. |
| 0.9 | Similar functional design validated by analysis. |
| 1.0 | Similar functional design not validated by analysis. |

PRODMF: Product design maturity factor.
First article: First item produced and qualified with validated technical data packages and certified production tooling.
Prototype: Item produced and qualified with validated technical data packages and development tooling.
Brassboard: Item identical in form, fit, and function to its production counterpart but has not been qualified.
Breadboard: Item identical to production item only in function.

Delta retains Analyst to tailor the product maturity factor rating schema so that the risk exposure estimating process is improved. In essence, Delta wishes Analyst to calibrate the schema to reflect the way the company does business.

Table 3.20 is the worksheet Analyst uses to tailor the product maturity factor rating schema. The first column in the table lists the original values of product maturity factor. The second column lists the average percent overrun values as decimal fractions. In the third column, Analyst adds one to each of the decimal fractions. In the fourth column, Analyst normalizes the average percent overrun values in the third column by dividing each of the sum values by 1.18, the greatest value in Table 3.20. The normalized values in Table 3.20 serve as the revised schema for rating PRODMF.

Delta questions the fact that the PRODMF value for the design status of "similar functional design validated by analysis (*viz.*, 1.000)" is greater than the PRODMF value for the design status "similar functional design not validated by analysis (*viz.*, 0.941)." Analyst replies that this is probably a case of a little bit of knowledge being dangerous.

## Table 3.19  Cost History for Attribute Weighting Example

| Design Status | Average Percent Overrun |
|---|---|
| Similar production first article tested successfully. | 6 |
| Similar production first article produced. | 9 |
| Similar prototype tested successfully. | 10 |
| Similar prototype fabricated. | 12 |

## 3.6 Rating Schema

**Table 3.19** *Cost History for Attribute Weighting Example (Cont.)*

| Design Status | Average Percent Overrun |
|---|---|
| Similar brassboard tested successfully. | 14 |
| Similar brassboard fabricated. | 19 |
| Similar breadboard tested successfully. | 23 |
| Similar breadboard fabricated. | 29 |
| Similar functional design completed. | 23 |
| Similar functional design validated by analysis. | 18 |
| Similar functional design not validated by analysis. | 11 |

**Table 3.20** *Worksheet for Attribute Weighting Example*

| PRODMF | Average Overrun | Sum | Normalized |
|---|---|---|---|
| 0.0 | 0.06 | 0.06 | 0.051 |
| 0.1 | 0.09 | 0.19 | 0.161 |
| 0.2 | 0.10 | 0.30 | 0.254 |
| 0.3 | 0.12 | 0.42 | 0.356 |
| 0.4 | 0.14 | 0.54 | 0.458 |
| 0.5 | 0.19 | 0.69 | 0.585 |
| 0.6 | 0.23 | 0.83 | 0.703 |
| 0.7 | 0.29 | 0.99 | 0.839 |
| 0.8 | 0.23 | 1.03 | 0.873 |
| 0.9 | 0.18 | 1.18 | 1.000 |
| 1.0 | 0.11 | 1.11 | 0.941 |

PRODMF: Product design maturity factor.
Average Overrun: Average percent overruns expressed as decimal fraction.
Sum: Sum of PRODMF and average overrun.
Normalized: Individual sum values divided by 1.18.

## 3.6 RATING SCHEMA

The derivation of quantitative risk determinant factors begins with the compilation and evaluation of checklists that are designed to reveal risk exposure. Table 3.21 is a typical checklist for product maturity factor. It concludes with the derivation of binary numbers or the construction of truth tables for determining logical states.

Logical states equal the equivalent decimal values of the binary numbers describing attributes of the products of interest. We use the quotients of product attribute states in decimal form and the largest possible attribute states in decimal form to derive risk determinant factors for the products of interest.

*Table 3.21   Product Maturity Factor*

| PRODMF | Event |
|---|---|
| 0.051 | Similar production first article tested successfully. |
| 0.161 | Similar production first article produced. |
| 0.254 | Similar prototype tested successfully. |
| 0.356 | Similar prototype fabricated. |
| 0.458 | Similar brassboard tested successfully. |
| 0.585 | Similar brassboard fabricated. |
| 0.703 | Similar breadboard tested successfully. |
| 0.839 | Similar breadboard fabricated. |
| 0.873 | Similar functional design completed. |
| 1.000 | Similar functional design validated by analysis. |
| 0.941 | Similar functional design not validated by analysis. |

PRODMF: Product design maturity factor.
First article: First item produced and qualified with validated technical data packages and certified production tooling.
Prototype: Item produced and qualified with validated technical data packages and development tooling.
Brassboard: Item identical in form, fit, and function to its production counterpart but has not been qualified.
Breadboard: Item identical to production item only in function.

### ■ 3.6.1 Attribute Checklist

Table 3.22 displays a checklist based on the three attributes A, B, and C. In technical risk management, the attributes A, B, and C could denote conditions such as funding adequacy, prototype completion, and material availability. For example, Questions 1, 2, and 3 might ask, "Is the funding adequate?" "Is the prototype completed?" or "Is the material available?"

*Table 3.22   Three-Attribute Checklist*

|  | Yes | No |
|---|---|---|
| 1. Is there A? | ✔ |  |
| 2. Is there B? |  | ✔ |
| 3. Is there C? | ✔ |  |

The questions are listed in the order of importance and answered with yes or no, as indicated by the checkmarks in Table 3.22. Next, you write the binary number that corresponds to the sequence of yes and no answers, with 1 equated to yes and 0 equated to no. For the answers in Table 3.22, the binary number is 101.

The equivalent decimal value of $101_2$ is $1 \cdot 2^2 + 0 \cdot 2^1 + 1 \cdot 2^0$, or 5. The equivalent decimal value of $111_2$ (*i.e.*, the maximum value) is $1 \cdot 2^2 + 1 \cdot 2^1 + 1 \cdot 2^1$, or 7. You can write the foregoing as $101_2 = 5_{10}$ and $111_2 = 7_{10}$. You would read these as, "101 to the base 2 equals 5 to the base 10," and "111 to the base 2 equals 7 to the base 10."

## 3.6 Rating Schema

Now, you derive the equivalent decimal value of $1111_2$, then read and write it as we just did.

The equivalent decimal value of $1111_2$ is $1\cdot 2^3 + 1\cdot 2^2 + 1\cdot 2^1 + 1\cdot 2^1$, or 15. You write the operation as $111_2 = 15_{10}$ and read it as, "1111 to the base 2 equals 15 to the base 10."

You use a scale of 0 to 1.0 for values of the risk determinant factor (RDF). The value 0 denotes the lowest degree of risk exposure and 1.0 the highest. Equation 3.29 is the generic form of the relationship we use to calculate the value of RDF.

$$RDF = \frac{\text{Maximum } EDV - \text{Actual } EDV}{\text{Maximum } EDV} \qquad (3.29)$$

where EDV denotes the equivalent decimal value of the binary word.

Substituting *Maximum EDV* = 7 and *Actual EDV* = 5 in Equation 3.29, we obtain

$$RDF = \frac{7-5}{7}$$

$$= 0.286 \qquad (3.30)$$

### ■ 3.6.2 Truth Table

A **truth table** consists of compound statements of basic propositions which can be formed from the truth values (*i.e.*, true or false, yes or no, or 1 and 0). The propositions are called conjunction, disjunction, conditional, and negation. Table 3.23 gives the definitions of these propositions. [7]

***Table 3.23***  *Basic Truth Table Propositions*

| Proposition | Logical Symbolism | Statement |
|---|---|---|
| Conjunction | $x\bullet y$: Read, "x and y." | The conjunction x and y is true, provided x and y is true; otherwise it is false. |
| Disjunction | $x+y$: Read, "x or y." | The disjunction x or y is true, provided x or y, or both, are true; otherwise it is false. |
| Conditional | $x\sim y$: Read, "if x, then y." | The conditional of x and y is true whenever x is true and y is true, x is false and y is true, or x is false and y is false. |
| Equivalence | $x\equiv y$: Read, "x if and only if y." | The equivalence of x and y is true if x then y and if y then x is true. |
| Negation | $x\bullet y'$: Read, "not x, not y." | The negation of x is *not* x. The negation of y is *not* y. |

The quality of the design of a given product is a function of the producibility, reliability, and testability of its design. Consider the three basic propositions in Table 3.24 regarding the quality of product design.

We can write two logical statements from the propositions in Table 3.24. The first is the conjunction logical statement that, "If a product were more producible, more reliable, and more testable, then the quality of the product design would be greater."

***Table 3.24*** *Basic Propositions for Quality of Product Design*

> 1. If a product were more producible, then the quality of the product design would be greater.
> 2. If a product were more reliable, then the quality of the product design would be greater.
> 3. If a product were more testable, then the quality of the product design would be greater.

The second is the disjunction logical statement that, "If a product were more producible, or more reliable, or more testable, or two or all of the foregoing, then the quality of the design would be greater."

The converse of the preceding statements are not universally true. The universally true statement is, "If the quality of a product were greater, then the product design would be in one of the eight logical states, which are functions of the three parameters producibility, reliability, and testability."

Table 3.25 gives the eight logical states for product quality that evolve from these logical statements.

***Table 3.25*** *Logical States for Product Quality*

> State 1: Product design is producible, reliable, and testable.
> State 2: Product design is producible, is reliable, and not testable.
> State 3: Product design is producible, is not reliable, and is testable.
> State 4: Product design is producible, is not reliable, and is not testable.
> State 5: Product design is not producible, is reliable, and is testable.
> State 6: Product design is not producible, is reliable, and is not testable.
> State 7: Product design is not producible, is not reliable, and is testable.
> State 8: Product design is not producible, is not reliable, and is not testable.

The number of possible logical states is a binary function (*i.e.*, yes or no) of the number of parameters ($n$) which are involved. Equation 3.31 gives this relationship.

$$\text{Number of states} = 2^n \qquad (3.31)$$

For $n = 3$, Equation 3.31 yields $2^3$, or 8. That is the same as saying that you need to consider eight propositions when there are three attributes.

Using the symbology $P$, $P'$, $R$, $R'$, $T$, and $T'$ for yes and no states of producibility, reliability, and testability, we can render the eight logical states in the simpler symbolic or binary forms given in Table 3.26. You read the notations $P'$ as *not P*, $R'$ as *not R*, and $T'$ as *not T*.

***Table 3.26*** *Symbolic and Binary Logical States for Product Quality*

| State | Symbolic | Binary | State | Symbolic | Binary |
|---|---|---|---|---|---|
| 1 | PRT | 111 | 5 | P'RT | 011 |
| 2 | PRT' | 110 | 6 | P'RT' | 010 |
| 3 | PR'T | 101 | 7 | P'R'T | 001 |
| 4 | PR'T' | 100 | 8 | P'R'T' | 000 |

## 3.6 Rating Schema

Given a specific binary number in Table 3.26, only the associated logical state is true. All other states in the table are false. For example, given the binary numbers $000_2$ and $111_2$, only State 0 and State 7 are true. States 1, 2, 3, 4, 5, and 6 are false. Note the subscript 2 after the binary numbers. We usually omit the subscripts, although they are still used in less frequently encountered number systems such as octal (*i.e.*, base 8).

Table 3.27 gives the positional values of digits in the binary numbers and decimal number systems.

**Table 3.27**  *Positional Values of Digits in Binary and Decimal Numbers*

| Position | 10 | 9 | 8 | 7 | 6 | 5 | 4 | 3 | 2 | 1 |
|---|---|---|---|---|---|---|---|---|---|---|
| Binary | $2^9$ | $2^8$ | $2^7$ | $2^6$ | $2^5$ | $2^4$ | $2^3$ | $2^2$ | $2^1$ | $2^0$ |
| Decimal | $10^9$ | $10^8$ | $10^7$ | $10^6$ | $10^5$ | $10^4$ | $10^3$ | $10^2$ | $10^1$ | $10^0$ |

Position 10 in the decimal number system has the decimal value of $10^9$, or one billion. Position 10 in the binary number has the decimal value of $2^9$, or 512. The equivalent binary number for decimal 512 is 100000000. The left-most digit in any number system is the most-significant digit because its positional value is the greatest. In a binary number, the bit in the left-most position is the most-significant bit. The bit in the right-most position of a binary number is the least-significant bit.

The decimal values of the binary numbers in a truth table can be used to weight the relative importance of logical states. The most important logical state in a system of three parameters would be State 7 equating to the binary number 111; the least important logical state would be State 0 equating to binary number 000.

### ■ 3.6.3 Example of Truth Table Design

Epsilon Agency specializes in the rental and maintenance of commercial and industrial buildings. The agency polls its tenants with the checklist given in Table 3.28. The yes and no answers in the checklist are the consensus of the answers of all the tenants to the particular questions.

Epsilon retains Analyst to design a truth table for displaying the various logical states of the consensus of answers, and to rate the agency's standing with its tenants on a scale of 0 to 1 with 0 denoting the highest rating. Analyst informs the Epsilon that it would be simpler to calculate the equivalent decimal value of the binary number describing the consensus of answers, but the agency instructs Analyst to proceed as directed.

Table 3.29 gives the technical approach Analyst follows in carrying out the assignment. The completed truth table in Table 3.30 contains 256 logical states, with State 0 = 00000000 and State 255 = 11111111. The sequence of answers is no, yes, no, yes, no, no, yes, yes, or binary 01010011. In Table 3.30, the EDV of the binary 01010011 and 11111111 are 83 and 255. Substituting these values in Equation 3.29, Analyst obtains

$$RDF = \frac{255 - 83}{255}$$

$$= 0.675. \tag{3.32}$$

**Table 3.28** *Survey Checklist for Truth Table Design Example*

|  | Yes | No |
|---|---|---|
| 1. Do you contemplate renewing your lease when it expires? |  | ✓ |
| 2. Are you satisfied with the space and facilities? | ✓ |  |
| 3. Do you believe that your rent is compatible with the space, facilities, and service provided? |  | ✓ |
| 4. Would you renew your lease if the rent were tied to the Consumer Price Index? | ✓ |  |
| 5. Would you recommend Epsilon Agency to your business associates? |  | ✓ |
| 6. Are you satisfied with the overall performance of the Epsilon Agency? |  | ✓ |
| 7. Are you satisfied with responses to your requests for service? | ✓ |  |
| 8. Do you find service and office personnel knowledgeable and courteous? | ✓ |  |

**Table 3.29** *Technical Approach for Truth Table Design Example*

1. Design the truth table.
2. Write the binary number for the consensus of answers to the questions in the checklist.
3. Look up the binary number in the truth table and determine the applicable logical state.
4. Rate the agency's standing with its clients.

On the scale of 0 to 1.0, the rating 0 would signify that the agency has the highest possible standing with its tenants. A rating of 0.5 signifies average and a rating of 0.675 is less than average. Needless to say, Epsilon does not like Analyst's finding.

> *If you know you are not going to like the answer, don't ask the question.*
> **Old New England saying**

Epsilon contemplates the effort Analyst expended in preparing the table and expresses the agency's appreciation. Analyst reiterates the contention that the job could be done by simply calculating the EDV of 01010011, the consensus of the responses, and the EDV of 11111111 and applying Equation 3.27 to these values.

This time the agency agrees with Analyst.

> *Be sure that all interested parties have grasped the essence and extent of the problem before proceeding too deeply into its solution. Above all, this should include you.*
> **Analyst**

## 3.6 Rating Schema

**Table 3.30** Truth Table for Truth Table Design Example

| EDV | Binary | EDV | Binary | EDV | Binary | EDV | Binary | EDV | Binary |
|---|---|---|---|---|---|---|---|---|---|
| 0 | 00000000 | 1 | 00000001 | 2 | 00000010 | 3 | 00000011 | 4 | 00000100 |
| 5 | 00000101 | 6 | 00000110 | 7 | 00000111 | 8 | 00001000 | 9 | 00001001 |
| 10 | 00001010 | 11 | 00001011 | 12 | 00001100 | 13 | 00001101 | 14 | 00001110 |
| 15 | 00001111 | 16 | 00010000 | 17 | 00010001 | 18 | 00010010 | 19 | 00010011 |
| 20 | 00010100 | 21 | 00010101 | 22 | 00010110 | 23 | 00010111 | 24 | 00011000 |
| 25 | 00011001 | 26 | 00011010 | 27 | 00011011 | 28 | 00011100 | 29 | 00011101 |
| 30 | 00011110 | 31 | 00011111 | 32 | 00100000 | 33 | 00100001 | 34 | 00100010 |
| 35 | 00100011 | 36 | 00100100 | 37 | 00100101 | 38 | 00100110 | 39 | 00100111 |
| 40 | 00101000 | 41 | 00101001 | 42 | 00101010 | 43 | 00101011 | 44 | 00101100 |
| 45 | 00101101 | 46 | 00101110 | 47 | 00101111 | 48 | 00110000 | 49 | 00110001 |
| 50 | 00110010 | 51 | 00110011 | 52 | 00110100 | 53 | 00110101 | 54 | 00110110 |
| 55 | 00110111 | 56 | 00111000 | 57 | 00111001 | 58 | 00111010 | 59 | 00111011 |
| 60 | 00111100 | 61 | 00111101 | 62 | 00111110 | 63 | 00111111 | 64 | 01000000 |
| 65 | 01000001 | 66 | 01000010 | 67 | 01000011 | 68 | 01000100 | 69 | 01000101 |
| 70 | 01000110 | 71 | 01000111 | 72 | 01001000 | 73 | 01001001 | 74 | 01001010 |
| 75 | 01001011 | 76 | 01001100 | 77 | 01001101 | 78 | 01001110 | 79 | 01001111 |
| 80 | 01010000 | 81 | 01010001 | 82 | 01010010 | 83 | 01010011 | 84 | 01010100 |
| 85 | 01010101 | 86 | 01010110 | 87 | 01010111 | 88 | 01011000 | 89 | 01011001 |
| 90 | 01011010 | 91 | 01011011 | 92 | 01011100 | 93 | 01011101 | 94 | 01011110 |
| 95 | 01011111 | 96 | 01100000 | 97 | 01100001 | 98 | 01100010 | 99 | 01100011 |
| 100 | 01100100 | 101 | 01100101 | 102 | 01100110 | 103 | 01100111 | 104 | 01101000 |
| 105 | 01101001 | 106 | 01101010 | 107 | 01101011 | 108 | 01101100 | 109 | 01101101 |
| 110 | 01101110 | 111 | 01101111 | 112 | 01110000 | 113 | 01111001 | 114 | 01111010 |
| 115 | 01110011 | 116 | 01110100 | 117 | 01110101 | 118 | 01110110 | 119 | 01110111 |
| 120 | 01111000 | 121 | 01111001 | 122 | 01111010 | 123 | 01111011 | 124 | 01111100 |
| 125 | 01111101 | 126 | 01111110 | 127 | 01111111 | 128 | 10000000 | 129 | 10000001 |
| 130 | 10000010 | 131 | 10000011 | 132 | 10000100 | 133 | 10000101 | 134 | 10000110 |
| 135 | 10000111 | 136 | 10001000 | 137 | 10001001 | 138 | 10001010 | 139 | 10001011 |
| 140 | 10001100 | 141 | 10001101 | 142 | 10001110 | 143 | 10001111 | 144 | 10010000 |
| 145 | 10010001 | 146 | 10010010 | 147 | 10010011 | 148 | 10010100 | 149 | 10010101 |
| 150 | 10010110 | 151 | 10010111 | 152 | 10011000 | 153 | 10011001 | 154 | 10011010 |
| 155 | 10011011 | 156 | 10011100 | 157 | 10011101 | 158 | 10011110 | 159 | 10011111 |
| 160 | 10100000 | 161 | 10100001 | 162 | 10100010 | 163 | 10100011 | 164 | 10100100 |
| 165 | 10100101 | 166 | 10100110 | 167 | 10100111 | 168 | 10101000 | 169 | 10101001 |
| 170 | 10101010 | 171 | 10101011 | 172 | 10101100 | 173 | 10101101 | 174 | 10101110 |
| 175 | 10101111 | 176 | 10110000 | 177 | 10110001 | 178 | 10110010 | 179 | 10110011 |
| 180 | 10110100 | 181 | 10110101 | 182 | 10110110 | 183 | 10110111 | 184 | 10111000 |
| 185 | 10111001 | 186 | 10111010 | 187 | 10111011 | 188 | 10111100 | 189 | 10111101 |
| 190 | 10111110 | 191 | 10111111 | 192 | 11000000 | 193 | 11000001 | 194 | 11000010 |
| 195 | 11000011 | 196 | 11000100 | 197 | 11000101 | 198 | 11000110 | 199 | 11000111 |
| 200 | 11001000 | 201 | 11001001 | 202 | 11001010 | 203 | 11001011 | 204 | 11001100 |
| 205 | 11001101 | 206 | 11001110 | 207 | 11001111 | 208 | 11010000 | 209 | 11010001 |
| 210 | 11010010 | 211 | 11010011 | 212 | 11010100 | 213 | 11010101 | 214 | 11010110 |
| 215 | 11010111 | 216 | 11011000 | 217 | 11011001 | 218 | 11011010 | 219 | 11011011 |
| 220 | 11011100 | 221 | 11011101 | 222 | 11011110 | 223 | 11011111 | 224 | 11100000 |
| 225 | 11100001 | 226 | 11100010 | 227 | 11100011 | 228 | 11100100 | 229 | 11100101 |
| 230 | 11100110 | 231 | 11100111 | 232 | 11101000 | 233 | 11101001 | 234 | 11101010 |
| 235 | 11101011 | 236 | 11101100 | 237 | 11101101 | 238 | 11101110 | 239 | 11101111 |
| 240 | 11110000 | 241 | 11110001 | 242 | 11110010 | 243 | 11110011 | 244 | 11110100 |
| 245 | 11110101 | 246 | 11110110 | 247 | 11110111 | 248 | 11111000 | 249 | 11111001 |
| 250 | 11111010 | 251 | 11111011 | 252 | 11111100 | 253 | 11111101 | 254 | 11111110 |
| 255 | 11111111 | | | | | | | | |

EDV: Equivalent decimal value.

### 3.6.4 Lookup Table

Using truth tables is a relatively simple process when you have relatively few questions to accommodate (*viz.*, four or less). Although straightforward, the construction of truth tables becomes cumbersome as the number of questions increase. Given a large number of questions, you should heed Analyst's advice to go directly to the EDV of the binary number describing the consensus of answers and apply Equation 3.29.

As an alternative, you can consider an event-driven lookup table such as the generic form in Table 3.31. The notations $A$, $A'$, $B$, $B'$, $C$, and $C'$ are events.

*Table 3.31  Generic Event-Driven Lookup Table*

| Factor | Event | Factor | Event |
|---|---|---|---|
| 0 | $A \cdot B \cdot C$ | 0.572 | $A' \cdot B \cdot C$ |
| 0.143 | $A \cdot B \cdot C'$ | 0.715 | $A' \cdot B \cdot C'$ |
| 0.286 | $A \cdot B' \cdot C$ | 0.858 | $A' \cdot B' \cdot C$ |
| 0.429 | $A \cdot B' \cdot C'$ | 1.0 | $A' \cdot B' \cdot C'$ |

In constructing such a table, you first determine the sequence of key events in the life cycle of the product of interest. You equate the event $A \cdot B \cdot C$ to 0 and $A' \cdot B' \cdot C'$ to 1.0. There are seven intervals in the table, so you divide 1 by 7 for 0.143 and use this value to increment the subsequent states.

Table 3.32 is an application of the generic lookup table for PRODMF. Here, events range from similar product produced, marketed, and serviced, which we equate to PRODMF = 0, to similar product not produced, not marketed, and not serviced, which we equate to PRODMF = 1.0.

*Table 3.32  Lookup Table for Product Maturity Factor*

| PRODMF | Event |
|---|---|
| 0 | Similar product produced, marketed, and serviced. |
| 0.143 | Similar product produced, marketed, and not serviced. |
| 0.286 | Similar product produced, not marketed, and serviced. |
| 0.429 | Similar product produced, not marketed, and not serviced. |
| 0.572 | Similar product not produced, marketed, and serviced. |
| 0.715 | Similar product not produced, marketed, and not serviced. |
| 0.858 | Similar product not produced, not marketed, and serviced. |
| 1.0 | Similar product not produced, not marketed, and not serviced. |

PRODMF: Product maturity factor.

It is not unusual to find suppliers and distributors that market and service products produced by others. These producers are referred to as "original equipment manufacturers" (OEM). Frequently, producers who market and service their own products will manufacture OEM products. You will find some producers who market but do not service their products. There are organizations that have built thriving businesses doing nothing but service work.

Table 3.33 is an example of using production events in the lookup table for PRODMF. In this case there are 11 events and the increment between events is 0.1. You will encounter a number of

## 3.7 Risk Determinant Factors

similar looking tables in Chapter 5 for hardware, software, and service product and process maturity, quality, complexity, and concurrency.

***Table 3.33***  *Hardware Product Maturity Factors*

| PRODMF | Event |
| --- | --- |
| 0.0 | Similar production first article tested successfully. |
| 0.1 | Similar production first article produced. |
| 0.2 | Similar prototype tested successfully. |
| 0.3 | Similar prototype fabricated. |
| 0.4 | Similar brassboard tested successfully. |
| 0.5 | Similar brassboard fabricated. |
| 0.6 | Similar breadboard tested successfully. |
| 0.7 | Similar breadboard fabricated. |
| 0.8 | Similar functional design completed. |
| 0.9 | Similar functional design validated by analysis. |
| 1.0 | Similar functional design not validated by analysis. |

PRODMF: Product design maturity factor.
First article: First item produced and qualified with validated technical data packages and certified production tooling.
Prototype: Item produced and qualified with validated technical data packages and development tooling.
Brassboard: Item identical in form, fit, and function to its production counterpart but has not been qualified.
Breadboard: Item identical to production item only in function.

## 3.7 RISK DETERMINANT FACTORS

Risk determinant factors are the measures used to quantify risk exposure. RDFs must reflect the operational environment and be descriptive of the products produced and the processes employed. These RDFs vary among hardware, software, and service products, although there is a fair degree of commonality among them.

Environmental attributes exert essentially the same influence on risk exposure in all products. These attributes are both intrinsic and extrinsic. The origin of **extrinsic factors**, such as climate and statutory regulations, are largely beyond the control of management. The intrinsic factors are indigenous to management philosophy and style and cut across the entire product line of the particular organization.

The attributes of maturity, quality, complexity, and concurrency are the bases for the other product and process RDFs you use in quantifying risk exposure. Table 3.34 lists the RDFs that should be considered in quantifying risk exposure. The management attribute and extrinsic attribute factors apply to both products and processes. Chapter 5 provides rating schema and step-by-step methodology for quantifying risk exposure in hardware, software, and service products.

Chapter 5 contains a number checklists and examples that can serve as role models for a wide range of risk management problems. You should, however, first consider the risk baselines in Chapter 4 as the background you need for undertaking the subject matter in Chapter 5.

**Table 3.34** *Risk Determinant Factors*

| Management Attribute | Extrinsic Attribute |
|---|---|
| Product Maturity | Process Maturity |
| Product Quality | Process Quality |
| Product Complexity | Process Complexity |
| Product Concurrency | Process Concurrency |

### ■ 3.7.1 Management Attribute Factor

Table 3.35 lists key contributors to the management attribute factor (**MAF**). MAF is an inverse measure of risk exposure due to management's lack of commitment to instituting aggressive control of the balance of quality, functionality, affordability, and profitability in its product line. You need to recognize this lack of commitment in your risk exposure estimate and be as forthright as possible in your findings and presentations.

> *Honesty is commended, and starves.*
> ***Juvenal***

**Table 3.35** *Contributors to Management Attribute Factor*

**Funding and budgeting policy**: Adequacy and consistency of budgeting and funding for research, development, production, and product support.
**Customer and user policy**: Adequacy and consistency of concern for customer's affordability limits and user's needs, applications, and expectations for products.
**Program continuity policy**: Adequacy and consistency of long-range planning and commitment to research and development, and product-line growth.
**Personnel retention policy**: Skill, adequacy, consistency, and longevity of the work force, and the maintenance of a system of employee motivation, recognition, and reward.

We rate MAF on a scale of 0 to 1.0. The greater the value of MAF, the greater the contribution to risk exposure.

### ■ 3.7.2 Extrinsic Attribute Factor

Extrinsic attributes, such as regulatory statutes and climatic conditions, are peripheral to given programs and, as such, are largely beyond the control of those programs. Nonetheless, they exert significant influence on risk exposure in all categories of products. Their impact can be mitigated with proper advance planning.

The **extrinsic attribute factor (EAF)** is the direct measure of the effect of these attributes on risk exposure. We rate EAF on a scale of 0 to 1.0. The greater the value of EAF, the greater the contribution to risk exposure.

One of the most difficult problems in program management is dealing with inflation and escalation. Although they are often viewed as one, inflation and escalation are distinctly different

## 3.7 Risk Determinant Factors

and the difference needs to be understood when attempting to estimate with realism and credibility. Chapter 4 addresses this subject.

### ■ 3.7.3 Product and Process Maturity Factors

Product maturity factor for products is an inverse measure of the current development status of the product of interest and is not a measure of how far along the actual development of the specific product has progressed. The current status of the product design (*i.e.,* design maturity) is the measure used to rate PRODMF.

By the same token, PRODMF is a direct measure of the probability of occurrence of a risk element during development. The greater the value of PRODMF, the greater the probability that risk time and risk cost will be expended.

**Process maturity factor (PROCMF)** is an inverse measure of the attribute of **process maturity** and of its readiness for production. By the same token, PROCMF is a direct measure of the risk exposure in the production process.

PROCMF is not a measure of how far along the production of a specific product has progressed. In addition, the notion of PROCMF only connotes that the process for given products has been proven and certified ready for production and does not, in any way, infer that the process produces products which are consistently uniform.

We rate PRODMF and PROCMF on a scale of 0 to 1.0. The greater the value of these factors, the greater the contribution to risk exposure.

### ■ 3.7.4 Product and Process Quality Factors

Quality means many things to many people; ranging from the popular perception of high-class products to the mathematically expressed notion that lack of quality is a loss to society. [8]

In the domain of technical risk management, the concern for quality centers about the potential need for corrective action in bringing products to the market place. For our purpose in technical risk management, we describe the **product quality factor (PRODQF)** as an inverse measure of the producibility, reliability, and testability of the product of interest.

Ordinarily, producibility is considered to be the ease in producing a given product but, in our context, it is the measure of **product quality**. Reliability is the measure of corrective actions which may be needed during the development of the product. Testability is the measure of ease in isolating failures for corrective action.

**Process quality factor (PROCQF)** is an inverse measure of process uniformity which we defined as the consistency with which the produced products stay within specified limits for functional, physical, and environmental requirements.

By the same token, PROCQF is a direct measure of the contribution to risk exposure of the process uniformity for products of interest. You can describe **process quality** by statistical measures of process states relative to specification requirements. The process state definitions are descriptive of how well processes control product tolerances. These definitions are the bases for deriving PROCQF.

We rate PRODQF and PROCQF on a scale of 0 to 1.0. The greater the value of these factors, the greater the contribution to risk exposure.

### 3.7.5 Product and Process Complexity Factors

**Product complexity factor (PRODCF)** is an inverse measure of the complexity of product and process design. By the same token, PRODCF is a direct measure of the risk exposure in the development of the particular design.

You use the complexity of the **generation breakdown (GB)** to rate PRODCF for the product of interest. Figure 3.6 illustrates the GB in conceptual form.

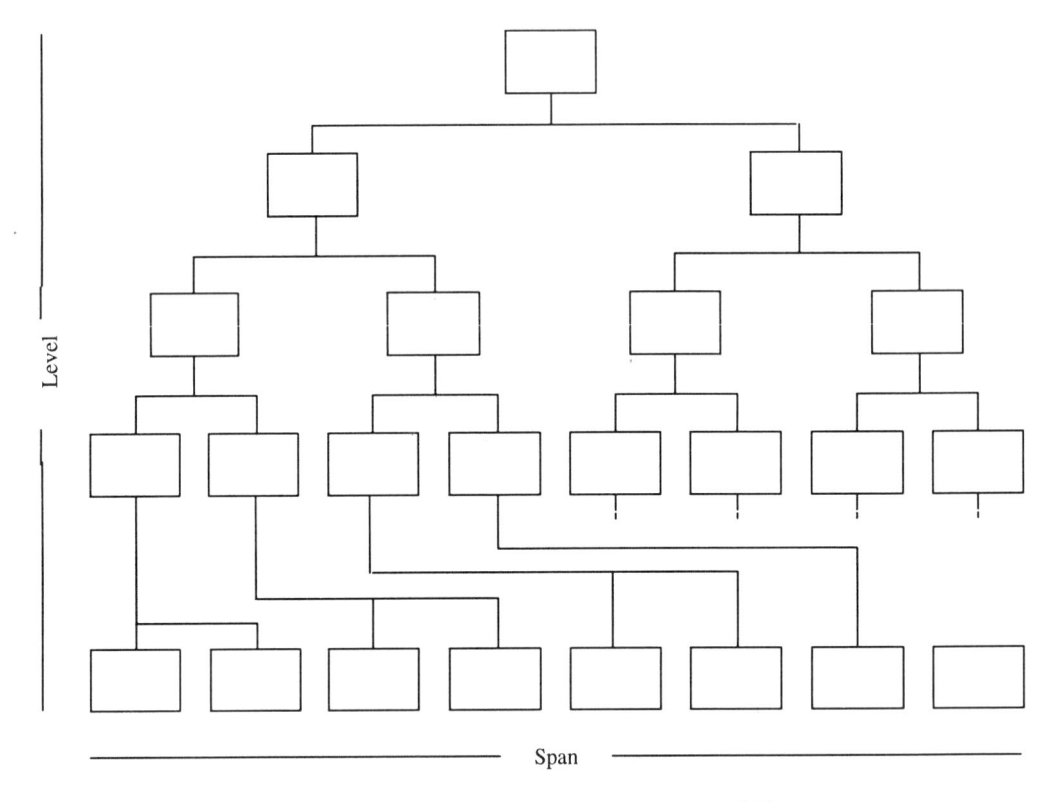

**Figure 3.6** Generation Breakdown in Conceptual Form

**Process complexity factor (PROCCF)** is an inverse measure of the complexity of process design. By the same token, PROCCF is a direct measure of the risk exposure in the production of the particular design.

There are two approaches for rating PROCCF. The simpler of the two is to equate PROCCF to the generation breakdown index of the product of interest, as with PRODCF.

The second approach equates PROCCF to the number of part numbers in the product. We use part numbers both to denote the number of parts in a given product and to account for the same parts being used a number of times. For example, we identify a certain capacitor that we use two times as Part Numbers C123-1 and C123-2. We refer to these notations as dash numbers.

Products consist of assemblies, subassemblies, details, and parts. Details are structural components, such as printed wire boards, that house parts. Raw material goes to make details. A num-

## 3.7 Risk Determinant Factors

ber of details, with parts installed, make up a subassembly, a number of subassemblies make up an assembly, and a number of assemblies make up a product. All raw material, parts, details, subassemblies, assemblies, and products have part numbers.

Table 3.36 gives suggested schema for rating hardware PROCCF that are keyed to the various categories of part numbers. We demonstrate the application of this table in Chapter 5.

**Table 3.36** *Hardware Process Complexity Factor*

| PROCCF | Part Numbers | PROCCF | Part Numbers |
|---|---|---|---|
| 0.0 | 2-5 Assemblies<br>2-5 Subassemblies per assembly<br>6-10 Details per subassembly<br>6-10 Parts per detail | 0.6 | 11-20 Assemblies<br>11-20 Subassemblies per assembly<br>11-20 Details per subassembly<br>11-20 Parts per detail |
| 0.1 | 2-5 Assemblies<br>6-10 Subassemblies per assembly<br>6-10 Details per subassembly<br>6-10 Parts per detail | 0.7 | 11-20 Assemblies<br>20-10 Subassemblies per assembly<br>11-20 Details per subassembly<br>11-20 Parts per detail |
| 0.2 | 6-10 Assemblies<br>6-10 Subassemblies per assembly<br>6-10 Details per subassembly<br>6-10 Parts per detail | 0.8 | 11-20 Assemblies<br>21-30 Subassemblies per assembly<br>21-30 Details per subassembly<br>11-20 Parts per detail |
| 0.3 | 6-10 Assemblies<br>11-20 Subassemblies per assembly<br>6-10 Details per subassembly<br>6-10 Parts per detail | 0.9 | 11-20 Assemblies<br>21-30 Subassemblies per assembly<br>21-30 Details per subassembly<br>11-20 Parts per detail |
| 0.4 | 6-10 Assemblies<br>11-20 Subassemblies per assembly<br>11-20 Details per subassembly<br>6-10 Parts per detail | 1.0 | 11-20 Assemblies<br>21-30 Subassemblies per assembly<br>21-30 Details per subassembly<br>21-30 Parts per detail |
| 0.5 | 6-10 Assemblies<br>11-20 Subassemblies per assembly<br>11-20 Details per subassembly<br>11-20 Parts per detail | | |

PROCCF: Process complexity factor.

### 3.7.6 Product and Process Concurrency Factors

Concurrency is the degree to which there is overlap among activities which are dependent upon each other and which, as a consequence, may contribute to risk exposure. Figure 3.7 illustrates concurrency of 0 percent to 100 percent between the Task i and Task j.

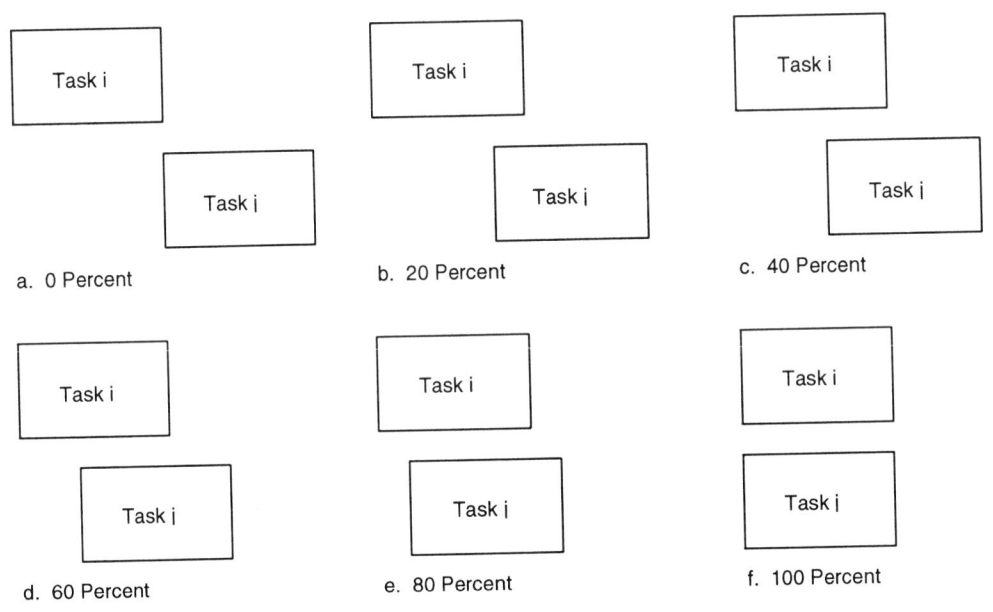

a. 0 Percent
b. 20 Percent
c. 40 Percent
d. 60 Percent
e. 80 Percent
f. 100 Percent

**Figure 3.7** Concurrency Between Hardware Task i and Task j

**Product concurrency factor (PROCYF)** is an inverse measure of the degree of overlap among dependent tasks and a direct measure of risk exposure as a function of concurrency among these tasks. Concurrency may exist among development and production tasks as well as among production tasks.

We rate PRODYF and PROCYF on a scale of 0 to 1.0. The greater the value of the factors, the greater the risk exposure.

### 3.7.7 Composite Factor

Risk determinant factors combine on a composite basis in contributing to risk exposure. The interactive relationship is governed by the order of the risk determinant factors involved. As we stated in Chapter 2, there are first-order and second-order risk determinant factors and the relationship between them is described by what is called the "$k$-factor."

The $k$-factor is equated to either the product or process maturity factor. The rationale is that if you have developed or produced a certain product before, then you can develop and produce a similar product with little risk exposure irrespective of the magnitude of any second-order factor. We illustrate the process in Chapter 5.

## 3.8
## SUMMARY

There are numerous terms in the vocabulary of technical risk management with very precise meanings. **Section 3.1 Definitions** provided definitions of the terms used in this chapter. We give definitions when terms are first used and repeat them in the glossary in Appendix A.

**Section 3.2 Risk Determinant Categories** expanded on the concepts of risk determinants and factors and addressed risk determinants as functions of the product categories (*viz.*, hardware, software, and service) along with the generic formulation used to quantify risk exposure. The approach to using risk formulation was illustrated with several examples.

**Section 3.3 Issues of Realism and Credibility** elaborated on the importance of perceived as well as realized realism and credibility in the derivation of risk determinant factors. The issue of heuristics vs. specifics was illuminated with an example based on reverse engineering. The issue of aggregation vs. disaggregation was described in the context of a cost element structure challenge. The issue of probabilistics vs. deterministics was addressed and it was concluded that the former is an embodiment of the principle, "An all probabilistic approach is the course of last resort."

**Section 3.4 Selection and Tailoring Process** explored the attributes making up risk determinants as functions of product categories. The categories are hardware, software, service, and investment. The attributes are classed as management and extrinsic attributes, and product and process maturity, product and process quality, product and process complexity, product and process concurrency.

**Section 3.5 Attribute Weighting** illustrated the manner in which risk determinant factors are derived from the various attributes describing products, processes, management of the products and processes, and external conditions surrounding the foregoing. The subjects covered were majority rule, weighted majority rule, and binary weighting. The section included an interesting example of attribute weighting.

**Section 3.6 Rating Schema** completed the kit of tools used to derive risk determinant factors and set the stage for the derivation of specific risk determinant factors in Chapter 4. The attribute checklist, truth table, and lookup table were defined and their relations were illustrated with an example of truth table design.

**Section 3.7 Risk Determinant Factors** enumerated the environmental, product, and process risk determinant factors that influence risk exposure. The section covered the attributes of product and process maturity, quality, complexity, and concurrency.

## 3.9
## EXERCISES

These exercise problems have been selected to reinforce key points and relationships in the preceding sections of the chapter. Step-by-step solutions to the problems are given in Appendix C of the book. We urge you to attempt the exercises without the solutions.

### 3.9.1 Metrics

State the metric terms for one millionth of a second and one billionth of a second.

### 3.9.2 Scientific Method

January 1, 1995, occurred on a Sunday. Use the scientific method to determine the day of the week on which the first day of January will occur in the years 2004 and 2104.

### 3.9.3 Confidence Level in Risk Exposure

Consider the example of risk exposure in highway and roadway construction in Section 3.2.2. The risk exposure, in terms of risk cost, was estimated at $15,475.

Estimate the risk cost at confidence levels of 0.80, 0.90, and 0.95. Use the rainfall statistics in Section 3.2.2, with an assumed standard deviation of 1.41 days. Select the probability density function and state your reason. On the basis of your findings, would you recommend the purchase of weather insurance?

### 3.9.4 Risk Determinant Factor Categories

Scientists of NASA decided to let the sun warm parts of the *Galileo* spacecraft (*v.*, Section 1.2) in an attempt to free its jammed main antenna. NASA hypothesizes that the antenna mast would extend from the heat of the sun to give sufficient additional leverage to the electric motors that deploy the antenna.

NASA hopes that repeating the process several times will free the antenna. It is also possible that the process will further degrade the antenna.

Assess the risk exposure in the process. In the process, should you be concerned with product or process risk determinant factors, or both categories of factors? Select the risk determinant factors to use and state your reasons for the selections.

### 3.9.5 Risk Determinant Factors for Trade Study

An electric utility company requests you to study and evaluate the relative risk exposure from investing in new facilities that would reduce operating cost versus investing in Treasury bonds that would increase operating revenue.

Select the risk determination factors from the categories given in Table 3.2 that you will need in your evaluation of risk exposure from the two alternatives. Cite the reasons for including and excluding the various risk determinant factors.

### 3.9.6 Comparative Realism and Credibility

Consider Table 3.37 that gives data on a product under development. The baseline cost estimate was derived both bottom-up and top-down. The corrective-action cost was derived bottom-up.

## 3.9 Exercises

**Table 3.37** Data for Exercise in Section 3.9.6

| Bottom-Up BCE | Top-Down BCE | Bottom-Up CAC |
|---|---|---|
| $720,000 | $640,000 | $180,000 |

BCE: Baseline cost estimate.
CAC: Corrective-action cost.

Design personnel consider the risk exposure to be low to medium. Quantify risk exposure using the guidelines in Table 2.7. Calculate the risk cost estimate as illustrated in the example in Section 3.2.3.

### ■ 3.9.7 Reverse Engineering

This exercise is a depiction of reverse engineering and requires you to use the history of engineering changes during a development program to derive values of product maturity factor which would have been applicable at the start of the program.

The systems described in Section 3.4.3 are developed under configuration control; meaning that design changes must be approved by a Configuration Control Board (CCB) which is comprised of representatives of the customer and the contractor. The board issues notices of revision (NOR) that authorize the implementation of changes, when and only if the changes are approved by the CCB. The number of NORs in Table 3.38 are typical for systems and subsystems of such magnitude and product maturity. [3]

The number of NORs as a function of time during development is plotted as the engineering change curve and is one of the many factors used to derive the estimate costs at completion. Allowances for NORs can range from a 10 percent of the development effort to more than 50 percent. You should scrutinize the allowances because the cumulative number of NORs during development is an inverse measure of product maturity at the onset of development.

**Table 3.38** Notice of Revision Data for Exercise 3.9.6

| System A | 540 | System B | 385 | System C | 265 |
|---|---|---|---|---|---|
| A1 | 105 | B1 | 100 | C1 | 65 |
| A2 | 150 | B2 | 85 | C2 | 40 |
| A3 | 70 | B3 | 70 | C3 | 45 |
| A4 | 110 | B4 | 80 | C4 | 55 |
| A5 | 105 | B5 | 50 | C5 | 60 |

In general, a relatively small number of NORs, by the end of development, signifies a relatively mature product at the start of development. On the other hand, a relatively large number of NORs signifies a relatively immature product at the start. Using the data in Table 3.38, construct a table of product maturity values, equating the subsystem with the smallest and largest number of NORs to PRODMF values of 0.1 and 1.0.

## 3.9.8 Attribute Weighting

Binary weighting is a form of positional weighting because of the influence of bit position on numerical values. Consider the binary weighting of a series of five questions.

Assume the questions are ranked in the inverse order of importance. Determine the relative weighting of the first question, which is in the most significant bit position, with respect to each successive question in the series. How does the number of binary weights vary as a function of the number of questions in a given series? Is it possible to assign equal weighting to two or more questions under binary weighting?

## 3.9.9 Risk Exposure in Cost Trades

An aluminum extrusion manufacturing firm needs to replace the primary power transformer that provides electricity to one of its facilities. The steady-state load of the machinery is 2,500 kilowatts (kw) with a 0.8 power factor (pf).

At the daily startup of the facility, the transient load is 5,500 kw with a pf of 0.65. It is customary to select power transformers with a 2:1 safety margin over the steady-state load, although a transient overload of 10 minutes or more could cause transformer failure

Large power transformers are rated in kilo-volt-amperes (kva). The relationship between kw and kva is given by

$$kw = (kva)(pf) \tag{3.33}$$

where the pf typically ranges from 0.80 to 0.95.

Assume the probability of transformer failure from transient overload is 5 percent and the relationships for the cost of buying and the cost of installing power transformers are:

$$\text{Cost of buying} = (\$100)(kva) \tag{3.34}$$

$$\text{Cost of installing} = (\$10)(kva) \tag{3.35}$$

Determine the relative cost advantage of buying and installing transformers sized for the steady-state vs. the transient load condition.

## 3.9.10 Number Systems

In the decimal number system, the largest digit value is 9. In the binary number system, the largest digit value is 1. In the ternary (*i.e.*, base or radix of 3), the largest digit value is 2. State the rule that governs these relationships.

The equivalent binary value of decimal 100 is $1100020_2$. Calculate the equivalent ternary value of decimal 100.

Convert decimal 12 to the equivalent octal value and the equivalent hexadecimal value.

## 3.10 REFERENCES

You can obtain referenced government documents from the issuing organizations and from:

Superintendent of Documents, U.S. Government Printing Office, Washington, DC 20402. Telephone: (202) 783-3238.

National Technical Information Service, U.S. Department of Commerce, Springfield, VA 22161. Telephone: (703) 487-4650.

1. K. H. Moller and D. J. Paulish, *Software Metrics*, IEEE Press, 1993.
2. U.S. National Oceanic and Atmospheric Administration, *Comparative Climatic Data*, Washington, DC, 1993.
3. Jack V. Michaels and William P. Wood, *Design to Cost*, John Wiley & Sons, Inc., 1989.
4. Ernest J. Henley and Hiromitsu Kumamoto, *Probabilistic Risk Assessment*, IEEE Press, 1992.
5. Mark L. Berenson and David M. Levine, *Statistics for Business and Economics*, Second Edition, Prentice Hall, 1993.
6. Jack V. Michaels and William P. Wood, *Design to Cost*, John Wiley & Sons, Inc., 1989.
7. Irving M. Copi, *Introduction to Logic*, Sixth Edition, Macmillan Publishing Company, Inc., 1982.
8. Madhav S. Phadke, *Quality Engineering Using Robust Design*, Prentice Hall, 1989.

> *There are lies, damn lies, and then there are statistics.*
> **Mark Twain**

# CHAPTER 4

# RISK BASELINES

> *The truth is rarely pure, and never simple.*
> **Oscar Wilde**

We characterize much of technical risk management as contingency analysis wherein we probe the what-if implications of future events and attempt to evaluate alternative courses of action. Such undertakings require some form of baseline to serve as a point of departure for the investigation. Technical risk management uses baselines of time and cost.

A **baseline** is the initial definition of the product to be developed and produced, the process used to produce the product, and the environment in which it is produced. The baseline serves as the means for exercising program control. We cannot overstress the importance of a well-documented baseline. [1]

The subject matter in this chapter addresses the baseline models used in technical risk management. These are the baseline time estimate model and the baseline cost estimate model. Figure 4.1 shows the organization of the chapter. Subjects are listed alongside the respective sections of the chapter.

**Section 4.1 Definitions** provides the definitions of key terms and abbreviations used in this chapter. These definitions are given when first used in the chapter and repeated in Appendix A.

**Section 4.2 Product Network** starts the exposition on baseline models used to describe the time-phased flow of activities and relationships for products of interest. The product network is evolved with techniques, such as PERT (*i.e.,* Program Evaluation Review Technique), CPM (*i.e.,* Critical Path Method), and precedence diagramming.

**Section 4.3 Baseline Time Estimate** introduces the concepts of standards and learning curves. Standards provide the building blocks for scheduling and cost estimating. Learning curves allow one to capitalize on the economy of scale (*e.g.,* large quantity production and procurement), especially in labor-intensive products.

**Section 4.4 Baseline Cost Estimate** addresses structure and content of cost estimating, cost estimating strategies, and cost estimating techniques. The strategies are top-down and bottom-up estimating; the techniques are expert opinion, analogy, parametric, and industrial engineering. This section introduces the concepts of aggregate vs. disaggregate cost estimates and explores the implications of these concepts with respect to realism and credibility.

**Section 4.5 Time Value of Money** illuminates the very important relationships underlying decisions for the future on the basis of return-on-investment. The subjects include present and future values involving sums of money and series of payments, economic analysis, escalation and

## 4.1 Definitions

inflation, and price indexes. The techniques are particularly useful in technical risk management for projecting baseline cost estimates into the future.

Chapter 4 concludes with **Section 4.6 Summary**, **Section 4.7 Exercises**, and **Section 4.8 References**. The summary serves to highlight the contents of the chapter, and the exercises reinforce the highlights.

|  |  |
|---|---|
| 4.1 Definitions | Key terms and abbreviations. |
| 4.2 Product Network | PERT and CPM; critical path definition; task flow analysis; network utilization; precedence diagramming. |
| 4.3 Baseline Time Estimate | Standards; standard data for job families; learning curves; probabilistic nature of learning curves; learning-curve discontinuity. |
| 4.4 Baseline Cost Estimate | Cost scenario; should cost; could cost; would cost; cost element structure; work breakdown structure; generation breakdown; cost estimating methodology; expert opinion; analogy; parametric; industrial engineering. |
| 4.5 Time Value of Money | Future value of a present single payment; present value of a future single payment; uniform series of payments for a future value; present value for a uniform series of payments; economic analysis; present value method; annual equivalent value method; benefit-cost method; internal rate of return; escalation and inflation; price indexes. |
| 4.6 Summary | Review of highlights. |
| 4.7 Exercises | Role models. |
| 4.8 References | Data sources. |

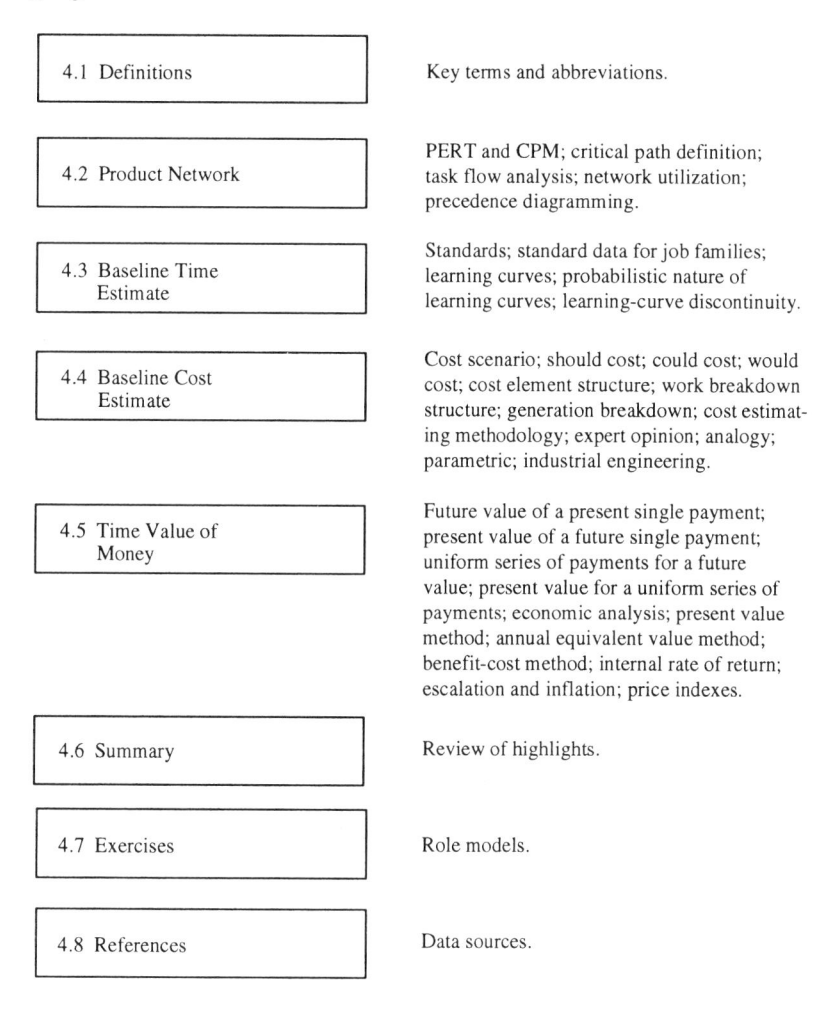

**Figure 4.1** Organization of Chapter 4

# 4.1 DEFINITIONS

Table 4.1 gives definitions of terms and abbreviations used in this chapter. Note, in particular, the meaning of *aggregation*, *disaggregation*, *baseline*, *baseline cost estimate*, and *baseline time esti-*

*mate*. Note the relationship among *task-duration time*, *path-duration time*, *network-duration time*, and *network-cycle time*.

We use a number of specialized terms in Section 4.5, which are defined in the section. However, note the terms in Table 4.1 that relate to the time value of money.

***Table 4.1*** *Terms and Abbreviations in Chapter 4*

**Aggregation**: Composition of component-related data into product-related data.
**Balanced production line**: Production line wherein no time is expended waiting for work to arrive at any work station in the line.
**Baseline**: Initial definition of the product to be developed, the process used to produce the product, and the environment within which the product is produced. The baseline serves as the means for exercising program control.
**Baseline cost estimate**: Estimated cost to complete development and production of the initial baseline.
**Baseline time estimate**: Estimated time to complete development and production of the initial baseline.
**Benefit-cost ratio**: Ratio of the present value of benefits to the present value of costs.
**Bivariate equation of regression**: Two-variable regression equation.
*Caveat emptor*: Latin for *let the buyer beware*.
**Coefficient of determination**: Statistical factor describing dependency among variables.
**Contingency analysis**: Definition of potential problems and solutions in development and production.
**Cost account**: Group of related work packages.
**CPM**: Critical path method.
**Critical path**: Path in multipath networks requiring the most time or money to complete the tasks comprising the path than the other paths.
**Critical path method**: Networking techniques that emphasize the critical path.
**Cycle time**: Same as network-duration time and run time. Amount of time needed to complete a production run.
**Deterministics**: Method of solution using a sequence of causes.
**Disaggregation**: Decomposition of product-related data into component-related data (*i.e.*, disaggregate parts).
**Extrinsic factors**: Factors, such as inflation, which are peripheral to, and largely beyond the control of, the given program.
**Generation breakdown:** Hierarchical rendition of how products are produced starting with raw material.
**Heuristic**: From the Greek word *heuriskein* meaning "to invent" or "to discover." The use of rules of thumb that leads to feasible though not necessarily optimal solutions.
**Heuristics**: Method of solution in which one proceeds along empirical lines using rules of thumb.
**Intangible property**: Non-physical property such as cash on hand, investments, accounts receivable, and prepaid services.
**Intrinsic factors:** Factors, which are part of a given program and, as such, are largely within the control of the program.
**Job family:** Group of similar products.
**Learning curve**: Graphical representation of the reduction in operation time as a function of learning from repetitive operations.
**Milestone**: Accomplishment signifying the completion of a task.
**Morphology**: Form and structure of baseline and risk estimates.
**Network-cycle time**: Same as network-duration time.
**Network-duration time**: Time to complete all tasks in network.
**Opportunity loss**: Return realized if money had been invested in the best possible investment opportunity.
**Path**: Series of tasks leading from start to finish milestones in product networks.
**Path-duration time**: Amount of time needed to complete tasks comprising a path.
**PERT**: Program evaluation review technique.
**Precedence**: Tasks which must be completed as prerequisites for other tasks to be started.
**Precedence diagram**: Networking method.
**Probabilistics**: Method of solution based on the probability of outcomes.
**Process**: Methodology, facility, equipment, and personnel for supplying a specific product.
**Product**: System or product consisting of hardware, software, or service components.
**RCE**: Risk cost estimate.

**Table 4.1**  Terms and Abbreviations in Chapter 4 (Cont.)

> **Risk cost**: Product of corrective-action cost and probability of needing corrective action.
> **Risk cost estimate**: Baseline cost estimate plus risk cost.
> **Risk time**: Product of corrective-action time and probability of needing corrective action.
> **Risk time estimate**: Baseline time estimate plus risk time.
> **RTE**: Risk time estimate.
> **Task-duration time**: Time to complete individual tasks in network.
> **Work-content time**: Amount of time needed to perform the work content of a work element.
> **Work element**: Smallest subdivision of manufacturing process which can be assigned to a single work station.
> **Work package**: Unit of work needed to complete a specific job which is assigned to a specific operator.

## 4.2 PRODUCT NETWORK

Figure 4.2 shows the **morphology** of baseline estimates with the product network at the center, providing the bridge from the baseline and technical and business approaches to the estimates. A product network is a conglomeration of tasks and milestones needed to (1) develop the product; (2) implement the process for producing the product; and (3) produce the product.

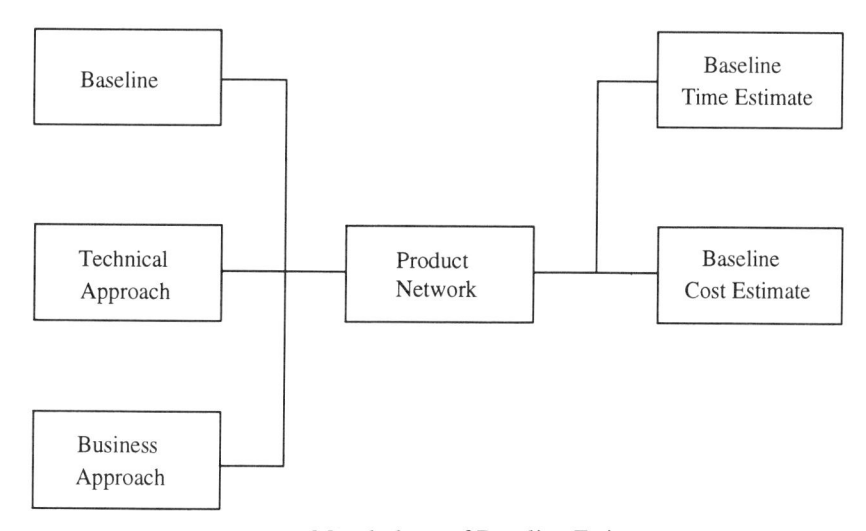

**Figure 4.2**  Morphology of Baseline Estimates

The baseline, technical approach, and business strategy drive the product network. The baseline is the initial definition of the product and process and is documented in the technical data package.

It is important to maintain the integrity of the technical data package. We do this with a system of configuration and data management.

The technical approach defines the what, how, and when of the product (*i.e.*, what is to be built, how is it to be built, and when is it to be built). The "what" of the product addresses its quality and functionality. The "how" of the product addresses the technology to be used in development and production. The "when" of the product addresses the time-phased relationships of tasks and their connectivity comprising the product network.

The business strategy defines the "who" and "where" of the product (*i.e.*, who is to build the product and where is it to be built). The "who" of the product addresses the issue of make vs. buy. The "where" of the product addresses the choice of facilities, equipment, and personnel.

The **baseline time estimate (BTE)** and **baseline cost estimate (BCE)**, which are shown as outputs in Figure 4.2, describe the time and money needed to complete the myriad tasks comprising the product network of interest. In technical terms, BTE is the time needed to traverse the product network. BCE is the budgeted cost to perform the scheduled work.

### ■ 4.2.1 PERT and CPM

Schedule and cost control are major elements in the management of complex programs. The concern of schedule control is the integrity of the time-phased flow of activities from the beginning to the completion of the program of interest. The concern of cost control is the integrity of the associate cost budget.

For years, the techniques used in schedule control were the well-known bar chart, **PERT** (*i.e.*, **Program Evaluation and Review Technique**), and **CPM** (*i.e.*, **Critical Path Method**). Today, the bar chart is used primarily for descriptive purposes such as showing the overall content and time phasing of a particular program, and the other techniques are in limited applications.

PERT and CPM, which are still in use, are the antecedents of precedence diagramming. Over the past decade, precedence diagramming has become the mainstay in schedule control. Precedence diagramming is particularly useful in manufacturing for achieving balanced production lines.

> *In a balanced production line, no time is expended waiting for work to arrive at any work station in the line.*
> **Analyst**

You need to understand PERT and CDM before attacking precedence diagramming. The U.S. Navy developed PERT in the 1950s for the POLARIS missile program. At about the same time, the I. E. duPont de Nemours Company developed CPM for planning and control of chemical plant maintenance. You can gauge the success of PERT and CPM by the two-year reduction in the Polaris development cycle and the reduction of more than 37 percent in maintenance downtime at the duPont Louisville works.

PERT and CPM are based on substantially the same concept, although there are some differences in the details. PERT uses so-called probabilistic estimates of task-duration times along the various paths comprising a product network. These time estimates are pessimistic, expected, and optimistic.

The use of pessimistic, expected, and optimistic times is the reason why PERT is considered probabilistic. CPM is characterized as being deterministic in that it uses single estimates of activity duration times. In actuality, CPM is also probabilistic, since these estimates are expected values.

## 4.2 Product Network

PERT and CPM generally appear in the forms shown in Figure 4.3. PERT is configured to show activity flow, whereas CPM is configured to emphasize the **critical path** in the product network.

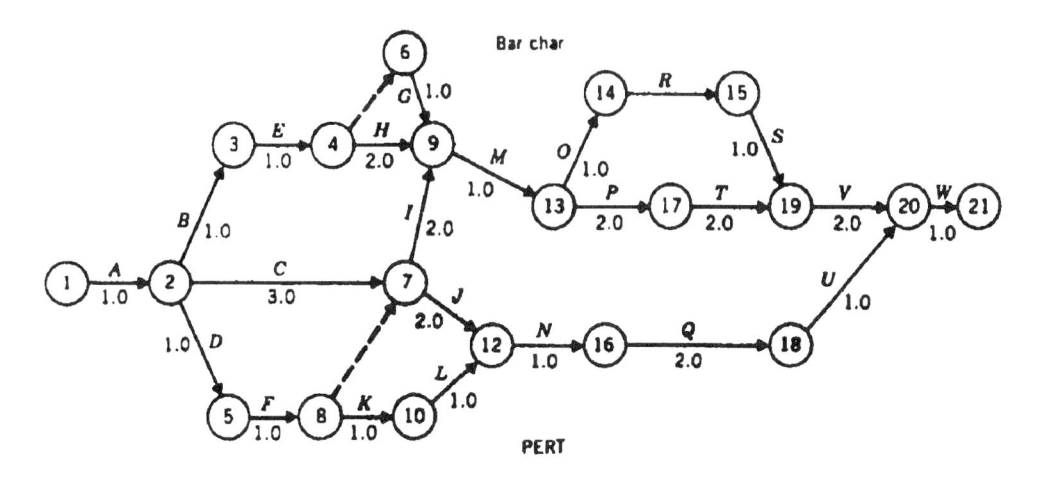

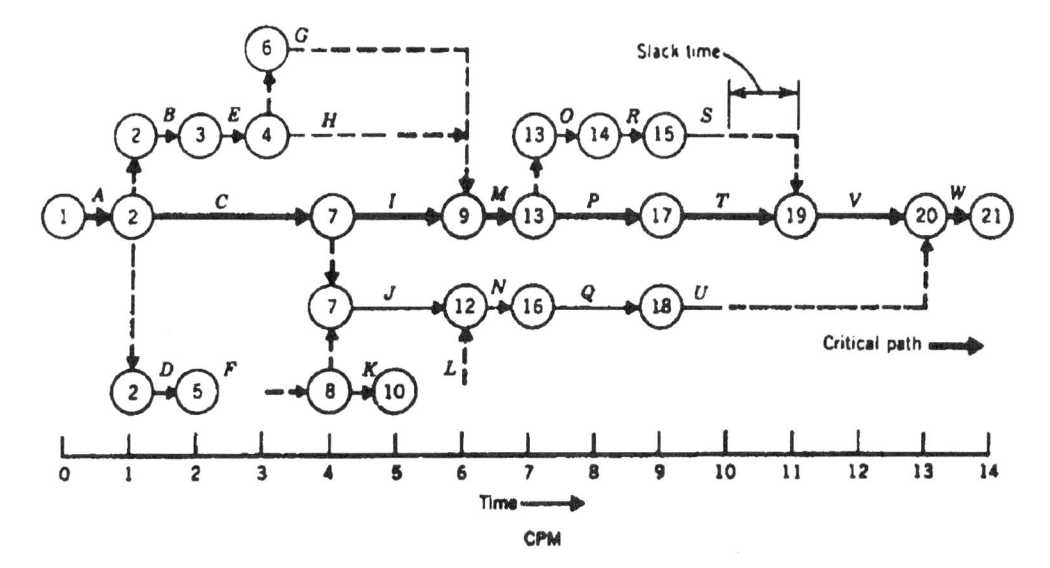

**Figure 4.3** General Forms of PERT and CPM Networks [1]
From Jack V. Michaels and William P. Wood, *Design to Cost*. Copyright© 1989, John Wiley & Sons, Inc. Reprinted by permission of John Wiley & Sons, Inc.

The procedure for developing any form of product network is the same. The steps are (1) network coding; (2) task flow analysis; and (3) network optimization.

Network coding ensures consistency in results. The initial task in Step 2 is the enumeration of the critical path in the network. The objective of Step 3 is to optimize the network with respect to the utilization of resources that include the time available to do the job, as well as labor, material, facilities, and equipment.

### ■ 4.2.2 Network Coding

Tasks in networks terminate at nodal points or milestones. To avoid confusion, it is important to establish coding conventions for tasks and milestones.

Table 4.2 gives typical coding conventions. These conventions can be altered to suit the purposes of individual products. Once established, however, it is important that you adhere to these conventions as consistently as possible.

**Table 4.2** *Product Network Coding Conventions*

1. Milestones (*i.e.*, start and finish of network) are designated by encircled Arabic numerals.
2. Tasks are designated by upper- or lower-case English letters.
3. Dummy tasks are designated by upper-case English letters or by Roman numerals.
4. Task-duration times are given in parentheses under the paths, in the order of pessimistic time, expected time, and optimistic time.

The simplified product network, shown in Figure 4.4, consists of ten tasks which are identified by lower-case English letters. A task is a work element that performs a single function (*e.g.*, punch hole in chassis). The tasks terminate or originate at the seven milestones indicated by encircled Arabic numbers.

A milestone is an accomplishment signifying the completion of a task. Series of tasks leading from the start to the finish milestones are **paths**.

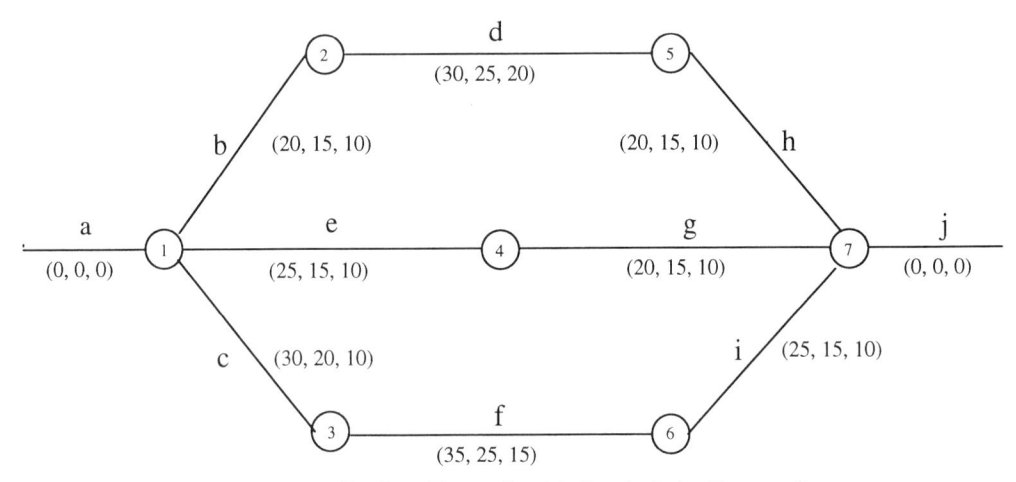

**Figure 4.4** Product Network with Pessimistic, Expected, and Optimistic Task-Duration Times

## 4.2 Product Network

Task-duration times are given in parentheses under the paths in the order of pessimistic, expected, and optimistic task-duration times. The parenthetical numbers in Figure 4.4 are values of unit time that can be seconds, minutes, or hours depending on the tasks of interest.

No time is allocated to Tasks a and b since they are the start and finish tasks. Consequently, the task-duration times for these tasks are indicated by the notation (0, 0, 0) in the figure. Usually, no time is allocated to milestones unless the review process is expected to be lengthy.

All product networks possess the properties given in Table 4.3. The slack-time properties can be used to equalize the network, as indicated in the table.

*Table 4.3    Network Properties*

| |
|---|
| 1. The path with the longest **path-duration** time is the critical path. The other paths in the network are noncritical paths.<br>2. The critical path time is the network-duration time.<br>3. The difference between the critical network-duration time and noncritical path-duration time is negative slack time in the critical path and the positive slack time in the respective noncritical paths.<br>4. Positive slack time in noncritical paths can be used to offset negative slack time in the critical path.<br>5. Decreasing the amount of positive slack time in noncritical paths can cause these paths to become the critical path. |

### ■ 4.2.3 Critical Path Definition

Table 4.4 gives the cumulative values of pessimistic, expected, and optimistic path-duration times for the unit task-duration times in Figure 4.4. The network path with the longest path-duration time is the critical path. It is critical from the viewpoint that taking more time to complete the task will impact the allocated time and money.

In Figure 4.4, Path a, c, f, i, j is the critical path with respect to both the expected and pessimistic path-duration times of 60 and 90 time units. With respect to the optimistic time, there are two critical paths (*viz.*, a, b, d, h, j and a, c, f, i, j), each with a path-duration time of 35 time units. In technical terms, noncritical paths possess positive slack whereas the critical path possesses negative slack. Positive slack may be indicative of spare resources which can be used to offset some of the negative slack, but it is also a measure of inefficiency in the network.

### ■ 4.2.4 Task Flow Analysis

The objective of task flow analysis is to illuminate the interrelationships of the activity tasks comprising the program. This step, which is unnecessary with simple networks, becomes increasingly important with an increasing number of paths and dependent tasks.

We conduct task flow analysis by asking the questions in Table 4.5. The redundant answers you may obtain to the third and fourth questions check the flow of the tasks.

*Table 4.4*  *Cumulative Path-Duration Times*

| Path | Cumulative Path-Duration Time | |
|---|---|---|
| **Optimistic Time** | | |
| a, b, d, h, j | 0 + 10 + 15 + 10 + 0 | = 35 |
| a, e, g, j | 0 + 10 + 10 + 0 | = 20 |
| a, c, f, i, j | 0 + 10 + 15 + 10 + 0 | = 35 |
| **Expected Time** | | |
| a, b, d, h, j | 0 + 15 + 25 + 15 + 0 | = 55 |
| a, e, g, j | 0 + 15 + 15 + 0 | = 30 |
| a, c, f, i, j | 0 + 20 + 25 + 15 + 0 | = 60 |
| **Pessimistic Time** | | |
| a, b, d, h, j | 0 + 20 + 30 + 20 + 0 | = 70 |
| a, e, g, j | 0 + 25 + 20 + 0 | = 45 |
| a, c, f, i, j | 0 + 30 + 35 + 25 + 0 | = 90 |

*Table 4.5*  *Task Flow Analysis Questions*

1. What tasks need to be performed?
2. What is the duration of each task?
3. Which tasks immediately precede other given tasks?
4. Which tasks immediately succeed other given tasks?

The answers to these questions are the bases for depicting the task flow network shown in Figure 4.5. The network consists of eight milestones, designated by encircled Arabic numerals, and twelve tasks, designated by lower-case English letters.

As the network develops we annotate each path with the optimistic, expected, and pessimistic times in parentheses. The annotation is not necessary, however, to judge the network efficiency.

At first glance the network would appear to have three alternate paths from start to finish but there are actually four paths. The fourth path is comprised of Tasks a, d, l, g, and k.

Depiction of the alternate paths is eased by using the task-precedence chart in Table 4.6. In the context of product networks, the word **precedence** denotes those tasks which must be completed as prerequisites for other tasks to be started. The table lists the tasks, their duration in unit times, and their respective predecessor tasks and successor tasks. Note that we annotate the start and finish tasks with zero unit time. Also note that the start task has no predecessor task and the finish task has no successor task. Task-precedence charts reveal the connectivity among tasks in terms of predecessor and successor tasks.

The usual practice in constructing the network is to work backward from the finish and delineate predecessor tasks until you reach the start of the network. You can work forward with a little more difficulty.

It is customary to include task-duration times in task-precedence charts. Note that time entries in Table 4.6 are in multiples of unit time. There is frequent ambiguity regarding the precedence of certain tasks, and we introduce a dummy task to eliminate such ambiguity. Tasks f and l in Figure 4.5 are dummy tasks, as indicated by the notation of (0) for task-duration times.

## 4.2 Product Network

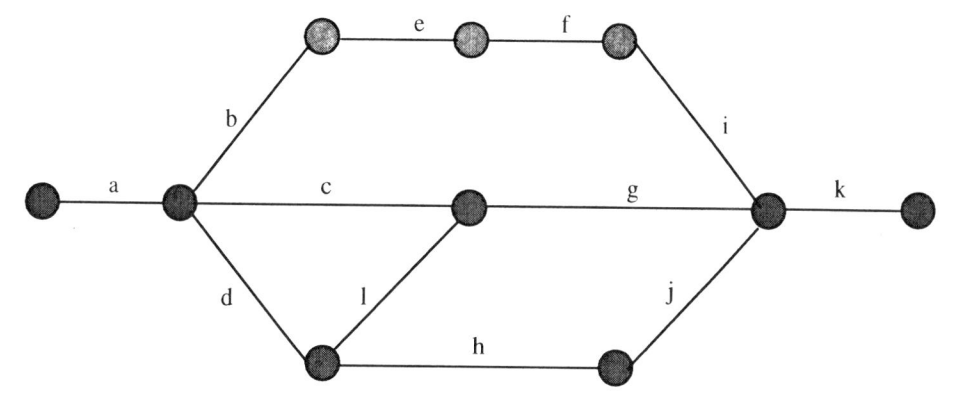

**Figure 4.5** Task Flow Network

**Table 4.6** Task-Precedence Chart

| Task | Unit Time | Predecessor | Successor |
|------|-----------|-------------|-----------|
| a | 0 | None | b, c, d |
| b | 5 | a | e |
| c | 5 | a | g |
| d | 5 | b | h, l |
| e | 10 | a | f |
| f | 0 | c | i |
| g | 5 | d | k |
| h | 15 | e, f | j |
| i | 5 | c | k |
| j | 5 | g | k |
| k | 5 | g, i, j | None |
| l | 0 | d | g |

Figure 4.5 shows that there are four paths that progress from starting Milestone 1 to finishing Milestone 8. The tasks in each task and path-duration times are

1. a, b, e, f, i, k:   20 time units
2. a, c, g, k:   15 time units
3. a, d, l, g, k:   15 time units
4. a, d, h, j, k:   25 time units

The critical path is a, d, h, j, k with the critical path time of 25 time units. There are five time units of positive slack in Path a, b, e, f, i, k (*i.e.*, 25 time units minus 20 time units) and ten units of positive slack in Path a, c, g, k (*i.e.*, 25 time units minus 15 time units). The positive slack in Path a, d, l, g, k amounts to ten time units (*i.e.*, 25 time units minus 15 time units).

As stated, the amount of slack in a network is a measure of the inefficiency of the network. We calculate the network-duration time by summing the four path-duration times for (20 + 25 + 20 + 15) time units, or 80 time units.

### ■ 4.2.5 Network Utilization

Network efficiency is the measure of network utilization. A network with no positive slack would be 100 percent efficient. The efficiency (E) of a network is given by:

$$E = \frac{\text{Network-duration time} - \text{total positive slack}}{\text{Network-duration time}} \quad (4.1)$$

In this case, the network efficiency is

$$E = \frac{80 \text{ time units} - 10 \text{ units}}{80 \text{ time units}}$$

$$= 0.875. \quad (4.2)$$

The critical-path time establishes the network-duration time. Where the product network is part of a recurring process (*e.g.*, production runs), run time and cycle time is the same as network-duration time.

### ■ 4.2.6 Example of Task Flow Analysis

The highway department of a certain state has 30 months to design a road project for submittal to the state legislature for approval and funding. The department's staff questions the adequacy of the allocated time for the design effort.

The department retains Analyst to develop the product network for the design effort, enumerate the critical path, and determine the product network efficiency. Table 4.7 gives the technical approach Analyst follows in carrying out the assignment.

***Table 4.7*** *Technical Approach for Task Flow Analysis Example*

1. Lay out product network showing task connectivity.
2. Derive task-precedence chart to include path-duration times.
3. Derive path-enumeration chart.
4. Designate critical path and determine slack in other paths.
5. Calculate the product network efficiency.

Analyst first lays out the product network shown in Figure 4.6 in accordance with the coding conventions given in Table 4.2. There are twenty-two tasks, three dummy tasks, and twenty milestones in the network.

Analyst designates the tasks by the letters *a* through *x*, the dummy tasks by the Roman numerals I through III, and the milestones by the numbers 1 through 20. As stated, the purpose of the dummy task is to eliminate ambiguity in viewing the network by showing the required task-to-task connectivity.

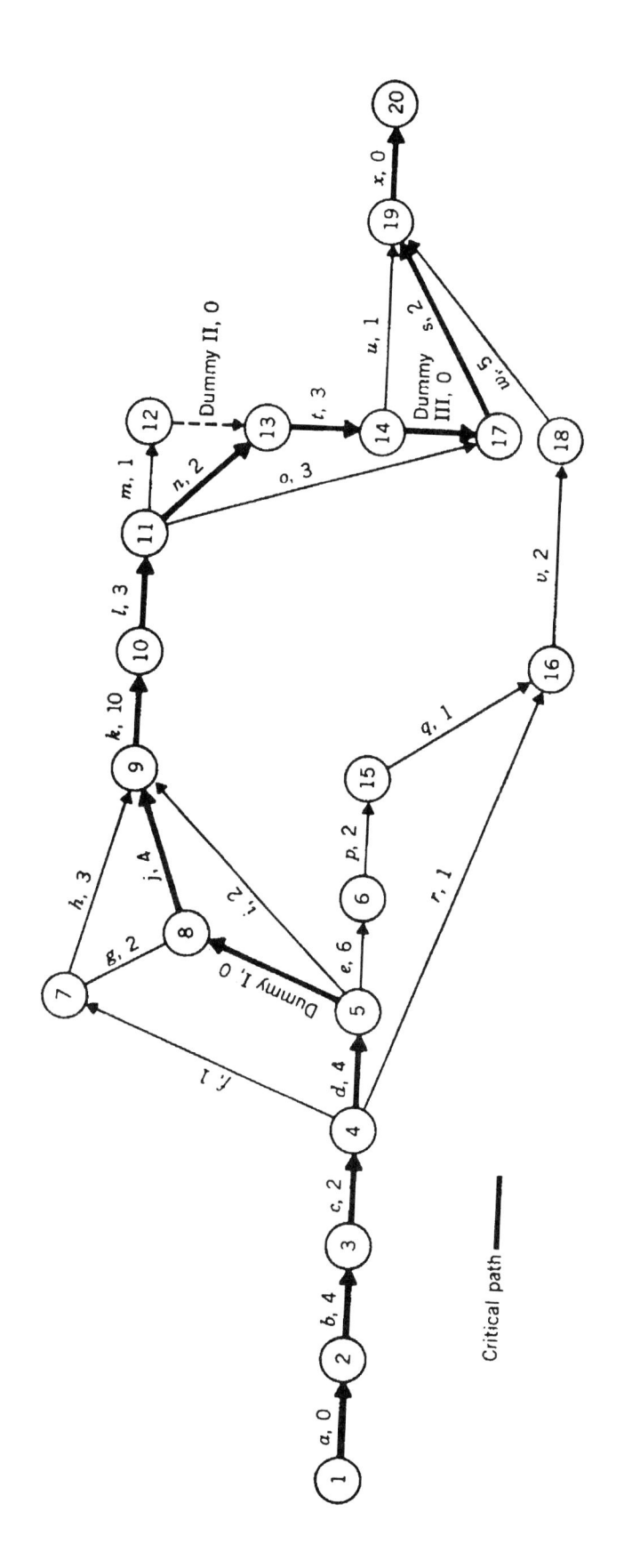

**Figure 4.6** Multiple Path Product Network for Task Flow Analysis Example [1]

From Jack V. Michaels and William P. Wood, *Design to Cost*. Copyright© 1989, John Wiley & Sons, Inc. Reprinted by permission of John Wiley & Sons, Inc.

123

Task-duration times, in time units, are given after the task designators in Figure 4.6. The time unit equals one month. Analyst assumes that Path a, b, c, d, I, j, k, l, n, t, III, s, x is the critical path in the network, and indicates the path by the heavier line in the figure. The critical-path time is 0 + 4 + 2 + 4 + 0 + 4 + 10 + 3 + 2 + 3 + 0 + 2 + 0, or 34 time units.

The value of the time unit is one month, and the critical-path time of 34 time units is thirty-four months, or four months more than the allocated time of thirty months. Analyst next prepares the task-precedence chart in Table 4.8, and the path-duration chart in Table 4.9.

Table 4.8 has a number of tasks with two and three predecessor and successor tasks, signifying a network with a fairly large number of paths. This statement is borne out by the complexity of Figure 4.6.

Table 4.9 indicates network-duration time of 651 months. This value is used in calculating the efficiency of the network after the calculation of the total path-slack time. Analyst prepares the path-slack chart in Table 4.10, enumerating critical-path time and slack in the other paths, and the network efficiency. The critical path is Path 15, the same as in Figure 4.6. The critical-path time is still thirty-four months or four months more than the allocated thirty months.

Analyst substitutes network-duration time of 651 months and total path-slack time of 97 months in Equation 4.1 and obtains

$$E = \frac{652 \text{ time units} - 97 \text{ time units}}{651 \text{ time units}}$$
$$= 0.851. \quad (4.3)$$

**Table 4.8** *Task-Precedence Chart for Task Flow Analysis Example [1]*

| Task | Duration | Predecessor | Successor |
|------|----------|-------------|-----------|
| a | 0 | None | b |
| b | 4 | a | c |
| c | 2 | b | d, f, r |
| d | 4 | c | e, i, j |
| e | 6 | d | p |
| f | 1 | c | g, h |
| g | 2 | f | j |
| h | 3 | f | k |
| i | 2 | d | k |
| j | 4 | d, g | k |
| k | 10 | i, j, h | l |
| l | 3 | k | m, n, o |
| m | 1 | l | r |
| n | 2 | l | r |
| o | 3 | l | s |
| p | 2 | e | q |
| q | 1 | p | v |
| r | 1 | c | v |
| s | 2 | o, t | x |
| t | 3 | m, n | s, u |
| u | 1 | t | x |
| v | 2 | q, r | w |
| w | 5 | v | x |
| x | 0 | s, u, w | None |

From Jack V. Michaels and William P. Wood, *Design to Cost*. Copyright© 1989, John Wiley & Sons, Inc. Reprinted by permission of John Wiley & Sons, Inc.

## 4.2 Product Network

The amount of effort that can be reallocated is a function of the network efficiency. In this case, the efficiency is 0.851, or 85.1 percent, and the department could reallocate 100 − 85.1 percent, or 14.9 percent of the effort toward reducing the critical path time by four months. On the basis of the findings, the department reallocates effort from tasks on noncritical paths to tasks on the critical path.

### ■ 4.2.7 Network Utilization

Network efficiency is a measure of how well you utilize resources in the development and production of products. Resources consist of the allocated material, facilities, and equipment. There are several ways whereby you can enhance the utilization of these resources.

If your intent were to reduce critical path time, you could simply use network compression. Network compression is the process of adding resources to the tasks comprising the critical path to accelerate performance along the path. If your intent is to improve efficiency as well, you would use network equalization. Network equalization is more economical than network compression.

*Table 4.9* Path-Duration Chart for Task Flow Analysis Example

| Path | Path-Duration Time | |
|---|---|---|
| 1. a, b, c, f, h, k, l, m, II, t, u, x. | 0 + 4 + 2 + 1 + 3 + 10 + 3 + 1 + 0 + 3 + 1 + 0 | = 28 |
| 2. a, b, c, f, h, k, l, m, II, t, III, s, x. | 0 + 4 + 2 + 1 + 3 + 10 + 3 + 1 + 0 + 3 + 0 + 2 + 0 | = 29 |
| 3. a, b, c, f, h, k, l, n, t, u, x. | 0 + 4 + 2 + 1 + 3 + 10 + 3 + 2 + 3 + 1 + 0 | = 29 |
| 4. a, b, c, f, h, k, l, n, t, III, s, x. | 0 + 4 + 2 + 1 + 3 + 10 + 3 + 2 + 3 + 0 + 2 + 0 | = 30 |
| 5. a, b, c, f, h, k, l, o, s, x. | 0 + 4 + 2 + 1 + 3 + 10 + 3 + 3 + 2 + 0 | = 28 |
| 6. a, b, c, f, g, j, k, l, m, II, t, u, x. | 0 + 4 + 2 + 1 + 2 + 4 + 10 + 3 + 1 + 0 + 3 + 1 + 0 | = 31 |
| 7. a, b, c, f, g, j, k, l, m, II, t, III, s, x. | 0 + 4 + 2 + 1 + 2 + 4 + 10 + 3 + 1 + 0 + 2 + 0 + 2 + 0 | = 31 |
| 8. a, b, c, f, g, j, k, l, n, t, u, x. | 0 + 4 + 2 + 1 + 2 + 4 + 10 + 3 + 2 + 3 + 1 + 0 | = 32 |
| 9. a, b, c, f, g, j, k, l, n, t, III, s, x. | 0 + 4 + 2 + 1 + 2 + 4 + 10 + 3 + 2 + 3 + 0 + 2 + 0 | = 33 |
| 10. a, b, c, f, g, j, k, l, o, s, x. | 0 + 4 + 2 + 1 + 2 + 4 + 10 + 3 + 3 + 2 + 0 | = 31 |
| 11. a, b, c, r, v, w, k. | 0 + 4 + 2 + 1 + 2 + 5 + 0 | = 14 |
| 12. a, b, c, d, I, j, k, l, m, II, t, u, x. | 0 + 4 + 2 + 4 + 0 + 4 + 10 + 3 + 1 + 0 + 3 + 1 + 0 | = 32 |
| 13. a, b, c, d, I, j, k, l, m, II, t, III, s, x. | 0 + 4 + 2 + 4 + 0 + 4 + 10 + 3 + 1 + 0 + 3 + 0 + 2 + 0 | = 33 |

**Table 4.9** *Path-Duration Chart for Task Flow Analysis Example (Cont.)*

| Path | Path-Duration Time | |
|---|---|---|
| 14. a, b, c, d, I, j, | 0 + 4 + 2 + 4 + 0 + 4 + | |
| k, l, n, t, u, x. | 10 + 3 + 2 + 3 + 1 + 0 | = 33 |
| 15. a, b, c, d, I, j, k, | 0 + 4 + 2 + 4 + 0 + 4 + 10 + | |
| l, n, t, III, s, x. | 3 + 2 + 3 + 0 + 2 + 0 | = 34 |
| 16. a, b, c, d, I, | 0 + 4 + 2 + 4 + 0 + 4 + | |
| j, k, l, o, s, x. | 10 + 3 + 3 + 2 + 0 | = 32 |
| 17. a, b, c, d, i, k, | 0 + 4 + 2 + 4 + 2 + 10 + | |
| l, m, II, t, u, x. | 3 + 1 + 0 + 3 + 1 + 0 | = 30 |
| 18. a, b, c, d, i, k, | 0 + 4 + 2 + 4 + 2 + 10 + | |
| l, m, II, t, III, s. | 3 + 1 + 0 + 3 + 0 + 2 + 0 | = 31 |
| 19. a, b, c, d, I, | 0 + 4 + 2 + 4 + 2 + | |
| n, t, k, l, u, x. | 10 + 3 + 2 + 3 + 1 + 0 | = 31 |
| 20. a, b, c, d, I, k, | 0 + 4 + 2 + 4 + 2 + 10 + | |
| l, n, t, III, s, x. | 3 + 2 + 3 + 0 + 2 + 0 | = 32 |
| 21. a, b, c, d, I, | 0 + 4 + 2 + 4 + 2 + | |
| k, l, o, s, x. | 10 + 3 + 3 + 2 + 0 | = 30 |
| 22. a, b, c, d, | 0 + 4 + 2 + 6 + | |
| e, p, v, w, x. | 2 + 1 + 2 + 5 + 0 | = 22 |

Network-duration time: 651 months.

The rationale for network compression is that there is a linear relationship between small increases in direct cost for accelerating critical path tasks and large savings from subsequent reduction in indirect cost (*i.e.*, overhead) from reduced periods of performance. The rationale for network equalization is that there is a linear relationship between task performance with resources expended at a given rate and task performance with the resources expended at an extended rate. At best, the assumption of linearity is tenuous in both approaches. More frequently, the increased costs exceed anticipated savings.

**Table 4.10** *Path-Slack Chart for Task Flow Analysis Example*

| Path | Duration | Slack | Path | Duration | Slack |
|---|---|---|---|---|---|
| 1 | 28 | 10 | 12 | 32 | 2 |
| 2 | 29 | 5 | 13 | 33 | 1 |
| 3 | 29 | 5 | 14 | 33 | 1 |
| 4 | 30 | 4 | 15 | 34 | 0 |
| 5 | 28 | 6 | 16 | 32 | 2 |
| 6 | 31 | 3 | 17 | 30 | 4 |
| 7 | 31 | 3 | 18 | 31 | 4 |
| 8 | 32 | 2 | 19 | 31 | 3 |
| 9 | 33 | 1 | 20 | 32 | 2 |
| 10 | 31 | 3 | 21 | 30 | 4 |
| 11 | 14 | 20 | 22 | 22 | 12 |

## 4.2 Product Network

### ■ 4.2.8 Example of Network Compression

This example illustrates network compression as a means for reducing periods of performance and, as a consequence, reducing cost.

The state legislature in the example of Section 4.2.6 approves funding of $5.1 million to be expended on the road design over thirty months. The example found that the network-duration time is thirty-four months, or four months more than the legislature specified. In addition, the path-duration time is more than thirty months in twelve of the twenty-two tasks comprising the network (v., Table 4.9).

The highway department believes that network compression may be the answer to the problem and again retains Analyst to evolve the network-compression algorithm for reducing thirty-four months network-duration time to thirty months. Table 4.11 gives the technical approach Analyst follows in carrying out the additional assignment.

*Table 4.11   Technical Approach for Network Compression Example*

---
1. Decrease the slack in noncritical and critical paths so that the path-duration time equals 30 months and delineate the slack reduction.
2. For each path with negative slack, calculate the additional effort needed to eliminate the negative slack.
3. Sum the foregoing amounts of additional effort and multiply the sum by burdened direct cost rate for the additional direct cost to be expended.
4. Multiply the indirect cost rate by the network compression for reduction in indirect cost.
5. Subtract the additional direct cost from the reduction in indirect cost.
---

Analyst investigates the cost structure of the department and finds that direct cost consists of burdened labor (*i.e.*, labor plus overhead burden): Labor is discrete cost keyed to the job to be done. Indirect cost is a constant monthly charge for general and administrative (G&A) support, plus other items such as capital cost of money: G&A support is level-of-effort cost keyed to the schedule.

Analyst subtracts from each path in the path-slack chart of Table 4.9 the number of months needed to reduce the respective path-duration times to 30 months and prepares the revised path-slack chart in Table 4.12. Note the negative values of slack in the table.

The negative value of network slack in Table 4.12 is the amount of compression required in the respective paths of the network. Analyst ascertains that the path-labor months equals the path-duration time for the respective paths.

Therefore, Paths 6, 7, 10, 18, and 19 each require 31 labor months to complete. Completing each path in 30 months would require the expenditure of (31 ÷ 30)(31 labor months), or 32.0333 labor months, which is 2.0333 labor months more than the original requirement for each path. The total additional requirement for the five paths is therefore (5)(2.0333) labor months, or 10.1665 labor months.

Analyst repeats these calculations for Paths 8, 12, 16, and 20; each requiring 32 labor months to complete. Completing each path in 30 months would require the expenditure of (32 ÷ 30)(32 labor months), or 34.1333 labor months, which is 2.1333 labor months more than the original requirement for each path. The total additional requirement for the four paths is (4)(2.1333 labor months), or 8.5332 labor months.

Paths 9, 13, and 14 each require 33 labor months to complete. Completing each path in 30 months would require the expenditure of (33 ÷ 30)(33 labor months), or 36.3 labor months, which is 3.3 labor months more than the original requirement for each path. The additional requirement for the three paths is (3)(3.3 labor months), or 9.9 labor months.

**Table 4.12** *Revised Path-Slack Chart for Network Compression Example*

| Path | Duration | Slack | Path | Duration | Slack |
|------|----------|-------|------|----------|-------|
| 1 | 28 | 2 | 12 | 32 | -2 |
| 2 | 29 | 1 | 13 | 33 | -3 |
| 3 | 29 | 1 | 14 | 33 | -3 |
| 4 | 30 | 0 | 15 | 34 | -4 |
| 5 | 28 | 2 | 16 | 32 | -2 |
| 6 | 31 | -1 | 17 | 30 | 0 |
| 7 | 31 | -1 | 18 | 31 | -1 |
| 8 | 32 | 2 | 19 | 31 | -1 |
| 9 | 33 | 3 | 20 | 32 | -2 |
| 10 | 31 | 1 | 21 | 30 | 0 |
| 11 | 14 | 16 | 22 | 22 | 8 |

Finally, Path 15, the critical path, requires 34 labor months to complete. Completing the path in 30 months would require the expenditure of (34 ÷ 30)(34 labor months), or 38.5333 labor months, which is 4.5333 labor months more than the original requirement for the path.

Analyst sums the foregoing additional requirements for 10.1665 + 8.5332 + 9.9 + 4.5333, or 31.1330 labor months. Analyst ascertains that the burdened direct cost of a labor month is $5,000. Multiplying $5,000 per labor month by 33.1330 labor months yields the additional direct cost requirement of $165,665.

Analyst also ascertains that the indirect cost rate is $125,000 per month. Compressing the network by four months reduces the indirect cost by (4)($125,000), or $500,000.

In reducing the network-duration time from thirty-four months to thirty months, Analyst was to determine whether the indirect cost saving from four months of network compression would be at least equal to the increased direct cost for accelerating the performance of tasks in paths with greater than thirty months duration time. It appears that network compression would yield a net saving of $500,000 − $165,665, or $334,335, provided the assumption of linearity were valid.

Analyst provides these findings to the agency, underscoring the need to validate the assumption of linearity before implementing the network compression. The agency validates the assumption and capitalizes on the opportunity provided by the study.

### ■ 4.2.9 Precedence Diagramming

**Precedence diagramming** is a popular method for schedule control, and is particularly useful for achieving balanced production lines in manufacturing operations. Most of the newer scheduling techniques use precedence diagramming. [1]

A product network consists of a number of production lines. With **balanced production lines**, no time is lost waiting for work to arrive at any work station in the network. Balanced production lines provide maximum efficiency in utilizing production resources.

The first step in precedence diagramming is to subdivide the manufacturing process into **work elements** which can be assigned to single work stations. The amount of work in each element is the work content and the time to do the work is the **work-content time**. The precedence diagramming process attempts to make work-content times as equal as possible throughout the network.

Production-line balancing involves redistributing work elements among the work stations and is usually approached on a heuristic basis. This involves a number of iterations until one attains the desired efficiency for the product network.

## 4.2 Product Network

### ■ 4.2.10 Example of Precedence Diagramming

Figure 4.7 shows the precedence diagram for a consumer product. The network consists of fourteen work elements and two dummy elements, (*i.e.*, S and F) for the network's start and finish.

There are three manufacturing work stations, which are labelled I, II, and III. The work elements in these stations fabricate the subassemblies and assemblies, which are fabricated elsewhere into complete products. The work-content times in Figure 4.7 are in time units. In this example, the total work-content time is 300 time units.

Table 4.13 gives the work elements and work-content times for the precedence diagram shown in Figure 4.7. Figure 4.7 and Table 4.13 describe the product network for a product produced by Rho Incorporated. The time unit is 0.1 minute, meaning that the total work-content time is (300 time units)(0.1 minute per time unit), or 30 minutes.

The critical path consists of Work Elements S, 2, 6, 11, F. The critical path time in Figure 4.7 is (15 + 20 + 30 time units)(0.1 minute per time unit) for (85 time units)(0.1 minute per time unit), or 8.5 minutes. The company wishes to ensure that the product network is as efficient as possible and retains Analyst for that purpose.

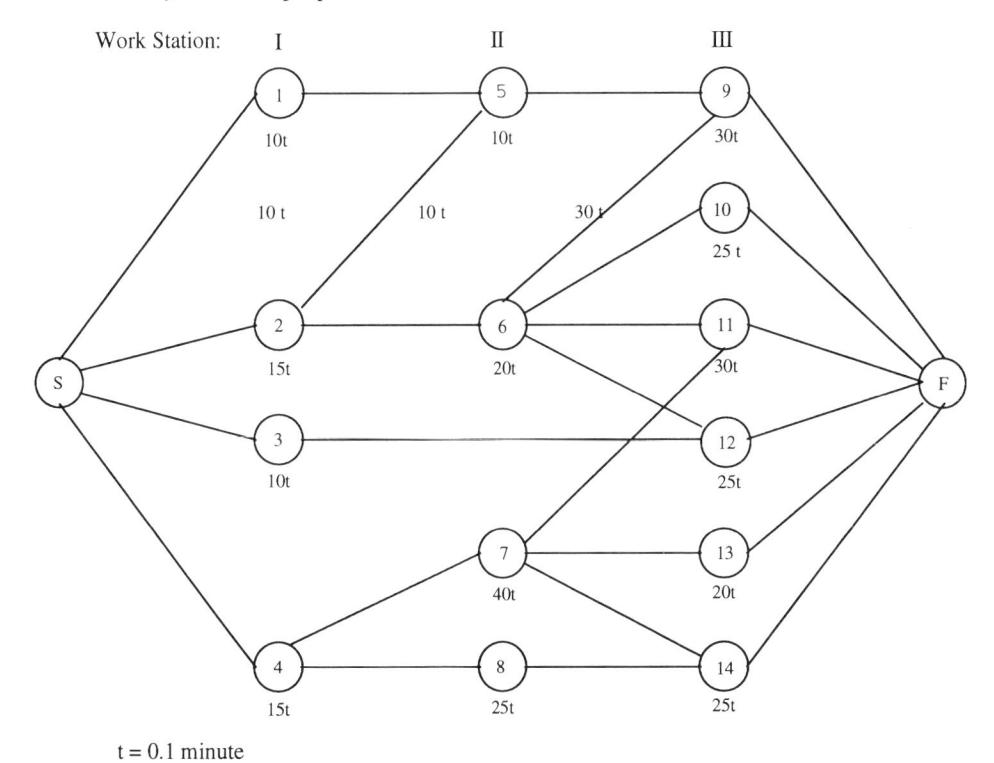

**Figure 4.7** Precedence Diagram

Table 4.14 gives the technical approach Analyst follows in carrying out the assignment. Analyst first delineates work elements and work-content time by work station by rearranging Figure 4.7 into the form given in Table 4.15.

*Table 4.13* Work-Content Times for Precedence Diagramming Example

| Work Element | Time Units | Work Element | Time Units | Work Element | Time Units |
|---|---|---|---|---|---|
| 1 | 10 | 6 | 20 | 11 | 30 |
| 2 | 15 | 7 | 40 | 12 | 25 |
| 3 | 10 | 8 | 25 | 13 | 20 |
| 4 | 15 | 9 | 30 | 14 | 25 |
| 5 | 10 | 10 | 25 | | |

Total work-content: 300 time units.

*Table 4.14* Technical Approach for Precedence Diagramming Example

1. Delineate work elements and work-content time by work stations.
2. Calculate product network efficiency.
3. Redistribute work elements among work stations.
4. Recalculate product network efficiency.
5. Repeat Steps 3 and 4 until at least 0.95 product network efficiency results.

Note that the work-content times in Table 4.15 are in time units ($tu$). The total work-content time of 300 $tu$ is (300)(0.1 minute), or 30 minutes. The total work-content time of 30 minutes is a constant in the precedence diagramming process. The objective is to attain equal work-content time at each work station.

*Table 4.15* Network Data for Precedence Diagramming Example

| Work Element | Work-Content Time, $tu$ | Work Element | Work-Content Time, $tu$ |
|---|---|---|---|
| Work Station 1 | | Work Station 3 | |
| 1 | 10 | 9 | 30 |
| 2 | 15 | 10 | 25 |
| 3 | 10 | 11 | 30 |
| 4 | 15 | 12 | 25 |
| | | 13 | 20 |
| | | 14 | 25 |
| **Total:** | 50 | **Total:** | 155 |
| Work Station 2 | | **Network-Content Time:** | 300 |
| 5 | 10 | | |
| 6 | 20 | | |
| 7 | 40 | | |
| 8 | 25 | | |
| **Total:** | 95 | $tu$: Time unit. | |

High values of product network efficiency signify that most of the work stations are fully occupied. Low values signify that only a few work stations are fully occupied and time is being wasted at other work stations waiting for work to arrive.

## 4.2 Product Network

The data in Table 4.15 signify that 105 (*i.e.*, 155 − 50) time units and 60 (*i.e.*, 155 − 95) time units, for a total of 165 time units, are wasted waiting for work to arrive at Work Stations 1 and 2. Analyst attempts to equalize the work load among work stations using product network efficiency as the measure of effectiveness.

The relationship for product network efficiency (E) is

$$E = \frac{\Sigma tu}{nc} \quad (4.4)$$

where $\Sigma tu$ denotes the network-content time in time units, $n$ the number of work stations, and $c$, which ordinarily denotes cycle time (*i.e.*, the time between production of successive units), in this case denotes the maximum work-content time at any of the work stations.

From Table 4.16, $tu = 300$, $n = 3$, and $c = 155$ time units at Work Station 3, the maximum work-content time at a work station. Applying these values to Equation 4.4, Analyst obtains

$$E = \frac{300 \ tu}{(3)(155 \ tu)}$$

$$= 0.6452. \quad (4.5)$$

Note that (3)(155 *tu*), or 465 *tu*, in the denominator of Equation 4.4 is the sum of work-content time and the idle time consumed in the product network and not just the work-content time that is only 300 *tu*. The product of 0.6452 and 465 *tu* is 300 *tu*.

**Table 4.16** *First Iteration for Precedence Diagramming Example*

| Work Element | Work-Content Time, *tu* | Work Element | Work-Content Time, *tu* |
|---|---|---|---|
| Work Station 1 | | Work Station 2 | |
| 1 | 10 | 7 | 40 |
| 2 | 15 | 8 | 25 |
| 3 | 10 | 9 | 30 |
| 4 | 15 | 10 | 25 |
| 5 | 10 | | |
| 6 | 20 | | |
| Total: | 80 | Total: | 120 |

| Work Element | Work-Content Time, *tu* | | |
|---|---|---|---|
| Work Station 3 | | Network-Content Time: | 300 |
| 11 | 30 | | |
| 12 | 25 | | |
| 13 | 20 | | |
| 14 | 25 | | |
| Total: | 100 | *tu*: Time unit. | |

Subsequent to each iteration of reallocating work elements, Analyst applies Equation 4.4 to assess the efficiency improvement in the product network efficiency. The next step in the balancing process is to reallocate work elements as uniformly as possible among the three work stations, meaning that each work station would be assigned (300 ÷ 4) time units, or 75 time units of work-content time. Table 4.16 gives the results of the first iteration of the balancing process.

Analyst takes Work Elements 5 and 6 from Work Station 2 and gives them to Work Station 1. Analyst next takes Work Elements 9 and 10 from Work Station 3 and gives them to Work Station 2. The work-content times load is now 80 time units for Work Station 1, 120 time units for Work Station 2, and 100 time units for Work Station 3. Work Station 2 now has the most work-content time.

Analyst examines the effect of the first iteration of reallocation on network efficiency. Substituting $\Sigma tu = 300$, $n = 3$, and $c = 120$ time units at Work Station 2 from Table 4.16 in Equation 4.4, Analyst obtains

$$E = \frac{300\ tu}{(3)(120 tu)}$$

$$= 0.8333. \tag{4.6}$$

The network efficiency of 0.8333 is still below the desired level of 0.95. This time, Analyst reallocates the work elements among the three work stations on the basis of 100 time units (*i.e.*, 300 time units divided by 3) of work-content time to each work station without concern for imposing bidirectional flow of work, meaning that work in process does flow continuously along the line.

Table 4.17 gives the results of the second iteration.

***Table 4.17*** *Second Iteration for Precedence Diagramming Example*

| Work Element | Work-Content Time, *tu* | Work Element | Work-Content Time, *tu* |
|---|---|---|---|
| Work Station 1 | | Work Station 3 | |
| 1 | 10 | 11 | 30 |
| 2 | 15 | 12 | 25 |
| 3 | 10 | 13 | 20 |
| 4 | 15 | 14 | 25 |
| 5 | 10 | | |
| 6 | 20 | | |
| 13 | 20 | | |
| **Total:** | 100 | **Total:** | 100 |
| Work Station 2 | | **Network-Content Time:** | 300 |
| 7 | 40 | | |
| 9 | 30 | | |
| 11 | 30 | | |
| **Total:** | 100 | *tu:* Time unit. | |

Substituting $\Sigma tu = 300$, $n = 3$, and $c = 100$ time units at Work Station 2 from Table 4.17 in Equation 4.4, Analyst obtains

$$E = \frac{300\ tu}{(3)(120\ tu)}$$

$$= 1.0. \tag{4.7}$$

## 4.3 Baseline Time Estimate

As expected from the second iteration of reallocating work elements, the network efficiency is 1.0, the maximum possible.

The value $E = 1.0$ signifies uniform distribution of the work elements among work stations in the network. Analyst provides this information to Rho, Incorporated. The company chooses to use the arrangement in Table 4.16 with the product-network efficiency of only 0.8333 because of the unidirectional flow of work.

# 4.3
# BASELINE TIME ESTIMATE

The baseline time estimate is the incarnation of the product network in the dimension of time. BTE provides the basic building block for time estimating and subsequent modeling for risk time estimates.

This section traces the evolution of BTE from standards and learning curves that reflect the way organizations do business, specifically estimating jobs in terms of set-up and operation times. The importance of standards stems from the fact that the labor cost is the predominant factor in competing in today's high-technology marketplace.

The theory of the learning curve allows us to capitalize on the economy of scale with high-volume production and procurement due to increased efficiency from repetitive jobs.

Careful selection and judicious use of standards and learning curves can ensure a manufacturer's preeminence in the field of interest. The examples in this section can serve as role models for a host of problems. We advise you to use a personal computer equipped with a spreadsheet program when emulating the more detailed examples.

### ■ 4.3.1 Standards

Standards are detailed data relating time and money as functions of jobs to be done. Standards support such applications as cost estimating and work measuring. Every organization needs and has standards for the profitable conduct of its business. Standards may be informal, residing in the personal archives or minds of managers and supervisors; however, the long-term need of even the smallest organizations dictate that standards be documented and maintained under configuration control.

Standards that reflect the way organizations do business are at the heart of all work measurement systems. Work measurement systems, in turn, provide positive feedback and reinforcement of standards for business success. In essence, work measurement is a business absolute. It tells you whether you are making or losing money.

We encounter two kinds of standards in practice. These are universal standard data based on minute elements of motion; and standard data for job families based on time values for major elements of jobs.

### ■ 4.3.2 Universal Standard Data

Universal standard data provide basic building blocks for product time and cost. Time data cover the minute-motion elements required by given tasks. Universal standard data are microdata, whereas standard data for job families are macrodata. You can see the parallel in the notions of disaggregation and aggregation.

Table 4.18 gives times for motion elements in the fabrication of electronic terminal boards. Set-up time is expended only once per production run; operation time is expended on each item in the run.

Consider a production run of 1,000 single-terminal boards. The set-up time would be 115.71 minutes and the operation time (2.02 minutes)(1,000), or 2,020 minutes, for a cycle time of

2,135.71 minutes, or 35.5952 hours. The deceptively simple appearance of fabricating 1,000 terminal boards nearly consumes a 40-hour work shift.

Table 4.19 gives universal standard data for a number of metals in the form of cost per pound. If you electroplate terminals with a conductive coating, the table allows cost trades among the more conductive metals. The prices in the table are contemporary spot quotations. You should obtain specific quotations for your requirements.

Candidate metals for conductive coatings are aluminum, copper, gold, and silver. The relative resistances are: 1.64 for aluminum; 1.00 for copper; 0.95 for silver; and 1.42 for gold, relative to the resistivity of copper which is $(1.7241)10^{-6}$ ohm-centimeter.

Aluminum and copper oxidize, and silver tarnishes readily, limiting selections to gold for high-reliability applications. If you were to use ten pounds of gold in electroplating terminals, the cost would be $47,138.40 according to Table 4.19.

*Table 4.18*  *Electronic Terminal Board Motion Elements [2]*

|  | Set-up | Operation |
|---|---|---|
| 1. Cut blank to size, 2 edges per inch | 8.08 | 0.02 |
| 2. Deburr 4 edges, per inch | 6.23 | 0.02 |
| 3. Drill holes set-up, per hole size | 23.82 |  |
| 4. Drill holes, per hole |  | 0.10 |
| 5. Deburr holes each side, per hole | 6.23 | 0.06 |
| 6. Silk screen | 63.30 | 0.73 |
| 7. Stake terminals set-up | 8.05 |  |
| 8. Stake terminals, per terminal |  | 0.04 |
| 9. Handle, 5 handling operations per board |  | 0.06 |
| Total Time in Minutes: | 115.71 | 2.02 |

From Rodney D. Stewart, *Cost Estimating*, Second Edition. Copyright© 1991, John Wiley & Sons, Inc. Reprinted by permission of John Wiley & Sons, Inc.

*Table 4.19*  *Universal Standard Data for Metal Prices*

|  | Dollars per Pound |  | Dollars per Pound |
|---|---|---|---|
| Aluminum | 0.74 | Nickel | 6.10 |
| Copper | 1.22 | Palladium | 154.50 |
| Silver | 65.88 | Platinum | 6736.00 |
| Gold | 4713.84 | Tin | 3.63 |
| Lead | 0.39 | Zinc | 0.49 |

### ■ 4.3.3 Standard Data for Job Families

Standard data for **job families** are common in production operations where distinct families of jobs have long-standing traditions. The advantage of standard data for job families is the quick response they allow in estimating time for short product runs.

Consider the sand-mold casting process. Sand combined with a binder suitable for casting metal is packed densely about a rigid pattern so that when the pattern is removed a cavity corresponding to the shape of the pattern remains. Molten metal is poured through the sprue into the cav-

## 4.3 Baseline Time Estimate

ity and, when solidified, forms a cast replica of the pattern. The sand used for casting is broken away for removal of the casting.

A large number of motion elements would need to be considered if universal standard data were used. In many cases, the job could be finished before estimates using universal standard data were completed.

Standard data for job families are based on variable characteristics of job families. In the case of sand-mold castings, the variable characteristics are pattern volume. In essence, normal times for motion elements increase with larger patterns.

Motion element data are collected over a number of sand-mold casting jobs with techniques such as methods-time-measurement. These data, together with volume data, are the subjects of regression analysis to derive an equation for estimating the normal motion-element time for sand-mold casting as a function of pattern volume.

Equation 4.8 is typical of the relationships used for estimating operation time in the job family of sand-mold casting. [3]

$$t = 2.5 + 7.5v \qquad (4.8)$$

where $t$ denotes time in minutes and $v$ the pattern volume in cubic meters.

For example, for a pattern volume of 0.5 cubic meters, Equation 4.8 yields:

$$t = 2.5 + (7.5)(0.5) \text{ minutes}$$
$$= 6.25 \text{ minutes}. \qquad (4.9)$$

The 6.25 minutes does not include set-up time, which is typically about 45 minutes for sand-mold casting. The time to produce the first casting is therefore 45 + 6.25, or 51.25 minutes. Set-up time is not included in the time to produce subsequent units, which also benefit from the applicable learning curves (v., Section 4.3.5).

### ■ 4.3.4 Example of Standard Data for Job Families

The Omicron Company is concerned about the amount of time spent on formulating cost estimates for small lots of sand-mold castings. It appears to the company that the estimating time is greater than the time spent on the actual jobs.

The data in Table 4.20 was amassed by the company's work measurement system on the past ten jobs. Typical orders were for about ten castings. Typical run times were about two hours including set-up and operation times, depending on the volume of the casting.

However, as much as four hours were spent on estimating the cost of such orders. Clearly, there is a need for developing standard data for estimating set-up and operation times as a function of pattern volume.

*Table 4.20  Data for Standard Data for Job Families Example*

| Job | Set-Up | Operation | Job | Set-Up | Operation |
|-----|--------|-----------|-----|--------|-----------|
| 1   | 94.15  | 2.25      | 6   | 99.75  | 2.95      |
| 2   | 100.95 | 3.15      | 7   | 103.50 | 3.25      |
| 3   | 96.90  | 2.50      | 8   | 90.65  | 2.05      |
| 4   | 92.35  | 2.15      | 9   | 95.05  | 2.40      |
| 5   | 109.15 | 3.50      | 10  | 100.25 | 3.05      |

Time in minutes.

**136**      *Chapter 4 • RISK BASELINES*

Omicron retains Analyst to derive standard data for the job family of sand-mold casting as a function of pattern volume to accelerate the estimating process. Table 4.21 gives the technical approach Analyst follows in carrying out the assignment.

Table 4.22 gives the results of annotating the job data with pattern volumes. Note that there is a general positive correlation between pattern volume and set-up and operation times.

***Table 4.21***    *Technical Approach for Standard Data for Job Families Example*

1. Annotate the job data in Table 4.20 with pattern volumes.
2. Derive the equation for the regression of set-up time on pattern volume.
3. Derive the equation for the regression of operation time on pattern volume.
4. Validate the regression equations by applying them to the data in Table 4.20.

***Table 4.22***    *Annotated Data for Standard Data for Job Families Example*

| Job | Set-Up | Operation | Pattern Volume |
|---|---|---|---|
| 1 | 94.15 | 2.25 | 100.25 |
| 2 | 100.95 | 3.15 | 102.50 |
| 3 | 96.90 | 2.50 | 99.50 |
| 4 | 92.35 | 2.15 | 102.25 |
| 5 | 109.15 | 3.50 | 102.75 |
| 6 | 99.75 | 2.95 | 100.00 |
| 7 | 103.50 | 3.25 | 102.30 |
| 8 | 90.65 | 2.05 | 101.98 |
| 9 | 95.05 | 2.40 | 100.25 |
| 10 | 100.25 | 3.05 | 102.79 |

Time in minutes.
Volume in cubic centimeters.

Analyst uses the data in Table 4.22 to derive regression equations for the job family of sand-mold castings in small lots. In this example, the dependent variables are set-up time and operation time, and the independent variable is pattern volume. The data in the table are samples of the respective populations. The equation of regression for samples uses the method of least squares that ensures the best fit of the line of regression to the data.

Figure 4.8 illustrates the plot of the line of regression of set-up time and operation time on volume for the data in this example. The independent variate, $x_i$, is entered on the abscissa of the plot and the dependent variable, $y_i$, on the ordinate.

Mathematically speaking, the method of least squares ensures that the sum of squared deviations of observed values of $y_i$, as functions of $x_i$, from the line of regression, is smaller than the sum of squared deviations of the observed values of $y_i$ from any other line which can be drawn through the observed values. In essence, the statement means that the square of the distances from the $y_i$ coordinates to the line are the shortest possible. [4]

The relative slopes of the plots in Figure 4.8 indicate that operation time is more sensitive to volume than set-up time is to volume. The values of set-up time range from about 94 to 102 min-

## 4.3 Baseline Time Estimate

utes. The values of operation time range from about 1.7 to 2.3 minutes. These relationships are typical in foundry operations for casting in such volume.

Analyst next derives the bivariate equations of regression for set-up and operation times. A variate is a specific value of a random variable. A **bivariate equation of regression** is a two-variable regression relationship.

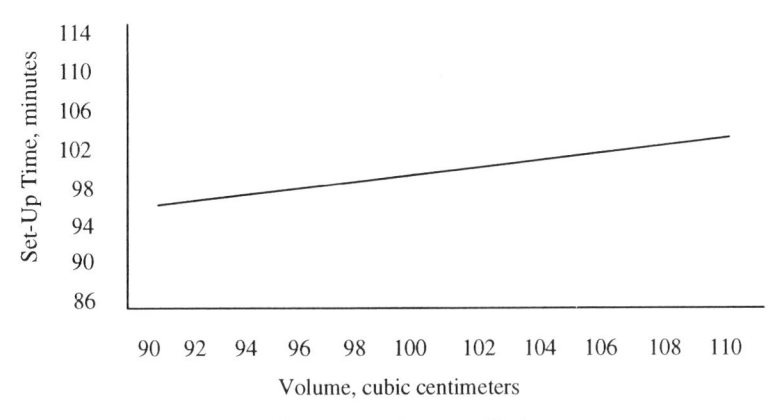

Regression of Set-Up Time on Volume

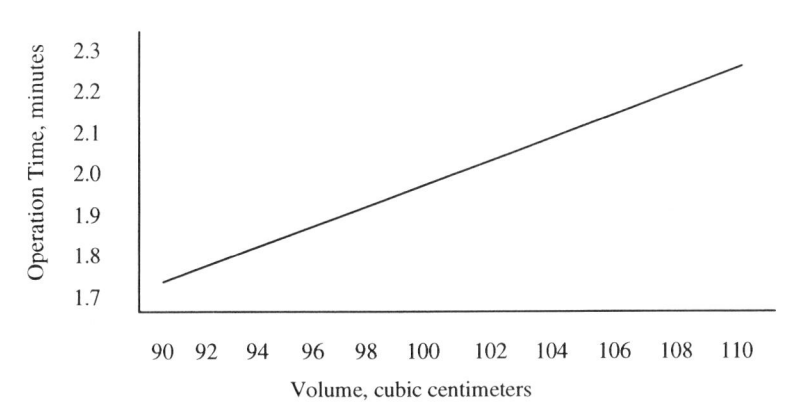

Regression of Operation Time on Volume

**Figure 4.8** Lines of Regression for Standard Data for Families Example

The bivariate equation of regression for sample data is given by

$$y_i = a + bx_i \qquad (4.10)$$

where $y_i$ denotes the $i$-th variate of the variable $y$, $a$ the regression constant, $b$ the regression coefficient, and $x_i$ the $i$-th variate of the variable $x$.

The solution of the equation of regression is straightforward, although tedious when a large number of variates are involved in the solution. Fortunately, spreadsheet programs for personal computers can afford you this capability. Reference 4, *The Essence of Statistics for Business,* gives a step-by-step procedure for calculating equations of regression.

In this example, there are ten sets of variates in the two equations (*i.e.*, set-up time and operation time). Analyst elects to use a spreadsheet program in the data regression mode on a personal computer to derive the two equations.

Entering the set-up time data from Table 4.22 in the spreadsheet program, Analyst obtains

$$y_i = (75.49 + 0.2495x_i) \text{ minutes} \qquad (4.11)$$

as the equation of regression for set-up time.

The spreadsheet program also provides the value 0.1933 for the coefficient of determination for the equation of regression.

The coefficient of determination is a measure of reliability of the equation of regression. We call the coefficient of determination "*r*-squared", where *r* is the symbol for the coefficient of correlation.

The value of *r*-squared ranges from 0 to 1, signifying the fraction of the time that the dependent variable is an exclusive function of the independent variate and not of some other random variable (*i.e.*, specific value of a random variable). In essence, the *r*-squared value of 0.19 means that 19 percent of the time, set-up time is a function of volume, whereas 81 percent of the time, set-up time is a function of some other random variable. Equation 4.11 is not a very reliable regression relationship.

Next, Analyst enters the operation time data from Table 4.22 into the spreadsheet program, and obtains

$$y_i = (-0.47 + 0.0246x_i) \text{ minutes} \qquad (4.12)$$

as the equation of regression for operation time with *r*-squared equal to 0.57, a more reasonable regression relationship.

Analyst calibrates Equations 4.11 and 4.12 with the observed low and high values of pattern volume in Table 4.22. These are $x_i = 99.5$ cubic centimeters and 102.79 cubic centimeters. Substituting these values in Equation 4.10, Analyst obtains

$$y_i = [75.49 + (0.2495)(99.5)] \text{ minutes}$$
$$= 100.32 \text{ minutes} \qquad (4.13)$$

as the estimated set-up time for the casting with the smaller volume,

$$y_i = [75.49 + (0.2495)(102.79)] \text{ minutes}$$
$$= 101.14 \text{ minutes} \qquad (4.14)$$

as the estimated set-up time for the casting with the larger volume,

$$y_i = [-0.47 + (0.0246)(99.5)] \text{ minutes}$$
$$= 1.98 \text{ minutes} \qquad (4.15)$$

as the estimated operation time for the casting with the smaller volume, and

$$y_i = [-0.47 + (0.0246)(102.79)] \text{ minutes}$$
$$= 2.06 \text{ minutes} \qquad (4.16)$$

as the estimated operation time for the casting with the larger volume.

## 4.3 Baseline Time Estimate

Table 4.23 compares the answers in Equations 4.13 through 4.16 to the observed values in Table 4.22 and provides the data to the Omicron Company. The company is pleased with both the ease of application and the relative accuracy afforded by this approach to estimating set-up and operation times.

> *Measure twice and cut once.*
> ***Finnish carpenter's rule***

**Table 4.23**  *Comparative Data for Standard Data for Job Families Example*

|  | **Set-Up Time** | | **Operation Time** | |
|---|---|---|---|---|
| **Volume** | **Observed** | **Estimated** | **Observed** | **Estimated** |
| 99.50 | 99.89 | 100.32 | 1.95 | 1.98 |
| 102.79 | 101.25 | 101.14 | 2.05 | 2.06 |

Time in minutes.
Volume in cubic meters.

### ■ 4.3.5 Learning Curves

**Learning curves** are graphical representations of the reduction in operation time as a function of learning from repetitive operations. Specifically, the theory is that, as quantities of units double, the time required to produce the last unit of the doubled quantity are reduced by a constant percentage. The graphical portrayal of this constant percentage is the learning curve.

For example, if the time needed to produce Unit 2 was 80 percent of the time needed to produce Unit 1, then, the time needed to produce Unit 4 would be 80 percent of the time or cost needed to produce Unit 2. Similarly, the time or cost needed to produce Unit 8 would be 80 percent of the time needed to produce Unit 4. The constant percentage of time reduction for successive octaves (*i.e.*, doubling of quantities) of units continues as long as the production of the same item continues without interruption.

We express learning curves in percentages, but we use learning curves expressed in decimal fractions for our calculations. A learning curve of 80 percent is the same as a learning curve of 0.80. The cumulative effect of reducing time or cost by a constant percentage is called compounding. We calculate the reduction factor due to compounding with the equation

$$RF = [1 + (1 - LC)]^{nso} \tag{4.17}$$

where $RF$ denotes reduction factor, $LC$ the learning curve expressed as a decimal fraction, and $nso$ the number of successive octaves.

For $LC = 0.80$ and $nso = 7$, Equation 4.17 yields

$$RF = [1 + (1 - 0.80)]^7$$
$$= 1.2^7$$
$$= 3.583. \tag{4.18}$$

Equation 4.18 has compounded the learning curve of 0.80 over seven octaves. Seven octaves means that quantity has doubled seven times to a total of 128. The time or cost to produce the 128th unit equals the time or cost to produce the first unit divided by the reduction factor of 3.583.

Figure 4.9 shows the plots of 80 percent and 90 percent learning curves.

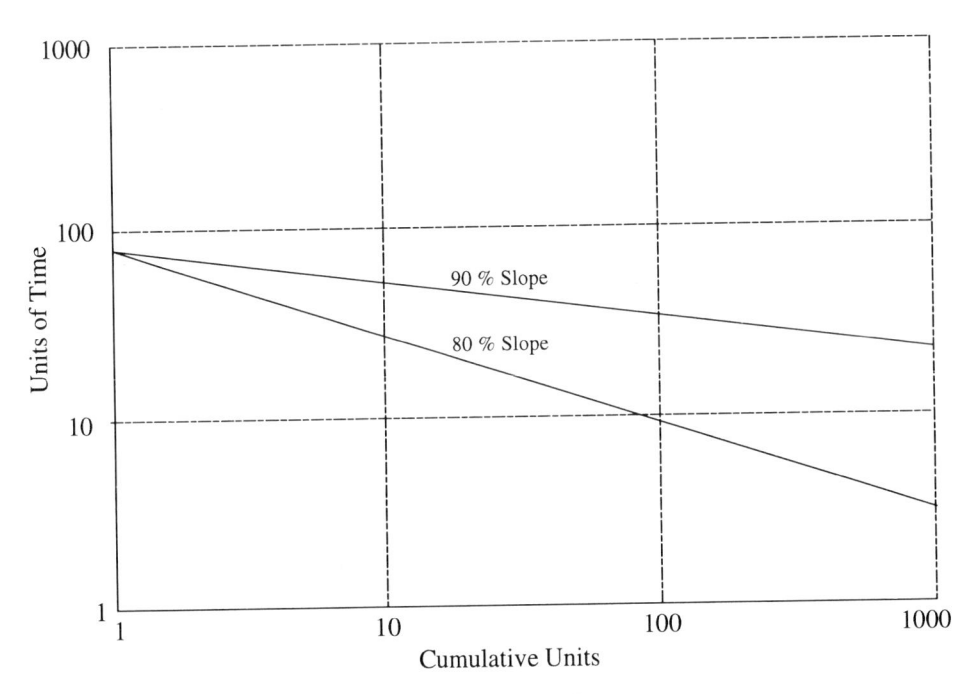

**Figure 4.9**  Learning Curves

The more acute slope for the 80 percent curve signifies that the improvement is greater at lower percentages. The reason why the curves appear as lines in Figure 4.9 is that the $x$ and $y$ axes are logarithmic. If you plotted the data on linear axes, the learning curves would be logarithmic in shape.

### ■ 4.3.6 Learning Curve Formulation

The usual relationship for calculating learning curve improvement is

$$y_x = ax^b \tag{4.19}$$

where $y_x$ is an amount of resource needed to produce unit $x$, $a$ is the amount of resource needed to produce the first unit, and $b$ is the slope of the learning curve.

Learning curve slopes are always negative, indicating that increased quantities result in accelerated performance. The slope $b = -1$ denotes that a one-unit increase in the abscissa causes a one-unit decrease in the ordinate. The slopes of learning curves are usually less acute.

The abscissa registers the number of the unit produced. The ordinate registers the number of time units required to produce the given unit. An increased number of units produced results in a decreased number of time units. For example, let us produce eight units on a learning curve with

## 4.3 Baseline Time Estimate

slope $b$ of $-0.5$. We know that we need four hours to produce the first unit. The following relationship indicates that we need 1.414 hours to produce Unit 8 on a learning curve with a slope of $-0.5$, given that we needed 8 hours to produce Unit 1:

$$y_8 = (4 \text{ hours})8^{-0.5}$$
$$= (4 \text{ hours})(0.3535)$$
$$= 1.414 \text{ hours.} \tag{4.20}$$

Equation 4.21 gives the relationship for the learning curve as a function of the slope $b$.

$$\text{Learning curve} = \text{Antilog } 0.30103b \tag{4.21}$$

where the value 0.30103 is the logarithm to the base 10 (*i.e.*, common logarithm) of 2.

For $b = -0.5$, the learning curve equals the antilogarithm of $(0.3013)(-0.5)$, or 0.7069. This is a learning curve of about 70.7 percent. The aforementioned reduction of four hours to produce the first unit to 1.414 hours to produce the eighth unit came from a learning curve of 70.7 percent.

Equation 4.22 gives the relationship for slope $b$ as a function of the learning curve. We use this relationship when we wish to plot learning curves as in Figure 4.9.

$$b = \frac{\log \text{learning curve}}{\log 2} \tag{4.22}$$

where the learning curve is expressed as a decimal fraction.

For example, the slope $b$ of a 95 percent learning curve is

$$b = \frac{\log 0.95}{\log 2}$$
$$= \frac{-0.02228}{0.30103}$$
$$= -0.0740. \tag{4.23}$$

The value $b = -0.0740$ describes a shallow slope, which is what you would expect from a 95 percent learning curve. Table 4.24 gives values of slope for a number of learning curves. The notion of unit time in a quantity of units is important to us. Unit time is the average time to produce each of the units in a given quantity. We use the following relationship to calculate the value of unit time:

$$y_u = \frac{a}{[1 + (1 - LC)]^{\log_2 x}} \tag{4.24}$$

where $y_u$ denotes average amount of time needed to produce each unit in the quantity $x$ of units, $a$ amount of time needed to produce the first unit, $LC$ learning curve expressed as a decimal fraction, and $\log_2$ logarithm to the base 2.

Equation 4.25 indicates that we reduce operation time from 10 minutes for the first unit to 7.23 minutes for the 100th unit, given that we are on a learning curve of 0.95.

$$y_u = \frac{10}{[1 + (1 - 0.95)]^{6.644}}$$
$$\frac{10}{(1 + 0.05)^{6.644}}$$
$$= 7.23 \text{ minutes} \tag{4.25}$$

where the exponent 6.644 is the logarithm to the base 2 of 100.

**Table 4.24** *Slopes of Learning Curves*

| LC | Slope | LC | Slope |
|------|--------|------|--------|
| 0.50 | −1.000 | 0.55 | −0.863 |
| 0.60 | −0.737 | 0.65 | −0.621 |
| 0.70 | −0.515 | 0.75 | −0.415 |
| 0.80 | −0.322 | 0.85 | −0.234 |
| 0.90 | −0.152 | 0.95 | −0.074 |
| 0.99 | −0.015 | | |

LC: Learning curve
The learning curve of 0.7071 has a slope of −0.500.

By operating on a 95 percent learning curve, we reduce operation time from 10 minutes for the first unit to 7.23 minutes for the 100th unit. The reduction in operation continues with decreasing percentage values of learning curves.

Table 4.25 lists a number of logarithms to the base 10 and base 2. Try converting from one base to the other.

> *The logarithm to the base 2 of a number equals the logarithm to the base 10 of that number divided by the logarithm to the base 10 of 2. The logarithm to the base 10 of a number equals the logarithm to the base 2 of that number divided by the logarithm to the base 2 of 10.*
> *Analyst*

### ■ 4.3.7 Learning Curve Applications

Learning curves range from 70 percent to 99 percent in high-technology applications. Assembly operations usually fall in the 70 percent to 89 percent range, and fabrication in the range of 80 percent to 99 percent. Procurement learning curves range from 90 percent to 99 percent for off-the-shelf items.

Improvement curves are composites of a number of contributing learning curves for both labor and other cost elements such as procured parts and material. Improvement curves are based on the postulate that efficiency improves by a constant rate as quantities double.

As you would expect, learning curve improvement opportunities are greater when you undertake the development production of new products in contrast to modifying or producing your basic products. Furthermore, opportunities are not as great in development as in productions because of the smaller quantities involved.

Learning curves are primarily functions of the amount of manual operations and the quantity of units. Table 4.26 is a guide for selecting learning curve values, the key determinant being the maturity of products and processes. Remember that lower percentage values yield greater opportunities than the higher values.

4.3 Baseline Time Estimate                                                                                       143

**Table 4.25**  *Logarithms to the Base 10 and Base 2*

| Number | Base 10 | Base 2 |
|---|---|---|
| 1 | 0.00000 | 0.00000 |
| 2 | 0.30103 | 1.00000 |
| 3 | 0.47712 | 1.58496 |
| 4 | 0.60206 | 2.00000 |
| 5 | 0.69897 | 2.32169 |
| 6 | 0.77815 | 2.58496 |
| 7 | 0.84510 | 2.80736 |
| 8 | 0.90309 | 3.00000 |
| 9 | 0.95424 | 3.16993 |
| 10 | 1.00000 | 3.32193 |
| 16 | 1.20412 | 4.00000 |
| 32 | 1.50515 | 5.00000 |
| 64 | 1.80618 | 6.00000 |
| 100 | 2.00000 | 6.64386 |
| 128 | 2.10721 | 7.00000 |
| 256 | 2.40824 | 8.00000 |
| 512 | 2.70927 | 9.00000 |
| 1000 | 3.00000 | 9.96578 |
| 1024 | 3.01030 | 10.00000 |

Table 4.27 offers general guidance on selecting learning curves. The guidance should be tempered somewhat when you contemplate a significant amount of automation or robotics in production. Automation, which provides dedicated functions such as the insertion of specific parts in specific assemblies, is referred to as hard automation. Robotics, that can provide a multitude of functions of a similar nature, is referred to as flexible or soft automation. Learning curves for automation and robotics are generally shallow.

The usual reasons for using robotics or hard automation is to reduce operation time. This is the reason why learning curves for processes involving automation and robotics are in the range of 90 percent or more depending upon the required degree of operator intervention. During start-up, operators become more familiar with products and processes; learning curves become steeper. Following this period of familiarization, learning curves become shallower, signifying that less learning opportunity is present.

### ■ 4.3.8 Example of Learning Curve Selection

Zeta Industries, Inc. manufactures a broad line of small household appliances. Zeta discerns that actual time for a certain process in manufacturing electric can openers exceeds estimated time based on a learning curve of 90 percent. Zeta retains Analyst to investigate the problem.

Table 4.28 gives the technical approach Analyst follows in carrying out the assignment. Analyst obtains the operation time data in Table 4.29. The sum of the operation times in Table 4.29 is 288 hours and the number of observations is 132. Therefore, the unit time is 288 hours ÷ 132, or 2.18 hours.

**Table 4.26**  *Learning Curves as a Function of Maturity*

|  | Percent |
|---|---|
| New Product Concept | |
|   New Process Concept | |
|     PROCMF or PRODMF: 0.0–0.5: | 75–80 |
|     PROCMF or PRODMF: 0.5–1.0: | 80–85 |
|   Basic Process Concept | |
|     PROCMF or PRODMF: 0.0–0.5: | 80–85 |
|     PROCMF or PRODMF: 0.5–1.0: | 85–90 |
| Basic Product Concept | |
|   New Process Concept | |
|     PROCMF or PRODMF: 0.0–0.5: | 85–90 |
|     PROCMF or PRODMF: 0.5–1.0: | 90–95 |
|   Basic Process Concept | |
|     PROCMF or PRODMF: 0.0–0.5: | 90–95 |
|     PROCMF or PRODMF: 0.5–1.0: | 95–99 |

PROCMF: Process maturity factor.
PRODMF: Product maturity factor.

**Table 4.27**  *Learning Curve Selection Guidelines*

1. When new products are produced by new processes, start-up efficiency is low but learning opportunity is high. When basic products are produced by basic processes, start-up efficiency is high but learning opportunity is low.
2. When both products and processes are new, use learning curves in the range of 75 to 85 percent.
3. When both products and processes are not fully mature, consider learning curves in the range of 80 to 90 percent because of somewhat reduced learning opportunity.
4. When either products or processes are not fully mature, use learning curves in the range of 85 to 95 percent.
5. When either products or processes are fully mature, use learning curves in the range of 90 to 99 percent.
6. When both products and processes are fully mature, do not apply learning curves.

**Table 4.28**  *Technical Approach for Learning Curve Selection Example*

1. Obtain historical data on operation times in the process.
2. Calculate the average value of the operation times.
3. Use this value as the unit time for the 132nd items produced.
4. Modify Equation 4.24 to yield the value of the learning curve as a function unit time, $a$, and $x$.
5. Calculate the learning curve.

## 4.3 Baseline Time Estimate

Analyst rearranges the terms in Equation 4.24 as follows:

$$LC = 1 - \left(\frac{a}{y_u}\right)^{\log_2 x} \quad (4.26)$$

where $LC$ denotes learning curve, $x$ quantity of units, $a$ amount of time needed to produce the first unit, and $y_u$ unit time.

**Table 4.29** *Operation Time Observations for Learning Curve Selection Example*

| Time | Time | Time | Time | Time | Time |
|---|---|---|---|---|---|
| 3.00 | 2.80 | 2.65 | 2.55 | 2.40 | 2.30 |
| 2.15 | 2.00 | 1.85 | 1.70 | 1.55 | 3.00 |
| 2.80 | 2.65 | 2.55 | 2.40 | 2.30 | 2.15 |
| 1.95 | 1.80 | 1.70 | 1.55 | 3.00 | 2.80 |
| 2.65 | 2.50 | 2.40 | 2.30 | 2.15 | 1.95 |
| 1.80 | 1.65 | 1.55 | 2.95 | 2.75 | 2.60 |
| 2.50 | 2.40 | 2.30 | 2.10 | 1.95 | 1.80 |
| 1.65 | 1.55 | 2.95 | 2.75 | 2.60 | 2.50 |
| 2.35 | 2.25 | 2.10 | 1.95 | 1.80 | 1.65 |
| 1.55 | 2.90 | 2.75 | 2.60 | 2.50 | 2.35 |
| 2.25 | 2.10 | 1.90 | 1.75 | 1.65 | 1.55 |
| 2.90 | 2.70 | 2.55 | 2.45 | 2.35 | 2.25 |
| 2.05 | 1.90 | 1.75 | 1.60 | 1.50 | 2.85 |
| 2.70 | 2.55 | 2.45 | 2.35 | 2.20 | 2.05 |
| 1.90 | 1.75 | 1.60 | 1.50 | 2.85 | 2.70 |
| 2.55 | 2.45 | 2.30 | 2.20 | 2.05 | 1.85 |
| 1.70 | 1.60 | 1.50 | 2.85 | 2.65 | 2.55 |
| 2.40 | 2.30 | 2.20 | 2.00 | 1.85 | 1.70 |
| 1.60 | 1.50 | 2.85 | 2.65 | 2.55 | 2.40 |
| 2.30 | 2.20 | 2.00 | 1.85 | 1.70 | 1.60 |
| 1.50 | 2.80 | 2.65 | 2.55 | 2.40 | 2.30 |
| 2.20 | 2.00 | 1.85 | 1.70 | 1.55 | 1.45 |

Time in hours.

Substituting $x = 132$, $\log_3 132 = 7.044$, $a = 3.00$ hours, and $y_u = 2.18$ hours in Equation 4.24, Analyst obtains

$$LC = 1 - \left(\frac{3.00}{2.18}\right)^{-\log_2 132}$$
$$= 1 - 1.376^{-7.044}$$
$$= 1 - 0.106$$
$$= 0.894. \quad (4.27)$$

Zeta had assumed a learning curve of 0.85 in its early deliberations. Analyst informs the company that the assumed value is too low.

### ■ 4.3.9 Probabilistic Nature of Learning Curves

We derive learning curves as point estimates that are the product of statistical inference drawn from historical data. The reliability of the data induces a degree of uncertainty in point estimates of learning curves. The learning curve finding of 0.894 in the example of Section 4.3.8 is a point estimate. No matter how repetitive, operations could never be repeated in exactly the same way and completed in exactly the same amount of time. This is a reflection of the probabilistic nature of learning curves.

Point estimates are expected values of the learning curve. This means that 50 percent of the time the values can be the expected value or less, and 50 percent of the time the values can be the expected value or more. Expected value is synonymous with mean, average, and nominal.

We prefer to express learning curves as interval estimates, which we provide with confidence intervals about the point estimates. Using confidence intervals about point estimates allows us to make such statements as, "Eighty percent of the time, the value of the learning curve will be within the limits 0.87 and 0.91." Figure 4.10 shows the lower and upper confidence limits bounding a 0.8 learning curve.

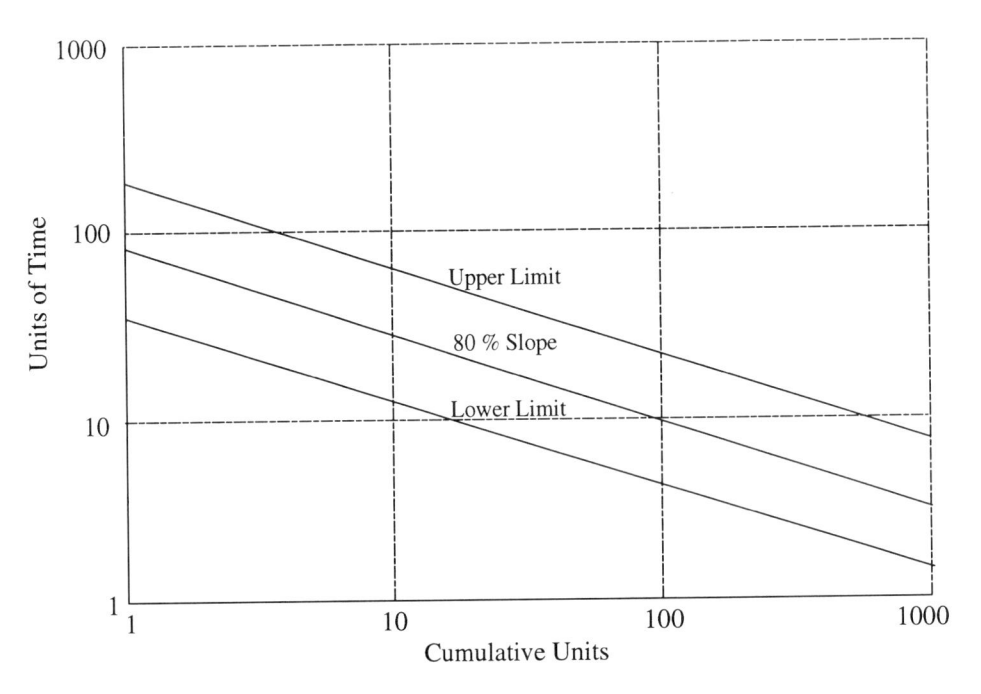

**Figure 4.10** Confidence Interval About Learning Curve

The breadth of the confidence intervals varies as a function of the confidence level we desire. Typically, we select confidence levels ranging from 80 percent to 95 percent. The higher the confidence level, the greater the breadth of the confidence interval about the point estimate and the greater the confidence that the true value of the learning curve falls within the limits.

> *Confidence intervals about estimates based on historical data are cornerstones of realism and credibility.*
> ***Analyst***

An adequate amount of carefully acquired historical data is the best way to ensure data reliability. Adequate data allows the assumption of normality that eases our calculations. As a minimum, you should have at least 30 data samples to justify the assumption of normality.

## 4.3 Baseline Time Estimate

The assumption of normality connotes that the normal density function governs sample distributions. Equation 4.28 is the relationship for calculating the confidence limits that bound the confidence intervals. Note the $z$-statistic in the equation [4]

$$CL = m \pm \frac{sz}{\sqrt{n}} \qquad (4.28)$$

where $CL$ denotes upper and lower confidence limits, $m$ mean, $s$ standard deviation of the data sample, $z$ the $z$-factor bounding the area under the curve of the normal probability density function, and $n$ size of the data sample.

The value of the $z$-factor is a function of the desired confidence level. Table 4.30 lists several values of $z$ as a function of confidence levels.

**Table 4.30** *Values of z-Factor as a Function of Confidence Level*

| Confidence Level | z-Factor |
|---|---|
| 0.60 | 0.84 |
| 0.70 | 1.04 |
| 0.80 | 1.28 |
| 0.90 | 1.64 |
| 0.95 | 1.96 |

Consider a learning curve of 0.85 with a standard deviation of 0.15 based on 30 data samples. The sample size, $n = 30$, justifies the assumption of normality in the data sample and the use of Equation 4.28. We wish to know the confidence interval about the point estimate of 0.85 with a confidence level of 80 percent, or 0.80.

From Table 4.30, we determine that the $z$-factor for the confidence level of 0.80 is 1.28. Substituting $m = 0.85$, $s = 0.15$, $z = 1.28$, and $n = 30$ in Equation 4.28, we obtain

$$CL = 0.85 \pm \frac{(0.15)(1.28)}{\sqrt{30}}$$

$$= 0.85 \pm 0.035$$

$$= 0.815, 0.885. \qquad (4.29)$$

Equation 4.29 indicates that 80 percent of the time the learning curve with the mean value of 0.85 will be within the limits of 0.815 and 0.885. To be conservative, you would choose the upper value.

### ■ 4.3.10 Example of Learning Curve Confidence Interval

In the example of Section 4.3.8, Analyst had determined for Zeta Industries, Inc. that the learning curve was 0.894. Zeta wishes to be more conservative in future estimates and asks Analyst to calculate the confidence intervals about the point estimate of 0.894 with a 0.99 confidence level. Table 4.31 gives the technical approach Analyst follows in carrying out the assignment.

In this example, Analyst goes back to the data in Table 4.29. The mean of the data samples is 2.183 hours, which is the unit time for the 132 observed operations. Analyst first calculates the lower and upper limits of the confidence interval for the unit time, then calculates the learning curves for these limits.

You may assume normality for data samples that are larger than thirty. On the basis of the sample size of 132, Analyst makes the assumption that the data sample is distributed normally. This allows the use of the $z$-statistic in Equation 4.28 to calculate the confidence limits of the unit time.

Analyst uses a spreadsheet program in a personal computer to obtain $m = 2.183$ hours and $s = 0.470$ hour. From Table 4.30, Analyst determines that $z$-statistic $= 2.58$ for a confidence level of 0.99.

**Table 4.31** *Technical Approach for Learning Curve Confidence Interval Example*

> 1. Use the observed operation data in Table 4.29.
> 2. Select the governing probability density function.
> 3. Use a spreadsheet computer program to calculate the standard deviation of the observed operation data.
> 4. Calculate the confidence limits of the confidence interval about the unit time point estimate of 2.183 minutes with a confidence level of 0.99.
> 5. Calculate the values of the learning curve for the lower and upper confidence limits for unit time.

Substituting $m = 2.183$ hours, $s = 0.470$ hour, $z = 2.58$, and $n = 132$ in Equation 4.28, Analyst obtains

$$CL = 2.183 \pm \frac{(0.470)(2.58)}{\sqrt{132}}$$

$$= 2.183 \pm 0.106$$

$$= 2.077, 2.289 \text{ hours.} \tag{4.30}$$

Analyst first calculates the learning curve for the unit time of 2.077 hours. Substituting $a = 3.00$ hours, $n = 132$, and $\log_2 132 = 7.044$, and $y_u = 2.077$ hours in Equation 4.26, Analyst obtains

$$LC = 1 - \left(\frac{3.00}{2.077}\right)^{-\log_2 132}$$

$$= 1 - 1.444^{-7.044}$$

$$= 1 - 0.0752$$

$$= 0.925. \tag{4.31}$$

The value of the upper confidence limit learning curve is 0.925. Analyst calculates the 0.925 learning curve for the unit time of 2.289 hours, substitutes $a = 3.00$ hours, $n = 132$, $\log_2 132 = 7.044$, and $y_u = 2.289$ hours, in Equation 4.26 and obtains

$$LC = 1 - \left(\frac{3.00}{2.289}\right)^{-\log_2 132}$$

$$= 1 - 1.311^{-7.044}$$

$$= 1 - 0.148$$

$$= 0.852. \tag{4.32}$$

## 4.3 Baseline Time Estimate

The value of the lower confidence limit learning curve is 0.852, or 85.2 percent. Analyst informs Zeta that 99 percent of the time the learning curve is between 0.852 and 0.925. To be conservative, the company chooses a learning curve of 0.925.

### ■ 4.3.11 Learning Curve Discontinuity

Breaks in development and production cause loss of learning, which we attribute to learning curve discontinuity. The customary approach to assessing loss of learning is to reapply the start-up efficiency to the first unit after disruption ceases. The magnitude of the start-up efficiency is a function of many factors, including how long the disruption in the process lasts, whether the process changes, and whether the same people operate the process.

Universal standard data and standard data for job families (v., Sections 4.3.2 and 4.3.3) provide the bases for estimating the time to produce a given number of units. To do so, we first have to contend with the start-up efficiency that makes the time to produce the first unit greater than the standard. We need to produce a number of units before the time to produce the subsequent unit equals the standard time.

> *The time to produce a quantity of units equals the time until standard time is reached plus the time from reaching standard time through production of the last unit.*
>
> ***Analyst***

Figure 4.11 shows the effect of start-up efficiency on time. The start-up line intercepts the learning curve at about the fifth unit. Consider a lot of ten units with a standard time of two hours on a 0.85 learning curve and a start-up efficiency of 0.667. The first unit time is two hours ÷ 0.667, or three hours. How many units do we need to produce before we reach the standard time of two hours? We use the following equation to determine the number

$$\log x = \frac{\log a - \log y_x}{-b} \tag{4.33}$$

where $x$ denotes number of units to reach standard time, $a$ time needed to produce the first unit, $y_x$ time to produce the $x$-th unit, and $b$ slope of the learning curve of 0.85.

The time needed to produce the first unit is $a = 3$ hours. The time to reach standard is $y_x = 2$ hours. From Table 4.21, the slope of the learning curve of 0.85 is $b = -0.234$. Substituting these values in Equation 4.33, we obtain

$$\log x = \frac{\log 3 - \log 2}{0.234}$$

$$= \frac{0.47712 - 0.30103}{0.234}$$

$$= 0.753. \tag{4.34}$$

We solve for $x$ by taking the antilogarithm of $\log x = 0.753$ with $10^{0.753}$, or 5.662. We round the answer 5.662 to closest whole number and state that we reach standard with the sixth unit.

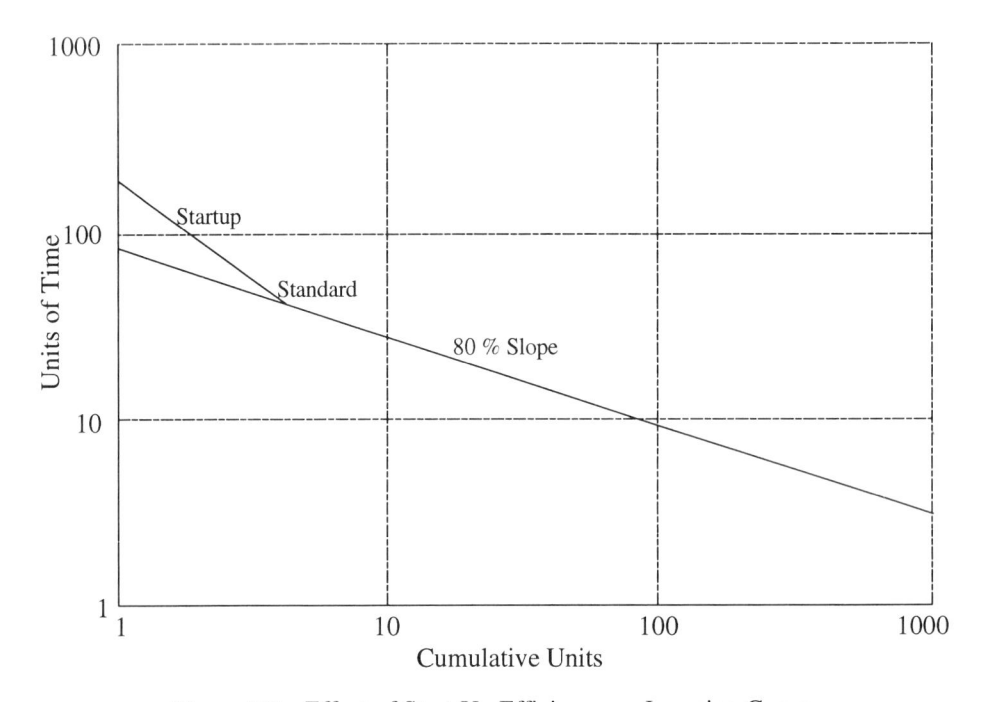

**Figure 4.11** Effect of Start-Up Efficiency on Learning Curve

> *The antilogarithm of a number to any base equals the base of the antilogarithm raised to the power of the number. The antilogarithm of x to the base 2 equals 2 raised to the power of x, or $2^x$. The antilogarithm of x to the base 10 equals 10 raised to the power of x, or $10^x$.*
> — *Analyst*

Assume that there is a break in production after the fifth unit and that the disruption is sufficiently long to warrant reapplying the start-up efficiency of 0.667 to the first unit after the disruption ceases. The standard time to produce the first of the five remaining units is two hours, which we reached at the last of the first five units. Start-up efficiency, however, increases the time to produce the first unit after the disruption ceases to three hours.

The operation is on the same learning curve as before the disruption and the relationship in Equation 4.33 still applies. We reach standard (*i.e.*, two hours) at the sixth unit, which is one more than the remaining quantity required. In short, we do not reach standard until after the tenth unit is produced.

### ■ 4.3.12 Example of Learning Curve Discontinuity

Zeta Industries, Inc. disrupts its small appliance production line for extensive repairs. Concurrently, Zeta receives an order to deliver 5,000 units over a period of one year. Zeta operates on a 40-hour per week, three-shift basis that yields 120 hours of weekly operation for a yearly total of (120 hours per week)(52 weeks per year), or 6,240 hours per year.

## 4.3 Baseline Time Estimate

The standard time per unit is 2.00 hours. Five thousand units at 2.00 hours per unit requires 10,000 hours of operation time, which is more than the 6,240 hours available in one year.

Zeta hopes that operating on a learning curve of 0.894 will allow completion of the order in one year and retains Analyst to address its expectation. Table 4.32 is the technical approach Analyst follows in carrying out the assignment.

**Table 4.32** *Technical Approach for Learning Curve Discontinuity Example*

1. Validate the standard time for the first unit and the start-up efficiency to apply.
2. Calculate the time to produce the first unit.
3. Validate the learning curve of the operation.
4. Calculate the number of the unit reaching the standard time.
5. Calculate the time from the first unit to the unit reaching standard time.
6. Calculate the time from the unit reaching standard time through the last unit.
7. Calculate the overall time to complete the order.

Analyst validates that the standard time is 2.00 hours and that the start-up efficiency is 0.30. Therefore, the time to produce the first unit is 2.00 hours divided by 0.30, or 6.67 hours.

Analyst also validates that the learning curve is 0.894 and uses this value to calculate which of the 5,000 units reaches the standard time of 2.00 hours. The reduction factor is 6.67 hours divided by 2.00 hours, or 3.335.

The reduction factor of 3.335 is equal to $[(1 + (1 - 0.894)]^{nso}$, where *nso* is the number of successive octaves until the operation reaches the standard time.

Analyst solves for *nso* with Equation 4.17. Note that Equation 4.34 yields a fractional value of *nso*. This allows us to pinpoint the number of the unit reaching standard time. The question now is at which unit does the operation reach standard time. Analyst calculates the number of the unit with Equation 4.35:

$$[1 + (1 - 0.894)]^{nso} = 3.335$$

$$nso \, \log 1.106 = \log 3.335$$

$$nso = \frac{0.52310}{0.04376}$$

$$= 11.954 \tag{4.35}$$

where 11.954 is the number of successive octaves it takes for the operation to reach the standard time of 2.00 hours.

$$n = 2^{11.954}$$

$$= 3,967.46 \tag{4.36}$$

where *n* is the number of the unit reaching the standard time of 2.00 hours.

Rounding the answer, Equation 4.36 indicates that the operation reaches standard time during unit 3,968, or before the order of 5,000 is completed. Turning to the operation time, $y_{3,968}$, for unit 3,968 and the time from the first unit through unit 3,968, Analyst substitutes the first unit time $a = 6.67$ hours, $x = 3,968$, $b = -0.074$ (*i.e.*, the slope of the 0.894 learning curve) in Equation 4.19 and obtains

$$y_{3,968} = (6.67)(3,968^{-0.074})$$
$$= (6.67)(0.542)$$
$$= 3.62 \text{ hours.} \qquad (4.37)$$

Zeta's primary interest, however, is in how many hours it will take to produce the quantity of 5,000 units. The answer is the product of the number of units and the unit time (*i.e.*, average unit time in the given quantity). Equation 4.24 gives the relationship for unit time or unit cost. Analyst substitutes $a = 6.67$ hours, $LC = 0.894$, and $x = 5,000$ in Equation 4.24 and obtains for the value of unit time ($y_u$):

$$y_u = \frac{6.67}{[1 + (1 - 0.894)]^{\log_2 5000}}$$
$$= \frac{6.67}{1.106^{12.288}}$$
$$= 1.93 \text{ hours.} \qquad (4.38)$$

Multiplying 1.93 hours per unit by 5,000 units, Analyst obtains 9,650 hours as the time to complete the order of 5,000 units. This is 9,650 – 6,240, or 3,410 hours more than the available yearly operation time.

Analyst provides the findings to Zeta. The company decides to set-up another production line for small appliances and to schedule repairs in smaller time increments.

## 4.4
## BASELINE COST ESTIMATE

The baseline cost estimate (BCE) is the incarnation of the product network in the dimension of money. BCE provides one of the building blocks for risk modeling in the next chapter.

It is necessary to ensure the consistency of the BCE, and the subsequent risk cost estimate, with regard to the cost scenarios, cost categories, cost estimating structures, and cost estimating methodology. These are the subjects of this section.

A number of detailed examples, chosen to serve as role models for a host of problems, are included in the section. Use a personal computer, equipped with a spreadsheet program, when emulating the examples.

### ■ 4.4.1 Cost Scenario

The cost scenario describes the cost estimating guidelines based on the statement of work, period of performance, items to be delivered, and the contemplated contractual vehicle. It includes schedules for the preparation of the estimate as well as the period of performance, and statements of ground rules and assumptions which must be observed in the cost estimating process.

Ground rules are requirements specified by the customer or user. Assumptions are boundary conditions that we select in the absence of applicable ground rules.

The cost scenario include the concepts of should cost, could cost, and would cost to describe the emphasis we place on cost estimates. These concepts allow different values of probability to be applied to cost estimates as a function of confidence levels.

## 4.4 Baseline Cost Estimate

Should cost, could cost, and would cost can serve as measures of the effectiveness of endeavors. The concept of could cost was originated in the military as the means for containing the cost of weapon system acquisition. [5]

### ■ 4.4.2 Should Cost, Could Cost, Would Cost

Cost estimating is a probabilistic process. Truly realistic estimates would consist of a range of values to account for the uncertainty in the process.

For example, when we speak of the probable cost of a product, we mean its should cost. When referring to the lowest possible cost of a product, we mean its could cost, inferring that everything will go right the first time in developing and producing the product. When referring to the highest possible cost of a product, we mean its would cost, inferring that everything will go wrong.

**Should Cost**
Should cost is the most likely cost for developing and producing a product in accordance with the development and production specifications. Should cost symbolizes the essence of well-run programs. We frequently express should cost as the 50-50 cost, meaning that there is a probability of 50 percent that the cost at the completion will equal the estimated cost.

Industrial engineering provides should cost estimates. Aside from normal production allowances for scrap and rework, the only allowance for changes is limited to those resulting from design enhancement rather than design deficiencies.

**Could Cost**
Could cost is the cost that results from eliminating all but essential requirements in developing and producing products and taking every possible step to prevent cost overrun. We frequently express could cost as the 80-20 cost, meaning that there is a probability of 80 percent that the cost at completion will not exceed the could cost estimate. Conversely, the probability is 20 percent that the cost will exceed the could cost estimate.

A could cost philosophy requires you to pursue every possible cost reduction opportunity and value engineering initiative. Typically, cost reduction provides savings of about 10 percent in complex programs. This is in contrast to savings of 30 percent and more that value engineering can provide. [5]

**Would Cost**
Would cost is at the other end of the spectrum and connotes the cost that results from not eliminating all but essential requirements in developing and producing products and not taking every possible step to prevent cost overrun. We frequently express would cost as the 20-80 cost, meaning that there is a probability of 20 percent that the cost at completion is less than the would cost estimate. Conversely, there is a probability of 80 percent that the cost is equal to or greater than the would cost estimate.

### ■ 4.4.3 Cost Categories

Cost categories of interest are direct and indirect. We class direct cost as a variable cost that is a function of the quantity of products provided. Direct cost includes touch labor, which adds value to products, parts and material, and subcontracts. We place an overhead burden on elements of direct cost. Burden rates usually differ among the elements.

We class indirect cost as a fixed cost that is essentially independent of the quantity of products produced. Indirect cost includes depreciation of facilities and equipment, general and administrative expenses (G&A), and capital cost of facility money (CCOFM), which is somewhat equivalent to opportunity loss.

> *Opportunity loss is the return you could have realized had you invested in the best possible investment opportunity.*
> **Analyst**

Direct costs and indirect costs make up the target cost of a given product. Profit is a percentage of the target cost. When dealing with the federal government, profit is a fixed amount and is called fixed fee. [5]

### ■ 4.4.4 Cost Element Structure

Cost traceability from early concept through final delivery is an essential element of successful management. To ensure traceability, you should prepare the BCE in accordance with a cost element structure (CES) that you maintain under configuration control.

Configuration control is the formal mechanism for ensuring that changes to baseline documentation follow prescribed change and approval procedures. The change control board, which consists of representatives of the customer and the supplier, is at the heart of configuration control.

The CES is the umbrella for cost estimating relationships (CER) we use to derive the BCE. You should select the CES and CER to support cost estimating and control over the life cycle of the product of interest.

We use top-down and bottom-up estimating approaches progressively as the product development and production progresses. The flow in the CES and CER should be from aggregate to disaggregate.

> *Aggregate cost estimating structures and cost estimating relationships provide estimates with very little detail below the work breakdown structure level of the item for which the estimate is derived (e.g., total product cost per unit of weight or power). Disaggregate cost estimating structures and cost estimating relationships provide details starting at the lowest level in the work breakdown structure for the particular item (e.g., unit time per manufacturing process and unit material cost).*
> **Analyst**

## 4.4 Baseline Cost Estimate

Figure 4.12 illustrates the challenge in constructing a CES that couples from top to bottom, the aggregate to the disaggregate, while we attempt to preserve the integrity of the cost estimating and control processes.

### ■ 4.4.5 Work Breakdown Structure

The work breakdown structure (WBS) is the cornerstone of program planning and control. The WBS is a task-oriented family tree for defining and assigning work, and for collecting costs that are related to all work activities. The WBS is concerned with both direct and indirect elements of cost.

The **generation breakdown** (**GB**) differs from the WBS in that the GB is product oriented. The GB is a hierarchical rendition of how a product is produced, starting with raw material and ending with the finished product. The GB is only concerned with direct elements of cost. In that respect, you can view the GB as the depiction of the value-added process.

Figure 4.13 is a partial rendition to the sixth level of a WBS for a value engineering workshop. Because of the partial rendition, you cannot see the pyramidal effect as you go down the WBS from the first level to the sixth level. In the full rendition of the WBS, there are a total of 1,871 elements.

Top-down cost estimating

High level of aggregation
Costs derived probabilistically
Emphasis is on functionality

Evolve cost element structures
that couple from top to bottom.

Low level of aggregation
Costs derived deterministically
Emphasis is on cost elements

Bottom-up cost estimating

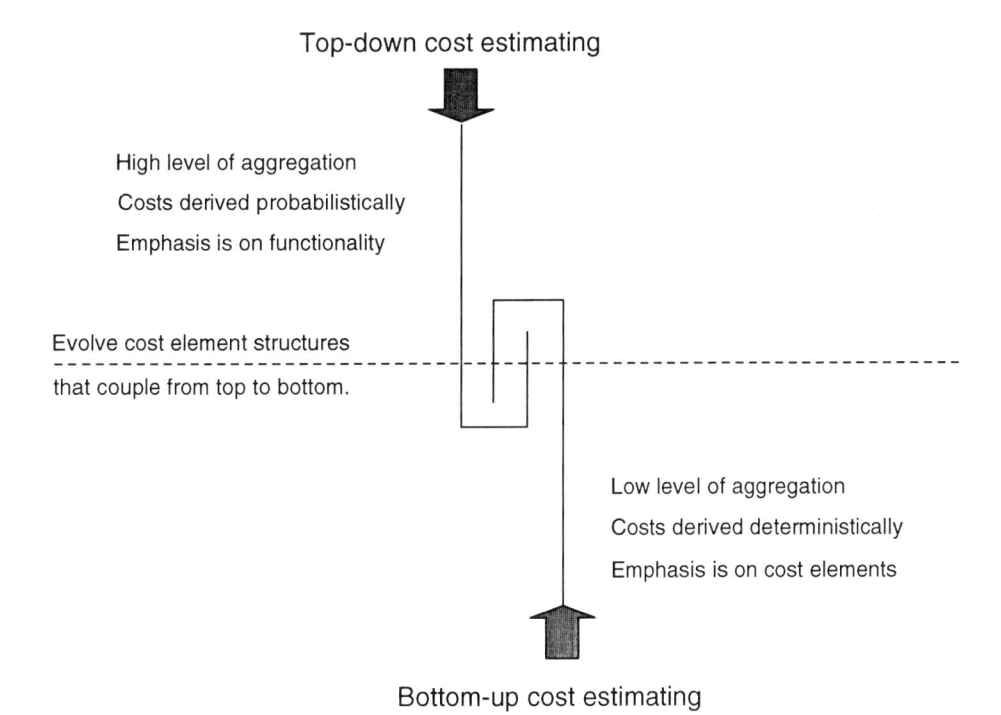

**Figure 4.12** The Cost Element Structure Challenge

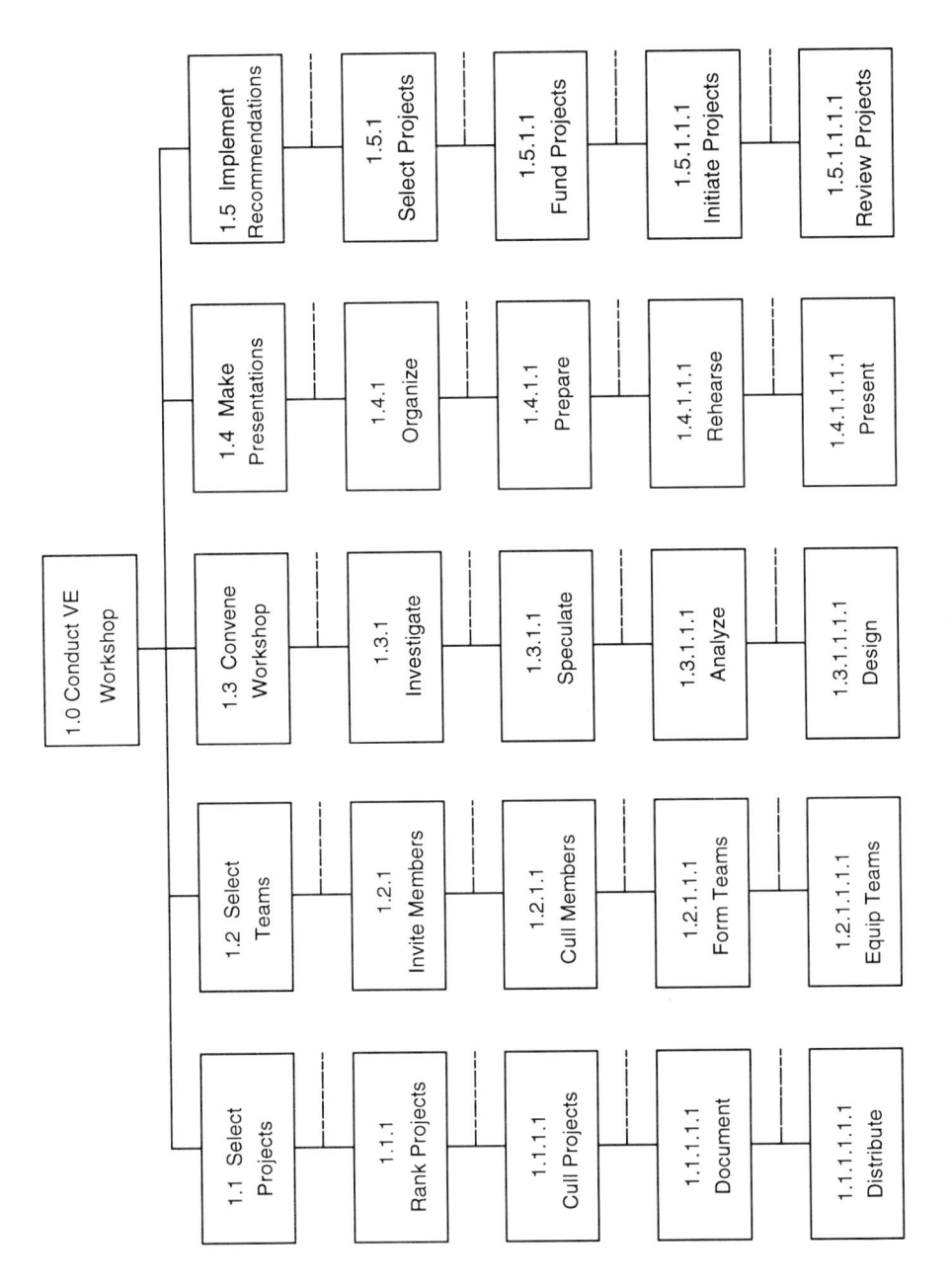

**Figure 4.13** Fourth-Level Work Breakdown Structure

## 4.4 Baseline Cost Estimate

The ratio of the number of elements to the number of levels is a measure of product complexity. The ratio in Figure 4.13 is 1,871:6, or about 311:1, which is moderately complex.

Many products have a WBS with eight or more levels and 10,000 or more elements for ratios of 1,250:1 or greater. We denote the top level in a WBS Level 1 although you may encounter Level 0 occasionally. We denote the next lower level of the WBS 2.1, 2.2, 2.3,..., 2.$n$, 2.1.1, 2.1.2, 2.1.3,..., 2.1.$n$, 2.2.1, 2.2.2, 2.2.3,...., 2.2.$n$, and 2.3.1, 2.3.2, 2.3.3,..., 2.3.$n$. The process is continued until all elements of costs are delineated. Eight or more levels in the WBS are commonplace for complex products.

WBS elements are broken down into work packages and cost accounts. A **work package** is a unit of work needed to complete a specific job and is assigned to a specific operator. A **cost account** is a group of related work packages.

### ■ 4.4.6 Generation Breakdown

The GB differs from the WBS in that the GB shows only the hierarchical relationship in developing or producing products and not the associated indirect cost elements. As we stated, the GB is a hierarchy of value-adding component parts that make up products and the way products are produced. Table 4.33 is the GB to the fourth level for producing automobiles.

We prefer the tabular format in Table 4.33 for the GB over the format in Figure 4.13 for the WBS since the former reveals the process flow. The activities in the table going from the bottom up of the table are in the order in which the manufacturer assembles the automobiles.

### ■ 4.4.7 Cost Estimating Methodology

The two basic estimating methodologies are top-down in the aggregate and bottom-up in the disaggregate. You may use most any cost estimating techniques with either of these methodologies, but you must use techniques that are compatible with the stage of product development.

Figure 4.14 shows how our choice of estimating techniques varies as a function of the phase of product development and production. The techniques are expert opinion, analogy, parametric, and industrial engineering. Table 4.34 gives their key attributes.

At the beginning of the conceptual phase, we rely heavily on the expert opinion and analogy estimates by comparing the concept to some other product we have designed. By the time the concept enters the development phase, we have enough performance data to use the parametric estimate and enough documented design effort to start using the industrial engineering estimate. We frequently use the parametric estimate as a check on the industrial engineering estimate.

> *The only certainty is uncertainty.*
> **Pliny the Elder**

**Table 4.33**  *Generation Breakdown for Producing Automobiles [6]*

**1.0 Automobile**
- 1.1 Chassis assembly
    - 1.1.1 Chassis
    - 1.1.2 Front suspension
    - 1.1.3 Rear suspension
    - 1.1.4 Steering gear
- 1.2 Running gear
    - 1.2.1 Wheels
    - 1.2.2 Brakes
    - 1.2.3 Tires
    - 1.2.4 Rear axle
- 1.3 Engine power train
    - 1.3.1 Engine
    - 1.3.2 Clutch
    - 1.3.3 Transmission
    - 1.3.4 Drive shaft and universal joints
- 1.4 Body and sheet metal
    - 1.4.1 Window assemblies
        - 1.4.1.1 Glass
        - 1.4.1.2 Molding
        - 1.4.1.3 Adhesive
        - 1.4.1.4 Clips and spacers
    - 1.4.2 Hood and deck lid
        - 1.4.2.1 Hood
        - 1.4.2.2 Weather stripping
        - 1.4.2.3 Hinges and brackets
        - 1.4.2.4 Latch and release mechanism
    - 1.4.3 Fenders and quarter panels
        - 1.4.3.1 Step panel
        - 1.4.3.2 Skirt panel
        - 1.4.3.3 Fenders
        - 1.4.3.4 Shield plates and seals
    - 1.4.4 Doors
        - 1.4.4.1 Door body shell
        - 1.4.4.2 Weather stripping
        - 1.4.4.3 Window regulator assemblies
        - 1.4.4.4 Locks, latches, strikers, and hinge assemblies
        - 1.4.4.5 Arm rest assemblies
        - 1.4.4.6 Door and window handle assemblies
        - 1.4.4.7 Trim and molding
    - 1.4.5 Roof and headliner
        - 1.4.5.1 Roof panel
        - 1.4.5.2 Roof cover
        - 1.4.5.3 Headliner
        - 1.4.5.4 Molding
    - 1.4.6 Instrument panel
        - 1.4.6.1 Central console
        - 1.4.6.2 Glove box
        - 1.4.6.3 Ashtray assembly
        - 1.4.6.4 Padding
    - 1.4.7 Exterior attachments
        - 1.4.7.1 Bumpers
        - 1.4.7.2 Bumper guards
        - 1.4.7.3 Shock mounts
        - 1.4.7.4 Tape stripes
- 1.5 Heating and cooling system
    - 1.5.1 Controls
    - 1.5.2 Heater
    - 1.5.3 Air conditioner
    - 1.5.4 Engine cooling system
- 1.6 Fuel system
    - 1.6.1 Fuel tank, lines, and filter
    - 1.6.2 Fuel pump
    - 1.6.3 Carburetor
    - 1.6.4 Accelerator assembly
- 1.7 Electrical system
    - 1.7.1 Ignition system
    - 1.7.2 Charging and battery system
    - 1.7.3 Starting system
    - 1.7.4 Lighting accessories

From Rodney D. Stewart, *Cost Estimating*, Second Edition. Copyright© 1991, John Wiley & Sons, Inc. Reprinted by permission of John Wiley & Sons, Inc.

## 4.4 Baseline Cost Estimate

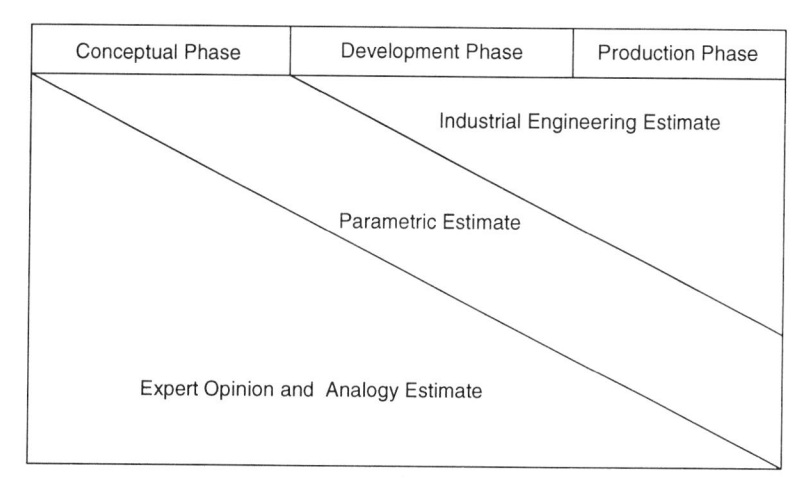

**Figure 4.14** Cost Estimating Techniques as a Function of Product Phase

*Table 4.34   Cost Estimating Techniques*

| Method | Advantages and Disadvantages |
|---|---|
| **Expert Opinion** | Suitable to a broad spectrum of estimates, easy and relatively inexpensive to use. |
|  | Difficult to substantiate or quantify estimates. |
| **Analogy** | Capitalizes on cost history and experience, very easy, and the most inexpensive method to use. |
|  | Limited to static technology and capability of the specific organization. |
| **Parametric** | Broad-based estimating and relatively inexpensive to use. |
|  | Relatively difficult to use and wrong conclusions from inapplicable extrapolations. |
| **Industrial Engineering** | Detailed and accurate estimates of broad range of products. |
|  | In-depth expertise needed, time consuming, and the most expensive technique to use. |

### ■ 4.4.8 Expert Opinion Estimate

Expert opinion is not too common for baseline cost estimates, unless programs find themselves either in technical difficulty or in highly competitive postures. In face of serious competition, consultants can provide insight into the customer's affordability limit.

What consultants provide in these competitive instances, however, are suggested selling prices that frequently bear little relationship to actual costs to deliver. In these instances, consultants represent an equalizing influence among competitors.

Programs facing technical problems that threaten schedule and cost, frequently turn to experts both from within and from without the organization. The use of experts, however, can lead to problems other than those which the organization expected the experts to solve.

The very presence of an expert tends to create an atmosphere of distrust and fear that, although usually unwarranted, proves counterproductive in both the problem area and normal operations. Very often, experts tend to overlook obvious solutions because of their preoccupation with favored approaches.

Although subject to bias, expert opinion may be the only alternative available when data are scarce or nonexistent or time is of the essence. In such cases, obtain data on analogous situations that support the position of the particular experts. In many respects, the use of expert opinion is similar to the use of analogy in estimating.

Bias can also be offset to some measure by retaining more than one expert on the same problem. The Delphi Technique can provide reliable conclusions and suggest means to quantify the certainty or uncertainty in the judgment rendered by experts. [7]

### ■ 4.4.9 Analogy Estimate

Analogy estimates derive costs for given products from cost histories from similar products. This technique often involves estimating the incremental or marginal cost associated with differences among products.

Estimating by analogy is relatively simple and estimates are usually inexpensive to obtain and provide reasonable accuracy for similar or related products. The key words are similar or related products. This poses the major disadvantage of analogy estimating because many estimators tend to ignore the warning these words impart.

Not only should you base analogy estimates on similar or related products, you should carefully notice the technology used to produce these items. The validity of analogy is also questionable when you apply analogy estimates to products produced by differing organizations. When estimating by analogy, you may use expert opinion to determine the similarity and differences among products of competitors and to offset the lack of knowledge about details that drive costs higher.

### ■ 4.4.10 Parametric Estimate

The parametric estimate is usually the only technique you can use to develop detailed cost estimates from the limited data available during concept formulation when only application and performance envelopes are defined. Understanding the application and performance aids in understanding the derivation of parametric relationships.

The parametric relationship may assume numerous forms, varying from rule-of-thumb to empirical relationships and mathematical relationships which you derive formally. Weight and volume relationships are particularly meaningful in parametric estimating. Figure 4.15 illustrates such a relationship in state-of-the-art electronic power supplies. In this relationship, the independent variable is output power in watts and the dependent variable is output power density in watts per cubic inch.

## 4.4 Baseline Cost Estimate

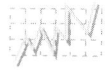

Figure 4.15 shows that the output power density of a power supply with an output power of 100 watts is between 8 and 22 watts per cubic inches.

The average is (8 + 22) ÷ 2, or 15 watts per cubic inch. Unit power density is one watt per cubic inch. We use the factor $80 per unit of power density to estimate the cost in the following relationship:

$$Cost = \frac{\$80 - \text{cubic inch}}{\text{watt}} \times \frac{15 \text{ watts}}{\text{cubic inch}}$$

$$= \$1,200. \qquad (4.39)$$

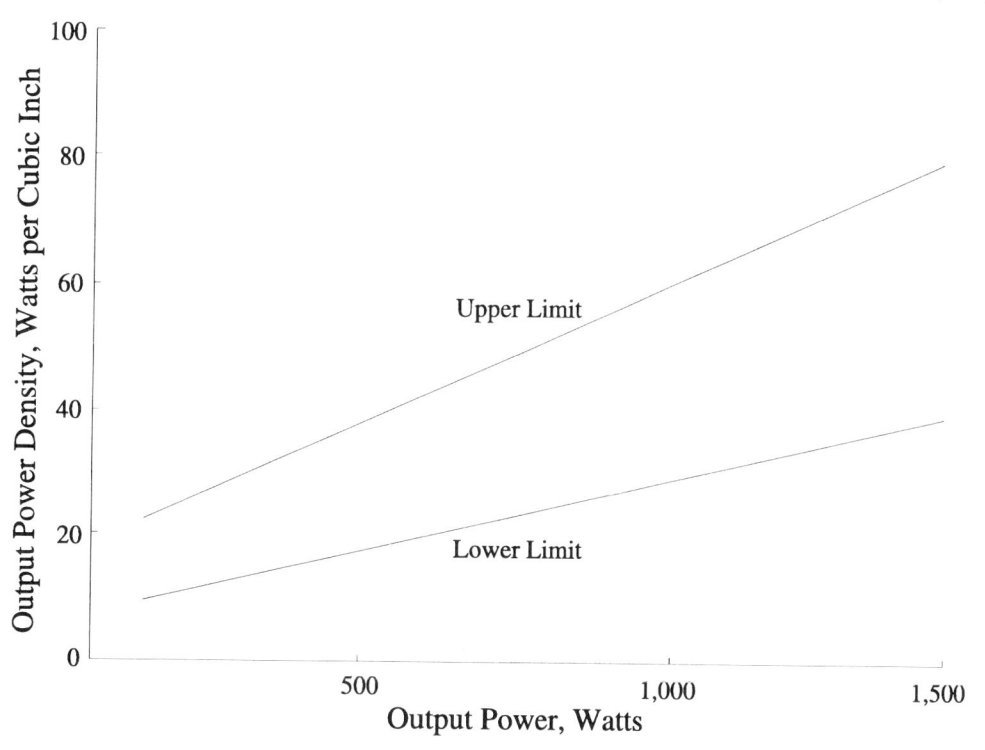

**Figure 4.15** Output Power Density vs. Output Power [8]

Adapted by courtesy of the U.S. Department of Navy from NAVMAT P4855-1, *Navy Power Supply Reliability*, 1982.

We derive factors such as the $80 per unit of power density from the cost of many similar products. The advantage of the parametric estimate is that it provides a relatively inexpensive means to examine the cost impact of changes in product performance requirements.

You can use statistical techniques such as regression and correlation to gauge the confidence in parametric estimates. Figure 4.16 shows the confidence interval about a parametric cost estimating relationship.

The notation *m* in Figure 4.16 locates the mean value of the independent variable. The plots of the lower and upper confidence limits are not linear because they are functions of the square root of the sample size *n*. Note the increasing spread between the lower and upper confidence limits at values of the independent variable that are less than and greater than the value of the *m*.

The ubiquitous personal computer has greatly increased our ability to do parametric estimates. We can investigate ranges of parametric variability that heretofore were impossible to even contemplate. You should not lose sight of the fact, however, that available data may be insufficient to form valid cost conclusions on the configurations of products that differ substantially from those used in deriving the parametric relationships.

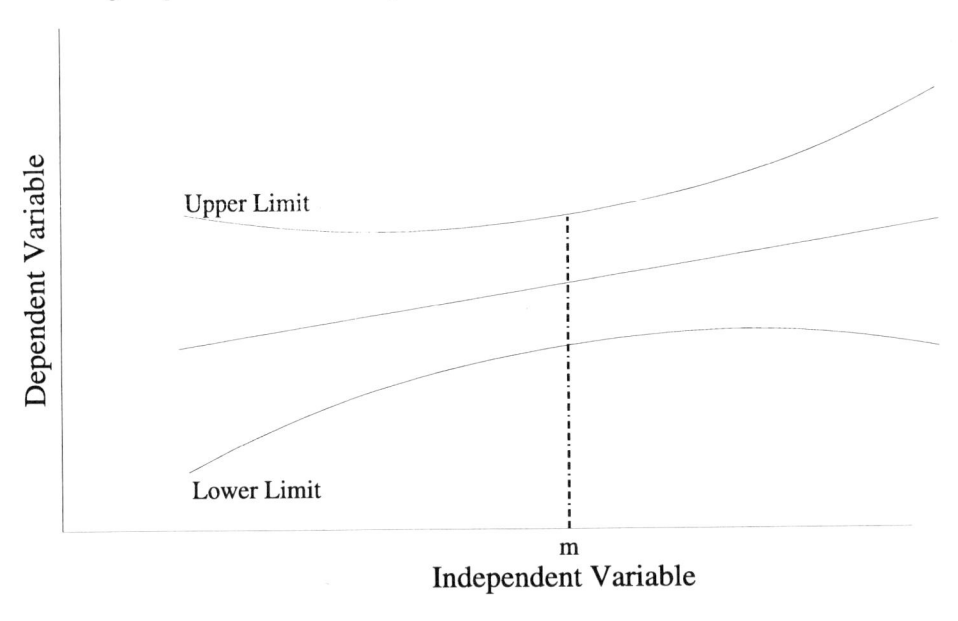

**Figure 4.16** Confidence Interval About Parametric Relationship

Parametric estimates are particularly sensitive to missing or inconsistent data. You should resist the temptation to forge ahead on the basis of inadequate data.

> *No mathematical technique can make up for missing or inconsistent data.*
> **Analyst**

### ■ 4.4.11 Example of Parametric Estimate

Sigma Products requests Analyst to estimate the cost of a conceptual, state-of-the-art, switching-mode power supply as a function of material cost. Table 4.35 gives the technical approach Analyst follows in carrying out the assignment.

## 4.4 Baseline Cost Estimate

**Table 4.35** *Technical Approach for Parametric Estimate Example*

1. Identify other manufacturers of a one kilowatt switching-mode power supply.
2. Obtain technical and pricing information.
3. Purchase several units from different manufacturers.
4. Estimate and deduct markup from purchase prices.
5. Conduct reverse engineering on units to delineate elements of direct cost in the manufacture of the power supplies.
6. Use largest element of direct cost to develop parametric relationship for power supply cost.
7. Prepare parametric estimate.

Analyst purchases units from three manufacturers. Table 4.36 is the worksheet for Analyst's reverse engineering of the units. Analyst obtains data on indirect costs of each manufacturer that, when subtracted from the purchase prices, yield total direct costs. Analyst then estimates the fractions of cost of labor, cost of material, and other direct cost (ODC) comprising the direct cost.

ODC includes direct cost charges for documentation and configuration control. ODC can amount to 25 percent of the cost of labor and material combined. Material cost and ODC, with the fraction of 0.56, is the largest element of direct cost. Analyst assumes a linear relationship between material and ODC and total direct cost, and derives the parametric relationship in Equation 4.40, the factor 0.56 from Table 4.36.

**Table 4.36** *Worksheet for Parametric Estimate Example*

|  |  |  | Direct Cost |  |  |
|---|---|---|---|---|---|
| Unit | Price | Markup | Labor | Materials & ODC | Total |
| 1 | $2,300 | $1,030 | $ 445 | $ 825 | $1,270 |
| 2 | 2,450 | 1,110 | 625 | 715 | 1,340 |
| 3 | 2,150 | 1,050 | 575 | 525 | 1,100 |
| Total | $6,900 | $3,190 | $1,645 | $2,065 | $3,710 |
| Average | $2,300 | $1,063 | $ 548 | $ 688 | $1,236 |
| Fraction of Total |  |  | 0.44 | 0.56 | 1.00 |

ODC: Other direct cost.

$$\text{Cost} = \frac{\text{Material} + \text{ODC}}{0.56} \qquad (4.40)$$

Analyst uses the client's historical data to estimate that the material cost and ODC for the conceptual power supply would be $1,250. Using the relationship in Equation 4.40, Analyst obtains $1,250 ÷ 0.56, or $2,232, as the parametric estimate for the conceptual power supply as a function of material cost and ODC.

Analyst recalls having used material weight raised to the three-half power in the parametric estimate of electronic products and estimates that the material, including enclosure, weight is 200 pounds. Raising 200 to the three-halves power (*i.e.*, $200^{3/2}$), yields 2,828. Therefore, the parametric estimate for the conceptual power supply as a function of material weight is $2,828.

> *To raise a number to the three-halves power without using a calculator, first multiply the number by itself twice; then take the square root of the product. For example, $4^3$ equals 64 and $4^{3/2}$ equals the square root of 64, or 8.*
> 
> *Analyst*

### ■ 4.4.12 Example of Parametric Estimate as a Function of Power Output and Volume

In this example, Sigma asks Analyst to estimate the cost as a function of power output and volume. Table 4.37 is the technical approach Analyst follows in continuing the assignment. The rationale for the second step in the table is that the more material, the greater the power output, and the smaller the volume the greater the cost. Cost is a direct function of material, a direct function of power output to the three-halves power, and an inverse function of volume to the fourth power.

**Table 4.37** *Technical Approach for Parametric Estimate as a Function of Power Output and Volume Example*

> 1. Ascertain power output and volume of conceptual power supply.
> 2. Derive parametric relationship for cost as direct function of material cost, direct function of power output raised to the three-halves power squared, and indirect function of volume raised to the fourth power.
> 3. Prepare parametric estimate.

Continuing the assignment, Analyst ascertains that the material cost is $550, the power output is one kilowatt and, the volume is 9 cubic feet. Analyst derives the following relationship for the parametric cost estimate of the conceptual power supply:

$$\text{Cost} = \frac{550(1000^{3/2})}{9^3}$$

$$= \frac{2,213,594}{6,651}$$

$$= 2,615. \quad (4.41)$$

The parametric cost estimate of $2,615 is $213 less than the previous estimate of $2,828. Analyst provides the findings to the client who elects to use the smaller estimate because it appears more realistic and credible.

> *Realism and credibility are in the eye of the beholder.*
> 
> *Analyst*

### ■ 4.4.13 Industrial Engineering Estimate

The industrial engineering estimate relies on detailed estimates of all the operations required to develop and produce a specifically defined system or product. It makes use of supplier quotations,

## 4.5 Time Value of Money

labor loading by work center and station, learning curves, and standards derived from time and motion studies. We refer to the industrial engineering approach as bottom-up estimating. The advantage of the industrial engineering estimate is that it provides accurate cost projections when detailed information is available. In addition, we can apply it to the various functional cost elements of products.

Thus, as more detailed information becomes available for specific elements, we can refine or replace earlier estimates with details such as those encountered in the form shown in Table 4.38. This detail is invaluable in implementing the disaggregate risk model in Chapter 6.

The chief disadvantage of industrial engineering estimating is that it cannot be used until detailed design data are available, by which time we have lost the opportunity to pursue attractive alternatives. In addition, the approach is more costly and time consuming than the other methods.

*Table 4.38* Industrial Engineering Cost Estimating

| Part No. | Name | NR Labor | NR Mtl | NR Sub | NR ODC | NR Total | R Labor | R Mtl | R Sub | R ODC | R Total |
|---|---|---|---|---|---|---|---|---|---|---|---|
| | | | | | | | | | | | |

NR: Nonrecurring   Mtl: Material   Sub: Subcontract   ODC: Other direct cost   R: Recurring

## 4.5 TIME VALUE OF MONEY

Economic feasibility is key in assessing alternative technical approaches and financial strategies such as long-term capital investment and short-term return-on-investment. The essence of economic feasibility in such issues is to ensure that benefits exceed costs with sufficient margin to warrant expenditures.

The **planning horizon** denotes the period of time over which we consider these issues. Typically, the planning horizon is at least five years, and sometimes ten or more years. In the case of five years or more, organizations document the resultant deliberations in the long-range operating plan. The plan governs all operational aspects of the particular organization from development through production and marketing.

Long-range operating plans are invaluable when guarded against changes for reasons of temporary expediency. Unfortunately, the meaning of long-range in some organizations is that the operating plan changes no more frequently than the frequency with which management convenes.

Plans for longer periods of time are more strategic in nature and are generally concerned with penetrating new marketplaces. The state of the overall economy is as much a decision criterion in carrying out these plans as the marketplaces of interest.

Irrespective of the extent of the planning horizon for a given product, expenditures and revenues addressed in long-range operating plans occur at different times. You need to consider the time value of money to make meaningful trades and render cogent judgment. The concept of equivalence is important in economic analysis and means simply that the value of a dollar today is equivalent to something more than the value of a dollar in the future. Conversely, the value of a dollar in the future is equivalent to something less than the value of a dollar today.

Table 4.39 gives a number of terms and abbreviations that you need to know to understand the time value of money.

*Table 4.39   Time Value of Money Terminology*

**Amortization**: Retirement of financial obligation over given term by uniform series of payments.
**Annual percentage rate**: Effective percentage rate of interest for period of one year.
**APR**: Annual percentage rate.
**Benefit-cost ratio**: Ratio of present value of benefits to present value of costs.
**Capital recovery**: Point at which expenditure, adjusted for the time value of money, is recovered.
**CIF**: Compound interest factor.
**Compound interest**: Interest on interest on principal.
**Compound interest factor**: One plus periodic interest rate raised to the power of the number of periods in the term.
**Constant-year dollars**: Fixed dollar value in baseline or reference year.
**CPI**: Consumer price index.
**Discount rate**: Factor used to calculate present value of future sum of money.
**Effective percentage rate**: Percentage rate of simple interest equivalent to compound interest rate for given term.
**EPR**: Effective percentage rate.
**Equation of regression**: Statistical techniques for deriving value of dependent variables from independent variables.
**Equivalence**: Equivalent present value of sum of money with given value in the future.
**FP**: Future payment.
**Future value**: Value of given sum of money at future time equivalent to value of the sum of money at present time at given interest rate.
**FV**: Future value.
**Interest rate**: Factor used to calculate future value of present sum of money.
**Internal rate of return**: Rate of return at which present value of benefits equals present value of costs.
**IRR**: Internal rate of return.
**Now dollars**: Value of given sum of dollars at current time.
**Opportunity cost**: Return that would have been realized had money been invested in a better opportunity.
**Period**: Time interval for compounding interest at periodic interest rates.
**Periodic interest rate**: Annual percentage rate divided by number of periods in year.
**Planning horizon**: Time period for long range planning.
**PPI**: Producer price index.
**Present value**: Value at present time of future payment or receipt at given discount rate.
**Principal**: Amount of money invested or borrowed.
**PV**: Present value.
**Rate of return**: Ratio of receipt to expenditure, adjusted for time value of money.
**Simple interest**: Interest without compounding earned on principal.
**Single payment**: Single receipt or expenditure.
**Sinking fund**: Fund to retire debt or acquire new equipment established by series of deposits at fixed time intervals.
**SP**: Single payment.
**Sunk cost**: Previously expended or committed money that is not considered in future economic analysis.
**Term**: Duration of financial transaction expressed by number of time intervals.
**Then dollars**: Value of given sum of dollars at future time.
**Uniform series of payments**: Series of payments or receipts of fixed amounts, at fixed time intervals and at fixed interest rate or discount rate.

## 4.5 Time Value of Money

### ■ 4.5.1 Time Value of Money Formulation

Table 4.40 gives the relationships used in time value of money calculations. The **compound interest factor** (**CIF**) is the first relationship in Table 4.40 and appears in all the other relationships in the table. It appears in both the numerators and denominators of the present value and the denominators of the future value relationships.

***Table 4.40*** *Time Value of Money Formulation [9]*

---

1. **Compound interest factor**: *CIF*

$$CIF = (1 + i)^n$$

where $i$ denotes interest rate and $n$ number of periods in term.

2. **Present value** of future payment: *PV*

$$PV = \frac{FP}{(1 + i)^n}$$

where **FP** denotes future payment, $i$ interest rate, and $n$ number of periods in term.

3. **Future value** of present payment: **FV**

$$FV = PP(1 + i)^n$$

where *PP* denotes present payment, $i$ interest rate, and $n$ number of periods in term.

4. Present value of **uniform series of payments**: *PV*

$$PV = SP \frac{1 - (1 + i)^{-n}}{i}$$

where *SP* denotes single payment, $i$ interest rate, and $n$ number of periods in term.

5. **Future value** of uniform series of payments: *FV*

$$FV = SP \frac{(1 + i)^n - 1}{i}$$

where *SP* denotes single payment, $i$ interest rate, and $n$ number of periods in term.

6. **Single payment** in uniform series of payments for present value: **SP**

$$SP = PV \frac{i}{1 - (1 + i)^{-n}}$$

where *PV* denotes present value, $i$ interest rate, and $n$ number of periods in term.

7. Single payment in uniform series of payments for future value: *SP*

$$SP = FV \frac{i}{(1 + i)^n - 1}$$

where *FV* denotes future value, $i$ interest rate, and $n$ number of periods in term.

---

Reprinted by permission of Management Science from Jack V. Michaels, *Understanding the Time Value of Money*, 1995.

Table 4.41 is an abstract of the table of compound interest factors in Reference 9 and gives values of CIF by period for an **Annual percentage rate** (**APR**) of 0.10. For interest compounded on a daily basis for a term of one month, you enter Table 4.40 at either $n = 30$ or $n = 31$ (*i.e.*, 30 or 31 days) and read CIF = 1.0082519133 or 1.0085281467 in the Daily column. For interest compounded on a monthly basis for a term of two years, you enter the table at $n = 24$ and read CIF = 1.2203909614 in the Monthly column.

For APR = 0.10 (*i.e.*, 10 percent) compounded on a daily basis, $i = 0.10 \div 365$, or 0.0002739726. For interest compounded on a monthly basis, $i = 0.10 \div 12$, or 0.008333333; compounded on a quarterly basis, $i = 0.10 \div 4$, or 0.0250; compounded on a semiannual basis, $i = 0.10 \div 2$, or 0.050; and compounded on an annual basis, $i = 0.10$.

For interest compounded on a quarterly basis for three years, you enter the table at $n = 12$ and read CIF = 1.3448888242 in the Quarterly column. For interest compounded on a semiannual basis for four years, you enter the table at $n = 8$ and read the value CIF = 1.4774554438 in the Semiannual column. For interest compounded on an annual basis for five years, you enter the table at $n = 5$ and read CIF = 1.6105100000 in the Annual column.

You can calculate values of the compound interest factor for values of $n$ not in Table 4.41 by raising the value of CIF for $n = 1$ to the power of the desired value of $n$. For example, the CIF for $n = 32$ is $1.0002739726^{32}$, or 1.0088044557. When dealing with large sums of money, use CIF = 1.00027397260273972726, which has 20 decimal places.

Table 4.42 is a useful variant of Table 4.41 and is also from Reference 9. The table gives CIF values for 10 to 10 7/8 percent interest in increments of one-eighth percent.

For example, consider an APR of 0.10125 (*i.e.*, 10 1/8 percent) compounded on a monthly basis for a term of one year. You enter Table 4.41 at $n = 12$ and read the value CIF = 1.10471 in the 0.10125 column. For an APR of 10 7/8 percent compounded on a monthly basis for a term of two years, you enter the table at $n = 24$ and read CIF = 1.24175 in the 0.10875 column.

### ■ 4.5.2 Number of Decimal Places

We express interest as an annual percentage rate but use interval values of $i$ in our calculations. For interest compounded on a daily basis, the interval is one day out of 365; on a monthly basis, the interval is one month out of twelve; on a semiannual basis the interval is one half-year out of two; and on an annual basis the interval is one year.

We just expressed the value of nine decimal places for daily and monthly **interest rates**, four places for quarterly interest rate, three places for semiannual interest rate, and two places for annual interest rate. How do we know the right number of places?

> *Except for exact values (e.g., 0.025, 0.05, 0.075, and 0.10), express interest rates to one decimal place more than the number of significant places (i.e., places to the left of the decimal point) in respective sums of the money.*
> 
> ***Analyst***

## 4.5 Time Value of Money

**Table 4.41** 10-Percent Compound Interest Factors by Period [9]

| n | Daily | Monthly | Quarterly | Semiannual | Annual |
|---|---|---|---|---|---|
| 1 | 1.0002739726 | 1.0083333333 | 1.0250000000 | 1.0500000000 | 1.1000000000 |
| 2 | 1.0005480203 | 1.0167361111 | 1.0506250000 | 1.1025000000 | 1.2100000000 |
| 3 | 1.0008221430 | 1.0252089120 | 1.0768906250 | 1.1576250000 | 1.3310000000 |
| 4 | 1.0010963409 | 1.0337523196 | 1.1038128906 | 1.2155062500 | 1.4641000000 |
| 5 | 1.0013706138 | 1.0423669223 | 1.1314082129 | 1.2762815625 | 1.6105100000 |
| 6 | 1.0016449619 | 1.0510533133 | 1.1596934182 | 1.3400956406 | 1.7715610000 |
| 7 | 1.0019193852 | 1.0598120909 | 1.1886857537 | 1.4071004227 | 1.9487171000 |
| 8 | 1.0021938837 | 1.0686438584 | 1.2184028975 | 1.4774554438 | 2.1435888100 |
| 9 | 1.0024684573 | 1.0775492238 | 1.2488629699 | 1.5513282160 | 2.3579476910 |
| 10 | 1.0027431062 | 1.0865288007 | 1.2800845442 | 1.6288946268 | 2.5937424601 |
| 11 | 1.0030178304 | 1.0955832074 | 1.3120866578 | 1.7103393581 | 2.8531167061 |
| 12 | 1.0032926298 | 1.1047130674 | 1.3448888242 | 1.7958563260 | 3.1384283767 |
| 13 | 1.0035675045 | 1.1139190097 | 1.3785110449 | 1.8856491423 | 3.4522712144 |
| 14 | 1.0038424545 | 1.1232016681 | 1.4129738210 | 1.9799315994 | 3.7974983358 |
| 15 | 1.0041174798 | 1.1325616820 | 1.4482981665 | 2.0789281794 | 4.1772481694 |
| 16 | 1.0043925805 | 1.1419996960 | 1.4845056207 | 2.1828745884 | 4.5949729864 |
| 17 | 1.0046677565 | 1.1515163601 | 1.5216182612 | 2.2920183178 | 5.0544702850 |
| 18 | 1.0049430080 | 1.1611123298 | 1.5596587177 | 2.4066192337 | 5.5599173135 |
| 19 | 1.0052183348 | 1.1707882659 | 1.5986501856 | 2.5269501954 | 6.1159090448 |
| 20 | 1.0054937371 | 1.1805448348 | 1.6386164403 | 2.6532977051 | 6.7274999493 |
| 21 | 1.0057692148 | 1.1903827084 | 1.6795818513 | 2.7859625904 | 7.4002499443 |
| 22 | 1.0060447681 | 1.2003025643 | 1.7215713976 | 2.9252607199 | 8.1402749387 |
| 23 | 1.0063203968 | 1.2103050857 | 1.7646106825 | 3.0715237559 | 8.9543024326 |
| 24 | 1.0065961010 | 1.2203909614 | 1.8087259496 | 3.2250999437 | 9.8497326758 |
| 25 | 1.0068718807 | 1.2305608861 | 1.8539440983 | 3.3863549409 | 10.834705943 |
| 26 | 1.0071477360 | 1.2408155601 | 1.9002927008 | 3.5556726879 | 11.918176538 |
| 27 | 1.0074236669 | 1.2511556898 | 1.9478000183 | 3.7334563223 | 13.109994191 |
| 28 | 1.0076996734 | 1.2615819872 | 1.9964950188 | 3.9201291385 | 14.420993611 |
| 29 | 1.0079757555 | 1.2720951704 | 2.0464073942 | 4.1161355954 | 15.863092972 |
| 30 | 1.0082519133 | 1.2826959635 | 2.0975675791 | 4.3219423752 | 17.449402269 |
| 31 | 1.0085281467 | 1.2933850965 | 2.1500067686 | 4.5380394939 | 19.194342496 |

Adapted by permission of Management Science from Jack V. Michaels, *Understanding the Time Value of Money*, 1995.

Let's look at several calculations involving different numbers of decimal places.
1. The product of $10,000,000 and $i = 0.123456789$ (*viz.*, nine places to the right of the decimal point) is $1,234,567.89. The product of $10,000,000 and $i = 0.12345$ (*viz.*, five places to the right of the decimal point) is $1,234,500, or $67.89 less than with the nine-place value of $i$.

2. The product of $1,000 and $i = 0.12345$ (*viz.*, five places to the right of the decimal point) is $123.45. The product of $1,000 and $i = 0.12$ (*viz.*, two places to the right of the decimal point) is $120, or $3.45 less than with the five-place value of $i$.

3. At the bottom of the spectrum, the product of $1 and $i = 0.12$ (*viz.*, two places to the right of the decimal point) is $0.12. The product of $1 and $i = 0.123$ (*viz.*, three places to the right of the decimal point) is $0.123, which you can round off to $0.12.

***Table 4.42*** *Monthly Compound Interest Factors by Interest Rate [9]*

| | \multicolumn{8}{c}{**Interest Rate**} |
|---|---|---|---|---|---|---|---|---|
| *n* | 0.10000 | 0.10125 | 0.10250 | 0.10375 | 0.10500 | 0.10625 | 0.10750 | 0.10875 |
| 1 | 1.00833 | 1.00844 | 1.00854 | 1.00865 | 1.00875 | 1.00885 | 1.00896 | 1.00906 |
| 2 | 1.01674 | 1.01695 | 1.01716 | 1.01737 | 1.01758 | 1.01779 | 1.01800 | 1.01821 |
| 3 | 1.02521 | 1.02553 | 1.02584 | 1.02616 | 1.02648 | 1.02680 | 1.02712 | 1.02743 |
| 4 | 1.03375 | 1.03418 | 1.03461 | 1.03503 | 1.03546 | 1.03589 | 1.03632 | 1.03675 |
| 5 | 1.04237 | 1.04291 | 1.04344 | 1.04398 | 1.04452 | 1.04506 | 1.04560 | 1.04614 |
| 6 | 1.05105 | 1.05170 | 1.05236 | 1.05301 | 1.05366 | 1.05431 | 1.05497 | 1.05562 |
| 7 | 1.05981 | 1.06058 | 1.06135 | 1.06211 | 1.06288 | 1.06365 | 1.06442 | 1.06519 |
| 8 | 1.06864 | 1.06953 | 1.07041 | 1.07130 | 1.07218 | 1.07307 | 1.07395 | 1.07484 |
| 9 | 1.07755 | 1.07855 | 1.07955 | 1.08056 | 1.08156 | 1.08257 | 1.08358 | 1.08458 |
| 10 | 1.08653 | 1.08765 | 1.08878 | 1.08990 | 1.09103 | 1.09215 | 1.09328 | 1.09441 |
| 11 | 1.09558 | 1.09683 | 1.09808 | 1.09932 | 1.10057 | 1.10182 | 1.10308 | 1.10433 |
| 12 | 1.10471 | 1.10608 | 1.10746 | 1.10883 | 1.11020 | 1.11158 | 1.11296 | 1.11434 |
| 13 | 1.11392 | 1.11542 | 1.11691 | 1.11842 | 1.11992 | 1.12142 | 1.12293 | 1.12444 |
| 14 | 1.12320 | 1.12483 | 1.12645 | 1.12808 | 1.12972 | 1.13135 | 1.13299 | 1.13463 |
| 15 | 1.13256 | 1.13432 | 1.13608 | 1.13784 | 1.13960 | 1.14137 | 1.14314 | 1.14491 |
| 16 | 1.14200 | 1.14389 | 1.14578 | 1.14768 | 1.14957 | 1.15147 | 1.15338 | 1.15528 |
| 17 | 1.15152 | 1.15354 | 1.15557 | 1.15760 | 1.15963 | 1.16167 | 1.16371 | 1.16575 |
| 18 | 1.16111 | 1.16327 | 1.16544 | 1.16761 | 1.16978 | 1.17196 | 1.17414 | 1.17632 |
| 19 | 1.17079 | 1.17309 | 1.17539 | 1.17770 | 1.18001 | 1.18233 | 1.18465 | 1.18698 |
| 20 | 1.18054 | 1.18299 | 1.18543 | 1.18788 | 1.19034 | 1.19280 | 1.19527 | 1.19774 |
| 21 | 1.19038 | 1.19297 | 1.19556 | 1.19815 | 1.20076 | 1.20336 | 1.20597 | 1.20859 |
| 22 | 1.20030 | 1.20303 | 1.20558 | 1.20851 | 1.21126 | 1.21401 | 1.21678 | 1.21954 |
| 23 | 1.21031 | 1.21318 | 1.21607 | 1.21896 | 1.22186 | 1.22477 | 1.22768 | 1.23060 |
| 24 | 1.22039 | 1.22342 | 1.22646 | 1.22950 | 1.23255 | 1.23561 | 1.23868 | 1.24175 |
| 25 | 1.23056 | 1.23374 | 1.23693 | 1.24013 | 1.24334 | 1.24655 | 1.24977 | 1.25300 |
| 26 | 1.24082 | 1.24415 | 1.24750 | 1.25085 | 1.25422 | 1.25759 | 1.26097 | 1.26436 |
| 27 | 1.25116 | 1.25465 | 1.25815 | 1.26167 | 1.26519 | 1.26872 | 1.27226 | 1.27582 |
| 28 | 1.26158 | 1.26524 | 1.26890 | 1.27258 | 1.27626 | 1.27996 | 1.28366 | 1.28738 |
| 29 | 1.27210 | 1.27591 | 1.27974 | 1.28358 | 1.28743 | 1.29129 | 1.29516 | 1.29904 |
| 30 | 1.28270 | 1.28668 | 1.29067 | 1.29468 | 1.29869 | 1.30272 | 1.30676 | 1.31082 |
| 31 | 1.29339 | 1.29753 | 1.30169 | 1.30587 | 1.31006 | 1.31426 | 1.31847 | 1.32270 |

Abstracted by permission of Management Science from Jack V. Michaels, *Understanding the Time Value of Money*, 1995.

Expressing interest rates to one decimal place more than the number of significant places in sums of money ensures accuracy to the nearest penny. Hand calculators typically have 9-digit preci-

## 4.5 Time Value of Money

sion; spreadsheet programs for personal computers typically provide 19-digit precision. This allows a digit followed by 18 decimal places. For example, $i = 0.008333333333333333$ for APR = 0.10 compounded on a monthly basis.

Nineteen-digit precision can provide precise solutions for sums of money with up to 19 significant places, or $1 quintillion (*viz.*, a one followed by 18 zeroes). Never use such precision to give the impression of accuracy.

> *Precision and accuracy are not synonymous.*
> **Analyst**

### 4.5.3 Present Value of a Future Payment

What is the value today of a sum of money received in the future? In the terminology of time value of money, you are asking, "What is the present value of a future payment?"

For example, a real-estate developer obtains an option to buy a parcel of commercially zoned land in three years for the price of $500,000. The question is how much of currently held property should the developer sell and invest at 10 percent compounded annually to ensure that the $500,000 is available when needed.

You can use tables to find a solution; however, you can provide the answer with the following relationship:

$$PV = \frac{FP}{(1+i)^n} \qquad (4.42)$$

where *PV* denotes present value, *FP* the future payment, *i* the interest rate, and *n* the number of periods in the term.

Substituting $FP = \$500{,}000$, $i = 0.10$ (*i.e.*, 10 percent), and $n = 3$ in Equation 4.42 yields

$$PV = \frac{\$500{,}000}{(1+0.10)^3} \qquad (4.43)$$

The realtor should sell up to $375,675 of the current holdings.

### 4.5.4 Future Value of a Present Payment

What will a certain sum of money invested today be worth several years from now? In the terminology of time value of money, you are asking, "What is the future value of a present payment?"

For example, a contractor considers an investment of $5 million in equipment that could lead to profit of $500 thousand in five years. The contractor wishes to know what the $5 million would be worth in five years if the money were invested at 10 percent interest compounded annually as an alternative to purchasing equipment.

You can use tables to find the answer, however, you can provide the answer with the following relationship:

$$FV = PP(1+i)^n \qquad (4.44)$$

where *FV* denotes future value, *PP* present payment, *i* interest rate, and *n* the number of time intervals in the term.

Substituting $PP = \$5$ million, $i = 0.10$, and $n = 5$ in Equation 4.44 yields the answer in Equation 4.45.

The answer may tempt the contractor to invest the money instead of purchasing equipment. However, if the contractor were to cease purchasing equipment, he or she would have to either lease equipment or cease being a contractor.

$$\begin{aligned} FV &= \$5,000,000(1 + 0.10)^5 \\ &= \$5,000,000(1.6105100000) \\ &= \$8,052,550. \end{aligned} \tag{4.45}$$

You can obtain the value for $(1 + 0.10)^5$ from Table 4.41 by entering the table at $n = 5$ and reading 1.6105100000 in the Annual column or solve the equation with a scientific calculator. In any event, the contractor would undoubtedly elect to invest the money at an APR of 10 percent.

Note how much the value of FP would increase if the interest were compounded daily instead of annually. The value of $n$ would be 1,825 days derived from five years multiplied by 365 days per year, leap years neglected.

Substituting $n = 1,825$ in Equation 4.44 yields:

$$\begin{aligned} FV &= \$5,000,000(1 + 0.0002739726)^{1,825} \\ &= \$5,000,000(1.64808361) \\ &= \$8,243,042. \end{aligned} \tag{4.46}$$

### ■ 4.5.5 Present Value of Uniform Series of Payments

A uniform series of payments is a sequence of payments of a fixed amount at periodic time intervals. This relationship is for the present value of a uniform series of payments and applies to situations where we know the periodic payments we can afford and need to know how much money we can borrow at the present.

For example, the aforementioned contractor needs to borrow $1 million but can only afford annual payments of $125,000 for a term of ten years. Within this limit, how much money can the contractor borrow at an interest rate of 10 percent compounded annually?

Again you can use tables; however, you can provide the answer with the following relationship:

$$PV = SP \frac{1 - (1 + i)^{-n}}{i} \tag{4.47}$$

where $PV$ denotes present value, $SP$ single payment, $i$ interest rate, and $n$ the number of time periods in the term.

Substituting $SP = \$125,000$, $i = 0.10$, and $n = 10$ in Equation 4.47 yields the answer in Equation 4.48.

$$\begin{aligned} PV &= \$125,000 \frac{1 - (1 + 0.10)^{-10}}{0.10} \\ &= 768,071. \end{aligned} \tag{4.48}$$

The amount of interest the contractor pays is $125,000(10) − $768,071, or $481,929.

## 4.5 Time Value of Money

### ■ 4.5.6 Future Value of Uniform Series of Payments

This relationship applies to situations where we know the amount of the periodic payments and need to know how much money will accumulate over a certain term. The most common applications are **sinking funds**.

For example, a turnpike authority commits its toll revenue to the redemption of $250 million of ten-year bonds. The authority deposits the annual toll revenue of $23 million in a sinking fund and wishes to know if the value of the sinking fund, compounded at 10 percent annually, will be sufficient to redeem the bonds by the end of the term of ten years.

You can find the answer in published tables; however, you can provide the answer with the following:

$$FV = SP\frac{(1+i)^n - 1}{i} \qquad (4.49)$$

where $FV$ denotes future value, $SP$ single payment, $i$ interest rate, and $n$ number of periods in the term.

Substituting $SP = \$23$ million, $i = 0.10$, and $n = 10$ in Equation 4.49 yields:

$$FV = \$23,000,000\,\frac{1 - (1+0.10)^{10} - 1}{0.10} \qquad (4.50)$$

The value of the sinking fund by the end of the term will be more than sufficient to redeem the $250 million of bonds.

### ■ 4.5.7 Single Payment in Uniform Series of Payments for Present Value

This relationship applies to situations where we know the present value and need to know the amount of the periodic payments. The most common applications are short-term loans and long-term mortgages. We refer to the process as **amortization** and there are many published compendia of amortization tables. [10]

For example, a contractor needs to borrow the sum of $100,000 for a term of two years and wishes to know the amount of the monthly payments at an interest rate of 10 percent compounded on a monthly basis. Let us use Table 4.43 to find the answer.

Table 4.43 is part of one page of the monthly amortization (*i.e.*, monthly payment) table for the sum of $100,000 in Reference 9.   Enter the table in the row labeled "Months = 24" in the column labeled "Term" and read $4,614.49 in the column labeled "0.10000 Interest."

You can use the table for sums other than $100,000 by factoring. For example, the monthly payment for the sum of $500,000 under the same conditions is ($500,000 ÷ $100,000)($4,614), or $9,228.98.

A complete version of Table 4.43 would be several hundred pages for just one sum of money. Consequently, you will usually encounter the abridged version in either Table 4.44 or Table 4.45. Note that the term is expressed in years and interest rate in increments of 0.0025 (*i.e.*, one-quarter percent) in both tables.

**Table 4.43**  Monthly Amortization Table: $100,000 [9]

|  | Interest Rate | | | | | | | |
|---|---|---|---|---|---|---|---|---|
| Term Months | 0.10000 | 0.10125 | 0.10250 | 0.10375 | 0.10500 | 0.10625 | 0.10750 | 0.10875 |
| • | | | | | | | | |
| • | | | | | | | | |
| 11 | 9551.74 | 9557.58 | 9563.42 | 9569.27 | 9575.11 | 9580.96 | 9586.81 | 9592.66 |
| 12 | 8791.59 | 8797.40 | 8803.22 | 8809.04 | 8814.86 | 8820.68 | 8826.51 | 8832.34 |
| 13 | 8148.47 | 8154.27 | 8160.07 | 8165.87 | 8171.67 | 8177.47 | 8183.28 | 8189.09 |
| 14 | 7597.31 | 7603.09 | 7608.88 | 7614.66 | 7620.45 | 7626.24 | 7632.04 | 7637.84 |
| 15 | 7119.72 | 7125.49 | 7131.26 | 7137.04 | 7142.82 | 7148.60 | 7154.38 | 7160.17 |
| 16 | 6701.89 | 6707.65 | 6713.42 | 6719.19 | 6724.96 | 6730.74 | 6736.52 | 6742.30 |
| 17 | 6333.29 | 6339.05 | 6344.81 | 6350.58 | 6356.35 | 6362.12 | 6367.89 | 6373.67 |
| 18 | 6005.71 | 6011.47 | 6017.23 | 6022.99 | 6028.76 | 6034.53 | 6040.30 | 6046.07 |
| 19 | 5712.67 | 5718.43 | 5724.19 | 5729.95 | 5735.71 | 5741.48 | 5747.26 | 5753.03 |
| 20 | 5448.99 | 5454.75 | 5460.51 | 5466.27 | 5472.04 | 5477.81 | 5483.59 | 5489.37 |
| 21 | 5210.48 | 5216.24 | 5222.00 | 5227.77 | 5233.54 | 5239.31 | 5245.09 | 5250.87 |
| 23 | 4795.83 | 4801.60 | 4807.37 | 4813.14 | 4818.92 | 4824.70 | 4830.49 | 4836.28 |
| 24 | 4614.49 | 4620.26 | 4626.04 | 4631.82 | 4637.60 | 4643.39 | 4649.19 | 4654.98 |
| 25 | 4447.71 | 4453.48 | 4459.27 | 4465.05 | 4470.84 | 4476.64 | 4482.44 | 4488.24 |
| 26 | 4293.80 | 4299.58 | 4305.37 | 4311.16 | 4316.96 | 4322.76 | 4328.57 | 4334.38 |
| 27 | 4151.33 | 4157.12 | 4162.91 | 4168.71 | 4174.52 | 4180.33 | 4186.14 | 4191.96 |
| 28 | 4019.08 | 4024.88 | 4030.68 | 4036.49 | 4042.30 | 4048.12 | 4053.94 | 4059.77 |
| 29 | 3895.99 | 3901.79 | 3907.60 | 3913.42 | 3919.24 | 3925.07 | 3930.90 | 3936.74 |
| 30 | 3781.14 | 3786.96 | 3792.78 | 3798.60 | 3804.43 | 3810.27 | 3816.11 | 3821.95 |

Adapted by permission of Management Science from Jack V. Michaels, *Understanding the Time Value of Money*, 1995.

**Table 4.44**  Abridged Monthly Amortization Table: $100,000 [9]

|  | Interest Rate | | | | | | | |
|---|---|---|---|---|---|---|---|---|
| Term Years | 0.10000 | 0.10125 | 0.10250 | 0.10375 | 0.10500 | 0.10625 | 0.10750 | 0.10875 |
| 1 | 8791.59 | 8797.40 | 8803.22 | 8809.04 | 8814.86 | 8820.68 | 8826.51 | 8832.34 |
| 2 | 4614.49 | 4620.26 | 4626.04 | 4631.82 | 4637.60 | 4643.39 | 4649.19 | 4654.98 |
| 3 | 3226.72 | 3232.59 | 3238.47 | 3244.35 | 3250.24 | 3256.14 | 3262.05 | 3267.96 |
| 4 | 2536.26 | 2542.27 | 2548.28 | 2554.31 | 2560.34 | 2566.38 | 2572.43 | 2578.49 |
| 5 | 2124.70 | 2130.86 | 2137.03 | 2143.20 | 2149.39 | 2155.59 | 2161.80 | 2168.01 |
| 6 | 1852.58 | 1858.89 | 1865.22 | 1871.55 | 1877.90 | 1884.26 | 1890.63 | 1897.01 |
| 7 | 1660.12 | 1666.58 | 1673.06 | 1679.56 | 1686.07 | 1692.59 | 1699.13 | 1705.68 |
| 8 | 1517.42 | 1524.04 | 1530.68 | 1537.33 | 1544.00 | 1550.69 | 1557.39 | 1564.11 |
| 9 | 1407.87 | 1414.65 | 1421.44 | 1428.26 | 1435.09 | 1441.93 | 1448.80 | 1455.68 |
| 10 | 1321.51 | 1328.44 | 1335.39 | 1342.36 | 1349.35 | 1356.36 | 1363.39 | 1370.43 |
| 11 | 1251.99 | 1259.07 | 1266.18 | 1273.30 | 1280.45 | 1287.61 | 1294.80 | 1302.01 |
| 12 | 1195.08 | 1202.31 | 1209.57 | 1216.84 | 1224.14 | 1231.46 | 1238.80 | 1246.17 |
| 13 | 1147.85 | 1155.23 | 1162.63 | 1170.05 | 1177.50 | 1184.97 | 1192.47 | 1199.99 |
| 14 | 1108.20 | 1115.72 | 1123.27 | 1130.84 | 1138.43 | 1146.05 | 1153.70 | 1161.36 |
| 15 | 1074.61 | 1082.27 | 1089.95 | 1097.66 | 1105.40 | 1113.16 | 1120.95 | 1128.76 |

Adapted by permission of Management Science from Jack V. Michaels, *Understanding the Time Value of Money*, 1995.

## 4.5 Time Value of Money

**Table 4.45** Abridged Monthly Amortization Table: 10 Percent Interest [9]

| Amount | \multicolumn{10}{c}{Years} |
| --- | --- | --- | --- | --- | --- | --- | --- | --- | --- | --- |
|  | 1 | 2 | 3 | 4 | 5 | 6 | 7 | 8 | 9 | 10 |
| 20,000 | 1758.32 | 922.90 | 645.34 | 507.25 | 424.94 | 370.52 | 332.02 | 303.48 | 281.57 | 264.30 |
| 30,000 | 2637.48 | 1384.35 | 968.02 | 760.88 | 637.41 | 555.78 | 498.04 | 455.22 | 422.36 | 396.45 |
| 40,000 | 3516.64 | 1845.80 | 1290.69 | 1014.50 | 849.88 | 741.03 | 664.05 | 606.97 | 563.15 | 528.60 |
| 50,000 | 4395.79 | 2307.25 | 1613.36 | 1268.13 | 1062.35 | 926.29 | 830.06 | 758.71 | 703.93 | 660.75 |
| 60,000 | 5274.95 | 2768.70 | 1936.03 | 1521.76 | 1274.82 | 1111.55 | 996.07 | 910.45 | 844.72 | 792.90 |
| 70,000 | 6154.11 | 3230.14 | 2258.70 | 1775.38 | 1487.29 | 1296.81 | 1162.08 | 1062.19 | 985.51 | 925.06 |
| 80,000 | 7033.27 | 3691.59 | 2581.37 | 2029.01 | 1699.76 | 1482.07 | 1328.09 | 1213.93 | 1126.29 | 1057.21 |
| 90,000 | 7912.43 | 4153.04 | 2904.05 | 2282.63 | 1912.23 | 1667.33 | 1494.11 | 1365.67 | 1267.08 | 1189.36 |
| 100,000 | 8791.59 | 4614.49 | 3226.72 | 2536.26 | 2124.70 | 1852.58 | 1660.12 | 1517.42 | 1407.87 | 1321.51 |

Adapted by permission of Management Science from Jack V. Michaels, *Understanding the Time Value of Money*, 1995.

You still get the same answer for the foregoing example by using Tables 4.44 and 4.45. Enter Table 4.44 at Year = 2 and read $4,614.49 in the 0.10000 column or enter Table 4.45 at Amount = $100,000 and read $4,614.49 in the 2 Years column.

In addition to using the tables, you can provide the answer with the following relationship:

$$SP = PV \frac{i}{1 - (1+i)^{-n}} \tag{4.51}$$

where $SP$ denotes single payment, $PV$ present value, $i$ periodic interest rate, and $n$ number of periods in the term.

Substituting $PV = \$100{,}000$, $i = 0.10 \div 12$, and $n = 24$ in Equation 4.51 yields

$$FV = \$100{,}000 \, \frac{0.10 \div 12}{1 - (1 + 0.10 \div 12)^{-24}}$$

$$= \$4{,}614.49. \tag{4.52}$$

To be accurate, we use $i = 0.10 \div 12$ instead of the repeating decimal 0.008333333... in Equation 4.52. Spreadsheet programs easily accommodate such fractions.

The amount of interest the contractor pays over the term of two years is the sum of the payments less the amount borrowed. This is $4,614.49(24) − $100,000, or $10,747.76.

### ■ 4.5.8 Single Payment in Uniform Series of Payments for Future Value

This relationship applies to situations where we know what the future value should be and need to know the amount of the periodic payments. Typical applications are annuities and sinking funds.

For example, a manufacturer wishes to retire certain equipment at the end of four years. Replacement cost will be $750,000, and the manufacturer needs to know the yearly contribution to a sinking fund at an interest rate of 10 percent compounded annually. Again, you can use tables; however, you can provide the answer with the relationship in Equation 4.53.

$$SP = FV \frac{i}{(1+i)^n - 1} \tag{4.53}$$

where $SP$ denotes single payment, $FV$ future value, $i$ interest rate, and $n$ number of time periods in the term.

Substituting $SP = \$750{,}000$, $i = 0.10$, and $n = 4$ in Equation 4.53 yields

$$SP = \$750{,}000 \frac{0.10}{(1+0.10)^4 - 1}$$

$$= \$161{,}603. \tag{4.54}$$

The annual contribution to the sinking fund is $\$161{,}603$. The contractor earns interest of $\$750{,}000 - \$161{,}603(4)$, or $\$103{,}588$.

> *Compound interest is the eighth wonder of the world.*
> *Analyst*

### ■ 4.5.9 Economic Analysis

The preceding calculations of time value of money are typical of those used in assessing alternative financial strategies. The issues are return-on-investment and capital recovery. The techniques used are present value, annual equivalent value, benefit-cost ratio, and internal rate of return.

### ■ 4.5.10 Present Value Method

We use net present value to measure the cost-effectiveness of alternative approaches. First, we determine the future values for the present values of the alternatives, then, we discount the future values to the same baseline year. We select the alternative that offers the greatest present value.

For example, consider two strategies in which you could realize savings of $\$500{,}000$ at the end of two years in the one and $\$550{,}000$ at the end of three years in the other. Which strategy would you choose?

In this application, we use the relationship for the present value of future payment ($PV$) in Equation 4.42 for terms of two years and three years. The greater value of PV indicates the preferred strategy.

Substituting $FV = \$500{,}000$, $i = 0.10$, and $n = 2$ in Equation 4.42 yields

$$PV = \frac{\$500{,}000}{(1+0.10)^2}$$

$$= \$413{,}223. \tag{4.55}$$

Substituting $FV = \$550{,}000$, $i = 0.10$, and $n = 3$ also in Equation 4.42 yields

$$PV = \frac{\$550{,}000}{(1+0.10)^3}$$

$$= \$413{,}223. \tag{4.56}$$

From a monetary viewpoint, the outcomes of the two strategies are the same. From a practical viewpoint the first strategy is preferred because of the shorter time for **capital recovery**.

### ■ 4.5.11 Annual Equivalent Value Method

The annual equivalent value approach considers alternative financial transactions on an annualized basis. The time for capital recovery is the selection criterion.

## 4.5 Time Value of Money

Consider the two strategies in Section 4.5.10. In the annual equivalent value approach, we use the formulation for single payment in uniform series of payments for future value (SP) in Equation 4.53. Substituting $FV = \$500{,}000$, $i = 0.10$, and $n = 2$ in Equation 4.53 yields

$$SP = \frac{\$500{,}000\,(0.10)}{(1 + 0.10)^2 - 1}$$
$$= \$238{,}095. \quad (4.57)$$

Substituting $FV = \$550{,}000$ and $n = 3$ years in Equation 4.53 yields

$$SP = \frac{\$550{,}000\,(0.10)}{(1 + 0.10)^3 - 1}$$
$$= \$166{,}163. \quad (4.58)$$

On an annualized basis, capital recovery occurs sooner with the first strategy.

### ■ 4.5.12 Benefit-Cost Ratio Method

**Benefit-cost ratio (BCR)** is the ratio of the monetary value of benefits to their costs. The monetary value of benefits can be in terms of present or future values. The associated costs can be lump-sum expenditures or annualized costs. The customary approach uses present value and annualized cost.

For the two strategies in Section 4.5.10, the annualized costs are \$84,000 and \$77,455. The relationship for BCR is

$$BCR = \frac{PV}{A} \quad (4.59)$$

where $PV$ denotes the present value and $A$ the annualized cost.

Substituting $PV = \$413{,}223$ and $A = \$84{,}000$ in Equation 4.59 yields

$$BCR = \frac{\$413{,}223}{\$84{,}000}$$
$$= 4.919. \quad (4.60)$$

Substituting $PV = \$413{,}223$ and $A = \$77{,}455$ in Equation 4.59 yields

$$BCR = \frac{\$413{,}223}{\$77{,}455}$$
$$= 5.335. \quad (4.61)$$

On the basis of BCR, you would select the second strategy.

### ■ 4.5.13 Internal Rate of Return Method

**Internal rate of return (IRR)** is the rate return at which the present value of benefits equals the present value of costs. The approach in calculating IRR is to equate the present values and solve for the **rate of return**.

For example, a company wishes to know the interest rate at which it would be advantageous to invest \$750,000 in a certain fund to replace equipment in seven years. The present value of the replacement equipment is \$1.0 million. Assume inflation remains constant over the seven years.

This is a simple problem in equality that we can formulate with the relationship for present value in Equation 4.44 as follows:

$$\$750{,}000(1 + i)^7 = \$1{,}000{,}000(1 + 0.04)^7 \tag{4.62}$$

where $i$ denotes the rate of return for the sinking fund.

Table 4.46 gives the steps we follow in solving for the value of $i$. Note that we use logarithms to the base 10 (*i.e.*, common logarithms) in the solution.

You can write $\log(1 + 0.04)^7$ as $7\log(1 + 0.04)$ and you can calculate the antilogarithm of $\log(1 + i)$ by raising 10 to the 0.08363 power. The final step in the calculation yields the value $i = 0.08363$.

***Table 4.46*** *Internal Rate of Return Calculations*

1. Equate: $\$750{,}000(1 + i)^7 = \$1{,}000{,}000(1 + i)^7$
2. Solve: $(1 + i)^7 = 1.315932$
3. Equate: $\$1{,}000{,}000(1 + i)^7 = \$1{,}315{,}932$
4. Solve: $(1 + i)^7 = \$1{,}315{,}933 \div \$750{,}000 = 17.54760$
5. Equate: $7\log(1 + i) = \log 17.54760$
6. Solve: $\log(1 + i) = 0.03488$
7. Solve: $(1 + i) = 1.08363$
8. Solve: $i = 0.08363$

The IRR is 0.08363, or 8.363 percent in this example. This value serves as a decision point for the company. The example in the next section illustrates the use of trial and error in calculating the value of IRR.

### ■ 4.5.14 Example of Trial and Error Solution for Internal Rate of Return

Omega Enterprises receives a proposal to participate in building and operating a shopping center with an estimated net annual return of $20 million over a term of ten years. The estimated investment for Omega would be $100 million. Omega retains Analyst to determine the IRR of the investment.

Table 4.47 is the technical approach Analyst follows in carrying out the assignment. Analyst selects the present value of the investment and the present value of uniform series of payments as the values to be equated.

***Table 4.47*** *Technical Approach for Trial and Error Example*

1. Select values to be equated.
2. Select the relationships for equating values.
3. Choose algebraic or trial and error solution.
4. Calculate the internal rate of return.

## 4.5 Time Value of Money

Analyst then selects Equation 4.47 as the relationship for equating these values. Substituting $PV = \$20{,}000{,}000$, $SP = \$20{,}000{,}000$, and $n = 10$ in Equation 4.47, Analyst obtains

$$\$100{,}000{,}000 = \$20{,}000{,}000 \, \frac{1 - (1 + i)^{-10}}{i} \tag{4.63}$$

where $i$ is the value of IRR to be determined.

Analyst chooses to solve Equation 4.62 by trial and error and substitutes $i = 0.15$ in the equation, obtaining the value $\$100{,}375{,}373$ for the right-hand side of the equation. This value is greater than $\$100{,}000{,}000$, whereby Analyst substitutes $i = 0.14$, and $i = 0.16$ in the equation, and obtains the values $\$104{,}322{,}313$ and $\$96{,}664{,}550$, which bracket $\$100{,}000$.

The value of IRR lies between 0.14 percent and 0.16 percent. You should not attempt to interpolate the value of IRR because of the nonlinear relationship in Equation 6.11. Analyst continues with trial and error, noting that increases in the value of $i$ decrease the value of the answer.

After several iterations, Analyst tries $i = 0.151$ and obtains

$$\$100{,}000{,}000 = \$20{,}000{,}000 \, \frac{1 - (1 + 0.151)^{-10}}{0.0831}$$

$$= \$99{,}993{,}971. \tag{4.64}$$

Analyst concludes that the IRR is slightly more than 15.1 percent.

### ■ 4.5.15 Escalation and Inflation

One of the most difficult problems in cost estimating is dealing with escalation and inflation. Although often viewed as one, they are different and you need to understand the difference.

Problems arise from either underestimating or overestimating future cost of labor or material. Contractors may recoup additional cost due to underestimates in cost-plus, fixed-fee contracts, but the fee is eroded. Overestimates result in the reduction of target cost of the contracts reducing the business base and increasing overhead in the company.

Contractors experience similar effects in fixed-price contracts due to underestimates except contractors cannot recoup additional cost due to underestimates unless the contracts contain economic price adjustment (EPA) clauses. You should be aware of the implications of improper selection of price indexes for EPA.

In general, underestimates impact contractors and customers at some future time. Overestimates impact contractors and customers in the near-term by erroneously limiting the size of orders to quantities less than what might be required and could be supplied.

**Escalation**

Escalation is both an intrinsic and an extrinsic cost driver. **Intrinsic factors** are essentially internal to organizations and, as such, can be controlled in large measure by the organizations.

**Extrinsic factors** are largely beyond the control of organizations. With the exception of climatic conditions, customers and regulatory bodies generally induce the extrinsic factors. No one takes credit for bad weather.

Table 4.48 is a partial list of intrinsic and extrinsic factors that may cause cost escalation. Note that such factors as budget instability, program stretchout, and program discontinuity are both intrinsic and extrinsic and are induced by both contractor and customer action.

You may think that supplier delinquency and labor problems are extrinsic factors, but remember, management selects suppliers and negotiates union contracts. Facility relocation can be an extrinsic factor when dealing with government organizations.

Can you add any other factors to the table?

*Table 4.48   Cost Escalation Factors*

| Intrinsic Factors | Extrinsic Factors |
| --- | --- |
| Budget instability | Budget instability |
| Program stretchout | Program stretch out |
| Program discontinuity | Program discontinuity |
| Management changes | Management changes |
| Personnel rotation | Personnel rotation |
| Inadequate preparation | Baseline changes |
| Supplier delinquency | Safety regulations |
| Long lead items | Zoning regulations |
| Labor problems | Environmental regulations |
| Facility relocation | Climatic conditions |

Budget instability and program discontinuity are perhaps the most severe factors of all, followed by climatic conditions. In any event, your approach should be to seek strategies that circumvent such factors. For example, if certain suppliers are continuously delinquent in delivering critical items, the preferred strategy would be to seek other suppliers.

**Inflation**

Inflation is the time-oriented decrease in purchasing power of a nation's money brought about by such factors as deficit spending and foreign trade imbalance. Inflation is an extrinsic cost driver induced by factors external to the program. The mode for dealing with inflation is primarily reactive, but certain steps can be taken to mitigate its effects.

For example, a countermeasure for inflationary pressure on raw materials is to stockpile material in accordance with the relative need for the various materials. Anticipated labor cost increases should be addressed both from the viewpoint of introducing robotics and automation and from revising the make or buy posture for the particular products.

### ■ 4.5.16 Price Indexes

The most commonly used indexes are the consumer price indexes and the producer price indexes. The primary sources of these data are monthly publications of the Bureau of Labor Statistics, U.S. Department of Commerce.

The **consumer price indexes** (**CPI**) are measures of average price changes over time of a fixed basket of goods and services. The U.S. Bureau of Labor Statistics publishes a CPI for all urban consumers, covering about 80 percent of the population, and a CPI for urban wage earners and clerical workers, covering about 32 percent of the population.

Beginning with the release of data for January 1988, the indexes were rebased to 1982–1983 = 100. This would infer that an item in the basket, costing one dollar in 1982–1983, would cost $1.40 in 1992 when the CPI was 140.3.

Figure 4.17 shows the indexes for all the items in the basket and for energy. Table 4.49 conveys the same data in tabular form.

## 4.5 Time Value of Money

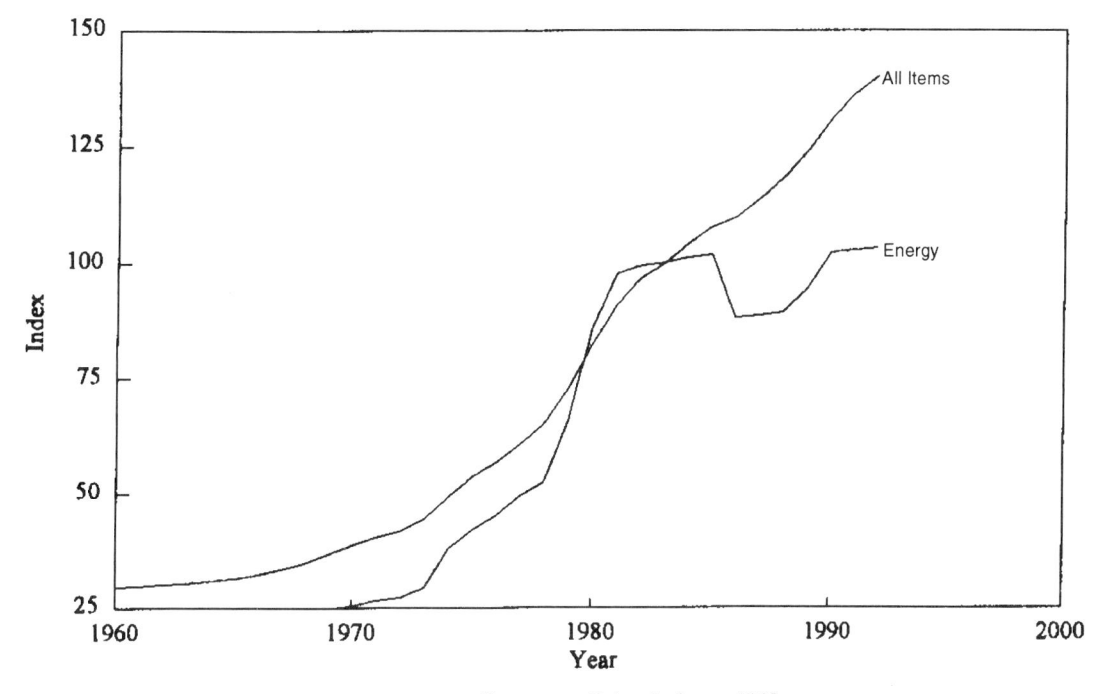

**Figure 4.17** Consumer Price Indexes [11]

Adapted by courtesy of the U.S. Department of Commerce from U.S. Bureau of the Census, *Statistical Abstract of the United States: 1993* (113th Edition), Washington, DC, 1993.

**Table 4.49** *Consumer Price Indexes [11]*

| Year | All | Energy Items | Year | All | Energy Items | Year | All | Energy Items |
|---|---|---|---|---|---|---|---|---|
| 1960 | 29.6 | 22.4 | 1971 | 40.5 | 26.5 | 1982 | 96.5 | 99.2 |
| 1961 | 29.9 | 22.5 | 1972 | 41.8 | 27.2 | 1983 | 99.6 | 99.9 |
| 1962 | 30.2 | 22.6 | 1973 | 44.4 | 29.4 | 1984 | 103.9 | 100.9 |
| 1963 | 30.6 | 22.8 | 1974 | 49.3 | 38.1 | 1985 | 107.6 | 101.6 |
| 1964 | 31.0 | 22.5 | 1975 | 53.8 | 42.1 | 1986 | 109.6 | 88.2 |
| 1965 | 31.5 | 22.9 | 1976 | 56.9 | 45.1 | 1987 | 113.6 | 88.6 |
| 1966 | 32.4 | 23.3 | 1977 | 60.6 | 49.4 | 1988 | 118.3 | 89.3 |
| 1967 | 33.4 | 23.8 | 1978 | 65.2 | 52.5 | 1989 | 124.0 | 94.3 |
| 1968 | 34.8 | 24.2 | 1979 | 72.6 | 65.7 | 1990 | 130.7 | 102.1 |
| 1969 | 36.7 | 24.8 | 1980 | 82.4 | 86.0 | 1991 | 136.2 | 102.5 |
| 1970 | 38.8 | 25.5 | 1981 | 90.9 | 97.7 | 1992 | 140.3 | 103.0 |

Adapted by courtesy of the U.S. Department of Commerce from U.S. Bureau of the Census, *Statistical Abstract of the United States: 1993* (113th Edition), Washington, DC, 1993.

The **producer price indexes** (**PPI**), dating from 1890, are the oldest continuous statistical series published by the Bureau of Labor Statistics. They measure average changes in producer prices of all commodities, at all stages of processing, produced in the United States.

Figure 4.18 shows the indexes for crude materials, intermediate materials (*i.e.*, work in process), and finished goods. Table 4.50 conveys the same data in tabular form.

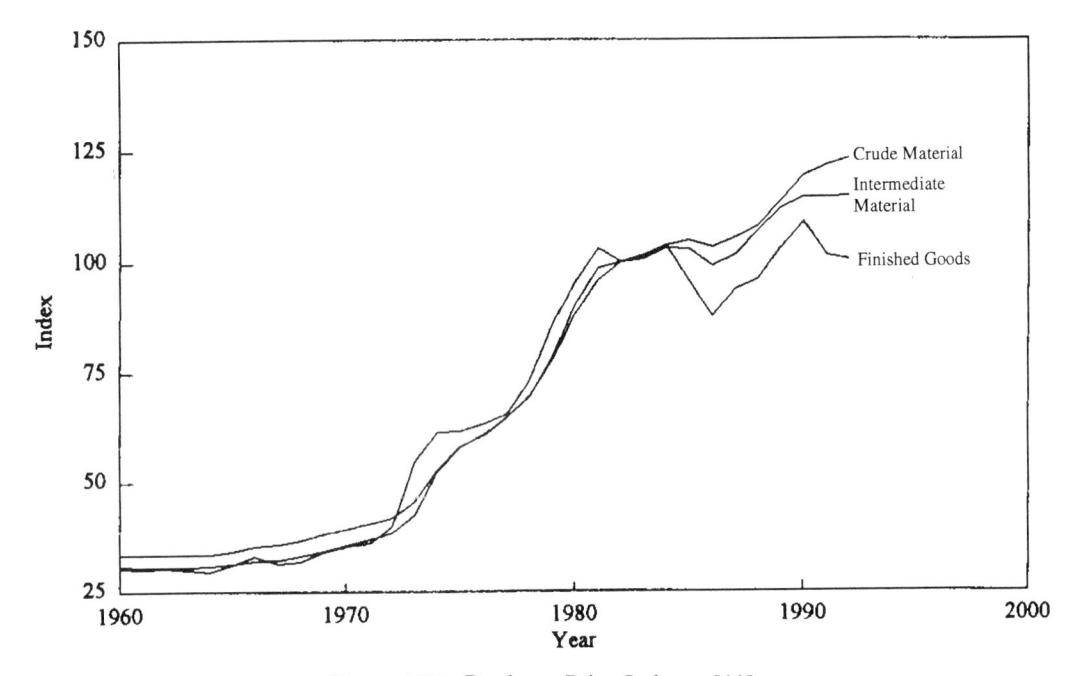

**Figure 4.18**   Producer Price Indexes [11]

Adapted by courtesy of the U.S. Department of Commerce from U.S. Bureau of the Census, *Statistical Abstract of the United States: 1993* (113th Edition), Washington, DC, 1993.

**Table 4.50**   *Producer Price Indexes [11]*

| Year | Crude Materials | Intermediate Materials | Finished Goods | Year | Crude Materials | Intermediate Materials | Finished Goods |
|---|---|---|---|---|---|---|---|
| 1960 | 30.4 | 30.8 | 33.4 | 1977 | 65.5 | 64.9 | 64.7 |
| 1961 | 30.2 | 30.6 | 33.4 | 1978 | 73.4 | 69.5 | 69.8 |
| 1962 | 30.5 | 30.6 | 33.5 | 1979 | 85.9 | 78.4 | 77.6 |
| 1963 | 29.9 | 30.7 | 33.4 | 1980 | 95.3 | 90.3 | 88.0 |
| 1964 | 29.6 | 30.8 | 33.5 | 1981 | 103.0 | 98.6 | 96.1 |
| 1965 | 31.1 | 31.2 | 34.1 | 1982 | 100.0 | 100.0 | 100.0 |
| 1966 | 33.1 | 32.0 | 35.2 | 1983 | 101.3 | 100.6 | 101.6 |
| 1967 | 31.3 | 32.2 | 35.6 | 1984 | 103.5 | 103.1 | 103.7 |
| 1968 | 31.8 | 33.0 | 36.6 | 1985 | 95.8 | 102.7 | 104.7 |

The Bureau of Labor statistics rebased the indexes to 1982–1983 = 100, beginning with the release of data for January 1988. This mean that a pound of crude material costing one dollar in 1982 would cost three mills more than one dollar in 1992.

## 4.5 Time Value of Money

**Table 4.50** Producer Price Indexes [11] (Cont.)

| Year | Crude Materials | Intermediate Materials | Finished Goods | Year | Crude Materials | Intermediate Materials | Finished Goods |
|---|---|---|---|---|---|---|---|
| 1969 | 33.9 | 34.1 | 38.0 | 1986 | 87.7 | 99.1 | 103.2 |
| 1970 | 35.2 | 35.4 | 39.3 | 1987 | 93.7 | 101.5 | 105.4 |
| 1971 | 36.0 | 36.8 | 40.5 | 1988 | 96.0 | 107.1 | 108.0 |
| 1972 | 39.9 | 38.2 | 41.8 | 1989 | 103.1 | 112.0 | 113.6 |
| 1973 | 54.5 | 42.4 | 45.6 | 1990 | 108.9 | 114.5 | 119.2 |
| 1974 | 61.4 | 52.5 | 52.6 | 1991 | 101.2 | 114.4 | 121.7 |
| 1975 | 61.6 | 58.0 | 58.2 | 1992 | 100.3 | 114.7 | 123.2 |
| 1976 | 63.4 | 60.9 | 60.8 |  |  |  |  |

Adapted by courtesy of the U.S. Department of Commerce from U.S. Bureau of the Census, *Statistical Abstract of the United States: 1993* (113th Edition), Washington, DC, 1993.

### ■ 4.5.17 Example of Forecasting Producer Price Index

There are two fundamental rules in attempting to forecast price indexes. The first rule is to avoid the use of outlier statistics (*i.e.*, extreme peaks and dips in data values). The second rule is to use the lowest level of aggregation possible. PPI for crude materials, intermediate materials, and finished good are aggregate indexes. These PPIs are composites of subindexes of commodities (*viz.*, approximately 3,200). The latter are disaggregate indexes. This example shows the consequences of ignoring the first rule.

Alpha Metals, Inc. deals in scrap metals reclamation and requests Analyst to forecast the PPI for scrap aluminum to the year 2000. Table 4.51 gives the technical approach Analyst follows in carrying out the assignment. Table 4.52 gives the historical data collected by Analyst. Note that the PPI for scrap aluminum was at a peak of 219.5 in 1988. The 1992 index is 138.3.

Equation 4.65 is the form of the **equation of regression** that Analyst intends to derive.

$$y_i = a + bx_i \tag{4.65}$$

where $y_i$ denotes *i*-th variate of dependent variable *y* (*i.e.*, PPI), *a* regression constant, *b* the regression coefficient, and $x_i$ the *i*-th variate of the independent variable *x* (*i.e.*, years).

**Table 4.51** Technical Approach for Aggregate vs. Forecasting Producer Price Indexes Example

1. Obtain historical producer price index data for aluminum scrap.
2. Calculate the regression constant and regression coefficient.
3. Derive the equation of regression for the time series.
4. Forecast the producer price index for the year 2000.

**Table 4.52** *Producer Price Index for Scrap Aluminum [11]*

| Year | Index | Year | Index |
|------|-------|------|-------|
| 1970 | 34.4  | 1989 | 204.4 |
| 1980 | 183.9 | 1990 | 172.6 |
| 1985 | 123.4 | 1991 | 143.1 |
| 1988 | 219.5 | 1992 | 138.3 |

Analyst next uses the following relationships to solve for the regression $a$ and regression coefficient $b$ in Equation 4.65:

$$b = \frac{n\Sigma x_i y_i - \Sigma x_i \Sigma y_i}{n\Sigma x_i^2 - (\Sigma x_i)^2} \qquad (4.66)$$

$$a = m_y + b m_x \qquad (4.67)$$

where $n$ denotes sample size, $\Sigma$ summation, and $m_y$ and $m_x$ means of variables of $y$ and $x$.

This particular application of the equation of regression is a time series because the independent variable $x$ is time. Since the independent variable is time, Analyst numbers the years with 1979 as the baseline. This means that 1979 is Year 1 in the regression operation. The resultant numbering is: 1979 – 1; 1989 – 20; 1980 – 11; 1990 – 21; 1985 – 21; 1988 – 16; 1991 – 22; and 1992 – 23.

Table 4.53 gives the worksheet for deriving the equation of regression. If there were entries in the table for the Years 2000, 2010, 2020, 2030, and 2040, the respective values of $x_i$ would be 31, 41, 51, 61, and 71.

Analyst now solves for the values of the regression constant $a$ and regression coefficient $b$. Substituting the values in Table 4.52 in Equations 4.66 and 4.67, Analyst obtains

$$b = \frac{8(22{,}916.2) - 133(1{,}209.9)}{8(2{,}964) - 17{,}689}$$

$$= 3.7212. \qquad (4.68)$$

$$a = 151.2375 + 3.7212(16.625)$$

$$= 157.424. \qquad (4.69)$$

**Table 4.53** *Worksheet for Forecasting Producer Price Indexes Example*

| $x_i$ | $y_i$ | $x_i y_i$ | $x_i^2$ |
|-------|-------|-----------|---------|
| 1     | 34.4  | 34.4      | 1       |
| 11    | 183.9 | 2,022.9   | 121     |
| 16    | 123.4 | 1,974.4   | 256     |
| 19    | 219.5 | 4,170.5   | 361     |
| 20    | 204.5 | 4,088.0   | 400     |
| 21    | 172.8 | 3,628.8   | 441     |
| 22    | 143.1 | 3,148.2   | 484     |
| 23    | 128.3 | 3,849.0   | 900     |
| Σ: 133 | 1,209.9 | 22,916.2 | 2,964   |

$m_x = 133 \div 8 = 16.625 \qquad m_y = 1{,}209.9 \div 8 = 151.2375$

## 4.6 Summary

Therefore, the equation of regression for the assignment is

$$y_i = 157.424 + 3.7212 x_i. \tag{4.70}$$

Relative to Year 1970, Year 2000 is year number 31. Substituting this value for $x$ in Equation 4.70, Analyst obtains

$$\begin{aligned} y_{2,000} &= 157.424 + 3.7212(31) \\ &= 272.7812. \end{aligned} \tag{4.71}$$

The forecasted PPI for aluminum scrap in the Year 2000 is 272.7812 based on the data in Table 4.52. Analyst cautions Alpha Metals to consider the coefficient of determination for the equation of regression, as you will in Exercise 4.7.13, before putting the finding to use.

# 4.6
# SUMMARY

**Section 4.1 Definitions** described the organization of Chapter 4 and the highlights of its sections. The section included the definitions of key terms and abbreviations used in the chapter. We gave these definitions when first used in the chapter and repeat them again in **Appendix A GLOSSARY**.

**Section 4.2 Product Network** started the exposition on baseline models used to describe the time-phased flow of activities and relationships for products of interest. The product network, which is evolved with techniques, such as PERT (*i.e.*, Program Evaluation Review Technique), CPM (*i.e.*, Critical Path Method), and precedence diagramming, were demonstrated in the section. Precedence diagramming is the basis for most current scheduling techniques and knowledge of PERT and CPM is a prerequisite.

**Section 4.3 Baseline Time Estimate** introduced the concepts of standards and learning curves and described their role in optimizing baseline time estimates. Standards provide the building blocks for scheduling and cost estimating. The use of learning curves, which allow one to capitalize on the economy of scale in repetitive operations, was illustrated. The impact of the probabilistic nature of learning curves on estimating realism was described.

**Section 4.4 Baseline Cost Estimate** addressed the baseline cost estimates as the second part of the foundation for the derivation of risk cost estimates. The subjects included cost estimating structures and cost estimating methodology. Methodology was discussed in the broad categories of top-down estimating and bottom-up estimating. Advantages and disadvantages of the various estimating techniques (*viz.*, expert opinion, analogy, parametric, and industrial engineering) were discussed.

**Section 4.5 Time Value of Money** illuminated the important subject of time value of money as a key element in long-range planning. The subjects included present value and future value of single payments and uniform series of payments, economic analysis with special emphasis on internal rate of return, escalation and inflation, and disaggregate and aggregate price indexes.

Many investigators rely on published tables for time value of money determinations. The section emphasized time value of money formulation you will need for combinations of terms and rates not found in published tables.

The techniques are particularly useful in technical risk management for projecting baseline cost estimates into the future. The section included an example on forecasting the producer price index.

## 4.7
## EXERCISES

Appendix C contains step-by-step solutions to the following exercises. Since the intent is to reinforce the subject matter covered in the chapter, we urge you to attempt the exercises before resorting to the solutions.

### ■ 4.7.1 Constructing Precedence Diagrams

Construct the precedence diagram for the tasks in Table 4.54. Unit time is one minute. Determine the critical path in the network and calculate the network efficiency.

*Table 4.54*  *Task-Precedence Chart for Exercise in Section 4.7.1*

| Task | Unit Time | Predecessor | Successor |
|------|-----------|-------------|-----------|
| a    | 0         | None        | b, c, e   |
| b    | 10        | a           | d         |
| c    | 15        | a           | f, i      |
| d    | 5         | b           | j         |
| e    | 15        | a           | h         |
| f    | 5         | c           | h         |
| g    | 10        | b           | k         |
| h    | 5         | e, f        | l         |
| i    | 15        | c           | k         |
| j    | 10        | g           | l         |
| k    | 5         | i           | l         |
| l    | 0         | h, j, k     | None      |

### ■ 4.7.2 Balancing Production Lines

Distribute the 12 tasks in Table 4.54 among four work stations for the best possible production-line balance. Calculate the resultant network efficiency.

### ■ 4.7.3 Deriving Standard Data for Job Families

Table 4.55 gives set-up and operation motion-element times which were observed during ten production runs for a certain product. Derive standard data for this particular job family using the equations of regression for set-up and operation.

Calibrate the data derived from the equations of regression against the observed data for Job Numbers 1, 5, and 10.

## 4.7 Exercises

**Table 4.55** *Motion-Element Time Data for Exercise in Section 4.7.3*

| Job | Setup | Operation | Job | Setup | Operation |
|---|---|---|---|---|---|
| 1 | 103.95 | 3.25 | 6 | 99.95 | 2.65 |
| 2 | 103.90 | 3.15 | 7 | 98.75 | 2.65 |
| 3 | 102.65 | 3.00 | 8 | 98.65 | 2.55 |
| 4 | 102.00 | 2.85 | 9 | 97.05 | 2.50 |
| 5 | 100.55 | 2.70 | 10 | 96.25 | 2.45 |

Set-up and operation times are in minutes.
Operation time is per-unit.

### ■ 4.7.4 Learning Curves in Service Products

The benefits of learning from repetitious operations are not the exclusive domain of the manufacturing sector of the economy. Service companies are beginning to dominate the gross national product of the world and could benefit considerably from employee learning.

According to Reference 12, the 1993 sales of the 100 largest diversified service companies in the world exceeded $2 trillion. On the other hand, the profit of these companies was only about $5 billion, which is less than 0.215 percent of sales. The average sales per employee of the companies amounted to $637,294.

Assume that labor is 60 percent of sales of these companies and that employees operate on a 99 percent learning curve. Calculate the increase in profit for the companies if employees were to operate on a learning curve of 95 percent. What value of learning curve would you apply to the service industry?

### ■ 4.7.5 Learning Curve Selection

Consider the lowest and highest values of operation time in Table 4.55 as the time needed to produce the last and first units in a lot. Derive the learning curve for the operation time.

### ■ 4.7.6 Learning Curve Confidence Interval

Repeat the example of Section 4.3.10 for a confidence level of 0.80. Under what circumstances would you use the upper confidence limit? Under what circumstances would you use the lower confidence limit?

### ■ 4.7.7 Learning Curve Discontinuity

Consider the manufacturer of high-technology products who experienced a prolonged labor strike. Prior to the time of the strike, the average unit cost of a particular product was $2,000 when produced in a continuous run of 1,000 units on a learning curve of 90 percent.

After the strike, the cost of the first unit produced was $7,250. Calculate the start-up efficiency that applied.

### 4.7.8 Parametric Estimate

A hypothetical parametric cost estimating relationship for production of a dual jet-engine aircraft, in a quantity of one, is given by

$$C = (V^2)(W^2) \tag{4.72}$$

where $C$ denotes estimated cost in thousands of dollars, $V$ cruising velocity in knots, and $W$ cargo weight in tons.

Assuming $V = 450$ knots and $W = 10$ tons, estimate the cost of the aircraft. Which of the two variables makes the greatest contribution to the cost of the aircraft?

### 4.7.9 Cost Projections

A recent news release cited discussions between the Boeing Company and members of the European consortium *Airbus Industrie* on futuristic aircraft that could transport 1,000 passengers over distances of 10,000 miles. The members of the consortium, which is headquartered in Toulouse, France, are Britain's *Aerospace*, France's *Aerospatiale*, Germany's *Deutche Aerospatz,* and Spain's *CASA*.

Boeing and *Airbus Industrie* call the jumbo aircraft Very Large Commercial Transport (VLCT). The VLCT will essentially double the payload of Boeing's 747. The VLCT will have a wing span of about 260 feet, length of 240 feet, and a height equal to that of two stacked 747s.

The principals estimate the development baseline cost estimate to be about $15 billion, and look to an international joint venture for the funding. They predict the aircraft might be ready for commercial service shortly after the turn of the century barring unforeseen problems.

Looking to the Pacific Rim region, Boeing sees a market of about 500 aircraft by the Year 2010. *Airbus Industrie* sees a market of about 1,000 aircraft in the same time frame. A number of airlines have expressed interest in the VLCT, but only British Airways and Singapore Airlines have stated that they would buy the aircraft.

Advocates of the VLCT claim that the large payload would alleviate traffic and loading-unloading problems at busy airports. What problems do you envision in accommodating the aircraft at departure and arrival gates?

Many people find the thought of being among 1,000 others in a single aircraft somewhat disconcerting. What problems do you envision in accommodating so many people and their luggage?

What major technical problems do you see hampering the development and production of the VLCT? What risk determinant factors do you see contributing to the risk exposure in the development and production of the VLCT?

Considering the history of the *Concorde* supersonic aircraft, do you think that the air transportation market in the next century will be large enough to support fleets of such massive aircraft? What kind of organizational structure do you envision and how many yearly passengers do you think are needed for successful operation?

*4.8 References* 189

Do you believe that an undertaking as large as the VLCT by an international joint venture would be successful? What risk determinant factors do you see at work in the areas of funding, management, and work division among the venture members?

On an intuitive basis, what do you believe the development and production risk time and cost estimates to be?

### ■ 4.7.10 Benefit-Cost Ratio

A certain public health institution wishes to issue $50 million of bonds for a new facility and contemplates a time period of 15 or 25 years for redeeming the bonds. Typically, interest on such bonds is paid semiannually. The prevailing interest rate is 8.0 percent compounded daily. Calculate and compare the benefit-cost ratios for the two time periods.

### ■ 4.7.11 Internal Rate of Return

Repeat the example of trial and error for internal rate of return (IRR) in Section 4.5.14 over a term of seven years. Account for the change in IRR.

### ■ 4.7.12 Cost of Inflation

Table 747 in the *1994 Statistical Abstract of the United States* gives consumer price indexes by groups for the time period of 1960 through 1993. Estimate what one dollar of energy in the Year 1993 would cost in the Year 2000.

### ■ 4.7.13 Coefficient of Determination

Define the coefficient of correlation and derive the equation of regression for the example of forecasting producer price index in Section 4.5.17.

## 4.8 REFERENCES

You can obtain referenced government documents from the issuing organizations and from:

Superintendent of Documents, U.S. Government Printing Office, Washington, DC 20402. Telephone: (202) 783-3238.
National Technical Information Service, U.S. Department of Commerce, Springfield, VA 22161. Telephone: (703) 487-4650.

1. Jack V. Michaels and William P. Wood, *Design to Cost*, John Wiley & Sons, Inc., 1989.
2. Rodney D. Stewart, *Cost Estimating*, Second Edition, John Wiley & Sons, Inc., 1991.
3. Jack V. Michaels and William P. Wood, *Design to Cost*, John Wiley & Sons, Inc., 1989.
4. Michael C. Fleming & Joseph G. Nellis, *The Essence of Statistics for Business*, Prentice Hall, 1991.

5. Jack V. Michaels and William P. Wood, *Design to Cost*, John Wiley & Sons, Inc., 1989.
6. Rodney D. Stewart, *Cost Estimating*, Second Edition, John Wiley & Sons, Inc., 1991.
7. Jack V. Michaels and William P. Wood, *Design to Cost*, John Wiley & Sons, Inc., 1989.
8. Department of the Navy, *Navy Power Supply Reliability*, NAVMAT P4855-1, 1982.
9. Jack V. Michaels, *Understanding the Time Value of Money*, Management Science, 1995.
10. Consumer Finance Institute, *The Amortization Handbook,* Longmeadow Press, 1896.
11. U.S. Bureau of the Census, *Statistical Abstract of the United States: 1993* (113th Edition), Washington, DC, 1991.
12. "The Fortune Service 500," *Fortune*, May 30, 1994.

> *All the rest is commentary.*
> **Paul Verlaine**

# CHAPTER 5

# RISK FORMULATION

> The theory of probability is at the bottom nothing but common sense reduced to calculus.
> **Pierre de Laplace**

Chapter 5 builds from the risk metrics in Chapter 3 by elaborating on risk formulation. The formulation is an extension of the relationships for baseline time and cost estimates covered in Chapter 4. Figure 5.1 illustrates the organization of the chapter

**Section 5.1 Definitions** provides an annotated perspective of the chapter with the definitions of key terms and abbreviations used in the chapter. These definitions are repeated when the terms are first used in the chapter and in Appendix A.

**Section 5.2 Perspective on Risk Determinant Factors** is pivotal to the application of the various risk determinant factors. Risk formulation is the essence of realistic, credible risk estimates, and the section addresses proper formulation in its generic form. The succeeding sections provide details on the specific risk determinant factors.

**Section 5.3 Management Attribute Factors** covers the influence of management attributes on risk exposure, as evidenced by company policies and management decisions. The attributes are funding and budgeting policy, customer and user policy, program continuity policy, and personnel recognition and retention policy. Management attribute factors vary primarily as functions of time.

**Section 5.4 Extrinsic Attribute Factors** addresses the influence on risk exposure of external attributes, such as escalation, inflation, and statutory regulations. The effects of extrinsic attribute factors also vary primarily as functions of time.

The next three sections address risk determinant factors as functions of product categories of hardware, software, and service. In each category, design maturity and process maturity dominate the other attributes in the contribution to risk exposure and is accounted for by $k$-factors equated to product maturity and process maturity.

**Section 5.5 Hardware Factors** develops schema for deriving hardware product and process risk determinant factors. We base the schema on the attributes of product and process design maturity, quality, complexity, and concurrency. Concurrency is an attribute of interdependent tasks that we perform concurrently. The dominant hardware factors are product design maturity and process design maturity.

|  |  |
|---|---|
| 5.1 Definitions | Key terms and abbreviations. |
| 5.2 Perspective on Risk Determinant Factors | Generic formulation. |
| 5.3 Management Attribute Factor | Attribute checklists, formulation. |
| 5.4 Extrinsic Attribute Factor | Attribute checklists, formulation. |
| 5.5 Hardware Factors | Product and process maturity, quality, complexity, concurrency, formulation. |
| 5.6 Software Factors | Product and process maturity, quality, complexity, concurrency, formulation. |
| 5.7 Service Factors | Product and process attribute checklist, formulation. |
| 5.8 Summary | Review of highlights. |
| 5.9 Exercises | Role models. |
| 5.10 References | Data sources. |

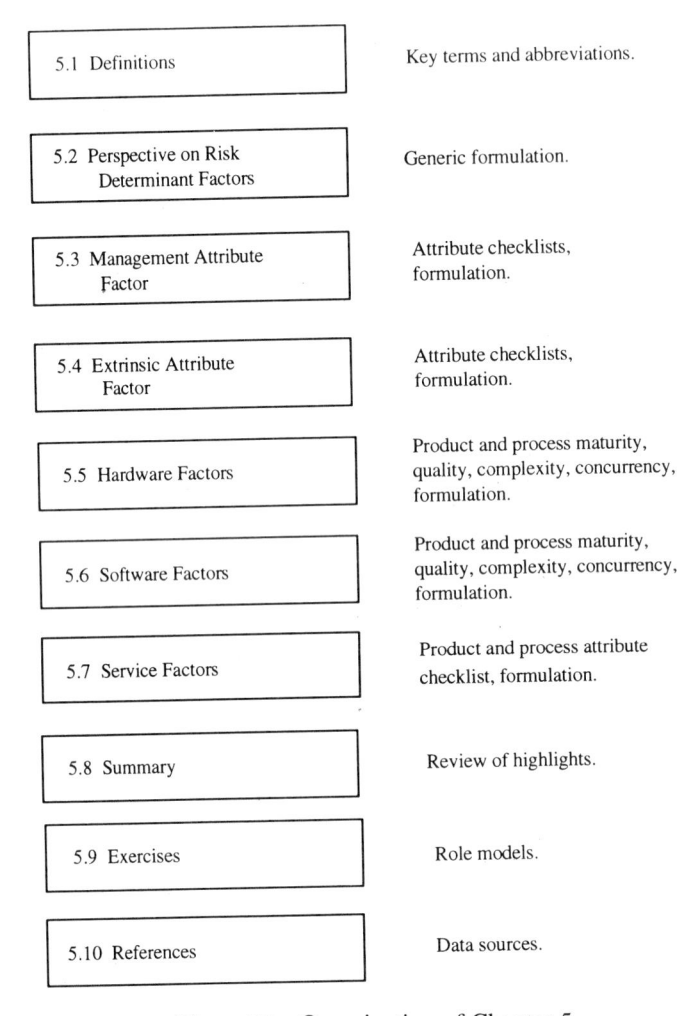

**Figure 5.1** Organization of Chapter 5

**Section 5.6 Software Factors** develops schema for deriving software risk determinant factors. We base the schema on the attributes of product and process design maturity, quality, complexity, and concurrency, and key the schema to the hierarchical processes in software development and production. The dominant software factors are product design maturity and process design maturity.

**Section 5.7 Service Factors** develops schema for deriving service risk determinant factors. In service work, products and process are one and the same. Therefore, we use the product attributes of complexity, concurrency, and maturity in deriving risk determinant factors for service products. The treatment of these attributes is similar to the treatment for hardware products and, as with hardware products, the dominant attribute is product maturity.

We discuss the management attributes of the service organization, including the attitude of users regarding the service rendered, as the bases for the service product quality factors. We treat service product quality as a first-order attribute.

Chapter 5 concludes with **Section 5.8 Summary**, **Section 5.9 Exercises**, and **Section 5.10 References**. The summary revisits the highlights of the chapter and the exercises reinforce the highlights.

# 5.1
# DEFINITIONS

Table 5.1 gives definitions of the key terms and abbreviations used in this chapter. Note, in particular, the abbreviations and the definitions of the various product and process risk determinant factors.

Note the relationship among *baseline, baseline cost estimate*, and *baseline time estimate*. Note the meaning of *majority rule, constant weighting*, and *binary weighting* used to derive risk determinant factors for estimating risk exposure.

Note also the meaning of *aggregation* and *disaggregation* and the distinction between the *management attribute factor* and *extrinsic attribute factor*. Note the distinction between *work breakdown structure* and *generation breakdown*.

# 5.2
# PERSPECTIVE ON RISK DETERMINANT FACTORS

Table 5.2 lists the risk determinant factors that we derive in this chapter. **Risk determinant factors** are quantified measures of management, extrinsic, product, and process attributes that contribute to risk exposure. We use risk determinant factors to estimate **risk time estimate** and **risk cost estimate**, the measures of **risk exposure**. Equations 5.1 and 5.2 are the preferred relationships for estimating these measures of risk exposure.

$$RTE = BTE + RT \cdot RDF \tag{5.1}$$

$$RCE = BCE + RC \cdot RDF \tag{5.2}$$

where RTE denotes **risk time estimate**, BTE **baseline time estimate**, RT **risk time**, RDF risk determinant factor, RCE risk cost estimate, BCE **baseline cost estimate**, and RC risk cost.

With the exception of the value of RDF, which is probabilistic, you can use deterministic or probabilistic values in Equations 5.1 and 5.2. Using deterministic values, these equations yield deterministic-deterministic-probabilistic solutions.

Equations 5.3 and 5.4 are alternative relationships for estimating the measures of risk exposure. These equations are heuristic (*i.e.,* rules of thumb) relationships, which you should use only when you are building from probabilistic estimates of baseline time and cost, and estimates of risk time and cost are unavailable.

$$RTE = BTE(1 + RDF) \tag{5.3}$$

$$RCE = BCE(1 + RDF) \tag{5.4}$$

RDF may be a composite risk determinant factor. In the case of dependency among the contributing factors (*viz.*, maturity, quality, complexity, concurrency), the value of RDF can be as high as four.

Substituting RDF = 4 in Equations 5.3 and 5.4 results in values of RTE and RCE that are five times the values of BTE and BCE. Such high values illustrate why probabilistic solutions generally lack realism and credibility.

*Table 5.1   Terms and Abbreviations in Chapter 5*

**Aggregation**: Assembling distinct components of products into an aggregate for estimating purposes.
**Baseline**: Initial definition of product to be developed and process to produce product.
**Baseline cost estimate**: Estimated cost to develop and produce product in accordance with baseline.
**Baseline time estimate**: Estimated time to develop and produce product in accordance with baseline.
**Binary weighting**: Method of weighting answers to questions with binary numbers.
**Brassboard**: Model of product, for use in design evaluation, identical in form, fit, and function to production items except it is not built to withstand environmental qualification.
**Breadboard**: Model of product consisting of details, subassemblies, and assemblies connected in unmounted form for use in concept demonstration and validation.
**Concurrency**: Degree of overlap among interdependent tasks.
**Constant weighting**: Weighting that changes at constant rate from sequence of questions.
**CPU**: Central processing unit.
**Cycle time**: Amount of time to complete production run.
**Disaggregation**: Disassembling product into component disaggregate parts for estimating time and cost to develop and produce product.
**EAF**: Extrinsic attribute factor.
**Extrinsic attribute factor**: Risk determinant factor for external conditions (*e.g.*, inflation and regulatory statutes) largely beyond control of organization.
**Field**: Task for collecting field data on use of product for purpose of product improvement.
**First article**: Denotes tasks that produce and test the first production item using LRIP tooling.
**Generation breakdown**: Hierarchical rendition of how product is produced.
**Hardware process complexity**: Hardware process attribute descriptor based on population of assemblies, subassemblies, details, and parts.
**Hardware process concurrency**: Hardware process attribute descriptor based on concurrence of interdependent tasks.
**Hardware product complexity**: Hardware product attribute descriptor based on expansiveness of generation breakdown.
**Hardware product concurrency**: Hardware product attribute descriptor based on concurrence of interdependent tasks.
**Hardware product maturity**: Hardware product attribute descriptor based on design maturity and readiness for production.
**Hardware product quality**: Hardware product attribute descriptor based on design producibility, reliability, and testability.
**Heuristics**: Method of solution along empirical lines using rules of thumb.
**Intrinsic attribute factor**: Risk determinant factor for internal conditions (*e.g.*, policy) largely within control of organization.
**Logical statement**: Statement in binary form (*i.e.*, 0 or 1 for yes or no, or vice versa).
**Low rate of initial production**: Production of items using soft (*i.e.*, multipurpose) tooling at the beginning of production.
**LRIP**: Low rate of initial production.
**MAF**: Management attribute factor.
**Majority rule**: Consensus of the answers is derived from the majority of the answers.
**Management attribute factor**: Risk determinant factor for management attributes (*e.g.*, funding and budgeting policy; customer and user policy; program continuity policy and personnel retention policy).

## 5.2 Perspective on Risk Determinant Factors

**Table 5.1** Terms and Abbreviations in Chapter 5 (Cont.)

---

**MPP**: Manufacturing process plan.
**PROCCF**: Process complexity factor.
**PROCMF**: Process maturity factor.
**PROCQF**: Process quality factor.
**PROCYF**: Process concurrency factor.
**Process maturity**: Maturity and production readiness of process design.
**Process quality**: Uniformity of process in producing products of consistent quality.
**Process uniformity**: Consistency with which process produces product within specified functional, physical, and environmental limits.
**PRODCF**: Product complexity factor.
**PRODMF**: Product maturity factor.
**PRODQF**: Product quality factor.
**PRODYF**: Product concurrency factor.
**Prototype**: Model of product, for use in formal design acceptance, which is identical to production items and is built to withstand environmental qualification.
**Rate production**: Production of items using hard (*i.e.*, dedicated, special purpose) tooling at a high rate.
**Risk**: Uncertainty surrounding loss from peril.
**Risk cost**: Product of probability of occurrence of peril and the corrective-action cost. Probabilistic-deterministic estimate.
**Risk cost estimate**: Sum of baseline cost estimate and risk cost.
**Risk determinant**: Attribute contributing to risk exposure.
**Risk determinant factor**: Quantified measure of risk determinant.
**Risk exposure**: Vulnerability to peril in terms of risk time and risk cost.
**Risk time**: Product of probability of occurrence of peril and corrective-action time. Probabilistic-deterministic estimate.
**Risk time estimate**: Sum of baseline time estimate and risk time.
**Root-sum-of-squares**: Square root of sum of squares of series of numbers.
**Service product complexity**: Service product attribute descriptor based on expanse of generation breakdown.
**Service product concurrency**: Service product attribute descriptor based on concurrence of interdependent tasks.
**Service product maturity**: Service product attribute descriptor based on design maturity.
**Service product quality factor**: Service product attribute descriptor based on management attributes.
**Software process complexity**: Software process attribute descriptor based on number of lines of code.
**Software process concurrency**: Software process attribute descriptor based on concurrency of interdependent tasks.
**Software process maturity**: Software process maturity descriptor based on software program maturity.
**Software process quality**: Software process attribute descriptor based on degree of control in software program.
**Software product complexity**: Software product attribute descriptor based on number of lines of code.
**Software product concurrency**: Software product attribute descriptor based on concurrency of interdependent tasks.
**Software product maturity**: Software product attribute descriptor based on design maturity.
**Software product quality**: Software product attribute descriptor based on degree of control in software program.
**Software program**: Set of instructions executed by computer.
**Statistics**: Branch of mathematics. Also, properties of samples.
**Tailoring**: Process of adapting procedures and criteria for certain applications to other applications.
**TDP**: Technical data package.
**Total procurement package**: Contractual instrument for development and production.
**Truth table**: Rendition of logical statements in binary form.
**Work breakdown structure**: Depiction of elements of cost for developing and producing product.

---

Figure 5.2 illustrates the alternative ways that you can use RDF to estimate risk exposure. The top path in the figure is deterministic-deterministic-probabilistic and is the preferred way. The bottom path is purely probabilistic and should be avoided.

```
┌──────────────┐     ┌──────────────┐     ┌──────────────┐
│Deterministic │     │Deterministic │     │Deterministic-│
│  Baseline    │─────│Risk Time and │─────│Deterministic-│
│  Estimates   │     │  Risk Cost   │     │Probabilistic Risk│
└──────────────┘     └──────────────┘     │  Estimates   │
                            │             └──────────────┘
                     ┌──────────────┐
                     │ Probabilistic│
                     │Risk Determinant│
                     │   Factors    │
                     └──────────────┘
                            │
┌──────────────┐     ┌──────────────┐     ┌──────────────┐
│ Probabilistic│     │ Probabilistic│     │Probabilistic-│
│  Baseline    │─────│Risk Time and │─────│Probabilistic-│
│  Estimates   │     │  Risk Cost   │     │Probabilistic Risk│
└──────────────┘     └──────────────┘     │  Estimates   │
                                          └──────────────┘
```

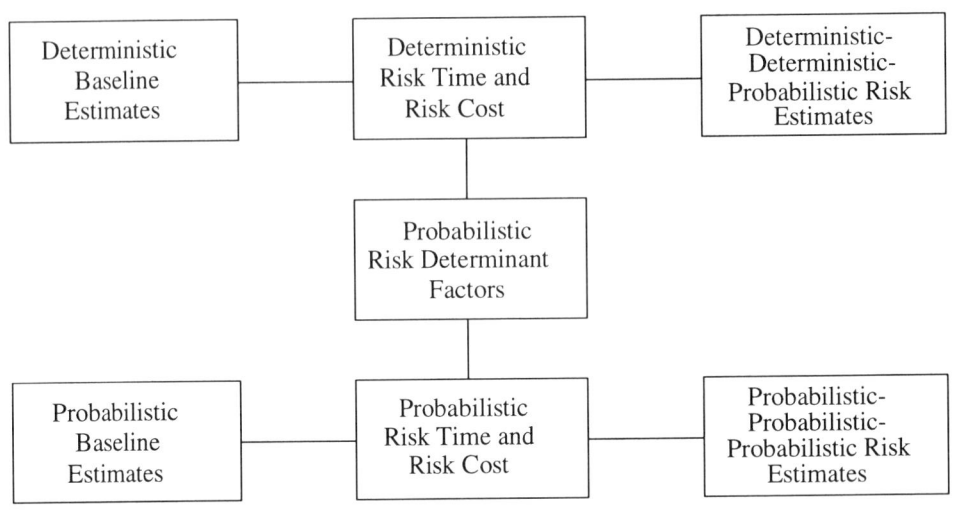

**Figure 5.2** Alternative Ways to Estimate Risk Exposure

For example, substituting $BTE = 24$ months, $RT = 2$ months, and $RDF = 0.4$ in Equation 5.1 yields

$$RTE = 24 \text{ months} + 0.4(2 \text{ months})$$
$$= 24.8 \text{ months} \qquad (5.5)$$
$$RTE = 24 \text{ months}(1 + 0.4)$$
$$= 33.6 \text{ months}. \qquad (5.6)$$

Which solution do you prefer? Equation 5.6 provides an answer which is about 26 percent more conservative than that of Equation 5.5, but it is far less realistic and credible.

> *Heuristic conclusions are self-fulfilling prophecies. Too much pessimism can be as deadly as too much optimism.*
> **Analyst**

We address the schema for deriving RDF values in the sections that follow. Table 5.2 lists attribute applicability for hardware, software, and service factors.

## 5.3 MANAGEMENT ATTRIBUTE FACTORS

The management attribute factors are first-order measures of the commitment to the quality, functionality, and affordability as well as the profitability of an organization's products. Specifically, the

## 5.3 Management Attribute Factors

**Table 5.2** Attribute Applicability for Risk Determinant Factors

| Risk Determinant Factor: | Hardware | Software | Service |
|---|---|---|---|
| Management Attributes | ✔ | ✔ | ✔ |
| Product Maturity | ✔ | ✔ | ✔ |
| Product Quality | ✔ | ✔ | ✔ |
| Product Complexity | ✔ | ✔ | ✔ |
| Product Concurrency | ✔ | ✔ | ✔ |
| Process Maturity | ✔ | ✔ | ✔ |
| Process Quality | ✔ | ✔ | ✔ |
| Process Complexity | ✔ | ✔ | ✔ |
| Process Concurrency | ✔ | ✔ | ✔ |
| Extrinsic Attributes | ✔ | ✔ | ✔ |

management attribute factor is a measure of the attributes that influence risk exposure in the products of interest.

Table 5.3 lists the key attributes contributing to the **management attribute factor** (**MAF**). These are funding and budgeting policy, customer and user policy, program continuity policy, and personnel growth and retention policy.

**Table 5.3** Attributes Contributing to Management Attribute Factor

> **Funding and budgeting policy**: Adequacy and consistency of budgeting and funding for research, development, production, and product support.
> **Customer and user policy**: Adequacy and consistency of concern for customer's affordability limits and user's needs, applications, and expectations for products.
> **Program continuity policy**: Adequacy and consistency of long-range planning and commitment to research and development, and product-line growth.
> **Personnel growth and retention policy**: Skill, adequacy, consistency, and longevity of the work force, and the maintenance of a system of employee motivation, recognition, and reward.

### ■ 5.3.1 Management Attribute Checklists

Tables 5.4 through 5.7 are suggested checklists that you can use to assess the respective management attributes. The checklists are suitable to a wide range of product categories with some amount of **tailoring**.

Each checklist consists of a series of questions which can be answered with a yes or no. The intent is to reach a conclusion on whether the respective management policies contribute to risk exposure in products of interest on the basis of a consensus of the answers to the questions in the respective checklists.

You can derive a consensus of the answers using a form of the **majority rule** or binary weighting. Be sure to list the questions in the order of importance in each sequence. In the interest of estimating realism and credibility, we recommend the use of binary weighting or majority rule with constant weighting over the use of the simple majority rule.

**Table 5.4** *Funding and Budgeting Policy Checklist*

|  | Yes | No |
|---|---|---|
| 1. Does the policy require return-on-investment to be considered over the life of given products? | | |
| 2. Is it the policy of the organization to fund product programs through completion? | | |
| 3. Is adequate early funding provided for critical research, design, and engineering activities? | | |
| 4. Are product programs provided adequate management reserve? | | |
| 5. Is production funding available during development for tooling and long-lead procurement? | | |
| 6. Does the policy require technical justification in support of fiscal decisions? | | |
| 7. Does the policy require the consideration of alternative approaches with different cost options? | | |
| 8. Is funding provided for alternative approaches? | | |

**Table 5.5** *Customer and User Policy Checklist*

|  | Yes | No |
|---|---|---|
| 1. Does the organization determine the users as well as the customers for the products? | | |
| 2. Does the organization solicit statements of user requirements in the user's own words? | | |
| 3. Is there a formal system for translating the voice of the user into product specifications? | | |
| 4. Are product warranties stated clearly and unambiguously? | | |
| 5. Is there easy access to the customer service organization? | | |
| 6. Does the organization facilitate the return of defective products? | | |
| 7. Does the organization automatically notify customers and users of product recalls and improvements? | | |

### ■ 5.3.2 Management Attribute Factor Formulation

We use constant and binary weighting of questions and subsequent answers in deriving values of the management attribute factor.

**Constant Weighting**

Table 5.8 gives the procedure for deriving the management attribute factor with the **constant weighting** approach. The approach weights the questions and answers in the order of their listing. The weighting effect is quite pronounced in long sequences. You should give as much thought to the order in which you list questions in sequences as you give to the questions.

## 5.3 Management Attribute Factors

**Table 5.6** *Program Continuity Policy Checklist*

|  | Yes | No |
|---|---|---|
| 1. Does the policy ensure continuity in multiyear programs subject to periodic performance, schedule, and cost reviews? | | |
| 2. Are specific accomplishments for the current reporting period reviewed at a minimum of every quarter? | | |
| 3. Are specific accomplishments planned for the next reporting period reviewed at a minimum of every quarter? | | |
| 4. Are reviews designed to give visibility to all disciplines and not just technical? | | |
| 5. Are performance, schedule, and cost monitored on a weekly basis? | | |
| 6. Are performance, schedule, and cost variance analyses required on a monthly basis? | | |
| 7. Are time and cost estimates required on a monthly basis? | | |

**Table 5.7** *Personnel Growth and Retention Policy Checklist*

|  | Yes | No |
|---|---|---|
| 1. Are assignments of key personnel made for the duration of programs? | | |
| 2. Are program directors and project managers responsible for only one major program or project at a time? | | |
| 3. Are career progressions defined so that every employee understands promotion opportunities? | | |
| 4. Do training programs in effect satisfy organizational and employee current and future needs? | | |
| 5. Are supervisors involved in the recruitment, training, and retention of key personnel? | | |

**Table 5.8** *Constant Weighting Procedure for Management Attribute Factor*

1. Ensure that questions and answers are listed in the descending order of importance.
2. Assign the weights $n, n-1, n-2, n-3, \ldots 1$, where $n$ equals the number of questions in the sequence, in the descending order of importance.
3. Sum the weights of all the questions for each sequence of questions, which is denoted by $\Sigma aqw$.
4. Sum the weights of all the sequences of questions, which is denoted by $\Sigma\Sigma aqw$.
5. Sum the weights of the questions with positive answers for each sequence of questions, which is denoted by $\Sigma paw$.
6. Sum the weights of all the sequences of questions with positive answers, which is denoted by $\Sigma\Sigma paw$.
7. Divide the sum of the positive-answer weights ($\Sigma\Sigma paw$) in Step 6 by the sum of the weights of all the questions ($\Sigma\Sigma aqw$) in Step 4.
8. Equate the value of MAF to $1 - \Sigma\Sigma paw \div \Sigma\Sigma aqw$.

For example, the first question in a sequence of eight questions would be weighted 8. The last question would be weighted 1. Consider Tables 5.4, 5.5, 5.6, and 5.7.

1. There are eight questions in Table 5.4. The weights for the sequence are 8, 7, 6, 5, 4, 3, 2, 1. The sum of the weights ($\Sigma aqw$) is 36.

2. There are seven questions in Tables 5.5. The weights for the sequence are each 7, 6, 5, 4, 3, 2, 1. The sum of the weights ($\Sigma aqw$) is 28.

3. There are seven questions in Table 5.6. The weights for the sequence are 7, 6, 5, 4, 3, 2, 1. The sum of the weights ($\Sigma aqw$) is 28.

4. There are five questions in Table 5.7. The weights for the sequence are 5, 4, 3, 2, 1. The sum of the weights ($\Sigma aqw$) is 15.

The total of the sums of the weights for the four sequences of questions ($\Sigma\Sigma aqw$) is 36 + 28 + 28 + 15 = 107.

Assume the following answers to the four sequences of questions:

1. Table 5.4: No, no, no, no, yes, yes, yes, yes
2. Table 5.5: No, no, no, no, yes, yes, yes
3. Table 5.6: No, no, no, no, yes, yes, yes
4. Table 5.7: No, no, no, yes, yes.

The sum of the weights of positive answers ($\Sigma paw$) in each sequence of questions are as follows:

1. Table 5.4: 4 + 3 + 2 + 1 = 10
2. Table 5.5: 3 + 2 + 1 = 6
3. Table 5.6: 3 + 2 + 1 = 6
4. Table 5.7: 2 + 1 = 3.

The sum of the sum of the weights of positive answers to the questions, $\Sigma\Sigma paw$, in each of the four sequences is 10 + 6 + 6 + 3 = 25.

From Table 5.8, Equation 5.7 is the relationship to use for deriving the value of the management attribute factor (*MAF*).

$$MAF = \frac{\Sigma\Sigma paw}{\Sigma\Sigma aqw} \qquad (5.7)$$

where $\Sigma\Sigma paw$ denotes sum of sum of weights of positive answers in each sequence of questions and $\Sigma\Sigma aqw$ sum of sum of weights of all questions in each sequence.

Substituting $\Sigma\Sigma paw$ = 25 and $\Sigma\Sigma aqw$ = 107 in Equation 5.7 yields

$$MAF = 1 - \frac{25}{107}$$
$$= 0.766. \qquad (5.8)$$

Next, we use the binary weighting approach to derive the value of *MAF*. Note the difference in answers from the constant weighting to the binary weighting approach.

**Binary Weighting**

Table 5.9 gives the procedure for deriving the management attribute factor with **binary weighting**. The procedure requires equivalent decimal values of the largest binary numbers which can be

## 5.3 Management Attribute Factors

formed with given numbers of bit positions. Table 5.10 gives equivalent decimal values for up to 12-bit positions.

**Table 5.9** *Binary Weighting Procedure for Management Attribute Factor*

1. Ensure that questions are listed in the descending order of importance.
2. Write the largest possible binary numbers for each sequence of questions in Step 1.
3. Calculate equivalent decimal number of largest possible binary number ($lpn$) in Step 2.
4. Sum equivalent decimal numbers of largest possible binary numbers ($\Sigma edvlpn$) in Step 3.
5. Write binary numbers for answers ($bna$) to sequences of questions in Step 1, equating yes to 1 and no to 0.
6. Calculate equivalent decimal values for binary number answers ($edvbna$) to sequences of questions in Step 5.
7. Sum equivalent decimal values for binary number answers ($\Sigma edvbna$) in Step 6.
8. Divide sum of equivalent decimal values for the binary number answers ($\Sigma edvbna$) in Step 7 by the sum of the equivalent decimal values of largest possible binary numbers ($\Sigma edvlpn$) in Step 4.
9. Equate the value of MAF to $1 - \Sigma edvbna \div \Sigma edvlpn$.

**Table 5.10** *Equivalent Decimal Values of Binary Numbers*

| Binary Number | Decimal Value | Binary Number | Decimal Value |
| --- | --- | --- | --- |
| 1 | 1 | 1111111 | 127 |
| 11 | 3 | 11111111 | 255 |
| 111 | 7 | 111111111 | 511 |
| 1111 | 15 | 1111111111 | 1023 |
| 11111 | 31 | 11111111111 | 2047 |
| 111111 | 63 | 111111111111 | 4095 |

Let us again consider the questions in Tables 5.4, 5.5, 5.6, and 5.7. There are eight questions in Table 5.4, seven questions in Tables 5.5 and 5.6, and five questions in Table 5.7.

If the four sequences of questions were to receive all positive responses, the four binary numbers would be

1. Table 5.4: 11111111
2. Table 5.5: 1111111
3. Table 5.6: 1111111
4. Table 5.7: 11111.

The equivalent decimal values of these binary numbers are 255, 127, 127, and 31. The sum of these equivalent decimal values is 540.

Next, we turn to the answers to the questions.

Again, assume the following answers to the four sequences of questions:

1. Table 5.4: No, no, no, no, yes, yes, yes, yes
2. Table 5.5: No, no, no, no, yes, yes, yes
3. Table 5.6: No, no, no, no, yes, yes, yes
4. Table 5.7: No, no, no, yes, yes.

The binary numbers for the answers to the foregoing sequences of questions are:

1. Table 5.4: 00001111
2. Table 5.5: 0000111
3. Table 5.6: 0000111
4. Table 5.7: 00011.

The equivalent decimal values for the binary number answers are 15, 7, 7, and 3. The sum of these equivalent decimal values is 32, which indicates a low value for the management attribute factor relative to the largest possible value of 540.

From Table 5.9, Equation 5.9 is the relationship to use in deriving the value of the MAF with binary weighting.

$$MAF = \frac{\Sigma edvbna}{\Sigma edvlpn} \qquad (5.9)$$

where $\Sigma edvbna$ denotes sum of equivalent decimal values of binary numbers of answers in sequences of questions and $\Sigma edvlpn$ sum of equivalent decimal values of largest possible binary numbers of answers in sequences of questions.

Substituting $\Sigma edvbna = 32$ and $\Sigma edvlpn = 540$ in Equation 5.9 yields

$$MAF = 1 - \frac{32}{540}$$
$$= 0.941. \qquad (5.10)$$

In most instances, the binary weighting approach paints a more pessimistic picture of the influence of MAF on risk exposure than does the constant weighting approach (*viz.*, 0.941 *vs.* 0.766 in Equation 5.8). You should base your choice on the desired degree of conservatism.

### ■ 5.3.3 Example of Management Attribute Factor for Funding and Budgeting Policy

Table 5.11 gives the checklist on funding and budgeting policy completed by the comptroller of Upsilon Publishers in anticipation of investing $10 million on the publication of a new trade magazine. The comptroller retains Analyst to ascertain the risk exposure as a function of the company's funding and budgeting policy. Table 5.12 gives the technical approach followed by Analyst in carrying out the assignment.

## 5.3 Management Attribute Factors

**Table 5.11** *Funding and Budgeting Policy Checklist for MAF Example*

| | Yes | No |
|---|---|---|
| 1. Does the policy require return-on-investment to be considered over the life of given products? | ✔ | |
| 2. Is it the policy of the organization to fund product programs through completion? | | ✔ |
| 3. Is adequate early funding provided for critical research, design, and engineering activities? | | ✔ |
| 4. Are product programs provided adequate management reserve? | ✔ | |
| 5. Is production funding available during development for tooling and long-lead procurement? | ✔ | |
| 6. Does the policy require technical justification in support of fiscal decisions? | ✔ | |
| 7. Does the policy require the consideration of alternative approaches with different cost options? | | ✔ |
| 8. Is funding provided for alternative approaches? | | ✔ |

**Table 5.12** *Technical Approach for MAF for Funding and Budgeting Policy Example*

1. Interview cost control personnel with respect to cost growth in similar undertakings.
2. Ensure that the checklist questions in Table 5.11 are listed in the descending order of importance.
3. Use both constant weighting and binary number weighting of the answers in Table 5.11 to derive the management attribute factor.
4. Derive the risk cost estimate with both the constant weighting approach and the binary weighting approach.

Analyst learns that funding discontinuities in the past undertakings of a similar nature have added approximately 25 percent to original estimates to complete (*i.e.*, BCE). Therefore, Analyst equates the **risk cost** (**RC**) to $10 million(0.25), or $2.5 million.

Analyst verifies that the checklist questions in Table 5.11 are listed in the descending order of importance. Analyst first uses the constant weighting approach and assigns the weights 8, 7, 6, 5, 4, 3, 2, and 1 to the questions.

The sum of all the weights is 36. The sum of the weight of the positive answers to the questions is 8 + 5 + 4 + 3, or 20.

Substituting the values $\Sigma\Sigma paw = 20$ and $\Sigma\Sigma aqw = 36$ in Equation 5.7, Analyst obtains

$$MAF = 1 - \frac{20}{36}$$
$$= 0.444. \tag{5.11}$$

Substituting *BCE* = $10 million, *RC* = $2.5 million, and *MAF* = 0.444 for the value of *RDF* in Equation 5.2, Analyst obtains

$$RCE = \$10 \text{ million} + \$2.5 \text{ million}(0.444)$$
$$= \$11.110 \text{ million.} \qquad (5.12)$$

Analyst next turns to the binary weighting approach. The binary number corresponding to the yes and no answers to the sequence of eight questions in Table 5.11 is 1011100. The decimal equivalent value of this binary number is $1 \cdot 2^7 + 0 \cdot 2^6 + 0 \cdot 2^5 + 1 \cdot 2^4 + 1 \cdot 2^3 + 1 \cdot 2^2 + 0 \cdot 2^1 + 0 \cdot 2^0$ for 128 + 16 + 8 + 4, or 156.

From Table 5.10, the largest possible equivalent decimal value is 255 for eight-bit binary number. Analyst substitutes the values of 156 and 255 in Equation 5.9 for MAF and obtains

$$MAF = 1 - \frac{156}{256}$$
$$= 0.391. \qquad (5.13)$$

Analyst substitutes *BCE* = $10 million, *RC* = $2.5 million, and *MAF* = 0.391 in Equation 5.2 and obtains

$$RCE = \$10 \text{ million} + \$2.5 \text{ million}(0.391)$$
$$= \$10.9775 \text{ million.} \qquad (5.14)$$

Analyst notes that the binary weighting approach yields a value of about one percent less than the finding of the constant weighting approach in Equation 5.12. Analyst forwards these findings to Upsilon who, because of the nature of the economy, uses the more conservative figure of $11.110 million.

## 5.4
## EXTRINSIC ATTRIBUTE FACTORS

Extrinsic attributes, such as regulatory statutes and climatic conditions, are peripheral to given programs and as such are largely beyond the control of those programs. One of the most difficult problems in program management is dealing with extrinsic attributes, just as dealing with inflation and escalation is one of the most difficult problems in cost estimating.

### ■ 5.4.1 Extrinsic Attribute Checklist

Table 5.13 is a suggested checklist that you can use to derive the **extrinsic attribute factor** (**EAF**). The checklist consists of a series of questions that you can answer with a yes or no. The intent is to reach a conclusion on the EAF contribution to risk exposure in products of interest with a consensus of answers to the questions.

You should find the checklist applicable to a wide range of products with some tailoring. With software products, for example, you would rarely need to consider stockpiles of price-sensitive material and environmentally compatible waste disposal.

## 5.4 Extrinsic Attribute Factors

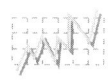

**Table 5.13** *Extrinsic Attribute Factor Checklist*

|  | Yes | No |
|---|---|---|
| 1. Are inflation, the producer price index, and the prime interest rate relatively stable? | | |
| 2. Do contracts contain economic price adjustment clauses? | | |
| 3. Are there adequate stockpiles of price-sensitive material? | | |
| 4. Is waste disposal compatible with environmental regulations? | | |
| 5. Are production processes compatible with industrial safety regulations? | | |
| 6. Can facilities operate under all weather conditions? | | |
| 7. Do personnel have all weather access to facilities? | | |
| 8. Can all weather receipt of supplies and delivery of finished goods be affected? | | |

### ■ 5.4.2 Example of Tailoring Extrinsic Attribute Factor Checklist

Upsilon Publishers requests Analyst to tailor the extrinsic attribute factor checklist in Table 5.13 as an extension to the assignment in the example of Section 5.3.3. Analyst's approach to the additional assignment is to confer with knowledgeable personnel on the applicability of the questions in the checklist with emphasis on whether other questions should be added to the list.

Table 5.14 gives the results of the investigation. Note the decrease in the number of questions and that Analyst has added a question to the beginning of the list.

**Table 5.14** *Tailored EAF Checklist for Tailoring Extrinsic Attribute Checklist Example*

|  | Yes | No |
|---|---|---|
| 1. Is the readership projection adequate for the desired return-on-investment? | | |
| 2. Are inflation, the producer price index, and the prime interest rate relatively stable? | | |
| 3. Are production processes compatible with industrial safety regulations? | | |
| 4. Can facilities operate under all weather conditions? | | |
| 5. Do personnel have all weather access to facilities? | | |
| 6. Can all weather receipt of supplies and delivery of finished goods be affected? | | |

### ■ 5.4.3 Extrinsic Attribute Factor Formulation

The procedure for using the constant weighting and binary weighting approaches in deriving the extrinsic attribute factor is essentially the same as the procedure for deriving the management attribute factor in Table 5.8. The similarity extends to the formulation we use.

**Constant Weighting**

Equation 5.15 is the relationship for deriving values of the extrinsic attributes factor with constant weighting.

$$EAF = 1 - \frac{\Sigma paw}{\Sigma aqw} \tag{5.15}$$

where $\Sigma paw$ denotes sum of positive-answers weights in sequence of questions and $\Sigma aqw$ sum of weights of all questions in sequence.

**Binary Weighting**

Equation 5.16 is the relationship for deriving values of the extrinsic attributes factor with the binary weighting approach.

$$EAF = 1 - \frac{\Sigma edvbna}{\Sigma edvlpn} \tag{5.16}$$

where $\Sigma edvbna$ denotes sum of equivalent decimal values of binary number answers to sequence of questions and $\Sigma edvlpn$ sum of equivalent decimal values of largest possible binary number answers to sequence of questions.

There are two forms of relationships for risk time estimate and risk cost estimate. Again, for estimating realism and credibility, use Equations 5.17 and 5.18, if at all possible.

$$RTE = BTE + RT \cdot EAF \tag{5.17}$$

$$RCE = BCE + RC \cdot EAF \tag{5.18}$$

$$RTE = BTE(1 + EAF) \tag{5.19}$$

$$RCE = BCE(1 + EAF) \tag{5.20}$$

where RTE denotes risk time estimate, BTE baseline time estimate, RT risk time, EAF extrinsic attribute factor, RCE risk cost estimate, BCE baseline cost estimate, and RC risk cost.

### ■ 5.4.4 Example of Composite Effect of MAF and EAF

Upsilon now asks Analyst to estimate the risk exposure in the proposed undertaking from the composite effect of MAF and EAF. Table 5.15 gives the technical approach Analyst follows in carrying out the additional assignment.

Analyst validates that the cost of the proposed undertaking is $10 million. Analyst ensures that the questions are in the proper order in Table 5.14, interviews appropriate personnel, and completes the checklist as given in Table 5.16.

Analyst first applies the constant weighting approach with Equation 5.15. The sum of the weights for questions with positive answers ($\Sigma paw$) is 6 + 4 + 3 + 2 + 1, or 16. The sum of the weights for all the questions ($\Sigma aqw$) is 6 + 5 + 4 + 3 + 2 + 1, or 21.

**Table 5.15** *Technical Approach for Composite Effect of MAF and EAF*

1. Validate the cost of the proposed undertaking.
2. Ensure that the checklist questions in Table 5.14 are in the descending order of importance.
3. Use Table 5.14 as the tailored checklist for extrinsic attribute factor as the basis for interviewing personnel.
4. Use both constant weighting and binary weighting approaches in deriving the value of *EAF*.
5. Using the root-sum-of-squares method combine the values of *MAF* from the example in Section 5.3.3 and *EAF* from Step 4.
6. Calculate risk cost estimates with *MAF* and *EAF* values from Step 5.

## 5.4 Extrinsic Attribute Factors

**Table 5.16** *Completed Intrinsic Attribute Checklist for Composite Effect Example*

|  | Yes | No |
|---|---|---|
| 1. Is the readership projection adequate for the desired return-on-investment? | ✔ |  |
| 2. Are inflation, the producer price index, and the prime interest rate relatively stable? |  | ✔ |
| 3. Are production processes compatible with industrial safety regulations? | ✔ |  |
| 4. Can facilities operate under all weather conditions? | ✔ |  |
| 5. Do personnel have all weather access to facilities? | ✔ |  |
| 6. Can all weather receipt of supplies and delivery of finished goods be affected? | ✔ |  |

Substituting $\Sigma paw = 16$ and $\Sigma aqw$ in Equation 5.15, Analyst obtains

$$EAF = 1 - \frac{16}{21}$$
$$= 0.238. \quad (5.21)$$

Analyst next applies the binary weighting approach and obtains from Table 5.10 the equivalent decimal value of 63 for the largest possible binary number which can be formed with a 6-bit number. The binary number for the positive answers in Table 5.16 is 101111. Its equivalent decimal value is $1 \cdot 2^5 + 0 \cdot 2^4 + 1 \cdot 2^3 + 1 \cdot 2^2 + 1 \cdot 2^1 + 1 \cdot 2^0$, or 47.

Substituting $\Sigma edvbna = 47$ and $\Sigma edvlpn = 63$ in Equation 5.16, Analyst obtains

$$EAF = 1 - \frac{47}{63}$$
$$= 0.254. \quad (5.22)$$

Table 5.17 summarizes the MAF and EAF findings from the examples of Sections 5.3.3 and 5.4.2. Note that the value of MAF is slightly more conservative (*i.e.*, greater values) with the constant weighting approach than from the binary weighting approach and that the reverse is true for the values of EAF.

**Table 5.17** *Summary of Findings for Examples of Sections 5.3.3 and 5.4.2*

|  | **Management Attribute Factor** | **Extrinsic Attribute Factor** |
|---|---|---|
| Constant Weighting | 0.444 | 0.238 |
| Binary Weighting | 0.391 | 0.254 |

Analyst now combines the values of MAF and EAF by the method of **root-sum-of-squares** (**RSS**) because of the independent relationship between these factors. For values from the constant weighting approach, Analyst obtains

$$RSS = \sqrt{(0.444)^2 = (0.238)^2}$$
$$= 0.504. \quad (5.23)$$

With values from the binary weighting approach, Analyst obtains

$$RSS = \sqrt{(0.391)^2 = (0.254)^2}$$

$$= 0.466. \tag{5.24}$$

For calculating the risk cost estimate (RCE) in the constant weighting approach, Analyst substitutes *BCE* = $10 million, *RC* = $2.5 million, *RSS* = 0.504 in place of *RDF* in Equation 5.2 and obtains

$$RCE = \$10 \text{ million} + \$2.5 \text{ million}(0.504)$$

$$= \$11.260 \text{ million}. \tag{5.25}$$

For calculating *RCE* in the binary approach, Analyst substitutes *BCE* = $10 million, *RC* = $2.5 million, and *RSS* = 0.466 in place of 0.504 in Equation 5.24 and obtains

$$RCE = \$10 \text{ million} + \$2.5 \text{ million}(0.466)$$

$$= \$11.165 \text{ million}. \tag{5.26}$$

Analyst forwards these findings to Upsilon. Because of the nature of the economy, the publisher uses the greater value in its deliberations.

# 5.5
# HARDWARE FACTORS

Gauging the risk exposure in developing or producing products requires the consideration of certain attributes which are specific to the products of interest. These attributes are the maturity, quality, complexity, and concurrency of product or process product designs.

These attributes vary among hardware, software, and service products, although there is similarity among them. For example, the attribute *concurrency* relates to the concurrent performance of tasks in the design process, and it is obvious that tasks differ somewhat among hardware, software, and service products.

Product maturity and process maturity are first-order attributes because of the influence they exert on the contribution to risk exposure by the other attributes of quality, complexity, and concurrency. The latter are second-order attributes.

The relationship between the first-order and second-order factors is described by the $k$-factor. The $k$-factor is equated to the product or process maturity factor as appropriate. The rationale is that if you have developed or produced certain products before, then you can develop or produce similar products with little risk exposure irrespective of the magnitude of any second-order factor such as quality, complexity, or concurrency. Remember, however, that product or process maturity alone does not connote any particular merit for the product or the process.

### ■ 5.5.1 Hardware Product Maturity Factor

**Hardware product maturity factor** (**PRODMF**) for hardware products is an inverse measure of how experienced you are in the approach for developing the particular product of interest. It is not a measure of how far along the actual development of the specific product has progressed.

## 5.5 Hardware Factors

The current status of product design maturity is the measure of PRODMF. The more mature the design, the smaller is the value of PRODMF. By the same token, PRODMF is a direct measure of the probability of occurrence of a risk element during development. The greater the value of PRODMF, the greater the probability that risk time and risk cost will be expended.

Table 5.18 gives suggested schema for values of PRODMF that range from 0 to 1.0. If PRODMF were to equal 0, there would be no risk exposure (*i.e.*, zero probability of facing risk recovery and the expenditure of additional time or cost) in the course of product development.

On the other hand, if PRODMF were to equal 1.0, there would be maximum risk exposure in the product development. We would be facing the need for risk recovery involving the expenditure of additional time and cost (*i.e.*, risk time and risk cost).

*Table 5.18*  Hardware Product Maturity Factors

| PRODMF | Level of Design Approach Maturity |
|---|---|
| 0.0 | Similar production first article tested successfully. |
| 0.1 | Similar production first article produced. |
| 0.2 | Similar prototype tested successfully. |
| 0.3 | Similar prototype fabricated. |
| 0.4 | Similar brassboard tested successfully. |
| 0.5 | Similar brassboard fabricated. |
| 0.6 | Similar breadboard tested successfully. |
| 0.7 | Similar breadboard fabricated. |
| 0.8 | Similar functional design completed. |
| 0.9 | Similar functional design validated by analysis. |
| 1.0 | No similar design approach used. |

PRODMF: Product design maturity factor.
First article: First item produced and qualified with validated technical data package and certified production tooling.
Prototype: Item produced and qualified with development technical data package and development tooling.
Brassboard: Item identical in form, fit, and function to its prototype counterpart but has not been qualified.
Breadboard: Item identical to prototype item only in function.

As stated, there are two forms of relationships you can use to derive risk time and cost estimates. Again, we recommend Equations 5.27 and 5.28 over Equations 5.29 and 5.30 in the interest of realism and credibility.

$$RTE = BTE + RT \cdot PRODMF \tag{5.27}$$

$$RCE = BCE + RC \cdot PRODMF \tag{5.28}$$

where RTE denotes risk time estimate, BTE baseline time estimate, RT risk time, PRODMF product maturity factor, RCE risk cost estimate, BCE baseline cost estimate, and RC risk cost.

With the exception of the value of PRODMF, which is probabilistic, you can use deterministic or probabilistic values in Equations 5.27 and 5.28. Using deterministic values, these equations yield deterministic-deterministic-probabilistic solutions.

Equations 5.29 and 5.30 are alternative relationships for estimating the measures of risk exposure. You should use these equations only when you are building from probabilistic estimates of baseline time, and cost and estimates of risk time and risk cost are unavailable.

$$RTE = BTE(1 + PRODMF) \tag{5.29}$$

$$RCE = BCE(1 + PRODMF) \tag{5.30}$$

Note that the $k$-factor does not appear in any of the foregoing relationships because PRODMF is a first-order risk determinant factor. The $k$-factor does appear, however, when the other product risk determinant factors are combined with PRODMF for composite values.

### ■ 5.5.2 Example of Hardware Product Maturity Factor

Rho Corporation has tested successfully a development product in brassboard form. Rho's comptroller believes that the company needs an additional expenditure of twenty-four months and $1.350 million to bring the product to the marketplace. Rho's designers believe that the risk exposure in one of the product's assemblies may cause the expenditure of six months on corrective action at a cost of $375,000.

The comptroller retains Analyst to determine the magnitude of risk exposure on the basis of the designers' allegations. Table 5.19 gives the technical approach Analyst follows in carrying out the assignment.

**Table 5.19**  *Technical Approach for Hardware Product Maturity Factor Example*

| |
|---|
| 1. Validate the baseline time estimate, baseline cost estimate, risk time, and risk cost.
2. Obtain the value of product maturity factor for a product which has been tested successfully in brassboard form from Table 5.18.
3. Use Equations 5.27 and 5.28 to derive the risk time estimate and risk cost estimate.
4. Calculate the additional indirect cost due to the extended time period for product development.
5. Calculate the total risk cost estimate. |

Analyst validates that $BTE = 24$ months, $RT = 6$ months, $BCE = \$1.35$ million, and $RC = \$0.375$ million. From Table 5.18, Analyst obtains $PRODMF = 0.4$ for a product which has been tested successfully in brassboard form.

Substituting these values in Equations 5.27 and 5.28, Analyst obtains:

$$RTE = 24 \text{ months} + 6 \text{ months}(0.40)$$

$$= 26.4 \text{ months} \tag{5.31}$$

$$RCE = \$1,350,000 + \$375,000(0.40)$$

$$= \$1,500,000. \tag{5.32}$$

The extended program duration of (26.4 − 24), or 2.4 months, adds the additional indirect cost to the development. Using the indirect cost rate of $75,000 per month provided by the comptroller, Analyst obtains the additional indirect cost of ($75,000 per month)(2.4 months), or $180,000. Adding $180,000 to the $1.500 million from Equation 5.32 yields $RCE = \$1.680$ million.

## 5.5 Hardware Factors

Analyst points out to the Rho Corporation comptroller that the additional indirect cost of $180,000 is greater than the additional direct cost of $150,000. Always consider elements of indirect cost as well as direct cost in your deliberations.

### ■ 5.5.3 Hardware Product Quality Factor

Quality is many things to many people, ranging from the popular perception of high-class products to the mathematically expressed notion in Reference 1 that lack of quality is a loss to society.

From the viewpoint of customers and users, product quality is defined by its performance, reliability, and maintainability. The rapid growth over the past few years of quality function deployment and total quality management as management techniques attests to the concern of producers and suppliers for the needs and perspectives of customers and users. [2]

In the domain of technical risk management, however, the concern for quality centers about the potential need for corrective action in the course of developing and producing the product. We define **hardware product quality factor** (**PRODQF**) as an inverse measure of the producibility, reliability, and testability of the product of interest. By the same token, it is a direct measure of risk exposure in the attribute of product quality.

Ordinarily, we view producibility as the ease in producing a given product. Producibility is a product attribute, however, that can serve as a measure of the quality of the product. Reliability is a product attribute that can serve as the measure of corrective actions which may be needed during the development of the product. Testability is a product attribute that can serve as the measure of ease in isolating failures for corrective action.

Tables 5.20, 5.21, and 5.22 are the checklists for the attributes of producibility, reliability, and testability. The tables list the sequences of questions in a suggested order of importance that you can tailor to products of interest.

*Table 5.20* *Producibility Checklist [1]*

|  | Yes | No |
|---|---|---|
| 1. Are specifications and standards consistent with the intended product environment? | | |
| 2. Does the design use the minimum possible number of different parts? | | |
| 3. Are nonstandard parts avoided? | | |
| 4. Is the design standardized to the proper degree? | | |
| 5. Have alternate design concepts been considered and the most producible one selected? | | |
| 6. Is the design within the manufacturing state-of-the-art? | | |
| 7. Does the design avoid the use of proprietary items or processes? | | |
| 8. Is the design simplified to the extent possible? | | |
| 9. Are unnecessary functions eliminated from the design? | | |
| 10. Does the design accommodate parts with slight differences as if they were identical? | | |
| 11. Are tolerances allocated properly? | | |

Adapted by courtesy of the Defense Systems Management College, Fort Belvoir, Virginia, from DSMC, *Test and Evaluation Management Guide*, March 1988.

**Table 5.21**  *Reliability Checklist [1]*

|  | Yes | No |
|---|---|---|
| 1. Has product reliability requirement been allocated to lower levels in the product? | | |
| 2. Is electronic stress screening used on all active components? | | |
| 3. Have parts been derated sufficiently to provide margin over design limits? | | |
| 4. Have parts control and standardization reduced the different number of parts to a minimum? | | |
| 5. Has the design complexity been reduced by using a minimum number of parts? | | |
| 6. Have thermal stresses been reduced by lowering component and terminal temperatures? | | |
| 7. Has redundancy been provided to offset component failures? | | |

Adapted by permission of the Defense Systems Management College, Fort Belvoir, Virginia, from DSMC, *Test and Evaluation Management Guide*, March 1988.

The relationship between hardware product quality factor (PRODQF) and the consensus of answers to questions on producibility, reliability, and testability is

$$PRODQF = PRT \oplus PRT' \oplus PR'T \oplus PR'T'$$
$$\oplus P'RT \oplus P'RT' \oplus P'R'T \oplus P'R'T' \qquad (5.33)$$

where $P$ denotes there is producibility, $P'$ there is not producibility, $R$ there is reliability, $R'$ there is not reliability, $T$ there is testability, and $T'$ there is not testability.

The symbol $\oplus$ in Equation 5.33 is the exclusive-OR logical function denoting that only one state at a time can exist. Equation 5.33 is the logical statement of PRODQF as we defined it.

**Table 5.22**  *Testability Checklist [2]*

|  | Yes | No |
|---|---|---|
| 1. Does the mechanical design provide a standard grid layout for component identification? | | |
| 2. Is enough space provided between components for testing? | | |
| 3. Are components oriented in the same direction? | | |
| 4. Are connector pins provided for test stimuli? | | |
| 5. Is the number of part types the minimum possible? | | |
| 6. Is built-in-test, *BIT*, incorporated in the design? | | |
| 7. Are program test sets available for the *BIT*? | | |
| 8. Can details be tested without integration into the subassembly level? | | |
| 9. Can subassemblies be tested without integration into the assembly level? | | |
| 10. Can assemblies be tested without integration into the product level? | | |
| 11. Can subsystems be tested without being integrated into the system level? | | |

Adapted by courtesy of the U.S. Department of Defense from MIL-STD-2165, *Military Standard-Testability Program for Electronic Systems and Equipments*, 1985.

## 5.5 Hardware Factors

> *PRODQF* exclusively equals producibility and reliability and testability, or exclusively equals producibility and reliability and not testability, or exclusively equals producibility and not reliability and testability, or exclusively equals producibility and not reliability and not testability, or exclusively equals not producibility and reliability and testability, or exclusively equals not producibility and reliability and not testability, or exclusively equals not producibility and not reliability and testability, or exclusively equals not producibility and not reliability and not testability.
>
> **Logical statement of product quality factor**

The notations *P*, *R*, and *T* are logical 1's, whereas the notations *P'*, *R'*, and *T'* are logical 0's. The 1's and 0's signify that the corresponding attribute either exists or does not exist. Table 5.23 gives the **truth table** for the logical states in Equation 5.33. Since there are three parameters (*i.e.*, producibility, reliability, and testability), eight 3-bit binary words can be formed.

Were you to reach the conclusion that a certain product is neither producible, reliable, nor testable (*i.e.*, *P'R'T'*), then the metric for PRODQF would be State 0. If the product were reliable and testable, but not producible (*i.e.*, *P'RT*), the metric would be State 3. If the product were producible, reliable, and testable (*i.e.*, *PRT*), the metric would be State 7.

*Table 5.23*   *Truth Table for Equation 5.33*

| State | Producibility | Reliability | Testability |
|-------|---------------|-------------|-------------|
| 0 | 0 | 0 | 0 |
| 1 | 0 | 0 | 1 |
| 2 | 0 | 1 | 0 |
| 3 | 0 | 1 | 1 |
| 4 | 1 | 0 | 0 |
| 5 | 1 | 0 | 1 |
| 6 | 1 | 1 | 0 |
| 7 | 1 | 1 | 1 |

The foregoing approach places the importance of producibility before reliability and testability, and the importance of reliability before testability. You can modify the relative importance by interchanging the positions of producibility, reliability, and testability in Table 5.23.

Table 5.24 gives the correlation between product quality states and values of PRODQF. Again, the assignments are suggestions that you can tailor as desired, although they are based on many years of experience.

*Table 5.24*   *Hardware Product Quality Factors*

| Factor | Product Quality State |
|--------|----------------------|
| 0 | 7 |
| 0.15 | 6 |
| 0.30 | 5 |
| 0.45 | 4 |
| 0.60 | 3 |
| 0.75 | 2 |
| 0.90 | 1 |
| 1.00 | 0 |

PRODQF equals 1.0 for products that are in product Quality State 0 and are neither producible, reliable, nor testable ($P'R'T'$). PRODQF equals 0 for products that are in Product Quality State 0 and are producible, reliable, and testable ($PRT$).

The binary weighting is the logical approach to use for deriving values of PRODQF. As stated previously, you begin by writing binary numbers that correspond to the answers to checklist questions. Next, you construct ratios of the binary numbers for the answers received to the binary number for all possible yes answers. The ratios are the values of PRODQF.

Consider the series of eleven, seven, and eleven questions in Tables 5.20, 5.21, and 5.22. All yes answers would be expressed by the following binary numbers:

Table 5.20: 11111111111

Table 5.21: 1111111

Table 5.22: 11111111111.

The equivalent decimal value of the maximum value of the two 11-bit binary words is $1 \cdot 2^{10} + 1 \cdot 2^9 + 1 \cdot 2^8 + 1 \cdot 2^7 + 1 \cdot 2^6 + 1 \cdot 2^5 + 1 \cdot 2^4 + 1 \cdot 2^3 + 1 \cdot 2^2 + 1 \cdot 2^1 + 1 \cdot 2^0$, or 2047. The equivalent decimal value of the 7-bit binary word is $1 \cdot 2^6 + 1 \cdot 2^5 + 1 \cdot 2^4 + 1 \cdot 2^3 + 1 \cdot 2^2 + 1 \cdot 2^1 + 1 \cdot 2^0$, or 127. The maximum possible composite equivalent decimal value in the dependent case is 2047 + 127 + 2047, or 4221.

Now, assume the answers no, yes, yes, yes, yes, yes, yes, yes, yes, yes, yes to the questions in Table 5.20. The binary number is 01111111111. Also, assume the answers no, no, yes, yes, yes, yes, yes to the questions in Table 5.21. The binary number is 0011111. Finally, assume the answers no, no, no, yes, no, no, yes, yes, yes, no, no to the questions in Table 5.22. The binary number is 00010011100.

For the binary number 01111111111, the equivalent decimal value is $0 \cdot 2^{10} + 1 \cdot 2^9 + 1 \cdot 2^8 + 1 \cdot 2^7 + 1 \cdot 2^6 + 1 \cdot 2^5 + 1 \cdot 2^4 + 1 \cdot 2^3 + 1 \cdot 2^2 + 1 \cdot 2^1 + 1 \cdot 2^0$, or 1023. For the binary number 0011111, the equivalent decimal number is $0 \cdot 2^6 + 0 \cdot 2^5 + 1 \cdot 2^4 + 1 \cdot 2^3 + 1 \cdot 2^2 + 1 \cdot 2^1 + 1 \cdot 2^0$, or 31. For the binary number 00010011100, the equivalent decimal value is $0 \cdot 2^{10} + 0 \cdot 2^9 + 0 \cdot 2^8 + 1 \cdot 2^7 + 0 \cdot 2^6 + 0 \cdot 2^5 + 1 \cdot 2^4 + 1 \cdot 2^3 + 1 \cdot 2^2 + 0 \cdot 2^1 + 0 \cdot 2^0$, or 156.

The composite equivalent decimal value for the foregoing values of 1023, 31, and 156 depends on the assumption of a dependent or independent relationship for producibility, reliability, and testability. In the dependent case, the composite equivalent decimal value is simply the arithmetic sum of the individual equivalent decimal values for 1023 + 31 + 156, or 1210.

Equation 5.34 gives the value of PRODQF for the dependent case.

$$PRODQF = \frac{4{,}221 - 1{,}210}{4{,}221}$$

$$= 0.713. \qquad (5.34)$$

In the independent case, the composite equivalent decimal value is the root-sum-of-squares (RSS) of the individual decimal values 1023, 31, and 255. Equation 5.35 gives the solution.

$$RSS = \sqrt{1{,}023^2 + 31^2 + 156^2}$$

$$= 1{,}035. \qquad (5.35)$$

## 5.5 Hardware Factors

The maximum possible composite equivalent decimal value is

$$RSS = \sqrt{2{,}047^2 + 127^2 + 2{,}047^2}$$
$$= 2{,}895. \qquad (5.36)$$

Equation 5.37 gives the value of PRODQF for the independent case. The constant weight and binary weighting approaches give approximately the same answer.

$$PRODQF = \frac{2{,}898 - 1{,}035}{2{,}898}$$
$$= 0.643. \qquad (5.37)$$

### ■ 5.5.4 Example of Hardware Product Quality Factor

Zeta Industries questions the hardware product quality of a product under development on the basis of the completed checklists in Tables 5.25, 5.26, and 5.27. Zeta requests Analyst to derive the value of PRODQF for the particular product. Table 5.28 gives the technical approach followed by Analyst in carrying out the assignment on the basis of the client's direction.

Analyst uses Tables 5.25, 5.26, and 5.27 to score producibility, reliability, and testability. Then, Analyst goes through three iterations in deriving PRODQF using the simple majority consensus, weighted consensus, and binary weighting.

The majority of answers are no in Table 5.25, yes in Table 5.26, and no in Table 5.27. The binary number for producibility, reliability, and testability is therefore 010 that equates to the equivalent decimal value 2.

Analyst looks up PRODQF for State 2 in Table 5.24 and obtains the value 0.75. Analyst records the value 0.75 for subsequent use, noting that the simple majority approach makes no allowance for dependent or independent relationship.

***Table 5.25*** *Producibility Checklist for Hardware Product Quality Factor Example*

| | Yes | No |
|---|---|---|
| 1. Are specifications and standards consistent with the intended product environment? | ✔ | |
| 2. Does the design use the minimum possible number of different parts? | | ✔ |
| 3. Are nonstandard parts avoided? | | ✔ |
| 4. Is the design standardized to the proper degree? | | ✔ |
| 5. Have alternate design concepts been considered and the most producible one selected? | | ✔ |
| 6. Is the design within the manufacturing state-of-the-art? | | ✔ |
| 7. Does the design avoid the use of proprietary items or processes? | ✔ | |
| 8. Is the design simplified to the extent possible? | | ✔ |
| 9. Are unnecessary functions eliminated from the design? | | ✔ |
| 10. Does the design accommodate parts with slight differences as if they were identical? | ✔ | |
| 11. Are tolerances allocated properly? | ✔ | |

**Table 5.26** *Reliability Checklist for Hardware Product Quality Factor Example*

|  | Yes | No |
|---|---|---|
| 1. Has product reliability requirement been allocated to lower levels in the product? | ✔ |  |
| 2. Is electronic stress screening used on all active components? |  | ✔ |
| 3. Have parts been derated sufficiently to provide margin over design limits? | ✔ |  |
| 4. Have parts control and standardization reduced the different number of parts to a minimum? |  | ✔ |
| 5. Has the design complexity been reduced by using a minimum number of parts? |  | ✔ |
| 6. Have thermal stresses been reduced by lowering component and terminal temperatures? | ✔ |  |
| 7. Has redundancy been provided to offset component failures? |  | ✔ |

**Table 5.27** *Testability Checklist for Hardware Product Quality Factor Example*

|  | Yes | No |
|---|---|---|
| 1. Does the mechanical design provide a standard grid layout for component identification? |  | ✔ |
| 2. Is enough space provided between components for testing? | ✔ |  |
| 3. Are components oriented in the same direction? |  | ✔ |
| 4. Are connector pins provided for test stimuli? | ✔ |  |
| 5. Is the number of part types the minimum possible? |  | ✔ |
| 6. Is built-in-test, *BIT,* incorporated in the design? | ✔ |  |
| 7. Are program test sets available for the *BIT*? |  | ✔ |
| 8. Can details be tested without integration into the subassembly level? | ✔ |  |
| 9. Can subassemblies be tested without integration into the assembly level? |  | ✔ |
| 10. Can assemblies be tested without integration into the product level? |  | ✔ |
| 11. Can subsystems be tested without being integrated into the system level? |  | ✔ |

**Table 5.28** *Technical Approach for Hardware Product Quality Factor Example*

1. Derive the simple majority consensus for the answers to checklist questions in Tables 5.25, 5.26, and 5.27.
2. Determine the logical state for producibility, reliability, and testability.
3. Look up simple majority PRODQF for logical state from Step 2 in Table 5.24.
4. Weight the checklist questions in the reverse order of their listing for weighted consensus approach.
5. Sum weighted values of yes answers and accept consensus yes for summed weighted values greater than one-half of maximum possible summed weighted values.
6. Derive constant-weighting composite value of PRODQF.
7. Write binary numbers that correspond to the answers to checklist questions in Tables 5.25, 5.26, and 5.27.
8. Calculate the equivalent decimal values of the binary numbers in Step 7.
9. Derive binary-weighting composite value of PRODQF.

## 5.5 Hardware Factors

Analyst weights the 11 questions in the producibility checklist of Table 5.25: Question 1 - 11; Question 2 - 10; Question 3 - 9; Question 4 - 8; Question 5 - 7; Question 6 - 6; Question 7 - 5; Question 8 - 4; Question 9 - 3; Question 10 - 2; and Question 11 - 1. The sum of the weighted values for all the questions is 11 + 10 + 9 + 8 + 7 + 6 + 5 + 4 + 3 + 2 + 1, or 66.

The weighted values of the yes answers in the producibility checklist of Table 5.25 are: Question 1 - 11; Question 7 - 5; Question 10 - 2; and Question 11 - 1. The sum of the weighted values for yes answers is 11 + 5 + 2 + 1, or 19.

Next, Analyst weights the seven questions in the reliability checklist of Table 5.26: Question 1 - 7; Question 2 - 6; Question 3 - 5; Question 4 - 4; Question 5 - 3; Question 6 - 2; and Question 7 - 1. The sum of the weighted values for all the questions is 7 + 6 + 5 + 4 + 3 + 2 + 1, or 28.

The weighted values of the yes answers in the reliability checklist of Table 5.26 are: Question 1- 7; Question 3 - 5; Question 6 - 2; and Question 7 - 1. The sum of the weighted values for yes answers is 7 + 5 + 2 + 1, or 15.

The weights of the 11 questions in the testability checklist of Table 5.27 are the same as the 11 questions in the producibility checklist of Table 5.25. The sum of the weighted values for all the questions is 11 + 10 + 9 + 8 + 7 + 6 + 5 + 4 + 3 + 2 + 1, or 66.

The weighted values of the yes answers in the testability checklist of Table 5.27 are: Question 2 - 10; Question 4 - 8; Question 6 - 6; and Question 8 - 4. The sum of the weighted values for yes answers is 10 + 8 + 6 + 4, or 28.

Analyst first assumes a dependent relationship for producibility, reliability, and testability. As stated, the composite value of the weights of yes answers, in the dependent case, is simply the arithmetic sum of the individual values, 19 + 15 + 28, or 62.

The maximum possible composite value for producibility, reliability, and testability is 66 + 28 + 66, or 160.

Therefore, the value of hardware PRODQF in the dependent case is

$$PRDOQF = 1 - \frac{160 - 62}{160}$$
$$= 0.388. \qquad (5.38)$$

Analyst records this value for subsequent use; noting the improvement over the hardware PRODQF value of 0.75 obtained with the simple majority approach. In the independent case, the composite value is the root-sum-of-squares (RSS) of the individual decimal values 19, 15, and 28, as given by

$$RSS = \sqrt{19^2 + 15^2 + 28^2}$$
$$= 37.014. \qquad (5.39)$$

The maximum possible composite equivalent decimal value is

$$RSS = \sqrt{66^2 + 28^2 + 66^2}$$
$$= 97.447. \qquad (5.40)$$

Therefore, the value of hardware PRODCF in the independent case is

$$PRODQF = 1 - \frac{97.447 - 37.014}{97.447}$$
$$= 0.380. \qquad (5.41)$$

The binary numbers for the three sequences of answers are 100000110011, 1010011, and 01010101000. The equivalent decimal value of the binary number for the sequence of questions in the producibility checklist of Table 5.25 is $1 \cdot 2^{10} + 0 \cdot 2^9 + 0 \cdot 2^8 + 0 \cdot 2^7 + 0 \cdot 2^6 + 0 \cdot 2^5 + 1 \cdot 2^4 + 0 \cdot 2^3 + 0 \cdot 2^2 + 1 \cdot 2^1 + 1 \cdot 2^0$ for $1024 + 16 + 2$, or 1,042.

The equivalent decimal value of the binary number for the sequence of questions in the reliability checklist of Table 5.26 is $1 \cdot 2^6 + 0 \cdot 2^5 + 1 \cdot 2^4 + 0 \cdot 2^3 + 0 \cdot 2^2 + 1 \cdot 2^1 + 1 \cdot 2^0$, for $64 + 16 + 2 + 1$, or 83.

The equivalent decimal value of the binary number for the sequence of questions in the testability checklist of Table 5.27 is $0 \cdot 2^{10} + 1 \cdot 2^9 + 0 \cdot 2^8 + 1 \cdot 2^7 + 0 \cdot 2^6 + 1 \cdot 2^5 + 0 \cdot 2^4 + 1 \cdot 2^3 + 0 \cdot 2^2 + 0 \cdot 2^1 + 0 \cdot 2^0$, for $512 + 128 + 32 + 8$, or 680.

Analyst assumes a dependent relationship for producibility, reliability, and testability. As stated, the composite equivalent decimal value of the binary answers in the dependent case is simply the arithmetic sum, for $1,042 + 83 + 680$, or 1,805. The maximum possible composite equivalent decimal value is $2,047 + 127 + 2,047$, or 4,221.

Therefore, the value of PRODQF for the dependent relationship is

$$PRODQF = 1 - \frac{4,221 - 1,805}{4,221}$$

$$= 0.428. \tag{5.42}$$

In the independent case, the composite equivalent decimal value is the root-sum-of-squares of the individual decimal values 19, 15, and 28, as given by

$$RSS = \sqrt{1,042^2 + 83^2 + 680^2}$$

$$= 1,247.018. \tag{5.43}$$

The maximum possible composite equivalent decimal value is

$$RSS = \sqrt{2,047^2 + 127^2 + 2,047^2}$$

$$= 2,897.680. \tag{5.44}$$

Therefore, the value of PRODCF for the independent relationship is

$$PRODQF = 1 - \frac{2,897.680 - 1,247.018}{2,897.680}$$

$$= 0.441. \tag{5.45}$$

Table 5.29 gives the calculated values of PRODQF. Pressed by the Zeta Industries, Analyst allows that the more realistic value of PRODQF is probably 0.559, derived from binary weighting with an assumption of independent relationship.

*Table 5.29*   *Comparative Values of Hardware Product Quality Factor Example*

| Approach | Dependent Case | Independent Case |
|---|---|---|
| Simple Majority | 0.750 | 0.750 |
| Constant Weighting | 0.606 | 0.615 |
| Binary Weighting | 0.563 | 0.559 |

## 5.5 Hardware Factors

### ■ 5.5.5 Hardware Product Complexity Factor

**Hardware product complexity factor** (**PRODCF**) is an inverse measure of the complexity of product design. By the same token, PRODCF is a direct measure of the risk exposure in the development of the particular design.

We use the complexity of the **generation breakdown** (**GB**) for the product of interest to rate PRODCF. Figure 5.3 illustrates the GB in conceptual form. The key properties of the GB are the number of levels and the span. The span is the number of elements at the lowest level of the GB.

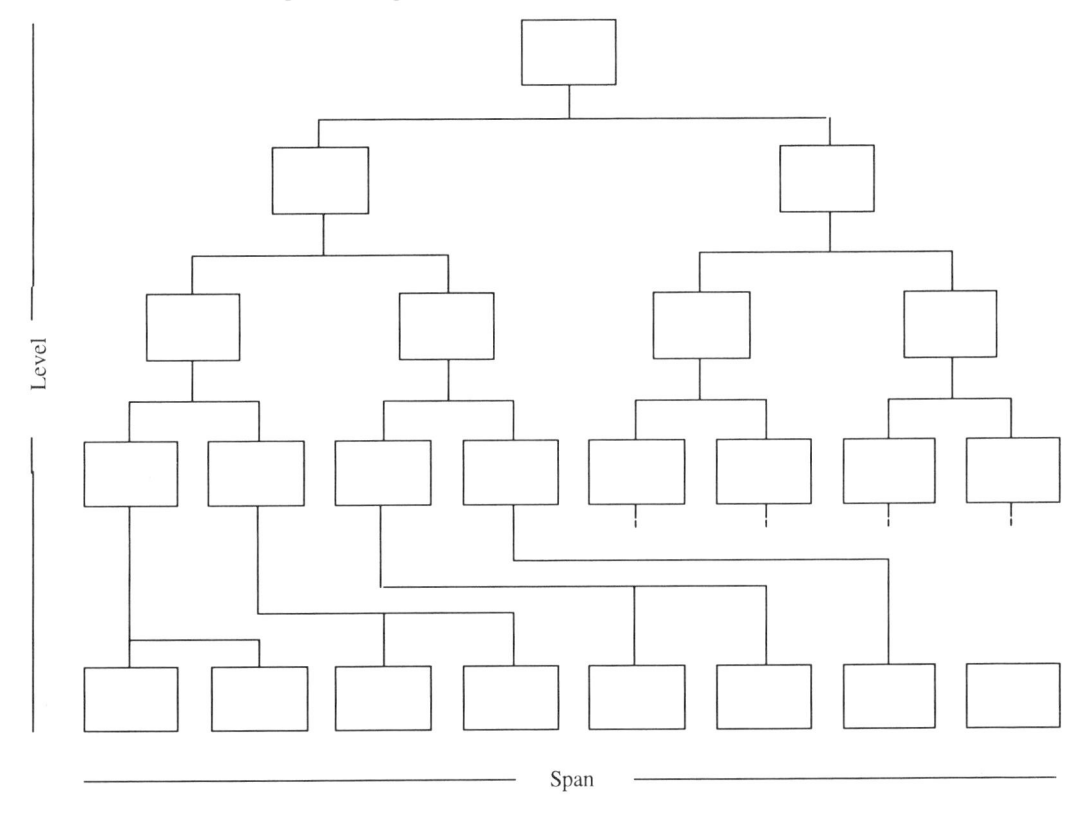

**Figure 5.3** Generation Breakdown in Conceptual Form

The product of the number of levels and the span in a given GB is the generation breakdown index (GBI). The value of the GBI in Figure 5.3 is (5)(16), or 80 (*n.b.*, each dotted line in the illustration goes to two elements). The value of 80 is a small value of GBI, denoting little product design complexity. Typical values of GBI for high-technology products range as high as 10,000 and greater.

Table 5.30 gives a suggested schema for rating PRODCF. The value of PRODCF is 0.1 for a product with a GBI of 1,000. PRODCF = 1.0 for GBI = 10,000.

A product with ten levels and a span of 120 in its GB has a GBI of (8)(120), or 1,200. In accordance with Table 5.30, the value of PRODCF would be little greater than 0.1. You can determine the precise value by interpolation. In this case, PRODCF equals $0.1 + 0.1(200 \div 1,000)$, or 0.12.

**Table 5.30** *Hardware Product Complexity Factor*

| Factor | GBI | Factor | GBI |
|---|---|---|---|
| 0.1 | 1,000 | 0.6 | 6,000 |
| 0.2 | 2,000 | 0.7 | 7,000 |
| 0.3 | 3,000 | 0.8 | 8,000 |
| 0.4 | 4,000 | 0.9 | 9,000 |
| 0.5 | 5,000 | 1.0 | 10,000 |

GBI: Generation breakdown index.

### ■ 5.5.6 Example of Hardware Product Complexity Factor

The Omega Organization wishes to sponsor the development of a primary time standard by one of its subsidiary companies. At Omega's request, the subsidiary describes the risk exposure for the development in terms of a risk cost (RC) of $150,000 on top of a baseline cost estimate (BCE) of $1.5 million.

The estimated product maturity factor is 0.50 and the product quality factor is 0.25. The generation breakdown for the proposed product has 11 levels and a span of 785.

Omega retains Analyst to estimate the composite risk determinant factor based on PRODMF, PRODQF, and PRODCF with the assumption of an independent relationship for these factors. Table 5.31 gives the technical approach Analyst follows in carrying out the assignment.

**Table 5.31** *Technical Approach for Hardware PRODMF, PRODQF, and PRODCF Example*

1. Derive generation breakdown index for proposed product.
2. Determine product complexity factor using Table 5.30.
3. Calculate composite risk determinant factor assuming independent relationships for individual risk determinant factors.
4. Derive risk cost estimate for proposed product.

The GBI equals the product of the number of levels and the span of the generation breakdown. For the proposed product, the value of the GBI is (11)(785), or 8,635.

From Table 5.30, Analyst obtains the PRODCF values of 0.8 and 0.9 for GBI values of 8,000 and 9,000. By interpolation, Analyst obtains $0.8 + 0.1(635 \div 1,000)$, or 0.8635 as the value of PRODCF for GBI = 8,635.

PRODMF is the dominating risk determinant factor and Analyst equates the $k$-factor to the value of PRODMF, or 0.50. The resultant factored values are

$$PRODCF = (0.50)(0.8635), \text{ or } 0.432$$

$$PRODQF = (0.50)(0.25) = 0.125.$$

Because of the assumption of an independent relationship, Analyst uses the method of root-sum-of-squares to derive the composite risk determinant factor (CRDF).

## 5.5 Hardware Factors

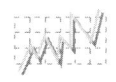

For $PRODMF = 0.50$, $PRODQF = 0.125$, and $PRODCF = 0.432$, Analyst obtains

$$RSS = \sqrt{0.50^2 + 0.125^2 + 0.432^2}$$
$$= 0.677. \qquad (5.46)$$

Substituting $BCE = \$1.5$ million, $RC = \$150,000$, and $CRDF = 0.677$ in Equation 5.2, Analyst obtains

$$RCE = \$1,500,000 + \$150,000(0.677)$$
$$= \$1,601,550. \qquad (5.47)$$

Analyst provides these findings to the Omega Organization, who elects to sponsor the development.

### ■ 5.5.7 Hardware Product Concurrency Factor

Concurrency is the degree to which there is overlap among activities which are dependent upon each other and which, as a consequence, may contribute to risk exposure. Figure 5.4 illustrates concurrency of various degrees between the two hypothetical development tasks, j and i.

Task j is the independent task and Task i the dependent one. The degree of concurrency ranges from 0 percent to 100 percent, the former being favorable to risk-free undertakings, the latter being conducive to high-risk ventures.

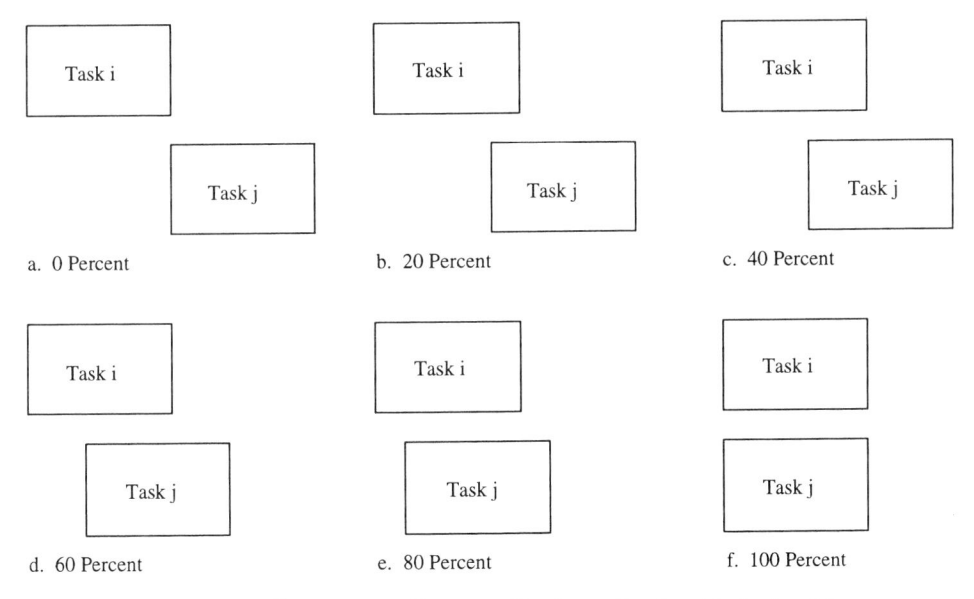

**Figure 5.4** Concurrency Between Hardware Product Tasks j and i

**Concurrency** has three components with respect to hardware products: concurrency in product development tasks; concurrency in product process tasks; and concurrency among product development tasks and product process tasks.

The risk exposure is greater in concurrency among product development tasks and product process tasks than in concurrency that is confined to product development tasks or product process tasks.

**Hardware product concurrency factor (PRODYF)** is an inverse measure of the degree of overlap among tasks which are dependent upon each other in product development. By the same token, PRODYF is a direct measure of risk exposure as a function of concurrency among tasks which are dependent on each other.

We suggest a simple, but realistic, rating schema for overlapping product development tasks. The decimal fraction of overlap serves as the value of PRODYF. Table 5.32 summarizes this schema.

*Table 5.32* Hardware Product Concurrency Factor

| Factor | Overlap | Factor | Overlap |
|--------|---------|--------|---------|
| 0      | 0       | 0.6    | 0.6     |
| 0.1    | 0.1     | 0.7    | 0.7     |
| 0.2    | 0.2     | 0.8    | 0.8     |
| 0.3    | 0.3     | 0.9    | 0.9     |
| 0.4    | 0.4     | 1.0    | 1.0     |
| 0.5    | 0.5     |        |         |

For 0 percent overlap of Tasks j and i, the decimal fraction is 0 and PRODYF equals 0. For 50 percent overlap of the tasks, the decimal fraction is 0.5 and PRODYF equals 0.5. For 100 percent overlap of the tasks, the decimal fraction is 0 and PRODYF equals 0. The greater the value of PRODYF, the greater the risk exposure due to concurrency of dependent tasks.

### ■ 5.5.8 Example of Expanded Hardware Product Concurrency Factor

Occasionally, there is some interest in the nature of the overlapping tasks. For example, we are more concerned about the overlap between a functional design task with a brassboard fabrication task than the overlap of a functional design task with a breadboard fabrication task.

Table 5.33 gives an abstract of the schema for PRODYF that accommodates such concerns by expanding the values in Table 5.32. The issue is the overlap of independent Task j for concept definition and a number of Tasks $i_n$ that depend on the findings of Task j. Tasks $i_n$ are for functional analysis, breadboard fabrication, brassboard fabrication, prototype fabrication, and production.

*Table 5.33* Expanded Hardware Product Concurrency Factor

| Task j | Tasks $i_n$ | Overlap | PRODYF |
|--------|-------------|---------|--------|
| Concept Definition | Functional Analysis | 0 – 1.0 | 0 – 0.2 |
|        | Breadboard Fabrication | 0 – 1.0 | 0.2 – 0.4 |
|        | Brassboard Fabrication | 0 – 1.0 | 0.4 – 0.6 |
|        | Prototype Fabrication  | 0 – 1.0 | 0.6 – 0.8 |
|        | Production             | 0 – 1.0 | 0.8 – 1.0 |

PRODYF: Product concurrency factor.

A 0.5 overlap of concept definition and functional analysis would receive the rating of PRODYF = 0 + 0.5(.2), or 0.1. A 0.5 overlap of concept definition and breadboard fabrication would receive the rating of PRODYF = 0.2 + 0.5(.2), or 0.3. A 0.5 overlap of concept definition and brassboard fabrication would receive the rating of PRODYF = 0.4 + 0.5(.2), or 0.5. A 0.5 overlap of concept definition and prototype fabrication would receive the rating of PRODYF = 0.6 + 0.5(.2), or 0.7. A 0.5 overlap of concept definition and production would receive the rating of PRODYF = 0.8 + 0.5(.2), or 0.9.

## 5.5 Hardware Factors

Concept definition denotes the task for specifying products to design and build. Function analysis denotes the task for analyzing product functions for conformance to specifications. **Breadboard** fabrication denotes the task for demonstrating and validating (*i.e.*, approval by customers) designs by bench test of unmounted details, subassemblies, and assemblies. **Brassboard** fabrication denotes the task for demonstrating designs by formal test of products or systems that are identical in form, fit, and function to the proposed production items except they are not built to withstand environmental tests. **Prototype** fabrication denotes the task for validating designs by performance and environmental testing of products that are identical in form, fit, and function to the ensuing production items. Production denotes the fabrication of products with certified tooling and processes.

The Gamma Group, who develops industrial property, questions the wisdom of spending $125,000 to fabricate a working-scale model of a large industrial complex while the concept definition is only one-quarter completed. Gamma requests Analyst to assess the risk exposure in terms of the risk cost estimate. Table 5.34 gives the technical approach Analyst follows in carrying out the assignment.

*Table 5.34   Technical Approach for Hardware Product Concurrency Factor Example*

---
1. Treat the working scale model as a brassboard.
2. Derive the amount of overlap and the value of PRODYF from Table 5.33.
3. Select the relationship for estimating risk cost estimate.
4. Derive risk cost estimate.
---

Fabricating the brassboard while the concept definition is one-quarter completed means the overlap is 0.75. An 0.75 overlap of concept definition and brassboard fabrication has the rating of PRODYF = 0.4 + 0.75(.2), or 0.55.

Lacking any knowledge of possible corrective action in the undertaking, Analyst selects the alternative relationship for *RCE* in Equation 5.2. Substituting *BCE* = $125,000 and *PRODYF* = 0.55 in Equation 5.2, Analyst obtains

$$RCE = \$125,000(1 + 0.55)$$

$$= \$193,750. \qquad (5.48)$$

Conservatism prevails at the Gamma Group. The company forgoes fabricating the working-scale model until such time as the staff has completed the concept definition of the industrial complex.

### ■ 5.5.9 Hardware Process Maturity Factor

**Hardware process maturity factor** (**PROCMF**) is an inverse measure of the attribute of **process maturity** and of its readiness for production. By the same token, PROCMF is a direct measure of the risk exposure in the production process.

PROCMF is not a measure of how far along the production of a specific product has progressed. In addition, the notion of PROCMF only connotes that the process for given products has been proven and certified ready for production, and does not infer in any way that the process produces products which are consistently uniform.

**Attribute Schema**
Table 5.35 gives suggested schema for choosing values of PROCMF with values ranging from 0 to 1.0. The greater the value of PROCMF, the greater is the contribution of the production process to risk exposure.

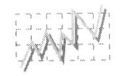

*Table 5.35  Hardware Process Maturity Factors*

| PROCMF | Current Level of Process Maturity |
|---|---|
| 0.0 | Identical rate units produced and tested. |
| 0.1 | Similar rate units produced and tested. |
| 0.2 | Rate first article produced and tested. |
| 0.3 | Rate tooling proofed. |
| 0.4 | Rate MPP validated. |
| 0.5 | Rate TDP validated. |
| 0.6 | LRIP first article produced and tested. |
| 0.7 | LRIP tooling proofed. |
| 0.8 | LRIP MPP validated. |
| 0.9 | LRIP TDP validated. |
| 1.0 | No related tooling, MPP, or TDP exists. |

**PROCMF**: Process maturity factor.
**LRIP**: Low rate of initial production.
**MPP**: Manufacturing process plan.
**Rate**: High-rate production.
**TDP**: Technical data package.

**Attribute Formulation**

The formulation for PROCMF is similar to that of hardware product maturity factor. Again, there are two groups of relationships for estimating the contribution of PROCMF to risk exposure.

We recommend Equations 5.49 and 5.50 over Equations 5.51 and 5.52.

$$RTE = BTE + RT \cdot PROCMF \tag{5.49}$$

$$RCE = BCE + RC \cdot PROCMF \tag{5.50}$$

where RTE denotes risk time estimate, RT risk time, PROCMF process maturity factor, RCE risk cost estimate, and RC risk cost.

You should consider Equations 5.51 and 5.52 only when it is impossible to obtain a gross estimate of risk time or risk cost.

$$RTE = BTE(1 + PROCMF) \tag{5.51}$$

$$RCE = BCE(1 + PROCMF) \tag{5.52}$$

Again, note that the *k*-factor does not appear in any of the foregoing equations because PROCMF, like its counterpart PRODMF, is a first-order **risk determinant**.

### ■ *5.5.10 Example of Hardware Process Maturity Factor*

Rho Corporation completes the development of the product in the example of Section 5.5.7. The comptroller now requests Analyst to determine the impact of PROCMF on the risk exposure in producing the product.

Table 5.36 gives the technical approach Analyst follows in carrying out the additional assignment.

## 5.5 Hardware Factors

**Table 5.36** *Technical Approach for Hardware Process Maturity Factor Example*

1. Use risk time and cost estimates from development phase as the baseline time and cost estimates for the production phase.
2. Determine current process design status.
3. Obtain value of PROCMF from Table 5.35.
4. Ascertain if risk time and risk cost have been estimated.
5. Select formulation and derive risk time and cost estimates.
6. Calculate the additional indirect cost due to the extended period of performance.
7. Calculate risk cost estimate for production.

The comptroller of the company provides the data in Table 5.37, informing Analyst that Task E is the integration task. Tasks A, B, C, and D are independent, concurrent, fabrication tasks followed by Task E. Thus, **cycle time** is the sum of the longest fabrication task time (*viz.*, 30 months for Assembly D) and the 12 months for integration, or 42 months. The table includes estimates of PROCMF for each task.

Analyst uses the worksheet in Table 5.38. Lacking values of risk time and risk cost, Analyst uses alternative Equations 5.3 and 5.4. The risk cost estimate is $3,850,000; however, additional indirect cost should be added to the risk cost estimate because of the extended period of performance.

As stated, the original cycle time is the sum of 30 months for assembly Task D and the 12 months for integration Task E, for a total of 42 months. The cycle RTE is the sum of the Task D, RTE of 57.0 months, and Task E, RTE of 24.0 months, or 81.0 months. The extended period of performance is the difference between the cycle RTE of 81.0 months and the original cycle time of 42.0 months, or 39 months. The additional indirect cost for these 39 months is the product of the indirect cost rate of $45,000 per month and 39 months, or $1,755,000.

**Table 5.37** *Data for Hardware Process Factor Example*

| Assembly | PROCMF | BTE | BCE |
|---|---|---|---|
| A | 0.5 | 12 months | $ 250,000 |
| B | 0.4 | 18 months | 375,000 |
| C | 0.5 | 24 months | 500,000 |
| D | 0.6 | 30 months | 750,000 |
| E | 0.9 | 12 months | 300,000 |
| Total: | | | $2,175,000 |

Overhead Rate: $45,000 per month.

PROCMF: Process maturity factor.
BTE: Baseline time estimate.
BCE: Baseline cost estimate.

*Table 5.38   Worksheet for Hardware Process Factor Example*

| Subsystem | BTE(1 + PROCMF) Months | BCE(1 + PROCMF) $ Thousand |
|---|---|---|
| A | (12)(1 + 0.3) = 15.6 | (250)(1 + 0.3) =   325 |
| B | (18)(1 + 0.6) = 28.8 | (375)(1 + 0.6) =   600 |
| C | (24)(1 + 0.8) = 43.2 | (500)(1 + 0.8) =   900 |
| D | (30)(1 + 0.9) = 57.0 | (750)(1 + 0.9) = 1,425 |
| E | (12)(1 + 1.0) = 24.0 | (300)(1 + 1.0) =   600 |
| Total: | | 3,850 |

BTE: Baseline time estimate.
PROCMF: Process maturity factor.
BCE: Baseline cost estimate.

The total risk cost estimate is therefore $1,755,000 plus $3,850,000, or $5.605 million.

### ■ 5.5.11 Hardware Process Quality Factor

**Hardware process quality factor (PROCQF)** is an inverse measure of process uniformity; that is the consistency with which the produced products stay within specified limits for functional, physical, and environmental requirements. By the same token, PROCQF is a direct measure of the contribution to risk exposure of the process uniformity for products of interest.

**Process quality** is also the consistency with which the produced products meet the functional, physical, and environmental requirements of pertinent specifications. Process quality can be described by statistical measures of process states relative to specification requirements.

The process state definitions are descriptors of how well processes control product uniformity in terms of tolerances. These definitions are the bases for deriving hardware PROCQF.

Table 5.39 provides a suggested schema for deriving PROCQF as a function of process control states that are descriptors of the uniformity with which products are produced. Specifically, the process control states are expressions of how the standard deviations of samples of the products fit within the lower and upper tolerance limits of product requirements. When viewed over time, they are descriptors of the stability of the processes.

It is customary to assume normality for product samples of size 30 or greater in the absence of a known probability density function (PDF). Figure 5.5 shows the PDF for the normal distribution, and illustrates the relationship between the upper and lower tolerance limits (LTL and UTL) and the standard deviation of the product sample. The number of standard deviations ($s$) range from $-6$ to $+6$. Note that LTL lies at approximately $-2.25-s$ and UTL at approximately $+3.6-s$. About $-3.75-s$ of the PDF lies below LTL, and about $+2.4-s$ above UTL.

We use the value of $s$ with the smaller magnitude to derive the value of PROCQF from Table 5.39. This is $2.4-s$, which is the amount of the PDF lying above UTL. Entering Table 5.39 with $\pm 2.4-s$, we read the value of PROCQF is between 0.6 and 0.7. By interpolation, we determine that PROCQF = $0.6 + (0.1)(0.1 \div 0.5)$, or 0.62.

Standard deviation is the universal measure of dispersion in statistical data. The smaller the standard deviation of process control states, the tighter is the probability distribution of the data. The tighter the probability distribution, the smaller is the risk exposure due to process quality.

## 5.5 Hardware Factors

*Table 5.39* Hardware Process Quality Factors

| PROCQF | Process Control State |
|---|---|
| 0 | ± 5.5-s of PDF fit within LTL and UTL |
| 0.1 | ± 5.0-s of PDF fit within LTL and UTL |
| 0.2 | ± 4.5-s of PDF fit within LTL and UTL |
| 0.3 | ± 4.0-s of PDF fit within LTL and UTL |
| 0.4 | ± 3.5-s of PDF fit within LTL and UTL |
| 0.5 | ± 3.0-s of PDF fit within LTL and UTL |
| 0.6 | ± 2.5-s of PDF fit within LTL and UTL |
| 0.7 | ± 2.0-s of PDF fit within LTL and UTL |
| 0.8 | ± 1.5-s of PDF fit within LTL and UTL |
| 0.9 | ± 1.0-s of PDF fit within LTL and UTL |
| 1.0 | ± 0.5-s of PDF fit within LTL and UTL |

PROCQF: Process quality factor.
s: Standard deviation.
PDF: Probability density function.
LTL: Lower tolerance limit.
UTL: Upper tolerance limit.

The derivation of the hardware PROCQF is retrospective in that you are looking to past performance to predict current performance. Hardware PROCQF is a second-order factor with respect to hardware product maturity factor in that allowances for rework and scrap are usually included in baseline time and cost estimates.

Figure 5.5 is also an illustration of tolerance centering, which is the fit of the PDF of products within the applicable tolerance limits. In these kinds of applications, it is only necessary to derive values of the standard deviation to use for looking up values of PROCQF in Table 5.39. You need not construct the PDF.

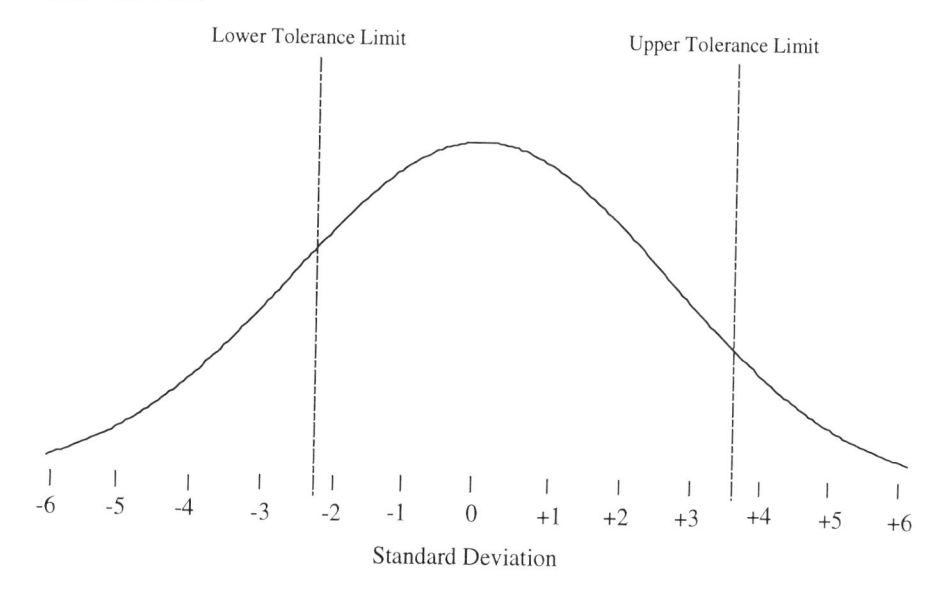

**Figure 5.5** Relationship Between Tolerance Limits and Probability Density Function

### 5.5.12 Example of Hardware Process Quality Factor

The production manager department of Delta Products, Inc., a manufacturer of electronic components, encounters an increase in the rejection rate on the production line for semiprecision resistors. The department requests Analyst to determine the process quality factor of the line. The company provides sample data from the current production run of 50-ohm, ± 1 ohm, resistors.

Table 5.40 gives the technical approach Analyst follows in carrying out the assignment. Table 5.41 gives the data for the analysis.

**Table 5.40** *Technical Approach for Hardware Process Quality Factor Example*

1. Calculate the standard deviation of the sample data.
2. Determine the process control state for the production run.
3. Derive the applicable value of PROCQF using Table 5.39.

Analyst calculates the mean of the sample data as the first step toward calculating the standard deviation.

The mean ($m$) of sample data in group form is

$$m = \frac{\Sigma (d_i f_i)}{n} \tag{5.53}$$

where $\Sigma(d_i f_i)$ denotes summation of products $d_i$ and $f_i$, or 5,710.90 ohms, and $n$ sample size that equals 114 (*i.e.*, the summation of $f_i$) in Table 5.41.

**Table 5.41** *Resistor Values in Ohms for Hardware Process Quality Factor Example*

| $c_i$ | $d_i$ | $f_i$ | $(d_i f_i)$ | $c_i$ | $d_i$ | $f_i$ | $(d_i f_i)$ |
|---|---|---|---|---|---|---|---|
| 49.0–49.1 | 49.05 | 1 | 49.05 | 50.0–50.1 | 50.05 | 10 | 500.50 |
| 49.1–49.2 | 49.15 | 2 | 98.30 | 50.1–50.2 | 50.15 | 10 | 501.50 |
| 49.2–49.3 | 49.25 | 2 | 98.70 | 50.2–50.3 | 50.25 | 8 | 402.00 |
| 49.3–49.4 | 49.35 | 3 | 148.05 | 50.3–50.4 | 50.35 | 9 | 453.15 |
| 49.4–49.5 | 49.45 | 5 | 247.25 | 50.4–50.5 | 50.45 | 8 | 403.60 |
| 49.5–49.6 | 49.55 | 4 | 198.20 | 50.5–50.6 | 50.55 | 7 | 353.85 |
| 49.6–49.7 | 49.65 | 5 | 248.25 | 50.6–50.7 | 50.65 | 6 | 303.90 |
| 49.7–49.8 | 49.75 | 7 | 348.25 | 50.7–50.8 | 50.75 | 5 | 253.75 |
| 49.8–49.9 | 49.85 | 8 | 392.40 | 50.8–50.9 | 50.85 | 3 | 152.55 |
| 49.9–50.0 | 49.95 | 9 | 449.55 | 50.9–51.0 | 50.95 | 2 | 101.90 |

$n = 114$
$\Sigma(d_i f_i) = 5,710.90$

$n$: Sample size, $\Sigma f_i$.
$c_i$: Cell interval of cell.
$d_i$: Midpoint of cell.
$f_i$: Frequency (*i.e.*, count) of variates in cell.

## 5.5 Hardware Factors

Substituting the $\Sigma(d_i f_i) = 5,710.90$ ohms and $n = 114$ in Equation 5.53, Analyst obtains

$$m = \frac{5,710.90}{114} \text{ ohms}$$
$$= 50.096 \text{ ohms.} \quad (5.54)$$

The variance $s^2$ of sample data in group form is given by

$$s^2 = \Sigma \frac{f(d_i - m)^2}{n-1} \quad (5.55)$$

where $f_i$ denotes frequency (*i.e.*, count) of variates in respective cells, $d_i$ midpoint value of *i*-th cell, $m$ mean, and $n$ sample size. [3]

Analyst uses the worksheet in Table 5.42 to calculate the variance and standard deviation of the sample distribution. The variance of the sample distribution is 0.1963 ohms². The standard deviation is simply the square root of the variance, or 0.443 ohms. Dividing the standard deviation into the tolerance limits of ± 1 ohm yields the number of standard deviations that fit into the tolerance limits, for (± 1 ohm) ÷ (0.443 ohm), or ± 2.257−$s$.

Analyst looks up the value of the hardware PROCQF for ± 2.257−$s$ in Table 5.39, and notes that the value falls between PROCQF = 0.6 and 0.7. By interpolation, Analyst determines that PROCQF equals 0.6 + 0.1(.257 ÷ 0.5), or 0.651, for the process of interest.

### ■ 5.5.13 Example of Composite Hardware Product and Process Quality Factors

Kappa Corporation contemplates the introduction of a new water purifier for use in restaurants. The company estimates that 48 months and $3.5 million are needed for product design and 24 months and $1.5 million for producing the first article.

Several officers of the firm question the estimates on the basis of the apparent deficiencies in product and process quality. Kappa retains Analyst for an independent assessment of the risk exposure contribution of product and process quality. Table 5.43 gives the technical approach Analyst follows in carrying out the assignment.

Analyst first reviews the proposed product design by interviewing key personnel and then completes the producibility, reliability and testability checklists for hardware product quality factor given in Tables 5.44, 5.45, and 5.46. The maximum possible equivalent decimal values of the 11-bit, 7-bit, and 10-bit binary numbers in the tables are 2,047, 255, and 1,023. The binary numbers corresponding to the yes and no answers in the checklists are 10101110111 for producibility; 1111011 for reliability; and 1101000111 for testability.

The equivalent decimal values of the binary number of the answers to the sequence of questions in the producibility checklist of Table 5.44 is $(1)(2^{10}) + (0)(2^9) + (1)(2^8) + (0)(2^7) + (1)(2^6) + (1)(2^5) + (1)(2^4) + (0)(2^3) + (1)(2^2) + (1)(2^1) + (1)(2^0)$, for 1,024 + 256 + 64 + 32 + 16 + 4 + 2 + 1, or 1,399.

The equivalent decimal values of the binary number of the answers to the sequence of questions in the reliability checklist of Table 5.45 is $(1)(2^6) + (1)(2^5) + (1)(2^4) + (1)(2^3) + (0)(2^2) + (1)(2^1) + (1)(2^0)$, for 64 + 32 + 16 + 8 + 2 + 1, or 123.

The equivalent decimal values of the binary number of the answers to the sequence of questions in the testability checklist of Table 5.46 is $(1)(2^{10}) + (1)(2^9) + (0)(2^8) + (1)(2^7) + (1)(2^6) + (0)(2^5) + (0)(2^4) + (1)(2^3) + (1)(2^2) + (1)(2^1) + (1)(2^0)$, for $1,024 + 512 + 128 + 64 + 8 + 4 + 2 + 1$, or 1,743.

**Table 5.42**  *Variance Worksheet for Hardware Process Quality Factor Example*

| $d_i$ | $f_i$ | $d_i m$ | $(d_i m)^2$ | $f(d_i m)^2$ |
|---|---|---|---|---|
| 49.05 | 1 | −1.046 | 1.094116 | 1.094116 |
| 49.15 | 2 | −0.946 | 0.894916 | 1.789832 |
| 49.25 | 2 | −0.846 | 0.715716 | 1.431432 |
| 49.35 | 3 | −0.746 | 0.556516 | 1.669548 |
| 49.45 | 5 | −0.646 | 0.417316 | 2.086580 |
| 49.55 | 4 | −0.546 | 0.298116 | 1.192464 |
| 49.65 | 5 | −0.446 | 0.198916 | 0.994580 |
| 49.75 | 7 | −0.346 | 0.119716 | 0.838012 |
| 49.85 | 8 | −0.246 | 0.060516 | 0.484128 |
| 49.95 | 9 | −0.146 | 0.021316 | 0.191844 |
| 50.05 | 10 | −0.046 | 0.002116 | 0.021160 |
| 50.15 | 10 | 0.054 | 0.002916 | 0.029160 |
| 50.25 | 8 | 0.154 | 0.023716 | 0.189728 |
| 50.35 | 9 | 0.254 | 0.064516 | 0.580644 |
| 50.45 | 8 | 0.354 | 0.125316 | 1.002528 |
| 50.55 | 7 | 0.454 | 0.206116 | 1.442812 |
| 50.65 | 6 | 0.554 | 0.306916 | 1.841496 |
| 50.75 | 5 | 0.654 | 0.427716 | 2.138580 |
| 50.85 | 3 | 0.754 | 0.568516 | 1.705548 |
| 50.95 | 2 | 0.854 | 0.729316 | 1.458632 |

$$\Sigma f_i i (d_i i - m)^2 = 22.1828$$
$$s^2 = 22.1828/(114-1) = 0.1963$$
$$s = 0.443$$

**Table 5.43**  *Technical Approach for Composite Hardware Product and Process Quality Factors Example*

1. Survey producibility, reliability, and testability of proposed product design.
2. Establish current state of process control for producing similar products.
3. Derive product quality factor.
4. Derive process quality factor.
5. Derive risk exposure for product and process quality factors.

## 5.5 Hardware Factors

**Table 5.44** *Producibility Checklist for Composite Hardware Product and Process Quality Factors Example*

| | Yes | No |
|---|---|---|
| 1. Are specifications and standards consistent with the intended product environment? | ✔ | |
| 2. Does the design use the minimum possible number of different parts? | | ✔ |
| 3. Are nonstandard parts avoided? | ✔ | |
| 4. Is the design standardized to the proper degree? | | ✔ |
| 5. Have alternate design concepts been considered and the most producible one selected? | ✔ | |
| 6. Is the design within the manufacturing state-of-the-art? | ✔ | |
| 7. Does the design avoid the use of proprietary items or processes? | ✔ | |
| 8. Is the design simplified to the extent possible? | | ✔ |
| 9. Are unnecessary functions eliminated from the design? | ✔ | |
| 10. Does the design accommodate parts with slight differences as if they were identical? | ✔ | |
| 11. Are tolerances allocated properly? | ✔ | |

**Table 5.45** *Reliability Checklist for Hardware Composite Product and Process Quality Factors Example*

| | Yes | No |
|---|---|---|
| 1. Has product reliability requirement been allocated to lower levels in the product? | ✔ | |
| 2. Is electronic stress screening used on all active components? | ✔ | |
| 3. Have parts been derated sufficiently to provide margin over design limits? | ✔ | |
| 4. Have parts control and standardization reduced the different number of parts to a minimum? | ✔ | |
| 5. Has the design complexity been reduced by using a minimum number of parts? | | ✔ |
| 6. Have thermal stresses been reduced by lowering component and terminal temperatures? | ✔ | |
| 7. Has redundancy been provided to offset component failures? | ✔ | |

Analyst assumes an independent relationship for producibility, reliability, and testability and calculates the RSS value of 1,399, 123, and 1,743 as follows:

$$RSS = \sqrt{1,399^2 + 123^2 + 1,743^2}$$
$$= 2,238. \tag{5.56}$$

As stated, the maximum possible decimal values of the 11-bit, 7-bit, and 10-bit binary numbers are 2,047, 255, and 1,023. Analyst now calculates RSS value of 2,047, 255, and 1,023 in Equation 5.57.

**Table 5.46** *Testability Checklist for Composite Hardware Product and Process Quality Factors Example*

|  | Yes | No |
|---|---|---|
| 1. Does the mechanical design provide a standard grid layout for component identification? | ✔ |  |
| 2. Is enough space provided between components for testing? | ✔ |  |
| 3. Are components oriented in the same direction? |  | ✔ |
| 4. Are connector pins provided for test stimuli? | ✔ |  |
| 5. Is the number of part types the minimum possible? |  | ✔ |
| 6. Is built-in test, *BIT*, incorporated in the design? |  | ✔ |
| 7. Are program test sets available for the *BIT*? |  | ✔ |
| 8. Can details be tested without integration into the subassembly level? | ✔ |  |
| 9. Can subassemblies be tested without integration into the assembly level? | ✔ |  |
| 10. Can assemblies be tested without integration into the product level? | ✔ |  |
| 11. Can subsystems be tested without being integrated into the system level? | ✔ |  |

$$RSS = \sqrt{2{,}047^2 + 255^2 + 1{,}023^2}$$

$$= 2{,}303. \tag{5.57}$$

On a scale of 0 to 1.0, the value of the hardware PROCQF is

$$PRODQF = \frac{2{,}303 - 2{,}232}{2{,}303}$$

$$= 0.031 \tag{5.58}$$

that represents a near risk-free condition.

Analyst sets this value aside while pondering how to derive the value of hardware process quality factor. Analyst concludes that the answer may lie in a model of the production line.

Production lines are complex organizations consisting of a number of sub-lines operating in parallel and coming together at various points in the production flow. Figure 5.6 shows an idealized version of a production line, consisting of i work stations on each sub-line and j sub-lines that come together at the end of the production line.

You can envision the production line as a matrix of a number of rows (**i**) and a number of columns (**j**). The notation **s(1,1)** denotes the process control state at Work Station 1 on Sub-line 1. The notation **s(i, j)** denotes the process control state at Work Station **i** on Sub-line **j**. The notation **s(Σ1,1-i, j)** denotes the composite production control state of all the work stations on all the sub-lines.

There is a dependent relationship for work stations on any given sub-line in that tolerance build-up is additive, just as process times are additive. Sub-lines are paths through the network. There are both dependent and independent relationships for sub-lines.

Production lines are networks and the concept of networks was covered in the preceding chapter. The relationship is dependent for sub-lines that comprise the critical path in the network, whereas the relationship is independent for sub-lines comprising noncritical paths.

## 5.5 Hardware Factors

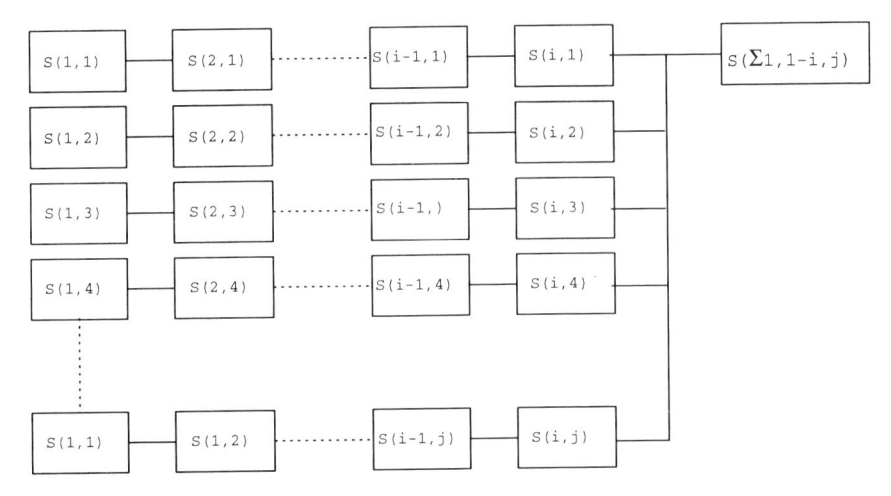

**Figure 5.6** Idealized Production Line for Composite Hardware Product and Process Quality Factors Example

The construction of risk networks is a tedious task and many analysts are prone to use their judgment in estimating a composite value of PROCQF. Analyst is no exception to this tendency and judges the value to be 0.350 for PROCQF. We will present a more objective schema in the next section.

Table 5.47 is the worksheet Analyst uses to derive risk time and cost estimates. Note that Analyst includes $150,000 per month for additional elements of indirect cost for the increased periods of performance during development and production.

Note the use of RSS in deriving composite risk time and risk cost estimates. This is necessary because of the assumption of independence among the attributes of producibility, reliability, and testability. The elements of cost would be additive if you were to assume that the attributes were dependent.

### ■ 5.5.14 Hardware Process Complexity Factor

**Hardware process complexity factor (PROCCF)** is an inverse measure of the complexity of process design. By the same token, PROCCF is a direct measure of the risk exposure in the production of the particular design.

There are two approaches for rating PROCCF, both of which are objective. The simpler of the two is to equate PROCCF to the generation breakdown index of the product of interest. The methodology is essentially the same as for product complexity factor, so we will elaborate on the alternative approach that equates PROCCF to the number of part numbers in the product.

We use the term *part numbers* to both denote the number of parts in a given product and to account for the same parts being used a number of times. For example, a certain capacitor, which is used two times, would be identified as Part Numbers C123-1 and C123-2. We refer to these notations as dash numbers.

Products consist of assemblies, subassemblies, details, and parts. Details are structural components, such as printed wire boards that house parts.

**Table 5.47** *Worksheet for Composite Hardware Product and Process Quality Factor Example*

| **Product Development Risk Time Estimate (RTE) and Risk Cost Estimate (RCE)** |
|---|
| $BTE$ = 48 months    $PRODQF$ = 0.031 |
| $RTE$ = (48 months)(1 + 0.031) = 49.488 months. |
| Additional indirect cost = (49.488 - 48 months)($150,000 per month) = $223,200. |
| $BCE$ = $3,500,000    $PRODQF$ = 0.031 |
| $RCE$ = ($3,500,000)(1 + 0.031) = $3,608,500. |
| Total development $RCE$ = $3,608,500 + $223,200 = $3,721,700. |
| **Product Production Risk Time Estimate (RTE) and Risk Cost Estimate (RCE)** |
| $BTE$ = 24 months    $PROCQF$ = 0.350 |
| $RTE$ = (24 months)(1 + 0.350) = 32.4 months. |
| Additional indirect cost = (32.4 − 24 months)($150,000 per month) = $1,260,000. |
| $BCE$ = $1,500,000    $PRODQF$ = 0.350 |
| $RCE$ = ($1,500,000)(1 + 0.350) = $2,025,000. |
| Total production $RCE$ = $2,025,000 + $1,260,000 = $3,285,000. |
| **Total Product Risk Cost Estimate (RCE)** |
| $RCE$ = $3,721,700 + $3,285,000 = $7,006,700. |

A number of details make up a subassembly, a number of subassemblies make up an assembly, and a number of assemblies make up a product. All parts, details, subassemblies, assemblies, and products have part numbers. Products may also have serial numbers. Table 5.48 gives suggested schema for rating hardware PROCCF which are keyed to the population of part numbers in each category.

Typical high-technology electronic products can have more than one-half million parts. Table 5.48 characterizes the processes for producing such products with the designation of PROCCF = 1.0. PROCCF = 1.0 equates to 540,000 parts.

### ■ 5.5.15 Example of Composite Hardware Process Maturity, Quality, and Complexity Factors

Sigma Specialties, Inc. estimates the unit production cost of a proposed time standard to be $2,500 and wishes to know the risk exposure from the hardware process attributes of maturity, quality, and complexity. The company has estimates for the hardware process maturity and quality factors *(viz.,* PROCMF = 0.30 and PROCQF = 0.60), but does not know how to derive PROCCF.

Sigma retains Analyst to derive the value of both PROCCF and the composite risk determinant factor for PROCMF, PROCQF, and PROCCF. Table 5.49 gives the technical approach Analyst follows in carrying out the assignment.

Analyst first addresses the part number population for the product of interest. There are eight assemblies per product and, on the average, fifteen subassemblies, eighteen details per subassembly, and fifteen parts per detail.

## 5.5 Hardware Factors

*Table 5.48* Hardware Process Complexity Factors

| PROCCF | Part Numbers | PROCCF | Part Numbers |
|---|---|---|---|
| 0.0 | 2-5 Assemblies<br>2-5 Subassemblies per assembly<br>6-10 Details per subassembly<br>6-10 Parts per detail | 0.6 | 11-20 Assemblies<br>11-20 Subassemblies per assembly<br>11-20 Details per subassembly<br>11-20 Parts per detail |
| 0.1 | 2-5 Assemblies<br>6-10 Subassemblies per assembly<br>6-10 Details per subassembly<br>6-10 Parts per detail | 0.7 | 11-20 Assemblies<br>20-10 Subassemblies per assembly<br>11-20 Details per subassembly<br>11-20 Parts per detail |
| 0.2 | 6-10 Assemblies<br>6-10 Subassemblies per assembly<br>6-10 Details per subassembly<br>6-10 Parts per detail | 0.8 | 11-20 Assemblies<br>21-30 Subassemblies per assembly<br>21-30 Details per subassembly<br>11-20 Parts per detail |
| 0.3 | 6-10 Assemblies<br>11-20 Subassemblies per assembly<br>6-10 Details per subassembly<br>6-10 Parts per detail | 0.9 | 11-20 Assemblies<br>21-30 Subassemblies per assembly<br>21-30 Details per subassembly<br>11-20 Parts per detail |
| 0.4 | 6-10 Assemblies<br>11-20 Subassemblies per assembly<br>11-20 Details per subassembly<br>6-10 Parts per detail | 1.0 | 11-20 Assemblies<br>21-30 Subassemblies per assembly<br>21-30 Details per subassembly<br>21-30 Parts per detail |
| 0.5 | 6-10 Assemblies<br>11-20 Subassemblies per assembly<br>11-20 Details per subassembly<br>11-20 Parts per detail | | |

PROCCF: Process complexity factor.

*Table 5.49* Technical Approach for Composite Hardware Process Maturity, Quality, and Complexity Factors Example

1. Establish part-number population for product.
2. Look up value of process complexity factor for part-number population in Table 5.48.
3. Assume independence in deriving value of composite risk determinant factor for process maturity, quality, and complexity.

The number of subassemblies, details, and parts in the product are averages. In accordance with Table 5.48, eight assemblies per product qualifies a factor of 0.2. An average of fifteen subassemblies per assembly qualifies the product for a factor of 0.3. An average of eighteen details per subassembly qualifies the product for a factor of 0.5. An average of fifteen parts per detail also qualifies the product for a factor of 0.5.

The larger value of PROCCF = 0.5 prevails. Because of the assumption of independence among the risk determinant factors, Analyst calculates the value of *RSS* for *PROCMF* = 0.3, *PROCQF* = 0.6, and *PROCCF* = 0.5, as follows

$$RSS = \sqrt{(0.3)^2 + [(0.3)(0.6)]^2 + [(0.3)(0.5)]^2}$$
$$= 0.381. \qquad (5.59)$$

Note $k = 0.3$, the value of PROCMF, factors the second and third term under the radical sign in Equation 5.59.

The maximum possible value of PROCMF, PROCQF, and PROCCF is one. The square root of $1^2 + 1^2 + 1^2$ is 1.732. Therefore, the value of CRDF for PROCMF, PROCQF, and PROCCF is

$$CRDF = \frac{0.381}{1.732}$$
$$= 0.220. \qquad (5.60)$$

Analyst provides the finding to the client who uses the factor to derive risk time and cost estimates for the particular production process.

### ■ 5.5.16 Hardware Process Concurrency Factor

**Hardware process concurrency factor (PROCYF)** describes the degree to which there is overlap among process tasks which are dependent upon each other and which, as a consequence, may contribute to risk exposure.

Figure 5.7, which is adapted from Figure 5.4, illustrates concurrency of various degrees between the two process tasks, j and i. As stated previously, concurrency has three components: (1) product concurrency; (2) process concurrency; and (3) concurrency between product and process. PROCCF describes the degree to which process tasks overlap and includes the overlap of development and process tasks.

Table 5.50, which is an expansion of Table 5.32, gives the schema for rating PROCYF for the overlap of only process tasks and for the overlap of development and process tasks.

Assume that Task j is the task to develop a breadboard of a certain product and Task i is the task to fabricate a first article of the product. The two tasks overlap by 10 percent, or 0.1. Task i is dependent task on Task j.

Enter Table 5.50 in the Task j column at Breadboard. Go right to the Task i column and down to Prototype. Continue right to the Concurrency and PROCYF columns.

The PROCYF value spread is 0.251 to 0.375 for concurrency 0.1 to 1.0. Therefore, for an overlap of 0.1 for the Tasks j and i, PROCYF = 0.251. You use interpolation for other values.

The degree of overlap among tasks, as shown in Figure 5.7, is measured on a scale of 0 to 1.0, the value 1.0 signifying 100 percent overlap between two tasks. Assume Tasks j and i are for rate production of two assemblies used in a certain product and that the production of the assembly in Task i depends on prior production of the assembly in Task j.

## 5.5 Hardware Factors

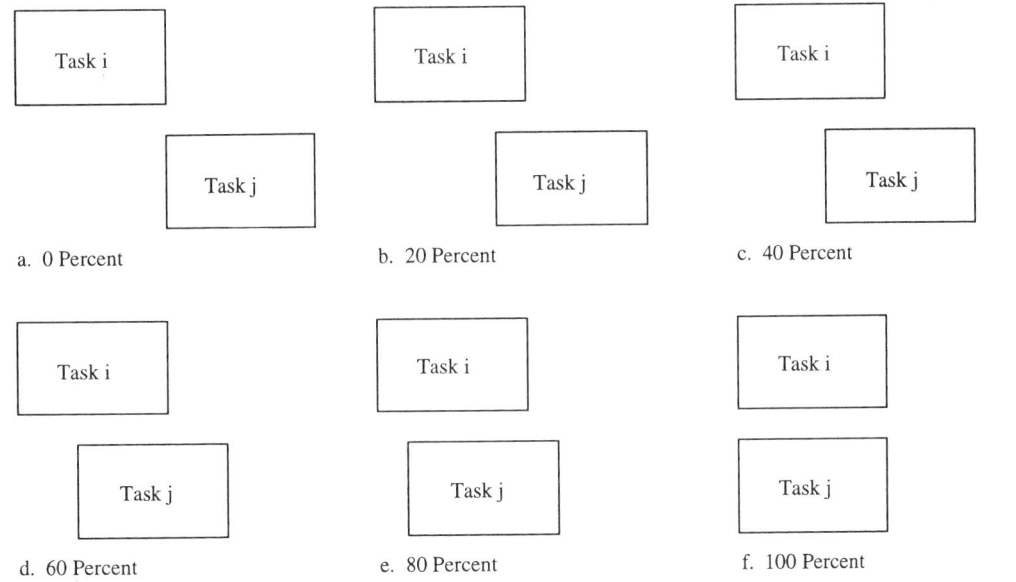

**Figure 5.7** Concurrency Between Hardware Process Tasks j and i

(a. 0 Percent, b. 20 Percent, c. 40 Percent, d. 60 Percent, e. 80 Percent, f. 100 Percent)

You enter Table 5.50 in the Task j column and go down to Rate. You continue to the right to the Task i column. If the overlap between Tasks j and i were 0.1, the concurrency factor would be 0.001. If the overlap were 1.0, the concurrency factor would be 0.125.

Concurrency factors for in-between values of overlap are obtained by interpolation. If Tasks j and i were for LRIP and rate production with an overlap of 0.4, you would enter Table 5.50 in the Task j column and go down to LRIP. You continue to the Task i column and go down to Rate.

The degree of concurrency factor would be [(0.250 − 0.126) ÷ 0.9](0.4), or 0.0551. The values 0.250 and 0.126 are the upper and lower values of the concurrency factor range for the concurrency range of 0.1 – 1.0, and 0.9 is the difference between 0.1 and 1.0.

### ■ 5.5.17 Example of Composite Hardware Process Maturity, Quality, Complexity, and Concurrency Factors

Sigma Specialities, Inc. now wishes to know the risk exposure from the hardware process attributes of maturity, quality, complexity, and concurrency. The company has the estimates PROCMF = 0.3, PROCQF = 0.6, and PROCCF = 0.5 and knows that there is an overlap of two process tasks for the product of interest. Sigma retains Analyst to derive the value of PROCYF and the composite risk exposure from PROCMF, PROCQF, PROCCF, and PROCYF. Table 5.51 gives the technical approach Analyst follows in carrying out the assignment.

Using Figure 5.7 as a guideline, Analyst determines that there is an overlap of 0.5 of two process tasks for the product of interest. Therefore, in accordance with Table 5.48, the value of PROCYF is 0.5.

Analyst calculates the RSS value for PROCMF, PROCQF, PROCCF, and PROCYF with Equation 5.56. Again, note the use of $k = 0.3$ in the right-hand side of Equation 5.61.

The maximum value of RSS results when the four risk determinant factors each equal one and RSS equals the square root of 4 or 2.0.

$$RSS = \sqrt{(0.3)^2 + [(0.3)(0.6)]^2 + [(0.3)(0.5)]^2 + [(0.3)(0.5)]}$$
$$= 0.409. \qquad (5.61)$$

Therefore, the value of CRDF for PROCMF, PROCQF, and PROCCF is

$$CRDF = \frac{0.409}{2.0}$$
$$= 0.205. \qquad (5.62)$$

*Table 5.50*    *Hardware Process Concurrency Factor*

| Task j | Task i | Concurrency | PROCYF |
|---|---|---|---|
| Concept | Concept | 0.1-1.0 | 0.001-0.125 |
| | Breadboard | 0.1-1.0 | 0.126-0.250 |
| | Brassboard | 0.1-1.0 | 0.251-0.375 |
| | Prototype | 0.1-1.0 | 0.376-0.500 |
| | First article | 0.1-1.0 | 0.501-0.675 |
| | LRIP | 0.1-1.0 | 0.676-0.750 |
| | Rate | 0.1-1.0 | 0.751-0.875 |
| | Field | 0.1-1.0 | 0.876-1.000 |
| Breadboard | Breadboard | 0.1-1.0 | 0.001-0.125 |
| | Brassboard | 0.1-1.0 | 0.126-0.250 |
| | Prototype | 0.1-1.0 | 0.251-0.375 |
| | First article | 0.1-1.0 | 0.376-0.500 |
| | LRIP | 0.1-1.0 | 0.501-0.675 |
| | Rate | 0.1-1.0 | 0.676-0.750 |
| | Field | 0.1-1.0 | 0.751-0.875 |
| Brassboard | Brassboard | 0.1-1.0 | 0.001-0.125 |
| | Prototype | 0.1-1.0 | 0.126-0.250 |
| | First article | 0.1-1.0 | 0.251-0.375 |
| | LRIP | 0.1-1.0 | 0.376-0.500 |
| | Rate | 0.1-1.0 | 0.501-0.625 |
| | Field | 0.1-1.0 | 0.626-0.750 |
| Prototype | Prototype | 0.1-1.0 | 0.001-0.125 |
| | First article | 0.1-1.0 | 0.126-0.250 |
| | LRIP | 0.1-1.0 | 0.251-0.375 |
| | Rate | 0.1-1.0 | 0.376-0.500 |
| | Field | 0.1-1.0 | 0.501-0.625 |
| First article | First article | 0.1-1.0 | 0.001-0.125 |
| | LRIP | 0.1-1.0 | 0.126-0.250 |
| | Rate | 0.1-1.0 | 0.251-0.375 |
| | Field | 0.1-1.0 | 0.376-0.500 |
| LRIP | LRIP | 0.1-1.0 | 0.001-0.125 |
| | Rate | 0.1-1.0 | 0.126-0.250 |
| | Field | 0.1-1.0 | 0.251-0.375 |
| Rate | Rate | 0.1-1.0 | 0.001-0.125 |
| | Field | 0.1-1.0 | 0.126-0.250 |

**Table 5.50** *Hardware Process Concurrency Factor (Cont.)*

PROCYF: Process concurrency factor.
Concept: Denotes tasks for concept formulation.
Breadboard: Denotes tasks for concept demonstration and validation (*i.e.*, approval by customers) by analysis and bench test of breadboard details, subassemblies, and assemblies.
Brassboard: Denotes tasks for design demonstration by formal test of products or systems that are identical in form, fit, and function to the proposed production items except they are not built to withstand environmental test.
Prototype: Denotes tasks for design validation by formal test (including environmental) of products or systems that are identical in form, fit, and function to proposed production items.
First article: Denotes tasks that produce and test the first production item using LRIP tooling.
LRIP: Low rate of initial production. Denotes tasks that produce and test production items using soft (*i.e.*, multipurpose) tooling in LRIP mode.
Rate: Full production rate. Denotes tasks that produce and test production items using hard (*i.e.*, dedicated, special purpose) tooling in full production rate mode.
Field: Denotes task that supports products in field, collects data on use of products for product improvement.

**Table 5.51** *Technical Approach for Hardware Composite Process Maturity, Quality, Complexity, and Concurrency Factors Example*

1. Determine the degree of process tasks overlap.
2. Obtain the value of PROCCF from Table 5.48.
3. Assume independence in deriving value of composite risk determinant factor.
4. Use the method of root-sum-of-squares to calculate composite risk determinant factor.

Analyst provides the finding to the client noting the small effect of the additional factor on the value of CRDF.

# 5.6
# SOFTWARE FACTORS

Computers and software pose a significant number of technical risk problems. This may be due, in part, to the somewhat limited knowledge on the subject matter. The ubiquitous nature of the effect, however, mandates a sound understanding of computers and software.

## ■ 5.6.1 Computer Operation

There are three major categories of computers: digital, analog, and hybrid. The digital computer functions exclusively with discrete digital techniques, whereas the analog computer uses continuously variable components (*e.g.*, rheostats, capacitors, and servomechanisms). The hybrid computer uses a combination of both of the aforementioned.

The emphasis in this book is on the digital computer and the software to make it function as intended. Figure 5.8 illustrates the organization of the digital computer. The input devices and output devices, shown separately in the figure, constitute the input-output unit. [4]

The digital computer contains the following basic components: (1) control unit; (2) arithmetic-logic unit; (3) primary memory; (4) secondary memory; (5) central processing unit; and (6) input-output unit.

The control unit, arithmetic-logic unit, and primary memory comprise the **central processing unit** (**CPU**) of the digital computer. The other components (*i.e.*, secondary memory and input-output unit) are referred to as peripheral devices.

The control unit initiates operations by retrieving instructions, from a sequence of instructions called the program, which are stored in primary memory. The control unit then instructs the other components when to function and monitors performance of the functions.

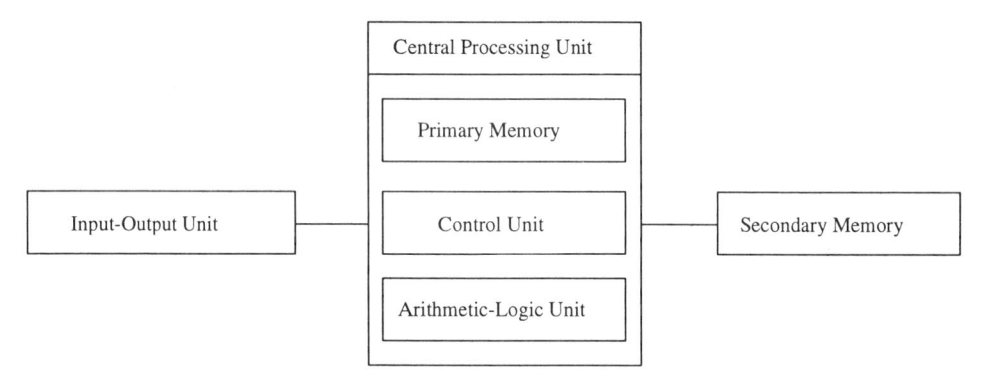

**Figure 5.8** Digital Computer Organization

Contained in the control unit is a precision clock that establishes the basic timing rate and distributes reference timing for the function initiation by the other components of the computer. Speed of operation is determined by the clock rate.

The arithmetic-logic unit operates on data and performs arithmetical calculations. The unit consists of many interconnected shift registers. They derive their name from the fact that data are shifted through series of memory devices during operations.

Operands of logical AND, OR, and NOT perform the mathematical operations. These operands are stored in primary memory. Primary memory stores data which must be retrieved quickly (*e.g.*, procedural instructions or routines) and not necessarily in any order. This random access governs many megabytes of primary storage.

Secondary memory stores data which are used less frequently. Secondary memory stores large batches of data which are retrieved sequentially when needed and are usually stored on hard and floppy disks and magnetic tape.

The input-output unit provides the interface between external data and the central processing unit. Input-output devices include keyboards, visual display units (*i.e.*, monitors), modems, and disk drives.

## 5.6 Software Factors

### 5.6.2 Software Program

A **software program** is a set of instructions which is executed by a computer. Software is expressed in precise notations called computer languages, so that the computer can literally respond to software instructions.

The basic categories of software programs are: (1) language; (2) operating system; (3) utility; and (4) application. Language programs are an important class of software. Machine-language programs are sequences of instructions in the form of numbers which can be read, understood, and executed by the computer.

Assembly-language programs attempt to approach human language by using abbreviated commands, instead of numbers, which require translation into machine language by assemblers. High-level language programs are quite close to human language, are easier to write than the lower-level languages, but require translation into machine language by compilers or interpreters.

Operating-system programs control the basic functions of a computer, such as loading, displaying, executing, and storing programs, as well as controlling input-output devices such as printers and modems. More sophisticated operating systems allocate and track computer time among users and programs. Utility programs develop and test other programs. The classes of utility programs are the editor, compiler, linker, loader, and debugger.

Editors make changes in other programs. Compilers translate programs into machine language. Linkers are used to combine a number of compiled programs. Loaders load linked programs into computer memory. Debuggers find errors in programs by stepping through programs one instruction at a time.

Application programs are the programs for specific applications such as word processing and spreadsheet. Application programs are either general purpose programs or dedicated.

General purpose application programs (*e.g.*, word processing, computer-aided design, and spreadsheet) can serve a broad spectrum of users. Dedicated programs (*e.g.*, machine control and diagnostics) serve only the application for which they are intended.

Dedicated software is frequently integrated with the hardware products supported by the computers. These are embedded computers, typical examples being the microprocessors in modern automobiles.

This section addresses risk determinant factors for software products (*i.e.*, programs). The topics are software product and process design maturity, quality, complexity, and concurrency factors. The emphasis is on dedicated software that is needed to make hardware products work. Software programming consists of eight sequential stages: requirements definition; functional design; design specification; code and unit test; program integration and test; acceptance test and evaluation; installation and operation; and maintenance. [5]

These stages provide the basis for deriving software risk determinant factors. However, the issue of hardware-software competition for resources first requires that the management attribute factor be revisited for software.

### 5.6.3 Software Management Attribute Factor

It is advisable to tailor the previously introduced checklists for the management attribute factor (*viz.*, Tables 5.4, 5.5, 5.6, and 5.7). Tables 5.52, 5.53, 5.54, and 5.55 are suggested checklists.

**Table 5.52**  *Software Funding and Budgeting Policy Checklist*

|  | Yes | No |
|---|---|---|
| 1. Does policy require return-on-investment to be considered over the life of given software products? | | |
| 2. Is it the policy of the organization to fund software product programs through completion? | | |
| 3. Is adequate early funding provided for critical research, design, and engineering activities? | | |
| 4. Are software product programs provided adequate management reserve? | | |
| 5. Does the policy require technical justification in support of financial decisions? | | |

**Table 5.53**  *Software Customer and User Policy Checklist*

|  | Yes | No |
|---|---|---|
| 1. Does the organization ascertain who are users as well as customers for software products? | | |
| 2. Does the organization solicit statements of user requirements in user's own words? | | |
| 3. Is there a formal system for translating voice of user into software product specifications? | | |
| 4. Are product warranties stated clearly and unambiguously? | | |
| 5. Is there easy access to the customer service organization? | | |
| 6. Does the organization facilitate return of defective software products? | | |
| 7. Does the organization automatically notify customers and users of software product improvements? | | |

**Table 5.54**  *Software Program Continuity Policy Checklist*

|  | Yes | No |
|---|---|---|
| 1. Does policy ensure continuity in multiyear software products programs subject to periodic performance, schedule, and cost reviews? | | |
| 2. Are specific accomplishments for the current reporting period reviewed at a minimum of every quarter? | | |
| 3. Are specific accomplishments planned for next reporting period reviewed at a minimum of every quarter? | | |
| 4. Are reviews designed to give visibility to all disciplines and not just technical? | | |
| 5. Are performance, schedule, and cost monitored on weekly basis? | | |
| 6. Are performance, schedule, and cost variance analyses required on monthly basis? | | |
| 7. Are time and cost estimates required on monthly basis? | | |

## 5.6 Software Factors

**Table 5.55** *Software Personnel Growth and Retention Policy Checklist*

|  | Yes | No |
|---|---|---|
| 1. Are assignments of key personnel made for the duration of software product programs? | | |
| 2. Are program directors and project managers responsible for only one major software product program at a time? | | |
| 3. Are career progressions defined so that every employee understands promotion opportunities? | | |
| 4. Do training programs satisfy organizational and employee current and future needs? | | |
| 5. Are software managers involved in recruitment, training, and retention of key personnel? | | |

Be very sensitive to the continuity of funding and the adequacy of management reserve. Software development invariably costs more than the baseline estimate. It is extremely important to know the requirements of the intended software user as well as those of the customer. You derive values of software product management attribute factor in the same manner as those for hardware products. The formulation for estimating the contribution of MAF to risk exposure is also the same (*v.*, Equations 5.7 through 5.14).

### ■ 5.6.4 Software Product and Process Maturity Factors

Software product and process maturity factors are keyed to software milestones and the documentation which marks the successful completion of these milestones. Tables 5.56 and 5.57 give suggested schema for deriving values of **software product maturity** factor and **software process maturity** factor.

Software PRODMF is an inverse measure of the maturity of the design approach of the software program being designed. By the same token, it is a direct measure of the contribution to risk exposure by lack of maturity.

**Table 5.56** *Software Product Maturity Factors*

| PRODMF | Level of Design Approach Maturity |
|---|---|
| 0.0 | Similar production maintenance software verified and validated |
| 0.1 | Similar production software verified and validated |
| 0.2 | Similar production software test drivers integrated and tested |
| 0.3 | Similar production modules integrated and tested |
| 0.4 | Similar production code and unit tests completed |
| 0.5 | Similar development modules integrated and tested |
| 0.6 | Similar development code and unit tests completed |
| 0.7 | Similar unit functional allocations and interfaces defined |
| 0.8 | HIPO of computer program modules specified |
| 0.9 | Functional requirements of computer program modules defined |
| 1.0 | Design approach not established |

PRODMF: Software product maturity factor.
HIPO: Hierarchical inputs, processes, and outputs.

**Table 5.57** *Software Process Maturity Factors*

| PROCMF | Current Level of Process Maturity |
|---|---|
| 0.0 | Similar software production document produced |
| 0.1 | Similar software user's manual produced |
| 0.2 | Similar software product specification produced |
| 0.3 | Similar software interface control document produced |
| 0.4 | Similar software subsystems specifications produced |
| 0.5 | Similar software requirements document produced |
| 0.6 | Similar software end-item acceptance plan produced |
| 0.7 | Similar software configuration management plan produced |
| 0.8 | Similar software quality plan produced |
| 0.9 | Similar software development produced |
| 1.0 | No similar software development plan produced |

PROCMF: Software process maturity factor.

Software PROCMF is an inverse measure of the design maturity of the process for producing the software program of interest. By the same token, it is a direct measure of the contribution to risk exposure by the lack of process maturity.

### ■ 5.6.5 Example of Composite Software Product and Process Maturity Factors

Iota, Incorporated, manufactures state-of-the-art production-line equipment and has a material-handling robot with a wide range of capability in development. Iota estimates that the remaining software development cost will be $300,000, but realizes that the cost can grow because of uncertainties in the software, which is embedded in the product.

Iota retains Analyst to estimate the risk cost. Table 5.58 gives the technical approach Analyst follows in carrying out the assignment.

**Table 5.58** *Technical Approach for Composite Software Product and Process Maturity Factors Example*

1. Determine software development status.
2. Derive values of software product and process maturity factors.
3. Establish dependency relationships among factors.
4. Calculate risk cost.

Table 5.59 summarizes Analyst's findings on the software development status. Analyst also finds that the relationship between software PRODMF and PROCMF is independent, meaning that Analyst should estimate the composite value of risk cost by taking the root-sum-of-squares of the individual risk cost values for PRODMF and PROCMF.

The RC value from PRODMF is simply the product of the development baseline cost estimate of $300,000 and PRODMF value of 0.6, for ($300,000)(0.6), or $180,000. The RC value from PROCCF is the product of the process BCE of $300,000 and the PROCMF value of 0.7, for ($300,000)(0.7), or $210,000.

## 5.6 Software Factors

Equation 5.63 gives $RSS$ = $276,586. If the relationship between the attributes of product and process maturity were dependent, the sum would equal $180,000 + $210,000, or $390,000.

**Table 5.59** *Status Data for Composite Software Product and Process Maturity Factors Example*

| Status | PRODMF | PROCMF |
|---|---|---|
| Development code and unit tests completed successfully | 0.6 | |
| Similar production unit folders compiled | | 0.7 |

PRODMF: Software product maturity factor.
PROCMF: Software process maturity factor.

Equation 5.63 gives the value of the RSS of the two individual values of risk cost.

$$RSS = \sqrt{(\$180{,}000)^2 + (\$210{,}000)^2}$$
$$= \$276{,}586. \qquad (5.63)$$

The RCE is, therefore, $300,000 + $276,586, or $576,000. Analyst provides the finding to Iota, Incorporated. The company remarks that, in its experience, it has not been unusual for software RCE to be almost twice the amount of the BCE.

### ■ 5.6.6 Software Product or Process Quality Factor

The quality of the development process establishes the quality of the software product. Therefore, you use **software product quality** factor or **software process quality** factor keyed to the control exercised during development and production.

PRODQF and PROCQF are inverse measures of the degree of control on the given program. By the same token, they are direct measures of the contribution to risk exposure from the lack of control. Table 5.59 gives suggested schema for deriving values of both PRODQF and PROCQF.

Reference 6 consist of extensive checklists which allow you to interpolate within the values of Table 5.60. In addition, the yes-no answers to the checklist allow you to apply binary weighting to the derivation of PRODQF and PROCQF values.

PRODQF and PROCQF are second-order risk determinant factors with respect to PRODMF and PROCMF that are first-order risk determinant factors. For example, if PRODQF or PROCQF were equal to 1.0, but PRODMF or PROCMF were equal to 0.2, then the latter would equal (0.2)(1), or 0.2. The fraction 0.1 is the $k$-factor.

Since the attributes of software product quality and software process quality have a dependent relationship, you treat composites of the two factors on an additive basis. The maximum possible value of two factors is 1 + 1, or 2. Given $k \cdot$ PRODQF = 0.2 and $k \cdot$ PROCQF = 0.4, for 0.2 + 0.6, or 0.8, the value of the composite risk determinant factor is 0.8 ÷ 2 = 0.4

> *Irrespective of its merit or value, do the job often enough and you will do it well.*
>
> *Analyst*

**Table 5.60** *Software Product Quality Factor or Software Process Quality Factor [4]*

| Factor | Level of Control |
|---|---|
| 0 | **Optimized**. Organization has not only achieved high degree of control over software development, it also has major focus on improving and optimizing its operation. This includes more sophisticated analyses of error and cost data gathered during process, and introduction of comprehensive error-cause analysis and prevention studies. |
| 0.2 | **Managed**. Organization bases its operating decisions on quantitative process data, and conducts extensive analysis of data gathered during software engineering tests and reviews. Tools are used increasingly to control and manage the design process as well as to support data gathering and analysis. The organization is learning to project expected errors with reasonable accuracy. |
| 0.4 | **Defined**. Organization not only defines its process in terms of software engineering standards and methods, it also has made series of organizational and methodological improvements. These include design and code reviews, training programs, and increased focus on software engineering. Major improvement in this control level is establishment and staffing of software engineering process groups that focus on software engineering and its adequacy. |
| 0.6 | **Repeatable**. Organization uses standard methods and practices for managing software development tasks such as cost estimating, scheduling, requirements changes, code changes, and status reviews. |
| 0.8 | **Initial**. Development environment has ill-defined procedures and controls. Organization does not consistently apply software engineering management to development process, nor does it use modern tools and technology. |
| 1.0 | **None**. Development environment has no defined procedures and controls. |

Adapted by courtesy of U.S. Air Force Electronic Systems Division from W. S. Humphrey and W. L. Sweet, *A Method for Assessing the Software Engineering Capability of Contractors*, ESD/TR-87-186, September 1987.

### ■ 5.6.7 Software Product or Process Complexity Factor

The attribute of software program size drives the complexity of both the software product and software process. Therefore, you use the **software product complexity** factor or **software process complexity** factor keyed to the number of lines of code.

PRODCF and PROCCF are inverse measures of software program size. By the same token, they are direct measures of the contribution to risk exposure from the size.

Table 5.61 gives suggested schema for deriving values of either PRODQF or PROCQF. Typical software programs for embedded computers in high-technology products use 5,000 to 10,000 thousand lines of code (KLOC).

## 5.6 Software Factors

You must use software product complexity factor or process complexity factor keyed to the size of the program. The metric used to describe the size of programs is the number of lines of code, excluding blank lines, which are required to implement the code. The number of lines of code are essentially equal to the number of instructions in the program. [5]

Table 5.61 gives the schema for deriving PRODCF or PROCCF as a function of number of lines of code. This metric is usually estimated prior to start of coding in thousands of lines of code (*i.e.*, KLOC).

*Table 5.61  Software Product Complexity Factor or Software Process Complexity Factor [7]*

| Factor | KLOC | Factor | KLOC |
|---|---|---|---|
| 0 | 0.1 | 0.6 | 100 |
| 0.1 | 0.5 | 0.7 | 500 |
| 0.2 | 1 | 0.8 | 1,000 |
| 0.3 | 5 | 0.9 | 5,000 |
| 0.4 | 10 | 1.0 | 10,000 |
| 0.5 | 50 | | |

**KLOC**: 1,000 lines of code

If each line of code were to consist of an average of five 4-byte words, 10,000 KLOC would require (5)(4)(10,000,000), or 200 megabytes (*i.e.*, 200,000,000 bytes) of data.

PRODCF and PROCCF are inverse measures of the complexity of the software program being designed and produced. By the same token, they are direct measures of the contribution to risk exposure by the lack of design and process complexity. PRODCF and PROCCF are second-order risk determinant factors with respect to PRODMF and PROCMF.

### ■ 5.6.8 Software Product or Process Concurrency Factor

You will use **software product concurrency** factor or **software process concurrency** factor that key to the overlap of dependent tasks. PRODYF and PROCYF are inverse measures of the degree of overlap. By the same token, they are direct measures of the contribution to risk exposure by the overlap. PRODYF is also a second-order risk determinant factor with respect to PRODMF and PROCMF.

Figure 5.9, which is adapted from Figure 5.4, illustrates concurrency of various degrees between software product Tasks j and i. Task j is the independent task and Task i the dependent one. The overlap ranges from 0 percent to 100 percent, or 0 to 1.0.

Again, we suggest a simple, but realistic, rating schema for PRODYF and PROCYF. The decimal fraction of overlap serves as the values of these factors. Table 5.62 gives the schema.

For example, for 0 percent overlap of Tasks j and i, the decimal fraction is 0 and PRODYF or PROCYF equals 0. For 100 percent overlap, the decimal fraction is 1.0 and PRODYF or PROCYF equals 1.0. The greater the value of PRODYF or PROCYF, the greater is the risk exposure from concurrency of dependent tasks.

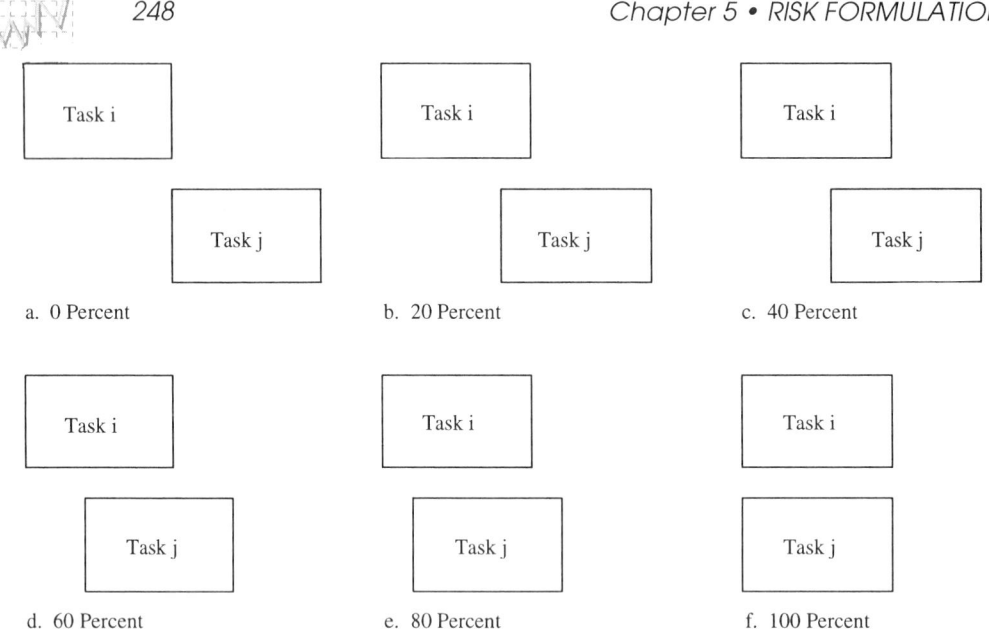

[Figure 5.9 shows six diagrams labeled a through f depicting two boxes (Task i and Task j) with varying degrees of overlap]

a. 0 Percent
b. 20 Percent
c. 40 Percent
d. 60 Percent
e. 80 Percent
f. 100 Percent

**Figure 5.9** Concurrency Between Software Product Tasks j and i

***Table 5.62*** *Software Product Concurrency or Software Process Concurrency Factor*

| Factor | Overlap | Factor | Overlap |
|---|---|---|---|
| 0 | 0 | 0.6 | 0.6 |
| 0.1 | 0.1 | 0.7 | 0.7 |
| 0.2 | 0.2 | 0.8 | 0.8 |
| 0.3 | 0.3 | 0.9 | 0.9 |
| 0.4 | 0.4 | 1.0 | 1.0 |
| 0.5 | 0.5 | | |

### ■ 5.6.9 Example of Composite Software Product and Process Maturity, Quality, Complexity, and Concurrency Factors

Delta Industries manufactures commercial and private jet aircraft that uses embedded computers. Delta contracts for the software for these computers and questions the ability of a software developer to deliver the program within the contracted time of two years. Delta is not overly concerned about cost because of the firm-fixed price contract.

Delta retains Analyst to investigate the software developer's attributes of product and process maturity, quality, complexity, and concurrency and to derive the risk-cost estimate for the undertaking. Table 5.63 give the technical approach Analyst follows in carrying out the assignment.

## 5.6 Software Factors

**Table 5.63** *Technical Approach for Composite Software Product and Process Maturity, Quality, Complexity, and Concurrency Factors Example*

1. Rate software developer for PRODMF, PROCMF, PRODQF, PROCQF, PRODYF, and PROCYF in accordance with Tables 5.56, 5.57, 5.60, 5.61, and 5.62.
2. Assume dependent relationship among product and process factors.
3. Equate $k$-factors to PRODMF and PROCMF.
4. Derive risk time estimate.

Analyst interviews top management, middle management, programmers, and support personnel at the software developer and gives the company the following ratings:

1. With respect to current level of design approach maturity (*v.*, Table 5.56), the company has integrated and tested similar production modules. PRODMF = 0.3.

2. With respect to current level of process maturity, (*v.*, Table 5.57), the company has produced similar software subsystems specifications. PROCMF = 0.4.

3. With respect to level of control (*v.*, Table 5.60), the company is "managed." PRODQF and PROCQF = 0.2.

4. With respect to complexity, (*v.*, Table 5.61), the software program will have 5,000 KLOC when completed. PRODCF and PROCCF = 0.9.

5. With respect to overlap of product and process tasks (*v.*, Table 5.62), product and process tasks overlap 50 percent. PRODYF and PROCYF = 0.5.

PRODCF and PRODYF are second-order tasks that Analyst multiplies by $k = 0.3$, the value of PRODMF. PROCCF and PROCYF are also second-order factors that Analyst multiplies by $k = 0.4$, the value of PROCMF. Table 5.64 gives the factored values.

**Table 5.64** *Factored Values for Composite Software Product and Process Maturity, Quality, Complexity, and Concurrency Factors Example*

| | |
|---|---|
| PRODMF = 0.3 | PROCMF = 0.4 |
| PRODQF = (0.2)(0.3) = 0.06 | PROCQF = (0.2)(0.4) = 0.08 |
| PRODCF = (0.9)(0.3) = 0.27 | PROCCF = (0.9)(0.4) = 0.36 |
| PRODYF = (0.5)(0.3) = 0.15 | PROCYF = (0.5)(0.4) = 0.20 |

The maximum value possible for each of the eight risk determinant factors is 1. Therefore, the maximum sum possible for all eight is 8. Equation 5.64 gives the value of the composite risk determinant factor (CRDF).

$$CRDF = 0.3 + 0.06 + 0.27 + 0.15 + 0.4 + 0.08 + 0.36 + 0.20$$
$$= 1.82 \tag{5.64}$$

where the risk determinant factor values in the numerator are from Table 5.64.

The value of CRDF equal to 1.82 is due to the assumption of dependency among the contributing factors. Since corrective-action specifics are unknown, Analyst uses Equation 5.3 for the value of RTE. Substituting $BTE = 2$ years, or 24 months, and $CRDF = 1.82$ in Equation 5.3, Analyst obtains

$$RTE = 24 \text{ months } (1 + 1.82)$$
$$= 67.68 \text{ months.} \quad (5.65)$$

Shocking? Not really. Such overruns of allotted time were commonplace in the early days of software development and still exist to some extent.

Analyst provides the finding to Delta Industries. The software for the embedded computer is in the critical path of the product network and the company will seek a second source.

## 5.7
## SERVICE FACTORS

Service is big business. According to Reference 8, the combined 1993 revenue of the world's 500 largest service corporations was in excess of 20.9 trillion U.S. dollars, and their profit increased by 28 percent from the prior year. These figures do not account for the myriad of smaller businesses in the service sector.

Table 5.65 gives the categories for the 500 largest service corporations. The category Diversified Service Companies includes the areas of wholesaling, trading, food engineering, construction, distribution, entertainment, gambling, marketing, broadcasting, home building, vehicle renting, food services, and information services. Table 5.65 also follows the revenue ranking of the corporations.

*Table 5.65* *Categories of the 500 Largest Service Corporations [6]*

| Category | Quantity | Revenue | Profit |
| --- | --- | --- | --- |
| Commercial Banking Companies | 100 | 1,866.3372 | 30.6167 |
| Retailing Companies | 50 | 491.0097 | 8.8021 |
| Diversified Service Companies | 100 | 436.9319 | 6.7810 |
| Savings Institutions | 50 | 352.5122 | 1.0334 |
| Diversified Financial Companies | 50 | 285.5711 | 21.543 |
| Life Insurance Companies | 50 | 262.0422 | 7.7924 |
| Utilities | 50 | 260.3123 | 12.0685 |
| Transportation Companies | 50 | 174.1274 | 6.6733 |

Revenue and profit in $ billion.
Adapted by permission of FORTUNE from *The Service 500*, FORTUNE, May 30, 1994.

We base service risk determinant factors on the attributes of service maturity, quality, complexity, and concurrency, with design maturity being the dominant attribute. The approach for rating service maturity factor is similar to that used for hardware products.

## 5.7 Service Factors

We use the management attribute factor for rating service quality because the quality is a function of management policy. We adapt the checklists in Tables 5.4, 5.5, 5.6, and 5.7 for capturing the essence of these policies.

The approach for rating service complexity is similar to that used for hardware products. We base the rating schema on the generation breakdown index that is a function of the number of levels and span in the generation breakdown of service products.

The approach for rating service concurrency is also similar to that used for hardware products. We base the rating schema on the overlap of dependent tasks in service products.

### ■ 5.7.1 Service Product or Process Maturity Factors

Product and process maturity are synonymous in service products. Service PRODMF and PROCMF are inverse measures of the experience and availability of the software provider. By the same token, they are direct measures of the contribution to risk exposure by the lack of experienced personnel.

Table 5.66 gives suggested schema for rating PRODMF or PROCMF. Note that we base ratings on the availability of experienced service teams.

*Table 5.66*  Service Product or Process Maturity Factor

| FACTOR | Level of Experienced Team Availability |
|---|---|
| 0 | Several experienced teams available for assignment. |
| 0.25 | One experienced team available for assignment. |
| 0.50 | Several experienced teams in organization but unavailable at present. |
| 0.25 | One experienced team in organization, but unavailable at present. |
| 1.0 | No experienced team employed in organization. |

Factor: PRODMF or PROCMF.

We suggest that you define *several* as "five," whereby each increment in Table 5.66 subdivides into five subincrements of 0.05 each. Given a service organization with two experienced teams available for assignment, PRODMF or PROCMF would equal two subincrements less than 0.25, for $0.25 - (2)(0.05)$, or 0.15.

### ■ 5.7.2 Service Product or Process Quality Factor

Product and process quality are also synonymous in service products. Service PRODQF and PROCQF are inverse measures of the management commitment to the service products offered. By the same token, they are direct measures of the contribution to risk exposure by lack of commitment.

The approach for deriving PRODQF or PROCQF for service products uses management attributes of service funding and budgeting policy, service customer and user policy, service program continuity policy, and service personnel growth and retention policy, and a survey of other customers. Tables 5.67, 5.68, 5.69, and 5.70 are the checklists for rating the management attributes. Table 5.70 lists questions for surveys of other customers of the service organization.

**Table 5.67**  *Service Funding and Budgeting Policy Checklist*

|  | Yes | No |
|---|---|---|
| 1. Is there sufficient funding for service equipment? | | |
| 2. Does the budget include funding for training? | | |
| 3. Does the budget include annual salary increases? | | |
| 4. Can the organization extend credit to customers? | | |
| 5. Is there sufficient financial reserve to repeat service rendered? | | |
| 6. Is equipment depreciation taken properly? | | |

Ask questions which you can answer with a yes or no, not those whose answers would need interpretation; for example, don't ask, "How often do you complain about the service?"

**Table 5.68**  *Service Customer Policy Checklist*

|  | Yes | No |
|---|---|---|
| 1. Does the organization survey customers after service products are rendered? | | |
| 2. Are service product warranties stated clearly and unambiguously? | | |
| 3. Is service repeated without charge if needed? | | |
| 4. Are customers automatically notified of service products improvements? | | |
| 5. Are performance, schedule, and cost monitored on a weekly basis? | | |

**Table 5.69**  *Service Personnel Growth and Retention Policy Checklist*

|  | Yes | No |
|---|---|---|
| 1. Are service personnel certified or licensed? | | |
| 2. Are service personnel required to take periodic refresher courses? | | |
| 3. Is there a specific individual in charge of each job? | | |
| 4. Are assignments of service personnel made for the duration of service contracts? | | |
| 5. Are career progressions defined so that every employee understands the promotion opportunities? | | |
| 6. Do training programs satisfy organizational and employee current and future needs? | | |
| 7. Are service managers involved in the recruitment, training, and retention of service personnel? | | |

## 5.7 Service Factors

**Table 5.70**  *Other Service Customers Checklist*

|  | Yes | No |
|---|---|---|
| 1. Has the original service contract been renewed? | | |
| 2. Is renewal of the service contract being contemplated? | | |
| 3. Is the service provided in a prompt, satisfactory manner? | | |
| 4. Are complaints handled promptly and at the expense of the service provider? | | |
| 5. Is there less than one complaint per month? | | |
| 6. Is billing for service accurate? | | |
| 7. Would you recommend the service provider to another company? | | |

### ■ 5.7.3 Service Product Quality Factor Example

Beta Industries, manufacturer of home appliances, is displeased with the quality of effort of its distributor and wishes to change to another. The company retains Analyst to rate the **service product quality** factor PRODQF for the proposed, new distributor.

Table 5.71 gives the technical approach Analyst follows in carrying out the assignment. Note that the approach uses the checklists in Tables 5.67, 5.68, 5.69, and 5.70.

**Table 5.71**  *Technical Approach for Service Product Quality Factor Example*

1. Obtain answers to checklist questions in Tables 5.67, 5.68, 5.69, and 5.70 for the proposed new distributor.
2. Use binary weighting to rate sequences of answers to checklist questions.
3. Calculate service product quality factor assuming dependent relationships among attributes comprising checklists.

Analyst interviews personnel in the proposed distributing company and surveys several organizations using its services presently. Table 5.72 is the worksheet Analyst uses to complete the assignment. The table gives the consensus of interview and survey findings in the first two columns.

**Table 5.72**  *Worksheet for Service Product Quality Factor Example*

| Table Number | Answers | Binary Number | Equivalent Decimal Value | Largest Possible Decimal Value |
|---|---|---|---|---|
| 5.67 | Yes, no, yes, no, yes, no | 101010 | 42 | 63 |
| 5.68 | No, no, yes, no, no | 00100 | 4 | 31 |
| 5.69 | No, no, no, no, no, no, yes | 0000001 | 1 | 127 |
| 5.70 | No, no, no, yes, no, no, no | 0001000 | 8 | 127 |
| | | Totals: | 55 | 348 |

The third, fourth, and fifth columns in Table 5.72 contain the binary numbers, the respective equivalent decimal values, and largest possible decimal values for the sequences of answers to the checklist questions. Note the sum of 55 for the equivalent decimal values and the sum of 348 for the largest possible decimal value.

Equation 5.66 gives the value of service product quality factor for a dependent relationship among the attributes comprising the checklists.

$$PRODQF = \frac{348 - 55}{348}$$
$$= 0.842. \qquad (5.66)$$

Analyst provides the finding to the Beta Industries. Beta notes that the values of PRODQF are about the same for the old and proposed, new distributor. This leaves the company in a quandary, or as Yogi Berra would say, "It's déjà vu, all over again."

### ■ 5.7.4 Service Product or Process Complexity Factor

**Service product** and process **complexity** are also synonymous. Service PRODCF and PROCCF are inverse measures of service complexity. By the same token, they are direct measures of the contribution to risk exposure by the complexity of the service.

Table 5.73 gives suggested schema for rating PRODCF. You first encountered GBI in Figure 5.3 that illustrated the concept.

**Table 5.73** *Service Product or Process Complexity Factor*

| Factor | GBI | Factor | GBI |
|--------|-----|--------|-----|
| 0.1 | 100 | 0.6 | 600 |
| 0.2 | 200 | 0.7 | 700 |
| 0.3 | 300 | 0.8 | 800 |
| 0.4 | 400 | 0.9 | 900 |
| 0.5 | 500 | 1.0 | 1000 |

Factor: PRODCF or PROCCF.
GBI: Generation breakdown index.

The value of GBI is a function of the number of levels in the GB and the span of the GB at the lowest levels. Typically, the range of values is 100 to 1,000 for the GBI of service products.

### ■ 5.7.5 Service Product or Process Concurrency Factor

Product and process concurrency are also synonymous in service products; therefore we use only **service product concurrency** factor. Service PRODYF is an inverse measure of service complexity. By the same token, it is a direct measure of the contribution to risk exposure by the concurrency among dependent tasks in the service product being tendered.

## 5.8 Summary

Table 5.74 gives suggested schema for rating PRODYF. Note that we base ratings on overlap of dependent tasks in the service product. You first encountered task overlap in Figure 5.4 that illustrated the concept.

*Table 5.74  Service Product or Process Concurrency Factor*

|        |         | Overlap | Factor    |
|--------|---------|---------|-----------|
| Task j | Task $i_1$ | 0 - 1.0 | 0   - 0.2 |
|        | Task $i_2$ | 0 - 1.0 | 0.2 - 0.4 |
|        | Task $i_3$ | 0 - 1.0 | 0.4 - 0.6 |
|        | Task $i_4$ | 0 - 1.0 | 0.6 - 0.8 |
|        | Task $i_5$ | 0 - 1.0 | 0.8 - 1.0 |

Factor: PRODYF or PROCYF.

We designed Table 5.74 for one independent task and five dependent tasks. The factor increment is 0.2. Given an overlap of 0.5 of one independent task and two dependent tasks, the value of the factor is 0.4 + (0.5)(0.2), or 0.5.

You accommodate a decrease in the number of dependent tasks by increasing the factor increment. Given two dependent tasks, the increment is 0.5. For a 0.5 overlap one independent task and two dependent tasks, the value of the factor is 0.5 + (0.5)(0.5), or 0.75. The exercise in Section 5.9.16 asks you to modify the table for four dependent tasks.

# 5.8
# SUMMARY

**Section 5.1 Definitions** described the organization of Chapter 5 and the highlights of its sections. The section included the definitions of key terms and abbreviations used in the chapter. These definitions were given when first used in the chapter and are repeated in Appendix A.

**Section 5.2 Perspective on Risk Determinant Factors** is pivotal to the application of the various risk determinant factors. Risk formulation is the essence of realistic, credible risk estimates, and the section addressed the proper formulation in its generic form. The section provided details on specific risk determinant factors.

**Section 5.3 Management Attribute Factors** covered the influence of management attributes, as evidenced by policies and decisions, on risk exposure. The effects of management attribute factors vary somewhat as functions of product categories. The section illustrated the use of checklists in deriving the values of the management attribute factor.

**Section 5.4 Extrinsic Attribute Factors** addressed the influence of extrinsic attributes, such as escalation, inflation, and statutory regulations, on risk exposure. The section illustrated the use of checklists in deriving values of the extrinsic attribute factor.

The next three sections addressed risk determinant factors as functions of the product categories; hardware, software, and service. In each category, maturity dominates over the other attributes in the contribution to risk exposure and we account for this domination by the $k$-factor equated to either product or process maturity.

**Section 5.5 Hardware Factors** developed schema for deriving hardware product and process risk determinant factors. We based these schema on the attributes of product and process design maturity, quality, complexity, and concurrency; the latter referring to the concurrent performance of interdependent design tasks. Again, the section illustrates the use of checklists and several weighting techniques in deriving values of hardware product risk determinant factors.

**Section 5.6 Software Factors** developed derivation schema for software product and process design maturity, quality, complexity, and concurrency factors. We keyed the schema to the hierarchical processes in software development and production. The derivation of software product risk determinant factors uses tailored versions of the management attribute checklist because of the general paucity of software knowledge at the upper-management level.

**Section 5.7 Service Factors** developed the derivation schema for the service product and process risk determinant factors. We based the schema on the availability of experienced service teams, tailored versions of the management attribute checklists plus a checklist for ratings by other customers of the service products, service task complexity, and the concurrency among dependent tasks of service products.

Chapter 5 concludes with the **Summary** in **Section 5.8**, **Exercises** in **Section 5.9**, and **References** in **Section 5.10**.

## 5.9
## EXERCISES

Appendix C contains step-by-step solutions to the following exercises. We urge you to attempt the exercises before resorting to the solutions. The intent is to reinforce the subject matter covered in the chapter.

### ■ 5.9.1 Risk Determinant Factor Dominance

Define the meaning of *first-order risk determinant factor*, *second-order risk determinant factor*, and k-*factor*. Give an example of the *k*-factor in operation.

### ■ 5.9.2 Hardware Risk Determinant Factors

Enumerate the risk determinant factors used to derive risk exposure in hardware products. Which factors are dominant?

### ■ 5.9.3 Extrinsic Attribute Checklist

Consider a tire manufacturing company, located in Ohio, that ships its products all over the world, all year round. What extrinsic attributes limit the company's ability to produce and ship its products?

## 5.9 Exercises

Tailor the extrinsic attribute checklists for use by the company in estimating the risk exposure due to the extrinsic attributes of tires for large trailer trucks and those for passenger vehicles. What steps would you take to reduce extrinsic attributes' contribution to risk exposure?

### ■ 5.9.4 Composite Management Attribute and Extrinsic Attribute Factors

Calculate the composite risk determinant factor for a management attribute factor of 0.3 and an extrinsic attribute factor of 0.5 for the company in the example of Section 5.4.4. Would you assume a dependent or independent relationship between the two factors and why?

### ■ 5.9.5 Risk Cost Estimate

Consider the following sets of values for hardware risk determinant factors and baseline cost estimates. Calculate and compare the two values of risk cost estimates.

PRODMF: 0.25    PRODQF: 0.50    BCE: $2.5 million
PRODMF: 0.50    PRODQF: 0.25    BCE: $2.5 million

### ■ 5.9.6 Revised Risk Cost Estimate

Assume the risk cost value of $500,000 in the preceding exercise. Recalculate the risk cost estimates using Equations 5.2 and 5.4. Which answers do you consider more realistic and credible?

### ■ 5.9.7 Hardware Product Complexity Factor

Values of the hardware product complexity factor are estimated from the number of levels and span of the generation breakdown. What do you call the product of the number of levels and the span in a GB? Given ten levels and a span of 250, estimate the PRODCF of a certain hardware product.

Assume a baseline cost estimate of $125,000 and risk cost estimate of $50,000. Calculate the risk cost estimate. Include *PRODMF* = 0.25 and recalculate the risk cost estimate. Explain the difference in the answers.

### ■ 5.9.8 Generation Breakdowns and Lists of Part Numbers

Computer-generated generation breakdowns and lists of part numbers usually appear in tabular form. Derive the computer-mechanized generation breakdown for a radial saw. Calculate the generation breakdown index and estimate the hardware product and process complexity factors.

Obtain the net selling price for a ten-inch radial saw. Derive the portion of the price attributable to risk exposure from product and process complexity.

### ■ 5.9.9 Hardware Product and Process Complexity Factors

Given the baseline cost estimate of $25 million, calculate the risk cost estimate for the PRODCF value of 0.6 and the PROCCF value of 0.8 with respective $k$-factors of 0.8 and 0.6.

## 5.9.10 Risk Exposure in Total Procurement Package

A total procurement package is a single contract for the sequential development and production of a given product. In the past, military aircraft were usually procured in this fashion. [7]

Consider the total procurement package described in Table 5.75. Estimate the risk exposure for the following values of hardware product risk determinant factors:

PRODMF = 0.2   PRODQF = 0.3   PRODCF = 0.2   PRODYF = 0.2
PROCMF = 0.1   PROCQF = 0.1   PROCCF = 0.1   PROCYF = 0.3.

*Table 5.75  Total Procurement Package Data*

|      | Development | Production Nonrecurring | Production Recurring | Total |
|------|-------------|-------------------------|----------------------|-------|
| BCE: | 250         | 150                     | 400                  | 800   |
| BTE: | 36          | 18                      | 48                   | 102   |
| AIC: | 3           | 3.5                     | 3.5                  | Per month |

BCE: Baseline cost estimate.
BTE: Baseline time estimate.
AIC: Additional indirect cost.
Costs are in $ million.

## 5.9.11 Software Risk Determinant Factors

Enumerate the risk determinant factors used to derive risk exposure in software products.
Which are the dominant factors? How many combinations can you form of first-order and second-order software risk determinant factors?

## 5.9.12 Software Management Attribute Factor

Describe the purpose of the software management attribute factor and how it is used. Does a dependent or independent relationship exist among the attributes of the software management factor?

## 5.9.13 Composite Software Risk Exposure

Given the data in Table 5.76, calculate the composite software risk exposure. Assume the baseline cost estimate to complete development is $3.75 million and derive the value of the risk cost estimate.

*Table 5.76  Software Development Status Data*

| Status | PRODMF | PROCMF |
|--------|--------|--------|
| Development code and unit tests completed successfully. | 0.4 | |
| Similar production unit folders compiled. | | 0.8 |

PRODMF: Product maturity factor.
PROCMF: Process maturity factor.

## 5.9 Exercises

### ■ 5.9.14 Service Risk Determinant Factors

Enumerate the risk determinant factors used to derive risk exposure in service products. Which are the first-order factors?

### ■ 5.9.15 Risk Exposure in Service Products

Estimate the software product quality factor using the methodology of the example in Section 5.7.3 with the following answers to the checklist questions in the example:

Table 5.67: Yes, yes, yes, no, yes, no
Table 5.68: No, no, yes, no
Table 5.69: No, yes, no, no, no, no, yes
Table 5.70: No, no, no, yes, yes, yes, yes

### ■ 5.9.16 Service Product or Process Concurrency Factor

Modify Table 5.74 to accommodate four dependent tasks. State the general relationship between the number of dependent tasks and the size of the factor increments.

### ■ 5.9.17 Risk Cost Retrospective

One way to ensure low risk cost is to start with low baseline cost. Aggressive cost reduction attacks time as the means for reducing elements of indirect cost.

Just as time is money, so is inventory. Over the past decade, thousands of companies adopted the concept of just-in-time (JIT) inventory to reduce the cost of carrying inventories in advance of sales. In theory, JIT should allow producers to buy only enough parts and material to fill near-term orders, and suppliers to move products from producers to customers almost immediately.

Zero inventory is the ultimate fulfillment of JIT as a procurement strategy. The concept of zero inventory is particularly appealing to high-technology enterprises because of the large investment in work-in-process. The classical example is Toyota's Kanban.

According to Kanban, inventories are both unnecessary and counterproductive in achieving low cost. The thrust is to eliminate the large runs by reducing set-up times on production lines. Toyota measures change-over time in minutes vs. hours in U.S. plants. In addition, Toyota eliminates buffer inventories that mask production problems. [8]

This is how JIT should work; however, according to the U.S. Department of Commerce, manufacturers' inventories grew faster in 1994 than at any time since 1987. The upward trend is pronounced since 1987.

What happened to the concept of JIT, which was supposed to have just the opposite effect on inventory? One explanation is that retail sales are erratic and companies do not want to be caught short of inventory to sell. Another explanation is that the price of commodities, such as steel and lumber, have surged upward, and companies that wait to buy commodities until they need the commodities will pay more and be unable to pass the price increase on to wholesalers and retailers.

Investigate manufacturer, wholesaler, retailer, and consumer data in the current issue of the *Statistical Abstract of the United States*. Do you detect correlation among the data? [9] State your reasons for any differences that you perceive. Do you think that concepts such as JIT can be as effective in the United States as it has been in Japan?

## 5.10
### REFERENCES

You can obtain referenced government documents from the issuing organizations and from:

> Superintendent of Documents, U.S. Government Printing Office, Washington, DC 20402. Telephone: (202) 783-3238.
> National Technical Information Service, U.S. Department of Commerce, Springfield, VA 22161. Telephone: (703) 487-4650.

1. Defense Systems Management College, *Test and Evaluation Management Guide*, Fort Belvoir, Virginia, March 1988.
2. U.S. Department of Defense, MIL-STD-2165, *Military Standard-Testability Program for Electronic Systems and Equipments*, 1985.
3. Mark L. Berenson and David M. Levine, *Statistics for Business and Economics*, Second Edition, Prentice Hall, 1993.
4. W. S. Humphrey and W. L. Sweet, *A Method for Assessing the Software Engineering Capability of Contractors*, ESD/TR-87-186, U.S. Air Force Electronic System Division, September 1987.
5. Möller, K. H. and D. J. Paulish, *Software Metrics*, IEEE Computer Society Press, 1993.
6. *The Service 500*, FORTUNE, May 30, 1994.
7. Jack V. Michaels and William P. Wood, *Design to Cost*, John Wiley & Sons, Inc., 1989.
8. Richard J. Schonberger, *Japanese Manufacturing Techniques: Nine Hidden Lessons in Simplicity*, The Free Press, 1982.
9. U.S. Bureau of the Census, *Statistical Abstract of the United States: 1994* (114th Edition), Washington, DC, 1994.

> *Experience is the name every one gives to their mistakes.*
> ***Oscar Wilde***

CHAPTER 6

# RISK MODELS

> *Probabilities direct the conduct of the wise.*
> **Cicero**

A model is a representation of an attribute of an object for the purpose of prediction of the particular attribute. A risk model is a representation of some attribute of a system or product for the prediction and control of the risk exposure contribution of that attribute. In general, interest lies in the attributes of time or money.

Figure 6.1 illustrates the organization of the chapter. Subjects are listed alongside the respective sections.

**Section 6.1 Definitions** provides an annotated perspective of the chapter with the definitions of key terms and abbreviations used in the chapter. These definitions are repeated when they are first used in the chapter and in the glossary in Appendix A.

**Section 6.2 Perspective on Risk Models** reveals the profusion of models that you can find in contemporary literature on risk analysis and in books on operations research. The section includes selection criteria and application guidelines to ensure that the risk model is compatible with the intended use of its output, the data available for its input, and the resources to run it.

The intriguing nature of these models may cause you to lose sight of the end objective of the application. Be sure that you are addressing the right problem before you even begin to seek a model to use.

> *Nothing is more inimical to credibility than a brilliant solution in search of a problem.*
> **Analyst**

**Section 6.3 Art of Simulation** reveals the intuitive and subjective nature of simulation and describes the various approaches to simulation. The section begins with a brief dissertation on sampling distributions as the basis for modeling. The subject matter includes the generation and use of random numbers in the popular Monte Carlo method.

**Sections 6.4 Aggregation vs. Disaggregation** completes the cycle that began with the discussion of risk metrics in Chapter 3. You will see that aggregation is essentially an embodiment of top-down estimating and disaggregation is one of bottom-up estimating.

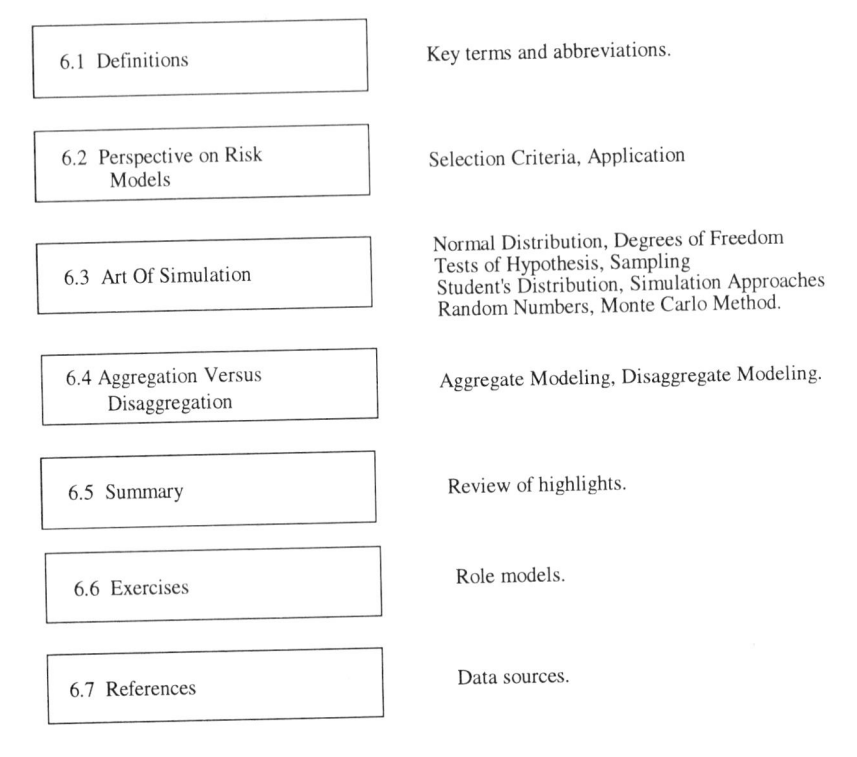

## Figure 6.1 Organization of Chapter 6

|  |  |
|---|---|
| 6.1 Definitions | Key terms and abbreviations. |
| 6.2 Perspective on Risk Models | Selection Criteria, Application |
| 6.3 Art Of Simulation | Normal Distribution, Degrees of Freedom, Tests of Hypothesis, Sampling, Student's Distribution, Simulation Approaches, Random Numbers, Monte Carlo Method. |
| 6.4 Aggregation Versus Disaggregation | Aggregate Modeling, Disaggregate Modeling. |
| 6.5 Summary | Review of highlights. |
| 6.6 Exercises | Role models. |
| 6.7 References | Data sources. |

You may employ either approach in any estimating methodology (*viz.*, expert opinion, analogy, parametric, or industrial engineering) or combinations of several methodologies. Aggregate modeling and disaggregate modeling denote the structure of the modeling approach, not the substance.

Chapter 6 concludes with **Section 6.5 Summary**, **Section 6.6 Exercises**, and **Section 6.7 References**. The summary serves to highlight the contents of the chapter and the exercises reinforce the highlights.

# 6.1
# DEFINITIONS

Table 6.1 gives definitions of the terms and abbreviations used in this chapter. Note the meaning of *aggregation* and *disaggregation* and the names of the various risk models. Note again the abbreviations of the risk determinant factors that we introduced in the previous chapters.

Note the meaning of the various statistical terms and statistical distributions, the *law of large numbers*, and the *central limit theorem*. Observe the relationships among confidence level, confidence limits, t-*statistic*, and z-*statistic*, and *test of hypotheses*. Note also the meaning of *Monte Carlo method*, *random number*, and *pseudorandom number*. The Monte Carlo method and pseudorandom numbers are at the heart of simulation.

## 6.1 Definitions

**Table 6.1**  *Terms and Abbreviations in Chapter 6*

**Aggregate model**: Top-down model with large granularity.
**Aggregation**: Assembling distinct components of products into aggregate for estimating purposes.
**Analog model**: Model representing properties of subject by other set of properties such as flow of electricity by flow of water.
**Baseline cost estimate**: Estimated cost to develop and produce product in accordance with baseline.
**Baseline time estimate**: Estimated time to develop and produce product in accordance with baseline.
**Central limit theorem**: Distributions of samples of populations approach normality with increased sample size.
**Chi-square distribution**: Sampling representation of variance of samples of population.
**Confidence level**: Degree of confidence desired in statistic of interest.
**Confidence limits**: Upper and lower boundaries of statistic of interest for desired confidence level.
**Degrees of freedom**: Number of variates in statistical distribution less number of dependent relationships among variates.
**Disaggregate model**: Bottom-up model with small granularity.
**Disaggregation**: Disassembling products into component parts for purpose of estimating the time and cost to produce products.
**EMV**: Expected monetary value.
**Equiprobability**: Equal probability.
***F*-distribution**: Statistical representation of ratios of samples of variances of several populations.
**GERT**: Graphical evaluation and review technique.
**Iconic model**: Model looking like subject.
**Law of large numbers**: Irrespective of probability distribution, the sample mean and variance converge on population mean and variance as random sample of size $n$ approaches population size.
**Moment-method**: Probabilistic modeling based on mean and variance of probability distributions.
**Mean**: Average value of statistical distribution.
**Monte Carlo method**: Method for simulating probability distributions with random numbers.
**Normal distribution**: Statistical representation of population of random variables.
**Null hypothesis**: Hypothesis that is subject of test of hypothesis.
**PAN**: Probabilistic analysis of network.
**Pseudorandom number**: Number picked at random from less than infinite uniform distribution of numbers.
**Random number**: Number picked at random from infinite uniform distribution of numbers.
**Risk cost**: Product of probability of occurrence of peril and the corrective-action cost. Probabilistic-deterministic estimate.
**Risk cost estimate**: Sum of baseline cost estimate and risk cost.
**Risk determinant factor**: Quantified measure of risk determinant.
**Risk exposure**: Vulnerability to peril in terms of risk time and risk cost.
**Risk time**: Product of probability of occurrence of peril and corrective-action time. Probabilistic-deterministic estimate.
**Risk time estimate**: Sum of baseline time estimate and risk time.
**RISNET**: Risk information system and network evaluation technique.
**SAM**: Stochastic aggregation model.
**Sampling distribution**: Statistical representation of samples of population.
**Standard deviation**: Measure of dispersion in statistical distribution. Square root of variance.
**Student's *t* distribution**: Statistical representation of small sample of population.
**Symbolic model**: Model representing its subjects by mathematical relationships.
**Test of hypotheses**: Statistical test of inferred values of means, standard deviations, and proportions.
**TRACE**: Total risk assessing cost estimate.
***t*-statistic**: Statistical measure for the area under the curve of the student's *t* distribution.
**Uniform distribution**: Statistical representation of variates with equiprobability of occurrence.
**Variance**: Measure of dispersion in statistical distribution. Square of standard deviation.
**VERT**: Venture evaluation and review technique.
***z*-statistic**: Statistical measure of the area under the curve of the normal distribution.

## 6.2
## PERSPECTIVE ON RISK MODELS

Risk models are not necessarily big, complex, or automated representations of systems or products. If you were to look at contemporary literature, it would appear that not only is the opposite true, but that there are as many approaches to modeling risk as there are practitioners who apply them. [1-3]

Table 6.2 lists a number of these models, or techniques, most of which have their roots in the defense community. Their use has spread in the private as well as the public sector to the point where practitioners refer to the majority of these techniques by their acronyms rather than by their full names. [1] [2]

### ■ 6.2.1 Selection Criteria

There are enough common threads weaving through the profusion of techniques in Table 6.2 to allow us to sort them into the three broad categories of network risk analysis, decision risk analysis, and cost risk analysis. Each of the categories serves a distinct purpose.

In addition, we can categorize the risk models in Table 6.2 by the classical models you encounter in operations research. These categories are the iconic model, analog model, and symbolic model.

*Table 6.2  Risk Modeling Techniques*

| |
|---|
| Cost Estimating Risk Analysis Technique |
| Cost Risk/WBS Simulation Model |
| Critical Path Method (CPM) |
| Decision Tree |
| Equirisk Contour Method |
| Expected Monetary Value (EMV) |
| Graphical Evaluation and Review Technique (GERT) |
| Probabilistic Analysis of Network (PAN) |
| Program Evaluation and Review Techniques (PERT) |
| Risk Factor Method |
| Risk Information System and Network Evaluation Technique (RISNET) |
| Stochastic Aggregation Model (SAM) |
| Total Risk Assessing Cost Estimate (TRACE) |
| Venture Evaluation and Review Technique (VERT) |

**Network Risk Analysis**

Network risk analysis concerns the **risk exposure** in the flow of activities for producing systems or products. The impact of perils on task performance time and cost and the effect of perils on the critical path activities equate to **risk time** and **risk cost**.

The models comprising the network risk analysis category are

1. Critical path method (CPM)
2. Graphical evaluation and review technique (**GERT**)
3. Probabilistic analysis of network (**PAN**)

## 6.2 Perspective on Risk Models

4. Risk information system and network evaluation technique (**RISNET**)
5. Venture evaluation and review technique (**VERT**).

We essentially use the foregoing models to find the shortest path through networks of risk time and risk cost. The product networks we develop in Chapter 4 fall in this category. We apply elements of network theory in the models. [3]

**Decision Risk Analysis**

The models comprising the decision risk analysis category are

1. Decision tree
2. Equirisk contour method
3. Expected monetary value (**EMV**).

We use these models to make optimal choices from alternative approaches and strategies. The examples in this chapter of aggregate and disaggregate modeling fall in this category. We apply elements of decision theory and game theory in these models. [3]

**Cost Risk Analysis**

The models comprising the cost risk analysis category are

1. Cost estimating risk analysis technique
2. Cost risk work breakdown structure model
3. Risk factor method
4. Stochastic aggregation model (**SAM**)
5. Total risk assessing cost estimate (**TRACE**).

We use these models when we are concerned with the inherent risk in making cost estimates. We apply a host of validating techniques in these models including statistical **tests of hypotheses**. [4]

As stated, it is also appropriate to try fitting the risk models in Table 6.2 to the classical models we encounter in operations research. These categories are the iconic model, analog model, and symbolic model. [5]

**Iconic Model**

The **iconic model** looks like the subject which it represents and may be as complex as a detailed, scale model of a high-performance aircraft or simply a photograph of the aircraft.

In the world of business, an industrial engineering cost estimate is an iconic model of the cost to produce the system or product of interest. Iconic models are perceived as being the most realistic of all extant models.

**Analog Model**

The **analog model** represents one set of properties by another set of properties such as a graph that uses scalar distances on the axes to represent the magnitude of the $x$ and $y$ variables. A typical analog model is the simulation of the flow of electricity by the flow of water.

Estimates by expert opinion are other examples of analog models in the business domain. Parametric estimates are combinations of analog models and symbolic models.

**Symbolic Model**

In the **symbolic model**, mathematical relationships describe the components and their inter-relationships in the form of an equation. As stated, the symbolic model is a form of parametric representation of objects of interest.

Where the object is cost, the symbolic model is a cost estimating relationship (CER). Typical relationships are cost as a linear function, or a direct or indirect power function of attributes such as weight, volume, and power. These relationships are particularly useful in estimating the cost of electrical and electronic products in their conceptual stages.

Three examples of parametric relationships follow. The first estimates cost as a linear function of material cost, the second and third as power functions of weight and volume.

> *A power function is a number raised to some power such as $x^n$. The power of that number defines the number of times you multiply the number by itself. For example, the value of the power function $2^4$ is (2)(2)(2)(2), or 16. The value of the power function $2^{1/2}$ is the square root of 2, or 1.4042. The value of the power function $2^{1/4}$ is the square root of the square root of 2, or 1.1892.*
> ***Analyst***

### ■ 6.2.2 Example of Cost as Function of Material

Sigma Products requests Analyst to estimate the cost of a state-of-the-art, switching-mode power supply as a linear function of material cost. Analyst uses a parametric relationship that equates the cost of such devices to a value of 2.5 to 5 times the cost of the bill of materials. [6]

Using an average of 2.5 to 5, or 3.75, Analyst derives Equation 6.1 as the cost estimating relationship (CER) for the power supply.

$$CER = 3.75 \text{ (Cost of bill of materials).} \tag{6.1}$$

From historical data, Analyst estimates that the bill of materials cost is $125 for a single unit. Substituting this value in Equation 6.1, Analyst obtains 3.75($125), or $468.75, as the estimated cost of the power supply.

Note that cost of $468.75 is the average estimated cost and can range as low as (2.5)($125), or $312.50, to as high as (5)($125), or $625.

### ■ 6.2.3 Example of Cost as Function of Weight

Reference 6 cites CER for a state-of-the-art, switching-mode power supply as its output power *P* multiplied by its weight *W* raised to the three-halves power. Equation 6.2 gives this relationship.

$$CER = \$P \cdot W^{3/2} \tag{6.2}$$

The power output and weight of the power supply are 5 watts and 20 pounds. Substituting these values in Equation 6.2, Analyst obtains ($5)($20^{3/2}$), or $447.21.

> *To raise the number 20 to the three-halves power, first take the cube of 20 for (20)(20)(20), or 8,000. Then take the square root of 8,000 for 89.4427.*
> ***Analyst***

## 6.2.4 Example of Cost as Function of Volume

As an alternative approach, Analyst equates the CER for the power supply to output power $P$ divided by the reciprocal of its volume $V$ raised to the third power.

Equation 6.3 gives the relationship for this CER.

$$CER = \frac{P}{(1/V)^3} \tag{6.3}$$

Analyst ascertains that the volume is 5 cubic inches for the 5-watt power supply. Substituting these values in Equation 6.3, Analyst obtains $5 \div (1 \div 5)^3$ (or, $625.00).

The following questions need to be answered before we can put to rest the issue of selecting risk models:

1. What resources can the program invest in analysis; what level of detail can the program provide?
2. Will the status of the program (*i.e.*, proposal, conceptual, development, or production) allow the investment of resources to conduct the analysis?
3. Will the status of the program afford the program the time to benefit from the analysis?

It would appear that approaches providing the most affirmative answers to these questions would be the most useful to the technical risk practitioner.

In situations where resources are ample and programs are still in an early enough phase of their life cycle to benefit from model findings, the detailed, bottom-up process that follows the work breakdown structure (WBS) would be the better approach. Disaggregate modeling provides this detailed, bottom-up and may involve either the parametric or industrial engineering approach to estimating.

Where resources are limited or programs are too far along in their life cycles to benefit greatly from the analytical findings, we recommend the relatively low-cost expert opinion or analogy approaches. Aggregate modeling provides this high-level, top-down process.

Table 6.3 provides a checklist for selecting the most appropriate technique for the problem at hand. Start with intended Applications of the analysis in column 3 and work toward the Inputs in column 1.

*Table 6.3*    *Modeling Technique Selection Checklist*

| **Inputs** | **Outputs** | **Applications** |
|---|---|---|
| Descriptive data | Level of detail | Long-range planning |
| Cost | Precision | Design guidance |
| Time | Accuracy | Status monitoring |
| Personnel | Aggregate | Problem solving |
| Facilities | Disaggregate | Proposal |

Consider the application of long-range planning. The output of the estimate need not have a great level of detail and can be in aggregate form. Precision and accuracy of the outputs, however, should be high enough to support planning conclusions. Similarly, the descriptive data and expenditures in the inputs should be sufficient to support planning conclusions.

Consider the application of proposal. You should assess the requirements for outputs and inputs in light of the proposal potential, the proposal cost, and the probable return-on-investment from the proposal.

In general, proposal originators expect high levels of detail in disaggregate form, all of which require substantial expenditures. The ratio of proposal cost to probable return-on-investment is the usual criterion that management uses in making proposal bid decisions. It is not uncommon to require at least ten to one.

If the application were detailed design guidance, the input and output would require a high level of detail with as much accuracy and precision as possible and the same level of detail, accuracy, and precision in the input. Typically, these are the characteristics of the outputs of **disaggregate models**. On the other hand, analysis in support of proposals generally requires less detail. This is the general characteristic of **aggregate models**.

There is always a question of availability of resources for the items listed in the Inputs column of Table 6.3. The importance of descriptive data (*e.g.*, performance requirements, design details, and test results) to the success of the modeling effort cannot be overstressed; however, the preparation of such data requires much effort.

> *Do not undertake risk modeling without a clear understanding of the intended application of the analytical findings and without complete assurance that adequate resources will be committed to the undertaking.*
> *Analyst*

### ■ 6.2.5 Application Guidelines

Irrespective of which techniques or approaches you select, you should have a clear understanding of the intended application of the analytical findings. The scope of the job and the resources to do the job should evolve from this understanding.

Figure 6.2 shows the typical flow of activities in the modeling process. The input box labeled Discern Need and the output box labeled Implement Findings are the boundary conditions for the process. The input box includes the statement of the problem in as concise, complete, and unambiguous terms as possible. The box labeled Formulate Problem includes the hypothesis of the problem regarding its root causes. You can note the iterative nature of the modeling process from the boxes labeled Run Model, Analyze Findings, and Rerun Model.

Discern Need → Formulate Problem → Construct Model → Validate Model → Run Model → Analyze Findings → Rerun Model → Implement Findings

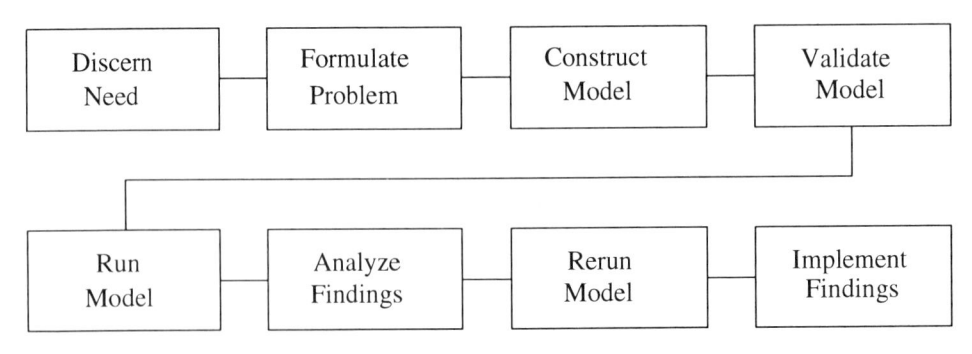

**Figure 6.2** Modeling Activity Flow

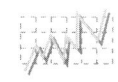

Table 6.4 is a checklist for choosing models to ensure that you not only choose the proper model to do the job but that you also do the job properly. The answers to the questions in the table should illuminate the scope of the job and the resources required.

***Table 6.4*** *Model Application Checklist*

> 1. Will the analysis support the decision to enter a marketplace?
> 2. Will the analysis reveal alternative approaches to reduce risk?
> 3. Will the analysis expose issues of functionality, affordability, and profitability?
> 4. Will the analysis evolve corrective actions?

Answers to the questions in Table 6.4 attest to the adequacy of the model of interest. For example, if the issue were simply one of corrective actions, then only the last question need be answered positively. On the other hand, if the issue were entry in a new marketplace, then answers to all four questions should be yes.

Risk models are derivatives of baseline models. For expediency, a lesser degree of complexity and detail may be used in constructing the risk model than that which is used in the corresponding baseline model. However, a greater degree of complexity and detail should not be used in the risk model than that which is used in the corresponding baseline model. This only provides an aura of increased precision which avails little.

If a baseline model were to use expert opinion, then the appropriate risk model should be other expert opinion and not an industrial engineering estimate. On the other hand, if the baseline model were to use industrial engineering, then the risk model could use industrial engineering or any of the other estimating methodologies that provide an equal or lower level of detail.

> *Risk models should be derivatives of models that produced the baseline estimates with equal or less, but not with more detail than the baseline.*
>
> *Analyst*

## 6.3 ART OF SIMULATION

The approaches to simulation are somewhat intuitive and subjective in nature, which is why we consider simulation an art. Strictly speaking, simulation is not a category of models, but a process.

Models are representations of some object, whereas simulation is a descriptive process that involves using models of real objects and performing experiments on these models to reach some understanding of the behavior of the object. These experiments are, in effect, similar to observing objects over sufficient time to reach some conclusion on their performance.

Simulation introduces specific values of the input variables in the model of interest and observes the effect on the output variables of the model, subject to the same laws of probability that govern the model.

Simulation builds from the precepts of sampling distributions, which is an important subject in probability and statistics. This section addresses normal distribution (*viz.*, the workhorse of simulation), tests of hypothesis, degrees of freedom, and the sampling distributions.

### ■ *6.3.1 Normal Distribution*

The **normal distribution** is the statistical representation of the normal probability density function. Figure 6.3 shows the normal probability density function in its standard form. The normal probability density function is symmetrical about the mean. In the standard form of the normal probability density function, **the mean** ($m$) = 0 and **standard deviation** ($s$) = 1. The area to the extreme left and right in Figure 6.3 are tails. Tails extend to minus and plus infinity. The point to remember is that parametric range of random variables in the normal probability distribution is minus infinity to plus infinity.

You see in Figure 6.3 percentages of the total area under the curve whose boundaries coincide with various plus and minus values of the *z*-**statistic**. We show these particular values of the *z*-statistic only because they are integers (*i.e.*, whole numbers). They could be partial integers and located anywhere on the abscissa (*i.e.*, horizontal axis of the illustration) from minus infinity to plus infinity.

If you wish to know the probability of occurrence relating to noninteger values of $z$, you should resort to tables. Table 6.5 is the table of areas under the normal probability density curve from $m = 0$ to $z = 1.99$. The table in Reference 6 extends through $z = 3.49$.

To determine the area under the normal probability density curve from the midpoint (*i.e.*, $m = 0$) to $z = -0.99$, enter Table 6.5 in the top row at .05. Go down the column to the row where $z = 0.90$ in the first column and read .2088 in the .09 column. The area under the curve from $m = 0$ to $z = -0.99$ is 0.3389. Therefore, the area in the right tail is $0.5 - 0.3389$, or 0.1611. Because of symmetry, the area under the curve from $m = 0$ to $z = 0.99$ is also 0.3389 and the area in the right tail is also 0.1611.

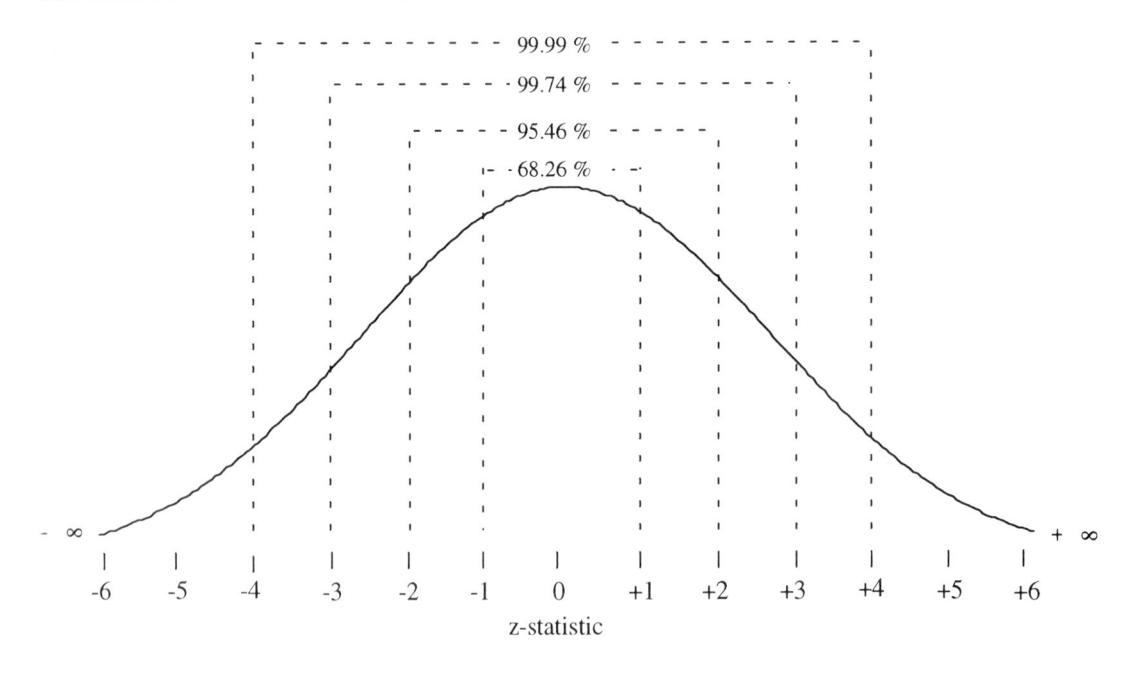

**Figure 6.3** Standard Form of Normal Probability Density Function

# 6.3 Art of Simulation

**Table 6.5** Areas Under Normal Probability Density Curve from m = 0 to z

| z | .00 | .01 | .02 | .03 | .04 | .05 | .06 | .07 | .08 | .09 |
|---|---|---|---|---|---|---|---|---|---|---|
| 0.00 | .0000 | .0040 | .0080 | .0120 | .0160 | .0199 | .0239 | .0279 | .319 | .0359 |
| 0.10 | .0398 | .0438 | .0478 | .0517 | .0557 | .0596 | .0636 | .0675 | .0714 | .0754 |
| 0.20 | .0793 | .0832 | .0871 | .0910 | .0948 | .0987 | .1026 | .1064 | .1103 | .1141 |
| 0.30 | .1179 | .1217 | .1255 | .1293 | .1331 | .1368 | .1406 | .1443 | .1480 | .1517 |
| 0.40 | .1554 | .1591 | .1628 | .1684 | .1700 | .1736 | .1772 | .1808 | .1844 | .1875 |
| 0.50 | .1915 | .1950 | .1985 | .2019 | .2054 | .2088 | .2123 | .2157 | .2190 | .2224 |
| 0.60 | .2258 | .2291 | .2324 | .2357 | .2389 | .2422 | .2464 | .2486 | .2518 | .2549 |
| 0.70 | .2580 | .2612 | .2642 | .2673 | .2704 | .2734 | .2764 | .2794 | .2823 | .2852 |
| 0.80 | .2881 | .2910 | .2939 | .2967 | .2996 | .3023 | .3051 | .3079 | .3106 | .3133 |
| 0.90 | .3159 | .3186 | .3212 | .3238 | .3264 | .3289 | .3315 | .3340 | .3365 | .3389 |
| 1.00 | .3413 | .3438 | .3461 | .3485 | .3508 | .3531 | .3564 | .3577 | .3599 | .3621 |
| 1.10 | .3643 | .3665 | .3688 | .3708 | .3729 | .3749 | .3770 | .3790 | .3810 | .3830 |
| 1.20 | .3849 | .3869 | .3888 | .3907 | .3925 | .3944 | .3962 | .3980 | .3997 | .4015 |
| 1.30 | .4032 | .4049 | .4066 | .4082 | .4099 | .4155 | .4131 | .4147 | .4162 | .4177 |
| 1.40 | .4192 | .4321 | .4222 | .4236 | .4251 | .4265 | .4279 | .4292 | .4319 | .4319 |
| 1.50 | .4332 | .4345 | .4357 | .4370 | .4382 | .4394 | .4406 | .4418 | .4430 | .4441 |
| 1.60 | .4452 | .4463 | .4474 | .4485 | .4495 | .4505 | .4515 | .4525 | .4535 | .4545 |
| 1.70 | .4554 | .4564 | .4573 | .4582 | .4591 | .4599 | .4608 | .4616 | .4625 | .4633 |
| 1.80 | .4641 | .4649 | .4656 | .4664 | .4671 | .4678 | .4686 | .4693 | .4700 | .4706 |
| 1.90 | .4713 | .4719 | .4726 | .4732 | .4738 | .4744 | .4750 | .4756 | .4762 | .4767 |

Now you try using Table 6.5. Determine the area under the curve from $z = -1.99$ to $z = 1.99$. Enter the table in the $z$ column at the 1.90 row, go right to the .09 column, and read .4767. The area under the curve from $z = -1.99$ to $z = 1.99$ is two times .4767, or 0.9534.

We use tables such as Table 6.5 in work on confidence intervals and tests of hypothesis at given significance levels. We usually express confidence as a percentage and confidence level as a decimal fraction. Significance level equals one unity minus the confidence level.

Confidence of 95 percent equals a confidence level of 0.95 and a significance level of 1 − 0.95, or 0.05.

The values of $z$ annotate the abscissa in Figure 6.3. We use the $z$-statistic in tests of hypothesis. Equation 6.4 is the relationship for deriving the $z$-statistic.

$$z = (m-\mu)\frac{\sqrt{n}}{\sigma} \tag{6.4}$$

where $m$ denotes mean of random sample of size $n$ of hypothesized normal population with mean $\mu$ and standard deviation $\sigma$.

### ■ 6.3.2 Tests of Hypothesis

Figure 6.4 illustrates the relationship between specific areas under the curve of probability density functions and tests of hypothesis. A one-tail test uses the area in one tail, either the left or right, which serves as the rejection region of the hypothesis. Two-tail tests use the sum of the areas in both tails of probability density functions, which also serves as the rejection region.

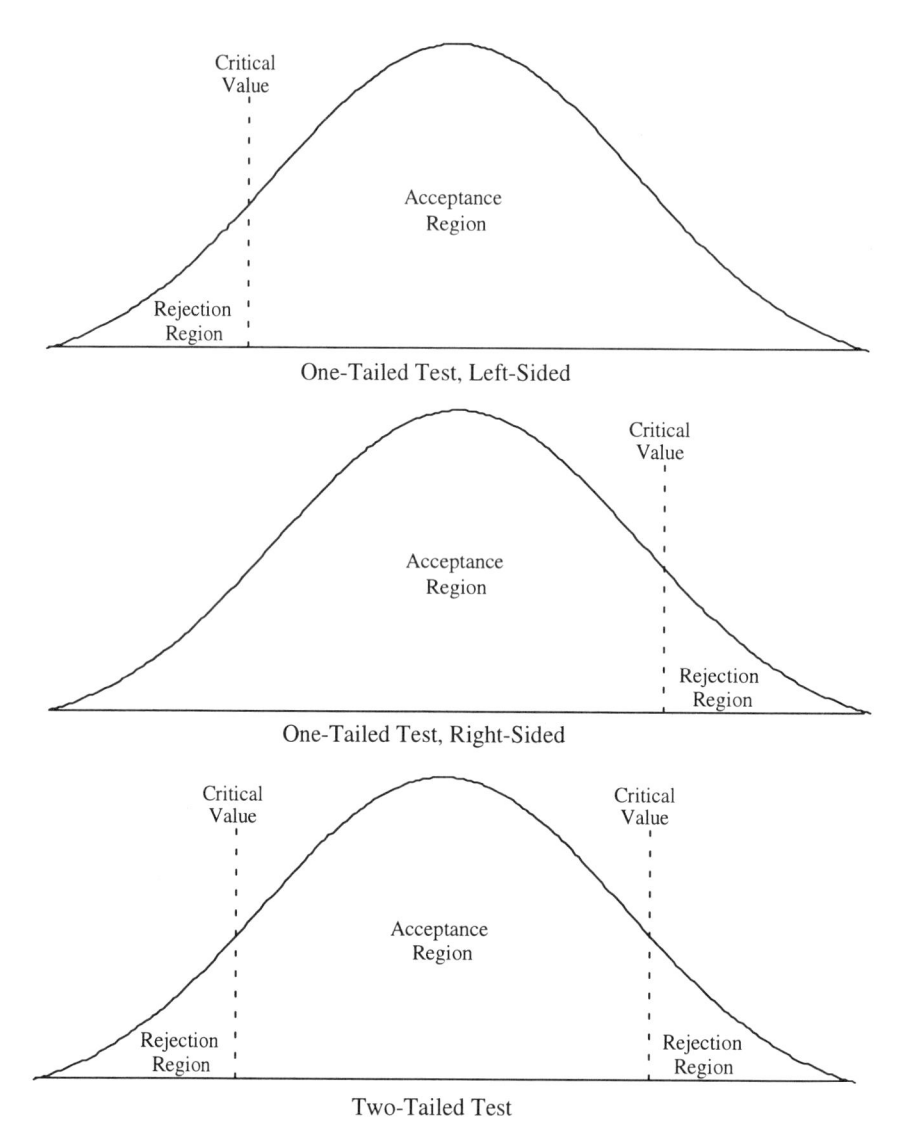

**Figure 6.4** Rejection and Acceptance Regions in Tests of Hypothesis

The **null hypothesis**, which we denote by the symbol $H_o$, is the hypothesis under test. Null implies that there would be no deleterious effect in not rejecting the hypothesis. We reject $H_o$ when our test statistic falls beyond some critical value. Critical values are the rejection region boundary values in Figure 6.4.

When we reject $H_0$, we accept some alternative hypothesis. We denote this alternative hypothesis with the symbol $H_1$.

We formulate decision rules for $H_0$ and $H_1$ in terms of significance levels that we denote with the Greek lower-case letter *alpha* ($\alpha$). Alpha is the area under the normal probability density

## 6.3 Art of Simulation

curve residing in the rejection region. The remaining area, $1 - \alpha$, resides in the acceptance region. We do not accept the null hypothesis if test statistics based on our samples fall in the rejection regions.

Tests of hypothesis concern means of populations, variance of populations, and ratios of variances of several populations. The essence of the tests is to ascertain if the mean and variance (and standard deviation) derived from samples are representative of the populations from which they are drawn to given significance levels.

We base the tests of hypothesis on the probability associated with areas under probability density curves. Equation 6.5 gives the relationship for probability ($P$) as a function of area ($A$).

$$P(\ 2 < z > 2) = 1 - [A(-\infty = z < 2) + A(2 > z = \infty)]. \tag{6.5}$$

### ■ 6.3.3 Example of Test of Hypothesis with Large Sample

The Zeta Company manufactures highway lighting components and claims that a certain light source has a mean life of 10,000 hours with a standard deviation of 400 hours. A state highway department wishes to test 30 samples from a large shipment of these light sources to know what the minimum mean life of the 30 samples should be to conclude with a significance level of 0.05 that the balance of the shipment is acceptable.

The department retains Analyst to do the investigation. Table 6.6 gives the technical approach Analyst follows in carrying out the assignment.

Analyst enumerates the decision rules by stating the null ($H_0$) and alternative ($H_1$) hypotheses and the significance level ($\alpha$):

1. $H_0$: $\mu$ = 10,000 hours
2. $H_1$: $\mu$ < 10,000 hours
3. $\alpha$ = 0.05.

The less-than symbol < in the rule $H_1$ signifies the need for a one-tailed, left-sided test. By the same token, the more-than symbol > would signify the need for a one-tailed, right-sided test.

The large sample size allows Analyst to assume normality and to use the $z$-statistic for the test of hypothesis. In one-tailed tests, the significance level of 0.05 means the area in the left tail is also 0.05 and the area under the curve from $m = 0$ to the tail boundary is $0.5 - 0.05$, or 0.45. The value of the boundary is the critical value of the $z$-statistic ($z_c$).

***Table 6.6*** *Technical Approach for Test of Hypothesis with Large Sample Example*

1. State null hypothesis indicating value of population parameter to be tested.
2. State alternative hypothesis indicating value of population parameter other than that of null hypothesis.
3. Determine from alternative hypothesis whether one-tailed or two-tailed test is required.
4. Determine critical value from significance level.
5. Calculate test statistic for random sample.
6. Reject null hypothesis if test statistic falls beyond critical value.

The value of the z-statistic for the area 0.45 is 0.1736 from Table 6.5. This is the critical value of the z-statistic ($z_c$). We accept $H_1$ when the calculated value of the test z-statistic falls beyond the value of $z_c$. Otherwise, we do not reject $H_0$.

Substituting $\mu = 10,000$ hours, $\sigma = 400$ hours, and $n = 100$ in Equation 6.4, and rearranging terms in the equation to solve for the limiting value of the mean (*m*) of the sample, Analyst obtains

$$m = 10,000 \text{ hours} - \frac{(0.1736)(400)}{\sqrt{30}} \text{ hours}$$

$$= 9,987.3 \text{ hours}. \qquad (6.6)$$

Analyst informs the state highway department that the shipment should not be rejected if the mean life of the 30 samples tested was 9,987.3 hours or more.

### ■ 6.3.4 Degrees of Freedom

Concern for **degrees of freedom** enters in the consideration of sampling distributions. Degrees of freedom equal the number of variates (*i.e.*, specific values of variables) less the number of dependent relationships among them such as the mean and variance or standard deviation.

If we were to estimate the mean of a population with a sample of ten, the degrees of freedom would be ten, since no statistic other than the mean is involved. There is no dependent relationship between the population and the mean of the population.

There is a difference when we extend our consideration to the variance or standard deviation (*i.e.*, the square root of variance). **Variance** is determined by dispersion of variates about the mean. We now have the case of one statistic (*i.e.*, the mean) governing another (*i.e.*, the variance) resulting in a dependent relationship between the mean and variance. The degrees of freedom for variance in a sample size ten is $10 - 1$, or 9.

This leads to the relationship in Equation 6.7 for degrees of freedom, symbolized by lower-case Greek letter nu ($\upsilon$).

$$= n - r \qquad (6.7)$$

where *n* denotes number of variates in sample and *r* number of dependent relationships.

In most applications, the $r = 1$, and we usually encounter Equation 6.8

$$v = n - 1 \qquad (6.8)$$

You see the right-hand term of Equation 6.8 in the denominator of equations when you have calculated the variance of a sample. There are a number of applications, however, where *r* is greater than 1. For example, $r = 2$ in calculating covariances because we are dealing with the variances of two distributions.

In essence, the greater the degrees of freedom, the closer we come to modeling population parameters by sample statistics. By knowing the true mean of an infinitely large population, we infer an infinitely large number of degrees of freedom in its estimation.

Equation 6.9 gives the relationship for probability (*P*) as a function of area (*A*) under the normal probability density curve.

$$P = 1 - [A(-\infty = z \leq -2) + A(+2 \geq z = +\infty)] \qquad (6.9)$$

where $A(-\infty = z \leq -2)$ denotes the area under the normal probability density curve from minus infinity to minus two standard deviations, and $A(+2 \geq z = +\infty)$ denotes the area under the normal probability density curve from plus two standard deviations plus infinity.

## 6.3 Art of Simulation

We use the $z$-statistic from Equation 6.9 as the test statistic in tests of hypothesis with the normal probability density function. To use the normal probability density function, you need a sample size of 30 or more.

For sample sizes of fewer than 30, we use the $t$-statistic. We use the $\chi^2$-statistic (*i.e.*, chi-square statistic) for tests of hypothesis about variances, and the $F$-statistic for tests of hypothesis about variances of different samples.

The value of the test statistic at the boundary of the tails in Figure 6.4 is the critical value. We calculate the test statistic from random samples and reject $H_0$ when the calculated value of the test statistic is either less (more negative) than or greater (more positive) than the critical value bounding the tails. Otherwise, we do not reject $H_0$.

### ■ 6.3.5 Sampling Distributions

**Sampling distributions** comprise an important class of probability distributions. They are statistical representations of various sampling processes and not of populations. The notion of large sample has special significance in sampling distributions because of the **central limit theorem**. [7]

> *Regardless of original population distributions, means and variances of samples approach normality with increased sample size.*
> **Central limit theorem**

In other words, the larger the sample size, the more applicable is the assumption of normality in the data sample of interest. As a matter of fact, most distributions can be approximately reliable by the normal distribution when sample sizes are large (*i.e.*, 30 or more). Mathematically, the normal distribution is the limit of sampling distributions as sample sizes of the sampling distributions approach infinity.

Classes of sampling distributions include **Student's *t* distribution**, **chi-square ($\chi^2$) distribution**, and ***F*-distribution**. The Student's *t* distribution is the statistical representation of small-size samples of populations. The $\chi^2$-distribution is the statistical representation of variances of populations. The *F*-distribution is the statistical representation of ratios of variances of several populations. For the most part, the normal and Student's *t* distributions will suffice for our work. Reference 6 gives details on the other sampling distributions.

> *The area under the curve of all probability density functions is unity.*
> **Analyst**

### ■ 6.3.6 Student's t Distribution

In general, a population will contain more extreme variates than a sample of that population. It can be expected, therefore, that the population standard deviation, $\sigma$ will be somewhat larger than the standard deviation, $s$, of any given sample.

Mathematically, we say that the standard deviation of the population is unknown. The assumption that $s = \sigma$ is only approximately correct for large samples and leads to erroneous conclusions.

This problem was studied by the turn-of-the-century Irish statistician William S. Gosset, who published under the pseudonym "Student," and promulgated the Student's *t* distribution. The Student's *t* distribution now ranks second only to the normal distribution in tests of hypothesis.

The Student's *t* distribution is the statistical representation of the sampling process where small-sized samples are involved. As a consequence, the values of degrees of freedom ($\upsilon$) are smaller. Figure 6.5 shows that with smaller values the Student's *t* probability density function has less central tendency (*i.e.*, less clustering of variates about the mean), less peakedness of the mean, and thicker tails than the probability density function of the normal probability distribution.

Like the normal probability density function, the mean of the Student's *t* probability density function has a value of zero. Note the influence of degrees of freedom on the peakedness of the curves. The curves approach the normal probability density function as a limit as degrees of freedom approach infinity.

Like the mean in the standard form of the normal probability density function, the mean of the Student's *t* probability density function also equals zero. Equation 6.10 is the relationship we use in deriving the *t*-**statistic**

$$t = (m - \mu)\frac{\sqrt{n}}{s} \tag{6.10}$$

where *m* denotes mean of random sample of size *n* of hypothesized normal population with mean $\mu$, and *s* is standard deviation of sample.

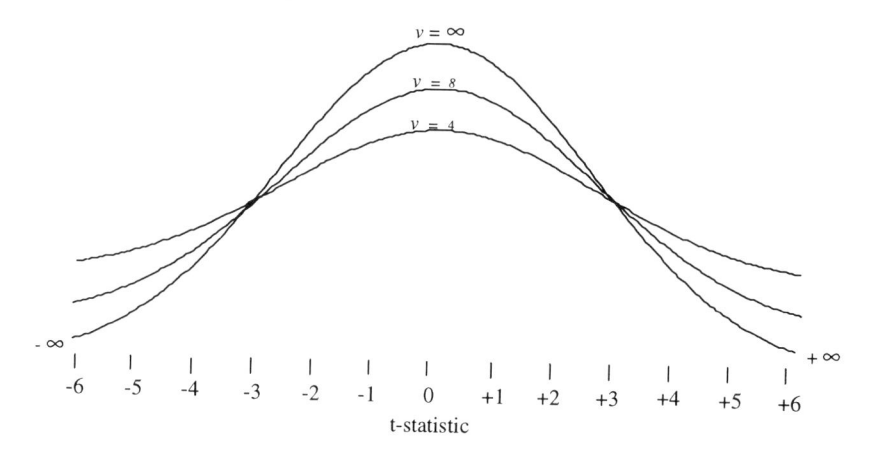

**Figure 6.5** Student's *t* Probability Density Function

The value we calculate for *t* in Equation 6.10 serves as the test statistic in our test of hypothesis.

### ■ 6.3.7 Example of Test of Hypothesis with Small Sample

We now assume that the light sources in the example of Section 6.3.3 are extremely costly. The state highway department wishes to consume no more than ten of them in our acceptance test. The department may still assume normality because of the large population from which the samples are drawn. We must, however, alter our approach for the small sample and use the Student's *t* distribution instead of the normal distribution.

## 6.3 Art of Simulation

The department completes the life test of ten light sources. The sample mean is 9,750 hours and the sample deviation is 350 hours. We ask Analyst to test the hypothesis that the mean life of the entire shipment is 10,000 hours.

Table 6.7 is the technical approach Analyst uses to carry out the assignment.

**Table 6.7** *Technical Approach for Test of Hypothesis with Small Sample Example*

1. State null hypothesis indicating value of population parameter to be tested.
2. State alternative hypothesis indicating value of population parameter other than that of null hypothesis.
3. Determine from alternative hypothesis whether one-tailed or two-tailed test is required.
4. Determine critical value from significance level.
5. Calculate test statistic for random sample.
6. Reject null hypothesis if test statistic falls beyond critical value.

Analyst enumerates the decision rules by stating the null ($H_0$) and alternative ($H_1$) hypotheses and the significance level ($\alpha$):

1. $H_0$: $\mu$ = 10,000 hours
2. $H_1$: $\mu$ < 10,000 hours
3. $\alpha$ = 0.05.

Again, the less-than symbol < in the rule $H_1$ signifies that Analyst needs a one-tailed, left-sided test. Analyst will accept $H_1$ when the calculated value of the test $z$-statistic falls beyond the value of $z_c$. Otherwise, Analyst will not reject $H_0$. Substituting $m$ = 9,750 hours, $\mu$ = 10,000 hours, $n$ = 10, and $s$ = 350 hours in Equation 6.10, Analyst obtains

$$t = (9{,}750 \text{ hours} - 10{,}000 \text{ hours}) \frac{\sqrt{10}}{350}$$
$$= 2.259. \tag{6.11}$$

Analyst next turns to Table 6.8, which is the table of areas under the curve for the Student's $t$ probability density function. Analyst enters the table at = 10 − 1, 09, goes right to the 0.05 column, and reads 2.228 as the area under the curve from $-t_c$ to $+t_c$. Since the test is one-tailed, left-sided, $t_c = -2.228 \div 2$, or $-1.114$.

The test $t$-statistic from Equation 6.11, $t = -2.259$, is more negative than the critical value, $t_c = -1.114$, signifying that $t$ falls in the rejection region. Analyst rejects the hypothesis that the mean life of the entire shipment is 10,000 hours. The state road department rejects the shipment.

### ■ 6.3.8 Simulation Approaches

You can utilize a number of approaches to simulation, the most common being the worst-case method, heuristic method, and probabilistic method. The **Monte Carlo method** is the embodiment of the probabilistic method. [8]

**Table 6.8**  *Area Under Student's **t** Probability Density Curve from -t to +t*

|    | α = 0.1 | 0.05   | 0.02   | 0.01   | 0.001   |
|----|---------|--------|--------|--------|---------|
| 1  | 6.314   | 12.706 | 31.821 | 63.657 | 636.619 |
| 2  | 2.920   | 4.303  | 6.965  | 9.925  | 31.598  |
| 3  | 2.353   | 3.182  | 4.541  | 5.841  | 12.941  |
| 4  | 2.132   | 2.776  | 3.747  | 4.604  | 8.610   |
| 5  | 2.015   | 2.571  | 3.365  | 4.032  | 6.859   |
| 6  | 1.943   | 2.447  | 3.143  | 3.707  | 5.959   |
| 7  | 1.895   | 2.365  | 2.998  | 3.499  | 5.405   |
| 8  | 1.860   | 2.306  | 2.898  | 3.355  | 5.041   |
| 9  | 1.833   | 2.262  | 2.821  | 3.250  | 4.781   |
| 10 | 1.812   | 2.228  | 2.764  | 3.169  | 4.587   |

In the worst-case method, extreme values of the input variables are introduced in the model to gauge the effect on the output variables. A typical example would be the estimate of sales of automotive vehicles over the next decade as a function of fuel costs. The approach would be to use regression analysis to project the relationship of sales and fuel costs and use, therein, extreme values of estimated fuel costs over the next decade.

The worst-case method would use the lowest conceivable fuel cost as well as the highest conceivable fuel cost and thus project a range of values.

The heuristic method, from the Greek word to invent or discover, denoting a methodology, proceeds along empirical lines and uses rules of thumb and the principle of the next-best rule to achieve good-enough solutions. A typical example is a computerized stock market that sells orders, the rationale being that stock quotations may go higher but sales at programmed quotations are good enough.

In the probabilistic approach, the input and output variables of the model are governed by some applicable probability distributions (*e.g.*, distributions of arrival and service rates in a queuing problem). The probabilistic method is encountered more frequently than the others because of its somewhat greater objectivity.

The **moment-method**, which uses the first and second moments (*i.e.*, mean and variance) of probability distributions, is a probabilistic approach. The approach derives the mean and variance of the statistics of interest *(e.g.*, risk time or risk cost) by operating on the means and variances of the input variables to the model and the correlation among the variables.

As stated, the most popular implementation of the probabilistic approach is the Monte Carlo method. The Monte Carlo method gets its name from the commune noted for its legendary gambling casinos in the Mediterranean coast principality of Monaco.

The Monte Carlo method uses random numbers to simulate probability distributions of the random variables that describe the performance of the statistics of interest. We address the Monte Carlo method following some comments on random numbers.

### ■ 6.3.9 Random Numbers

A **random number** is a number picked at random from a uniform distribution of numbers. **Uniform distribution** of numbers is a distribution in which every number in the distribution has an equal probability of being selected.

## 6.3 Art of Simulation

The totality of the numbers in the distribution comprises a population. The **equiprobability** (*i.e.*, equal probability) of the numbers is the reciprocal of the population size $n$ comprising the distribution, or $1 \div n$. Thus, the probability of randomly selecting any one of 1,000 random numbers would be $1 \div 1,000$, or 0.001.

The governing assumption is the applicability of the uniform distribution in generating tables of random numbers. The result of this assumption is the relatively easy computation of cumulative probability values, values of required subranges of random numbers, and random number values used in simulation models. In addition, we can assume normality in the variates that we simulate by the random numbers.

Except for certain applications like failure mode propagation and reliability prediction, the uniform probability distribution is a reasonable assumption because of the **law of large numbers**. [9]

> *If random samples of size* n *are drawn from populations of size* N *irrespective of probability distributions, sample means and variances converge on population means and variances as* n *approaches* N.
> ***Law of large numbers***

The law of large numbers is also known as Bernoulli's or Tchebycheff's theorem. As stated, sample sizes of 30 or greater are usually sufficient to support the assumption of normality. This situation is quite convenient because the mean and variance uniquely define the normal probability distribution.

Random numbers can consist of any number of digits depending on the parametric ranges of the variates to be simulated. Consider, for example, a sample of ten items which you first draw from a lot of 500 and next draw from a lot of 5,000. The required precision of the random number increases from three places to four places.

The lot of 500 requires 500 three-digit random numbers ranging from 0 to 499 irrespective of the sample size. Similarly, a sample lot of 5,000 requires 5,000 random numbers ranging from 0 to 4,999.

Table 6.9 is an abstract of the random table that we generated on a personal computer with a pseudorandom number algorithm. The full table consists of 1,000 **pseudorandom numbers** ranging from 0 to 999 and is suitable for a sample lot of 1,000.

***Table 6.9*** *Abstract of Pseudorandom Number Table*

| 296 | 662 | 999 | 447 | 452 | 551 | 352 | 253 | 365 | 010 |
| 779 | 038 | 314 | 068 | 309 | 370 | 075 | 955 | 457 | 602 |
| 232 | 694 | 022 | 634 | 456 | 247 | 049 | 216 | 652 | 178 |

The pseudorandom number algorithm is finite and eventually repeats numbers. Note that numbers with values less than 100 are preceded with zeros which were supplied manually. The reason for this will become obvious when you select numbers to represent samples from the lot of 5,000. If zeros are not supplied by the pseudorandom number algorithm in the computer, you should add them.

> *In mathematics, an algorithm is a method for solving a specific kind of problem.*
> ***Analyst***

The customary practice is to select numbers sequentially by row. Therefore, you select 3-digit numbers in the top row of Table 6.9 to represent the sample size ten from the lot of 500.

On the other hand, you need 4-digit numbers to represent samples from the lot of 5,000. The procedure here is simply to borrow digits from the successive numbers in the rows. Therefore, the ten 4-digit numbers selected to represent the sample size ten from the lot of 5,000 would be: 2966, 6299, 9447, 4525, 5135, 2253, 3651, 0779, 0383, and 1468. Note that there are two numbers that start with zero.

The precision of a number should not be confused with the accuracy of a number. In digital communication, for example, accuracy is a function of such factors as the signal-plus-noise-to-noise ratio in the channel over which communication is attempted, whereas precision is strictly a function of the digitizing process used to encode the number.

### ■ 6.3.10 Monte Carlo Method

The process of defining the subranges of random numbers in accordance with some governing probability distribution is called "encoding." Encoding is the essence of the Monte Carlo method. Any probability distribution may be assumed to govern, provided the sample adequately represents the population of the assumed probability distribution. Reference 10 contains an extensive table of random numbers for the normal distribution.

Figure 6.6 shows the sequential flow of activities in the Monte Carlo method. Next, we describe the steps in the activities and tie them together in the example of Section 6.3.11.

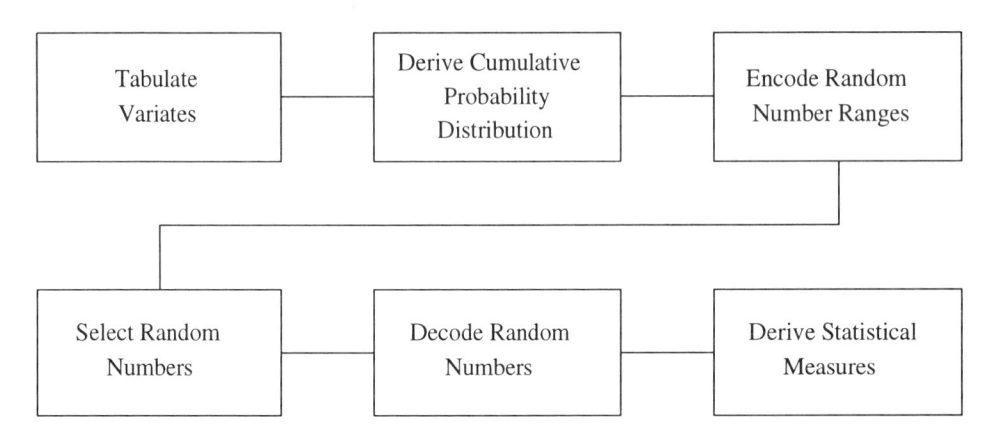

**Figure 6.6** Monte Carlo Method Activity Flow

**Tabulate Variates**

Assume that process times in a certain production line are the variates of interest. These variates are listed in the first column of Table 6.10.

Note that the parametric range of the variates is 1.25 to 2.50 minutes, which means that the precision of the observed data is 0.25 minute, or three places. We use the same precision to encode the random number ranges.

## 6.3 Art of Simulation

**Table 6.10** Variates for Monte Carlo Method

| Process Time | Frequency | Probability | Cumulative Probability | Random Number Subrange |
|---|---|---|---|---|
| 1.25 | 10 | 0.141 | 0.141 | 000 - 140 |
| 1.50 | 11 | 0.155 | 0.296 | 141 - 295 |
| 1.75 | 12 | 0.169 | 0.465 | 296 - 464 |
| 2.00 | 14 | 0.197 | 0.662 | 465 - 661 |
| 2.25 | 13 | 0.183 | 0.845 | 662 - 844 |
| 2.50 | 11 | 0.155 | 1.000 | 845 - 999 |
| Totals: | 71 | 1.000 | | |

The frequency (*i.e.*, number of observations) of the respective variates are listed in the second column of Table 6.10. The probability values in the third column of the table are simply the relative frequency of the respective individual values of the production process time which is obtained from dividing the individual values by the sum of the individual values.

### Derive Cumulative Probability Distribution

The cumulative probability values in the fourth column of Table 6.10 are obtained from sequentially summing the individual probability values in the third column. The first entry in the fourth column is simply the first probability entry in the third column, or 0.141. The second entry in the fourth column is 0.141 plus the second probability entry in the third column, or 0.296.

The second cumulative probability value in the fourth column is 0.141 + 0.155, or 0.296; the third is 0.296 + 0.169, or 0.465; the fourth is 0.465 + 0.197, or 0.662; the fifth is 0.662 + 0.183, or 0.845; and the sixth is 0.845 + 0.155, or 1.000.

### Encode Random Number Ranges

The respective cumulative probability values are then represented by the 3-digit random numbers ranging from 0 to 999 in the last column of Table 6.10. Note that there are as many subranges of random numbers as there are variates. In this example, there are six variates for process time. Consequently, six subranges of random numbers are required.

Note also in the fifth column of Table 6.10 that the first subrange of random numbers starts with 000 and extends to 140. We obtain the upper value of this subrange by multiplying the cumulative probability value for the variate 0.125 minutes by 1,000 (*viz.*, 0.141 × 1,000) for 141 and then subtracting the value 1 from 141 that yields 140.

The lower value of the next subrange of random numbers starts with the value of 141 and extends to 295, which we obtain by multiplying the cumulative probability value for the variate 0.150 minutes by 1,000 (*viz.*, 0.296 × 1000) for 296, and then subtracting 1 from 296 for 295.

This process is continued until subranges of random numbers are assigned to the remaining variates. Note in Table 6.10 that the subrange for the variate 2.50 minutes is 845 to 999.

### Generate Random Numbers

The next step in the methodology is either to generate random numbers with a random number generator or to select random numbers from a table of random numbers. You can apply the table of random numbers in Reference 10 to almost any situation.

You can generate tables of pseudorandom numbers on a personal computer with algorithms in spreadsheet programs. Again, be sure to add zeros at the beginning of the those numbers with fewer than all the digits. In a 3-digit number, they are those under 100.

**Decode Random Numbers**

This step decodes the random numbers generated in the previous step into values of variates which you may use to derive statistical measures. For example, assume that the random numbers generated are 085, 199, 987, 303, 815, 234, 542, 609, 720, and 963.

The decoded values of the variates in Table 6.10 are listed in Table 6.11. The variates range in value from 125 to 250 and comprise a simulated random sample.

*Table 6.11   Decoded Random Numbers*

| Random Number | Variate | Random Number | Variate |
|---|---|---|---|
| 085 | 1.25 | 234 | 1.50 |
| 199 | 1.50 | 542 | 2.00 |
| 987 | 2.50 | 609 | 2.00 |
| 303 | 1.75 | 720 | 2.25 |
| 815 | 2.25 | 963 | 2.50 |

**Derive Statistical Measures**

We use the decoded random numbers in Table 6.11 to calculate statistical measures of interest, the most popular being the mean and the standard deviation. We demonstrate this final step in the example of Section 6.3.11 along with the preceding four steps of the Monte Carlo method.

### ■ 6.3.11 Example of the Monte Carlo Method

The marketing director of Zeta Company asks the production director to estimate the cost for producing 100 units of a certain product. There is a problem in that Zeta has manufactured only 10 of these units in the past and the production manager is reluctant to estimate the cost by extrapolating to 100.

The production manager retains Analyst to estimate the unit cost of the product in a quantity of 100 with a confidence level of 0.90 with the instruction to exclude learning curves in the interest of a conservative estimate. Table 6.12 is the technical approach Analyst follows in carrying out the assignment.

*Table 6.12   Technical Approach for Monte Carlo Method Example*

1. Obtain historical cost data.
2. Derive cumulative probability distribution for the variates in historical cost data.
3. Encode cumulative probability distribution into random number ranges for variates.
4. Generate a pseudorandom number table of 100 numbers on a personal computer with precision to match precision of the variates.
5. Decode 100 pseudorandom numbers into 100 simulated variates.
6. Derive mean of simulated variates and 0.90 confidence interval about mean.
7. Use mean value as unit cost for estimate.

Table 6.13 gives the cost history of the ten units manufactured to date. Analyst derives the cumulative probability distribution and encodes it into the random number subranges given in Table 6.14.

## 6.3 Art of Simulation

Analyst then derives the pseudorandom numbers in Table 6.15 using a computer algorithm to generate 3-digit pseudorandom numbers with values ranging from 0 to 999. Analyst adds zeros at the front of numbers containing fewer than three digits.

*Table 6.13*   Cost History for Monte Carlo Method Example

| Unit | Cost Dollars | Unit | Cost Dollars |
|---|---|---|---|
| 1 | 985 | 6 | 915 |
| 2 | 965 | 7 | 895 |
| 3 | 975 | 8 | 905 |
| 4 | 930 | 9 | 885 |
| 5 | 905 | 10 | 850 |

*Table 6.14*   Encoded Random Number Subranges for Monte Carlo Method Example

| Cost Dollars | Frequency | Probability | Cumulative Probability | Random Number Subrange |
|---|---|---|---|---|
| 850 | 1 | 0.10 | 0.10 | 000 - 099 |
| 885 | 1 | 0.10 | 0.20 | 100 - 199 |
| 895 | 1 | 0.10 | 0.30 | 200 - 299 |
| 905 | 2 | 0.20 | 0.50 | 300 - 499 |
| 915 | 1 | 0.10 | 0.60 | 500 - 599 |
| 930 | 1 | 0.10 | 0.70 | 600 - 699 |
| 965 | 1 | 0.10 | 0.80 | 700 - 799 |
| 975 | 1 | 0.10 | 0.90 | 800 - 899 |
| 985 | 1 | 0.10 | 1.00 | 900 - 999 |
|  | 10 | 1.00 |  |  |

*Table 6.15*   Pseudorandom Number Table for Monte Carlo Method Example

| | | | | | | | | | |
|---|---|---|---|---|---|---|---|---|---|
| 358 | 799 | 624 | 176 | 975 | 740 | 196 | 203 | 266 | 429 |
| 687 | 262 | 595 | 578 | 569 | 559 | 496 | 337 | 010 | 965 |
| 326 | 943 | 306 | 711 | 734 | 553 | 637 | 862 | 586 | 591 |
| 562 | 314 | 502 | 510 | 985 | 596 | 021 | 692 | 492 | 716 |
| 020 | 353 | 869 | 189 | 426 | 468 | 113 | 121 | 787 | 423 |
| 174 | 613 | 685 | 119 | 351 | 015 | 041 | 193 | 568 | 402 |
| 390 | 215 | 395 | 112 | 611 | 724 | 930 | 980 | 728 | 965 |
| 501 | 716 | 910 | 498 | 494 | 751 | 293 | 464 | 052 | 568 |
| 981 | 020 | 029 | 831 | 180 | 375 | 396 | 658 | 863 | 223 |
| 136 | 152 | 475 | 479 | 891 | 403 | 180 | 177 | 697 | 184 |

*Use the precise amount of data required for solving the problem, no more, no less. Extraneous information causes you to digress from the essence of the problem leading to confusion, argument, and needless expense.*

*Analyst*

284                                                                         Chapter 6 • RISK MODELS

Analyst generates precisely 100 three-digit numbers, no more, no less. Analyst then decodes the random numbers into simulated variates. This is a tedious job with 100 random numbers needing to be equated with variates and use of a personal computer is recommended. Table 6.16 gives the results of Analyst's effort.

**Table 6.16**   *Decoded Random Numbers for Monte Carlo Method Example*

| P | V | P | V | P | V | P | V | P | V |
|---|---|---|---|---|---|---|---|---|---|
| 358 | 905 | 799 | 965 | 624 | 930 | 176 | 885 | 975 | 985 |
| 559 | 915 | 496 | 905 | 337 | 905 | 010 | 850 | 965 | 985 |
| 326 | 905 | 943 | 985 | 306 | 905 | 711 | 965 | 734 | 965 |
| 596 | 915 | 021 | 850 | 692 | 930 | 492 | 905 | 716 | 965 |
| 468 | 905 | 113 | 885 | 121 | 885 | 787 | 885 | 423 | 905 |
| 015 | 850 | 041 | 850 | 193 | 885 | 568 | 915 | 402 | 905 |
| 724 | 965 | 930 | 985 | 980 | 885 | 728 | 965 | 965 | 985 |
| 501 | 915 | 716 | 965 | 910 | 985 | 498 | 905 | 494 | 905 |
| 981 | 985 | 020 | 850 | 029 | 850 | 831 | 975 | 180 | 885 |
| 136 | 885 | 152 | 885 | 475 | 905 | 479 | 905 | 891 | 975 |
| 740 | 965 | 196 | 885 | 203 | 895 | 266 | 895 | 429 | 905 |
| 687 | 930 | 262 | 895 | 595 | 915 | 578 | 915 | 569 | 915 |
| 553 | 915 | 637 | 930 | 862 | 975 | 586 | 915 | 591 | 915 |
| 562 | 915 | 314 | 905 | 502 | 915 | 510 | 915 | 985 | 985 |
| 020 | 850 | 353 | 905 | 869 | 975 | 189 | 885 | 426 | 905 |
| 174 | 885 | 613 | 930 | 685 | 930 | 119 | 885 | 351 | 905 |
| 390 | 905 | 215 | 895 | 395 | 905 | 112 | 885 | 611 | 930 |
| 751 | 965 | 293 | 895 | 464 | 905 | 052 | 850 | 568 | 915 |
| 375 | 905 | 396 | 905 | 658 | 930 | 863 | 975 | 223 | 895 |
| 403 | 905 | 180 | 885 | 177 | 885 | 697 | 930 | 184 | 885 |

*P:* pseudorandom number
*V:* Variate

Table 6.17 lists the values of the variates in the Table 6.16. Analyst is now ready to calculate the mean and standard deviation of the simulated sample.

**Table 6.17**   *Simulated Sample for Monte Carlo Method Example*

| 905 | 965 | 624 | 885 | 985 | 965 | 885 | 895 | 895 | 905 |
|---|---|---|---|---|---|---|---|---|---|
| 915 | 905 | 905 | 850 | 985 | 930 | 895 | 915 | 915 | 915 |
| 905 | 985 | 905 | 965 | 965 | 915 | 930 | 975 | 915 | 915 |
| 915 | 850 | 930 | 905 | 965 | 915 | 905 | 915 | 915 | 985 |
| 905 | 885 | 885 | 885 | 905 | 850 | 905 | 975 | 885 | 905 |
| 850 | 850 | 885 | 915 | 905 | 885 | 930 | 930 | 885 | 905 |
| 965 | 985 | 885 | 965 | 985 | 905 | 895 | 905 | 885 | 930 |
| 915 | 965 | 985 | 905 | 905 | 965 | 895 | 905 | 850 | 915 |
| 985 | 850 | 850 | 975 | 885 | 905 | 905 | 930 | 975 | 895 |
| 885 | 885 | 905 | 905 | 975 | 905 | 885 | 885 | 930 | 885 |

The values in Table 6.17 are in dollars and the sum of the variates in the table are $91,249. This is the estimated cost for producing 100 units.

## 6.3 Art of Simulation

Analyst needs the values of the mean and standard deviation to calculate the confidence interval about the mean. The mean of the simulated sample is $91,249 ÷ 100, or $912.49.

The variance of sample data ($s^2$) is given by

$$s^2 = \frac{(x_1 - m)^2}{n - 1} \qquad (6.12)$$

where $\Sigma(x_i - m) = 219{,}454.75$ (*i.e.*, the summation of the squares of the individual variates $x_i$ minus the mean $m$) and $n = 100$.

Substituting these values in Equation 6.12, Analyst obtains $219{,}454.75 ÷ 99$, or $2{,}216.71$ for the variance. The standard deviation is the square root of the variance, or $47.08.

Analyst can now address the confidence interval about the mean of $912.49 at a confidence level of 0.90. Analyst first makes the assumption that the sample data is from a normally distributed population, which is reasonable considering the sample size 100.

Equation 6.13 is the relationship for deriving confidence limits (CL) about means of samples with 30 or more variates drawn from a normally distributed population.

$$CL = m \pm z\frac{s}{\sqrt{n}} \qquad (6.13)$$

where $m$ denotes mean, $z$ values of the standard deviation on the abscissa (*i.e.*, $x$ axis) of normal probability density function, $s$ standard deviation, and $n$ sample size.

Analyst uses Table 6.18, which is designed specifically for looking up values of $z$ for given areas under the curve of the normal probability density function. Entering the table at $A = 0.90$, Analyst reads the values $\pm 1.64$.

**Table 6.18**  *z Values as Functions of Area Under Curve for Monte Carlo Method Example*

| A | z | A | z |
|---|---|---|---|
| 0.50 | 0.0 | 0.85 | ± 1.44 |
| 0.55 | ± 0.06 | 0.90 | ± 1.64 |
| 0.60 | ± 0.84 | 0.95 | ± 1.96 |
| 0.65 | ± 0.94 | 0.99 | ± 2.58 |
| 0.70 | ± 1.04 | 0.995 | ± 2.81 |
| 0.75 | ± 1.15 | 0.999 | ± 3.27 |
| 0.80 | ± 1.28 | | |

*A*: Area under curve of normal probability density function.
*z*: Number of standard deviations on abscissa of curve.

Substituting $m = \$912.49$, $s = \$47.08$, and $n = 100$ in Equation 6.13, Analyst obtains

$$CL = \$912.49 \pm 1.64\frac{47.08}{\sqrt{100}}$$

$$= \$912.49 \pm 7.72$$

$$= \$904.77, \$920.21. \qquad (6.14)$$

Analyst forwards this information and the estimated cost of $91,249 to the production manager of Zeta Company. Adding a margin of 10 percent to the estimated cost, the production manager informs the marketing director that the cost for 100 units is $101,223. The marketing director adds another 10 percent margin making the cost $111,345. The finance department adds a general and administrative burden of 75 percent that raises the cost to $194,854. Adding a profit of 15 percent, the marketing director informs the prospective customer that the selling price for 100 units of the product is $224,086.

The customer declines the offer. The production manager and marketing director fail to recognize that the narrow confidence interval about the estimate precludes the need for large margins, and Zeta Company loses the sale.

> *Base your margin for error on historical data, not on arbitrary percentages.*
> ***Analyst***

## 6.4
## AGGREGATION VS. DISAGGREGATION

**Aggregation** is an embodiment of top-down estimating and **disaggregation** is an embodiment of bottom-up estimating. Either may employ any estimating methodology (*viz.*, expert opinion, analogy, parametric, or industrial engineering), or combinations of the methodologies.

The designations of aggregate modeling and disaggregate modeling are assigned to modeling approaches on the basis of structure not substance. You will encounter modeling approaches that use combinations of aggregation and disaggregation.

An aggregate is an assemblage or collection of distinct component parts. A building is an aggregate of concrete, steel beams, and other building material. Conversely, a disaggregate is a component part of an aggregate assemblage or collection. Concrete and steel beams are disaggregates of a building.

Table 6.19 gives the disaggregation of the Level 1 aggregation of industrial and commercial machinery and computer equipment in two sequential levels. In turn, each lower level is an aggregation to the next lower level.

***Table 6.19*** *Disaggregation of Industrial and Commercial Machinery and Computer Equipment [11]*

| | |
|---|---|
| Level 1: | Industrial and Commercial Machinery and Computer Equipment |
|     Level 2: | Engines and Turbines |
|         Level 3: | Steam, Gas, and Hydraulic Turbines and Turbine Generator Set Units |
|         Level 3: | Internal Combustion Engines |
| Level 1: | Computer and Office Equipment |
|     Level 2: | Electronic Computers |
|         Level 3: | Computer Storage Devices |
|         Level 3: | Computer Terminals |
|         Level 3: | Computer Peripheral Equipment |
|         Level 3: | Calculating and Accounting Machines |
|         Level 3: | Office Machines |

Adapted by courtesy of Executive Office of the President, from Office of Management and Budget, *Standard Industrial Classification Manual*, 1987.

## 6.4.1 Aggregate Modeling

The distinguishing feature between aggregate modeling and disaggregate modeling is bottom-up estimating with total adherence to the detailed work breakdown structure (WBS) or generation breakdown (GB) in the latter and top-down estimating with adherence to the summary level WBS in the former.

Consider the summary of WBS in Table 6.20 for constructing a building for a computer processing center. The first level in the WBS is the building. The costs for each WBS element in the table are industrial engineering estimates derived from the lowest level in the WBS and summarized at the second level. Irrespective of how the estimator derived the costs, the WBS in the table is an aggregate model.

There are two approaches to estimating risk exposure in the foregoing cost elements:

1. Require the people who prepared the original estimates of time and cost to judge what may go wrong. Use the same methodology to estimate the corrective-action time and cost which may be required, and predict the probability that the problem will occur.

    The products of the probability of occurrence and the corrective-action time and cost are risk time and risk cost. Add these to the **baseline time** and **baseline cost estimates** to yield the **risk time** and **risk cost estimates**.

2. Require those who prepared the original estimates of time and cost to estimate **risk determinant factors** for each element in the WBS or GB.

    The products of the original baseline time and baseline cost estimates and one plus risk determinant factor (*i.e.*, 1 + RDF) are the risk time and risk cost estimates.

*Table 6.20* Summary Work Breakdown Structure for Computer Processing Center Building [12]

| Level | Element | Estimated Cost |
|---|---|---|
| 100 | Total building | $2,742,500 |
| 101 | General requirements | 345,000 |
| 102 | Site work | 118,000 |
| 103 | Concrete | 235,000 |
| 104 | Masonry | 105,000 |
| 105 | Metals | 372,000 |
| 106 | Wood and plastic | 33,000 |
| 107 | Thermal and moisture | 142,000 |
| 108 | Doors and windows | 66,500 |
| 109 | Finishes | 95,000 |
| 110 | Specialties | 360,000 |
| 120 | Conveying systems | 102,000 |
| 130 | Mechanical | 542,000 |
| 140 | Electrical | 227,000 |

From Alphonse J. Dell'Isola and Stephen J. Kirk, *Life Cycle Costing for Design Professionals*. Copyright©1981 McGraw-Hill Book Company. Material reproduced with permission of McGraw-Hill, Inc.

Equations 6.15 and 6.16 are the recommended relationships for estimating risk exposure in terms of risk time and risk cost. For general contractors and subcontractors who are experienced in such buildings, it is reasonable to assume risk determinant factors of 0.50 or less.

$$RTE = BTE + (RT)(CRDF) \tag{6.15}$$

$$RCE = BCE + (RC)(CRDF) \tag{6.16}$$

where CRDF denotes composite risk determinant factor.

Substituting $BTE$ = 16 months, $RT$ = 6 months, and the assumed value of $CRDF$ = 0.5 in Equation 6.15 yields $RTE$ = 16 + (6)(0.5), or 19 months.

Substituting $BCE$ = \$2,742,550, $RC$ = \$450,000, and the assumed value of $CRDF$ = 0.5 in Equation 6.16 yields $RCE$ = \$2,742,550 + (\$450,000)(0.5), or \$2,967,550.

### ■ 6.4.2 Example of Aggregate Modeling

The general contractor estimated the cost of the new building in the Chi-Square Center at \$2,742,550 in 1985. Funding, however, was not available until 1988, at which time the director of the center suggested that the contractor use the change in the producer price index (PPI) from 1985 to 1988 to update the quotation.

The general contractor is uncomfortable with this suggestion. On the one hand, the contractor does not wish to incur the cost of another industrial engineering estimate. On the other hand, the contractor does not wish to chance losing the building contract. The contractor retains Analyst to resolve the issue.

Table 6.21 gives the technical approach Analyst follows in carrying out the assignment.

*Table 6.21   Technical Approach for Aggregate Modeling Example*

1. Obtain producer price indexes for 1985 through 1988 from the *Statistical Abstract of the United States*.
2. Calculate ratio of the 1985 index to the 1988 index.
3. Multiply baseline cost estimate by ratio of indexes.

Analyst pursues the director's suggestion that the 1985 estimate be updated by the ratio of the 1988 PPI to the 1985 PPI. From Table 6.22 the ratio of the two values 106.9 ÷ 103.2 is 1.035853. The product of 1.035853 and the 1985 estimate of \$2,742,550 is \$2,840,827.

*Table 6.22   Producer Price Index Data for Aggregate Modeling Example [13]*

|  | 1985 | 1986 | 1987 | 1988 |
|---|---|---|---|---|
| Producer price index | 103.2 | 100.2 | 102.8 | 106.9 |
| Construction materials index | 107.6 | 107.3 | 109.5 | 115.7 |
| Construction labor percent change | 3.2 | 3.6 | 4.2 | 5.2 |

Adapted by courtesy of U.S. Department of Commerce, Bureau of the Census from *Statistical Abstract of the United States: 1990* (110th Edition), Washington, DC, 1990.

## 6.4 Aggregation vs. Disaggregation

The updated figure pleases the director of the Chi-Square Center, but not the contractor who feels it is too low. The contractor informs Analyst that the material-labor split in the estimate is 0.25-0.75, and asks Analyst to approach the issue on this basis.

On this basis, the amount of material in the 1985 estimate is (0.25)($2,742,550), or $685,625. The amount of labor is (0.75)($2,742,550), or $2,056,875.

Analyst updates the material portion of the 1988 estimate with the ratio of the 1988 construction material index of 115.7 to the 1985 construction material index of 107.6, obtaining 115.7 ÷ 107.6, or 1.0752788. The product of 1.0752788 and the 1985 material value of $685,625 is $737,238.

Analyst next compounds the annual percent change for construction labor from 1985 to 1988 in Table 6.22, obtaining (1.032)(1.036)(1.042)(1.052), or 1.172. The product of 1.172 and $2,056,875 (*i.e.*, the labor-portion of the 1985 estimate) is $2,410,658.

The sum of the updated material estimate and updated labor estimate is $737,238 + $2,410,658, or $3,147,896. Analyst provides this finding to the general contractor and the director of the Chi-Square Center. The contractor is pleased with the figure, but the director feels that the figure is too high. Analyst leaves the issue to the two individuals to resolve.

### ■ 6.4.3 Disaggregate Modeling

As stated, the major difference between disaggregate modeling and aggregate modeling is bottom-up estimating with total adherence to the WBS or GB in the former and top-down estimating with adherence to the summary level WBS in the latter. Table 6.23 is the six-level WBS for the computer processing center building in the Chi-Square Center.

Starting with the lowest element in the WBS, estimators used industrial engineering to compile the costs. The total cost at the first level is the same as the total cost at the first level in Table 6.20.

***Table 6.23*** *Six-Level Work Breakdown Structure for Computer Processing Center Building [14]*

| WBS | Element | Estimated Cost |
|---|---|---|
| 100000 | Total building | $2,742,500 |
| 101000 | General requirements | 345,000 |
| 101001 | Mobilization expenses | 10,000 |
| 101002 | Job site overhead | 125,000 |
| 101003 | Demobilization | 5,000 |
| 101004 | Office expense | 205,000 |
| 102000 | Site work | 118,000 |
| 102001 | Clearing and demolition | 4,000 |
| 102002 | Grading and earthwork | 24,500 |
| 102003 | Excavation and backfill | 2,000 |
| 102004 | Below slab fill | 6,500 |
| 102005 | Drainage and utilities | 32,000 |
| 102006 | Paving and landscaping | 49,000 |
| 103000 | Concrete | 235,000 |
| 103001 | Foundation forms and reinforcement | 30,500 |
| 103002 | Slab forms and reinforcement | 34,500 |

**Table 6.23** *Six-Level Work Breakdown Structure for Computer Processing Center Building [14] (Cont.)*

| WBS | Element | Estimated Cost |
|---|---|---|
| 103003 | Floor forms and reinforcement | $ 40,000 |
| 103004 | Roof forms and reinforcement | 35,000 |
| 103005 | Walls forms and reinforcement | 95,000 |
| 103006 | Walls finish | 10,000 |
| 104000 | Masonry | 105,000 |
| 104001 | Exterior walls | 40,000 |
| 104002 | Interior partitions | 25,000 |
| 104003 | Interior paving and finish | 40,000 |
| 105000 | Metals | 372,000 |
| 105001 | Floor structural framing | 140,000 |
| 105002 | Roof structural framing | 100,000 |
| 105003 | Floor joists and decking | 42,000 |
| 105004 | Roof joists and decking | 45,000 |
| 105005 | Stairs | 16,000 |
| 105006 | Exterior ornamental | 14,000 |
| 105007 | Interior ornamental | 15,000 |
| 106000 | Wood and plastic | 33,000 |
| 106001 | Floors rough carpentry | 3,000 |
| 106002 | Roof rough carpentry | 2,000 |
| 106003 | Exterior wall rough carpentry | 5,000 |
| 106004 | Partitions rough carpentry | 10,000 |
| 106005 | Finished carpentry and cabinets | 13,000 |
| 107000 | Thermal and moisture | 142,000 |
| 107001 | Water and damp proofing | 19,000 |
| 107002 | Slab thermal insulation | 9,000 |
| 107003 | Exterior walls thermal insulation | 27,000 |
| 107004 | Membrane roofing and topping | 54,000 |
| 107005 | Roof sheet metal | 2,000 |
| 107006 | Skylights | 30,000 |
| 107007 | Sealants and caulking | 1,000 |
| 108000 | Doors and windows | 66,500 |
| 108001 | Exterior doors and frames | 4,000 |
| 108002 | Exterior windows and curtain walls | 14,000 |
| 108003 | Interior doors and frames | 14,000 |
| 108004 | Interior glass and glazing | 22,000 |
| 108005 | Hardware and specialties | 12,500 |
| 109000 | Finishes | 95,000 |
| 109001 | Gypsum wallboard | 20,000 |
| 109002 | Tile and terrazzo | 11,000 |
| 109003 | Acoustical ceiling and treatment | 46,000 |
| 109004 | Interior paint and wall covering | 18,000 |
| 110000 | Specialties | 360,000 |
| 110001 | Toilet, bath, wardrobe accessories | 4,000 |
| 110002 | Access flooring | 350,000 |

## 6.4 Aggregation vs. Disaggregation

**Table 6.23**  Six-Level Work Breakdown Structure for Computer Processing Center Building [14] (Cont.)

| WBS | Element | Estimated Cost |
|---|---|---|
| 110002 | Miscellaneous specialties | $    6,000 |
| 120000 | Conveying systems | 102,000 |
| 120001 | Elevators, dumbwaiters, & lifts | 102,000 |
| 130000 | Mechanical | 542,000 |
| 130001 | Exterior mechanical | 19,000 |
| 130002 | Water supply & treatment | 36,000 |
| 130003 | Waste water disposal & treatment | 52,000 |
| 130004 | Plumbing fixtures | 30,000 |
| 130005 | Fire protection systems & equipment | 65,000 |
| 130006 | Heat generation equipment | 20,000 |
| 130007 | Refrigeration | 20,000 |
| 130008 | HVAC piping, ductwork, & terminals | 210,000 |
| 130009 | Controls & instrumentation | 61,000 |
| 130010 | Insulation (Plumbing) | 4,000 |
| 130011 | Insulation (HVAV) | 26,000 |
| 140000 | Electrical | 227,000 |
| 140001 | Utilities & service entries | 1,000 |
| 140002 | Substations & transformers | 2,000 |
| 140003 | Distribution & panel boards | 45,000 |
| 140004 | Lighting fixtures | 60,000 |
| 140005 | Branch wiring & devices | 80,000 |
| 140006 | Special electric systems | 20,000 |
| 140007 | Communications | 19,000 |

From Alphonse J. Dell'Isola and Stephen J. Kirk, *Life Cycle Costing for Design Professionals*. Copyright© 1981 McGraw-Hill Book Company. Material reproduced with permission of McGraw-Hall, Inc.

### ■ 6.4.4 Example of Disaggregate Modeling

The general contractor for the building in Chi-Square Center has had substantial personnel turnover and retains Analyst to assess the risk cost in undertaking the construction job. Table 6.24 is the worksheet which Analyst uses in carrying out the assignment.

**Table 6.24**  Technical Approach for Disaggregate Modeling Example

1. Select the work breakdown structure level for estimating risk exposure.
2. Obtain judgment of personnel on potential corrective-action cost and corrective-action probability.
3. Equate risk cost to product of corrective-action cost and corrective action probability.
4. Derive values of risk cost.

The effort for disaggregate modeling is great compared to that for aggregate modeling, which causes the latter to be favored over the former in most circumstances. Where accuracy is essential, you should use the lowest possible level in the WBS. A reasonable compromise is the second-level WBS in Table 6.23, with the knowledge that second-level costs are compilations of bottom-up estimates.

> *In estimating, use the lowest level of aggregation that time and money will allow, or spend the time and money later when initial findings prove inconclusive.*
> **Analyst**

Analyst proceeds on the basis of estimating risk exposure in the building at the second-level of the WBS. Analyst interviews the lead personnel on the potential for corrective action, corrective-action costs, and corrective-action probability in the second-level WBS elements. Table 6.25 is the worksheet Analyst uses in completing the assignment.

*Table 6.25  Worksheet for Disaggregate Modeling Example*

| Element | BCE | CAC | P(CA) | Product | RCE |
|---|---|---|---|---|---|
| 101000 | 345,000 | 52,000 | 0.20 | 10,400 | 355,400 |
| 102000 | 118,000 | 13,500 | 0.30 | 4,050 | 122,050 |
| 103000 | 235,000 | 36,400 | 0.15 | 5,460 | 240,460 |
| 104000 | 105,000 | 9,800 | 0.35 | 3,430 | 108,430 |
| 105000 | 372,000 | 69,900 | 0.40 | 27,960 | 399,960 |
| 106000 | 33,000 | 5,500 | 0.10 | 550 | 33,550 |
| 107000 | 142,000 | 18,300 | 0.25 | 4,575 | 146,575 |
| 108000 | 66,500 | 8,100 | 0.10 | 810 | 67,310 |
| 109000 | 95,000 | 10,400 | 0.25 | 2,600 | 97,600 |
| 110000 | 360,000 | 63,800 | 0.30 | 19,140 | 379,140 |
| 120000 | 102,000 | 7,600 | 0.10 | 760 | 102,760 |
| 130000 | 542,000 | 101,000 | 0.35 | 35,350 | 577,350 |
| 140000 | 227,000 | 30,100 | 0.25 | 7,525 | 234,525 |
|  |  |  |  | Total: | 2,865,110 |

*BCE*: Baseline cost estimate.
*CAC*: Corrective-action cost.
*P(CA)*: Probability of corrective action.
Product: Product of CAC and P(AC).
*RCE*: Risk cost estimate.

The title Product in the fifth column of Table 6.25 denotes the multiplication of the respective corrective-action cost (CAC) by the probability of corrective action (P(CA)). The respective risk cost estimate (RCE) is the sum of the baseline cost estimates (BCE) and the product of CAC and P(CA).

The sum of the RCE values in Table 6.25 is $2,865,110. This is about 4.47 percent greater than the total building baseline cost estimate of $2,742,500 in Table 6.20, suggesting that risk exposure in the new building is low.

## 6.5 SUMMARY

**Section 6.1 Definitions** provided an annotated perspective of the chapter with the definitions of key terms and abbreviations used in the chapter. These definitions were repeated when we first used them in the chapter.

**Section 6.2 Perspective on Risk Models** illuminated the profusion of risk models which can be found in contemporary literature. We compared these to the classical categories of models which we encounter in operations research as well as in the methodology used in estimating baseline time and cost. Estimators constantly relate cost to material, weight, and volume, and we gave examples on using each of the three parameters.

The section included selection criteria and application guidelines to ensure that the risk model is compatible with its environment and the resources available to run it. We pointed out that the intriguing nature of these models might cause you to lose sight of the end objective of the application and end up with a brilliant solution in search of a problem. As the eminent information theorist Robert Hamming said, "The purpose of computing is insight, not numbers."

**Section 6.3 Art of Simulation** presented approaches to simulation. The subject matter included the normal distribution and sampling distributions, with emphasis on the Student's $t$ distribution, as the bases for modeling. We introduced the important subjects of degrees of freedom and tests of hypothesis. We also addressed the generation and use of random numbers in the popular Monte Carlo method.

**Sections 6.4 Aggregation vs. Disaggregation** completed the cycle that began with the discussion of risk metrics in Chapter 3. You learned that aggregation is essentially an embodiment of top-down estimating and disaggregation an embodiment of bottom-up estimating. We reinforced the section with examples of modeling.

Chapter 6 concludes with **Section 6.5 Summary**, **Section 6.6 Exercises**, and **Section 6.7 References**. The summary serves to highlight the contents of the chapter and the exercises reinforce the highlights.

## 6.6 EXERCISES

Appendix C contains step-by-step solutions to the following exercises. We urge you to attempt the exercises without first resorting to the solutions, since the intent is to reinforce the subject matter covered in the chapter.

### ■ 6.6.1 Parametric Relationship

Given the data in Table 6.26, derive the parametric relationship for estimating the list price of vehicles as a function of weight.

*Table 6.26   Vehicle Data for Exercise in Section 6.6.1*

| Vehicle | List Price Dollars | Weight Pounds | Vehicle | List Price Dollars | Weight Pounds |
|---------|-------------------|---------------|---------|-------------------|---------------|
| A | 19,500 | 4,550 | F | 22,230 | 4,120 |
| B | 15,690 | 3,990 | G | 31,600 | 5,500 |
| C | 22,000 | 5,300 | H | 12,590 | 3,200 |
| D | 28,000 | 4,900 | I | 42,000 | 6,100 |
| E | 36,000 | 5,600 | J | 16,990 | 2,850 |

### ■ 6.6.2 Law of Large Numbers

State the law of large numbers. What is the significance of the law to the modeling process? Give an example.

### ■ 6.6.3 Central Limit Theorem

State the central limit theorem. What is the significance of the theorem to the modeling process? Give an example.

### ■ 6.6.4 Area Under Normal Probability Density Curve

What are the $z$-statistics bounding the areas about the mean for confidence levels of 0.80, 0.90, 0.95, and 0.99? How does the magnitude of confidence intervals vary as a function of the value of $z$?

### ■ 6.6.5 Area in Tails of Normal Probability Density Function

What are the areas in both tails for the following values of the $z$-statistic: $\pm 1$, $\pm 2$, $\pm 3$, and $\pm 4$? What are the areas in a single tail?

### ■ 6.6.6 Degrees of Freedom

Define *degrees of freedom*. How do degrees of freedom enter into probability distributions and statistics? Give three examples.

### ■ 6.6.7 Mean and Standard Deviation

Calculate the value of the mean and standard deviation for the dependent data in Table 6.27. What probability distribution would you use to model the data?

*Table 6.27   Data for Exercise in Section 6.6.7*

| | | | | |
|---|---|---|---|---|
| 120 | 260 | 245 | 390 | 155 |
| 425 | 690 | 670 | 210 | 320 |
| 635 | 405 | 710 | 400 | 655 |
| 175 | 410 | 250 | 600 | 310 |

## 6.6.8 Confidence Limits

Given a sample of 100 bolts with a mean of 3.05 inch and a standard deviation of 0.10 inch, calculate the confidence limits about the mean for a 90 percent confidence level.

## 6.6.9 Sampling Distributions

Name the sampling distributions. What are the tests of hypothesis using these distributions?

## 6.6.10 Area Under Student's t Probability Density Function

What are the $t$-statistics bounding the areas under the Student's $t$ curve for confidence levels of 0.80, 0.90, 0.95, and 0.99 and a sample size of ten? How does the shape of the curve vary as a function of degrees of freedom? What is the meaning of the statement that the normal distribution is the limit of the Student's $t$ distribution with increasing sample size?

## 6.6.11 Student's t Distribution

Repeat the exercise in Section 6.6.8 for a confidence level of 0.90 and a sample size of ten bolts.

## 6.6.12 Test of Hypothesis

Automobile manufacturers typically test a few of each year's models for extended periods of time to validate gas mileage performance. Miles per gallon for a particular model were 28, 31, 34, 30, 27, and 29.

The design goal for a certain model is 30 miles per gallon. At a confidence level of 90 percent, test the null hypothesis that the sample mean is representative of the population mean. Derive the 90-percent confidence interval about the sample mean.

## 6.6.13 Random Numbers

What is the difference between a random number and a pseudorandom number (PRN)? How many PRNs consisting of how many digits do you need to simulate lots of size 10,000, 5,000, 1,000, 500, 100, 50, and 10?

## 6.6.14 Monte Carlo Method

Describe the steps comprising the Monte Carlo method. What probability distribution would you use to simulate a sample of ten variates?

## 6.6.15 Simulation

Emulate the simulation in the example of Section 6.3.11 for a sample size of 30 with the cost data in Table 6.28.

*Table 6.28    Cost History for Exercise in Section 6.6.15*

| Unit | Cost Dollars | Unit | Cost Dollars |
|------|--------------|------|--------------|
| 1 | 9,850 | 6 | 8,790 |
| 2 | 9,650 | 7 | 8,580 |
| 3 | 9,750 | 8 | 8,150 |
| 4 | 9,300 | 9 | 7,750 |
| 5 | 9,050 | 10 | 7,300 |

Calculate the confidence interval about the mean for significance levels of 0.20, 0.10, and 0.05.

### ■ 6.6.16 Aggregate Model

Repeat the example in Section 6.4.2 with the data in Table 6.29.

*Table 6.29    Producer Price Index Data for Aggregate Modeling Example [15]*

|  | 1980 | 1985 | 1986 | 1987 | 1988 |
|---|---|---|---|---|---|
| Intermediate producer price index | 90.3 | 102.7 | 99.1 | 101.5 | 107.1 |
| Construction materials price index | 92.5 | 107.6 | 107.3 | 109.5 | 115.7 |
| Construction weekly dollar earnings | 397 | 520 | — | — | — |

|  | 1989 | 1990 | 1991 | 1992 | 1993 |
|---|---|---|---|---|---|
| Intermediate producer price index | 112.0 | 114.5 | 114.4 | 114.7 | 116.2 |
| Construction materials price index | 119.5 | 119.6 | 120.4 | 122.5 | 128.6 |
| Construction weekly dollar earnings | 513 | 526 | 533 | 535 | 551 |

Intermediate producer price index: Table No. 753.
Construction materials price index: Table No. 1193.
Construction weekly dollar earnings: Table No. 654.
Adapted by courtesy of U.S. Department of Commerce, Bureau of the Census from *Statistical Abstract of the United States: 1994* (114th Edition), Washington, DC, 1994.

### ■ 6.6.17 Disaggregation

Using the current edition of the *Statistical Abstract of the United States*, delineate the disaggregation of the producer price index for metals. [15]

How does the producer price index for primary metals correlate with producer price indexes for nonferrous metals and ferrous metals over a period of five years?

How does the producer price index for individual metals correlate with the producer price index for primary metals? How does the producer price index for primary metals correlate with producer price index for crude material and the consumer price index for energy?

### ■ 6.6.18 Disaggregate Modeling

Compare the updated baseline cost estimate from the example in Section 6.4.4 with the risk cost estimate from the example in Section 6.4.2.

Which of the two estimates do you think is more realistic and credible?

# 6.7 References

You can obtain referenced government documents from the issuing organizations and from:

Superintendent of Documents, U.S. Government Printing Office, Washington, DC 20402. Telephone: (202) 783-3238.

National Technical Information Service, U.S. Department of Commerce, Springfield, VA 22161. Telephone: (703) 487-4650.

1. Analytical Sciences Corporation, *Risk Management Concepts and Guidance*, Defense Systems Management College, 1988.
2. Robert G. Batson and Gerald R. McNichols, *Cost Risk Analysis Methodology: A State-of-the-Art Review*, First Joint National Conferences of the Institute of Cost Analysis and the National Estimating Society, 1988.
3. Effraim Turban and Jack R. Meredith, *Fundamentals of Management Science*, Fourth Edition, Business Publications, Inc., 1988.
4. Irwin Miller, John E. Freund, and Richard A. Johnson, *Probability and Statistics for Engineers*, Fourth Edition, Prentice Hall, 1990.
5. Jack V. Michaels, *Lectures on Operation Research*, Naval Ordinance Station, Indian Head, Maryland, 1968.
6. NAVMAT P4855-1, *Navy Power Supply Reliability*, Department of the Navy, 1982.
7. Irwin Miller, John E. Freund, and Richard A. Johnson, *Probability and Statistics for Engineers*, Fourth Edition, Prentice Hall, 1990.
8. Jack V. Michaels, *Lectures on Operation Research*, Naval Ordinance Station, Indian Head, Maryland, 1968.
9. Irwin Miller, John E. Freund, and Richard A. Johnson, *Probability and Statistics for Engineers*, Fourth Edition, Prentice Hall, 1990.
10. The Rand Corporation, *A Million Random Digits with 100,000 Normal Deviates*, The Free Press, 1956.
11. Office of Management and Budget, *Standard Industrial Classification Manual*, Executive Office of the President, 1987.
12. Alphonse J. Dell'Isola and Stephen J. Kirk, *Life Cycle Costing for Design Professionals*, McGraw-Hill Book Company, 1981.
13. U.S. Department of Commerce, Bureau of the Census, *Statistical Abstract of the United States: 1990* (110th Edition), Washington, DC, 1990.
14. Alphonse J. Dell'Isola and Stephen J. Kirk, *Life Cycle Costing for Design Professionals*, McGraw-Hill Book Company, 1981.
15. U.S. Bureau of the Census, *Statistical Abstract of the United States: 1994* (114th Edition), Washington, DC, 1994.

> *What we anticipate seldom occurs; what we least expect generally happens.*
>
> **Benjamin Disraeli**

# CHAPTER 7

# RISK CONTROL

> Most problems are self imposed and usually can be traced to lack of discipline. The foremost attribute of successful programs is discipline: Discipline to evolve and proclaim realistic cost goals; discipline to forego appealing but nonessential features; discipline to minimize engineering changes; discipline to do thorough failure analyses; discipline to abide by test protocols; and discipline to persevere in the face of problems that will occur in even the best-managed programs.
>
> **Norman R. Augustine**

The passage from the classic *Augustine's Laws* epitomizes the essence of this book. [1] The key message is: "Give people the responsibility, means, and authority to do the job you assign them; hold them accountable for their actions; and reward them commensurately with their performance."

You can never eliminate risk completely. It is contrary to the nature of the world, society, and people. As Thornton Wilder said, "Every good thing in the world stands on the razor-edge of danger."

You can, however, reduce risk to an acceptable and affordable level, given the proper environment, know-how, and discipline to do so. The proper environment is a function of your company and organization. This book can supply the know-how. Only you can supply the discipline.

We equate effective technical risk management to company policy, procedures, and motivation, and the discipline of the company and its personnel to adhere to the foregoing. Figure 7.1 bears out the stark simplicity of this statement.

The process begins with the chief executive officer's (CEO) statement of technical risk management policy. Responsibility, authority, accountability, and funding must flow directly from the CEO to those charged with carrying out risk control. Responsibility, authority, accountability, and finding must then flow from those charged with carrying out risk control to product and service managers. Everyone in the company must know that those people speak for the CEO and that reward or punishment will be commensurate with performance.

Chapter 7 • Risk Control 299

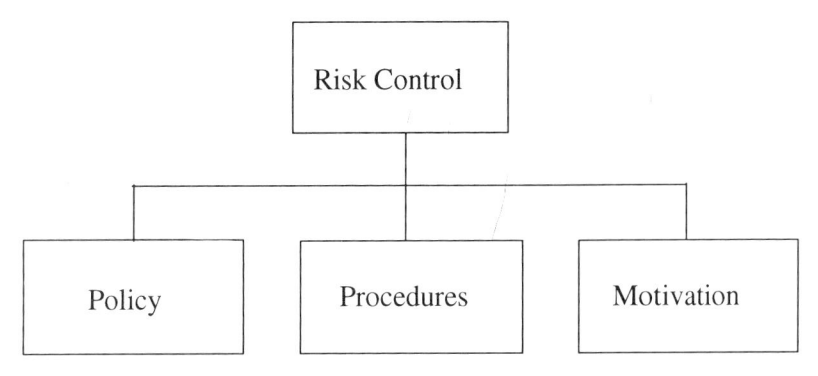

**Figure 7.1** Technical Risk Management Elements

Chapter 7 represents a capsule summary of the book in the form of organizational, procedural, and motivational guidelines, risk perspectives and principles, and some real-world examples of risk in action. Figure 7.2 illustrates the organization of the chapter.

**Section 7.1 Definitions** provides an annotated perspective of the chapter with the definitions of key terms and abbreviations used in the chapter. These definitions are repeated when we first use them in the chapter and in the glossary in Appendix A.

You can lessen risk by the way you approach a job and **Section 7.2 Organizational Guidelines** offers you guidance on how to organize for minimizing risk exposure. The key element is the direct chain-of-command from the CEO or product director to those charged with risk management.

**Section 7.3 Procedural Guidelines** stresses the smooth transition from development into production. The section draws from costly lessons learned by the U.S. Department of Defense.

**Section 7.4 Motivational Guidelines** offers some suggestions on motivating personnel and suppliers to help in controlling risk. The section illustrates the difference between award fees and incentives.

**Section 7.5 Risk Perspectives** describes the philosophical outlook that we evolved over many years of risk control and the outlook of several prominent people. The section includes a warning regarding the margin of error in opinion polls on which you may base long-range planning and shows you how to discern systematic errors and sampling bias errors.

**Section 7.6 Risk Examples** describes the experiences of a number of large corporations and governmental organizations; some of which have done well; some of which should have known better. See if you can relate to these examples.

We sprinkled a number of quotations throughout the book with the intent of highlighting certain points as well as holding your interest. **Section 7.7 Risk Principles** repeats some of these earlier remarks and adds a few more for your consideration.

The chapter concludes with **Section 7.8 Summary**, **Section 7.9 Exercises**, and **Section 7.10 References**. We drew the exercises from events that made headlines in the news. They should interest and challenge you.

Analyst and I hope that you have found *Technical Risk Management* easy to read and interesting as well as a useful guide and reference book. Above all, we hope it launches you into a career of

technical risk management. Treat this book with care and respect, and it will take care of you throughout your career.

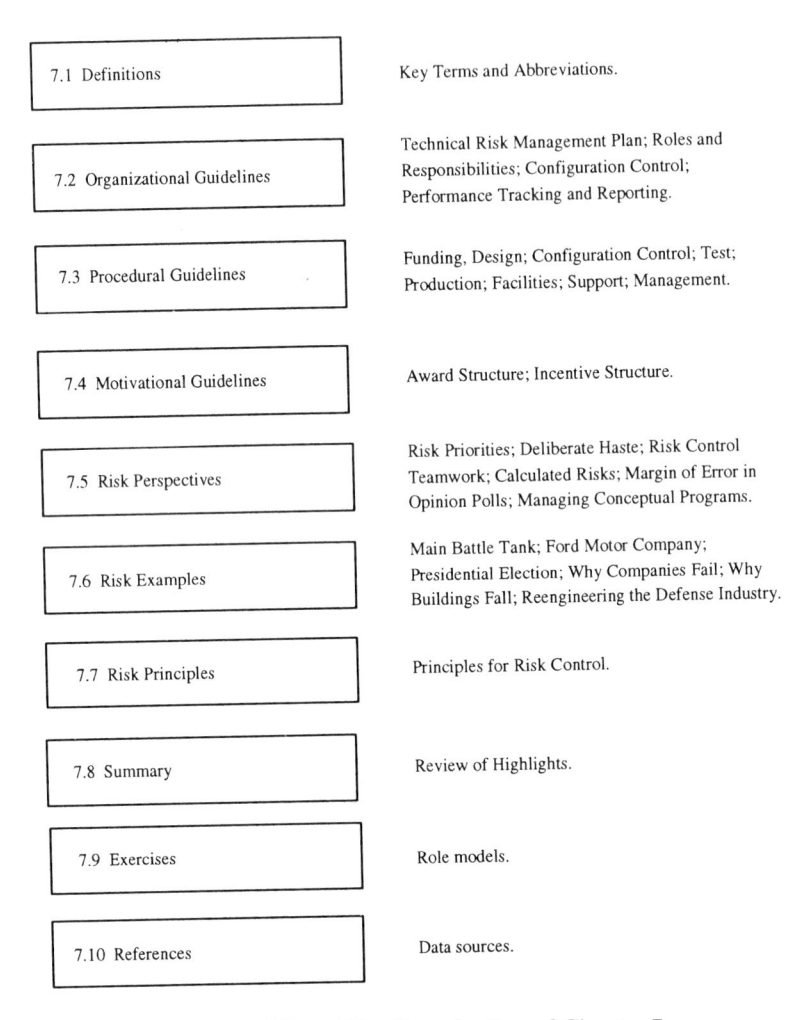

|  |  |
|---|---|
| 7.1 Definitions | Key Terms and Abbreviations. |
| 7.2 Organizational Guidelines | Technical Risk Management Plan; Roles and Responsibilities; Configuration Control; Performance Tracking and Reporting. |
| 7.3 Procedural Guidelines | Funding, Design; Configuration Control; Test; Production; Facilities; Support; Management. |
| 7.4 Motivational Guidelines | Award Structure; Incentive Structure. |
| 7.5 Risk Perspectives | Risk Priorities; Deliberate Haste; Risk Control Teamwork; Calculated Risks; Margin of Error in Opinion Polls; Managing Conceptual Programs. |
| 7.6 Risk Examples | Main Battle Tank; Ford Motor Company; Presidential Election; Why Companies Fail; Why Buildings Fall; Reengineering the Defense Industry. |
| 7.7 Risk Principles | Principles for Risk Control. |
| 7.8 Summary | Review of Highlights. |
| 7.9 Exercises | Role models. |
| 7.10 References | Data sources. |

**Figure 7.2** Organization of Chapter 7

The hours are long, the concentration is high, and the responsibility is great in technical risk management. Risk control requires commitment and dedication that not too many are willing to share. However, as Augustine points out, "The *sine qua non* of successful program execution is the participation of highly competent and highly motivated people. Carefully selected but small groups of individuals can contribute far beyond their numbers and should be rewarded accordingly, if for no other reason than that it is a sound business investment." Risk control is a tough job, but the rewards are great.

# 7.1 Definitions

> *For many are called, but few are chosen.*
> Matthew XXII: 14

Table 7.1 gives definitions of terms and abbreviations used in the chapter. Note the definitions of *award fee*, *incentive*, *sampling bias*, and *sampling error*.

***Table 7.1** Terms and Abbreviations in Chapter 7*

**Affordability**: Characteristic of product with selling price that approaches its functional worth and is within the limit of what customer is both able and willing to pay.
**Award fee**: Form of recognition for performance on contract.
**First article test**: Test of first production unit of product.
**Functionality**: Form, fit, and function of product relative to intended use.
**Incentive**: Form of recognition for performance on contract.
**Life-cycle cost**: Cost of production acquisition, operation, support, and disposal.
**Margin for error**: Statement of statistical confidence in opinion surveys.
**Mission success**: Development and production of product that gains widespread customer and user acceptance.
**Pegasus**: In Greek mythology, the winged horse of the Muses.
**Point of total assumption**: Dollar amount above which contractor assumes responsibility for additional cost on contract.
**Product manager**: Individual responsible for development and production of product within time and money constraints.
**Profitability**: Return-on-investment commensurate with resources expended on producing product.
**Quality**: Degree to which product provides required functionality over expected periods of time with expected level and frequency of maintenance and repair.
**RFP**: Request for proposal.
**Risk**: Uncertainty surrounding loss from perils.
**Risk cost**: Product of the probability of corrective action and corrective-action cost.
**Risk determinant factor**: Quantified measure that serves to estimate risk exposure.
**Risk exposure**: Susceptibility of product to perils in terms of risk time and risk cost.
**Risk time**: Product of corrective action and corrective-action time.
**ROI**: Return-on-investment.
**Sampling bias**: Error resulting from design of sampling plan.
**Sampling error**: Error that is either a function of sample size and confidence level or of sampling bias.
**Service manager**: Individual responsible for development and performance of service within time and money constraints.
*Sine qua non*: Latin for *an absolute prerequisite*.
**Stratified random sampling**: Division of populations into subgroups, or strata, from which samples are drawn.
**Systematic random sampling**: Selection of first sample at random and subsequent samples with some periodicity.
**Template**: Depiction of critical events in design, test, and production of product.

## 7.2 ORGANIZATIONAL GUIDELINES

Technical risk management begins with the CEO's policy statement on risk control. Table 7.2 is a sample of such a statement. The statement should be brief but explicit so that no one can question its meaning.

Risk control must be structured to be effective. This section describes the initial planning necessary to provide this structure. Table 7.3 lists the elements of a structured technical risk management program.

*Table 7.2   Policy Statement on Risk Control*

> *In accordance with the Company's commitment to the quality, functionality, affordability, and profitability of its products and services, all operating units in the Company shall conduct risk control on new products and services and on redesigns of existing products and services under direction of the Company's Technical Risk Manager.*
>
> *The Technical Risk Manager shall be vested with the responsibility, authority, and accountability to implement, fund, and direct risk control programs.*
>
> *Any deviations from, or exceptions to, this policy require advance approval of my office.*
>
> **Chief Executive Officer**

*Table 7.3   Elements of Structured Technical Risk Management*

1. Generate technical risk management plan:
   - Place plan under configuration control from program onset
   - Apply plan to all program phases.
2. Define roles and responsibilities:
   - Appoint technical risk manager
   - Place manager under the program director
   - Include manager in approval chain for design and cost changes
   - Define interfaces with other program managers
   - Promulgate program elements responsibility matrix.
3. Institute configuration control:
   - Document baseline configuration and technical data package
   - Establish Change Control Board
   - Incorporate approved changes in baseline documentation
   - Separate requirement changes from corrective-action changes.
4. Track and report progress:
   - Prepare initial risk time and risk cost estimates
   - Provide monthly performance and cost variance analyses reports
   - Institute corrective action as required
   - Update risk time and risk cost estimates.

## 7.2 Organizational Guidelines

Note the second item Define Roles and Responsibilities in Table 7.3. Effective risk control requires a direct chain-of-command and a direct reporting channel between the technical risk manager and the product and **service managers**.

### ■ 7.2.1 Technical Risk Management Plan

A comprehensive management plan is a key element of strong technical risk management and **requests for proposals** (**RFP**) from customers often require such plans. RFPs from most governmental organizations usually require technical risk management plans. The plan should be conceived and documented under configuration control early in the program deliberations and should be applicable through all program phases.

The elements of the technical risk management program plan are essentially the definitions of organizational roles and responsibilities, baseline design control, and performance tracking and reporting requirements. Make sure that the technical risk management program schedule is compatible with the schedule for the products of interest.

### ■ 7.2.2 Roles and Responsibilities

**Product managers** should report directly to the technical risk manager. The technical risk manager has the responsibility to ensure a cohesive working relationship among product, functional, and mission success managers in the product organization.

Functional managers (*i.e.*, engineering, finance, manufacturing, planning, procurement, and quality) should be those who are already in the product organization. This ensures that technical risk management is a part of their normal work function. Product organizations also include the allied disciplines of concurrent engineering, design to cost, quality function deployment, system engineering, total quality management, and value engineering to ensure the **mission success** of products. [2]

### ■ 7.2.3 Configuration Control

Program baseline documentation for performance, schedule, and cost should be placed under formal configuration control. This includes authorization to pursue design alternatives and submit data to customers. The program director should issue a directive that names lead personnel responsible for specific activities.

It is at this point that the configuration control organization establishes an audit trail that documents baseline changes and their effects. Changes to the baseline are incorporated through the formal change control process. The technical risk management organization reviews engineering change proposals (ECP) and value engineering change proposals (VECP) for schedule and cost impact. The configuration control organization incorporates approved ECPs and VECPs for the baseline design.

### ■ 7.2.4 Performance Tracking and Reporting

Formal baseline tracking and reporting provide the audit trail for assessing and directing technical risk management performance. The tracking and reporting process provides the status of **risk expo-**

sure in terms of current risk time and risk cost estimates and variances as well as various internal and customer reports. The requirement for internal technical risk management reporting should be at least monthly. The frequency of customer reports should be in accordance with contract requirements.

When there is a variance between current and initial risk time and risk cost estimates, corrective action should be taken immediately. These actions may result in an ECP or a VECP. Only approved ECPs and VECPs are incorporated into the baseline.

## 7.3
## PROCEDURAL GUIDELINES

After all is said and done, the name of the game is production. Production supplies the needs of the public sector and of the private sector. Production is where profits are reaped by contractors who strike the right combination of **functionality**, **quality**, and **affordability**.

Too often in the past, when faced with funding and schedule constraints, the technical integrity of programs has been compromised by deleting or deferring vital program elements that contribute to system performance, producibility, and supportability. This has added unintentionally to the life cycle cost and postponed operational capability dates by pursuing development programs which did not yield producible designs and supportable configurations in a timely manner.

The U.S. Department of Defense (DoD) experienced the foregoing in a number of costly programs. These experiences led to the promulgation of DoD Directive 4245.7, *Transition from Development to Production*. The directive mandates the use of DoD 4245.7-M, *Transition from Development to Production* manual as the basis for structuring technically sound programs, assessing their risk and identifying areas needing corrective action. Appendix B provides amplifying details for those contemplating business with the military. We recommend that you consider the procedures in the manual because they are worthy of emulation in other sectors of the economy.

In essence, the major thrust of the manual is directed toward identifying and establishing critical engineering processes and their control methods. This leads to more organized accomplishment of these tasks, and places much more significance and accountability on the tasks.

The most critical events in the design, test, and production elements of the industrial process are transformed into product **templates**. There are product templates for funding, design, configuration control, test, production, facilities, support, and management.

### ■ 7.3.1 Funding

Aside from the issue of the amount of money devoted to programs, the major technical risk stems from the time-phasing of the money. You exacerbate risk exposure by authorizing development without production in mind.

You should accompany the development decision by adequate and timely development funding. In addition, the development decision is a commitment to production that you must support by properly phased funding.

### ■ 7.3.2 Design

You need accurate and complete specification of the usage profile to support the design process. The degree to which the usage profile corresponds to ultimate usage directly determines the risk exposure. In large products (*e.g.*, buildings), we translate design requirements from operational requirements and frequently negotiate the requirements during the design process. You can only verify these design requirements by post-development assessment and as such they are a common cause of risk exposure.

Trade studies are both essential and expected elements of development programs. However, reducing production risk is not a usual subject of trade studies and this is another element of risk exposure.

The existence or absence of documented corporate policies, backed up by controlled engineering practices manuals has a direct bearing on risk in production. The design process should reflect a sound design policy and proper engineering disciplines and practices.

Design analysis by specialty engineering is critical to low risk design for production. Low risk design should allow parts and materials to operate well below maximum allowable stress levels. Stress derating policies must be in place at the start of hardware development.

Failure to allocate system requirements clearly between hardware and software greatly increases the difficulty in isolating and correcting design problems. Experience shows that more than 60 percent of software errors are traceable to functional or logical design.

Many modern design tools, such as computer-aided design, are not used to the proper extent because they appear to be time consuming and costly. This short-sightedness results in overall longer schedules and costs.

In particular, design for testing is one of the many areas frequently neglected. You cannot afford to ignore the cost advantage of built-in tests in today's marketplace.

### ■ 7.3.3 *Configuration Control*

A common source of risk in the transition from development to production is the lack of adequate configuration control. The lack of specific direction and discipline in design reviews is another significant contributor to risk.

The most critical area in design, however, is the issue of released engineering. The requirements for completely checked engineering cannot be compromised for timely release to the factory without severe time and cost consequences.

### ■ 7.3.4 *Test*

The absence of a carefully integrated test plan is conducive to a high level of risk exposure. This is exacerbated by introducing production changes without requiring recertification.

The objective of failure reporting and corrective action is to prevent failure recurrence. Failure to flow-down such requirements to suppliers is a major contributor to risk exposure, along with indiscriminate uses of non-uniform test reports.

The cost for correcting software design errors after the design phase of programs multiplies at a much greater rate than the cost for correcting hardware design errors. This should be recognized in the course of establishing design limits and requirements for testing.

### ■ 7.3.5 *Production*

Involvement of production and manufacturing engineering only after the design process has been completed is a fundamental error and a major source of risk exposure during the transition from development to production.

Failure to certify manufacturing processes as well as product designs is a frequent contributor to the risk profile. Piece-part control, subcontractor control, and defect control are other areas that are conducive to high levels of risk exposure.

Planning for tooling and special test equipment should be initiated early in development. Similarly, early implementation of computer-aided manufacturing in conjunction with computer-aided design will facilitate the development and debugging of the technical data package for production.

Manufacturing screening, in particular environmental stress screening, can reduce field failure rates by as much as 90 percent and in-plant failure rates by as much as 75 percent. Electronic stress screening requirements should be established early in development.

### ■ 7.3.6 Facilities

There is a strong tendency to ignore facility needs when contemplating new products. In addition, current government contracting policy inhibits industry investment for modernization for prime contractors and their suppliers.

On the other hand, you can attribute many product failures in usage to outmoded manufacturing processes. You should provide motivation for contractors to adopt the productivity center approach, wherein they blend together technology and skilled workers.

### ■ 7.3.7 Support

Make customer support analysis an integral part of the design process to minimize operation and support costs of products in the hands of customers and users. You should design products with as complete an understanding as possible of customers and users.

You should develop support and test equipment in concert with prime mission equipment both for design efficiency and to ensure that the equipment is available when user training begins. You should treat training materials and equipment and spare parts and technical manuals used for operations and repairs in the same manner as support and test equipment.

### ■ 7.3.8 Management

Development management strategies should be supportive of the goals of both the customer and the contractor. You can never expend too much effort on tracking and reporting. Your guideline should be to ensure accuracy, completeness, and integrity. Last minute surprises are the most devastating events from the viewpoint of schedule and cost, in particular if your schedule requires deliveries from suppliers, be they subcontractors or vendors.

Breaks in production impact costs in two fashions, the first being the effect of inflation and, the second, being the loss of learning. Reductions in rate of production have the same deleterious effects.

## 7.4
## MOTIVATIONAL GUIDELINES

The judicious use of awards and incentives can motivate personnel and suppliers to make significant technical contributions to their work, their products, and to the reduction of risk. An effective

## 7.4 Motivational Guidelines

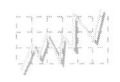

motivational technique has been put forth by the Martin Marietta Corporation in its value engineering programs.

Very simply, the company awards the originator of a successful value engineering changes proposal a sum of money equal to the company's share of the savings raised to the two-thirds power. On a saving share of $1 million, the sum amounts to $10,000, a tidy sum.

The cash award is, of course, accompanied by appropriate recognition and publicity. But, the gleam in the recipient's eye is from the sight of the money.

> *Professionals thrive on recognition, but live on money. Effective recognition programs are those that balance the two.*
> **Analyst**

The same situation applies to suppliers, subcontractors, or vendors. Nothing motivates like **award fees** and **incentives** that strike right at the bottom line. There are, however, salient differences between award fees and incentives, as well as the normal contract fee, which you should understand to realize their full potential.

You can use award fees and incentives with any form of contract whether it be fixed price or cost reimbursable. You can use award fees and incentives separately or together; however, they are completely apart from the normal fee on contracts and you should never associate the former with the latter.

As a matter of fact, it is advisable not to use the expressions *award fee* or *incentive fee* to avoid any association with government regulations that limit the maximum fee which contractors may earn on government contracts. The preferred expressions are *award structure* or *incentive structure*.

### ■ 7.4.1 Award Structure

Contractors and subcontractors regard award fees more favorably than incentive fees because of their somewhat benevolent-appearing nature. An award clause in a contract says in essence, "Achieve the parameter of interest and we will reward you accordingly. Should you not achieve the parameter to the extent required, you will be rewarded on the basis of our perception of your performance toward achieving the parameter."

The parameter of interest need not be technical, such as some property of mass. The parameter may be time, such as delivery date. The parameter may be economic, such as total acquisition cost or unit production cost. The amount of money allocated for award is a reflection of the importance of the particular parameter to the program.

Typically, amounts range from about 0.5 percent of the target cost of large-sized contracts (*i.e.*, hundreds of millions of dollars), to about 1 percent of the target cost in moderately sized subcontracts (*i.e.*, several million dollars), and to about 1.5 percent of the target cost in small-sized contracts (*i.e.*, hundreds of thousands of dollars or less).

Table 7.4 gives suggested schema that use both objective and subjective criteria. You use the objective criteria to reward achievement and the subjective criteria to reward effort.

We use Equation 7.1 to calculate the amount of an award ($-award) on the basis of the amount of money allocated for awards ($-allocated) and the average of the objective rating ($O$) and subjective rating ($S$).

$$\text{\$-award} = (\text{\$-allocated}) \frac{O + S}{2} \tag{7.1}$$

*Table 7.4* Award Structure

| Objective Criteria | Rating |
|---|---|
| Portion achieved of the technical parameter of interest. | 0 - 1.0 |
| **Subjective Criteria** | |
| **Outstanding**. Performance exceeds general level of competence expected of qualified contractor by wide margin approaching highest achievable standard, and demonstrates pattern of meritorious and noteworthy accomplishment. | 0.9 - 1.0 |
| **Above average**. Performance significantly exceeds general level of competence expected of qualified subcontractor. Areas of deficient performance are few and low in importance. | 0.8 < 0.9 |
| **Average**. Performance achieves general level of competence expected of qualified subcontractor. Areas of deficient performance are of the same number and importance as areas of performance that exceed the average competence level. | 0.7 < 0.8 |
| **Below average**. Performance is adequate on overall basis but does not achieve general level of competence expected of qualified contractor. | 0 |

Equation 7.1 provides that the full amount of the allocation is awarded when $O = 1$ and $S = 1$. Consider $100,000 as award money allocated to a particular contract. The contractor has completed one-half of the effort; therefore, the objective rating is $O = 0.5$. The award committee perceives the contractor's performance to be between below average and average; therefore, the subjective rating is $S = (0 + 0.70) \div 2$, or 0.35.

Substituting $-allocated = $100,000, $O = 0.5$, and $S = 0.35$ in Equation 7.1, we obtain $-award = $100,000[(0.5 + 0.35) \div 2]$, or $42,500.

You should select members of the award committee from each discipline involved in the program in which the particular contract resides. Typically, contractors may appeal the rulings of the award through the normal appeal channel of the contract.

We usually pay awards incrementally in conjunction with key milestones such as preliminary design review, critical design review, and **first article test**. Incremental allocations are not cumulative usually. We do not carry over funds remaining from each allocation at any given milestones for possible award at the next milestone.

Incremental award allocations at the various milestones are not of usually equal magnitude, but rather are shaped to match the effort required to reach the respective milestones. In contracts involving high technology, you may encounter arrangement of 60 percent of the total allocation at the preliminary design review, 20 percent at the critical design review, and 20 percent at first article test.

### ■ 7.4.2 Incentive Structure

Awards are used to motivate contractors toward specific achievements such as technological breakthroughs and substantial time savings. The primary objective of the incentive structure is to save costs.

Contractors generally do not view incentive structures with the same high regard as they do award structures because of the punitive aspect of the latter in the event of cost overrun. Nonetheless, they usually accept incentive structures willingly because of the potential at the other end of the spectrum for sharing in cost savings. Incentives are keyed to the cost at completion of the contract relative to the target cost at the inception of the contract.

## 7.4 Motivational Guidelines

Incentives may be paid incrementally within the context of the progress payment schema for the particular contract. In this case, incentives are keyed to the estimated cost at completion relative to the target cost.

Unlike awards, the process with incentives is cumulative until the final accounting takes places at the end of the contract. There have been numerous occasions where problems completely eroded early incentive payments based on the estimated cost at completion before the end of the contract. This resulted in cost overruns that contractors were obliged to share at the end of the contract.

Table 7.5 is an incentive structure that you will encounter in contracts involving high technology. We generally see the range of the cost variance of the target cost limited to plus or minus 20 percent.

Cost variances greater than this amount usually lead to redetermination of both the cost and the statement of work. The rationale is that neither the customer or contractor had understood the scope of work.

*Table 7.5   Incentive Structure*

| Fraction of Target Cost | Customer's Share | Contractor's Share |
|---|---|---|
| Less than 0.85 | 0 | 1.0 |
| 0.85 to less than 0.90 | 0.25 | 0.75 |
| 0.9 to less than 0.95 | 0.50 | 0.50 |
| 0.95 to less than 1.0 | 0.75 | 0.25 |
| 1.0 | 0 | 0 |
| More than 1.0 to 1.05 | 0.75 | 0.25 |
| More than 1.05 to 1.10 | 0.50 | 0.50 |
| More than 1.10 to 1.15 | 0.25 | 0.75 |
| More than 1.15 | 0 | 1.0 |

We calculate the fraction of the target cost by dividing the cost at completion by the target cost. Consider an estimated cost at completion of $225 million and a target cost of $250 million for a cost underrun of $25 million. The governing fraction would be ($225 million) ÷ ($250 million), or 0.9.

The cost underrun of $25 million would be shared by the customer and contractor in accordance with Table 7.5. For the governing factor of 0.90, the cost distribution would be 0.5 to the customer and 0.5 to the contractor, or $12.5 million to each.

Conversely, if the estimated cost of completion were $260 million for a cost overrun of $10,000, the governing factor would be ($260 million) ÷ ($250 million), or 1.04. For the governing factor of 1.04 (v., Table 7.5), the cost distribution would be 0.75 to the customer, or $7,500, and 0.25 to the contractor, or $2,500.

Factors in Table 7.5 which are less than 0.85 or more than 1.15 are the **points of total assumption**. The contractor keeps all of the cost underrun at factors below 0.85 but assumes all the cost overrun at factors above 1.15.

These unexpected costs are strong motivators and underscore the importance of negotiating target costs that truly reflect the should cost of products of interest.

> *Dig the well before you are thirsty.*
> *Old Chinese saying*

## 7.5
## RISK PERSPECTIVES

There is risk in every walk of life. There is risk in making decisions and in not making decisions. There is risk every time an instruction is given. There is risk every time an instruction is carried out.

Risk cannot be avoided, but it can be anticipated, quantified, and managed to a large measure. The most important thing is to maintain a balanced outlook on the job you have to do.

### ■ 7.5.1 Risk Priorities

Dining-out critic Duncan Hines used to say, "I've run less risk driving my way across country than eating my way across it." He never knew what to expect on entering an establishment. We never have known what to expect in taking on a technical risk management job. Hines' goal was to reduce the public's risk in dining out. Our goal has been to reduce our clients' risk exposure in bringing products to the marketplace.

We have learned to examine our priorities on a continuing basis. Priorities have a remarkable way of changing as programs mature. Even driving has become less hazardous with the advent of air bags.

Rank problems by impact and go after them in the descending order of their impact on risk exposure. Make sure that you identify all possible root causes before attacking problems. Again, rank root causes by impact and go after them in the descending order of their impact on the particular problems.

### ■ 7.5.2 Deliberate Haste

Thomas J. Watson, Jr., the former head of IBM, claimed, "I never varied from the managerial rule that the worst possible thing we could do would be to lie dead in the water with any problem. Solve it, solve it quickly, solve it right or wrong. If you solved it wrong, it would come back and slap you in the face and then you could solve it right. Doing nothing is a comfortable alternative because it is without immediate risk but it is an absolutely fatal way to manage a business."

You will frequently encounter the need for haste in risk control, but let it be deliberate haste on the basis of calculated risks. Do the best job you can in estimating relative risk exposure in the available alternatives. Rank the alternatives and give facts to support the rankings.

### ■ 7.5.3 Risk Control Teamwork

Dr. W. Edwards Deming, dean of quality, would make this point in his seminars: "People want to work but they want to take joy in their work. American managers still insist on managing people instead of the system—creating fear and mistrust in the workplace, removing joy, rewarding themselves at the top with bonuses and perks, punishing those at the bottom. It is destructive, and it prevents companies from functioning efficiently as a system."

The scope of technical risk management is enormous. You cannot know all there is to know; you cannot do all there is to do; you must rely on teamwork. General George C. Patton put it succinctly when he said, "Never tell people how to do things. Tell them what to do and they will surprise you with their ingenuity."

## 7.5.4 Calculated Risks

Lee J. Iacocca, in an address before the American Management Association, lamented, "A small company in Virginia that made driving aids for handicapped people went out of business because it couldn't afford the liability insurance. Too risky. Hardly anyone makes gymnastics or hockey equipment anymore. Too risky. We've virtually stopped making light aircraft in this country; the biggest cost is the product liability. Too risky. One day, we're going to wake up and say, 'The hell with it—competing is just too risky!' Why even try to build a better mousetrap? Let somebody else do it—and then sue him."

Nonetheless, Iacocca took the calculated risk of introducing the minivan to the motoring public by weighing the odds that it would not sell against the potential payoff. Chrysler's minivan has become a winner. The triumph is a tribute to superior market research and Iacocca's remarkable instinct for consumer interest. Successful entrepreneurs are not risk takers; they are calculated risk takers.

A calculated risk is the course of action you select from the available alternatives on the basis of **return-on-investment** (**ROI**) and relative risk exposure (RRE). Rating RRE on a scale of 0 to 1.0, a course of action with $ROI = 5$ and $RRE = 0.25$ would have a probable $ROI$ of $5(1 - 0.25)$, or 3.75. On the same scale, another course of action with $ROI = 10$ and $RRE = .75$ would have a probable $ROI$ of $10(1 - 0.75)$, or 2.50.

Which course of action should you pick? It is obvious that you should pick the first one. Suppose, however, that the ROI for the second course of action were 20. Which one should you pick now?

The expected ROI of the second course of action is now $20(1 - 0.75)$, or 5.0. You should take the calculated risk of picking the second course of action.

The great Indian leader Jawaharal Nehru once proclaimed, "The policy of being too cautious is the greatest risk of all." Entrepreneurs would say, "Calculated risks are the road to wealth."

## 7.5.5 Margin for Error in Opinion Polls

The objective of statistics is to make inferences about populations based on information contained in samples of the populations. Specifically, statistical inference is concerned with making inferences about population parameters such as the mean, standard deviation area under the curve of the probability density function above or below or between some variates (*i.e.*, specific values of random variables). We feel obliged to caution you about the **margin for error** claimed for the findings. Many organizations base long-range planning on such polls without understanding the risk exposure in the margin for error.

What would Chrysler have done if the company had listened to an opinion poll predicting the next decade's sale of minivans would decline to less than 5 percent of vehicles sold with a margin of error of ± 3 percent? Chrysler probably would not have introduced the highly successful vehicle.

There are two components in the margin for error in opinion polls. The first, and easiest to accommodate, is the systematic error that is primarily a function of sample size and confidence level you desire in the conclusions.

The second, and more insidious error, is a function of how you design the sampling plan for the opinion poll. We refer to this error as sampling bias.

**Systematic Error**

We express systematic error as the margin for error in statistical inferences in terms of plus or minus so many percent. There is a common misconception that the margin for error is an immutable thing. On the contrary, the margin for error is nothing more than one part of an expression of the goodness of the inferential procedures used in surveys.

The other part of the measure of goodness is the confidence level desired by the investigators. If we were to predict that next year's spot price of a certain commodity would be $12.50, plus or minus $2.25, we should add what our confidence level is. Typical opinion polls use a confidence level of 0.95.

The assumption of normality underlies most opinion polls. This assumption connotes that the normal density function governs the distribution of the survey samples and allows the use of the $z$-statistic that you encountered in Chapter 6 in bounding the area under the normal probability density curve.

Equation 7.2 relates the **sampling error** to the sampling statistics and sample size.

$$\varepsilon = z\sqrt{\frac{pq}{n}} \qquad (7.2)$$

where $\varepsilon$ denotes error, $z$ area under normal probability density curve, $p$ proportion of responders who prefer objects of survey, $n$ sample size, and $q$ equaling $1 - p$. Conversely, $q$ equals the proportion of responders who do not prefer the objects of survey.

You can usually assume normality for sample distributions in opinion polls because of the large sample sizes you encounter.

Questions about objects of surveys take the following forms: "Would you buy Brand A?" "Would you vote for Candidate B?" and "Do you approve of the performance of Individual C?" Assume that in an opinion poll of 1,000 adults, 40 percent approved the performance of Candidate B.

The value of $p$ in Equation 7.2 is therefore 0.4 and $q = 1 - 0.4$, or 0.6. We wish to know the error about $p = 0.4$ with a confidence level of 0.95. We recall from Table 4.30 that $z = \mp 1.96$ for the confidence level of 0.95.

Substituting these values and $n = 1,000$ in Equation 7.2 we obtain:

$$\varepsilon = 1.96\sqrt{\frac{(0.4)(0.6)}{1,000}}$$
$$= 0.0304. \qquad (7.3)$$

Equation 7.3 allows us to say, "Forty percent of adults approve of Candidate B's performance with an error of plus or minus 3 percent." When prompted, we would add, "on the basis of a sample of 1,000 adults." When prompted further, we might add, "with a confidence level of 95 percent."

Table 7.6 repeats the data in Table 4.30. Try your hand at estimating the error with a confidence of 90 percent and 99 percent and compare it to the value in Equation 7.3.

**Table 7.6** *Values of z-Factor as a Function of Confidence Level*

| Confidence Level | z-Factor |
|---|---|
| 0.60 | 0.84 |
| 0.70 | 1.04 |
| 0.80 | 1.28 |
| 0.90 | 1.64 |
| 0.95 | 1.96 |

## 7.5 Risk Perspectives

The error at 90 percent is simply the error at 95 percent multiplied by the ratio of the value of $z$ at 90 percent confidence to the value of $z$ at 95 percent confidence. Carry this out and you will obtain $\mp 0.0304(1.64 \div 1.96)$, or $\mp 0.0254$. The error at 99 percent is the error at 95 percent confidence multiplied by the ratio of the value of $z$ at 99 percent confidence to the value of $z$ at 95 confidence. Carrying this out you will obtain $\mp 0.0304(2.58 \div 1.96)$, or $\mp 0.040$. By this time, you will have also noticed that the margin for error increases with increased confidence level.

Equation 7.4 is a variation of Equation 7.2 that we use when we wish to determine the minimum sample size for a specified allowable error.

$$n = pq\left(\frac{z}{\varepsilon}\right)^2 \tag{7.4}$$

where $\varepsilon$ now denotes specified allowable error and the other units are the same as those in Equation 7.2.

We make the assumption that $p = q = 0.5$, when we apply Equation 7.4. The product of $p = 0.5$ and $q = 0.5$ is 0.25 and is greater than the product of any other values of $p$ and $q$, where $q = 1 - p$. Multiply 0.51 by 0.49 and get 0.2499. Multiply 0.99 by 0.01 and get 0.0099. The result is that the assumption that $p = q = 0.5$ yields the largest value of $n$ in Equation 7.4.

Now we wish to determine the minimum sample size that will yield the specified allowable error of 3 percent with a confidence of 95 percent (*n.b.*, $z = 1.96$). Substituting $p = q = 0.5$, $z = 1.96$, and $\varepsilon = 0.03$ in Equation 7.4, we obtain

$$n = (0.5)(0.5)\left(\frac{1.96}{0.03}\right)^2$$

$$= 1{,}067.111 \tag{7.5}$$

which we round off to 1,068.

Try your hand at estimating the minimum sample size for an allowable error of 5 percent in Equation 7.5. We'll let you in on a little trick; the square of the ratio of the old to the new allowable errors will give you the answer. Multiply $n = 1{,}068$ by $(0.03 \div 0.05)^2$, for $1{,}068(0.36)$, or 385.

### Sampling Bias

The two approaches to sampling populations of interest are systematic random sampling and stratified random sampling. Your choice should be a function of the patterns in the population of interest. Systematic random sampling and stratified random sampling frequently use the Monte Carlo method we discussed in Chapter 6.

In **systematic random sampling**, we choose the first sample at random and subsequent samples systematically. We arrange members of the populations in some fashion (*e.g.*, alphabetically, chronologically, or numerically), which we sample with some periodicity.

We can draw systematic samples with random numbers. For example, if we were to draw a sample from 5,000 purchase orders, we would first number the purchase orders 0001 through 5000 and then select them with a table of five-digit random numbers.

In **stratified random sampling**, we first divide populations into subgroups, or strata, and then draw samples from each stratum. For example, the 5,000 purchase orders we wish to sample could be from 250 different suppliers. We would first sort the vendors into strata (*e.g.*, electrical or mechanical) and then systematically draw samples from each stratum.

Done properly, stratified random sampling produces the least **sampling bias** and consequential error. On the other hand, incorrect stratified random sampling can be disastrous. The example in Section 7.6.4 corroborates this statement.

> *Never use systematic random sampling if there are predetermined patterns in populations of interest.*
> 
> **Analyst**

In general it is far better to let your own people do the forecasting and to trust their judgment rather than that of some survey organization. Give them freedom of choice and action.

### ■ 7.5.6 Managing Conceptual Programs

People frequently ask us, "How do we estimate the risk exposure in purely conceptual programs?" We would be tempted to answer, "Very carefully," were it not for the magnitude of cost overruns we witnessed over the past four decades in high-technology programs.

Many of these programs were not even conceptual. You need only look at the before and after of the annual budget of the United States to corroborate this remark.

Suppose an organization came to you with the proposition to develop nuclear power generators for use in homes and vehicles, provided you were to support the effort with $100 million and allow five years for the development. How would you attempt to model the **risk time** and **risk cost** in the undertaking?

Table 7.7 lists the **risk determinant factors** we discussed in the previous chapters. We would begin to depart from the deterministic approach that we favored throughout the book.

We would assume that every factor in Table 7.7 applies and that they apply in an additive manner. Assuming the rating of 1 for each of the ten risk determinant factors in Table 7.7, we obtain a multiplier of 10 for time and cost. The initial estimate of risk time is 10(5 years), or 50 years, and 10($100 million), or $1 billion for risk cost. Shocking? Take a hard look at the history of the annual budget of the United States.

*Table 7.7*  *Risk Determinant Factors*

| | |
|---|---|
| Management Attribute Factor | Extrinsic Attribute Factor |
| Product Maturity Factor | Process Maturity Factor |
| Product Quality Factor | Process Quality Factor |
| Product Complexity Factor | Process Complexity Factor |
| Product Concurrency Factor | Process Concurrency Factor |

Next, look at the organization making the proposal and the environment with which it proposes to do the job. Would you reduce the ratings for management attribute factor and extrinsic attribute factor?

Address product and process risk determinant factors the way we did in the risk formulation in Chapter 5. Finally, use a confidence level of at least 0.95 in your conclusion.

> *For precise estimates of risk exposure, you need to know what could go wrong, the probability that it could go wrong, and the corrective-action time and cost to recover. Without such knowledge, you should assume the worst will happen because it will.*
>
> *Analyst*

We have witnessed overruns of 500 to 1,000 percent in baseline cost estimates of a few thousands of dollars to $100 million and overruns of 200 to 500 percent in baseline cost estimates of more than $100 million. This would suggest that composite risk determinant factors of 2 to 10 were at play in these programs.

# 7.6 Risk Examples

The history of high technology is replete with both enormous successes and dismal failures. Lessons should be learned from everything you observe and from every job you undertake. If not, history is sure to repeat itself but with you as the player.

### ■ 7.6.1 Main Battle Tank

The history of the weapons system acquisition program for the main battle tank covers the 12-year period from 1964 through 1976. It was in 1976 that the program entered the full-scale engineering development phase for the third and final time.

Lessons were learned, but at an enormous cost and at a point too late to benefit the original participants in the program. In addition, the military was denied the use of the tank for more than a decade. [3]

The technical objective of the program was to develop a more combat-effective tank than was available at that time. The financial goal was that the tank would be sufficiently low in acquisition and operating cost to be affordable in quantities needed to equip first line armored forces in the 1980s.

The evolution of the design started in 1964 as a joint effort of the United States and what was then the Federal Republic of Germany (*i.e.*, West Germany). The approach proved to be far too costly for either country, and a more austere version was needed.

The estimated production cost of the latter was still more than the Congress was willing to approve, and the Congress terminated the program, as originally constituted, about seven years after it had been started. A scaled-down version of the tank entered development in 1976.

The military had learned several lessons, in particular the importance of conducting cost vs. performance trades early in the programs. Unfortunately, recognition had come too late to provide the battlefield asset to the extent it was needed.

Cost vs. performance trades proved invaluable in establishing requirements for a less complex and less costly tank.

Again, the design of the predecessor had progressed too far to allow significant cost saving. The military ordered a significantly smaller number of tanks than required.

The most expensive lesson learned on the Main Battle Tank program related to the formulation of the design approaches. The original design concept included a three-member crew in the turret of the tank along with an automatic gun loader.

The automatic gun loader proved to be far too complex and costly. An attempt was made to replace it with a manual loader operated by a fourth crew member in the turret.

The configuration, however, would not allow this substitution and, thus, the automatic loader could not be replaced by a manual version, albeit a third crew member could be squeezed in. The state of the art was not ready for the implementation of the automatic approach and many other aspects of the design. Problems with suspension, propulsion, night vision, and fire control, as well as with ammunition loading literally buried the program. The successor program, based on the then current state of the art, succeeded.

> *Technology should be well in hand before full-scale engineering development is undertaken.*
> *Analyst*

### ■ 7.6.2 Pegasus

In Greek mythology, **Pegasus** was the winged horse of the Muses. With the aid of a golden bridle from the goddess Athena, the youth Bellerophon tamed Pegasus. Bellerophon attempted to ride Pegasus to heaven. Pegasus, however, threw Bellerophon to his death and continuing the ascent to the heavens became the star constellation bearing the name Pegasus.

The modern version of the winged horse is the three-stage Pegasus rocket, developed and built by the Orbital Sciences Corporation. Pegasus recently placed a Brazilian environmental spacecraft in a 450-nautical mile orbit about the earth. The spacecraft performed its mission in an eminently satisfactory manner.

The interesting part of the story is that Pegasus was launched from an aircraft at an altitude of about 43,000 feet rather than from ground level. By this simply contrivance, Pegasus gained the capability to launch a heavier payload at one-third of the cost of a larger vehicle such as the Delta rocket. In addition, the launching from an aircraft is more gentle than from the ground, reducing risk exposure during the launch environment by an order of magnitude. We consider Pegasus as the embodiment of the corollary that the line is the shortest distance between two points.

### ■ 7.6.3 Ford Motor Company

By the end of the 1970s, the Ford Motor Company, which had already lost billions of dollars from failure to respond to the motoring public's demand for performance, style, and quality, was facing dim prospects.

However, a dramatic turnaround started in 1980 when Ford recognized its failure in responding to market pressure. Despite prior-year losses, the company invested billions of dollars in advanced technology, focusing on what the motoring public wanted. By 1989 Ford was being hailed as first in sales of vehicles manufactured in the United States. [4]

The company listened to its own employees as well as to automotive consultants. Innovative design was combined with affordable quality which has given Ford the image of design leader and has led to the domination of the automotive marketplace. Prior-year losses were more than offset by the increased sales.

### ◼ 7.6.4 Presidential Election

The *Literary Digest* conducted what it claimed to be a highly scientific opinion poll on the 1936 presidential election. The competing candidates were Democrat Franklin D. Roosevelt and Republican Alfred M. Landon. Based on a sample of more than 3 million responses, the *Literary Digest* predicted that Landon would defeat Roosevelt by a very wide margin.

Well, exactly the opposite happened. Roosevelt won one of the most one-sided elections in American history, gathering in almost 70 percent of the popular vote. The *Literary Digest*, which ultimately ceased publishing, attributed the erroneous results to sampling bias.

The *Literary Digest* used the wrong stratified random sample in its opinion poll. Its investigators selected samples from names in telephone directories and on magazine subscription lists. These are hallmarks of prosperous individuals favoring the Republican platform.

The vast majority of the voters were still recovering from the economic effects of the depression of 1929 and favored the Democratic platform. After the election, it became obvious to the *Literary Digest* that most of these voters did not have telephones and did not subscribe to magazines; therefore, they were not represented in the sample.

Some political analysts attempted to rationalize the outcome of the opinion poll citing sampling bias of nonresponders. The sampling bias of nonresponders connotes that many of the voters favoring the Democratic platform would not have responded even if they were polled. What do you think?

### ◼ 7.6.5 Why Companies Fail

Every corporate disaster tells its own awful story. According to Kenneth Labich in the November 14, 1994, issue of Fortune, most debacles are the result of managers making one or more of the six big mistakes listed in Table 7.8. The author cites statistics showing that about 50,000 U.S. companies had reached the point of ultimate failure in 1989 and the number had nearly doubled by 1992.

The article includes fascinating accounts of the travails of Scott Paper, Digital Equipment Corporation (DEC), Maytag, Commerce Clearing House, Mack Truck, and IBM. The author identifies which mistakes these companies made and what steps, if any, they took to rectify them.

Labich introduces Albert Dunlop, whose job was to restructure the financially crumbled Scott Paper. He proceeded to unload the company's campus-like headquarters near Philadelphia and eliminate much of the staff. Dunlop says, "I see no point in sacrificing 100 percent of the employees for the 35 percent who ought to leave."

In discussing the troubles of DEC and Maytag, Labich notes that DEC's net income fell from a high of $1.3 billion to a loss of $2.8 billion in 1992. DEC executives failed to see that the marketplace was embracing a new kind of desktop computer. Attempts to restructure are going slowly.

Maytag's net income fell from a high of $159 million in 1988 to a loss of $315 million in 1992. Maytag's problem was excessive debt caused by acquisition of other companies. Maytag is recovering, but slowly.

The other accounts are equally fascinating.

**Table 7.8**  *Mistakes Made by Corporate Managers [5]*

| | |
|---|---|
| Identity Crisis | Senior executives too often don't understand the fundamentals of their business. In their competitive situation, they neglect to ask central questions, such as what precisely is the company's core expertise, what are reasonable long- and short-term goals, and what are the key drivers of profitability? |
| Failures of Vision | Too many senior executives are content to prepare their companies for only likely problems. They should ask themselves if their strategy is flexible enough to deal with wildest-case scenario. They should contemplate and include the absurd in their planning. |
| Big Squeeze | Too many senior executives allow their companies to become overextended financially by overpaying for an acquisition or overreacting to the predations of corporate raiders. They allow their companies to be robbed of two of its most essential attributes: the strength to weather market downturns and the flexibility to respond to market challenges. |
| The Glue Sticks, and Sticks | Too many senior executives allow their companies to rely on past glories and vainly try to recapture past glories. Complacency and bloat settle in. Nobody works too hard, and employment is guaranteed, for a while. |
| Anybody Out There? | Too many senior executives fail to stay close with the customer. Smart managers increasingly zero in on key customers who no longer want their product or service. Too many managers fail to install any system for distilling and interpreting information from salespeople. |
| Enemies Within | Too many senior executives take a narrow view of their employees resulting in hostility that can sink companies. Too many managers preach one doctrine and practice another. These actions are tantamount to managerial malpractice. |

Adapted by permission of FORTUNE from Kenneth Labich, *Why Companies Fail*, FORTUNE, November 14, 1994.

### ■ 7.6.6 Why Buildings Fall Down

Only one of the Seven Wonders of the World survives today, the Pyramid of Khufu in the Egyptian desert. The pyramids resisted the rigors of time and forces of nature for so long only because the Egyptians learned to stabilize soils and design foundations. [6]

People do violate good design practices and the principle of risk management, and disasters ultimately strike. The worst structural disaster in the United States occurred during the evening of July 17, 1981, at the Hyatt Regency Hotel in Kansas City, Missouri. The hotel consisted of three buildings, a tower at one end, and a function block at the south end. The function block contained

## 7.6 Risk Examples

meeting and dining rooms and kitchens. The tower was connected to the function block by three walkways overlooking an atrium.

There were more than 1,700 people in the atrium of the hotel when two of the walkways collapsed resulting in the death of 114 and injuries to more than 200. The initial investigation attributed the immediate cause of the collapse to people on the walkways stomping their feet in rhythm with the dance music from below.

The final investigation revealed that the walkways were both underdesigned and lacked redundancy. This is contrary to the risk management mandate of prudent reserve of strength in public structures.

*Why Buildings Fall Down* [6] gives fascinating accounts of how structures fail and why buildings fall down. The authors describe the first structural failure in the world (*viz.*, Tower of Babel) and the miracle on Thirty-fourth Street in New York City when an airplane collided with the Empire State Building.

### ■ 7.6.7 Reengineering the Defense Industry

We leave this risk example section on a somewhat happier note by describing how defense and aerospace contractors have responded to massive cutbacks in military spending and what the DoD is doing to aid the process. There have been two main thrusts in the attempt.

Companies like Martin Marietta and Lockheed have joined together to augment their expertise and their competitive posture in the aerospace marketplace. Lockheed Martin is now the world's largest aerospace contractor. The union followed Martin Marietta's acquisition of General Electric's Aerospace Division.

Other companies, like Hughes Aircraft, McDonnell Douglas, and TRW are attempting to become competitive in the commercial marketplace by changing their management style and forming alliances with specialty firms to develop new product lines. In keeping with sound risk management, they are sticking to what they do best, high technology.

The DoD, through its Advanced Research Projects Agency (ARPA), has initiated the Defense Technology Conversion, Reinvestment, and Transition Assistance Program as the means for reengineering the defense industry. The DoD will provide funds for activities which develop technologies that enable new products and processes, deploy existing technology on to commercial and military products and processes, and stimulate the integration of commercial and military research and production areas. Table 7.9 lists the technology development focus areas that the ARPA will support financially. There is a small business set-aside called the Small Business Innovation Research Program.

For information on either program, contact Technology Reinvestment Project, 3701 North Fairfax Drive, Arlington, Virginia 22203-1714. Ask for the names, addresses, and telephone numbers of points of contact with the various components of the DoD for the technology focus areas listed in Table 7.9.

*Table 7.9  Technology Development Focus Areas*

| | |
|---|---|
| Information Infrastructure | Environmental Technology |
| Electronic Design & Manufacturing | Aeronautical Technology |
| Mechanical Design & Manufacturing | Vehicular Technology |
| Materials & Structures Manufacturing | Shipbuilding Industrial Infrastructure |
| Health Care Technology | Advanced Battery Technology |
| Training & Instruction Technology | |

> *Good examples are like bells calling us to worship.*
> ***Old Scandinavian saying***

## 7.7
## RISK PRINCIPLES

In the coming millennium, the high-technology marketplace will be dominated by those industrial organizations that know how to balance quality, functionality, affordability, and profitability and are committed to achieving and sustaining the balance which customers not only need but also demand. [7]

Most customers expect contractors to make a fair and reasonable profit on their products and contracts. Procurement organizations in government bodies use their requests for proposals as the vehicle for conveying such convictions. The federal government spells this out in the Federal Acquisition Regulation, which allows up to 15 percent profit on contracts.

The preceding pages encapsulate our experience from the more than 40 years in the construction, defense, and aerospace industries. We have participated in creating literally hundreds of proposals to various agencies and supported scores of programs with the tools and techniques described in this book.

Be wary of statements such as, "We were the best technically but lost on price." The statement is a classic example of rationalization and is intrinsically contradictory. We witnessed only a few instances where this statement was true. Usually, the technical proposals were as ill-conceived as the cost proposals.

If you were truly best technically, you would know not only the precise needs of the customer but also how to satisfy those needs at a cost which the customer could afford, and at a fair profit to yourself. The common thread in winning proposals is the customer's perception of the contractor's commitment to the balance of quality, functionality, affordability, and **profitability**.

It should not come as a surprise to you that this perceived commitment is usually a proposal strategy on the part of the would-be contractor, tendered with the best of intentions but frequently abandoned in competition for resources after contract award. We have seen numerous instances of this strategy go awry.

The common thread in programs which were successful over the long haul was that commitment was not just perceived, but was sustained with highly visible management participation. Such programs have an air of discipline that seems to emanate from the top. You need such an ambience to be consistently successful in achieving goals.

Be equally wary of situations where experts and consultants are brought in at moments of crisis. They may offer good counsel and guidance, but you should weigh their inputs against those of your own people who have far more experience and insight in the subject matter, provided they are permitted to be objective in what they say.

Carry with you the words of Bertrand Russell who said, "Even when experts agree, they may well be mistaken." Remember too, that many organizations bring in consultants at the last moment in an attempt to share the blame.

The challenge is to motivate your people so that they are objective in the counsel and guidance they offer. This is difficult in the presence of outside experts whose very appearance may strike fear throughout the ranks of an organization.

## 7.7 Risk Principles

**Table 7.10** *Some Principles for Technical Risk Management*

- A dollar of risk avoidance is worth many dollars of risk recovery.
- An equitable balance of the principle of risk-benefit equity and the principle of risk cost is necessary for technical risk management to prevail in the long term.
- Professionals thrive on recognition, but live on money. Effective recognition programs are those that balance the two.
- Responsibility, authority, accountability, and funding must flow directly from the CEO to those charged with carrying out risk control for it to succeed.
- Give people the responsibility, means, and authority to do the job you assign them; hold them accountable for their actions; and reward them commensurately with their performance.
- Be as direct in your expressions as in your thinking. Do not equivocate, vacillate, obfuscate, understate, or overstate.
- Patience is a sound business practice as well as a virtue.
- Do not lose sight of the product's use. Failure to recognize user requirements as well as those of the customer will invariably affect its acceptance.
- Do not undertake risk modeling without a clear understanding of the intended application of the analytical findings and without complete assurance that adequate resources are available and, furthermore, will be committed to the undertaking.
- Do not summarily reject estimates of risk time or risk cost because they seem too high. The higher the estimate, the greater is the need for deliberation on the message it conveys.
- Use the precise amount of data required for the solution of the given problem; no more, no less. Extraneous information leads to confusion, arguments, and extra expense. Above all, it causes one to digress from the mainstream concentration needed to solve problems expeditiously and cost effectively.
- In modeling, use the lowest possible level of aggregation as time and money will allow, or spend the time and money later after your initial findings prove to be inconclusive.
- Risk models should be derivatives of models that produced baseline estimates with equal or less, but not with more, detail than the baseline.
- Confidence intervals about estimates based on reliable, historical data are the cornerstones of realism and credibility.
- Nothing is more inimical to credibility than a brilliant solution in search of a problem.
- Technology should be well in hand before full-scale development is undertaken.
- Base your margin for error on historical data, not arbitrary percentages.
- Do not confuse desire for reality.
- Know the subject before undertaking the activity.
- Precise estimates of risk exposure require knowledge of what could go wrong, the probability of it going wrong, and corrective-action time and cost to recover from what went wrong.
- Risk avoidance is *a priori* corrective action.

We have sprinkled a number of quotations and principles throughout the book with the intent of maintaining your interest as well as driving home key points. Table 7.10 is an abbreviated list of these principles to which we added a few new ones.

We do not preach against risk taking. On the contrary, the theme of the book is that risk taking with knowledge can be profitable. Above all, it is quite challenging.

Take care to ensure the realism and credibility of your findings. Rely on disaggregate, bottom-up estimates to the extent possible. Always test your findings with common sense. Weigh the alternatives as carefully as we did in considering calculated risk. Your criteria for taking risks should include the timing of alternative courses of action as well as the potential return-on-investment and relative risk exposure. We cannot overstress the importance of timing. Strike while the window of opportunity is open. The best possible decision when the window is closed is worse than the worst possible decision when the window is open.

The shadow of what could have been only yields grief.

> *In delay there lies no plenty.*
> **William Shakespeare**

## 7.8
## SUMMARY

**Section 7.1 Definitions** provided an annotated perspective of the chapter with the definitions of key terms and abbreviations used in the chapter. We repeated these definitions when we first used them in the chapter and in the glossary in Appendix A.

**Section 7.2 Organizational Guidelines** offered guidance on how to organize for minimizing risk exposure. The key element is the direct chain-of-command from the CEO or product director to those charged with risk management. The section covered the technical risk management plan, roles and responsibilities, configuration control, and performance tracking and reporting.

**Section 7.3 Procedural Guidelines** stressed the smooth transition from development to production. The section drew from costly lessons learned by the U.S. Department of Defense that resulted in the promulgation of DoD 4245.7-M, *Transition from Development to Production*, 1985. The section gave guidelines for funding, design, configuration control, test, production, facilities, support, and management. [7]

**Section 7.4 Motivational Guidelines** offered some suggestions on motivating personnel and suppliers to help in controlling risk. The section described the technique used by a major corporation to motivate its employees and illustrated the difference between award fees and incentives with quantitative examples.

**Section 7.5 Risk Perspectives** described the philosophical outlook that we evolved over many years of risk control and the outlook of several prominent people. The section covered the notions of risk priorities, deliberate haste, risk control teamwork, and calculated risks. The section included a warning regarding the margin for error opinion polls on which you may base long-range planning and shows you how to discern systematic errors and sampling bias errors. The section offered some guidance on estimating risk exposure in conceptual programs.

**Section 7.6 Risk Examples** described the experiences of a number of companies and organizations; some of which have done well; some of which should have known better. The examples were based on the Main Battle Tank, Pegasus, Ford Motor Company, the presidential election of 1936, and the questions of why companies fail and why buildings fall. See if you can relate to these examples.

**Section 7.7 Risk Principles** repeats some of these earlier remarks and adds a few more for your consideration. Keep a copy of these principles before you when you undertake your next assignment. They work.

We conclude the chapter with **Section 7.8 Summary**, **Section 7.9 Exercises**, and **Section 7.10 References**. We drew the exercises from events that made news headlines all over the nation and the world. You should find them interesting and they should challenge you.

# 7.9
## EXERCISES

Appendix C contains step-by-step solutions to the following exercises. We urge you to attempt the exercises without resorting to the solutions, since the intent is to reinforce the subject matter covered in the chapter.

### 7.9.1 Lloyd's of London

The history of Lloyd's can be traced back to its founding in the late seventeenth century. [8] We associate Lloyd's with large insurance policies underwritten on things which other companies would not even consider. Lloyd's is an association of more than 7,000 insurance underwriters organized into some 250 syndicates specializing in such categories as marine, motor, and aviation insurance. The members, also known as *names,* are the people who back the policies financially. Many of the members now face financial ruin.

On June 25, 1992, Lloyd's of London reported a loss of $3.82 billion on policies underwritten in 1989, the latest year under Lloyd's three-year accounting system. This was the worst loss in its history and followed a reported loss of $944.8 million in 1988.

Although there were major disasters, such as the Exxon oil spill in Alaska, Hurricane Hugo, and the San Francisco earthquake, members claim that the losses were due to poor self-regulation and they are now contemplating litigation. State the management and extrinsic attributes that may have contributed to the risk exposure in the insurance policies underwritten by Lloyd's.

### 7.9.2 Corporate Losses

Nineteen ninety-two was a banner year for corporate losses. General Motors Corporation posted a record loss of $23.5 billion on sales of $123 billion and Ford Motor Company a loss of $7.4 billion on sales of $100.1 billion.

General Motors claimed that the loss was due mostly to charges for retiree health-care costs and that, without these charges, the company would have made a profit of more than $273 million. Ford claimed that the loss was due mostly to revised accounting practices and that the company would be profitable in 1993.

State the management and extrinsic attributes that may have contributed to risk exposure in the financial losses of the two companies. What risk determinant factors are significant in these cases? What do you consider to be the major difference between the two companies?

### 7.9.3 Standardized Risk Measure

The chairman of the Securities and Exchange Commission (SEC) recently advocated a standardized measure of risk in investing in mutual funds to replace the current rating practice. The current practice uses the relative mix in funds, U.S. Treasury bills, common stocks, and bonds.

The U.S. Treasury bills are the least risky securities, but provide the smallest return over time. Common stocks are the most risky and provide the greatest return. The risk and return fall in between the bills and stocks. All in all, the SEC considers the practice difficult for the average investor to comprehend. The chairman of the SEC recommended a rating system based on the mean and standard deviation of the rate of return for the securities comprising the funds.

Table 7.11 is a list of annual returns for a hypothetical mutual fund. Calculate the mean and standard deviation of the returns. Using the guidelines of low risk equals $\mp$one standard deviation, medium risk equals $\mp$two standard deviations, and high risk equals $\mp$three standard deviations, what risk rating would you ascribe to the fund?

**Table 7.11** *Annual Rate of Return for Hypothetical Mutual Fund*

| Year | Rate Percent | Year | Rate Percent |
|------|--------------|------|--------------|
| 1    | 16.7         | 6    | 20.1         |
| 2    | 13.6         | 7    | 19.0         |
| 3    | 6.7          | 8    | 12.3         |
| 4    | −1.3         | 9    | 14.8         |
| 5    | −2.7         | 10   | 10.9         |

Assume the hypothetical mutual fund of Table 7.11 belongs to a class of funds with an average yield of 9.25 percent and a mean rating of medium risk. Test the hypothesis that the sample mean is representative of the mean of this class for confidence of 80 percent, 90 percent, 95 percent, and 99.9 percent. Show your calculations for deriving the test statistic that you used in the test of the hypothesis regarding the mean.

What probability distribution did you choose for deriving the test statistic? State the reason for your choice. What other probability distribution could you have chosen and what would be the significance of the choice?

### 7.9.4 Consumer Price Index

The Congressional Budget Office announced recently that the Consumer Price Index (CPI) overstates inflation by 0.2 to 0.8 percentage point per year. Every 1 percentage point increase in the CPI raises the federal budget deficit by approximately $6.5 billion, primarily by increasing government benefit payments.

The U.S. Department of Labor, the keeper of the CPI, has overhauled the government's measure of inflation to shave about 0.1 percent off the CPI. What has changed is the way the Department of Labor measures the price of food consumed at home, shelter, and name-brand prescription drugs. Apparently, generic drugs are taking a larger share of sales.

Obtain budget deficit data since the last time the Labor Department changed the CPI baseline from the current edition of the *Statistical Abstract of the United States*. [9] Calculate what the deficit would be currently, if the CPI had reflected the deduction of 0.1 percent.

### 7.9.5 Short-Term Interest Rates

The Federal Reserve System uses short-term interest rates as the means for controlling inflation. Paradoxically, excessive economic growth equates to runaway inflation.

*7.9 Exercises*

The Federal Reserve System expressed surprise at the strength of the economy despite the recent series of five increases in short-term interest rates by Federal Reserve Banks. In addition, the housing market, which is typically the first to feel the effect of higher rates, remains buoyant. The banks are expected to increase short-term interest rates by 1.5 percent in trying to contain inflation as measured by the CPI.

Using the current edition of *Statistical Abstract of the United States*, establish the correlation between Federal Reserve Bank's discount rates and the CPI. [9].

### ■ *7.9.6 Conflicting Requirements*

Recent news releases say that manufacturers of refrigerators and air conditioners are in a race against time to develop a suitable substitute for ozone-damaging chlorofluorocarbons (CFC). CFC destroys the ozone through the following process.

Ultraviolet rays from the sun dislodge chlorine atoms from CFC molecules. Chlorine atoms attract oxygen atoms from ozone molecules. Other single oxygen atoms break chlorine-oxygen bonds and form oxygen molecules. Oxygen molecules do not block ultraviolet rays. The process is iterative.

By international agreement, production of CFC coolants must cease by 1996. The agreement allows recycling of these coolants for repair purposes, however, new units will require alternative coolants. Some refrigerator and air conditioning manufacturers are considering hydrochlorofluorocarbons (HCFC), which are less harmful to the environment. The reaction of the environmentalists to HCFC is as yet unknown.

Some air conditioning manufacturers are considering the return to ice, the coolant of more than 50 years ago. Environmentalists have yet to state their position on ice.

What do you consider the cost impact will be from using HCFC in air conditioners? Consider yourself an analyst for a company such as Carrier Corporation. How would you rate management attribute factor, extrinsic attribute factor, product maturity factor, and process maturity factor for the undertaking? State your reasons.

The U.S. Bureau of the Census estimates that 99.9 percent of U.S. households have refrigerators and 50 percent of U.S. households have central air conditioning or window units. Using the current edition of the *Statistical Abstract of the United States*, estimate the cost impact of replacing these units with environmentally acceptable units. [9]

### ■ *7.9.7 Nuclear Energy*

In the half century since the discovery of nuclear fission, nuclear power has become a major source of the world's electric energy. The United States is the world's largest producer of nuclear power. Nuclear power is now the second largest source of U.S. electricity, exceeded only by coal that provides about 55 percent of the country's electricity. The nuclear energy portion is expected to reach about 25 percent by the end of the twentieth century.

In general, nuclear plants are more complex and costly to build than plants using fossil fuels; however, the cost of fuel for nuclear plants is significantly lower. Many see nuclear energy as the source of inexpensive, clean power. Many others feel that it may not be a viable energy alternative to the use of fossil fuels or solar energy because of the hazardous radiation emitted and the radioactive waste produced in the nuclear fission process.

The nuclear fusion process is the safe alternative to the fission process. A fusion reaction is one in which two atomic nuclei merge to form a heavier nucleus and, in most cases, an accompanying product such as a free nucleon. This process, which has been energizing the stars for billions of years, has clear potential as a power source on earth.

Nuclear fusion reactors require temperatures in the range of 100 – 250 million degrees, several times the temperature of the center of the sun. At these temperatures, matter can exist only in the plasma state, consisting of electrons, positive ions, and very few neutral atoms. Thermonuclear plasma is self-limiting because contact with the containment vessel walls causes extinction of the plasma within a few thousandths of a second.

In addition to being an almost inexhaustible fuel supply, fusion is environmentally benign. The resulting ash is harmless helium and hydrogen, and the heat in the fusion reactors is much less than in a fission reactor and dissipates through larger thermal masses. Nuclear fusion is not a chain reaction and it cannot run out of control. Perturbations cause the plasma to extinguish itself. It would also be far more difficult to produce nuclear-weapons materials surreptitiously at a fusion plant than at a fission plant, because fissionable material should not be present at fusion plants, and it is a simple matter to detect characteristic gamma rays from such sources.

The goal of nuclear fusion researchers is to create and contain the equivalent of a small star. The scientific community views this goal as the greatest technological challenge ever undertaken. A recent announcement by Princeton University energized the search for safe nuclear energy. Researchers at Princeton successfully tested a fuel with commercial promise and ready availability. These researchers used a mixture of equal parts of deuterium and tritium, which are isotopes of oxygen.

Researchers at Princeton University, Argonne National Laboratory, and Massachusetts Institute of Technology now forecast the completion of a full-power nuclear fusion generator by the year 2035.

What industry do you believe will produce the full-power generator? Should nuclear fusion power become commonplace, what would become of power utilities and manufacturers of conventional power generators? Identify the attributes of the extrinsic attribute factor influencing the proliferation of nuclear fusion power.

### ■ 7.9.8 Sample Space

Three missiles are fired at a target, each having a hit probability of 0.90. Describe the sample space and determine the probability of two or more missiles hitting the target.

## 7.10
## REFERENCES

You can obtain referenced government documents from the issuing organizations and from:

> Superintendent of Documents, U.S. Government Printing Office, Washington, DC 20402. Telephone: (202) 783-3238.
> National Technical Information Service, U.S. Department of Commerce, Springfield, VA 22161. Telephone: (703) 487-4650.

## 7.10 References

1. Norman R. Augustine, *Revised and Enlarged Augustine's Laws*, American Institute of Aeronautics and Astronautics, 1983.
2. Jack V. Michaels and William P. Wood, *Design to Cost*, John Wiley & Sons, Inc., 1989.
3. Gerald T. Croskery and Cyril F. Horton, *XM-1 Main Battle Tank*, Defense Management Journal, September 1974.
4. Motor Vehicle Manufacturers Association, *MMVA Motor Vehicle Facts and Figures*, 1989.
5. Kenneth Labich, *Why Companies Fail*, FORTUNE, November 14, 1994.
6. Matthys Levy and Mario Salvadori, *Why Buildings Fall Down*, W. W. Norton & Company, 1992.
7. Department of Defense DoD 4245.7-M, *Transition from Development to Production*, 1985.
8. Ralph Straus, *LLOYD'S, The Gentlemen at the Coffee House*, Carrick & Evans, Inc., 1938.
9. U.S. Department of Commerce, Bureau of the Census, *Statistical Abstract of the United States: 1994* (114th Edition), Washington, DC, 1994.

> *Few things are impossible to diligence and skill. Great works are performed not by strength, but by perseverance.*
> **Samuel Johnson**

# EPILOGUE

The two questions we hear most frequently are, "How do I get started in technical risk management?" and "How do I deal with apathy and downright opposition?" Having gotten this far in the book, you know enough to get started. You just need a little encouragement and direction. Table E.1 repeats the steps in technical risk management. They are easy to follow.

*Table E.1   Steps in Technical Risk Management*

1. Rank order the cost drivers in the generation breakdowns of the products of interest.
2. Select candidates for technical risk management from the top ranking cost drivers.
3. Determine what problems could occur in development and production of these cost drivers.
4. Estimate the probability of these problems occurring.
5. Ascertain the corrective action for these problems.
6. Estimate the probability of needing corrective action for these problems.
7. Calculate the risk time and risk cost with the products of corrective-action time and cost and the probability of needing corrective action.
8. Estimate additional cost of schedule extension by risk time, and add to risk cost for the risk cost exposure.
9. Determine up-front risk avoidance that could prevent the problems from occurring.
10. Estimate the cost of risk avoidance and subtract the cost of risk avoidance from risk cost exposure.
11. Present the cost difference to upper management as the additional profit from technical risk management.

We can guarantee that you will never get the chance to carry out the steps in Table E.1 without management support. We can also guarantee that you will never get management support for technical risk management unless you ask for it. Ask for it, but in the way that favors consent.

Get the experts involved; make them your allies. Upper management listens to their experts. That is why they hired them in the first place. The support of these experts is essential to a successful launching of technical risk management.

Start with the financial organization in your company. With the comptroller, who acts as the conscience of an organization, rank order the cost drivers in the work breakdown structures or generation breakdowns.

*Epilogue*

Work with the design and manufacturing people to determine what could go wrong in development and production of the products of interest. With them, establish the potential corrective actions and corrective-action time and cost. Get them to help you estimate the probability of needing corrective action.

Now you are in the position of being able to estimate the risk exposure in terms of risk time and risk cost. With the finance department, estimate the additional indirect cost due to the prolongation of the schedule from corrective action. Add the additional indirect cost from schedule prolongation to risk cost for the total risk cost exposure.

Now, you are ready to go to upper management with your message. But wait. First find out the cost of up-front risk avoidance, which could prevent problems from occurring, and indicate the savings over the amount of risk cost exposure. Work with design, manufacturing, and finance people to quantify the saving. Now you are ready to carry your message to upper management.

Be positive in your presentation. Do not stress how much money is being lost in the absence of risk control but emphasize how much more profit there will be from implementation of risk control.

Don't let one refusal discourage you. Above all, don't take it as a personal rebuff; management has other priorities to consider. Exercise multiple point penetration. This will allow you to take advantage of changing priority profiles and ultimately succeed in gaining management support.

Next, bring this message to the marketing organization. Marketing is probably the most influential element in an organization and you are well on your way if you can gain marketing's support. Marketing will view the cost saving as additional profit, which is its *raison d'être*.

Priorities change in all programs; the change is greatest in high-technology programs. Consider Table E.2 that lists the technical reviews of military conduct which many high-technology companies practice. The reviews are milestones in the acquisition of systems and products. Companies practice these reviews either formally or in a *de facto* fashion.

*Table E.2*  *Technical Reviews*

**System Requirements Review**
 To ascertain adequacy of technical requirements definition.
**System Design Review**
 To evaluate completeness and risks associated with technical requirements.
**Preliminary Design Review**
 To evaluate technical adequacy, compatibility, and risk resolution.
**Critical Design Review**
 To determine that detail design satisfies technical and specialty engineering requirements.
**Functional Configuration Audit**
 To validate that development has been completed satisfactorily.
**Physical Configuration Audit**
 To verify that as-built system or product conforms to defining technical documentation.
**Formal Qualification Review**
 To verify that system or product has met contractual requirements.
**Production Readiness Review**
 To verify completion of specific action prior to executing production decision.

Adapted by courtesy of the U.S. Department of Defense from MIL-STD-1521A, *Technical Reviews and Audits; Equipments and Computer Programs*. Available from National Technical Information Service, U.S. Department of Commerce, Springfield, VA 22161. Telephone: (703) 487-4650.

Priorities change and concern shifts toward risk exposure with each successive milestone. We have witnessed numerous instances of contractors who have been unsuccessful in bids for development contracts become the winning contractors in bids for production follow-on. The winning contractors recognized the change in priorities. Losing the first bid and winning the second solicitation is the essence of multiple point penetration.

Let multiple point penetration be your hallmark. Whatever you do or say, however, make sure you know the product line and that you can document the benefits you claim for technical risk management. Don't be afraid to ask for the management support if you know you are right.

> *Many things are lost for the want of asking.*
> ***Old English saying***

With regard to apathy and opposition, we have encountered more of these roadblocks than we care to mention. You have to approach apathy and opposition on a case-by-case basis.

Apathy usually stems from ignorance. Analyst is a long-time observer of the passing parade. Analyst says, "There are three kinds of people: those who make things happen; those who understand what happened; and those who wonder what happened when some event occurs." Your challenge is to educate, but on a personal basis. Stress what the program has to offer the individual in the way of recognition and reward.

Opposition stems from insufficiency or resentment. Many people fear being exposed as incompetent in their work. Others resent the implication that their work is not perfect. Their reaction is symptomatic of the not-invented-here (NIH) syndrome. NIH has killed many a good idea and suggestion.

Make sure the people to whom you are appealing understand that technical risk management is not a threat to their work but rather a benefit to them as well as the company. Treat these people as experts, praise their work, and solicit their ideas. Give them credit for risk avoidance strategies that prove successful. Make sure the risk control motivational plan is in place at the start of programs and reward performance generously, promptly, and publicly. Remember that people like to be praised but live on money.

Avoid the lean-machine syndrome when it comes to technical risk management as well as allied disciplines such as design to cost, total quality management, and value engineering. Companies need these disciplines all the more during lean years. Regrettably, these disciplines are usually the first to go. This is an important lesson to learn.

You constantly hear about lessons learned. When did you learn your lessons? You learned them after the fact. Wouldn't it be nice if could learn them before the fact? You could do so in a *de facto* fashion by remembering the lessons you learned and getting others to remember them as well. This may very well prevent the same or similar perils from recurring.

Be sure to read the section on the technical risk management plan in Appendix B. Before you undertake the job, make sure you have a plan under configuration control.

Configuration control is your contract with management. Don't make a move without it. Stick to the plan. Resist the temptation to allow yourself or others to depart from the plan even for a moment. Expediency ends up the long way around.

The French expression *embarras du choix* ("burden of too many choices") epitomizes the problem of choosing optimal approaches from available alternatives. From a technical risk management perspective, optimal approaches are those with the least amount of risk exposure. From an overall management perspective, however, optimality is also a function of profit and return-on-investment.

If you need to present the interaction of these factors, decision tables and trees are effective presentation media and easy to use. Mather and Solow illustrate the use of these techniques in their book *Management Science: The Art of Decision Making*, Prentice Hall, Inc., 1994. The book comes with a computer diskette with numerous in-text examples.

Whatever you do, be dispassionate and objective in your presentation. Stick to the facts and allow management to render judgment and make the decisions. Above all, remember that your stock in trade is reality and credibility. Management will adopt the more credible approach; the more realistic approach will come closest to meeting management's goals.

> *Round numbers are always false.*
> **Samuel Johnson**

# APPENDIX A

# GLOSSARY

**Affordability**: Characteristic of a system or product with a selling price that approaches its functional worth and is within the limit of what the customer is both able and willing to pay.
**Aggregate model**: Top-down model with large granularity.
**Aggregation**: Act of assembling distinct components of products into aggregates for purpose of top-down estimating of time and cost to produce the products.
**Amortization**: Retirement of financial obligation over given term by uniform series of payments.
**Analog model**: Model representing properties of subject by other set of properties such as flow of electricity by flow of water.
**Annual percentage rate**: Effective percentage rate of interest for period of one year.
**Application program**: Software that provides computational functions on computers.
**APR**: Annual percentage rate.
**Attribute**: Characteristic of risk determinants.
**Award fee**: Form of recognition for performance on contract.
**Balanced production line**: Production line wherein no time is expended waiting for work to arrive at any work station in the line.
**Baseline**: Initial specification of product to be developed, process to produce the product, and environment within which product is produced.
**Baseline cost estimate**: Estimated cost to develop and produce product in accordance with baseline.
**Baseline time estimate**: Initial estimated time to complete the development and production of products.
**BCE**: Baseline cost estimate.
**Benefit-cost ratio**: Ratio of the present value of benefits to the present value of costs.
**Binary weighting**: Method of weighting answers to questions with binary numbers.
**Bit**: Binary digit.
**Bivariate equation of regression**: Two-variable regression equation.
**Brassboard**: Model of product, for use in design evaluation, identical in form, fit, and function to production items except it is not built to withstand environmental qualification.
**Breadboard**: Model of product consisting of details, subassemblies, and assemblies connected in unmounted form for use in concept demonstration and validation.
**BTE**: Baseline time estimate.
**Capital recovery**: Point at which an investment or loan, adjusted for the time value of money, is recovered.

**Cause and effect diagram**: Depiction of risk network. Also called "fishbone diagram."
*Caveat emptor*: Latin for *let the buyer beware*.
**Central limit theorem**: Distributions of samples of populations approach normality with increased sample size.
**Chi-square distribution**: Sampling representation of variance of samples of population.
**CIF**: Compound interest factor.
**Coefficient of determination**: Statistical factor describing dependency among variables.
**Commitment to excellence**: Philosophy of doing things right the first time.
**Compound interest**: Interest on interest on principal.
**Compound interest factor**: Factor equal to one plus interest rate raised to the power of the number of terms that interest is applied to principal.
**Concurrency**: Degree of overlap among dependent tasks.
**Conditional probability**: Probability of occurrence of event given the occurrence of another event.
**Constant weighting**: Weighting that changes at constant rate in sequence of questions.
**Constant year dollars**: Fixed dollar value in baseline or reference year.
**Contingency analysis**: Definition of potential problems and solution in development and production.
**Corrective action**: Action taken to offset performance degradation or schedule or cost perturbations in programs, due to perils, so that the programs may continue as planned. Also called "work-around of risk recovery."
**Cost account**: Group of related work packages.
**CPI**: Consumer price index.
**CPM**: Critical path method.
**CPU**: Central processing unit.
**Critical path**: Path in multipath networks requiring more time or money to complete activities comprising the path than to complete the other paths.
**Critical path method**: Networking techniques that emphasize the critical path.
**Cycle time**: Amount of time to complete production run. Same as network-duration time and run time.
**Degrees of freedom**: Number of variates in statistical distribution less number of dependent relationships among variates.
**Deterministics**: Method of solution using a sequence of causes.
**Disaggregate model**: Bottom-up model with small granularity.
**Disaggregation**: Disassembling product into component disaggregate parts for estimating time and cost to develop and produce product.
**Discount rate**: Factor used to calculate present value of future sum of money.
**DOS**: Disk operating system.
**Dummy activity**: Activity inserted in a path of a network to complete the path in a depiction of the network.
**EAF**: Extrinsic attribute factor.
**Effective percentage rate**: Percentage rate of simple interest equivalent to compound interest rate for given term.
**EMV**: Expected monetary value.
**EPR**: Effective percentage rate.
**Equation of regression**: Statistical techniques for deriving value of dependent variables from independent variables.
**Equiprobability**: Equal probability.

**Equirisk**: Equal risk.
**Equivalence**: Equivalent present value of sum of money with given value in the future.
**Extrinsic attribute**: Source of risk exposure from forces such as inflation and statutory regulation that are external to given program and largely beyond control of the program.
**Extrinsic attribute factor**: Quantified extrinsic attribute on a scale of 0 to 1.0.
**Extrinsic factors**: Factors, such as inflation, which are peripheral to, and largely beyond the control of, the given program.
**Factorial**: Product of a positive integer and all positive integers less than that integer. By definition, factorials 1 and 0, denoted by 1! and 0!, are both equal to 1.
**Failure rate**: Number of failures per unit time of a particular item.
***F*-distribution**: Statistical representation of ratios of samples of variances of several populations.
**Field**: Task for collecting field data on use of product for purpose of product improvement.
**First article**: First production item produced and tested with LRIP tooling.
**First article test**: Test of first production unit of product.
**Fit**: Property of products given by static and dynamic interfaces with other products.
**Form**: Property of products given by the physical attributes of shape, weight, material, and packaging of the components.
**FP**: Future payment.
**Function**: Property of products given by operations performed by products.
**Functionality**: Form, fit, and function of products relative to intended use for products.
**Functional worth**: Cost of least expensive way to perform the intended function.
**Future value**: Value of given sum of money at future time equivalent to value of the sum of money at present time at given interest rate.
**FV**: Future value.
**Generation breakdown**: Hierarchical rendition of how products are produced starting with raw material.
**GERT**: Graphical evaluation and review technique.
**Hardware process complexity**: Hardware process attribute descriptor based on population of assemblies, subassemblies, details, and parts.
**Hardware process concurrency**: Risk determinant based on concurrence of dependent tasks.
**Hardware process maturity**: Risk determinant based on maturity and production readiness of process design.
**Hardware process quality**: Risk determinant based on uniformity of process in producing products of consistent quality.
**Hardware product complexity**: Risk determinant based on expansiveness of generation breakdown.
**Hardware product concurrency**: Risk determinant based on concurrence of interdependent tasks.
**Hardware product maturity**: Risk determinant based on design maturity and readiness for production.
**Hardware product quality**: Risk determinant based on design producibility, reliability, and testability.
**Hazard**: Condition or action that may result in perilous conditions.
**HDI**: Human development index.
**Heuristic**: From the Greek word *heuriskein* meaning to invent or discover.
**Heuristics**: Method of solution in which one proceeds along empirical lines using rules of thumb that leads to feasible though not necessarily optimal solutions.
**Human development index**: Measure of the quality of life based on longevity, literacy, and command over resources needed for a decent living.
**Iconic model**: Model looking like subject.

# Appendix A • Glossary

**Incentive**: Form of recognition for performance on contract.
**Intangible property**: Non-physical property such as cash on hand, investments, accounts receivable, and prepaid services.
**Interest rate**: Ratio, expressed as a percentage, of interest earned or paid at the end of a given period of time to the money invested or borrowed at the beginning of the given period of time.
**Internal rate of return**: Rate of return at which present value of benefits equals present value of costs.
**Intrinsic attribute**: Source of risk exposure from forces internal to given program and largely within control of the program.
**Intrinsic attribute factor**: Quantified intrinsic attribute on a scale of 0 to 1.0.
**Intrinsic factors**: Factors, which are part of a given program and, as such, are largely within the control of the program.
**IR&D**: Independent research and development.
**IRR**: Internal rate of return.
**Job family**: Group of similar products.
**Joint probability**: Probability of a succession of events.
**Law of large numbers**: Irrespective of probability distribution of the sample mean and variance converge on population mean and variance as random sample of size $n$ approaches population size.
**Learning curve**: Graphical representation of reduction in operation time as function of learning from repetitive operations.
**Life cycle cost**: Cost of product acquisition, operation, support, and disposal.
**Limited warranty**: Guaranty covering product replacement but not cost consequences of product malfunction.
**Logical statement**: Statement in binary form (*i.e.*, 0 or 1 for yes or no, or vice versa).
**Low-rate of initial production**: Production of items using soft (*i.e.*, multipurpose) tooling at the beginning of production.
**LRIP**: Low rate of initial production.
**MAF**: Management attribute factor.
**Majority rule**: Consensus of answers is derived from majority of the answers. If yes, the logical statement of the question is yes. Conversely, if consensus is no, the statement is no.
**Management attribute factor**: Risk determinant factor for management attributes (*e.g.*, funding and budgeting policy; customer and user policy; program continuity policy and personnel retention policy).
**Management science**: Body of techniques used to model and improve operations that include decision theory, utility and game theory, queuing theory, forecasting, linear and dynamic programming, distribution modeling, network modeling, inventory modeling, and simulation. Also called "operations research."
**Margin for error**: Statement of statistical confidence in opinion surveys.
**Mean**: Average value of statistical distribution.
**Mean-time-between failures**: Average time interval of successive failures of a particular item.
**Measure of effectiveness**: Quantitative measure of the effectiveness of a given strategy.
**Milestone**: Accomplishment signifying the completion of a task.
**Mission success**: Development and production of product that gains wide spread customer and user acceptance.
**Moment-method**: Probabilistic modeling based on mean and variance of probability distributions.
**Monte Carlo method**: Method for simulating probability distributions with random numbers.
**Morphology**: Form and structure of baseline and risk estimates.

**MPP**: Manufacturing process plan.
**NASA**: National Aeronautics and Space Administration.
**Network**: System of activities and events annotated with time.
**Next-best rule**: Rule advocating the use of good-enough solutions.
**NFA**: Need for aid.
**Normal distribution**: Statistical representation of population of random variables.
**Now dollars**: Value of given sum of dollars at current time.
**Now value of money**: Value of money at the current time.
**Null hypothesis**: Hypothesis that is subject of test of hypothesis.
**Operating system**: Software used to run computer-mechanized processes.
**Opportunity loss**: Return that would have been realized had money been invested in the best possible investment opportunity.
**Outcome**: An event with a unique probability of occurrence.
**PAN**: Probabilistic analysis of network.
**Pareto's law**: The bulk of wealth, influence, and power in the world resides mostly in the hands of a few people (*i.e.*, the vital few), and if distributed evenly among all the people of the world (*i.e.*, the trivial many), would inevitably return to the hands of the few.
**Path**: Series of tasks leading from start to finish milestones in product networks.
**Path-duration time**: Amount of time needed to complete tasks comprising a path.
**Pegasus**: In Greek mythology, the winged horse of the Muses.
**Peril**: Undesirable event resulting from hazard.
**Peril probability**: Probability of occurrence of a given peril.
**Period**: Time interval for compounding interest at periodic rate.
**PERT**: Program evaluation review technique.
**Planning horizon**: Time period for long-range planning.
**Point of diminishing return**: Dollar point at which rate of saving potential decreases.
**Point of total assumption**: Dollar amount above which contractor assumes responsibility for additional cost on contract.
**PPI**: Producer price index.
**Precedence**: Tasks which must be completed as prerequisites for other tasks to be started.
**Precedence diagram**: Networking method.
**Present value**: Value at present time of a future payment or receipt at given discount rate.
**Principal**: Amount of money invested or borrowed.
**Probabilistics**: Method of solution based on the probability of outcomes.
**Problem formulation**: Transformation of statements of perceived problems into precise, concise, and complete mathematical descriptions.
**PROCCF**: Process complexity factor.
**Process complexity**: Expanse of components of the product to be produced by the process.
**Process maturity**: Maturity and production readiness of process design.
**Process quality**: Uniformity of process in producing products of consistent quality.
**Process uniformity**: Consistency with which process produces product within specified functional, physical, and environmental limits.
**PROCMF**: Process maturity factor.
**PROCQF**: Process quality factor.

# Appendix A • Glossary

**PROCYF**: Process concurrency factor.
**PRODCF**: Product complexity factor.
**PRODMF**: Product maturity factor.
**PRODQF**: Product quality factor.
**Product**: Tangible or intangible item, or number of items called "system," including hardware and software, or service items.
**Product complexity**: Expanse of the generation breakdown for the product design.
**Product concurrency**: Concurrency of dependent product design activities.
**Product manager**: Individual responsible for development and production of product within time and money constraints.
**Product maturity**: Maturity and production readiness of the product design.
**Product quality**: Producibility, reliability, and testability of the product design.
**PRODYF**: Product concurrency factor.
**Profitability**: Return-on-investment commensurate with resources expended on producing products.
**Prototype**: Model of product, for use in formal design acceptance, which is identical to production items and is built to withstand environmental qualification.
**Pseudorandom number**: Number picked at random from less than infinite uniform distribution of numbers.
**PV**: Present value.
**QFAP**: Quality, functionality, affordability, and profitability.
**Quality**: Degree to which products provide intended functionality over expected periods of time with expected levels and frequencies of maintenance and repair.
**Random number**: Number picked at random from infinite uniform distribution of numbers.
**Rate of return**: Ratio of receipt to expenditure, adjusted for time value of money.
**Rate production**: Production of items using hard (*i.e.*, dedicated, special purpose) tooling at a high rate.
**RCE**: Risk cost estimate.
**RFP**: Request for proposal.
**Risk**: Uncertainty surrounding loss from perils.
**Risk avoidance**: Action taken to reduce risk exposure. Also called "risk reduction."
**Risk cost**: Product of corrective-action cost and probability of needing corrective action.
**Risk cost estimate**: Sum of baseline cost estimate and risk cost.
**Risk determinant**: Attribute serving as measure of risk exposure.
**Risk determinant factor**: Quantified measure of risk determinant on a scale of 0 to 1.0.
**Risk dominance**: Attribute of risk elements that influences or mitigates the contribution of other risk elements to risk exposure.
**Risk exposure**: Susceptibility of product to perils in terms of risk time and risk cost.
**Risk management**: Executive function of controlling hazards whose consequential perils cause property loss, personal loss, or legal liability.
**Risk metrics**: System of measurements for quantifying risk exposure.
**Risk morphology**: Antecedents, form, and structure of risk exposure from hazards and perils.
**Risk network**: Hierarchy of hazards and perils, or causes and effects.
**Risk recovery**: Corrective action to offset performance, schedule, or cost perturbations in programs due to perils so that programs may continue as planned. Also called "work-around" or "corrective action."

**Risk reduction**: Same as "risk avoidance."
**Risk time**: Product of corrective-action time and probability of needing corrective action.
**Risk time estimate**: Sum of baseline time estimate and risk time.
**RISNET**: Risk information system and network evaluation technique.
**ROI**: Return-on-investment.
**Root-sum-of-squares**: Square root of sum of squares of series of numbers.
**RSS**: Root-sum-of-squares.
**RTE**: Risk time estimate.
**SAM**: Stochastic aggregation model.
**Sampling bias**: Error resulting from design of sampling plan.
**Sampling distribution**: Statistical representation of samples of population.
**Sampling error**: Error that is either a function of sample size and confidence level or of sampling bias.
**Scientific method**: Formalized reasoning process that consists of observation, problem formulation, formulation of hypotheses, test of hypotheses, and verification.
**Service**: Intangible product consisting of business and personal services.
**Service manager**: Individual responsible for development and performance of service within time and money constraints.
**Service product concurrency**: Risk determinant based on concurrency of dependent service activities.
**Service product complexity**: Risk determinant based on expanse of the service generation breakdown.
**Service product maturity**: Risk determinant based on maturity and provisioning readiness of service design.
**Service product quality**: Risk determinant based on repeatability, reliability, and inspectability of the service activities.
**Should cost**: Probable cost of well-run program wherein nothing unforeseen happens. Also called "50-50 cost."
**Simple interest**: Interest without compounding earned on principal.
*Sine qua non*: Latin for *an absolute prerequisite*.
**Single payment**: Single receipt or expenditure.
**Sinking fund**: Fund to retire debt or acquire new equipment established by series of deposits at fixed time intervals.
**Software process complexity**: Risk determinant based on number of lines of code.
**Software process concurrency**: Risk determinant based on concurrency of interdependent tasks.
**Software process maturity**: Risk determinant based on software program maturity.
**Software process quality**: Risk determinant based on degree of control in software program.
**Software product complexity**: Risk determinant based on the expansiveness of the generation breakdown of the software.
**Software product concurrency**: Risk determinant for software products based on the degree of concurrence among interdependent software design tasks.
**Software product maturity**: Risk determinant based on software design maturity and readiness for production.
**Software product quality**: Software product attribute descriptor based on degree of control in software program.
**Software program**: Set of instructions executed by computer.
**SP**: Single payment.

Appendix A • Glossary

**Specifics**: Use of specific details of individual elements of cost based on historical data from the same or similar products. Provides maximum realism and credibility but requires maximum expenditure of resources.
**Standard deviation**: Measure of dispersion about the mean of a probability distribution.
**Statistics**: Branch of mathematics. Also, properties of samples.
**Stratified random sampling**: Division of populations into subgroups, or strata, from which samples are drawn.
**Student's $t$ distribution**: Statistical representation of small sample of population.
**Sunk cost**: Previously expended or committed money that is not considered in future economic analysis.
**Supplier**: Producer or supplier of systems, products, or services, or both.
**Symbolic model**: Model representing its subjects by mathematical relationships.
**Systematic random sampling**: Selection of first sample at random and subsequent samples with some periodicity.
**Tailoring**: Process of adapting procedures and criteria for certain applications to other applications.
**Tangible property**: Physical property with intrinsic value.
**Taxonomy**: Laws and principles governing the classification of objects.
**TDP**: Technical data package.
**Technical risk management**: Executive function of controlling technical hazards and perils.
**Template**: Depiction of critical events in design, test, and production of product.
**Term**: Duration of financial transaction expressed by number of time periods for compounding interest.
**Test of hypothesis**: Statistical test of inferred values of means, standard deviations, and proportions.
**Then dollars**: Value of given sum of dollars at a future time.
**Total procurement package**: Contractual instrument for development and production.
**TRACE**: Total risk assessing cost estimate.
**Truth table**: Rendition of logical statements in binary form.
***t*-statistic**: Statistical measure for the area under the curve of the Student's $t$ distribution.
**Uniform distribution**: Statistical representation of population of variables with equiprobability of occurrence.
**Uniform series of payments**: Series of payments or receipts of fixed amounts, at fixed time intervals and at fixed interest rate or discount rate.
**User**: Customer, user, or both.
**Variance**: Measure of dispersion in data comprising a probability distribution. Square of standard deviation.
**VERT**: Venture evaluation and review technique.
**VOA**: Value of aid.
**Window of opportunity**: Period of time for pursuing an opportunity without loss of potential.
**Work breakdown structure**: Depiction of elements of cost for developing and producing product.
**Work-content time**: Amount of time needed to perform the work content of a work element.
**Work element**: Smallest subdivision of manufacturing process which can be assigned to a single work station.
**Work package**: Unit of work needed to complete a specific job which is assigned to a specific operator.
***z*-statistic**: Statistical measure of the area under the curve of the normal distribution.

# APPENDIX B

# RISK MANAGEMENT IN THE DEPARTMENT OF DEFENSE

The approach to technical risk management by the U.S. Department of Defense (DoD) and its components is worthy of emulation by producers and suppliers of high-technology products and services.

The approach is characterized by the way they acquire systems and products, and by the way they attempt to manage risk in the process. Appendix B addresses the acquisition policy of the DoD and planning for risk management as promulgated by the Defense Systems Management College.

## ■ B.1 Acquisition Policy

The DoD recently revised the 5000 series documents that govern defense acquisition policy and procedures (*i.e.*, the way the DoD and its components do business with industry). Table B.1 lists these documents.

*Table B.1*    *U.S. Department of Defense 5000 Series Documents*

> Directive Number 5000.1, *Defense Acquisition*, 23 February 1991.
> Instruction Number 5000.2, *Defense Acquisition Management Policies and Procedures*, 23 February 1991.
> Manual Number 5000.2-M, *Defense Acquisition Management Documents and Reports*, 23 February 1991.

> Available from National Technical Information Service, U.S. Department of Commerce, Springfield, VA 22161. Telephone: (703) 487-4650.

The intent of the revisions is to (1) provide a single uniform acquisition system for all DoD acquisition programs; (2) forge an interface among the DoD's systems for generating requirements, planning, programming, and budgeting; (3) and ensure event-driven acquisition strategies based on objective assessment of status at each milestone in the program and the management of risk in subsequent phases of the program.

Figure B.1 illustrates the intent of the DoD for successful systems acquisition. Toward that end, the DoD and its components conduct in-depth reviews at a series of milestones in the process.

342     *Appendix B • Risk Management in the DoD*

Figure B.2 depicts the five major milestones in the DoD's revised acquisition process. Note the objectives of the five milestones in the illustration. Each objective must be achieved before the project can proceed to the next phase. Figure B.3 shows that risk management is at the heart of each milestone decision point in the overall acquisition strategy. The exit criteria serve as gates to go to the next phase in system acquisition.

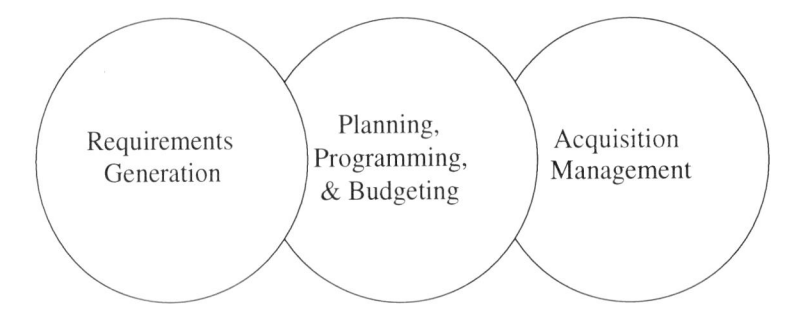

**Figure B.1**    Effective Interaction of Decision Making Essential for Success

Adapted by courtesy of the Defense Systems Management College, Fort Belvoir, Virginia from Charles B. Cochrane, *Defense Acquisition Policy: A New Set of Directives for a Disciplined Management Approach*, Program Manager, May-June 1991.

| | Phase 0 | Phase I | Phase II | Phase III | Phase IV |
|---|---|---|---|---|---|
| Determination of Mission Need | Concept Exploration & Definition | Demonstration & Validation | Engineering & Manufacturing Development | Demonstration & Validation | Operation & Support |

Milestone 0    Milestone I    Milestone II    Milestone III    Milestone IV

Milestone 0: Concept Studies Approval
    Milestone I: Concept Demonstration
        Milestone II: Development Approval
            Milestone III: Production Approval
                Milestone IV: Major Modification Approval

**Figure B.2**    Acquisition Milestones and Phases

Adapted by courtesy of the U.S. Department of Defense from DoD Instruction Number 5000.2, *Defense Acquisition Management Policies and Procedures*, 23 February 1991. Available from National Technical Information Service, U.S. Department of Commerce, Springfield, VA 22161. Telephone: (703) 487-4650.

At each milestone decision point, assessments are conducted on the status of program execution and the plans for the next phases and the remainder of the program. The risks associated with

Appendix B • Risk Management in the DoD

the program and the adequacy of risk management planning are expressed explicitly. Additionally, program-specific results called "exit criteria" must be accomplished before transition to the next acquisition phase is permitted. Exit criteria can be viewed as gates through which a program must pass during the particular phase. In particular, significant effort must be devoted to risk management to ensure that the milestones in Figure B.3 are achieved.

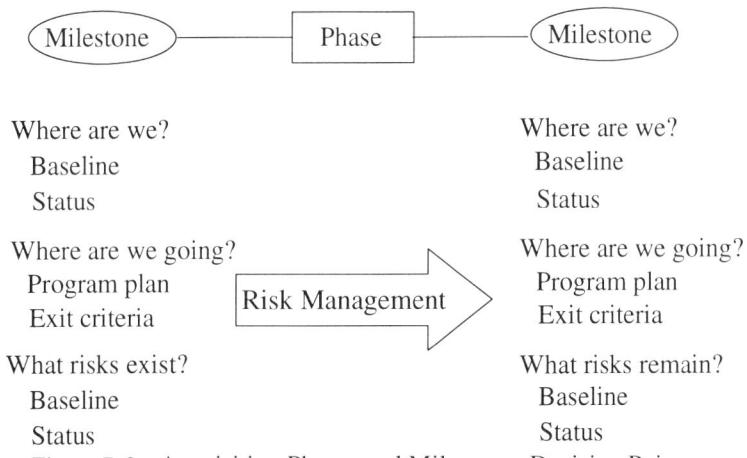

```
   (Milestone) ──── [Phase] ──── (Milestone)

Where are we?                          Where are we?
   Baseline                               Baseline
   Status                                 Status

Where are we going?                    Where are we going?
   Program plan     ══Risk Management══▶  Program plan
   Exit criteria                          Exit criteria

What risks exist?                      What risks remain?
   Baseline                               Baseline
   Status                                 Status
```

**Figure B.3**  Acquisition Phases and Milestones Decision Points

Adapted by courtesy of the U.S. Department of Defense from DoD Instruction Number 5000.2, *Defense Acquisition Management Policies and Procedures*, February 23, 1991. Available from National Technical Information Service, U.S. Department of Commerce, Springfield, VA 22161. Telephone: (703) 487-4650.

Too often in the past, when faced with funding and schedule constraints, the technical integrity of programs has been compromised by deleting or deferring vital program elements that contribute to system performance, producibility, and supportability. This has added to the life-cycle cost and postponed operational capability dates by pursuing development programs which did not yield producible designs and supportable configurations in a timely manner.

This experience led DoD to promulgate Directive Number 4245.7 in January 1984. Directive Number 4245.7 mandated the use of DoD Manual Number 4245.7-M, *Transition from Development to Production Manual*, September 1985, for structuring technically sound programs, assessing their risk, and identifying areas needing corrective action. The thesis of the manual is that the true causes of acquisition risk are technical, not managerial, in nature, and that the DoD's emphasis on management, when seeking corrective measures, should be refocused on technical performance, in particular technical risk assessment.

The manual was produced by the Defense Science Task Force on the Transition from Development to Production, and copies are available from the National Technical Information Service, U.S. Department of Commerce, Springfield, VA 22161. The telephone number is (703) 487-4650.

Figure B.4 illustrates the manual's perspective of the transition problem and the level of special risk evaluation which must be reached in order to lower product transition risk. The thrust of the manual is to identify critical engineering events in the acquisition management of defense products; the initial event being funding and money phasing. These events are transformed into what are referred to as "templates."

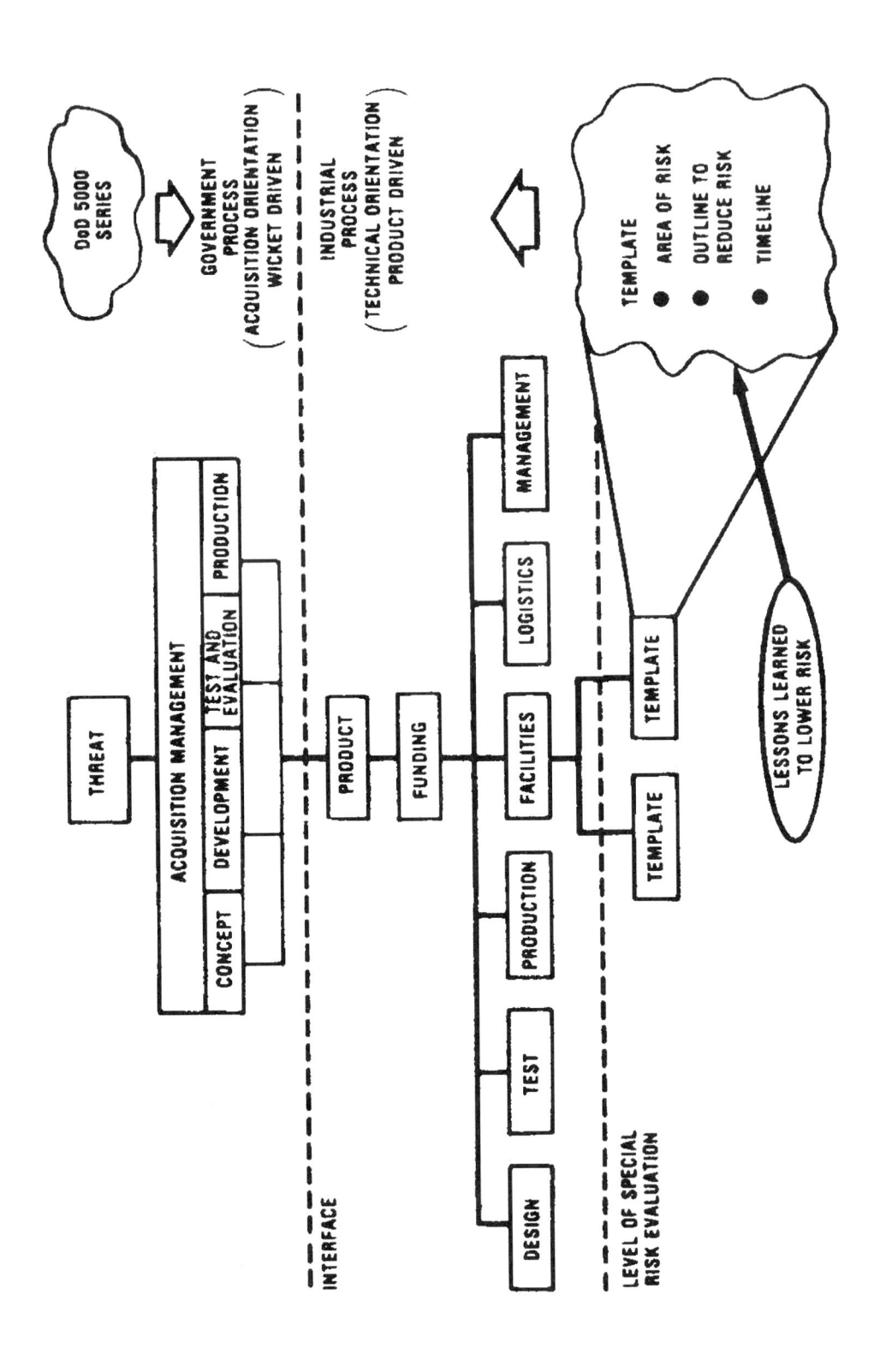

**Figure B.4** Transition Problem Perspective

## Appendix B • Risk Management in the DoD

The Defense Science Task Force declared that the most critical event in program life cycles is the transition from development to production. Figure B.5 identifies the critical path templates needed to reduce risk in the transition.

The Defense Science Task Force averred that the track record of major defense systems acquisitions had been poor over the past several years, as manifested by length of acquisition cycles, unsatisfactory effectiveness, and life-cycle cost. Numerous attempts to improve the defense systems' acquisition process were fruitless.

The major areas addressed by the task force were funding, design, test production, facilities, logistics, and management. Within the funding area, the task force found that both government and industry project managers realize the importance of adequate and timely funding to ensure project success. However, few appreciate the complexity of the defense authorization and appropriation process.

In addition, few project managers possess sufficient knowledge of the DoD Planning, Programming, and Budgeting System (PPBS), or understand the relationship between the PPBS and the DoD acquisition process. As a result, many projects begin with inadequate allocation of research, development, test, and evaluation funding for the initial design and engineering effort. This causes further aggravation as early production money is unavailable to support production line start-up.

Within the management area, the task found that numerous decisions were made under uncertainty. Since uncertainty and risk are synonymous, the task force questioned, "Why have so many years of alleged emphasis on technical risk assessment by government and industry program managers achieved so few results?"

The task force concluded that the essence of acquisition problems in the management area was ignorance of technical risk assessment. The task force outlined a sequence of steps addressing this lack of knowledge. Table B.2 is the outline put forth by the task force. You will note the similarity to what we advocate in this book.

The steps were accompanied with many checklists to ensure proper action in a timely manner to reduce risk. The sheer number of the checklist areas in Table B.3 attest to the seriousness with which the DoD views the problems in its system acquisition process.

Table B.3 is a testimonial to DoD's attempt to improve its system acquisition process. It appears, however, that the DoD has omitted two important measures from the outline.

Do you know what they are? We spoke previously about the importance of these measures to cost-effective risk control:

1. Early in the life cycle of programs, give organizations and people the authority and the tools that are commensurate with the job you expect them to do.
2. Set up and publicize a system of recognition and awards. Review their performance on a near real-time basis. Reward and publicize their performance accordingly.

---

Footnote for Figure B.4 appearing on facing page:

Reprinted by courtesy of the U.S. Department of Defense from DoD 4275.7-M, *Transition from Development to Production*, September 1985. Available from National Technical Information Service, U.S. Department of Commerce, Springfield, VA 22161. Telephone: (703) 487-4650.

**Figure B.5** Critical Path Templates

Reprinted by courtesy of the U.S. Department of Defense from DoD 4275.7-M, *Transition from Development to Production*, September 1985. Available from National Technical Information Service, U.S. Department of Commerce, Springfield, VA 22161. Telephone: (703) 487-4650.

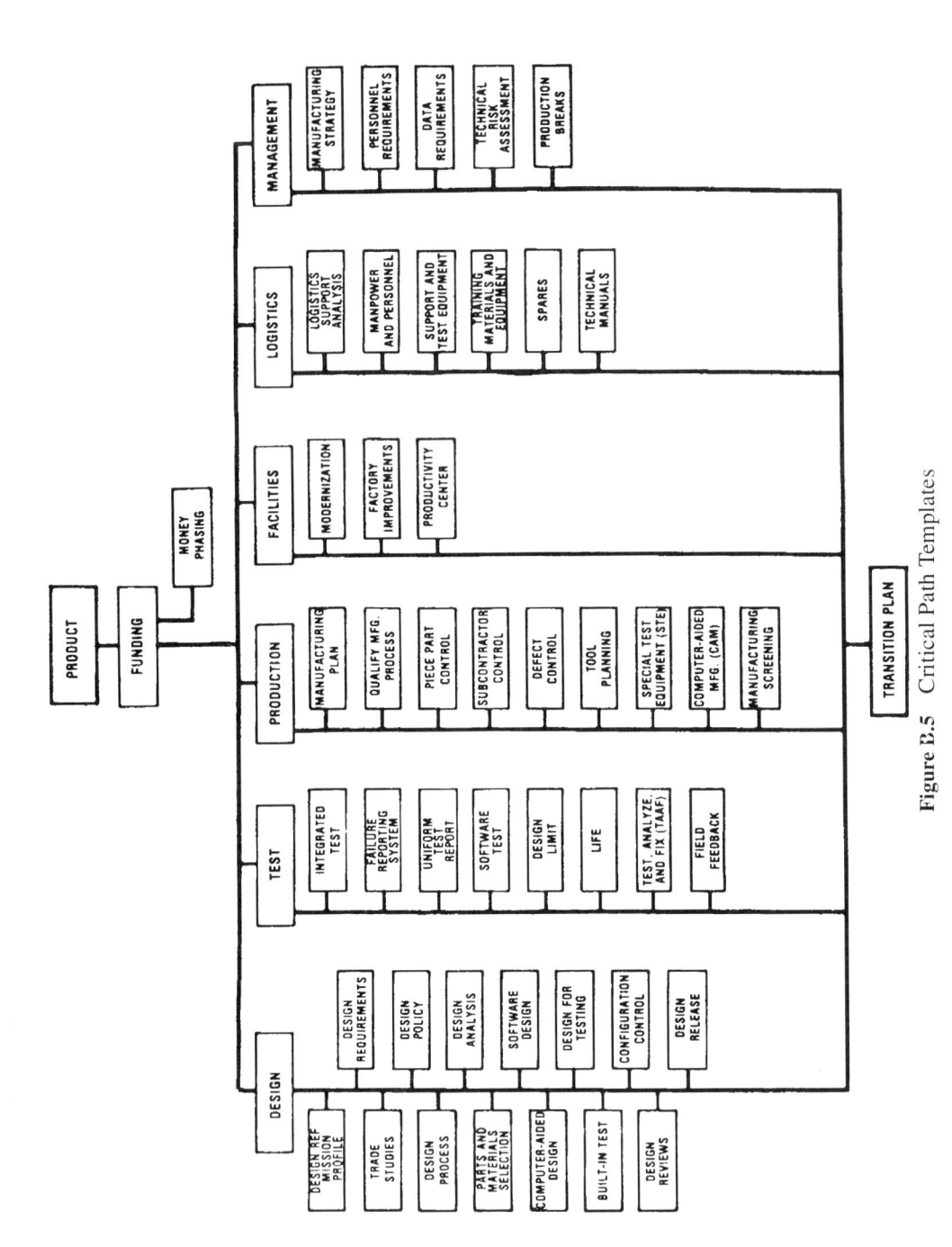

## Appendix B • Risk Management in the DoD

**Table B.2**  *Outline for Reducing Risk*

1. Specify technical risk management as a contractual requirement for early implementation in the development process.
2. Identify areas of risk as early as possible in the development cycle. Determine a specific set of tracking indicators for each major technical element (*i.e.*, design, test, and production) as well as for cost and management.
3. Develop plans to track, measure, assess, and adjust for identified risks using a disciplined system that can be applied by managers from a variety of positions within the government and contractor organizations. This system should provide continuous assessment of program health against quantifiable parameters.
4. Ensure that risk drivers are understood adequately by contractors, using qualified design and production engineers knowledgeable of the risk drivers to identify and reduce program technical risk.
5. Highlight technical problems before they become critical.
6. Avoid hasty shortcuts, review mission profiles, and use existing analysis tools while implementing the technical risk assessment system.
7. Structure test programs to verify that high risk design areas have been resolved.

Adapted by courtesy of the U.S. Department of Defense from DoD 4275.7-M, *Transition from Development to Production*, September 1985. Available from National Technical Information Service, U.S. Department of Commerce, Springfield, VA 22161. Telephone: (703) 487-4650.

The objective of the checklists listed in Table B.3 is to avoid the traps that program managers face in development and production.

**Table B.3**  *Checklists for Reducing Risk*

| | | |
|---|---|---|
| Money Phasing | Design Reference Mission Profile | Design Requirements |
| Trade Studies | Design Policy | Design Process |
| Design Analysis | Parts and Materials Selection | Software Design |
| Computer-Aided Design | Design for Testing | Built-In Test |
| Configuration Control | Design Reviews | Design Release |
| Integrated Test | Failure Reporting | Uniform Test Report |
| Software Test | Design Limits | Life Test |
| Test, Analyze, and Fix | Field Feedback | Manufacturing Plans |
| Quality Process | Piece Part Control | Subcontractor Control |
| Defect Control | Tool Planning | Special Test Equipment |
| Manufacturing Process | Manufacturing Screening | Transition Plan |
| Modernization | Factory Improvements | Productivity Center |
| Logistics Support | Manpower and Personnel | Support and Test Equipment |
| Training Equipment | Training Material | Spares |
| Technical Manuals | Manufacturing | Data Requirements |
| Technical Risk | Production Breaks | |

Adapted by courtesy of the U.S. Department of Navy from NAVSO P-6071, *Best Practices*, March 1987. Available from National Technical Information Service, U.S. Department of Commerce, Springfield, VA 22161. Telephone: (703) 487-4650.

The task force enumerated the following major traps and consequences in the area of funding:

1. Technical issues are not adequately presented to justify funding requirements. As a consequence, funding decisions are based primarily on cost, schedule, and bureaucratic considerations.
2. Project managers believe that major decisions are made by people with sufficient technical background. As a consequence, project status may be in jeopardy.
3. Funding is skewed, as described in DoD 4245.7-M. One consequence is inadequate design effort due to poor allocation of funds.
4. Procurement of long-lead items and proof of manufacturing is started late. One consequence is production start-up problems are magnified.

The task force enumerated the following major traps and consequences in the area of technical risk assessment:

1. Contractors claim to have a technical risk assessment and reporting system. As a consequence, time delay occurs in recognizing factors driving cost and schedule.
2. Technical problems are formally reported only at the project management level. As a consequence, engineers hope to solve problems before management is alerted.
3. Top-level requirements are not interpreted and passed on to in-house engineers or subcontractors. As a consequence, many technical issues are not considered during development.
4. The only indicators used for technical risk management are test results. As a consequence, unanticipated design and manufacturing problems surface during tests, resulting in significant cost and schedule impact.

Table B.4 is the checklist for technical risk assessment.

*Table B.4* Technical Risk Assessment Checklist

1. Does the contractor have a specific technical risk assessment and reporting program?
2. Are periodic reports provided to all levels of management on the technical status, problems, corrective actions, and subsequent project impact?
3. Have technical risk indicators been generated for design, test, manufacturing, and management?
4. Does each technical risk indicator have a projection of where it should be during its phase of the project?
5. Have all top level requirements been allocated to the lowest design and test levels for both the prime and subcontractors?

## ■ B.2 Technical Risk Management Plan

Programs are guided by a series of plans that provide the processes whereby programs are executed. A technical risk management plan is a sensible part of this suite.

This section of Appendix B is adapted by the courtesy of the Defense Systems Management College, Fort Belvoir, Virginia, from *Task Management Concepts and Guidance*, 1989. The approach is worthy of emulation by producers and suppliers of high-technology products and services.

**Table B.5** *Technical Risk Management Plan*

1. Program Description
    1.1 Objective
    1.2 Product
        1.2.1 Product Description
        1.2.2 Key Functions
    1.3 Required Operational Characteristics
    1.4 Required Technical Characteristics
2. Program Summary
    2.1 Requirements
    2.2 Management
    2.3 Schedule
3. Approach
    3.1 Definitions
        3.1.1 Technical Risk
        3.1.2 Programmatic Risk
        3.1.3 Supportability Risk
        3.1.4 Cost Risk
        3.1.5 Schedule Risk
    3.2 Structure
    3.3 Methods Overview
4. Application
    4.1 Risk Assessment
        4.1.1 Risk Identification
        4.1.2 Risk Quantification
    4.2 Risk Analysis
    4.3 Risk Control
        4.3.1 Risk Reduction Milestones
        4.3.2 Risk Quantification
        4.3.3 Risk Budgeting
        4.3.4 Contingency Planning
5. Summary
    5.1 Risk Process Summary
    5.2 Technical Risk Summary
    5.3 Programmatic Risk Summary
    5.4 Supportability Risk Summary
    5.5 Schedule Risk Summary
    5.6 Cost Risk Summary
    5.7 Conclusions
6. Bibliography
7. Approval

Adapted by courtesy of the Defense Systems Management College, Fort Belvoir, Virginia, from *Risk Management Concept and Guidance*, 1989. Available from National Technical Information Service, U.S. Department of Commerce, Springfield, VA 22161. Telephone: (703) 487-4650.

Table B.5 is the general outline for generating technical risk management plans. The program description and program summary sections of the plan provide the bases of reference to understand the need and major functions of the product. The material should include operational and technical characteristics, description of organizational relationships, responsibility and authority, and an integrated program schedule.

The approach section of the plan describes the intended approach for risk assessment, analysis, and control. The material includes definitions, measurement techniques, and risk rating methods for technical risk, programmatic risk, supportability (*i.e.*, service and repair) risk, cost risk, and schedule risk.

The application section of the plan includes the procedures and processes for identifying risk, quantifying risk, using tools to analyze risk, and applying specific actions to control risk. The material includes interfaces with other governing plans. These include program management plan, system management plan, procurement plan, quality plan, test and evaluation plan, manufacturing plan, and supportability plan.

These plans provide insight to items of risk. Typically, they are not written from the viewpoint of risk, but when they are read with an eye to questions about risk, they provide valuable insight.

The technical risk management plan should be maintained under configuration control. This means that there can be no change to the plan without specific, documented Change Control Board action.

Adherence to the technical risk management plan should be monitored as carefully and frequently as every aspect of design, schedule, and cost. Deviations from the plan should be reported immediately to management along with recommendations for corrective action. Approved corrective actions should also be placed under configuration control.

The technical risk management plan coalesces the requirements for developing a cost-effective technical risk management capability. The plan should stress the following key points:

1. Agencies and companies must organize for technical risk management.
2. Technical risk management is a team function.
3. Proper and prompt communication of risk information is as important as the process.
4. Delineate technical risk management responsibility and authority commensurate with the responsibility at the organizational and personnel levels.
5. Establish a recognition and reward system early in program life cycles and reward organizations and personnel promptly and publicly, commensurate with their performance.

# APPENDIX C

# SOLUTIONS TO EXERCISE PROBLEMS

Appendix C contains step-by-step solutions to the exercises in Chapters 1 through 7. Since our intent is to reinforce the subject matter covered in each chapter, we urge you to attempt the exercises before resorting to the following solutions.

By the way, be sure to read the postscripts following the solutions to Exercises 1.5.1, 3.9.9, 6.6.6, and 7.9.7.

### ■ 1.5.1 Planning Disasters

Planning disasters are projects that go awry, costing monumental sums of money but without fulfilling their intended purposes. Identify three such planning disasters and cite the driving forces behind the disasters.

**SOLUTION**

The Anglo-French Concorde, the Bay Area Rapid Transit System in San Francisco, and the Opera House in Sydney, Australia, are the three planning disasters that intrigue us the most.

**Anglo-French Concorde**

The Concorde is perhaps the costliest commercial blunder in history. The cost to develop and produce the aircraft was almost an order of magnitude more than estimates, and the revenue has been a fraction of the expectation.

The Concorde flies subsonically until it achieves the cruising altitude of 55,000 feet. The aircraft then goes supersonic at a speed of Mach 2 (*i.e.*, twice the speed of sound), at which point the aircraft emits an excruciatingly loud sonic boom. The Concorde is essentially *persona non grata* in the vicinity of airports that can accommodate the aircraft, adding to the problem of acceptance by other communities.

**Bay Area Rapid Transit System**

The Bay Area Rapid Transit (BART) System in San Francisco, California, is another costly blunder and a case of mistaking desire for reality. The planners perceived the 71-mile system as the primary means of transportation for people living and working in the Bay area. What the planners did not recognize was that in the Bay area residents and business were dispersed over a wide area and that the dispersion would increase as the area developed. Patronage came mostly from bus riders, exacerbating the economic problems of the bus systems.

The majority of the residents continued to drive. With patronage being 50 percent less than the forecast, fares produced less than 50 percent of the required revenue. Operating cost was about 500 percent greater than the estimate. The balance is subsidized by taxpayers who already had to contend with the capital cost that was 150 percent more than the estimate.

**Sydney Opera House**
The Sydney Opera House is another blunder of immense dimensions. The stage was set in 1957, when the planners selected a design featuring interlocking concrete shells connected side by side.

The opera house was not completed until late 1973, by which time the estimated cost had multiplied by a factor of fifteen. Indeed, the cost overrun would have been much greater, had the design not been scaled down considerably.

As a matter of fact, the design was scaled down to the point where the opera house cannot accommodate productions of the scale of operas. Thus the Sydney Opera House qualifies as both a financial and operational blunder.

**POSTSCRIPT**
We would be remiss in leaving this exercise if we were to make no mention of the Bhopal and Chernobyl disasters. Bhopal has the tragic distinction of being the site of the world's worst industrial accident. Chernobyl has the equally tragic distinction of being the site of the world's worst nuclear reactor accident.

Bhopal is the capital of the State of Madhya Pradesh in central India. It is a rail, agricultural, and industrial region with a population of more than one million. On December 3, 1984, about 2,500 people died and about 20,000 were injured when a toxic methyl isocyanate leaked from a pesticide plant in the region. The disaster challenged the safety of the chemical industry and raised serious questions about the legal and moral responsibilities of multinational companies operating in third world countries.

Chernobyl is a city in Ukraine about 130 kilometers north of the city of Kiev. On April 26, 1986, a reactor exploded in Chernobyl's nuclear power plant. There was neutron build-up in the core causing the nuclear reaction to go out of control. A steam-induced explosion followed, blowing the lid off the reactor. A chemical explosion followed, scattering fragments over a wide area. Radioactivity spread over the Northern Hemisphere. Thirty-one people were killed and more than 500 were injured. Despite clean-up efforts, several million people still live on contaminated ground. Two of the three remaining reactors remain in operation because of Ukraine's need for electrical power.

### ■ 1.5.2 Scientific Method

In the example of Section 1.2.7, Analyst calculated the number of positions that various configurations of unit cubes could occupy. Given a built-up cube with the dimensions of eight unit cubes by six unit cubes by four unit cubes, follow Analyst's technical approach and calculate the number of positions that various configurations of these unit cubes could occupy.

**SOLUTION**
Analyst used the following relationship for the number of positions that $n$ cubes could occupy:

$$n = x^3 + (x - 1)^3 + (x - 2)^3 + ... + (x - n + 1)^3. \tag{C.1}$$

The axes in the example are symmetrical. The axes in this exercise are eight unit cubes by six unit cubes by four unit cubes. Designating the axes by $x$, $y$, and $z$, we replace Equation C.1 with Equation C.2.

Appendix C • Solutions

$$n = [x + (x - 1) + (x - 2) + ... + (x - n + 1)] \cdot$$
$$[y + (y - 1) + (y - 2) + ... + (y - n + 1)] \cdot$$
$$[z + (z - 1) + (z - 2) + ... + (z - n + 1)]. \quad (C.2)$$

Substituting $x = 8$, $y = 6$, and $z = 4$ in Equation C.2, we obtain Equation C.3 that gives 7,560 as the number of positions that various configurations of these unit cubes could occupy. Equation C.3 appears lengthy, but it saves much effort in trying to position built-up cubes from the size of 8 by 6 by 4 down to the size of 1 by 1 by 1.

$$n = [8 + (8 - 1) + (8 - 2) + (8 - 3)$$
$$+ (8 - 4) + (8 - 5) + (8 - 6) + (8 - 7)]$$
$$\cdot [6 + (6 - 1) + (6 - 2) + (6 - 3)$$
$$+ (6 - 4) + (6 - 5)]$$
$$\cdot [4 + (4 - 3) + (4 - 2) + (4 - 1)]$$
$$= (36)(21)(10)$$
$$= 7,560. \quad (C.3)$$

Specifically, you would need to construct and position cubes measuring 8 by 6 by 4, 8 by 6 by 3, 8 by 6 by 2, 8 by 6 by 1, 8 by 5 by 4, 8 by 5 by 3, 8 by 5 by 2, 8 by 5 by 1, 8 by 4 by 4, 8 by 4 by 3, 8 by 4 by 2, 8 by 3 by 4, 8 by 3 by 3, 8 by 3 by 2, 8 by 3 by 1, 8 by 2 by 4, 8 by 2 by 3, 8 by 2 by 2, 8 by 2 by 1, 8 by 1 by 4, 8 by 1 by 3, 8 by 1 by 2, 8 by 1 by 1, 7 by 6 by 4, 7 by 6 by 3, 7 by 6 by 2, 7 by 6 by 1, 7 by 5 by 4, 7 by 5 by 3, 7 by 5 by 2, 7 by 5 by 1, and so on until you reached 1 by 1 by 1. I think you get the point about the value of the scientific method.

### ■ 1.5.3 Greek Alphabet

Which English letters do not have roots in the Greek alphabet? What are the roots of these letters?

**SOLUTION**

English letters $g$ and $w$ do not have their roots in the Greek alphabet. The respective roots are the Latin and Anglo-Saxon alphabets.

### ■ 2.7.1 Risk Principles

Section 2.7.1 gives background information on this exercise. The exercise asks you to identify the conflicting risk principles in this situation and the protagonists who are engaged in the conflict. Discuss the significance of the situation to DoD contractors and the defense budget.

**SOLUTION**

The conflicting risk principles are the risk benefit-equity principle and the risk cost-effectiveness principle. The chief protagonists are the environmental and health advocates on the one hand and members of the military-industrial complex on the other.

The defense budget has been reduced considerably with the relaxation of the cold war. The number of DoD contractors is dwindling and this will cause problems should defense mobilization be needed in the future.

Requirements to adopt more expensive manufacturing techniques will exacerbate the funding problem. Many contractors would elect not to convert to the new technology.

### ■ 2.7.2 Risk Continuum

In a certain production facility, there are six hazards involving inspection, of which any two can induce the peril of a faulty part eluding inspection. Calculate the number of combinations which are possible in the problem of interest.

Increase the number of hazards to seven and note the increase in the number of combinations. Next, increase the number of perils to three and note how the number of combinations have multiplied.

**SOLUTION**
We calculate the number of combinations $c$ which can be formed from $n$ items taken $r$ at a time with Equation C.4.

$$c = \frac{n!}{r!(n-r)!} \tag{C.4}$$

where $n!$ and $r!$ denote the factorials of $n$ and $r$.

Substituting $n = 7$ and $r = 2$ in Equation C.4, we obtain

$$c = \frac{7!}{2!(7-2)!}$$
$$= \frac{5,040}{2(120)}$$
$$= 21. \tag{C.5}$$

Substituting $n = 7$ and $r = 3$ in Equation C.4, we obtain

$$c = \frac{7!}{3!(7-3)!}$$
$$= \frac{5,040}{6(24)}$$
$$= 35. \tag{C.6}$$

### ■ 2.7.3 Risk Hierarchy

Section 2.7.3 gives background information on this exercise. The exercise asks you to develop a hierarchical system of hazards and perils for this particular case along the lines of Table 2.12.

**SOLUTION**
The peril in this case was the fraudulent conversion of the company's assets by some individuals. The initial hazard in Table C.1 is inadequate resources.

Appendix C • Solutions

**Table C.1**  Hierarchy of Computer Fraud Hazards and Perils

| Hazards | Perils |
|---|---|
| Inadequate resources | Inadequate training |
| Inadequate training | Inadequate security |
| Inadequate security | Unauthorized access |
| Unauthorized access | Asset loss |
| Asset loss | Inadequate cash flow |
| Inadequate cash flow | Business failure |

### 2.7.4 Multiprocess Risk Probability

Table C.2 gives suggested values of process maturity factor (PROCMF) as a function of the level of maturity in the related process. Consider three processes, one of which has been used to produce and test similar LRIP first articles and two of which have had their similar LRIP rate tooling proofed. Calculate the composite multiprocess PROCCF with the assumptions of dependence and independence among the processes.

Under what circumstances would the assumptions of dependence and independence among the three processes be valid?

**Table C.2**  Process Maturity Factors for Multiprocess Risk Probability Exercise

| Factor | Level of Process Maturity |
|---|---|
| 0.0 | Similar rate units produced and tested. |
| 0.1 | Similar rate first article produced and tested. |
| 0.2 | Similar rate tooling proofed. |
| 0.3 | Similar LRIP first article produced and tested. |
| 0.4 | Similar LRIP tooling proofed. |
| 0.5 | Similar prototype produced and tested. |
| 0.8 | Similar brassboard produced and tested. |
| 0.9 | Similar breadboard produced and tested. |
| 1.0 | No similar experience possessed. |

Rate: Full production rate.
LRIP: Low rate of initial production.

**SOLUTION**

The PROCMF for the process used to produce and test similar LRIP first articles is 0.3. The PROCMF used to proof similar LRIP tooling is 0.4.

Assuming dependence among the processes, the value of composite PROCMF is the sum of the individual factors. This equates to (0.3 + 0.4 + 0.4), or 1.1. Note that we do not divide the value by 3, the number of individual values of PROCMF, as we would when different factors are operating on the same product.

Assuming independence among the three processes, the value of the composite PROCMF is the root-sum-of-squares of the values of the individual PROCMF. This equates to the square root of $(0.3^2 + 0.4^2 + 0.4^2)$, or 0.41.

The assumption of dependence among the three processes would be valid if one process were an input to the second process and the second process were an input to the third. The assumption of independence among the three processes would be valid if the three processes were not inputs to each other.

### ■ 2.7.5 Risk Network

Section 2.7.5 gives background information on this exercise. The exercise asks you to assume product maturity factors of 0.8 for brassboard status and 0.9 for breadboard status. Use the technical approach for the example in Section 2.4.7 to construct the risk network. Calculate the risk cost estimate for each path in the network and the composite risk cost estimate for the overall network.

Which path is the critical path of the network? How much slack is there in the noncritical paths? Repeat the exercise with the assumption that the tasks are dependent on each other and they overlap 50 percent. How does your finding change with the assumption of independence among the tasks?

Table C.3 gives the precedence data for a hypothetical IRAD program. The IRAD program consists of ten tasks that are being proposed by an aerospace company to a certain agency. The tasks are interrelated and therefore comprise a network.

Tasks a and j are the starting and finish tasks. Table C.3 also gives corresponding baseline time estimates and the design status for the programs which were started during the previous year.

*Table C.3* Precedence, Time, and Design Data for Risk Network Exercise

| Activity | Precedent | Successor | BTE | Design Status |
|---|---|---|---|---|
| a | None | b, c, d, e | N/A | N/A |
| b | a | f | 1 month | Brassboard |
| c | a | g | 2 months | Brassboard |
| d | a | h | 4 months | Breadboard |
| e | a | i | 3 months | Breadboard |
| f | b | j | 1 month | Brassboard |
| g | c | h | 2 months | Brassboard |
| h | d | j | 1 month | Brassboard |
| i | e | j | 1 month | Brassboard |
| j | f | None | N/A | N/A |

BTE: Baseline time estimate.
N/A: Not applicable.

**SOLUTION**

We first construct the product network in Figure C.1. Activities a and j are the start and finish of the network and take no time.

Appendix C • Solutions

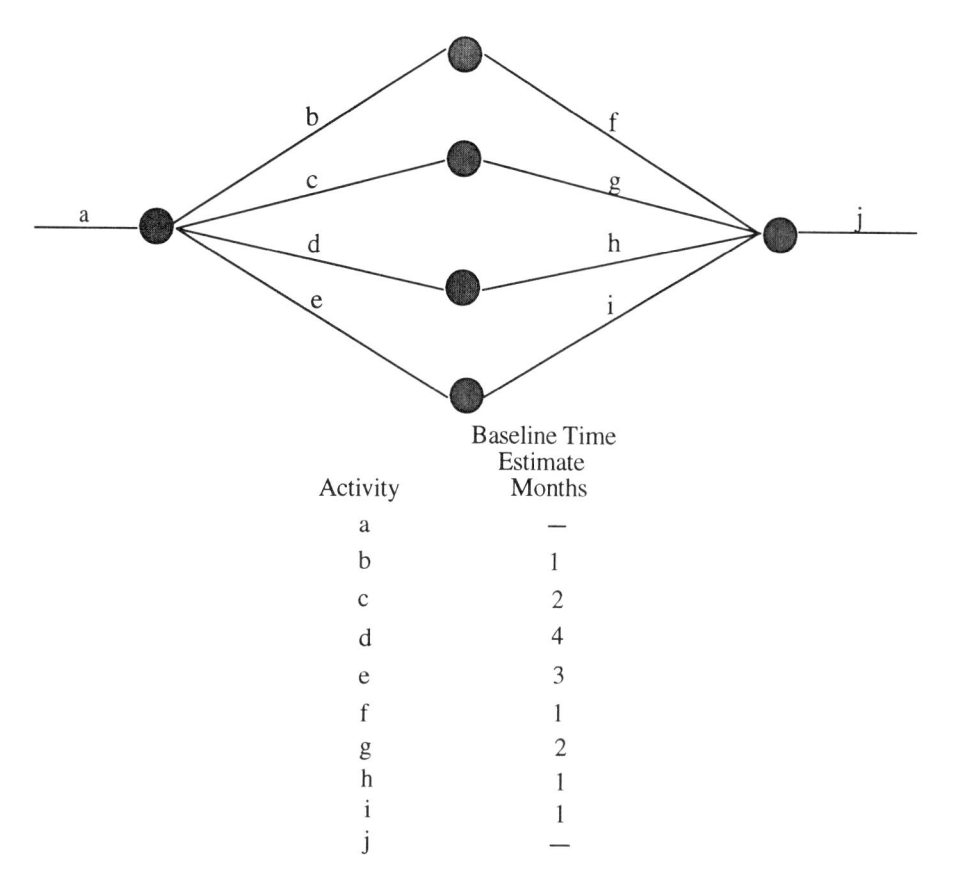

**Figure C.1** Product Network for Risk Network Exercise

| Activity | Baseline Time Estimate Months |
|---|---|
| a | — |
| b | 1 |
| c | 2 |
| d | 4 |
| e | 3 |
| f | 1 |
| g | 2 |
| h | 1 |
| i | 1 |
| j | — |

We use the worksheet in Table C.4 to calculate the risk time estimates for the paths in Figure C.1. We are dealing with a simple product, which accounts for the low values of baseline time estimate in contrast to the high values of product maturity factor.

**Table C.4** Worksheet for Risk Network in Manufacturing Exercise

| Path | Baseline Time Estimate Months | PRODMF | Risk Time Estimate Months |
|---|---|---|---|
| a, b, f, j | 0 + 1 + 1 + 0 = 2 | 0.8, 0.8 | 1(1 + 0.8) + 1(1 + 0.8) = 3.60 |
| a, c, g, j | 0 + 2 + 2 + 0 = 4 | 0.8, 0.8 | 2(1 + 0.8) + 2(1 + 0.8) = 7.20 |
| a, d, h, j | 0 + 4 + 1 + 0 = 5 | 0.9, 0.8 | 4(1 + 0.9) + 1(1 + 0.8) = 9.40 |
| a, e, i, j | 0 + 3 + 1 + 0 = 4 | 0.9, 0.8 | 3(1 + 0.9) + 1(1 + 0.8) = 7.50 |

We use the quantity (1 + PRODMF) as the multiplier of baseline time estimate to obtain risk time estimate (RTE). The values of path RTE range from 3.60 months to 9.40 months.

Path a, d, h, j with the risk time estimate of 9.40 months is the critical path. Path a, b, f, j has 9.40 − 3.60, or 5.80 months of slack. Path a, c, g, j has 9.40 − 7.20, or 2.20 months of slack. Path a, e, i, j has 9.40 − 7.50, or 1.90 months of slack.

If we assume the three paths in the network are dependent on each other, the network RTE is the sum of the values of path RTE for 3.6 + 7.2 + 9.4 + 7.5, or 27.7 months. If we assume that three paths in the network are independent of each other, we derive network risk time estimate with the root-sum-of-squares method. Equation C.7 gives the calculation of the root-sum-of-squares (RSS) of the values of RTE in Table C.4.

$$RSS_{RT} = \sqrt{(3.60\,months)^2 + (7.20\,months)^2 + (9.40\,months)^2 + (7.50\,months)^2}$$

$$= 14.47\ months. \tag{C.7}$$

We next consider an overlap of 50 percent of the tasks in each path. An overlap of 50 percent yields a product concurrency factor (PRODYF) of 0.5. Section 2.5 describes the dominance of PRODMF over PRODYF, meaning that the value of PRODYF is factored by the value of PRODMF. We use the quantity (1 + PRODMF • PRODYF) as an additional multiplier of BTE to calculate RTE.

Table C.5 gives the results of including PRODYF in the calculations. The critical path is still Path a, d, h, j, but the critical path time is now 16.60 months instead of 9.4 months.

*Table C.5* *Worksheet with Concurrency for Risk Network in Manufacturing Exercise*

| Path | Baseline Time Estimate Months | PRODMF | Risk Time Estimate Months |
|---|---|---|---|
| a, b, f, j | 0 + 1 + 1 + 0 = 2 | 0.8, 0.8 | 1(1 + 0.8) + 1(1 + 0.8•0.5) + 1(1 + 0.8) + 1(1 + 0.8•0.5) = 6.40 |
| a, c, g, j | 0 + 2 + 2 + 0 = 4 | 0.8, 0.8 | 2(1 + 0.8) + 2(1 + 0.8•0.5) + 2(1 + 0.8) + 2(1 + 0.8•0.5) = 12.80 |
| a, d, h, j | 0 + 4 + 1 + 0 = 5 | 0.9, 0.8 | 4(1 + 0.9) + 4(1 + 0.9•0.5) + 1(1 + 0.8) + 1(1 + 0.8•0.5) = 16.60 |
| a, e, I, j | 0 + 3 + 1 + 0 = 4 | 0.9, 0.8 | 3(1 + 0.9) + 3(1 + 0.9•0.5) + 1(1 + 0.8) + 1(1 + 0.8•0.5) = 13.25 |

Path a, b, f, j has 16.60 − 6.40, or 10.20 months of slack. Path a, c, g, j has 16.60 − 12.80, or 3.80 months of slack. Path a, e, g, j has 16.60 − 13.25, or 3.35 months of slack. If we again assume the three paths in the network are dependent on each other, the network RTE is the sum of the values of path RTE for 6.4 + 12.8 + 16.6 + 13.25, or 49.05 months.

If we assume that three paths in the network are independent of each other, we again use the root-sum-of-squares method to derive the value of the network risk time estimate. Equation C.8 gives the calculation of the root-sum-of-squares for the values of RTE in Table C.5.

Appendix C • Solutions

$$RSS_{RT} = \sqrt{(6.40 \text{ months})^2 + (12.80 \text{ months})^2 + (16.60 \text{ months})^2 + (13.25 \text{ months})^2}$$

$$= 25.61 \text{ months}. \tag{C.8}$$

### 2.7.6 Risk Dominance

Alpha-Omega Company has a contract to produce several million quartz clocks which will be used as a give-away in an advertising campaign. The unit cost of the clocks is estimated to be $0.75. The product and process quality, complexity, and concurrency factors are estimated to be 0.9.

Alpha-Omega has already produced millions of quartz clocks of a similar design, and the product and process maturity factors are estimated to be 0.1. Estimate the unit risk cost of the quartz clocks.

Repeat the exercise with the assumption that Alpha-Omega has completed only a prototype of the clock and that the product and process maturity factors are estimated to be 0.5.

**SOLUTION**

The values of the product maturity factor (PRODMF) and process maturity factor (PROCMF) establish the value of the $k$-factors to use in the exercise. In the first case, PRODMF = 0.1, and PROCMF = 0.1, and $k = 0.1$.

Equation C.9 gives the calculation of unit risk cost (RC) for the unit cost of $0.75 with PRODMF and PROCMF equal to 0.1, $k = 0.1$, and other risk determinant factors equal to 0.9.

$$RC = 2(\$0.75)(0.1 + 0.1 \cdot 0.9 + 0.1 \cdot 0.9 + 0.1 \cdot 0.9)$$

$$= \$0.56. \tag{C.9}$$

The factor 2 in the right-hand side of the equation is the multiplier that accounts for the fact that both PRODMF and PROCMF affect the risk cost.

Note that the amount in Equation C.9 is only the risk cost. The risk cost estimate (RCE) is the sum of the baseline cost and the risk cost for $0.75 + $0.56, or $1.31.

Equation C.10 gives the calculation of RC with PRODMF and PROCMF equal to 0.5, $k = 0.5$, and the other risk determinant factors equal to 0.9.

$$RC = 2(\$0.75)(0.5 + 0.5 \cdot 0.9 + 0.5 \cdot 0.9 + 0.5 \cdot 0.9)$$

$$= \$2.78. \tag{C.10}$$

The value of RCE is $0.56 + $2.78, or $3.34.

### 2.7.7 Risk Exposure in Product Development

Risk exposure is significantly lower in developing and producing products with low values of product maturity factor (PRODMF) and process maturity factor (PROCMF) irrespective of the values of the other risk determinant factors. Consider a product with a development cost of $1.5 million and production cost of $3.0 million. PRODMF and PROCMF equal 0.8. Estimate the risk exposure in terms of risk cost for PRODMF and PROCMF.

What are the other pertinent risk determinant factors that affect risk cost? Calculate the increase in risk cost if you were to consider these risk determinant factors equal to 0.8. Repeat the exercise with PRODMF and PROCMF equal to 0.5 and the other risk determinant factors equal to 0.8.

**SOLUTION**

Table C.6 is the worksheet for calculating risk cost with consideration of PRODMF and PROCMF alone. The risk exposure in terms of risk cost is $3,600,000. The RCE is $4,500,000 + $3,600,000, or $8,100,000.

*Table C.6  Risk Cost Calculations Worksheet*

| Development Cost | PRODMF | Development Risk Cost |
|---|---|---|
| $1,500,000 | 0.8 | 0.8($1,500,000) = $1,200,000 |
| Production Cost | PROCMF | Production Risk Cost |
| $3,000,000 | 0.08 | 0.8($3,000,000) = $2,400,000 |
| Total Cost |  | Total Risk Cost |
| $4,500,000 |  | $3,600,000 |

The other pertinent risk cost determinant factors affecting risk cost are product quality factor (PRODQF), product complexity factor (PRODCF), product concurrency factor (PRODYF), process quality factor (PROCQF), process complexity factor (PROCCF), and process concurrency factor (PROCYF). Table C.7 is the worksheet for calculating risk cost with consideration of all the pertinent risk determinant factors.

*Table C.7  Risk Cost Calculations with All Pertinent Risk Determinant Factors Worksheet*

| Development Cost |  | Development Risk Cost |
|---|---|---|
| $1,500,000 | **PRODMF:** 0.8<br>**PRODQF, PRODCF, PRODYF:**<br>0.8, 0.8, 0.8 | (0.8 + 0.8 • 0.8 + 0.8 • 0.8 +<br>0.8 • 0.8) • ($1,500,000) =<br>$4,080,000 |
| **Production Cost** |  | **Production Risk Cost** |
| $3,000,000 | **PROCMF:** 0.8<br>**PRODQF, PRODCF, PROCYF:**<br>0.8, 0.8, 0.8 | (0.8 + 0.8 • 0.8 + 0.8 • 0.8 +<br>0.8 • 0.8) • ($3,000,000) =<br>$8,160,000 |
| **Total Cost** |  | **Total Risk Cost** |
| $4,500,000 |  | $12,240,000 |

We repeat the exercise for PRODMF, PROCMF, and the other pertinent risk determinant factors with PRODMF and PROCMF equated to 0.5 and the other factors to 0.8. Table C.8 is the worksheet for the repeated calculations.

Note the use of the values of PRODMF and PROCMF (*i.e.*, 0.5) as the values of the *k*-factor. The *k*-factors are applied to the values of PRODQF, PRODCF, PRODYF, PRODQF, PRODCF, and PROCYF.

Appendix C • Solutions

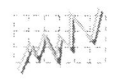

**Table C.8** *Risk Cost Repeated Calculations with All Pertinent Risk Determinant Factors Worksheet*

| Development Cost | | Development Risk Cost |
|---|---|---|
| $1,500,000 | **PRODMF**: 0.5 | (0.8 + 0.5 • 0.8 + 0.5 • 0.8 + |
| | **PRODQF, PRODCF, PRODYF**: | 0.5 • 0.8) • ($1,500,000) = |
| | 0.8, 0.8, 0.8 | $3,000,000 |
| Production Cost | | Production Risk Cost |
| $3,000,000 | **PROCMF**: 0.5 | (0.8 + 05 • 0.8 + 0.5 • 0.8 + |
| | **PRODQF, PRODCF, PROCYF**: | 0.5 • 0.8) • ($3,000,000) = |
| | 0.8, 0.8, 0.8 | $6,000,000 |
| Total Cost | | Total Risk Cost |
| $4,500,000 | | $9,000,000 |

### ■ 2.7.8 Risk Exposure in Manufacturing Process

Consider an item with a process maturity factor (PROCMF) of 0.2, process quality factor (PROCQF) of 0.4, process complexity factor (PROCCF) of 0.6, and process concurrency factor (PROCYF) of 0.8. Calculate the composite risk determinant factor ($\Sigma$RDF) for the manufacturing process. Would you assume dependence or independence among these factors and how would the assumptions affect results?

**SOLUTION**

The relationship among these factors can be dependence or independence. Were you to assume dependence, you would simply add the individual values of the factors. For the values in this exercise, the $\Sigma$RDF is 0.2 + (0.2)(0.4) + (0.2)(0.6) + (0.2)(0.8), or .56.

This value establishes the risk cost at 2.2 times the baseline cost estimate and the risk cost estimate at 3.3 times the baseline cost estimate, which is probably unrealistically high. Unless you are applying $\Sigma$RDF to corrective-action time or cost, and not product cost, we would advise the assumption of independence and the use of the root-sum-of-squares method. This is not farfetched. Given enough opportunity, you can become quite proficient at doing complex, concurrent jobs of low quality.

Equation C.11 gives the calculation of the composite $\Sigma$RDF with the RSS method.

$$\Sigma RDF = \sqrt{(0.2)^2 + (0.2 \bullet 0.4)^2 + (0.2 \bullet 0.6)^2 + (0.2 \bullet 0.8)^2}$$
$$= 0.29. \quad \text{(C.11)}$$

The factors are generally independent of each other. Given enough opportunities, we can become very proficient at doing a poor quality job. Note the use of the root-sum-of-squares method in Equation C.11.

The exercise also asks you to repeat the calculation for PROCMF of 0.4 and 0.1, PROCQF of 0.2 and 0.6, PROCCF of 0.6 and 0.8, and PROCYF of 0.8 and 1.0 and to describe the sensitivity of

ΣRDF to changes in the value of PROCMF compared to value changes in the other risk process determinant factors.

Equations C.12 and C.13 repeat the calculation for: (1) *PROCMF* = 0.3, and *PROCQF*, *PROCCF*, and *PROCYF* unchanged; and (2) *PROCMF* = 0.2, *PROCQF* = 0.6, *PROCCF* = 0.8, and *PROCYF* = 1.0.

$$\Sigma RDF = \sqrt{(0.3)^2 + (0.3 \cdot 0.4)^2 + (0.3 \cdot 0.6)^2 + (0.3 \cdot 0.8)^2}$$
$$= 0.44. \tag{C.12}$$

$$\Sigma RDF = \sqrt{(0.2)^2 + (0.2 \cdot 0.6)^2 + (0.2 \cdot 0.8)^2 + (0.2 \cdot 0.1)^2}$$
$$= 0.28 \tag{C.13}$$

Table C.9 gives the comparison of values of ΣRDF as functions of values of PROCMF and the other risk process determinant factors.

**Table C.9**  *Comparison of Composite Risk Determinant Factors*

| PROCMF | PROCQF | PROCCF | PROCYF | RDF |
|--------|--------|--------|--------|------|
| 0.2    | 0.4    | 0.6    | 0.8    | 0.29 |
| 0.2    | 0.6    | 0.8    | 1.0    | 0.35 |
| 0.3    | 0.4    | 0.6    | 0.8    | 0.44 |

The data in the first data line of Table C.9 are the reference values. In the second data line, holding the value of PROCMF constant and increasing the other values by 50 percent increases the value of ΣRDF to 0.35, which is about 21 percent more than the reference value.

In the third data line, increasing the value of PROCMF by 50 percent and holding the other values constant increases the value of ΣRDF to 0.44, which is about 52 percent more than the reference value. For these data, the sensitivity of ΣRDF to changes in the value of PROCMF is almost two and one-half times more than the sensitivity to changes in the other risk determinant factors.

### ■ 2.7.9 Risk Exposure in Investment

Table C.10 is an updated version of Table 2.24. Using U.S. Treasury 10-year note yield data from the current edition of the *Statistical Abstract of the United States*, recalculate the risk exposure in the example of Section 2.5.5.

**SOLUTION**

Repeat the exercise with U.S. Treasury 3-year note yield data. Tabulate the results from using 10-year note and 3-year note data with the mutual fund data in Table C.10. How has the risk exposure changed from the example in Section 2.5.5? Which U.S. Treasury instrument yield has the greatest variability? Which U.S. Treasury instrument would you recommend as an investment on the basis of risk exposure? State your reasons for the recommendation.

Table C.11 lists the percentage yield of U.S. Treasury notes for periods of three years, five years, and ten years from 1984 through 1993. The data are from Table 810 on page 527 of U.S. Bureau of the Census, *Statistical Abstract of the United States: 1994* (114th Edition), Washington, DC, 1994.

Appendix C • Solutions

**Table C.10** Mutual Fund Data for Risk Exposure in Investment Exercise

| Year | Percent | Year | Percent |
|------|---------|------|---------|
| 1984 | 11.70   | 1989 | 9.75    |
| 1985 | 9.83    | 1990 | 9.30    |
| 1986 | 8.37    | 1991 | 8.68    |
| 1987 | 7.91    | 1992 | 8.90    |
| 1988 | 8.56    | 1993 | 6.10    |

**Table C.11** Treasury Note Data for Risk Exposure in Investment Exercise

|               | 1984  | 1985  | 1986 | 1987 | 1988 |
|---------------|-------|-------|------|------|------|
| 3-Year Notes  | 11.92 | 9.62  | 7.06 | 7.68 | 8.26 |
| 5-Year Notes  | 12.26 | 10.12 | 7.30 | 7.94 | 8.47 |
| 10-Year Notes | 12.46 | 10.62 | 7.67 | 8.39 | 8.85 |
|               | 1989  | 1990  | 1991 | 1992 | 1993 |
| 3-Year Notes  | 8.55  | 8.26  | 6.82 | 5.30 | 4.44 |
| 5-Year Notes  | 8.50  | 8.37  | 7.37 | 6.19 | 5.14 |
| 10-Year Notes | 8.49  | 8.55  | 7.86 | 7.01 | 5.87 |

Adapted by courtesy of the U.S. Bureau of the Census from *Statistical Abstract of the United States: 1994* (114th Edition), Washington, DC, 1994.

Table C.12 gives suggested values of product maturity factor as functions of the standard deviation ($s$) divided by the mean ($m$). You can derive in-between values of PRODMF with interpolation.

**Table C.12** Product Maturity Factors for Risk Exposure in Investment Exercise

| PRODMF | $s \div m$ | PRODMF | $s \div n$ |
|--------|------------|--------|------------|
| 0.1    | <1         | 0.6    | ≥5<6       |
| 0.2    | ≥1<2       | 0.7    | ≥6<7       |
| 0.3    | ≥2<3       | 0.8    | ≥7<8       |
| 0.4    | ≥3<4       | 0.9    | ≥8<9       |
| 0.5    | ≥4<5       | 1.0    | ≥9         |

PRODMF: Product maturity factor.
$s \div m$: Standard deviation divided by the mean.
<: Less than.
≥: Equal to or more than.

Table C.13 is the worksheet we use to derive the risk exposure from investing in the mutual fund relative to 10-year U.S. Treasury notes.

***Table C.13*** *10-Year Note Worksheet for Risk Exposure in Investment Exercise*

| Year | Mutual Fund | 10-Year Notes | Difference |
|---|---|---|---|
| 1984 | 11.78 | 12.46 | −0.68 |
| 1985 | 9.83 | 10.62 | −0.79 |
| 1986 | 8.37 | 7.67 | +0.70 |
| 1987 | 7.91 | 8.39 | −0.48 |
| 1988 | 8.56 | 8.85 | −0.29 |
| 1989 | 9.75 | 8.49 | +1.26 |
| 1990 | 9.30 | 8.55 | +0.75 |
| 1991 | 8.68 | 7.86 | +0.82 |
| 1992 | 8.90 | 7.01 | +1.89 |
| 1993 | 6.10 | 5.87 | +0.23 |

Sum of differences: 3.41

The mean ($m$) of the sample in Table C.13 is 3.41 ÷ 10, or 0.341. We use Equation C.14 to calculate the variance ($s^2$) of the variates $x_i$ (*i.e.*, differences) with sample size $n = 10$.

$$s^2 = \frac{\Sigma (x_i - m)^2}{n - 1} \tag{C.14}$$

Substituting values of $x_i$ and $n$ in Equation C.14, we obtain

$$s^2 = [(-0.68 - 0.341)^2 + (-0.79 - 0.341)^2 + (0.70 - 0.341)^2 + (-0.48 - 0.341)^2 + (-0.29 - 0.341)^2$$
$$+ (1.26 - 0.341)^2 + (0.75 - 0.341)^2 + (0.82 - 0.341)^2 + (1.89 - 0.341)^2 + (0.23 - 0.341)^2] \div (10 - 1)$$
$$= 0.797. \tag{C.15}$$

The standard deviation is the square root of the variance, or 0.893 percent. The value of $s \div m$ is 0.893 ÷ 0.341, or 2.619.

In accordance with Table C.12, the corresponding value of PRODMF is between 0.3 and 0.4. With interpolation, we obtain

$$PRODMF = 0.3 + 0.1(2.619 - 2)$$
$$= 0.3619. \tag{C.16}$$

For every $100 invested in the mutual fund, the risk exposure in terms of risk cost is $100(0.3619), or $36.19, relative to investing the $100 in 10-year U.S. Treasury notes.

The exercise also asked you to repeat the exercise with U.S. Treasury 3-year note yield data and to compare the results from using 10-year and 3-year note data. Table C.14 is Table C.13 with 10-year note data replaced by 3-year note data.

*Appendix C • Solutions* 365

**Table C.14**  3-Year Note Worksheet for Risk Exposure in Investment Exercise

| Year | Mutual Fund | 3-Year Notes | Difference |
|------|-------------|--------------|------------|
| 1984 | 11.78 | 11.92 | −0.14 |
| 1985 | 9.83 | 9.62 | +0.21 |
| 1986 | 8.37 | 7.06 | +1.31 |
| 1987 | 7.91 | 7.68 | +0.23 |
| 1988 | 8.56 | 8.26 | +0.30 |
| 1989 | 9.75 | 8.55 | +1.20 |
| 1990 | 9.30 | 8.26 | +1.04 |
| 1991 | 8.68 | 6.82 | +1.86 |
| 1992 | 8.90 | 5.30 | +3.60 |
| 1993 | 6.10 | 4.44 | +1.66 |
|      |      |      | Sum of differences: 11.27 |

The mean ($m$) of the sample in Table C.14 is $11.27 \div 10$, or 1.127. Equation C.17 gives the results of using Equation C.14 to calculate the variance ($s^2$) of the variates $x_i$ (i.e., differences) with sample size $n = 10$.

$$s^2 = \frac{[(-0.14 - 1.127)^2 + (0.21 - 1.127)^2 + (1.31 - 1.127)^2 (0.23 - 1.127)^2 + (0.30 - 1.127)^2}{10 - 1}$$

$$\frac{+ (1.20 - 1.127)^2 + (1.04 - 1.127)^2 + (1.86 - 1.127)^2 + (3.60 - 1.127)^2 + (1.66 - 1.127)^2]}{10 - 1}$$

$$= 10.92. \tag{C.17}$$

The standard deviation is simply the square root of the variance, or 3.305 percent. The value of $s \div m$ is $3.305 \div 1.127$, or 2.933.

In accordance with Table C.12, the corresponding value of PRODMF is between 0.3 and 0.4. With interpolation, we obtain

$$PRODMF = 0.3 + 0.1(2.933 - 2)$$
$$= 0.3933. \tag{C.18}$$

For every $100 invested in the mutual fund, the risk exposure in terms of risk cost is $100(0.3933), or $39.33, relative to investing the $100 in 3-year U.S. Treasury notes.

Table C.15 compares yields and risk costs relative to 3-year and 10-year U.S. Treasury notes. The mean yield of A (i.e., mutual fund described in the example in Section 2.5.5) is 10.54 percent. One hundred dollars invested in A would yield $100(0.1054), or $10.54, without considering compound interest. The risk cost is $11.00 for the 10-year note, or about the same as the yield.

The mean yield of B (i.e., mutual fund described in this exercise) is 10.54 percent. One hundred dollars invested in fund B would yield $100(0.1054), or $10.54, without considering compound interest. The risk cost of B is $39.33 for the 3-year note and $34.96 for the 10-year note.

*Table C.15  Comparison of Mutual Fund Yields and Risk Costs*

| Instrument | Mean Yield Percent | 3-Year Note Risk Cost | 10-Year Note Risk Cost |
|---|---|---|---|
| Mutual fund A | 10.54 | | $11.00 |
| Mutual fund B | 8.92 | $39.33 | $34.96 |

Mutual fund A is described in the example of Section 2.5.5.
Mutual fund B is described in this exercise.
Risk costs are for investments of $100.00.

What do you recommend? We recommend the 3-year U.S. Treasury note in Table C.14, with a mean yield of 7.79 percent or the 10-year U.S. Treasury note in Table C.13, with a mean yield of 8.58 percent.

### ■ 2.7.10 Risk Exposure in Construction

Review the example of risk exposure in construction in Section 2.5.6. Calculate the risk cost for the other work packages in the example.

Under what circumstance would you assume dependence or independence among these work packages? What approach would you use to derive composite risk determinant factors as functions of your assumptions?

Derive the composite risk determinant factors for both assumptions.

**SOLUTION**

Table C.16 lists data for the other work packages in the example of Section 2.5.6. The total for all the other work packages is £30 million. The maximum possible value for CRDF is 4 — the number of RDF inputs to the values of CRDF. We divide the CRDF values by 4 and obtain the following values normalized with respect to unity:

| | |
|---|---|
| Demolition CRDF: | 0.5 |
| Piling CRDF: | 1.3 |
| Diaphragm Wall CRDF: | 1.6 |
| Superstructure CRDF: | 1.2 |
| Fire Protection CRDF: | 1.1 |
| Drylining CRDF: | 1.3 |
| Air Handling Pods CRDF: | 2.4 |
| Toilet Pods CRDF: | 2.3 |
| Suspended Ceilings CRDF: | 2.4 |
| Raised Floors CRDF: | 1.8 |

## Appendix C • Solutions

We multiply the values of CRDF and the respective values of factored BCE, and obtain the following values of risk cost (**RC**):

| | |
|---|---|
| Demolition RC: | £1.0 |
| Piling RC: | £5.2 |
| Diaphragm Wall RC: | £4.8 |
| Superstructure RC: | £3.6 |
| Fire Protection RC: | £4.4 |
| Drylining RC: | £6.5 |
| Air Handling Pods RC: | £7.2 |
| Toilet Pods RC: | £6.9 |
| Suspended Ceilings RC: | £4.8 |
| Raised Floors RC: | £1.8 |

The total RC equals £46.2 million. The sum of this value of RC and the value of RC from the example in Section 2.5.6 is £46.2 million + £43.175 million, or £89.375 million. Risk cost estimate is the sum of BCE and RC. The total project RCE is £125 million + £89.375 million, or £214.375 million.

***Table C.16*** *Worksheet for Other Work Packages in Risk Exposure in Construction Exercise*

| Work Package | BCE £M | RDF-1 | RDF-2 | RDF-3 | RDF-4 | CRDF | Factored £BCE |
|---|---|---|---|---|---|---|---|
| Demolition | 2 | – | – | – | 0.5 | 0.5 | 1.0 |
| Piling | 4 | 0.4 | 0.3 | – | 0.6 | 1.3 | 5.2 |
| Diaphragm Wall | 3 | 0.6 | 0.4 | – | 0.6 | 1.6 | 4.8 |
| Superstructure | 3 | 0.5 | 0.4 | – | 0.3 | 1.2 | 3.6 |
| Fire Protection | 4 | 0.4 | 0.3 | – | 0.4 | 1.1 | 4.4 |
| Drylining | 5 | 0.6 | 0.4 | – | 0.3 | 1.3 | 6.5 |
| Air Handling Pods | 3 | 0.6 | 0.7 | 0.8 | 0.3 | 2.4 | 7.2 |
| Toilet Pods | 3 | 0.6 | 0.7 | 0.7 | 0.3 | 2.3 | 6.9 |
| Suspended Ceilings | 2 | 0.7 | 0.5 | 0.5 | 0.7 | 2.4 | 4.8 |
| Raised Floors | 1 | 0.3 | 0.4 | 0.6 | 0.5 | 1.8 | 1.8 |
| Totals: | 30 | | | | | | 46.2 |

RDF-1: Complexity of design risk determinant factor.
RDF-2: Level of technological innovation risk determinant factor.
RDF-3: Complexity of off-site construction risk determinant factor.
RDF-4: Complexity of on-site construction risk determinant factor.
CRDF: Composite risk determinant factor.
Factored BCE: Product of baseline cost estimate and composite risk determinant factor.
Adapted by permission of AACE International, P.O. Box 1557, Morgantown, WV 26507-1557 from David H. Buchan, *Risk Analysis-Some Practical Suggestions*, Cost Engineering, January 1994.

### ■ 2.7.11 Scientific Method

Revise the configuration of 24 circles in Figure C.2 to consist only of circles at locations on the axes that are prime numbers. Determine how many rectangles or squares can be formed from the revised configuration with the four corners of each rectangle or square on four of the circles in the figure.

Review the example in Section 1.2.6 and the exercise in Section 1.5.3 of the previous chapter. Apply the methodology used therein to the solution of this exercise.

Reword this exercise so that it applies to the number of triangles that can be formed with the three corners of the triangle on three of the circles in the figure.

**Figure C.2** Configuration for Scientific Method Exercise

### SOLUTION

A prime number is an integer that has no integral factors except unity and itself, as 2, 3, 5, 7, or 11; 1 is usually excluded. Figure C.3 shows the result of revising Figure C.2 to consist only of circles at locations on the axes that are prime numbers.

The axes in this exercise are four circles by three circles. We designate the axes by $x$ and $y$, and use Equation C.19 to solve for the number of positions that could be occupied by squares or rectangles. As an aside, a square is nothing but a rectangle with four equal sides.

$$n = [(x-1) + (x-2) + ... + (x-n+1)]$$
$$\cdot [(y-1) + (y-2) + ... + (y-n+1)]. \tag{C.19}$$

Substituting $x = 4$ and $y = 3$ in Equation C.19, we obtain Equation C.20 that gives 6 · 3, or 18 as the number of positions that could be occupied.

$$n = [(4-1) + (4-2) + (4-3)] \cdot [(3-1) + (3-2)]$$
$$= 18. \tag{C.20}$$

Appendix C • Solutions

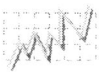

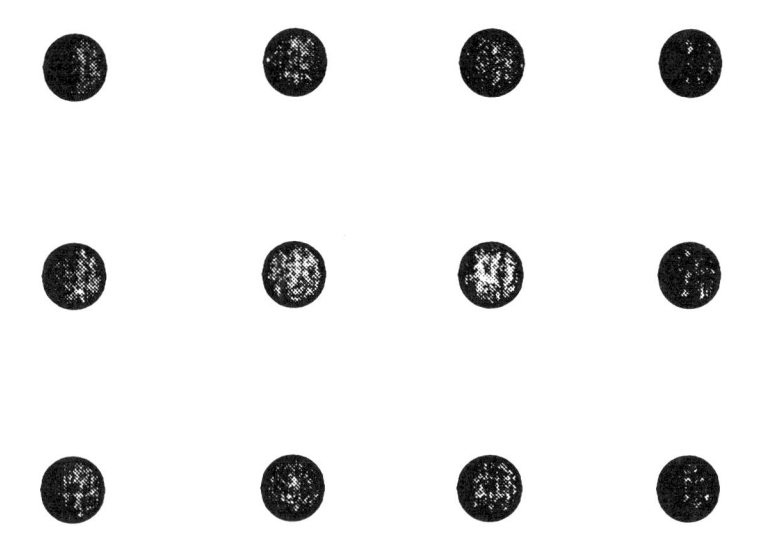

**Figure C.3** Revised Configuration for Scientific Method Exercise

We are not finished yet. Look at Figure C.4 and you will see that there are two more positions that could be occupied. But you knew that.

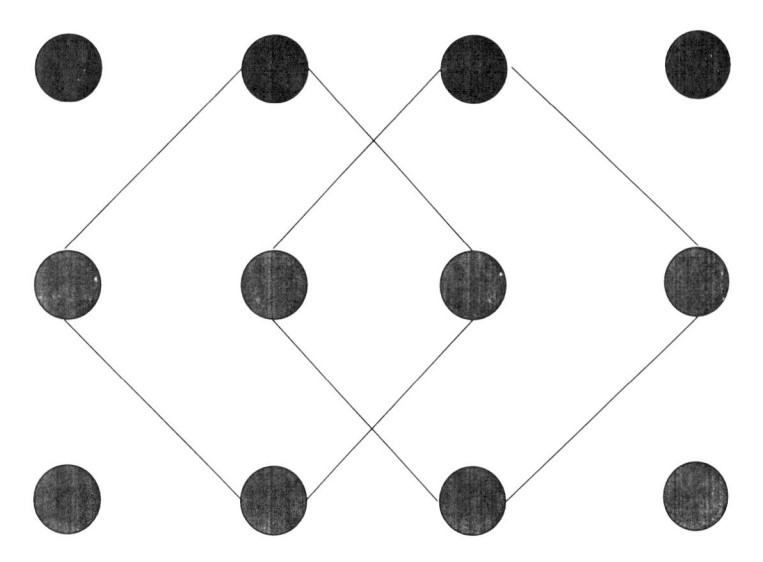

**Figure C.4** Diagonal Position

The exercise asked you to reword this exercise so that it applies to the number of triangles that can be formed with the three corners of the triangle on three of the circles in the figure. First look at the basic triangle configurations in Figure C.5.

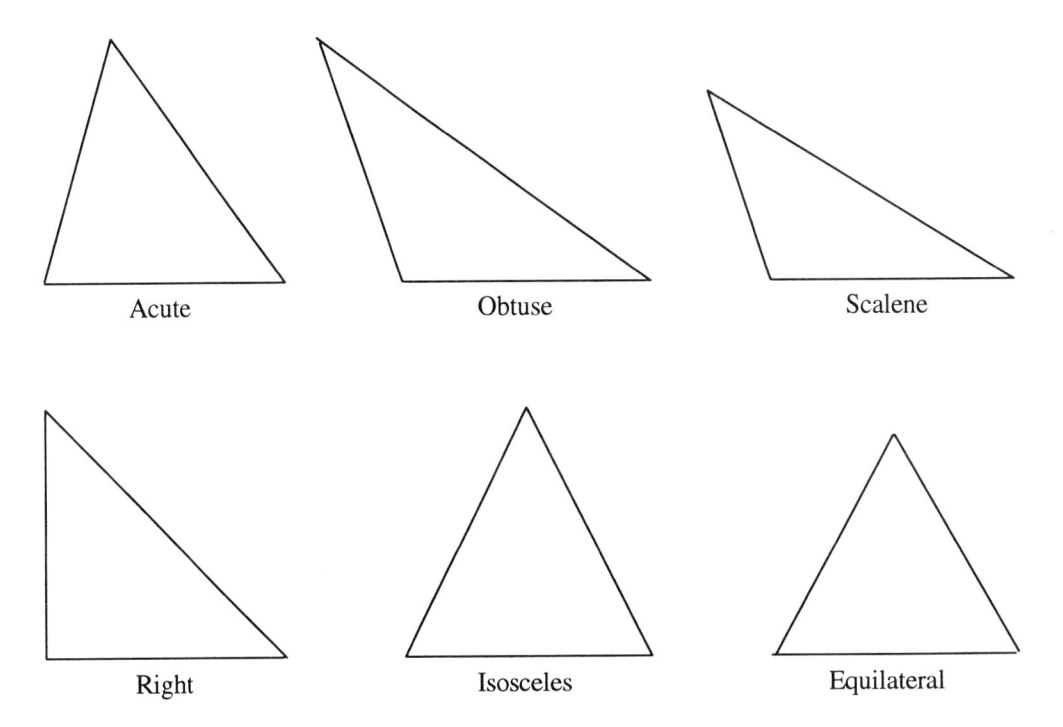

**Figure C.5** Triangle Configurations

An acute triangle is a triangle whose interior angles are all acute. An obtuse triangle contains an obtuse interior angle. A scalene triangle is a triangle with no two sides equal. A right triangle contains a 90-degree interior angle. An isosceles triangle has two sides equal. An equilateral triangle has all sides equal.

The triangle configurations have two common properties. The sum of the interior angles equals 180 degrees, and the area of triangles is one half the area of rectangles in which the triangles can be circumscribed. The latter property means that you can fit four like triangles in a circumscribing rectangle: one triangle upright; one triangle inverted; and two triangles the left images of the other two.

Your challenge in rewording this exercise so that it applies to triangles is to bring out the relationship of triangles to rectangles as a hint. The consequences of not including this hint are awesome.

### ■ 2.7.12 Probability and Statistics

Proficiency with probability and statistics is useful in technical risk management. Test your knowledge with this exercise.

Appendix C • Solutions

# SOLUTION

1. Define *combination, permutation, population, sample, parameter, statistic, statistics, large sample, continuous variable, discrete variable, small sample, normal distribution, Student's t distribution, probability density function*, and *probability distribution function*.

   **Combination**: A selection of one or more items from a set of items without regard to order.
   **Permutation**: An ordered selection of one or more items from a set of items.
   **Population**: The total set of items defined by some characteristic of the items.
   **Sample**: A finite portion of a population.
   **Parameter**: A characteristic of a population.
   **Statistic**: An estimate from a sample of a parameter of a population.
   **Statistics**: Methods for obtaining and analyzing quantitative data.
   **Large sample**: Sample of 30 or more.
   **Continuous variable**: Random variable with infinitely continuous values.
   **Discrete variable**: Random variable with step values.
   **Small sample**: Sample of fewer than 30.
   **Normal distribution**: Probability density function of random variables of a population.
   **Student's *t* distribution**: Probability density of small samples of random variables of a population.
   **Probability density function**: A function whose integral over a set gives the probability that a random variable has values in this set.
   **Probability distribution function**: A function giving the cumulative frequency corresponding to the various values of a variable.

2. Define the *central limit theorem* and the *law of large numbers*.

   **Central limit theorem**: Distributions of samples of populations approach normality with increased sample size.
   **Law of large numbers**: Irrespective of probability distribution, the sample mean and sample variance converge on population mean and variance as a random sample of size $n$ approaches population size.

3. Define *mean, median, mode, variance,* and *standard deviation*.

   **Mean**: Average value of variables in a statistical distribution.
   **Median**: Most frequently occurring variable in a statistical distribution.
   **Mode**: The largest valued variable occurring in a statistical distribution.
   **Variance**: Measure of dispersion in data comprising a statistical distribution.
   **Standard deviation**. The standard deviation is the statistical measure of dispersion.

4. Define and enumerate *tests of hypothesis*.

   **Tests of hypothesis**: Tests of the validity of assumptions about population parameters to specified confidence levels. The hypothesis relates to means and variances.

5. What are the statistical measures of central tendency and dispersion?

   **Mean and standard deviation**

6. Calculate the mean, median, mode, variance, and standard deviation for the sample data in Table C.17.

**Table C.17** *Sample Data for Probability and Statistics Exercise*

| 16 | 41 | 29 |
|----|----|----|
| 14 | 36 | 20 |
| 25 | 12 | 18 |
| 42 | 49 | 17 |
| 23 | 26 | 35 |
| 10 | 15 | 42 |
| 33 | 25 | 19 |
| 18 | 42 | 27 |

**SOLUTION**

Table C.18 is the worksheet for calculating the mean, median, mode, and standard deviation for the sample data. We begin by arranging the data in descending order.

The mean ($m$) of the sample in Table C.18 is 634 ÷ 24, or 26.42. We use Equation C.14 to calculate the variance ($s^2$) with $\Sigma(x_i - m) = 2,880.72$ and $n = 24$, and obtain

$$s^2 = \frac{2,880.72}{24 - 1}$$
$$= 125.25. \qquad (C.21)$$

The standard deviation is the square root of 125.25, or 11.19.

7. Which statistical distribution would you use to model the sample data in Table C.18? State your reason.

**SOLUTION**

Use the Student's $t$ distribution because the sample size is less than 30.

**Table C.18** *Worksheet for Probability and Statistics Exercise*

| $x_i$ | $(x_i - m)^2$ | $x_i$ | $(x_i - m)^2$ |
|-------|---------------|-------|---------------|
| 10 | 269.62 | 25 | 2.02 |
| 12 | 207.94 | 26 | 0.18 |
| 14 | 154.26 | 27 | 0.34 |
| 15 | 130.42 | 29 | 6.66 |
| 16 | 108.58 | 33 | 43.30 |
| 17 | 88.74  | 35 | 73.62 |
| 18 | 70.90  | 36 | 91.78 |
| 18 | 70.90  | 41 | 212.58 |
| 19 | 55.06  | 42 | 242.74 |
| 20 | 41.22  | 42 | 242.74 |
| 23 | 11.96  | 42 | 242.74 |
| 25 | 2.02   | 49 | 509.86 |

$\Sigma x_i = 634$

$m = 634 \div 24 = 26.42$
$(x_i - m)^2 = 2,880.72$

*Appendix C • Solutions*

8. Calculate the 95 percent confidence limits about the mean of the sample data in Table C.17.

**SOLUTION**

We use Equation C.22 to calculate the 95 percent confidence limits (CL) about the mean.

$$CL = m \mp \frac{ts}{\sqrt{n}} \quad (C.22)$$

where $m$ denotes the mean, $t$ the $t$-statistic, and $s$ the standard deviation.

The value of the $t$-statistic is a function of the degrees of freedom and the required significance level. We obtain values of the $t$-statistic from tables of the Student's $t$ distribution in statistics books such as Berenson, Mark L., David M. Levine, *Statistics for Business and Economics*, Second Edition, Prentice Hall, 1993.

Although the significance level equates to the area in both tails of the Student's $t$ probability density function, most statistical tables are based on the area in one tail. Because of the symmetry of the density function, we enter the table at one-half the value of the required significance level.

The degrees of freedom equal $n - 1$, the sample size minus one. In this case, $n = 24$ and the degrees of freedom are $24 - 1$, or 23. The significance level is equal to one-half of one minus confidence level. This equates to the area in one tail of the Student's $t$ probability density function.

At a confidence level of 0.95, $1 - 0.95$ equals 0.05. One-half of 0.05 equals 0.025. We enter the table of the Student's $t$ distribution at degrees of freedom equal to 23 and significance level equal to 0.025 and read $t$ equals 2.069. This is the value of the $t$-statistic we use in Equation C.23.

Substituting $m = 26.42$, $t = 2.069$, $s = 11.19$, and $n = 23$ in Equation C.22, we obtain the answer in Equation C.23. The confidence interval equals 4.82. The confidence limits about the mean are 26.42 $\mp$ 4.82, or 21.60 or 31.24.

$$CL = 26.42 \mp \frac{(2.069)(11.19)}{\sqrt{23}}$$

$$= 26.42 \mp 4.82$$

$$= 21.60, 31.24. \quad (C.23)$$

The meaning of Equation C.23 is that 95 percent of the time the value of the mean of other samples drawn from the governing population will fall between 21.60 and 31.24.

### ■ *3.9.1 Metrics*

State the metric form for one millionth of a second and one billionth of a second.

**SOLUTION**

The metric form for one millionth of a second and one billionth of a second are the microsecond and the nanosecond. You might be interested in Table C.19.

*Table C.19   Metric Prefixes and Multipliers*

| Prefix | Symbol | Multiplier |
|---|---|---|
| atto | a | 0.000000000000000001: $10^{-18}$ |
| femto | f | 0.000000000000001: $10^{-15}$ |
| pico | p | 0.000000000001: $10^{-12}$ |
| nano | n | 0.000000001: $10^{-9}$ |
| micro | $\nu$ | 0.000001: $10^{-6}$ |
| milli | m | 0.001: $10^{-3}$ |
| centi | c | 0.01: $10^{-2}$ |
| deci | d | 0.1: $10^{-1}$ |
| deka | da | 10: $10^{1}$ |
| hecto | h | 100: $10^{2}$ |
| kilo | k | 1,000: $10^{3}$ |
| mega | M | 1,000,000: $10^{6}$ |
| giga | G | 1,000,000,000: $10^{9}$ |
| tera | T | 1,000,000,000,000: $10^{12}$ |
| peta | P | 1,000,000,000,000,000: $10^{15}$ |
| exa | E | 1,000,000,000,000,000,000: $10^{18}$ |

### ■ 3.9.2 Scientific Method

January 1, 1995, occurred on a Sunday. Use the scientific method to determine the day of the week on which the first day of January will occur in the years 2004 and 2104.

**SOLUTION**

If there were 364 days in each year, each day of the month would occur on the same day of the week in each successive year. There are, however, 365 days in each year, and each day of the week occurs a day later in each successive year. Each day of the week occurs two days later in successive leap years.

You could labor on a solution as follows: January 1, 1995, occurred on a Sunday. January 1, 1996, will occur on a Monday. The year 1996 is a leap year, therefore January 1, 1997, will occur on a Wednesday. January 1, 1998, will occur on a Thursday. January 1, 1999, will occur on a Friday. January 1, 2000, will occur on a Saturday. The year 2000 is a leap year, therefore January 1, 2001, will occur on a Monday. January 1, 2002, will occur on a Tuesday. January 1, 2003, will occur on Wednesday. Finally, January 1, 2004, will occur on a Thursday.

This is a lot of work; imagine how much more there would be in calculating the day of the week on which January 1, 2104, will occur. We can avoid much of this ordeal with the day of the week algorithm in Table C.20.

Before we address the algorithm, let us consider leap years. Leap years occur every four years in years exactly divisible by four, but years ending in the digits 00 must be divisible by 400 to be leap years. Thus the years 1996, 2000, 2004, 2104 are leap years, whereas the years 2100 and 2500 are not. We insert a leap day, February 29, after February 28 in the leap years. Each century has 25 leap days.

Appendix C • Solutions

**Table C.20** Day of the Week Algorithm

1. Call the earlier day, month, and year the referenced date, and the later day, month, and year the shifted date.
2. Calculate the number of lapsed years by subtracting the reference year from the shifted year.
3. Calculate the number of lapsed days by multiplying the number of lapsed years by 365 and adding to the answer the number of leap days in the lapsed years.
4. Calculate the number of lapsed weeks by dividing the number of lapsed days by seven.
5. The answer consists of an integer and a fraction. The numerator of the fraction is the number of days to shift from the referenced day of the week to the shifted day of the week.

Our referenced date is January, 1, 1995. The shifted dates are January 1, 2004, and January 1, 2104. Subtracting 1995 from 2004, we obtain nine lapsed years. Multiplying 9 by 365, we obtain 3,285. There are two leap years between the referenced and shifted dates (*i.e.*, 1996 and 2000) so we add two leap days to the 3,285 lapsed days for a total of 3,287 lapsed days. We divide 3,287 lapsed days by seven and obtain 469-4/7 weeks. We shift the referenced day of the week, Sunday, four (*i.e.*, the numerator in 4/7) days to Thursday, the day of the week on which January 1, 2004, will occur.

Next we subtract 1995 from 2104, and obtain 109 lapsed years. Multiplying 109 by 365, we obtain 39,785 lapsed days. There are 27 leap years between the referenced and shifted dates so we add 27 leap days to the 39,785 lapsed days for a total of 39,812 lapsed days. We divide 39,812 lapsed days by seven and obtain 5687-3/7. We shift the referenced day of the week, Sunday, three (*i.e.*, the numerator in 3/7) days to Wednesday, the day of the week on which January 1, 2104, will occur.

### ■ 3.9.3 Confidence Level in Risk Exposure

Consider the example of risk exposure in highway and roadway construction in Section 3.2.2. The risk exposure, in terms of risk cost, was estimated at $15,475.

Estimate the risk cost at confidence levels of 0.80, 0.90, and 0.95. Use the rainfall statistics in Section 3.2.2, with an assumed standard deviation of 1.41 days. Select the probability density function and state your reason. On the basis of your findings, would you recommend the purchase of weather insurance?

**SOLUTION**

We use the normal distribution to model the exercise because of the large size sample of 50 years of data. We use Equation C.24 to calculate the confidence limits (CL) about the mean.

$$CL = m \mp \frac{zs}{\sqrt{n}} \qquad (C.24)$$

where $m$ denotes the mean of the data, $z$ the $z$-statistic in the normal probability density function, $s$ the standard deviation, and $n$ the sample size.

The value of $m$ is 5.74 days and is the average number of days that rainfall during the month of May exceeded 0.01 inch over the past 50 years in Mobile. The value of the $z$-statistic is a function of the required significance level.

We obtain values of the $z$-statistic from tables of the normal distribution in statistics books such as Berenson, Mark L., David M. Levine, *Statistics for Business and Economics*, Second Edition, Prentice Hall, 1993. Although the significance level equates to the area under the curve of the normal probability density function between the minus and plus values of the $z$-statistic, most statistical tables are based on the area under the curve from the mean to the plus value of the $z$-statistic. Because of the symmetry of the density function, we enter the table at one-half the value of the required significance level.

At a confidence level of 0.80, $1 - 0.80$ equals 0.20. One-half of 0.20 equals 0.10. We enter the table of the normal distribution at the area under the curve of 0.10, and discover to our chagrin that there are entries for 0.0987 and 0.1026, but not 0.10. To avoid the need to interpolate, we generated Table C.21 that gives values of the $z$-statistic as functions of the area ($A$) under the curve of the normal probability density function between the minus and plus values of the $z$-statistic.

**Table C.21**    z-Statistic as a Function of Area Under the Curve

| A | z | A | z |
|---|---|---|---|
| 0.50 | 0.0 | 0.80 | 1.28 |
| 0.55 | 0.06 | 0.85 | 1.44 |
| 0.60 | 0.84 | 0.90 | 1.64 |
| 0.65 | 0.94 | 0.95 | 1.96 |
| 0.70 | 1.04 | 0.99 | 2.58 |
| 0.75 | 1.15 | | |

We first address the confidence level of 0.80, which from Table C.21 yields $z = 1.28$. Substituting $m = 5.74$ days, $z = 1.28$, $s = 1.41$ days, and $n = 50$ (*i.e.*, the number of years of data) in Equation C.24, we obtain

$$CL = 5.74 \mp \frac{(1.28)(1.41)}{\sqrt{50}}$$

$$= 5.74 \mp 0.26$$

$$= 5.48, 6.00 \text{ days.} \quad (C.25)$$

We repeat the calculations in Equations C.26 and C.27 with $z = 1.64$ for a confidence level of 0.90 and $z = 1.96$ for a confidence interval of 0.95.

$$CL = 5.74 \mp \frac{(1.64)(1.41)}{\sqrt{50}}$$

$$= 5.74 \mp 0.33$$

$$= 5.41, 6.07 \text{ days.} \quad (C.26)$$

$$CL = 5.74 \mp \frac{(1.96)(1.41)}{\sqrt{50}}$$

$$= 5.74 \mp 0.39$$

$$= 5.35, 6.13 \text{ days.} \quad (C.27)$$

## Appendix C • Solutions

In calculating risk cost, we use the upper values of the confidence limits, 6.00, 6.07, and 6.13 days, that correspond to confidence intervals of 0.80, 0.90, and 0.95. The baseline cost estimate of indirect elements of cost in Gulf Construction will be $25,000 per day during the month of May. This is the cost that will continue irrespective of whether or not the company places the roadway foundation. The values of the risk cost are the products of the probability of rainfall exceeding 0.01 inch on each of the five days and $25,000.

Equation C.28 is the relationship for calculating the probability of a day with excessive rain, given that it has not rained during the month of May. Equations C.29 through C.32 are the relationships for calculating the probability of a day with excessive rainfall given that it has already rained on one, two, three, and four days.

$$P = \frac{6.00}{31 \, \text{days}}$$
$$= 0.194. \quad (C.28)$$

$$P = \frac{5.00}{30 \, \text{days}}$$
$$= 0.167. \quad (C.29)$$

$$P = \frac{4.00}{29 \, \text{days}}$$
$$= 0.138. \quad (C.30)$$

$$P = \frac{3.00}{28 \, \text{days}}$$
$$= 0.107. \quad (C.31)$$

$$P = \frac{2.00}{27 \, \text{days}}$$
$$= 0.074. \quad (C.32)$$

Note the successive change in the sample space in the numerators and denominators of Equations C.28 to C.32.

The risk cost for the first day of rain, for a confidence level of 0.80, is the product of $P = 0.194$ and $25,000, or $4,850. The risk cost values for the second, third, fourth, and fifth days are in the first column of Table C.22, the worksheet for our risk cost calculations. The risk exposure is the sum of the individual risk cost for each of the five days.

**Table C.22**  *Worksheet for Risk Exposure with Confidence Intervals*

| 0.80 Significance Level | 0.90 Significance Level | 0.95 Significance Level |
|---|---|---|
| **Day 1**: (0.194)($25,000) = $ 4,850 | **Day 1**: (0.196)($25,000) = $ 4,900 | **Day 1**: (0.198)($25,000) = $ 4,950 |
| **Day 2**: (0.167)($25,000) =    4,175 | **Day 2**: (0.169)($25,000) =    4,225 | **Day 2**: (0.171)$25,000) =    4,275 |
| **Day 3**: (0.138)($25,000) =    3,450 | **Day 3**: (0.140)($25,000) =    3,500 | **Day 3**: (0.142)($25,000) =    3,550 |
| **Day 4**: (0.107)($25,000) =    2,675 | **Day 4**: (0.110)($25,000) =    2,750 | **Day 4**: (0.112)($25,000) =    2,800 |
| **Day 5**: (0.074)($25,000) =    1,850 | **Day 5**: (0.077)($25,000) =    1,925 | **Day 5**: (0.079)($25,000) =    1,975 |
| **Total**:              $17,000 | **Total**:              $17,300 | **Total**:              $17,550 |

*378*  Appendix C • Solutions

Note the risk cost values in Table C.22. Would you spend $15,000 for weather insurance? I don't know about you, but Gulf Construction probably would not.

### ■ 3.9.4 Risk Determinant Factor Categories

Scientists of the National Aeronautics and Space Administration (NASA) decided to let the sun warm parts of the *Galileo* spacecraft (*v.*, Section 1.2) in an attempt to free its jammed main antenna.

NASA hypothesizes that the antenna mast would extend sufficiently from the heat of the sun to give sufficient additional leverage to the electric motors that deploy the antenna. NASA hopes that repeating the process several times will free the antenna. It is also possible that the process will further degrade the antenna.

Assess the risk exposure in the process. In the process, should you be concerned with product or process risk determinant factors, or both categories of factors? Select the risk determinant factors to use and state your reasons for the selections.

**SOLUTION**

Heat will change the process not the product design. Therefore, we only use the process risk determinant factors to assess the risk exposure. Because of unknowns, we assign a value of unity to the composite process risk determinant factor. This means that if NASA were to invest $1 million in the attempt, the risk cost would also be $1 million and the attempt might cost $2 million before it was finished.

### ■ 3.9.5 Risk Determinant Factors for Trade Study

An electric utility company requests you to study and evaluate the relative risk exposure from investing in new facilities that would reduce operating cost versus investing in Treasury bonds that would increase operating revenue.

**SOLUTION**

Select the risk determinant factors from the categories given in Table C.23 that you will need in your evaluation of risk exposure from the two alternatives. Cite the reasons for including and excluding the various risk determinant factors.

*Table C.23*  Risk Determinant Categories

| Management Attributes | Extrinsic Attributes |
|---|---|
| Product Maturity | Process Maturity |
| Product Quality | Process Quality |
| Product Complexity | Process Complexity |
| Product Concurrency | Process Concurrency |

You would need the risk determinant factors for all the categories in Table C.23 to estimate the risk exposure in acquiring new facilities. To estimate the risk exposure in the Treasury bonds investment, you would only need the extrinsic attributes factor since your concern would be the uncertainty of the return-on-investment.

### ■ 3.9.6 Comparative Realism and Credibility

Table C.24 gives data on a product under development. The baseline cost estimate (BCE) was derived both bottom-up and top-down. The corrective-action cost (CAC) was derived bottom-up.

## Appendix C • Solutions

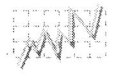

Design personnel consider the risk exposure to be low to medium. Quantify risk exposure using the guidelines in Table C.25. Calculate the risk cost estimate as illustrated in the example in Section 3.2.3.

*Table C.24* Data for Comparative Realism and Credibility Exercise

| Bottom-Up BCE | Top-Down BCE | Bottom-Up CAC |
|---|---|---|
| $720,000 | $640,000 | $180,000 |

BCE: Baseline cost estimate.
CAC: Corrective-action cost.

*Table C.25* Verbal Expressions vs. Quantified Measures of Risk Exposure

| Verbal Expression | Quantified Measure | Verbal Expression | Quantified Measure |
|---|---|---|---|
| Certain | 1.0 | Medium | 0.50 |
| Extremely High | 0.99 | Low | 0.25 |
| Very High | 0.90 | Very low | 0.10 |
| High | 0.75 | Impossible | 0 |

**SOLUTION**

As stated, design personnel consider the risk exposure to be low to medium. From Table C.25, this equates to 0.25 + 0.25 ÷ 2, or 0.375. We use this value as the risk determinant factor (RDF) in Equation C.33 to calculate the risk cost estimate (RCE) when we have a bottom-up (*i.e.*, disaggregate) baseline cost estimate (BCE).

$$RCE = BCE + (CAC)(RDF) \qquad (C.33)$$

where CAC denotes corrective-action cost.

Consider first the bottom-up BCE of $720,000 and CAC of $180,00 from Table C.24. Substituting these values in Equation C.33, we obtain

$$RCE = \$720{,}000 + (\$180{,}000)(0.375)$$

$$= \$787{,}500. \qquad (C.34)$$

We use Equation C.35 to calculate RCE when we have a top-down (*i.e.*, aggregate) BCE.

$$RCE = BCE(1 + (RDF)). \qquad (C.35)$$

Substituting the top-down BCE of $640,000 from Table C.24 in Equation C.35, we obtain

$$RCE = \$640{,}000(1 + 0.375)$$

$$= \$880{,}000. \qquad (C.36)$$

We like to think that the RCE of $787,500 is more realistic than the RCE of $880,000. It is certainly more credible.

## 3.9.7 Reverse Engineering

Sections 3.4.3 and 3.8.7 give background information on this exercise. The exercise requires you to derive values of product maturity factor which would have been applicable at the start of a development program consisting of five systems.

The systems are developed under configuration control; meaning that design changes must be approved by a Configuration Control Board (CCB) which is comprised of representatives of the customer and the contractor. The board issues notices of revision (NOR) that authorize the implementation of changes, when and only if the changes are approved by the CCB.

In general, a relatively small number of NORs, by the end of development, signifies a relatively mature product at the start of development. On the other hand, a relatively large number of NORs signifies a relatively immature product at the start. Using the data in Table C.26, construct a table of product maturity values, equating the subsystem with the smallest and largest number of NORs to PRODMF values of 0.1 and 1.0.

**Table C.26** *Notice of Revision Data for Reverse Engineering Exercise*

| System A | 540 | System B | 385 | System C | 265 |
|---|---|---|---|---|---|
| A1 | 105 | B1 | 100 | C1 | 65 |
| A2 | 150 | B2 | 85 | C2 | 40 |
| A3 | 70 | B3 | 70 | C3 | 45 |
| A4 | 110 | B4 | 80 | C4 | 55 |
| A5 | 105 | B5 | 50 | C5 | 60 |

**SOLUTION**

The number of NORs goes from 40 to 150, which is a range of 110. We equate 40 or fewer NORs to PRODMF = 0.1. There are nine more values of PRODMF that we need to consider. Dividing nine into 110 yields $12.222^+$. We use twelve NORs per increment of PRODMF and account for the cumulative fractions by equating 137 to 150 NORs to PRODMF = 1.0.

Table C.27 is the rating schema that evolves.

**Table C.27** *Product Maturity Factor Rating Schema for Reverse Engineering Exercise*

| PRODMF | NORs | PRODMF | NORs |
|---|---|---|---|
| 0.1 | 0–40 | 0.6 | 89–100 |
| 0.2 | 41–52 | 0.7 | 101–112 |
| 0.3 | 53–64 | 0.8 | 113–124 |
| 0.4 | 65–76 | 0.9 | 125–136 |
| 0.5 | 77–88 | 1.0 | 137–150 |

PRODMF: Product maturity factor.
NOR: Notice of revision.

Appendix C • Solutions

### 3.9.8 Attribute Weighting

Binary weighting is a form of positional weighting because of the influence of bit position on numerical values. Consider the binary weighting of a series of five questions.

Assume the questions are ranked in the inverse order of importance. Determine the relative weighting of the first question, which is in the most-significant bit position, with respect to each successive question in the series. How does the number of binary weights vary as a function of the number of questions in a given series? Is it possible to assign equal weighting to two or more questions under binary weighting?

**SOLUTION**

The equivalent decimal value (EDV) of a five-digit binary number of all 1s equals $1 \cdot 2^4 + 1 \cdot 2^3 + 1 \cdot 2^2 + 1 \cdot 2^1 + 1 \cdot 2^0$, or 31. Starting from the left of the sequence, the decimal positional weights are 16, 8, 4, 2, and 1.

The decimal positional weights signify that the first question is twice as important than the second, four times as important than the third, eight times as important as the fourth, and sixteen times as important as the fifth question. Ranking the questions in the inverse order of importance merely inverts the decimal position weights. The first question is still sixteen times more important than the fifth.

The number of binary weights vary directly with the number of questions in the sequence. A sequence of ten questions requires a ten-bit binary number.

The question of whether it is possible to assign equal weighting to two or more questions under binary weighting is somewhat tricky. The answer is no if the questions are part of the same sequence.

### 3.9.9 Risk Exposure in Cost Trades

An aluminum extrusion manufacturing firm needs to replace the primary power transformer that provides electricity to one of its facilities. The steady-state load of the machinery is 2,500 kilowatts (kw) with a 0.8 power factor (pf).

At the daily start-up of the facility, the transient load is 5,500 kw with a pf of 0.65. It is customary to select power transformers with a 2:1 safety margin over the steady-state load, although a transient overload of ten minutes or more could cause transformer failure.

Large power transformers are rated in kilo-volt-amperes (kva). The relationship between kw and kva is given by

$$kw = (kva)(pf) \tag{C.37}$$

where the pf typically ranges from 0.80 to 0.95.

Determine the relative cost advantage of buying and installing transformers sized for the steady-state vs. the transient load condition. Assume the probability of transformer failure from transient overload is 5 percent and the relationships for the cost of buying and the cost of installing power transformers are as follows:

$$\text{Cost of buying} = (\$100)(kva) \tag{C.38}$$

$$\text{Cost of installing} = (\$10)(kva) \tag{C.39}$$

## SOLUTION

The steady-state load of the machinery is 2,500 kw with pf = 0.8. The equivalent kva is 2,500 ÷ 0.8, or 3,125 kva. The start-up load is 5,500 kw with pf = 0.65 for the equivalent kva of 5,500 ÷ 0.65, or 8,462 kva.

Consider first, the cost of buying and installing the transformer on the basis of the steady-state load. Substituting 3,125 kva in Equations C.38 and C.39, we obtain ($100)(3,125), or $312,500 for buying, and ($10)(3,125), or $31,250 for installing. The total cost is $312,500 + $31,250, or $343,750.

The probability of failure from transient overload is 5 percent. We treat this probability as a risk determinant factor of 0.05 in calculating risk cost. The risk cost in buying and installing a transformer on the basis of steady-state load is $343,750(0.05), or $17,188, making the total cost $343,750 + $17,188, or $360,938.

Consider next the cost of buying and installing the transformer on the basis of the transient load. Substituting 8,462 kva in Equations C.38 and C.39, we obtain ($100)(8,462), or $846,200 for buying, and ($10)(8,462), or $84,620 for installing. The total cost is $846,200 + $84,620, or $930,820.

Most utilities would elect to buy and install the transformer on the basis of the steady-state load and depend on networking with other utilities for the transient load. This practice frequently leads to power blackouts over wide regions.

## POSTSCRIPT

Intel Corporation, the world's largest producer of microprocessor chips, and International Business Machines Corporation, one of the world's largest producer of personal computers, are at odds over the Pentium® chip produced by Intel. This event has drawn unprecedented reactions from computer manufacturers, suppliers, customers, users, and government.

A microprocessor is at the heart of every personal computer. The Pentium® chip, the most advanced device on the market, is capable of operating at speeds up to 90 megahertz. Earlier this year, Intel discovered that on rare occasions the chip would produce incorrect answers in double precision division. Intel elected to continue sales of the chip while correcting the anomaly because few people would be affected by the rare error.

The problem came to light when a mathematics professor discussed the anomaly on a computerized information network. One must consider just how rare is rare.

Intel claims that the chances of error are one in 9 billion for the average user of spreadsheet programs. Intel bases its contention on the typical spreadsheet program usage of 1,000 division computations per day per computer. International Business Machine claims that the typical spreadsheet program user calculates 5,000 divisions per second for 15 minutes per day increasing the error rate to one every 24 days.

International Business Machine has halted shipments of computers with the Pentium® chip. Other computer manufacturers are continuing to use the chip, but many suppliers, retailers, and customers are hesitant about buying personal computers with the chip.

The Attorney General's office in Florida informed Intel that the company may have violated the state's ban on deceptive trade practices, but that the problem would be solved if Intel were to replace the defective chip. Intel had offered to replace the chip, provided the user could demonstrate that the anomaly was inimical to the user's application. Placing the burden of proof on the user raised such an outcry that Intel changed its offer to replace the chip on request.

Appendix C • Solutions

Meanwhile, a whole new cottage industry has sprung up. A number of software developers are producing utility programs as interim solutions to the anomaly. As members of the Order of the Christophers would say, "It is better to light one little candle than to curse the darkness."

### ■ 3.9.10 Number Systems

In the decimal number system, the largest digit value is 9. In the binary number system, the largest digit value is 1. In the ternary (*i.e.*, base or radix of 3), the largest digit value is 2. State the rule that governs these relationships.

The equivalent binary value of decimal 100 is $110020_2$. Calculate the equivalent ternary value of decimal 100.

Convert decimal 12 to the equivalent octal value and the equivalent hexadecimal value.

### SOLUTION

A number system consists of a radix and base. The radix is any number that is made the base of a number system. The base of a number system evolves from the radix and is the number of units, in a given digit's place or decimal place, which must be taken to enter a 0 in the least significant place (*i.e.*, extreme right position) and a 1 in the next higher place.

**Decimal Number System**

The radix of the decimal number system is 10. The least significant place (*i.e.*, right position) is called the $10^0$, or units place, the next higher place the $10^1$, or tens place, the next higher place the $10^2$, the hundreds place, and so on. Nine, the base of 10 minus 1, is the largest permissible digit in any place.

Ten is denoted by a 1 in the tens place and a 0 in the units place. One hundred units are denoted by a 1 in the hundreds place, a 0 in the tens place, and a 0 in the units place. One hundred and nine is denoted by a 1 in the hundreds place, a 0 in the tens place, and a 9 in the units place.

**Binary Number System**

The radix and base of the binary number system are 2. The least significant place is called the $2^0$ place, the next higher place the $2^1$ place, the next higher place the $2^2$ place, and so on. One, the base of 2 minus 1, is the largest permissible digit in any place.

The equivalent binary number for the decimal number 2 is a 1 in the $2^1$ place and a 0 in the $2^0$ place for $10_2$. The equivalent binary number for decimal 100 is a 1 in the $2^6$ place, a 1 in the $2^5$ place, a 0 in the $2^4$ place, a 0 in the $2^3$ place, a 1 in the $2^2$ place, a 0 in the $2^1$ place, and a 0 in the $2^0$ place, for $1100100_2$.

Try converting the decimal numbers 128 and 1,024 to binary numbers. The subscript 2 after binary numbers is optional if the context in which binary numbers are discussed makes the use clear.

**Ternary Number System**

The radix and base of the ternary number system are 3. The least significant place is called the $3^0$ place, the next higher place the $3^1$ place, the next higher place the $3^2$ place, and so on. Two, the base of 3 minus 1, is the largest permissible digit in any place.

The equivalent ternary number for the decimal number 2 is a 2 in the $3^0$ place for $2_3$. The equivalent ternary number for the decimal number 4 is a 1 in the $3^1$ place, and a 1 in the $3^0$ place for $11_3$. The equivalent ternary number for decimal 100 is a 1 in the $3^4$ place, a 0 in the $3^3$ place, a 2 in the $3^2$ place, a 0 in the $3^1$ place, and a 0 in the $3^1$ place, and a 1 in the $3^0$ place, for $102001_3$.

## Octal Number System

The radix and base of the octal number system are 8. The least significant place is called the $8^0$ place, the next higher place the $8^1$ place, the next higher place the $8^2$ place, and so on. Seven, the base of 8 minus 1, is the largest permissible digit in any place.

The equivalent octal number for the decimal number 7 is a 7 in the $8^0$ place for $7_8$. The equivalent octal number for decimal 100 is a 1 in the $8^2$ place, a 4 in the $8^1$ place, and a 0 in the $8^0$ place, for $140_8$.

Try converting the decimal numbers 128 and 1,024 to octal numbers. The subscript 8 after octal numbers is optional if the context in which they are used makes the use clear.

## Hexadecimal Number System

The radix and base of the hexadecimal number system are 16 and the count is 1, 2, 3, 4, 5, 6, 7, 8, 9, A, B, C, D, E, F, 10, 11, 12, 13, 14, 15, 16, 17, 18, 19, 1A, 1B, 1C, 1D, 1E, 1F, 20, 21, 22, 23, and so on. The least-significant place is called the $16^0$ place, the next higher place the $16^1$ place, the next higher place the $16^2$ place, and so on. Fifteen, the base of 16 minus 1, is the largest permissible digit in any place.

The equivalent hexadecimal number for the decimal number 2 is a 2 in the $16^0$ place. The equivalent hexadecimal number for decimal 100 is a 6 in the $16^1$ place and a 4 in the $16^0$ place for $64_{16}$.

Try converting the decimal numbers 128 and 1,024 to hexadecimal numbers. The subscript 16 after hexadecimal numbers is optional if the context in which they are used makes the use clear.

### ■ 4.7.1 Constructing Precedence Diagrams

Construct the precedence diagram for the tasks in Table C.28. Determine the critical path in the network and calculate the network efficiency.

*Table C.28  Task-Precedence Chart for Constructing Precedence Diagram Exercise*

| Task | Unit Time | Predecessor | Successor |
|---|---|---|---|
| a | 0 | None | b, c, e |
| b | 10 | a | d, g |
| c | 15 | a | f, i |
| d | 5 | b | j |
| e | 15 | a | h |
| f | 5 | c | h |
| g | 10 | b | k |
| h | 5 | e, f | l |
| i | 15 | c | k |
| j | 10 | g | l |
| k | 5 | i | l |
| l | 0 | h, j, k | None |

Appendix C • Solutions

## SOLUTION

Figure C.6 is the product network for the tasks in Table C.28. The time unit is 0.1 minute, meaning that the total work-content time is (300 time units)(0.1 minute per time unit), or 30 minutes.

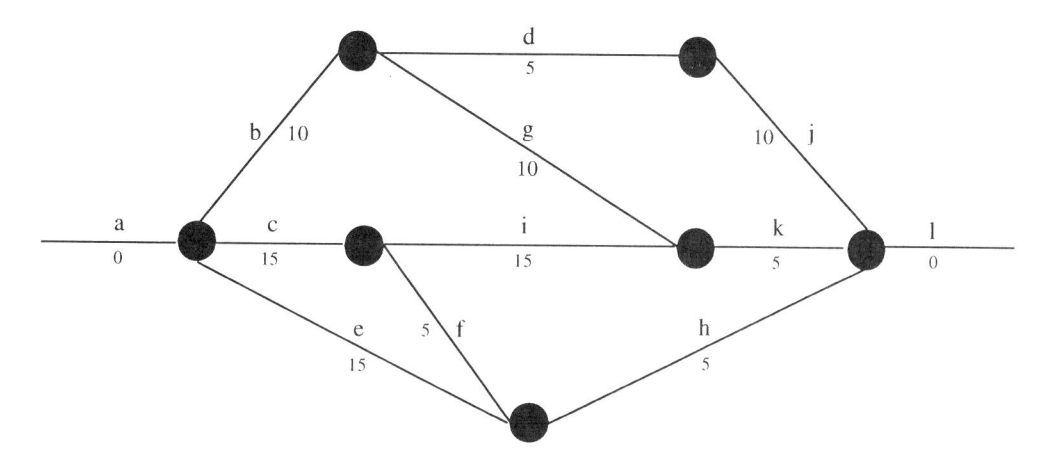

**Figure C.6** Precedence Diagram for Constructing Precedence Diagram Network

The path duration time enumeration is

Path a, b, d, j, l: 0 + 10 + 5 + 10 + 0 = 25 time units.
Path a, b, g, k, l: 0 + 10 + 10 + 5 + 0 = 25 time units.
Path a, c, i, k, l: 0 + 15 + 15 + 5 + 0 = 35 time units.
Path a, c, f, h, l: 0 + 15 + 5 + 5 + 0 = 25 time units.
Path a, e, h, l: 0 + 15 + 5 + 0 = 20 time units.

The total path duration time is 25 + 25 + 35 + 25 + 20, or 130 time units. The critical path consists of Activities a, c, i, k, l, and the critical path time is 35 time units. The path slack time enumeration is

Path a, b, d, j, l: 0 + 10 + 5 + 10 + 0 = 35 − 25, or 10 time units.
Path a, b, g, k, l: 0 + 10 + 10 + 5 + 0 = 35 − 25, or 10 time units.
Path a, c, i, k, l: 0 + 15 + 15 + 5 + 0 = 35 − 35, or 0 time unit.
Path a, c, f, h, l: 0 + 15 + 5 + 5 + 0 = 35 − 25, or 10 time units.
Path a, e, h, l: 0 + 15 + 5 + 0 = 35 − 20, or 15 time units.

The total slack time is 10 + 10 + 0 + 10 + 15, or 45. Equation C.40 gives the efficiency of the network.

$$E = \frac{(\text{Total path time} - \text{total slack time})}{(\text{Total path time})}$$

$$= \frac{130 - 45}{130}$$

$$= 0.65. \tag{C.40}$$

## 4.7.2 Balancing Production Lines

Distribute the twelve tasks in Table C.29 among four work stations for the best possible production-line balance. Calculate the resultant network efficiency.

**SOLUTION**

The natural tendency is to establish as many work stations as there are paths in the network and to assign to each work station the activities on the respective paths. Table C.29 is the result of such action.

Note that we maintain the activity flow at work stations by indicating 0 time units for activities performed at other work stations. For example, Activity b requires 10 time units at Work Station 1 and 0 time units at Work Station 2.

Equation C.41 is the relationship for calculating network efficiency (E) with respect to production line balance.

$$E = \frac{\Sigma tu}{nc} \tag{C.41}$$

where $\Sigma tu$ denotes the total work-content time in time units, $n$ the number of work stations, and $c$, which ordinarily denotes cycle time (*i.e.*, the time between production of successive units), in this case denotes the maximum work-content time at the work stations.

Low values of product network efficiency signifies that only a few work stations are fully occupied and time is being wasted at other work stations waiting for work to arrive.

*Table C.29  Work Station Assignments for Balancing Production Lines Example*

| Activities at Work Station 1 | Time Units | Activities at Work Station 4 | Time Units |
|---|---|---|---|
| a | 0 | a | 0 |
| b | 10 | c | 0 |
| d | 5 | f | 5 |
| j | 10 | h | 5 |
| l | 0 | l | 0 |
| Total: | 25 | Total: | 10 |
| Work Station 2 | | Work Station 5 | |
| a | 0 | a | 0 |
| b | 0 | e | 15 |
| g | 10 | h | 0 |
| k | 5 | l | 0 |
| l | 0 | | |
| Total: | 15 | Total: | 15 |
| Work Station 3 | | | |
| a | 0 | | |
| c | 15 | | |
| i | 15 | | |
| k | 0 | | |
| l | 0 | | |
| Total: | 30 | Total work content: | 95 |

Appendix C • Solutions

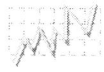

Substituting $\Sigma tu = 95\ tu$, $n = 5$, and $c = 30\ tu$ (i.e., the work content at Work Station 3) in Equation C.41, we obtain

$$E = \frac{95\ tu}{(5)(30\ tu)}$$

$$= 0.63. \qquad (C.42)$$

In the first iteration of reassigning activities to work stations, we begin by reducing the number of work stations to two. Table C.30 gives the result of the action.

Substituting $\Sigma tu = 95\ tu$, $n = 2$, and $c = 50\ tu$ (i.e., the work content at Work Station 3) in Equation C.41, we obtain

$$E = \frac{95\ tu}{(2)(50\ tu)}$$

$$= 0.95. \qquad (C.43)$$

You could improve the production line further by dividing an activity such as k in half and assigning a half to each work station. This action would increase $E$ to 1.0.

*Table C.30* Work Station Assignments for Balancing Production Lines Example

| Activities at Work Station 1 | Time Units | Activities at Work Station 2 | Time Units |
| --- | --- | --- | --- |
| a | 0 | a | 0 |
| b | 10 | c | 15 |
| c | 0 | e | 15 |
| d | 5 | f | 5 |
| g | 10 | h | 5 |
| i | 15 | i | 0 |
| j | 10 | k | 5 |
| k | 0 | l | 0 |
| l | 0 | | |
| **Subtotal:** | 50 | **Subtotal:** | 45 |
| | | **Total work content:** | 95 |

### ■ 4.7.3 Deriving Standard Data for Job Families

Table C.31 gives set-up and operation motion-element times which were observed during ten production runs for a certain product. Derive standard data for this particular job family using the equation of regression for set-up and operation. Calibrate the standard data against the observed data.

**SOLUTION**

The exercise asks you to derive equations for the regression of set-up time and operation time. Essentially, the exercise wants you to examine the learning from job to job.

In this exercise the dependent variables are set-up time and operation time, and the independent variable is the job number. The data in Table C.31 are samples of the respective populations. The equation of regression for samples uses the method of least squares that ensures the best fit of the line of regression to the data.

The solution of the equation of regression is straightforward, although tedious when a large number of variates are involved in the solution. Fortunately, spreadsheet programs for personal computers can afford you this capability.

We enter the job number as the independent variable, and set-up time as the dependent variable. The spreadsheet program we use gives us the equation of regression for set-up time on job number in Equation C.44. Next we enter the job number as the independent variable, and set-up time as the dependent variable. The spreadsheet program we use gives us the equation of regression for operation time on job number in Equation C.45.

*Table C.31  Motion-Element Time Data for Deriving Standard Data for Job Families*

| Job | Set-Up | Operation | Job | Set-Up | Operation |
|-----|--------|-----------|-----|--------|-----------|
| 1 | 103.95 | 3.25 | 6 | 99.95 | 2.65 |
| 2 | 103.90 | 3.15 | 7 | 98.75 | 2.65 |
| 3 | 102.65 | 3.00 | 8 | 98.65 | 2.55 |
| 4 | 102.00 | 2.85 | 9 | 97.05 | 2.50 |
| 5 | 100.55 | 2.70 | 10 | 96.25 | 2.45 |

Set-up and operation times are in minutes.
Operation time is per-unit.

$$y_i = (105.29 - 0.89x_i) \text{ minutes.} \tag{C.44}$$

$$y_i = (3.26 - 0.09x_i) \text{ minutes.} \tag{C.45}$$

Table C.32 compares the observed data and the data calculated with the equations of regression. For Job 1, the observed set-up and operation times are within 0.43 percent and 2.52 percent of the regression times. For Job 5, the observed set-up and operation times are within 0.59 percent and 4.07 percent of the regression times. For Job 10, the observed set-up and operation times are within 0.15 percent and 3.81 percent of the regression times.

*Table C.32  Comparison Data for Deriving Standard Data for Job Families*

| | Observed | | Regression | |
|---|---|---|---|---|
| Job | Set-Up | Operation | Set-Up | Operation |
| 1 | 103.95 | 3.25 | 104.40 | 3.17 |
| 5 | 100.55 | 2.70 | 100.84 | 2.81 |
| 10 | 96.25 | 2.45 | 96.39 | 2.36 |

Set-up and operation times are in minutes.
Operation time is per-unit.

### ■ 4.7.4 Learning Curves in Service Products

The benefits of learning from repetitious operations are not the exclusive domain of the manufacturing sector of the economy. Service companies are beginning to dominate the gross national product of the world and could benefit considerably from employee learning.

Appendix C • Solutions

According to an article in *The Service 500*, May 30, 1994, FORTUNE, the 1993 sales of the 100 largest diversified service companies in the world exceeded $2 trillion. On the other hand, the profit of these companies was only about $5 billion, which is less than 0.215 percent of sales. The average sales per employee of the companies amounted to $637,294.

Assume that labor is 60 percent of sales of these companies and that employees operate on a 99 percent learning curve. Calculate the increase in profit for the companies if employees were to operate on a learning curve of 95 percent. What value of learning curve would you apply to the service industry?

**SOLUTION**

This exercise does not give you too much information and you can only obtain an approximation of the increase in profit from reducing labor cost. Nonetheless, approximations are useful, but should be identified clearly as such.

The exercise tells you that sales exceeded $2 trillion, profit was $5 billion, and labor is 60 percent of sales. Therefore, labor cost was ($2 trillion)(0.6), or $1.2 trillion. Overall cost was $2 trillion − $5 billion, or $1.995 trillion.

In essence, the exercise asks you to determine how much labor cost would be reduced if personnel were to operate on a learning curve of 95 percent instead of 99 percent. The simplest approach is to apply the ratio of the two percentages to the labor cost for (95 ÷ 99)($1.2 trillion), or $1.1515$^+$ trillion. The symbol $^+$ denotes a repeating decimal fraction.

Try using the ratio of the slopes of the two learning curves. Equation C.46 gives the relationship for slope $b$ as a function of the learning curve.

$$b = \frac{\text{Log learning curve}}{\log 2} \quad \text{(C.46)}$$

where the learning curve is expressed as a decimal fraction.

The slope $b$ of 95 percent and 99 percent learning curves are:

$$b = \frac{\text{Log } 0.95}{\log 2}$$

$$= \frac{-0.02228}{0.30103}$$

$$= -0.0740 \quad \text{(C.47)}$$

$$b = \frac{\text{Log } 0.99}{\log 2}$$

$$= \frac{-0.004365}{0.30103}$$

$$= -0.0145 \quad \text{(C.48)}$$

Applying the ratio of the two slopes to the labor cost yields an answer of (0.0145 ÷ 0.07409)($1.2 trillion), or $235.135 billion. Which value of reduced labor cost would you present to your management, $235.135 billion or $1.1515$^+$ trillion?

Present the larger figure. Using the ratio of learning curve percentages is the right thing to do when estimating cost improvement.

The exercise also asks what value of learning curve would you apply to the service industry. The service industry is very labor intensive despite the use of computers and machinery. In general, you should apply learning curves in the range 75 to 85 percent.

## 4.7.5 Learning Curve Selection

Consider the lowest and highest values of operation time in Table 4.55 as the time needed to produce the last and first units in a lot. Derive the learning curve for the operation time.

**SOLUTION**
Equation C.49 gives the relationship for calculating learning-curve improvement.

$$y_x = ax^b \tag{C.49}$$

where $y_x$ is an amount of resource needed to produce Unit $x$, $a$ the amount of resource needed to produce the first unit, and $b$ the slope of the learning curve.

Substituting $y_x = 2.45$ time units, $x = 10$, and $a = 3.25$ time units in Equation C.49, we obtain

$$2.45 \text{ time units} = (3.25 \text{ time units})10^{-b}$$

$$b = -(\log 3.25 + \log 2.45)$$

$$= -0.13. \tag{C.50}$$

Equation C.51 gives the relationship for the learning curve as a function of the slope $b$.

$$\text{Learning curve} = \text{Antilog } 0.30103b \tag{C.51}$$

where the value 0.30103 is the logarithm to the base 10 (*i.e.*, common logarithm) of 2.

For $b = -0.13$, the learning curve equals the antilogarithm of $(0.3013)(-0.13)$, or 0.9138. This is a learning curve of 91.38 percent.

## 4.7.6 Learning Curve Confidence Interval

Repeat the example in Section 4.3.10 for a confidence level of 0.80. Under what circumstances would you use the lower and upper confidence limits?

**SOLUTION**
We use the following information from the example in Section 4.3.10:

1. The large sample is from a normally distributed population allowing the use of the $z$-statistic.
2. The sample size ($n$) is 132.
3. The mean ($m$) equals 2.183 hours.
4. The standard deviation ($s$) equals 0.470 hour.
5. The time ($a$) to produce the first unit is 3.000 hours.

We first calculate the lower and upper confidence limits (CL) about the mean ($m$) with Equation C.52.

$$CL = m \mp \frac{sz}{\sqrt{n}} \tag{C.52}$$

From Table 4.30, we determine that $z = 1.28$ for the confidence level of 0.8. Substituting $m = 2.183$ hours, $s = 0.470$ hour, $z = 1.28$, and $n = 132$ in Equation C.52 we obtain

$$CL = 2.183 \mp \frac{(0.470)(1.28)}{\sqrt{132}}$$

$$= 2.183 \pm 0.0524$$

$$= 2.131, \ 2.235 \text{ hours.} \tag{C.53}$$

Appendix C • Solutions

We next solve for the slope of the learning curve $b$ for the lower limit of 31 hours with Equation C.49.

$$2.131 \text{ time units} = (3.000 \text{ time units})10^b$$
$$b = (\log 2.131 - \log 3.000)$$
$$= -0.149 \qquad (C.54)$$

We then solve for the learning curve for $b = -0.149$ with Equation C.51.

$$\text{Learning curve} = \text{Antilog } 0.30103\,(-0.149)$$
$$= 0.902 \qquad (C.55)$$

The learning curve for 2.131 hours is 0.902, or 90.2 percent.

We now calculate the learning curve for the upper limit of 2.235 hours. Replacing 2.131 hours in Equation C.54 with 2.235 hours, we obtain the value $b = -0.128$. Replacing $-0.149$ with $-0.128$ in Equation C.55, we obtain 0.915, or 91.5 percent, as the learning curve for 2.235 hours.

Did you notice that more hours for the last unit yields a learning curve percentage that is greater than the learning curve percentage for fewer hours? Of course you did.

### ■ 4.7.7 Learning Curve Discontinuity

Consider the manufacturer of high-technology products who experienced a prolonged labor strike. Prior to the time of the strike, the average unit cost of a particular product was $2,000 when produced in a continuous run of 1,000 units on a learning curve of 90 percent. After the strike, the cost of the first unit produced was $7,250. Calculate the start-up efficiency which applied.

**SOLUTION**

We first calculate the cost to produce the first unit under the initial conditions. We do this with Equation C.56, which is Equation 4.24 with the terms rearranged.

$$a = y_u[1 + (1 - LC)]^{\log_2 x} \qquad (C.56)$$

where $a$ denotes cost to produce the first unit, $y_u$ unit cost, $LC$ learning curve, and $x$ quantity produced.

Substituting $y_u = \$2{,}000$, $LC = 0.90$, and $x = 1{,}000$ in Equation C.56, we obtain

$$a = \$2{,}000[1 + (1 - 0.90)]^{\log_2 1{,}000}$$
$$= \$2{,}000(1.1)^{9.966}$$
$$= \$5{,}171. \qquad (C.57)$$

The cost of the first unit produced after the strike was $7,250. Therefore, the start-up efficiency was ($7,250 − $5,171) ÷ 5,171, or 0.402.

### ■ 4.7.8 Parametric Estimate

A hypothetical, parametric, cost-estimating relationship for production of a dual jet-engine aircraft, in a quantity of one, is given by

$$C = \$(V^2)(W^2) \qquad (C.58)$$

where $C$ denotes estimated cost in thousands of dollars, $V$ cruising velocity in knots, and $W$ cargo weight in tons.

Assuming $V = 450$ knots and $W = 10$ tons, estimate the cost of the aircraft. Which of the two variables makes the greatest contribution to the cost of the aircraft?

**SOLUTION**
Substituting $V = 450$ knots and $W = 10$ tons in Equation C.58, we obtain

$$\begin{aligned} C &= \$(450^2)(10^2) \\ &= \$(202,500)(100) \\ &= \$20,250,000. \end{aligned} \tag{C.59}$$

The contribution to cost from velocity is greater than that of weight.

### ■ 4.7.9 Cost Projections

Section 4.7.9 gives background information on this exercise regarding the proposition of a very large commercial transport (VLCT). The exercise asks you to envision:

1. Problems in accommodating the aircraft at departure and arrival gates.
2. Problems in accommodating so many people and their luggage.
3. Major technical problems and risk determinant factors hampering the development and production of the VLCT.
4. Commercial viability in the next century's air transportation market.
5. The kind of organizational structure to operate the system.
6. The number of yearly passengers for successful operation.
7. The possibility for success of such a large undertaking by an international joint venture.
8. Risk determinant factors in the areas of funding, management, and work division among the venture members.
9. The development and production of risk time and cost.

**SOLUTION**
Problems of accommodating aircraft of the size and speed of the VLCT, the number of passengers, and amount of luggage will be orders of magnitude greater than those with jumbo jets. The VLCT will require dedicated runways, multi-lane gates, and mammoth luggage conveyors. The issues would be suitable locations and cost.

Reliability, maintainability, human factors, and safety will offer the greatest risk exposure in development and production. Test and evaluation will be extensive. The issue of noise suppression will be enormous.

Commercial viability of the VLCT will depend on convenience as well as cost. The cost problems of the Concorde come from the few airports allowing it to operate. The VLCT will not be successful with a fare structure similar to that of the Concorde.

The ideal organizational structure would be similar to that of the more successful American airlines. Irrespective of how the system is funded or owned, the chain of command should be short and direct from the policy-making level to the operational level. Boeing Company Airbus Industrie sees a market of about 1,500 aircraft by the year 2010. The 1,000-passenger aircraft would have to

*Appendix C • Solutions*

fly at least once weekly with at least 90 percent capacity to be commercially successful. This suggests the need of about 70 million passengers per year for successful operation.

Just about every attribute in the extrinsic attribute factor and management attribute factor will be at work contributing to risk exposure. Funding and control will be primary issues. Governments view contractual awards as the means for reducing unemployment. Work division will be contested severely.

VLCT principals estimate the development baseline cost estimate to be about $15 billion. It is not unreasonable to expect this estimate to grow by a factor of two to four as time goes by. With regard to production cost, it is also not unreasonable to expect the unit cost of production models to be two to four times the cost of today's jumbo jet.

### ■ 4.7.10 Benefit-Cost Ratio

A certain public health institution wishes to issue $50 million of bonds for a new facility and contemplates a time period of 15 or 25 years for redeeming the bonds. Typically, interest on such bonds is paid semi-annually. The prevailing interest rate is 8.0 percent compounded daily. Calculate and compare the benefit-cost ratios for the two time periods.

**SOLUTION**

We use Equation C.60 to calculate the present value of a future single payment.

$$PV = \frac{FP}{(1+i)^n} \quad (C.60)$$

where $PV$ denotes present value, $FP$ future payment, $i$ interest rate, and $n$ number of time intervals in the term.

For the time period of 15 years, we substitute $FP = \$50,000,000$, $i = 0.08 \div 365$, or $0.000219178$, and $n = (15)(365) + 4$ for leap years, or 5,479 days, in Equation C.60 and obtain the answer in Equation C.61.

For the time period of 25 years, we replace the value $n = 5,479$ in Equation C.61 with $n = (25)(365)$ plus six days for leap years, or 9,131, and obtain the answer in Equation C.62

$$PV = \frac{\$50,000,000}{(1+0.00021918)^{5,479}}$$
$$= \frac{\$50,000,000}{3.32259026}$$
$$= \$15,048,500. \quad (C.61)$$

$$PV = \frac{\$50,000,000}{(1+0.00021918)^{9,131}}$$
$$= \frac{\$50,000,000}{7.3971518}$$
$$= \$6,759,358. \quad (C.62)$$

The benefit is the amount received from the sales of the bonds less the present value of the amount to be redeemed at the end of the appropriate time period. For the time period of 15 years, the benefit is $50,000,000 − $15,048,500, or $34,951,500. For the time period of 25 years, the benefit is $50,000,000 − $6,759,358, or $43,240,642.

We now turn to the cost part of the benefit-cost ratio. The cost is the present value of the series of uniform semi-annual interest payments. The amount of the semi-annual interest payment is ($50,000,000)(0.08 ÷ 2), or $2,000,000.

We use Equation C.63 to calculate the amount of the present value of the uniform series of semi-annual interest payments.

$$PV = SP \frac{1 - (1 + i)^{-n}}{i} \tag{C.63}$$

where $PV$ denotes present value, $SP$ single payment, $i$ interest rate, and $n$ the number of time intervals in the term.

For the time period of 15 years, we substitute $SP$ = $2,000,000, $i$ = 0.08 ÷ 2, or 0.04, and $n$ = (15)(2) or 30 half-years, in Equation C.63 and obtain the answer in Equation C.64

$$PV = \$2,000,000 \; \frac{1 - (1 + 0.04)^{-30}}{0.04}$$

$$= \$34,584,067. \tag{C.64}$$

For the time period of 15 years, the benefit-cost ratio is $34,951,500 ÷ $34,584,067, or 1.011.

For the time period of 25 years, we replace of the value $n$ = 30 in Equation C.64 with the value $n$ = (25)(2) or 50 half-years, and obtain the answer in Equation C.65.

$$PV = \$2,000,000 \; \frac{1 - (1 + 0.04)^{-50}}{0.04}$$

$$= \$42,964,369. \tag{C.65}$$

For the time period of 25 years, the benefit-cost ratio is $43,240,642 ÷ $42,964,369, or 1.006.

What do you conclude from this exercise? The longer the time period for redemption of the bonds, the greater is the benefit-cost ratio.

### ■ 4.7.11 Internal Rate of Return

Repeat the example of trial and error for internal rate of return (IRR) in Section 4.5.14 over a term of seven years. Account for the change in IRR.

### SOLUTION

Specifically, the exercise asks you to determine the IRR of an investment of $100 million with an estimated net annual return of $20 million over a term of seven years.

We use Equation C.66 as the relationship for equating these values and solve for IRR by trial and error.

$$\$100,000,000 = \$20,000,000 \; \frac{1 - (1 + i)^{-7}}{i} \tag{C.66}$$

where $i$ is the value of IRR to be determined.

The fractional term in the right-hand side of Equation C.66 must equal 5 for the equation to be an equality. We substitute $i$ = 0.10 in the fractional term and obtain the value 5.13158 for the

Appendix C • Solutions

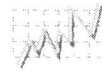

fractional term. We next substitute $i = 0.101$ in the fractional term, obtaining 5.04856, and $i = 0.102$, obtaining 4.96739.

The value of IRR lies between 0.101 and 0.102, and it usually suffices to say that the IRR is 0.101, or 10.1 percent. Equation C.67 gives a precise value by interpolation.

$$IRR = 0.101 + (0.102 - 0.101)\frac{4.96739}{5.04856}$$
$$= 0.10198. \quad (C.67)$$

### ■ 4.7.12 Cost of Inflation

Table 747 in the *Statistical Abstract of the United States: 1994* gives consumer price indexes by groups for the time period of 1960 through 1993. Estimate what one dollar of energy in the Year 1993 would cost in the Year 2000.

**SOLUTION**

We use the regression of energy price indexes only on the Years 1986 through 1993 because of the abnormally high prices in previous years. Table C.33 lists the data we use in a spreadsheet program.

*Table C.33*  Energy Price Indexes for Cost of Inflation Exercise

| Year | Index | Year | Index |
|------|-------|------|-------|
| 1986 | 88.2  | 1990 | 102.7 |
| 1987 | 88.6  | 1991 | 102.5 |
| 1988 | 89.3  | 1992 | 103.0 |
| 1989 | 94.3  | 1993 | 104.2 |

The years, numbered 1 through 8 for the spreadsheet program, are the independent variates $x_i$ and the price indexes are the dependent variates $y_i$. Equation C.68 is the equation of regression produced by the program.

$$y_i = 84.17 + 2.76x_i. \quad (C.68)$$

Year 2000 is number 15. We substitute $x_i = 15$ in Equation C.68, and obtaining 84.17 + 2.76(15), or 125.57 we find the forecasted energy price index for Year 2000.

### ■ 4.7.13 Coefficient of Determination

Derive the coefficient of determination for the equation of regression in the example of the forecasting producer price index in Section 4.5.17. Compare the coefficient of determination to the coefficient of correlation and describe the significance of the coefficient of determination in this exercise.

**SOLUTION**

The aforementioned spreadsheet program also calculates the coefficient of determination along with the derivation of the equation of regression. We use the data in Table C.34 for this purpose.

**Table C.34**  *Producer Price Indexes for Coefficient of Determination Example*

| Year | Index | Year | Index |
|------|-------|------|-------|
| 1970 | 34.4  | 1989 | 204.4 |
| 1980 | 183.9 | 1990 | 172.6 |
| 1985 | 123.4 | 1991 | 143.1 |
| 1988 | 219.5 | 1992 | 138.3 |

Year 1970 is number 1, year 1980 is number 11, year 1985 is number 16, and years 1988 through 1992 are numbers 19 through 23 for the spreadsheet program. The program calculates the coefficient of determination as 0.429, or 42.9 percent.

This value means that 42.9 percent of the time, the equation of regression governs price indexes as functions of year numbers. The other 57.1 percent of the time, the price indexes are being driven by some other variable. The coefficient of correlation is a factor describing the correlation between price indexes and year numbers and is the square root of the coefficient of determination. In this exercise, the value of the coefficient of correlation is the square root of 0.429, or 0.655.

### ■ 5.9.1 Risk Determinant Factor Dominance

Define the meaning of *first-order risk determinant factor*, *second-order risk determinant factor*, and k-*factor*. Give an example of the *k*-factor in operation.

**SOLUTION**
A first-order risk determinant factor is a quantified risk determinant that is dominant over other risk determinants. A second-order risk determinant factor is the quantified risk determinant that is dominated. The *k*-factor describes the degree of dominance on a scale of 0 to 1.0 and is equated to the product or process maturity factor.

For a product maturity factor (PRODMF) of 0.3 for a particular item, the *k*-factor equals 0.3. Given a product quality factor (PRODQF) of 0.8, the factored PRODQF is (0.3)(0.8), or 0.24. PRODMF is a measure of job familiarity. The rationale for the *k*-factor is that if you do a job often enough you will do it well, irrespective of the other attributes of the job.

### ■ 5.9.2 Hardware Risk Determinant Factors

Enumerate the risk determinant factors used to derive risk exposure in hardware products. Which factors are dominant?

**SOLUTION**
The hardware risk determinant factors are product and process maturity, product and process quality, product and process complexity, and product and process complexity. Product and process maturity are the dominant hardware factors.

Appendix C • Solutions

## 5.9.3 Extrinsic Attribute Checklist

Consider a tire manufacturing company, located in Ohio, that ships its products all over the world, all year round. What extrinsic attributes limit the company's ability to produce and ship its products?

Tailor the extrinsic attribute checklists for use by the company to estimate the risk exposure due to the extrinsic attributes of tires for large trailer trucks and those for passenger vehicles. What steps would you take to reduce the contribution of extrinsic attributes to risk exposure?

**SOLUTION**
Table C.35 is the extrinsic attribute factor checklist that we use in exercises such as this.

*Table C.35   Extrinsic Attribute Factor Checklist*

|  | Yes | No |
|---|---|---|
| 1. Are inflation, the producer price index, and the prime interest rate relatively stable? | | |
| 2. Do contracts contain economic price adjustment clauses? | | |
| 3. Are there adequate stockpiles of price-sensitive material? | | |
| 4. Is waste disposal compatible with environmental regulations? | | |
| 5. Are production processes compatible with industrial safety regulations? | | |
| 6. Can facilities operate under all weather conditions? | | |
| 7. Do personnel have all weather access to facilities? | | |
| 8. Can all weather receipt of supplies and delivery of finished goods be affected? | | |

Every attribute in Table C.35 applies to the tire manufacturing company and we do not recommend tailoring of the checklist. The steps we would take to reduce the contribution of extrinsic attributes to risk exposure is to ensure activities can be performed under all weather conditions.

## 5.9.4 Composite Management Attribute and Extrinsic Attribute Factors

Calculate the composite risk determinant factor for a management attribute factor of 0.3 and an extrinsic attribute factor of 0.5 for the company in the example of Section 5.4.4. Would you assume a dependent or independent relationship between the two factors and why?

**SOLUTION**
We calculate the composite risk determinant factor (CRDF) on either an additive or root-sum-of-squares (RSS) basis depending on whether the relationship between the management attribute factor and extrinsic attribute factor is dependent or independent. In general, management philosophy and policy are functions of extrinsic attributes and the relationship is one of dependency.

Therefore, we calculate CRDF on an additive basis for 0.3 + 0.4, or 0.0.7. On an RSS basis, CRDF equals the square root of 0.3 square plus 0.4 square, or 0.5.

### ■ 5.9.5 Risk Cost Estimate

Consider the following sets of values for hardware risk determinant factors and baseline cost estimates (BCE). Calculate and compare the two values of risk cost estimates.

PRODMF: 0.25    PRODQF: 0.50    BCE: $2.5 million
PRODMF: 0.50    PRODQF: 0.25    BCE: $2.5 million

**SOLUTION**
PRODMF is dominant over PRODQF. For *PRODMF* = 0.25, k-*factor* = 0.25 and *PRODQF* equals (0.25)(0.5), or 0.125. For *PRODMF* = 0.50, k-*factor* = 0.50 and *PRODQF* equals (0.50)(0.25), or 0.125.

Since both sets of values have the same value of BCE, we need make only one calculation. The value of the composite RDF is (0.125 + 0.125) ÷ 2, or 0.125. We are obliged to use Equation C.69 because we have no estimate of corrective-action cost

$$RCE = BCE(1 + RDF). \tag{C.69}$$

Substituting $BCE$ = $2.5 million and $RDF$ = 0.125 in Equation C.69, we obtain $2,500,000 • (1 + 0.125), or $2,812,500.

### ■ 5.9.6 Revised Risk Cost Estimate

Assume the risk cost value of $500,000 in the preceding exercise. Recalculate the risk cost estimates using Equations C.69 and C.70. Which answer do you consider more realistic and credible?

**SOLUTION**
Given $RC$ = $500,000, we can use Equation C.70.

$$RCE = BCE + RC \cdot RDF. \tag{C.70}$$

Substituting $BCE$ = $2,500,000, $RC$ = $500,000, and $RDF$ = 0.125 in Equation C.70, we obtain $2,500,000 + ($500,000)(0.125), or $2,562,500.

Not knowing the circumstances, we do not know which of the two answers is more realistic. The smaller value of RCE will probably be more likeable, if not more credible, to management. It is worthwhile repeating the dictum that analysts should only provide facts. Management should provide judgment and opinion.

### ■ 5.9.7 Hardware Product Complexity Factor

Values of the hardware product complexity factor are estimated from the number of levels and span of the generation breakdown (GB). What do you call the product of the number of levels and the span in a GB? Given ten levels and a span of 250, estimate the PRODCF of a certain hardware product.

Appendix C • Solutions

Assume a baseline cost estimate of $125,000 and risk cost of $50,000. Calculate the risk cost estimate. Include PRODMF = 0.25 and recalculate the risk cost estimate. Explain the difference in the answers.

**SOLUTION**

The product of the number of levels and the span of the GB is called the generation breakdown index (GBI). A GB with ten levels and a span of 250 has a GBI of (10)(250), or 2,500. In accordance with Table C.36, the value of PRODCF would be midway between 0.2 and 0.3, or 0.25.

*Table C.36*  *Hardware Product Complexity Factor*

| Factor | GBI | Factor | GBI |
| --- | --- | --- | --- |
| 0.1 | 1,000 | 0.6 | 6,000 |
| 0.2 | 2,000 | 0.7 | 7,000 |
| 0.3 | 3,000 | 0.8 | 8,000 |
| 0.4 | 4,000 | 0.9 | 9,000 |
| 0.5 | 5,000 | 1.0 | 10,000 |

GBI: Generation breakdown index.

We use Equation C.70 to calculate the risk cost estimate. Substituting *BCE* of $125,000, *PRODCF* of 0.25 for RDF, and *RC* of $50,000 in the equation, we obtain $125,000 + $50,000(0.25), or $137,500.

We again use Equation C.70 to calculate the risk cost estimate. The PRODMF of 0.25 serves as the *k*-factor. Substituting *BCE* of $125,000, *PRODCF* of 0.25, or 0.125 for *RDF*, and *RC* of $50,000, we obtain $125,000 + $50,000(0.125), or $131,250. The dominance of PRODMF accounts for the difference in this case.

### ■ 5.9.8 Generation Breakdowns and Lists of Part Numbers

Computer-mechanized generation breakdowns and list of part numbers usually appear in tabular form. Derive the computer-mechanized generation breakdown for a radial saw. Calculate the generation breakdown index and estimate the hardware product and process complexity factors.

Obtain the net selling price for a ten-inch radial saw. Derive the portion of the price attributable to risk exposure from product and process complexity.

**SOLUTION**

The net selling price for a certain ten-inch radial saw is $450.00. The GB has eight levels and a span of 200 for a GBI of (8)(250), or 2,000. In accordance with Table C.36, the GBI of 2,000 equates to *PRODCF* = 0.2.

The hardware process complexity factor (PROCCF) is a function of the number of assemblies, the number of subassemblies per assembly, the number of details per subassembly, and the number of parts per detail. An exploded view of the saw shows that there are eight assemblies. The maximum number of subassemblies per assembly is six, the maximum number of details per subassembly is nine, and the maximum number of parts per detail is ten. In accordance with Table C.37, the value of PROCCF is 0.40.

*Table C.37  Hardware Process Complexity Factors*

| PROCCF | Part Numbers | PROCCF | Part Numbers |
|---|---|---|---|
| 0.0 | 2-5 Assemblies<br>2-5 Subassemblies per assembly<br>6-10 Details per subassembly<br>6-10 Parts per detail | 0.6 | 11-20 Assemblies<br>11-20 Subassemblies per assembly<br>11-20 Details per subassembly<br>11-20 Parts per detail |
| 0.1 | 2-5 Assemblies<br>6-10 Subassemblies per assembly<br>6-10 Details per subassembly<br>6-10 Parts per detail | 0.7 | 11-20 Assemblies<br>20-10 Subassemblies per assembly<br>11-20 Details per subassembly<br>11-20 Parts per detail |
| 0.2 | 6-10 Assemblies<br>6-10 Subassemblies per assembly<br>6-10 Details per subassembly<br>6-10 Parts per detail | 0.8 | 11-20 Assemblies<br>21-30 Subassemblies per assembly<br>21-30 Details per subassembly<br>11-20 Parts per detail |
| 0.3 | 6-10 Assemblies<br>11-20 Subassemblies per assembly<br>6-10 Details per subassembly<br>6-10 Parts per detail | 0.9 | 11-20 Assemblies<br>21-30 Subassemblies per assembly<br>21-30 Details per subassembly<br>11-20 Parts per detail |
| 0.4 | 6-10 Assemblies<br>11-20 Subassemblies per assembly<br>11-20 Details per subassembly<br>6-10 Parts per detail | 1.0 | 11-20 Assemblies<br>21-30 Subassemblies per assembly<br>21-30 Details per subassembly<br>21-30 Parts per detail |
| 0.5 | 6-10 Assemblies<br>11-20 Subassemblies per assembly<br>11-20 Details per subassembly<br>11-20 Parts per detail | | |

PROCCF: Process complexity factor.

## ■ 5.9.9 Hardware Product and Process Complexity Factors

Given the baseline cost estimate of $25 million, calculate the risk cost estimate for the PRODCF value of 0.6 and the PROCCF value of 0.8 with respective *k*-factors of 0.8 and 0.6.

**SOLUTION**

We assume an independent relationship between PRODMF and PROCMF and use Equation C.71 to calculate the risk cost estimate (RCE).

$$RCE = BCE\sqrt{(k \bullet PRODCF)^2 + (k \bullet PROCCF)^2} \tag{C.71}$$

Appendix C • Solutions

Substituting $BCE = \$25,000,000$, $PRODCF = 0.6$ with $k = 0.8$, and $PROCCF$ of 0.8 with $k = 0.6$ in Equation C.71, we obtain

$$RCE = \$25,000,000 \left(1 + \sqrt{(0.8 \bullet 0.6)^2 + (0.6 \bullet 0.8)^2}\right)$$

$$= \$41,970,563. \qquad (C.72)$$

### ■ 5.9.10 Risk Exposure in Total Procurement Package

Section 5.9.10 gives background information for this exercise. Consider the total procurement package in Table C.38.

*Table C.38*   *Total Procurement Package Data*

|      | Development | Production Nonrecurring | Production Recurring | Total |
|------|-------------|-------------------------|----------------------|-------|
| BCE: | 250         | 150                     | 400                  | 800   |
| BTE: | 36          | 18                      | 48                   | 102   |
| AIC: | 3           | 3.5                     | 3.5                  | Per month |

BCE: Baseline cost estimate.
BTE: Baseline time estimate.
AIC: Additional indirect cost.
Costs are in $ million.

Estimate the risk exposure for the following values of hardware product risk determinant factors:

PRODMF = 0.2   PRODQF = 0.3   PRODCF = 0.2   PRODYF = 0.2
PROCMF = 0.1   PROCQF = 0.1   PROCCF = 0.1   PROCYF = 0.3.

**SOLUTION**

We assume dependent relationships among the hardware product factors and among the hardware process factors. We first apply $k$-factors to the appropriate risk determinant factors. For PRODMF = 0.2, $k = 0.2$ for the product factors or PROCMF = 0.1, $k = 0.1$ for the process factors.

The resultant factors are

PRODMF = 0.2                    PROCMF = 0.1
PRODQF = (0.2)(0.3) = 0.06      PROCQF = (0.1)(0.3) = 0.03
PRODCF = (0.2)(0.2) = 0.04      PROCCF = (0.1)(0.2) = 0.02
PRODYF = (0.2)(0.2) = 0.04      PROCYF = (0.1)(0.2) = 0.02.

The value of the product CRDF is 0.2 + 0.06 + 0.04 + 0.04, or 0.34. The value of the process CRDF is 0.1 + 0.03 + 0.02 + 0.02, or 0.17.

We assume independence between product and process CRDFs in this exercise. We begin by calculating their individual risk time estimates (RTE) and risk cost estimates (RCE).

For the product CRDF of 0.34, RTE equals (3 months)(1 + 0.34), or 4.02 months. RCE equals ($250,000,000)(1 + 0.34), or $335,000,000. The additional indirect cost of $3,000,000 per month for the increased period of (4.02 − 3) months, or 1.02 months is ($3,000,000 per month)(1.02 months), or $3,060,000.

For the process CRDF of 0.17 during the production nonrecurring phase, RTE equals (18 months)(1 + 0.17), or 21.06 months. RCE equals ($150,000,000)(1 + 0.17), or $175,500,000. The additional indirect cost of $3,500,000 per month for the increased period of (21.06 − 18) months, or 3.06 months is ($3,500,000 per month)(3.06 months), or $10,710,000.

For the process CRDF of 0.17 during the production recurring phase, RTE equals (48 months)(1 + 0.17), or 56.16 months. RCE equals ($400,000,000)(1 + 0.17), or $468,000,000. The additional indirect cost of $3,500,000 per month for the increased period of (56.16 − 48) months, or 8.166 months is ($3,500,000 per month)(8.16 months), or $28,560,000.

Under the assumption of dependency between development and production, the total value of RCE is $335,000,000 + $3,060,000 + $175,000,000 + $10,710,000 + $468,000,000 + $28,560,000, or $1,020,330,000. This is 27.5 percent more than the BCE of $800 million in Table C.38.

### ■ 5.9.11 Software Risk Determinant Factors

Enumerate the risk determinant factors used to derive risk exposure in software products. Which are the dominant factors? How many combinations of first-order and second-order software risk determinant factors can you form?

**SOLUTION**

The first-order risk determinant factors (RDFs) are management attribute, extrinsic attribute, and product and process maturity. The dominant RDFs are product maturity and process maturity. The second-order RDFs are product quality, complexity, and concurrency, and process quality, complexity, and concurrency.

Remember that development and production RDFs are mutually exclusive, meaning one or the other can apply at the same time, but not both. The exercise wants you to calculate the number of combinations you can form from the three development and three process second-order RDFs and then add the numbers to account for the two dominant first-order RDFs.

We use Equation C.73 to calculate the number of combinations $c$ which can be formed from $n$ items taken $r$ at a time.

$$c = \frac{n!}{r!\,(n-r)!} \tag{C.73}$$

where $n!$ and $r!$ denote the factorials of $n$ and $r$.

We solve Equation C.73 first for combinations of one, two, and three for the three second-order RDFs. Substituting $r = 1$ and $n = 3$ we obtain

$$\begin{aligned} c &= \frac{3!}{1!\,(3-1)!} \\ &= \frac{6}{1\,(2)} \\ &= 3. \end{aligned} \tag{C.74}$$

For $r = 2$ and $n = 3$, we obtain

$$\begin{aligned} c &= \frac{3!}{2!\,(3-2)!} \\ &= \frac{6}{2\,(1)} \\ &= 3. \end{aligned} \tag{C.75}$$

Appendix C • Solutions

For $r = 3$ and $n = 3$, we obtain

$$c = \frac{3!}{3!(3-3)!}$$
$$= \frac{6}{6(1)}$$
$$= 1. \tag{C.76}$$

Note that by mathematical convention, $0! = 1$.

We sum the foregoing number of combinations, obtaining $3 + 3 + 1$, or 7 for each of the second-order RDFs. Doubling 7 to account for the two first-order dominant RDFs, the number of combinations are 14.

### ■ 5.9.12 Software Management Attribute Factor

Describe the purpose of the software management attribute factor and how it is used. Does a dependent or independent relationship exist among the attributes of the software management factor?

**SOLUTION**

The purpose of the software management attribute factor is to assess the contribution of management's policy on software funding and budgeting, customer and user support, program continuity, and personnel growth and retention. Generally, we assume an independent relationship among these attributes.

### ■ 5.9.13 Composite Software Risk Exposure

Given the data in Table C.39, calculate the composite software risk exposure. Assume the baseline cost estimate to complete development is $3.75 million and derive the value of the risk cost estimate.

*Table C.39* Software Development Status Data

| Status | PRODMF | PROCMF |
|---|---|---|
| Development code and unit tests completed successfully. | 0.4 | |
| Similar production unit folders compiled. | | 0.8 |

PRODMF: Product maturity factor.
PROCMF: Process maturity factor.

**SOLUTION**
We assume a dependent relationship, meaning the values of PRODMF and PROCMF are additive. The value of the risk cost estimate is $3,750,000(1 + 0.4 + 0.8), or $8,250,000.

### ■ 5.9.14 Service Risk Determinant Factors

Enumerate the risk determinant factors used to derive risk exposure in service products. Which are the dominant factors?

## SOLUTION

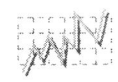

The product is the process and the process is the product in the service industry. Consequently, product and process are synonymous in the respective risk determinant factors (RDF). These are maturity, quality, complexity, and concurrency, in addition to the management attribute and extrinsic attribute RDFs.

The maturity, management attribute, and extrinsic attribute RDFs are first-order. Maturity is the dominant RDF.

### ■ 5.9.15 Risk Exposure in Service Products

Estimate the software product quality factor using the methodology of the example of Section 5.7.3 with the following answers to the checklist questions in the example:

Table 5.67: Yes, yes, yes, no, yes, no.

Table 5.68: No, no, yes, no.

Table 5.69: No, yes, no, no, no, no, yes.

Table 5.70: No, no, no, yes, yes, yes, yes.

## SOLUTION

We use binary weight to rate the sequences of answers to the aforementioned tables. We then calculate the product quality factor (PRODQF) assuming a dependent relationship among the attributes comprising the checklists.

The binary number for the answers in Table 5.67 is 111010 with the equivalent decimal value of $2^5 + 2^4 + 2^3 + 0^2 + 2^1 + 2^0$, or 58.

The binary number for the answers in Table 5.68 is 0010 with the equivalent decimal value of $0^3 + 0^2 + 2^1 + 0^0$, or 2.

The binary number for the answers in Table 5.69 is 0100001 with the equivalent decimal value of $0^6 + 2^5 + 0^4 + 0^3 + 0^2 + 0^1 + 2^0$, or 33.

The binary number for the answers in Table 5.70 is 0001111 with the equivalent decimal value of $0^6 + 0^5 + 0^4 + 2^3 + 2^2 + 2^1 + 2^0$, or 15.

The sum of the EDVs is 58 + 2 + 33 + 15, or 108.

The largest possible EDVs for Tables 5.67 through 5.70 (*i.e.*, all 1s) are 127, 63, 255, and 255 for a total of 700.

Equation C.77 gives the value of service product quality factor (PRODQF) for a dependent relationship among the attributes comprising the checklists.

$$PRODQF = \frac{700 - 100}{700}$$
$$= 0.857. \qquad (C.77)$$

Appendix C • Solutions

## ■ 5.9.16 Service Product Concurrency Factor

Modify Table 5.74 to accommodate four dependent tasks. State the general relationship between the number of dependent tasks and the size of PRODQF increments.

### SOLUTION
Table C.40 is Table 5.74 modified to accommodate four dependent tasks.

*Table C.40*   *Service Product or Process Concurrency Factor*

|  |  | Overlap | Factor |
|---|---|---|---|
| Task j | Task $k_1$ | 0 – 1.0 | 0 – 0.25 |
|  | Task $k_2$ | 0 – 1.0 | 0.25 – 0.50 |
|  | Task $k_3$ | 0 – 1.0 | 0.50 – 0.75 |
|  | Task $k_4$ | 0 – 1.0 | 0.75 – 1.00 |
| Factor: PRODYF or PROCYF. | | | |

The general relationship between increment size and the number ($n$) of tasks is $1.00 \div n$. In this case, the increment is $1.00 \div 4$, or 0.25.

## ■ 5.9.17 Risk Cost Retrospective

Section 5.9.17 gives background information on this exercise. The exercise asks you to investigate manufacturer, wholesaler, retailer, and consumer data in the *Statistical Abstract of the United States 1994*. Do you detect correlation among the data? Do you think that concepts such as just-in-time (JIT) can be as effective in the United States as it has been in Japan? State your reasons for any differences that you perceive.

### SOLUTION
There is correlation, but generally there is sufficient lag among the different sectors of the economy to make difficult the application of concepts such as JIT. JIT can be successful in vertical organizations where companies are their own suppliers.

Suppliers and buyers need assurance that concepts like JIT will not impose economic penalties. The biggest unknown is the buying habits of the American public.

## ■ 6.6.1 Parametric Relationship

Given the data in Table C.41, derive the parametric relationship for estimating the list price of vehicles as a function of weight.

**Table C.41** *Vehicle Data for Parametric Relationship Exercise*

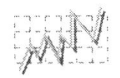

| Vehicle | List Price Dollars | Weight Pounds | Vehicle | List Price Dollars | Weight Pounds |
|---------|-------------------|---------------|---------|-------------------|---------------|
| A | 19,500 | 4,550 | F | 22,230 | 4,120 |
| B | 15,690 | 3,990 | G | 31,600 | 5,500 |
| C | 22,000 | 5,300 | H | 12,590 | 3,200 |
| D | 28,000 | 4,900 | I | 42,000 | 6,100 |
| E | 36,000 | 5,600 | J | 16,990 | 2,850 |

**SOLUTION**

We use the equation of regression for the parametric relationship and a spreadsheet computer program to derive the equation of regression. We equate weight to the independent variate ($x_i$) and dollars to the dependent variate ($y_i$) for the following:

$$y_i = -6,351.65 + 5.749650 x_i. \tag{C.78}$$

By the way, the coefficient of determination is 0.215519, which is rather poor. The interpretation is that more than 78 percent of the time the price of a vehicle is a function of factors other than weight.

### ■ 6.6.2 Law of Large Numbers

State the law of large numbers. What is the significance of the law to the modeling process? Give an example.

**SOLUTION**

Law of large numbers: "If random samples of size $n$ are drawn from populations of size $N$, irrespective of probability distributions, sample means and variances converge on population means and variances as $n$ approaches $N$."

The law of large numbers allows you to assume normality given a sample size of thirty or more. The assumption of normality allows you to use well-known statistical techniques and readily available tables of the normal distribution.

Surveys of customer preferences are typical examples of the law of large numbers in action. Other examples are the design of sampling plans for the test and evaluation of products.

### ■ 6.6.3 Central Limit Theorem

State the central limit theorem. What is the significance of the theorem to the modeling process? Give an example.

**SOLUTION**

Central limit theorem: "Regardless of original population distributions, means and variances of samples approach normality with increased sample size."

The central limit theorem allows you to assume that means and variances are from normally distributed populations given a sample size of 30 or more. The assumption of normality allows you

Appendix C • Solutions

to use well-known statistical techniques and readily available tables of the normal distribution. The examples for the law of large numbers apply to the central limit theorem.

### ■ 6.6.4 Area Under Normal Probability Density Curve

What are the $z$-statistics bounding the areas about the mean for confidence levels of 0.80, 0.90, 0.95, and 0.99? How does the magnitude of confidence intervals vary as a function of the value of $z$?

**SOLUTION**
The values of $z$ are as follows:

    Confidence level 0.80:   $\mp 1.28$
    Confidence level 0.90:   $\mp 1.64$
    Confidence level 0.95:   $\mp 1.96$
    Confidence level 0.99:   $\mp 2.58$.

The magnitude of the confidence interval varies directly with the value of the $z$-statistic.

### ■ 6.6.5 Area in Tails of Normal Probability Density Function

What are the areas in both tails for the following values of the $z$-statistic: $\mp 1$, $\mp 2$, $\mp 3$, and $\mp 4$? What are the areas in a single tail?

    $z = \mp 1$: Area = 0.6826
    $z = \mp 2$: Area = 0.9546
    $z = \mp 3$: Area = 0.9974
    $z = \mp 4$: Area = 0.9999

The areas in a single tail for any value of the $z$-statistic is one half of one minus the area within the $\mp z$ values. For example for $z = \mp 1$, area equals $(1 - 0.6826) \div 2$, or 0.1587.

### ■ 6.6.6 Degrees of Freedom

Define *degrees of freedom*. How do degrees of freedom enter into probability distributions? and statistics? Give three examples.

**SOLUTION**
Degrees of freedom are the sample size minus one. For example, a sample of size 30 has $30 - 1$, or 29, degrees of freedom.

Examples of where we use degrees of freedom are in the tables of the Student's $t$ distribution, chi-square distribution, and $F$-distribution. Areas under the curves of the respective probability density functions are functions of the number of degrees of freedom.

**POSTSCRIPT**
You saw the Student's $t$ probability density function in Figure 6.4. Figures C.7 and C.8 show the chi-square distribution and $F$-distribution probability density functions. The curves approach normality with increasing degrees of freedom. Note that there are no negative values.

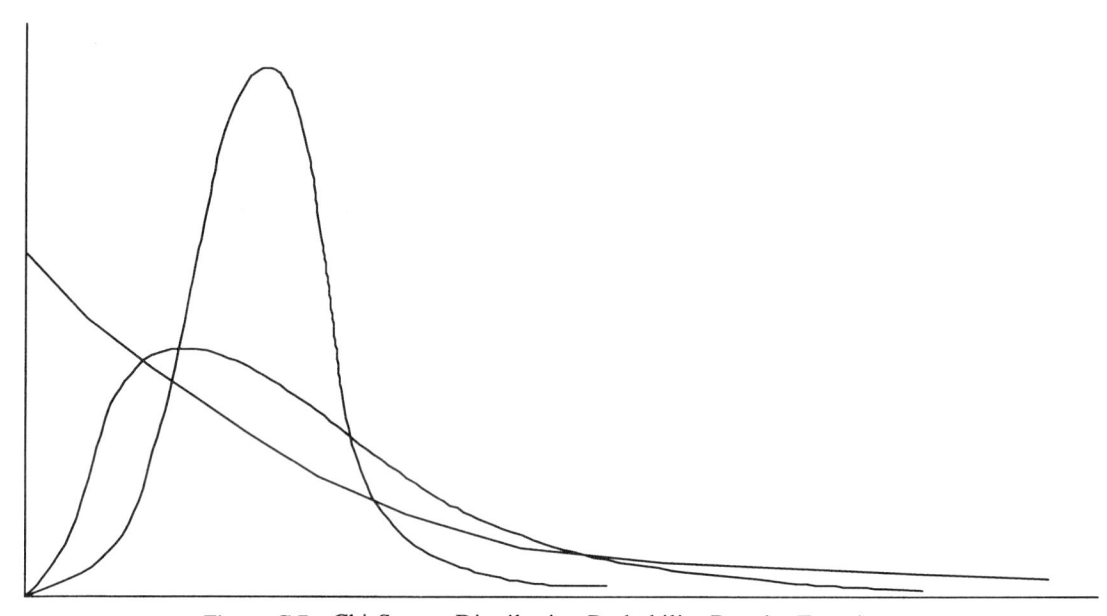

**Figure C.7** Chi-Square Distribution Probability Density Function

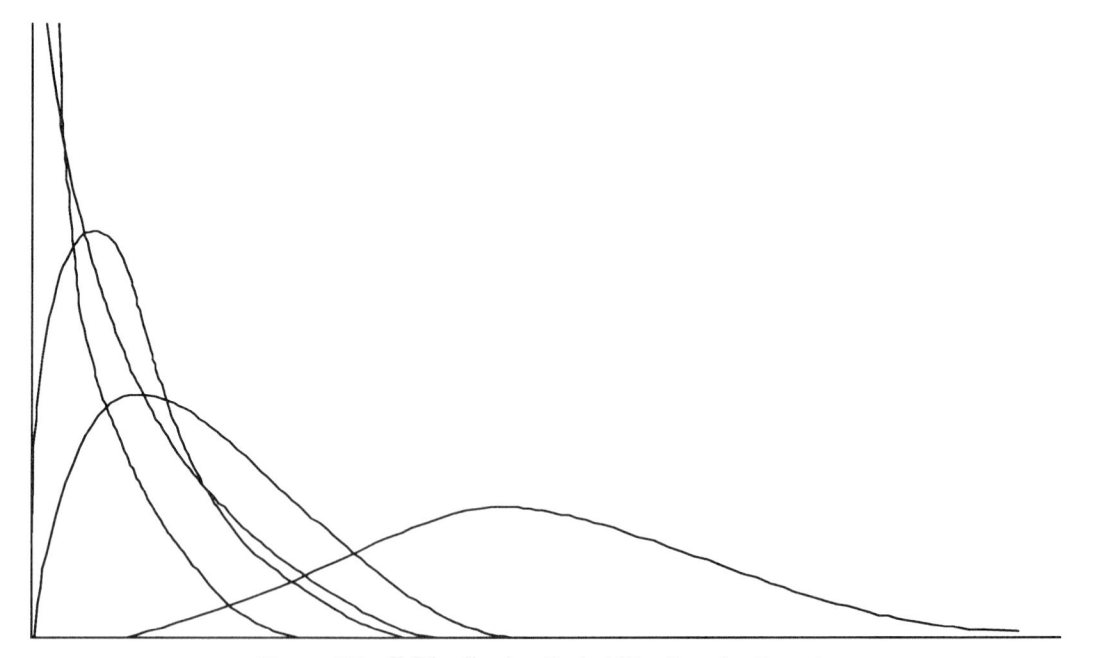

**Figure C.8** $F$-Distribution Probability Density Function

## 6.6.7 Mean and Standard Deviation

Calculate the value of the mean and standard deviation for the dependent data in Table C.42. What probability distribution would you use to model the data?

**Table C.42** Data for Mean and Standard Deviation Exercise

| 120 | 260 | 245 | 390 | 155 |
| 425 | 690 | 670 | 210 | 320 |
| 635 | 405 | 710 | 400 | 655 |
| 175 | 410 | 250 | 600 | 310 |

**SOLUTION**

We use a spreadsheet program to calculate the mean and standard deviation of the data in Table C.42. The mean equals 496.75. The standard deviation equals 433.636.

We assume the data sample is from a normal distribution. However, since the sample size is less than 30, we model the data with the Student's $t$ distribution.

## 6.6.8 Confidence Limits

Given a sample of 100 bolts with a mean of 3.05 inch and a standard deviation of 0.10 inch, calculate the confidence limits (CL) about the mean for a 90 percent confidence level.

**SOLUTION**

We assume the sample is from a normally distributed population and use Equation C.79 to calculate the confidence limits (CL) about the mean.

$$CL = m \mp \frac{sz}{\sqrt{n}} \quad \text{(C.79)}$$

where $m$ denotes means, $s$ standard deviation, $z$ the $z$-statistic, and $n$ sample size.

Substituting $m = 3.05$ inch, $s = 0.10$ inch, $z = 1.64$ for 90 percent confidence level, and $n = 100$ we obtain

$$CL = 3.05 \mp \frac{(0.10)(1.64)}{\sqrt{100}}$$

$$= 3.05 \mp 0.0164$$

$$= 3.0336 \text{ inches}, 3.0664 \text{ inches}. \quad \text{(C.80)}$$

## 6.6.9 Sampling Distributions

Name the sampling distributions. What are the tests of hypothesis using these distributions?

**SOLUTION**

The sampling distributions are the Student's $t$ distribution, chi-square distribution, and $F$-distribution. The tests of hypothesis are about means, proportions of means, variances, and proportions of variances.

410    Appendix C • Solutions

## 6.6.10 Area Under Student's t Probability Density Function

What are the *t*-statistics bounding the areas under the Student's *t* curve for confidence levels of 0.90, 0.95, 0.99, and 0.999 and a sample size of 10? How does the shape of the curve vary as a function of degrees of freedom? What is the meaning of the statement that the normal distribution is the limit of the Student's *t* distribution with increasing sample size?

### SOLUTION
For a sample size of 10, the degrees of freedom are 10 − 1, or 9. The values of the *t*-statistic as a function of confidence level are available in most probability and statistics books. They are

Confidence level 0.90:    $\mp 1.833$
Confidence level 0.95:    $\mp 2.262$
Confidence level 0.99:    $\mp 3.250$
Confidence level 0.999:   $\mp 4.781$.

The shape of the curve becomes increasingly more like the curve of the normal probability density function with increasing numbers of degrees of freedom. The practical meaning of the statement is that you can use the normal distribution instead of the Student's *t* distribution for sample sizes of 30 or more.

## 6.6.11 Student's t Distribution

Repeat the exercise in Section 6.6.8 for a confidence level of 0.90 and a sample size of 10 bolts.

### SOLUTION
We assume that the Student's *t* distribution governs because of the small sample size. The number of degrees of freedom are 10 − 1, or 9. The value of the *t*-statistic is 1.833 for 9 degrees of freedom and a confidence level of 0.90.

We replace the value $z = 1.64$ with $t = 1.833$ in Equation C.80, and obtain

$$CL = 3.05 \mp \frac{(0.10)(1.8333)}{\sqrt{100}}$$

$$= 3.05 \mp 0.018333$$

$$= 3.031667 \text{ inches}, 3.068333 \text{ inches}. \qquad (C.81)$$

## 6.6.12 Test of Hypothesis

Automobile manufacturers typically test a few of each year's models for extended periods of time to validate gas mileage performance. Miles per gallon for a particular model were 28, 31, 34, 30, 27, and 29.

The design goal for a certain model is 30 miles per gallon. With a confidence of 90 percent, test the null hypothesis that the sample mean is representative of the population mean. Derive the 90 percent confidence interval about the sample mean.

### SOLUTION
The mean of the test miles per gallon is (28 + 31 + 34 + 30 + 27 + 29) ÷ 6, or 29.833 miles per gallon. The exercise asks you to determine if the sample mean ($m$) is representative of the population mean ($\mu$) of 30 miles per gallon with a confidence level of 0.90. The significance level ($\alpha$) is one minus the confidence level for 1 − 0.90, or 0.10.

*Appendix C • Solutions* 411

The exercise is a test of hypothesis with a small sample. We enumerate the decision rules by stating the null ($H_0$) and alternative ($H_1$) hypotheses and the significance level ($\alpha$), as follows:

1. $H_0$: $\mu = 30$ miles per gallon
2. $H_1$: $\mu < 30$ miles per gallon
3. $\alpha = 0.10$.

The "less than" symbol (<) in the rule $H_1$ signifies that we need a one-tail, left-sided test. We accept $H_1$ when the calculated value of the test statistic ($t$) falls beyond the value of the critical value of $t$ ($t_c$). Otherwise, we do not reject $H_i$, which in practical terms means that we accept it.

We calculate the value of the test statistic ($t$) with Equation C.82

$$t = (m - \mu)\frac{\sqrt{n}}{s} \tag{C.82}$$

where $t$ denotes the $t$-statistic, $m$ sample mean, $\mu$ population mean, $n$ sample size, and $s$ standard deviation.

The standard deviation ($s$) is the square root of the variance ($s^2$), which we calculate with Equation C.83.

$$s^2 = \frac{(28-29.833)^2 + (31-29.833)^2 + (34-29.833)^2 + (30-29.833)^2 + (27-29.833)^2 + (29-29.833)^2}{6-1}$$

$$= 6.167. \tag{C.83}$$

The value of $s$ is the square root of 6.167, or 2.483. Substituting $m = 29.833$ miles per gallon, $\mu = 30$ miles per gallon, $n = 6$, and $s = 2.483$ miles per gallon in Equation C.82, we obtain the answer in Equation C.84.

$$t = (29.833 \text{ miles per gallon} - 30 \text{ miles per gallon}) \frac{\sqrt{6}}{2.483}$$

$$= -0.1647. \tag{C.84}$$

We next turn to the table of the Student's $t$ probability density function in most probability and statistics books. For degrees of freedom $= 6 - 1$, or 5, and $\alpha = 0.10$, we read 2.015 as the area in both tails of the curve.

Our test of hypothesis is one-tail, left-sided, so we divide 2.015 by 2 and make it negative for $-1.0075$ as the value of $t_c$. The test $t$-statistic of $-0.1647$ in Equation C.85 is less negative than $-1.0075$. Therefore, we do not reject the hypothesis that the sample mean of 29.833 is representative of the population mean of 30 miles per gallon with a confidence level of 0.90.

### ■ 6.6.13 Random Numbers

What is the difference between a random number and a pseudorandom number (PRN)? How many PRNs consisting of how many digits do you need to simulate lots of size 10,000, 5,000, 1,000, 500, 100, 50, and 10?

**SOLUTION**

A random number is a number picked at random from an infinitely long uniform distribution of numbers. A PRN is a number picked at random from a less than infinitely long uniform distribution of numbers. The probability of randomly selecting any one PRN from a distribution of size $n$ is $1 \div n$.

The lot of 10,000 requires 10,000 five-digit numbers ranging from 0 to 10,000. The lot of 5,000 requires 5,000 four-digit numbers ranging from 0 to 5,000. The lot of 1,000 requires 1,000 four-digit numbers ranging from 0 to 1,000. The lot of 500 requires 500 three-digit numbers ranging from 0 to 50. The lot of 100 requires 100 three-digit numbers ranging from 0 to 100. The lot of 50 requires 50 two-digit numbers ranging from 0 to 50. The lot of 10 requires 10 two-digit numbers ranging from 0 to 10.

### ■ 6.6.14 Monte Carlo Method

Describe the steps comprising the Monte Carlo method. What probability distribution would you use to simulate a sample of ten variates?

**SOLUTION**
The steps comprising the Monte Carlo Method are as follows:

1. Tabulate variates.
2. Derive cumulate probability distribution.
3. Encode random number ranges.
4. Select random numbers.
5. Decode random numbers.
6. Derive statistical measures.

We use the Student's $t$ distribution to model a sample of ten variates. For simulation, however, we recommend sample sizes of 30 so that you may assume normality for derived statistical measures.

### ■ 6.6.15 Simulation

Emulate the simulation in the example of Section 6.3.11 for a sample size of 30 with the cost data in Table C.43.

*Table C.43   Cost History for Simulation Exercise*

| Unit | Cost Dollars | Unit | Cost Dollars |
|---|---|---|---|
| 1 | 9,850 | 6 | 8,790 |
| 2 | 9,650 | 7 | 8,580 |
| 3 | 9,750 | 8 | 8,150 |
| 4 | 9,300 | 9 | 7,750 |
| 5 | 9,050 | 10 | 7,300 |

Calculate the confidence interval about the mean for significance levels of 0.20, 0.10, and 0.05.

**SOLUTION**
Table C.44 lists the encoded random number subranges for the data in Table C.43.

## Appendix C • Solutions

**Table C.44** Encoded Random Number Subranges for Monte Carlo Method Exercise

| Cost Dollars | Frequency | Probability | Cumulative Probability | Random Number Subrange |
|---|---|---|---|---|
| 7,300 | 1 | 0.10 | 0.10 | 0000–0999 |
| 7,750 | 1 | 0.10 | 0.20 | 1000–1999 |
| 8,150 | 1 | 0.10 | 0.30 | 2000–2999 |
| 8,580 | 1 | 0.10 | 0.40 | 3000–3999 |
| 8,700 | 1 | 0.10 | 0.50 | 4000–4999 |
| 9,050 | 1 | 0.10 | 0.60 | 5000–5999 |
| 9,300 | 1 | 0.10 | 0.70 | 6000–6999 |
| 9,750 | 1 | 0.10 | 0.80 | 7000–7999 |
| 9,650 | 1 | 0.10 | 0.90 | 8000–9999 |
| 9,850 | 1 | 0.10 | 1.0 | 9000–9999 |
|  | 10 | 1.00 |  |  |

Table C.45 lists the sequence of 30 four-digit random numbers generated with a spreadsheet program on a personal computer.

**Table C.45** Pseudorandom Number Table for Monte Carlo Method Exercise

| | | | | |
|---|---|---|---|---|
| 0462 | 0812 | 9585 | 5838 | 6296 |
| 2720 | 9604 | 3452 | 0976 | 2629 |
| 8444 | 0332 | 1821 | 9996 | 8239 |
| 5716 | 0111 | 0348 | 5677 | 9708 |
| 6548 | 0262 | 6183 | 7227 | 6665 |
| 5949 | 5264 | 5453 | 0978 | 8700 |

We next decode the random numbers into simulated variates. Table C.46 gives the results.

**Table C.46** Decoded Random Numbers for Monte Carlo Method Exercise

| P | V | P | V | P | V | P | V | P | V |
|---|---|---|---|---|---|---|---|---|---|
| 0462 | 7,300 | 0812 | 7,300 | 9585 | 9,850 | 5838 | 9,050 | 6296 | 9,300 |
| 2720 | 8,150 | 9604 | 9,850 | 3452 | 8,580 | 0976 | 7,300 | 2629 | 8,150 |
| 8444 | 9,650 | 0332 | 7,300 | 1821 | 7,750 | 9996 | 9,850 | 8239 | 9,650 |
| 5716 | 9,050 | 0111 | 7,300 | 0348 | 7,300 | 5677 | 9,050 | 9708 | 9,850 |
| 6548 | 9,300 | 0262 | 7,300 | 6183 | 9,300 | 7227 | 9,750 | 6665 | 9,300 |
| 5949 | 9,050 | 5264 | 9,050 | 5453 | 9,050 | 0978 | 7,300 | 8700 | 9,650 |

P: Pseudorandom number.
V: Variate.

Table C.47 lists the values of the variates in Table C.46. The variates comprise simulated sample.

**Table C.47** *Simulated Sample for Monte Carlo Method Exercise*

| | | | | |
|---|---|---|---|---|
| 7,300 | 7,300 | 9,850 | 9,050 | 9,300 |
| 8,150 | 9,850 | 8,580 | 7,300 | 8,150 |
| 9,650 | 7,300 | 7,750 | 9,850 | 9,650 |
| 9,050 | 7,300 | 7,300 | 9,050 | 9,850 |
| 9,300 | 7,300 | 9,300 | 9,750 | 9,300 |
| 9,050 | 9,050 | 9,050 | 7,300 | 9,650 |

The sum of the variates in Table C.47 is 260,630. The mean is 260,630 ÷ 30, or 8,687.67, or rather $8,687.67.

We also need the value of the standard deviation to calculate the confidence interval about the mean. We use a spreadsheet program on a personal computer to calculate the standard deviation and obtain $s = \$990.87$.

The exercise asks you to calculate the confidence interval about the mean for significance levels of 0.20, 0.10, and 0.05. Equation C.85 is the relationship we use to derive confidence limits (CL) for samples of size 30 or more variates drawn from a normally distributed population.

$$CL = m \mp s\frac{z}{\sqrt{n}} \tag{C.85}$$

where $m$ denotes mean, $z$ the $z$-statistic, $s$ standard deviation, and $n$ sample size.

Significance levels of 0.20, 0.10, and 0.05 are the same as confidence levels of 0.80, 0.90, and 0.95. We first solve Equation C.86 with the $z$ value of 1.28 for the confidence level of 0.80.

Substituting $m = \$8,687.67$, $s = \$990.87$, $z = 1.28$, and $n = 30$ in Equation C.85, we obtain

$$CL = \$8,687.67 \mp \$990.87\frac{1.28}{\sqrt{30}}$$

$$= \$8,687.67 \mp 231.56$$

$$= \$8,456.11, \$8,919.23. \tag{C.86}$$

Replacing $z = 1.28$ by $z = 1.64$ in Equation C.86, we obtain the confidence limits of $11,124.06 and $11,138.10 for the confidence level of 0.90. Replacing $z = 1.28$ by $z = 1.96$ in Equation C.86, we obtain the confidence limits of $13,294.60 and $13,311.39 for the confidence level of 0.90.

### ■ 6.6.16 Aggregate Model

Repeat the example in Section 6.4.2 with the data in Table C.48.

Appendix C • Solutions

**Table C.48**  *Producer Price Index Data for Aggregate Modeling Example*

|  | 1980 | 1985 | 1986 | 1987 | 1988 |
|---|---|---|---|---|---|
| Intermediate producer price index | 90.3 | 102.7 | 99.1 | 101.5 | 107.1 |
| Construction materials price index | 92.5 | 107.6 | 107.3 | 109.5 | 115.7 |
| Construction weekly dollar earnings | 397 | 520 | - | - | - |
|  | 1989 | 1990 | 1991 | 1992 | 1993 |
| Intermediate producer price index | 112.0 | 114.5 | 114.4 | 114.7 | 116.2 |
| Construction materials price index | 119.5 | 119.6 | 120.4 | 122.5 | 128.6 |
| Construction weekly dollar earnings | 513 | 526 | 533 | 535 | 551 |

Intermediate producer price index: Table No. 753.
Construction materials price index: Table No. 1193.
Construction weekly dollar earnings: Table No. 654.
Adapted by courtesy of U.S. Department of Commerce, Bureau of the Census from *Statistical Abstract of the United States: 1994* (114th Edition), Washington, DC, 1994.

**SOLUTION**

Section 6.4.2 gives background information on this exercise. The exercise wants you to update the 1985 baseline cost estimate (BCE) of $2,742,500 with the data in Table C.48 from the *Statistical Abstract of the United States: 1994*.

The numbers in Table C.48 identify data source locations in the statistical abstract. The exercise wants you to do the update in two ways. First, update the 1985 BCE with the ratio of the 1993 intermediate producer's price index (PPI) to the 1985 intermediate PPI. Second, update the 1985 BCE by the inflation in material and labor.

The intermediate PPI for 1993 is 106.9 and 103.2 for 1985. The ratio of the two values of intermediate PPI is 106.9 ÷ 103.2, or 1.0358527. The updated BCE is the product of 1.0358527 and the 1985 BCE of $2,742,500, and is $2,840,826.

The growth in the construction material price index is 128.6 ÷ 115.7, or 1.1114952. The growth in construction weekly dollar earnings is 551 ÷ 520, or 1.0596153.

The updated BCE is the product of the construction material price index growth of 1.1114952, construction weekly dollars earnings growth of 1.0596153, and the BCE of $2,742,500, and is $3,229,999.

Which amount do you think is more realistic and credible? We think $3,229,999 is more realistic and certainly more credible.

### ■ 6.6.17 Disaggregation

Using the current edition of the *Statistical Abstract of the United States*, delineate the disaggregation of the producer price index for metals.

How does the producer price index for individual metals correlate with the producer price index for primary metals? How does the producer price index for primary metals correlate with the producers price index for nonferrous metals and ferrous metals over a period of five years?

## SOLUTION

Table C.49 lists metal producer price indexes (PPI) for the Years 1985 and 1993, and the percent difference between the years, from Table 1164 in the *Statistical Abstract of the United States: 1994*.

***Table C.49*** *Metal Producer Price Indexes for Disaggregation Exercise*

|  | 1985 | 1993 | Percent Difference |
|---|---|---|---|
| Primary metals | 101.8 | 106.4 | 4.52 |
| Nonferrous | 96.5 | 99.5 | 3.11 |
| Copper | 99.8 | 117.7 | 18.05 |
| Aluminum | 104.7 | 110.5 | 5.54 |
| Iron and steel | 104.5 | 111.5 | 6.70 |

The correlation is quite poor, highlighting the advantage of disaggregate price indexes.

### ■ 6.6.18 Disaggregate Model

Compare the updated baseline cost estimate from the example in Section 6.4.4 with the risk cost estimate from the example in Section 6.4.2. Which of the two estimates do you think is more realistic and credible?

## SOLUTION

The updated baseline cost estimate (BCE) of $3,147,896 from the example in Section 6.4.2 is an aggregate estimate. The risk cost estimate (RCE) of $2,922,835 from the example in Section 6.4.4 is a disaggregate estimate. The difference between the two estimates is 7.70 percent.

In general, disaggregate estimates are more realistic and credible than aggregate estimates. Choose the value of RCE over that of BCE in this exercise.

### ■ 7.9.1 Lloyd's of London

Section 7.9.1 gives background information on this exercise. The exercise asks you to state the management and extrinsic attributes that may have contributed to risk exposure in the insurance policies underwritten by Lloyd's.

## SOLUTION

The key management attribute contributor to risk exposure was funding and budgeting policy. Lloyd's did not have sufficient financial reserve for the policies it wrote. The key extrinsic attribute contributor was climatic conditions that were very severe for the time period of interest.

### ■ 7.9.2 Corporate Losses

Section 7.9.2 gives background information on this exercise. The exercise asks you to state the management and extrinsic attributes that may have contributed to risk exposure in the financial losses of the two companies. What risk determinant factors are significant in these cases? What do you consider to be the major difference between the two companies?

Appendix C • Solutions

**SOLUTION**

The key management attribute contributors were funding and budgeting policy and customer and user policy. Accounting practices contributed to the problems in both companies. This was accompanied by failure to recognize change in the motoring public's buying trend. The key extrinsic attribute was the motoring public.

The significant risk determinant factors were the management attribute factor and extrinsic attribute factor. The major difference between the two companies was the timing in reacting to the motoring public.

### ■ 7.9.3 Standardized Risk Measure

Section 7.9.3 gives background information on this exercise. The exercise asks you to develop a standardized risk measure for investing in mutual funds based on the mean and standard deviation of a hypothetical fund.

Table C.50 is a list of annual returns for a hypothetical mutual fund. Calculate the mean and standard deviation of the returns. Using the guidelines of low risk equals $\mp 1$ standard deviation, medium risk equals $\mp 2$ standard deviations, and high risk equals $\mp 3$ standard deviations, what risk rating would you ascribe to the fund? Derive a table for risk rating on the scale of 0 to 1.0.

*Table C.50* Annual Rate of Return for Hypothetical Mutual Fund

| Year | Rate Percent | Year | Rate Percent |
|------|--------------|------|--------------|
| 1    | 16.7         | 6    | 20.1         |
| 2    | 13.6         | 7    | 19.0         |
| 3    | 6.7          | 8    | 12.3         |
| 4    | −1.3         | 9    | 14.8         |
| 5    | −2.7         | 10   | 10.9         |

Assume the hypothetical mutual fund of Table C.50 belongs to a class of funds with an average yield of 9.25 percent and a mean rating of medium risk. Test the hypothesis that the sample mean is representative of the mean of this class.

**SOLUTION**

We use the Student's $t$ distribution to model the data because of the small sample size. Given a sample of size thirty or more, we could use the normal distribution.

We calculate the value of the test statistic ($t$) with Equation C.87.

$$t = (m - \mu)\frac{\sqrt{n}}{s} \tag{C.87}$$

where $t$ denotes the $t$-statistic, $m$ sample mean, $\mu$ population mean, $n$ sample size, and $s$ standard deviation.

The value of $\mu$ is given as 9.25 percent. We use a spreadsheet program on a personal computer to derive the mean ($m$) and standard deviation ($s$) of the data in Table C.50.

The calculated value of $m$ is 11.01 percent and the value of $s$ is 7.886 percent. This represents an extremely high risk compared to a medium risk of $\mp 2.5s$.

Substituting $m = 11.01$ percent, $\mu = 9.25$ percent, $n = 10$, and $s = 7.886$ percent in Equation C.88, we obtain

$$t = (11.01 - 9.25)\% \frac{\sqrt{10}}{7.886\%}$$
$$= 0.706. \quad \text{(C.88)}$$

We assume a desired confidence level of 0.995 for $\alpha$ equals $1 - 0.995$, or 0.005. We turn to any probability or statistics book for the value of the critical $t$-statistic. Since our concern is for the yield to be equal to or greater than the average of the class of funds, we use a one-sided, right-tail test.

For degrees of freedom equal to $10 - 1$, or 9, and equal to 0.005, the critical $t$-statistic equals 3.250. The test $t$-statistic of 0.706 is less than 3.250, so we reject the hypothesis that the sample mean is representative of the mean of this class.

### ■ 7.9.4 Consumer Price Index

The Congressional Budget Office announced recently that the consumer price index (CPI) overstates inflation by 0.2 to 0.8 percentage points per year. Every 1 percentage point increase in the CPI raises the federal budget deficit by approximately $6.5 billion, primarily by increasing government benefit payments.

The U.S. Department of Labor, the keeper of the CPI, has overhauled the government's measure of inflation to shave about 0.1 percent off the CPI. What has changed is the way the Department of Labor measures price of food consumed at home, shelter, and name-brand prescription drugs. Apparently, generic drugs are taking a larger share of sales.

Obtain budget deficit data since the last time the Labor Department changed the CPI baseline from the current edition of the *Statistical Abstract of the United States*. Calculate what the deficit would be currently, if the CPI had reflected the deduction of 0.1 percent.

**SOLUTION**

The U.S. Department of Labor last changed the CPI baseline in 1960. Table No. 504 in the *Statistical Abstract of the United States: 1994* indicates that from 1960 to 1994 the budget deficit grew from $290,525 million to $4,676,029 million, or $4,385,504.

The deduction of 0.1 percent annually, over the period of 25 years, would have been compounded to the value of $(1 + 0.01)^{25}$, or 1.282431995. Dividing the budget deficit growth by this value yields $4,385,504 million ÷ 1.282431995, or $3,419,677.626 million as the current deficit.

### ■ 7.9.5 Short-Term Interest Rates

The Federal Reserve System uses short-term interest rates as the means for controlling inflation. Paradoxically, excessive economic growth equates to runaway inflation.

Appendix C • Solutions

The Federal Reserve System expressed surprise at the strength of the economy despite the recent series of five increases in short-term interest rates by Federal Reserve Banks. In addition, the housing market, which is typically the first to feel the effect of higher rates, remains buoyant. The banks are expected to increase short-term interest rates by 1.5 percent in trying to contain inflation as measured by the consumer price index (CPI).

Using the current edition of *Statistical Abstract of the United States*, establish the correlation between Federal Reserve Bank's discount rates and the CPI.

**SOLUTION**

Table C.51 lists the highest annual rates of the Federal Reserve Bank of New York and values of CPI from 1988 to 1993 from Tables Nos. 747 and 806 of the *Statistical Abstract of the United States: 1994*. Compare the values.

*Table C.51  Federal Reserve Bank Rates and Consumer Price Indexes*

| Year | Rates Percent | CPI |
|---|---|---|
| 1988 | 6.50 | 118.3 |
| 1989 | 7.00 | 124.0 |
| 1990 | 6.50 | 130.7 |
| 1991 | 6.00 | 136.2 |
| 1992 | 3.00 | 140.3 |
| 1993 | 3.00 | 144.5 |

There is no correlation between the discount rates and the CPI.

### ■ 7.9.6 Conflicting Requirements

Section 7.9.6 gives background information on this exercise. The exercise asks you to consider what the cost impact will be from using HCFC in air conditioners. Consider yourself an analyst for a company such as Carrier Corporation. How would you rate management attribute factor, extrinsic attribute factor, product maturity factor, and process maturity factor for the undertaking? State your reasons.

The U.S. Bureau of the Census estimates that 99.9 percent of U.S. households have refrigerators and 50 percent of U.S. households have central air conditioning or window units. Using the current edition of the *Statistical Abstract of the United States*, estimate the cost impact of replacing these units.

**SOLUTION**

We would rate the management attribute factor close to 0.0 because of the company's commitment to stay in the marketplace. We would rate the extrinsic attribute factor at about 0.50 because of uncertainties regarding statutory regulations and the reaction of customers. Similarly, we would rate product and process maturity factors no higher than 0.05 because of unfamiliarity with HCFC.

According to Table No. 1217 in the *Statistical Abstract of the United States: 1994*, there are 44,918 housing units in the United States. The number of units with refrigerators is (44,918)(0.999), or 44,873. The number of units with central air conditioning are (44,918)(0.50), or 22,459.

We assume the average cost of a refrigerator is $500.00 and that a replacement with HCFC would cost 25 percent more, or $625.00. The refrigerator cost impact will be (44,873)($625.00), or $28,045,625. We assume the average cost of central air is $5,000.00 and that a replacement with HCFC would cost 25 percent more, or $6,250.00. The central air conditioning cost impact will be (22,459)($6,250.00), or $14,036,875. The total cost impact will be $42,082,500.

### ■ 7.9.7 Nuclear Energy

Section 7.9.7 gives background information on this exercise. The exercise asks you what industry you believe will produce the nuclear fusion full-power generator? Should nuclear fusion power become commonplace? What would become of power utilities and manufacturers of conventional power generators? Identify the attributes of the extrinsic attribute factor influencing the proliferation of nuclear fusion power.

**SOLUTION**

The exercise poses very complex questions. The answers depend more on political and economic factors than technical factors.

The larger entities in the conventional power generator manufacturing industry will probably produce the first full-power generator. Power utilities will remain operative to distribute the electric power.

The automotive industry may produce smaller units to power vehicles, provided safety and regulatory issues are resolved. Smaller units for home and business use will probably not be seen until the fourth millennium.

The extrinsic attributes influencing the proliferation of nuclear fusion power are safety and control.

**POSTSCRIPT**

Electric power utilities have been offering customers financial inducements to install more energy efficient appliances and equipment and conserve energy by reducing consumption. Now, after many years, a number of utilities are attempting to withdraw from these arrangements which are subject to the approval of the public utility commission of the state in which the utility operates.

The utilities claim that these measures have not been effective enough to warrant the cost of the programs. The outcome of these attempts will be interesting.

### ■ 7.9.8 Sample Space

Three missiles are fired at a target, each having a hit probability of 0.90. Describe the sample space and determine the probability of two or more missiles hitting the target.

## Appendix C • Solutions

### SOLUTION

The solution to this exercise is adapted from Jack V. Michaels, *Lectures on Operation Research*, Naval Ordinance Station, Indian Head, Maryland, 1968, by courtesy of the U.S. Navy.

Figure C.9 shows the model of the sample space using unit vectors for each of the three missiles. The numerals 0 and 1 denote miss and hit. The common origin of the unit vectors (*i.e.*, binary number 000) denotes three misses.

Table C.52 lists the eight logical states with their respective binary number and state probability. Since the probability of a hit is 0.9, the probability of a miss is 1 − .9, or 0.1.

The probability of three misses is (0.1)(0.1)(0.1). or 0.001. The probability of three hits is (.9)(.9)(.9), or 0.729. The sum of the eight state probabilities is 1, as we expected.

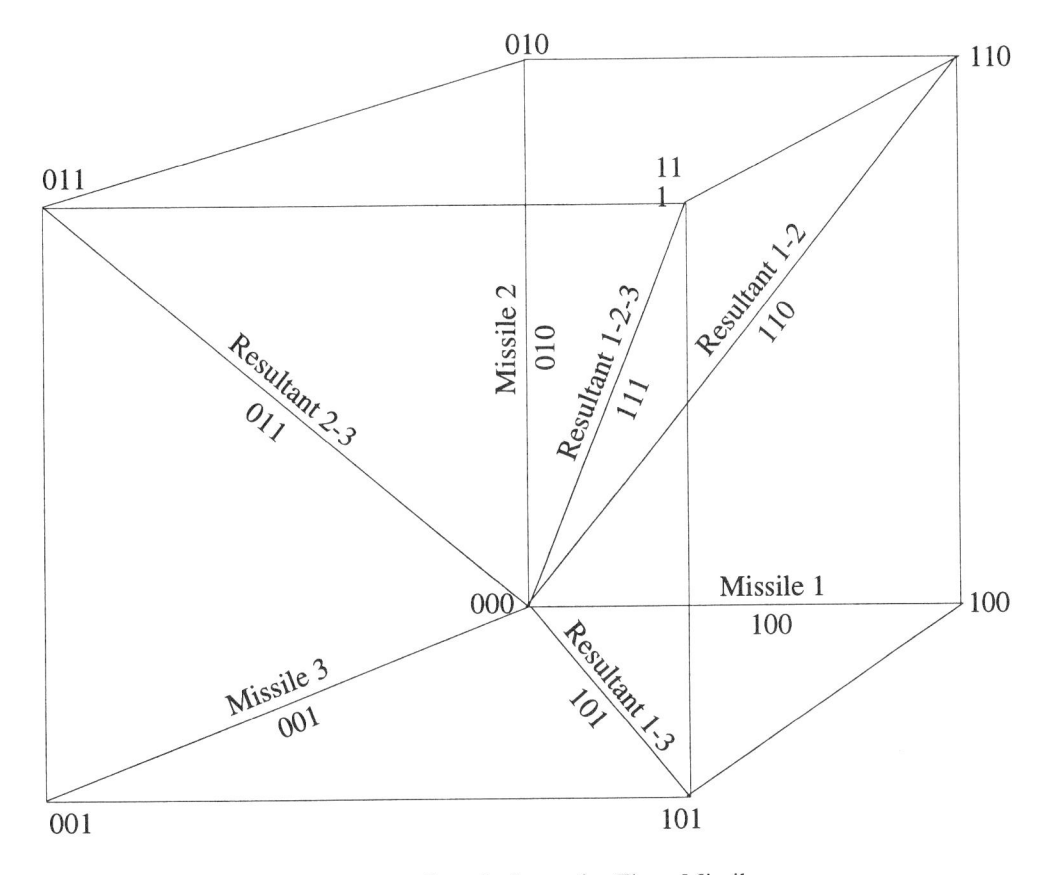

**Figure C.9** Sample Space for Three Missiles

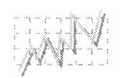

***Table C.52***  *Logical States and Probabilities for Three Missiles*

| Logical State | Event | Binary Representation | State Probability |
|---|---|---|---|
| 0 | Missile 1 miss<br>Missile 2 miss<br>Missile 3 miss | 000 | $(0.1)(0.1)(0.1) = 0.001$ |
| 1 | Missile 1 hit<br>Missile 2 miss<br>Missile 3 miss | 100 | $(0.9)(0.1)(0.1) = 0.009$ |
| 2 | Missile 1 miss<br>Missile 2 hit<br>Missile 3 miss | 010 | $(0.1)(0.9)(0.1) = 0.009$ |
| 3 | Missile 1 miss<br>Missile 2 miss<br>Missile 3 hit | 001 | $(0.1)(0.1)(0.9) = 0.009$ |
| 4 | Missile 1 hit<br>Missile 2 hit<br>Missile 3 miss | 110 | $(0.9)(0.9)(0.1) = 0.081$ |
| 5 | Missile 1 hit<br>Missile 2 miss<br>Missile 3 hit | 101 | $(0.9)(0.1)(0.9) = 0.081$ |
| 6 | Missile 1 miss<br>Missile 2 hit<br>Missile 3 hit | 011 | $(0.9)(0.9)(0.1) = 0.081$ |
| 7 | Missile 1 hit<br>Missile 2 hit<br>Missile 3 hit | 111 | $(0.9)(0.9)(0.9) = 0.729$ |
|   |   |   | Sum = 1.000 |

The probability of two or more missiles hitting the target is the sum of the probabilities for States 4 through 7 for 0.081 + 0.081 + 0.081 + 0.729, or 0.972. The probability of exactly two missiles hitting the target is the sum of the probabilities of States 4 through 6 for 0.081 + 0.081 + 0.081, or 0.243.

> *Further deponent sayeth not.*
> ***Old courtroom saying***

# INDEX

*Ask, and it shall be given you; seek, and ye shall find; knock, and it shall be opened unto you.*
— **Matthew VII, 7**

## A

Acceptance region, 272
Acquisition milestones and phases, 342
Acquisition policy, 341
Advanced Research Projects Agency, 319
Aerospace, 188
*Aerospatiale,* 188
Affordability, 7, 320
Aggregate cost, 154
Aggregate model, 287, 296, 414
Aggregation, 286
*Airbus Industrie,* 188
Aldrin Jr., Edwin E, 38
Algorithm, 279
Allied disciplines, 6
Alpha Metals, Inc., 183
Amortization, 173
Analog model, 265
Analogy estimate, 160
Anglo-French Concorde, 351
Annual equivalent value method, 176
Annual rate of return, 324, 417
Antilogarithm, 142, 150
*Apollo* 1, 6, 37
Armstrong, Neil, 38

ARPA (Advanced Research Projects Agency), 319
Atlantis, 5
Attribute:
 checklist, 94
 extrinsic, 27, 68
 formulation, 224
 intrinsic, 47
 order, 47
 rating schema, 93
 weighting, 89, 110, 381
Augustine, Norman R., xviii, 298
*Augustine's Laws,* 298
Automobiles, 158
Award structure, 307

## B

Balanced production line, 116
BART (Bay Area Rapid Transit System), 351
Baseline, 133, 152
Bay Area Rapid Transit System, 351
Belize, 24
Benefit-cost ratio method, 177, 393
Best Manufacturing Practices Program, 10

Beta Industries, 34, 253
Bhopal, 352
Binary numbers, 91, 97, 200, 383
    equivalent decimal values, 201
    positional values of digits, 97
Binary weighting, 91, 200
Boeing Company, 188
British Honduras, 25
Built-up cube, 12

## C

Carrier Corporation, 325, 419
Cause and effect diagram:
    lower-level, 33
    top-level, 33
CCA (circuit card assembly), 57
Central America, 24
Central limit theorem, 275, 294, 371, 406
CFC (chlorofluorocarbon), 325
Chaffee, Roger B., 37
*Challenger*, 10, 6, 38
Chief executive officer, 302
Chernobyl, 352
Chi-Square Center, 288
Chi-square distribution, 407
Chlorofluorocarbon, 325
Chrysler Corporation, 311
Cicero, 261
Circuit card assembly, 57
Coefficient of determination, 189, 395
Collins, Michael, 38
Columbus, iii
Combinations, 30, 371
Commerce Clearing House, 317
Compound interest factor, 169
Computer fraud, 273, 355
Computer operation, 239
Computer processing center, 289
*Concorde*, 188
Concurrent engineering, 6
Confidence:
    interval, 162

limits, 295, 409
Configuration control, 303
Confucius, 63
Congressional Budget Office, 324, 418
Constant weighting, 90, 198, 418
Consumer price index, 180, 324, 418
Continuous variable, 371
Conventions, 16
Coolidge, William D., 40
Corporate losses, 323, 416
Cost:
    at completion, 79
    categories, 153
    element structure, 154
    escalation factors, 180
    material, 266
    projections, 188, 392
    risk analysis, 265
    scenario, 152
    should, could, and would, 153
Costa Rica, 24
Cost-benefit ratio method, 189
Cost estimating, 79
    analogy, 160
    baseline, 152
    confidence, 80
    expert opinion, 159
    function of volume and weight, 267
    industrial engineering, 164
    methodology, 157
    parametric, 160, 188, 293, 391, 405
    techniques, 159
CPM (critical path method), 116
CPM network, 117
Credibility, 75, 108, 261, 378
Critical path, 119, 345
Cunningham, Walter, 38
Customer and user policy, 198, 242, 252

## D

Day of the week algorithm, 375
Decimal number system, 383

positional values of digits, 97
Decision:
  continuum, 10
  milestones, 342
  process, 10
  product, 10
  program, 10
  risk analysis, 265
  theory, 12
Defense industry, 319
Defense Sciences Board, 10
Degrees of freedom, 274, 294, 407
Deliberate haste, 310
Delta Industries, 44, 248
Delta Products, 91
Deming, Dr. W. Edwards, 310
Department of Defense, 7, 57, 341
Department of Labor, 418
Design, 304
Design to cost, 6
Design of experiments, 6
*Deutche Aerospatz*, 188
Digital Equipment Corporation, 317
Disaggregate cost, 154
Disaggregate modeling, 289, 296
Disaggregation, 76, 286, 415
Disraeli, Benjamin, 297
DoD 5000 Series Documents, 341
Dunlop, Albert, 317
DuPont (I. E. DuPont de Nemours), 116

### E

Economic Analysis, 176
  annual equivalent value method, 176
  benefit-cost ratio method, 177
  internal rate of return method, 177
  present value method, 176
Eisele, Donn F., 38
El Salvador, 24
Empire State Building, 319
Endeavor, 5
Energy price index, 395

Epilogue, 328
Epsilon Agency, 97
Epsilon Enterprises, Inc., 49
Equiprobability, 279
Escalation, 179
Expected task duration time, 118
Expert Opinion, 159
Experts, 29
Exponential plots, 85
Extrinsic attribute, 27, 102, 205, 256, 397

### F

Facilities, 306
Factorial, 30
Failure rate, 41
$F$-distribution probability density function, 408
Federal Reserve Bank, 419
Federal Reserve System, 418
Ferdinand and Isabella, xvii
Fishbone diagram, 33
Ford, Henry, 7
Ford Motor Company, 316, 323
Forecasting, 12, 183
FORTUNE, 317
Functionality, 7, 320
Funding, 304
Funding and Budgeting Policy, 198, 203, 242, 252
Future Value, 173

### G

Gagarin, Yuri, 37
Galileo, 5
Gamma Group, 223
Gamma Products, Inc., 40
*Gemini*, 37
General Motors Corporation, 323
Generation breakdown, 104, 158, 219, 257, 399

Greek alphabet, 16, 353
Grissom, Virgil I. "Gus," 37
Guatemala, 24
Gulf Construction Company, 70

**H**

Hardware:
   factors, 208
   process complexity factor, 233, 237, 400
   process concurrency factor, 236
   process maturity factor, 223, 234
   process quality factor, 226, 234, 237
   product complexity factor, 219, 257, 398
   product concurrency factor, 221
   product maturity factor, 208
   product quality factor, 211, 229
   risk determinant factors, 256, 396
Hazards and perils, 29
HCFC (hydrochlorofluorocarbon), 325
Heuristics, 196
Hexadecimal number system, 110, 384, 395
Hierarchy of hazards and perils, 32
Highway and roadway construction, 69
Hines, Duncan, 310
Honduras, 24
*Hubble*, 5
Hughes Aircraft, 319
Human development index, 25
Hyatt Regency Hotel, 318
Hydrochlorofluorocarbon, 325
Hypothesis:
   alternative, 272
   null, 272

**I**

I. E. DuPont de Nemours, 116
Iacocca, Lee J., 311
IBM (International Business Machine Corporation), 317

Iconic model, 265
Incentive Structure, 308
Independent research and development, 3
Industrial Engineering, 164
Inflation, 179, 189, 395
Initial operational capability, 8
Insurability, 2
Intel Corporation, 382
Internal rate of return method, 177, 189, 394
International Business Machines Corporation, 382
Iota, Incorporated, 244
Iota Industries, Inc., 86
IR&D (independent research and development), 3

**J**

Jarvis, Gregory, 38
JIT(Just-in-time), 259
Johnson, Samuel, 327
Jupiter, 5
Juvenal, 102
Just-in-time inventory, 259

**K**

$k$-factor, 48
Kanban, 259
Kappa Corporation, 229
Karr, Alphonse, 20
Kennedy, John F., 37
King's messenger, 9

**L**

Labich, Kenneth, 317
Laplace, Pierre de, 199
Law of large numbers, 279, 294, 371, 406

# Index

Learning curve, 139
   applications, 142
   confidence interval, 146, 187, 390
   discontinuity, 149, 187, 391
   function of maturity, 144
   formulation, 140
   probabilistic nature, 145
   selection, 143, 187, 390
   service products, 187, 388
   startup efficiency, 150
Limited warranty, 41
Linearity of scale, 84
Linear programming, 12
Lines of regression, 137
Lloyd's of London, 323, 416
Lockheed, 319
Lockheed Martin Corporation, iii
Logarithm, 142, 150
Logarithmic plots, 85
Logical statement, 213
Logical states, 96
   three missiles, 421
Longfellow, Henry Wadsworth, 432
Lookup table, 100

## M

Mack Truck, 317
Main battle tank, 315
Majority rule, 89
Management, 306
Management attribute factor, 27, 102, 196
   checklists, 197
   customer and user policy, 198
   formulation, 198
   funding and budgeting policy, 198
   personnel growth and retention policy, 199
   program continuity policy, 199
Management science, 12
Managing conceptual programs, 314
Margin for error, 286
   opinion polls, 311

Martin Marietta Corporation, 319
Matthew, 301, 423
Maytag, 317
McAuliffe, Christa, 38
McNair, Ronald, 38
McDonnell Douglas, 319
Mean, 294, 371, 409
Mean-time-between-failures, 40
Median, 371
Mercury, 37
Metric prefixes and multipliers, 374
Metrics, 108, 373
Miracle on Thirty-Fourth Street, 319
Mistakes by corporate managers, 318
Mode, 371
Modeling, 269
Moment method, 278
Monte Carlo method, 280, 295, 412
Montreal Protocal, 57
Morphology, 115
Motion elements, 134
Motion-element time, 187, 388
Motivational guidelines, 306
MTBF (mean-time-between-failures), 40
Mutual fund, 52, 60, 324, 363, 366, 417

## N

NASA (National Aeronautics and Space Administration), 5, 37, 108
National Aeronautics and Space Administration, 5, 37, 108
National Technical Information Service, 18, 62, 189, 260, 297, 326, 341
Need for aid, 25
Nehru, Jawaharial, 311
Network
   coding, 118
   compression, 127
   risk analysis, 264
   utilization, 122
Nicaragua, 24

Normal distribution, 270, 371
  probability density function, 271, 285, 294, 407
Notice of revision, 109, 380
Nuclear energy, 325, 420
  fission, 325
  fusion, 325
Null hypothesis, 272
Number of decimal places, 168
Number systems, 110, 383
  binary, 91, 200, 383
  decimal, 110, 383
  hexadecimal, 110, 383
  octal, 110, 383
  ternary, 110, 383

## O

Objective criteria, 308
Objective risk, 36
Octal number system, 110, 383
Omega Organization, 220
Onizuka, Ellison, 38
Opportunity loss, 154
Optimistic task duration time, 118
Organizational guidelines, 302
Organization of digital computer, 240
Oscar, Wilde, 112
Output power density, 161
Ozone, 325

## P

Pacific Rim, 189
Panama, 24
Paper work, 74
Parametric estimate, 160, 188, 293, 391, 405
  function of power output and volume, 164
Pareto analysis, 34
Part numbers, 233, 257, 399
Path-duration times, 121

Path slack time, 121
Patton, General George C., 310
Pegasus, 316
Pentium® chip, 382
Performance tracking and reporting, 303
Permutation, 371
Personnel growth and retention policy, 199, 243, 252
PERT (program evaluation and review technique), 116
Pessimistic task duration time, 118
Planning disasters, 18, 351
Pliny the Elder, 157
PODR (point of diminishing return), 35
Point of diminishing return, 35
Population, 371
Postcripts, 352, 382, 407, 420
PRA (probabilistic risk assessment), 38
Precedence, 59, 356
  diagram, 129, 186, 384
Precision and accuracy, 171
Present value of future payment, 171
Present value method, 176
Present value of uniform series of payments, 172
Presidential election, 317
Price indexes, 180
Probabilistic nature of risk, 38
Probabilistic risk assessment, 38
Probabilistics vs. Deterministics, 76
Probability, 62, 191, 261, 370, 422
Probability density function:
  chi-square distribution, 408
  $F$-distribution, 408
  normal distribution, 271, 285. 294, 407
  student's $t$ distribution, 275, 295, 371, 409
Procedural guidelines, 304
Process complexity factor, 27, 104
  hardware, 233
  service, 254
  software, 246
Process concurrency factor, 27, 106
  hardware, 222
  service, 254

# Index

software, 245
Process maturity factor, 27, 103
   hardware, 223
   service, 250
   software, 245
Process quality factors, 27, 103
   hardware, 226
   service, 254
   software, 246
Producer price index, 182, 288, 296, 396, 415
Producibility, 211, 231
Product categories, 86
Product complexity factor, 27, 104
   hardware, 219
   service, 254
   software, 245
Product concurrency factor, 27, 104
   hardware, 221
   service, 254
   software, 249, 250
Production, 305
   hazards and perils, 32
   line, 233
   line balancing, 186, 386
Product maturity factor, 27, 73, 103
   hardware, 208
   service, 250
   software, 245
Product network, 118, 357
Product quality factor, 27, 103, 213
   hardware, 211
   service, 254
   software, 246
Profitability, 7, 32
Program continuity policy, 199, 241
Pseudorandom numbers, 279, 413
Pyramid of Khufu, 318

## Q

QFAP (quality, functionality, affordability, and profitability), 7, 32, 320

Quality, 7, 32, 320
Quality function deployment, 6
Quantified risk measures, 28

## R

Rabelais, François, 19
Rainfall, 70
Random numbers, 278, 295, 411
Rating schema, 93
Realism, 74, 108, 378
Recognition, 307
Reengineering, 319
Rejection region, 271
Reliability, 212, 231
Required operational capability, 8
Requirements, conflicting, 325, 419
Resistor values, 228
Resnik, Judith, 38
Reverse engineering, 109, 380
Reviews, technical, 329
Rho Corporation, 210
Risk:
   applicability, 51
   avoidance, 1, 5, 8
   baselines, 112
   calculated, 311
   categories, 36
   continuum, 57
   control, 298
   dominance, 46, 59, 359
   examples, 315
   formulation, 71, 191
   fundamentals, 20
   hierarchy, 32, 58, 354
   management, 1, 431
   metrics, 64
   models, 262
   morphology, 26
   order, 47
   perspective, 193, 310
   priorities, 310

Risk: (continued)
    probability, 58, 355
    recovery, 1
    reducing, 347
    policy statement, 302
    systems, 30
    taxonomy, 11
Risk cost, 34, 39, 362, 360
    development, 73
    estimate, 257, 398
    perspective, 405
    retrospective, 259
Risk determinant factor, 101, 314, 362
    attribute applicability, 197
    categories, 66, 88, 108, 378
    dominance, 256, 396
    first order, 47
    second order, 47
    selection, 82
    tailoring, 82
    trade study, 108, 378
Risk exposure, 315
    component level, 40
    confidence intervals, 377
    confidence level, 108
    construction, 54, 61, 366
    cost trades, 110, 381
    estimating, 78, 83
    highway and roadway construction, 69
    investment, 52, 60, 362
    manufacturing process, 60, 361
    product development, 60, 359
    quantified measures, 28, 379
    service products, 259, 404
    software, 258, 402
    standardized measure, 323, 417
    taxonomy, 11
    total procurement package, 258, 401
    verbal expressions, 28, 379
Risk models, 261
Risk network, 42, 59, 356
    dependent, 42
    hybrid, 43
    independent, 43
    manufacturing, 44, 357

Risk principles, 23, 57, 320
    risk benefit-equity, 23
    risk cost-effectiveness, 24
Risk time, 39
    dominance, 49
    network, 49
Roles and responsibilities, 302
Root-sum-of-squares, 43,
RSS (root-sum-of squares), 43
Russell, Bertrand, 320


S


Sample, 371
    small, 371
    large, 371
Sample space, 326, 420
Sampling:
    bias, 313
    distributions, 275, 295, 409
    error, 312
Schirra Jr., Walter M., 38
Scientific method, 11, 18, 61, 108, 352, 367, 374
Scobbee, Francis, 38
Scott Paper, 317
SEC (Security and Exchange Commission), 323
Security and Exchange Commission, 323
Service:
    corporations, 250
    customer policy, 252
    customers, 253
    factors, 250
    funding and budgeting policy, 252
    learning curves, 187, 388
    management attributes, 251
    personnel growth and retention policy, 252
    process complexity factor, 254
    process concurrency factor, 254
    process maturity factor, 251
    process quality factor, 251
    product complexity factor, 254
    product concurrency factor, 254, 259, 405

Index

product maturity factor, 251
product quality factor, 251
risk determinant factors, 258, 402
risk exposure 259, 404
Seven Wonders of the World, 318
Shakespeare, William, 49, 322
Shaw, George Bernard, 16
Short-term interest rates, 324, 418
Should cost, 153
Sigma Products, 162
Sigma Specialties, Inc., 234
Simulation, 269, 295, 412
Single Payment:
   uniform series of payments for future value, 175
   uniform series of payments for present value, 173
Slack time, 119
Smith, Michael, 38
Software:
   development, 258, 403
   factors, 239
   management attribute factor, 241, 258, 403
   process and product maturity factors, 243, 251
   process or product complexity factor, 246
   process or product concurrency factor, 247
   process or product quality factor, 245
   programs, 241
   risk determinant factors, 258, 402
Soviet Union, 37
*Soyuz*, 37
Space shuttle, 38
Speculative risk, 36
*Sputnik*, 37
Standard data for job families, 134, 180, 387
Standard deviation, 62, 294, 371, 409
Standards, 133
Statistic, 371
Statistics, 62, 111, 371
Student's *t* distribution, 275, 295, 371
   probability density function, 82, 275, 295, 409
Subjective criteria, 308
Subjective engineering, 37

Subjective risk, 36
Superintendent of Documents, 18, 62, 111, 189, 260, 297, 326
Support, 306
Sydney Opera House, 352
Symbolic model, 266
Symbology, 16
Symbols, 17
Systematic error, 311
System engineering, 6

T

Tacking and Data Relay Spacecraft, 5
Task concurrency, 106, 221, 236, 247
Task flow analysis, 120
Task precedence, 121, 186, 384
Technical risk management, 4, 10, 299, 349
   absolutes, 4, 26
   plan, 349
   processes, 4
   steps, 328
   structure, 303
Technology development focus areas, 319
Technology Reinvestment Project, 319
Ternary number system, 110, 383
Test, 305
Testability, 216, 232
Test of hypothesis, 271, 295, 371, 410
   large sample, 273
   small sample, 276
Time Value of Money, 165
   formulation, 167
   future value, 171
   present value, 171
   single payment, 173
   uniform series of payments, 173
Tolerance limits, 227
Total procurement package, 258, 401
Total quality management, 6
Tower of Babel, 319
Transition, 345
Treasury notes, 362
Trial and error, 178

Truth table, 95, 213
  basic propositions, 95
  design, 97
TRW, 319

## U

Uniform series of payments for future value, 175
Uniform series of payments for present value, 173
Union of Soviet Socialist Republics, 37
Universal standard data, 133
  metal prices, 134
Upsilon Publishers, 203
U.S. Army:
  Combat Development Command, 8
  Materiel Command, 8
U.S. Department of Defense, 7, 57, 341
User Requirements, 7
U.S. Navy, 10, 116
  best manufacturing practices program, 10
USSR (Union of Soviet Socialist Republics), 37

## V

Value of aid, 25
Value engineering, 6
Variable:
  continuous, 371
  discrete, 371
Variance, 229, 371
Verlaine, Paul, 190
Very Large Cargo Transport, 188
VLCT (Very Large Cargo Transport), 188

Von Schiller, Johann, 72
*Vostok,* 37

## W

Warranty, 41
Watson, Jr., Thomas J., 310
WBS (work breakdown structure), 155, 287, 289
Weighting:
  binary, 91, 200
  constant, 90, 198
White II, Edward H., 37
Why buildings fall, 319
Why companies fail, 317
Wilde, Oscar, 260
Wilder, Thornton, 298
Window of opportunity, 8, 9
Work breakdown structure, 155, 287, 289
Would cost, 153

## X

X-ray tube, 40

## Z

$z$-factor, 147, 312
$z$-statistic, 376
Zero inventory, 259
Zeta Company, 273, 282
Zeta Corporation, 73
Zeta Industries, Inc., 144, 216

---

*Though the mills of God grind slowly; yet they grind exceedingly small;*
*Though with patience He stands waiting, with exactness grinds He all.*

***Henry Wadsworth Longfellow***